FEDERAL INCOME TAXATION

A Law Student's Guide to the Leading Cases and Concepts

FOURTEENTH EDITION

MARVIN A. CHIRELSTEIN
Late Professor of Law
Columbia University

LAWRENCE ZELENAK
Professor of Law
Duke University

CONCEPTS AND INSIGHTS SERIES®

FOUNDATION
PRESS

Concepts and Insights Series is a trademark registered in the U.S. Patent and Trademark Office.

ISBN: 978-1-64020-824-7

To Boris

MARVIN CHIRELSTEIN

This Fourteenth Edition of *Federal Income Taxation* is the first since the death of Marvin Chirelstein in 2015. From its original publication in 1977, Chirelstein's "little book" (as he liked to call it) about the income tax has had a deep influence on generations of law students, and perhaps an even deeper influence on their teachers (including, in both capacities, the co-author of the present edition). Chirelstein's guide to the law of contracts, *Concepts and Case Analysis in the Law of Contracts*, has been similarly influential in its field. He was much more, however, than the author of the two books for which he is best known. He knew everything about the history of boxing and baseball, seemed to have the complete works of Gerard Manley Hopkins committed to memory, and enjoyed playing in string quartets. He cared passionately about the integrity of the income tax, which he continued to defend long after his official retirement. He wrote in an unmistakable voice, with clarity, grace and wit (and not just about tax and contracts—take a look at his last published essay, "Bork, Dworkin, and the Constitution," 17 Green Bag 2d 17 (2013)). He belongs on the short list of funniest law professors of all time (despite, or perhaps because of, his almost never cracking a smile). And underneath a somewhat gruff exterior, he was one of the kindest persons his co-author has ever met.

PREFACE

This book is intended as a study aid for law students taking the basic course in federal income taxation, and it is therefore largely an explanation of how the income tax affects individuals. A systematic treatment of the taxation of corporations and shareholders—usually the subject of an advanced course, and in any event requiring an entire volume to itself—is not included. Certain fundamental elements of the corporate-shareholder system are referred to at various points, but this is done only as an incident of some other discussion and never in any real detail. The focus here is on the individual income tax and on the case and statutory materials that are likely to be covered in an introductory law-school course.

Our approach, we should also state, is anything but comprehensive. All sorts of topics are omitted which the student may encounter in the classroom and desire more information about, while other topics of no greater intrinsic importance are discussed at length. But we have not attempted to write a treatise, or a summary of Code sections, or a manual which can be used to answer specific questions about the tax law. Instead, the aim, which has not changed since the senior author's writing of the First Edition several decades ago, is to disclose the structural characteristics of the income tax mechanism—how the plumbing works, what's at stake in the controversies that arise, what elements of internal consistency or inconsistency can be detected, and so on. Accordingly, we have used whatever legal materials seemed best to illustrate the technical components of the system. We have tried to sketch the outline of the house—or at least one wing of it—but have made no effort to furnish all the rooms. This concept has led to a selective coverage of the law (to put it mildly), but it has also made possible a higher level of coherence and connectedness than could have been attained if more detail had been included.

The organization of the work—Income, Deductions, Attribution, etc.—roughly mirrors that of the various casebooks in use in the law schools. Although they differ among themselves in many ways, the casebooks also exhibit a great many elements of similarity, and it seems safe to say that the resemblances outnumber the differences. Large subject-matter headings are, of course, alike. In addition, the casebooks generally employ the same "great" landmark cases to carry the tax story from one topic to another: a few dozen well-known Supreme Court decisions are always featured, and even the lesser gleanings from the lower courts and the Internal Revenue Service are often the same. The notes that follow the cases, as well as the independent editorial materials, are very different in emphasis and style, and there are many differences in organization which are of real importance. But, again, there is considerable overlap in the lists of leading cases and administrative rulings.

This aspect of agreement among the editors, on cases as well as subject matter, has made it possible to write a book which tracks the casebooks—follows them like a reproach, as it were—without really having to develop a closer relationship to any one than to any other. We have used the landmark decisions as vehicles for explanation whenever possible, because the casebooks do so. Where the casebooks diverge, we have tried to invent hypotheticals which abstract from the cases in such a way as to merge the elements that seem to be common to all. Our hope is that this book can be used as a kind of universal supplement, therefore, and that the discussions it contains will have roughly equal relevance for all law students taking the basic tax course, no matter what the identity of their primary course materials. So as not to seem to claim too much, however, we should state again that not every casebook subject is taken up in detail; and some are omitted entirely.

This Fourteenth Edition reflects the more significant (in terms of the purposes of this book) statutory, regulatory, and judicial developments since the publication of the Thirteenth Edition. Of those various developments, the most significant by far is the Tax Cuts and Jobs Act of 2017.

LAWRENCE ZELENAK
Duke University

March 15, 2018

TABLE OF CONTENTS

TABLE OF CONTENTS

FEDERAL INCOME TAXATION

A Law Student's Guide to the
Leading Cases and Concepts

FOURTEENTH EDITION

Introduction

TERMINOLOGY, TIMING AND RATES

(a)   Tax Terminology

A brief presentation of income tax terminology may be useful by way of introduction:

The computation of an individual's tax liability begins with a determination of his *gross income*. This term is defined in Code § 61 as encompassing "all income from whatever source derived" except as otherwise provided by the statute. For most individual taxpayers gross income is made up of wages and salaries, dividends, interest and rents, and gains from the sale of investments such as securities and real estate. The definition of gross income is broad enough, however, to include receipts from other, less familiar sources as well. The statutory exceptions to the reach of § 61, which are fairly numerous, are usually referred to as *exclusions* from gross income (sometimes the term *exemption* is used). A well-known example is interest on state and municipal bonds, which is specifically excluded from gross income by Code § 103(a). Excluded items simply do not enter into the computation of tax. Thus, an individual with $50,000 of salary plus $5,000 of interest on bonds issued by the State of New York has a gross income of only $50,000. Quite obviously, the effect of the exclusion is to tax the excluded item at a rate of zero. The benefit to an individual taxpayer depends on her own applicable tax bracket, which in turn depends on how much income she receives from taxable sources. If the taxpayer just mentioned would otherwise be taxed at a rate of (say) 32% on the last $5,000 of non-excludable income, the dollar value of the exclusion from her standpoint is 32% of $5,000, or $1,600. If her bracket rate were only 10%, the dollar value of the exclusion would be only $500.

Having determined her gross income under § 61, the taxpayer next subtracts all the outlays and expenditures that are allowed by the Code as *deductions*. Deductible items include the taxpayer's business expenses—wages paid to employees, depreciation on business equipment, fees paid to investment advisers, etc.—which represent the cost of earning the gross income determined above. In addition, while personal living expenses (food, apartment rent) are generally disallowed, the Code does permit certain items—for example, charitable contributions—to be deducted, even though plainly in the category of personal rather than business expense. As a matter of tax arithmetic the dollar value of a deduction from gross income is the same as that of an exclusion. If a 32% bracket taxpayer

1

contributes $5,000 to charity, the value of the deduction from her standpoint is obviously $1,600. The effect is just the same whether the amount of the charitable gift is excluded from her gross income in the first instance, or included but then allowed as a deduction.

A major complicating factor in the federal income tax is the special treatment accorded to long-term *capital gains.* In computing gain (or loss) from the sale of property, the taxpayer subtracts her cost, or *basis,* for the property sold from the *amount realized* on the transaction. The gain, if any, is recognized and included in her gross income under § 61. If the property sold is a *capital asset*—for example, securities or real estate acquired for investment—and if the property has been held for more than 1 year, the gain will be taxed at a lower tax rate—now, generally, 15% or 20%—than the rate that applies to wages, salaries, business profits and other kinds of *ordinary* income. As capital gains are thus more to be desired than income that does not qualify for the lower rate, the scope of the capital asset definition becomes a matter of considerable importance.

Once gross income has been reduced by allowable deductions, including personal and dependency exemptions, the figure that remains is the taxpayer's *taxable income.*[1] Taxable income is the residual or net amount on which the taxpayer's tax liability is based. Having selected the appropriate rate schedule from § 1 (depending on whether she is married, single, or a "head of household"), the taxpayer then determines her tax by fitting her taxable income into the schedule in the manner indicated below. The tax liability that results may be reduced by statutory *credits*—*e.g.,* the child tax credit (7.07). Tax credits are subtracted directly from the tax due. While the dollar-value of a *deduction* depends on the particular taxpayer's applicable tax rate (so that the value is greater for higher than for lower-bracket taxpayers), a credit has the same dollar-value for all taxpayers entitled to use it. This is so because a credit is a dollar-for-dollar reduction of the tax itself rather than being a subtraction from gross income.

Income tax returns are filed and taxes are paid on an *annual* basis, which for almost all individual taxpayers simply means the calendar year. Accounting rules are employed to allocate income and deduction items to one taxable year or another, with most individuals using the *cash method* of accounting and most businesses using the *accrual method.* The timing of income and deductions is important, because taxpayers strongly prefer to pay their taxes later rather than sooner. Money in the bank or invested in government bonds earns

---

[1] An intermediate calculation between gross income and taxable income called *adjusted gross income* is necessary in computing the various personal expense allowances and for certain other purposes. See discussion at 7.06.

interest—until recently quite a bit—so that if given a choice between paying $1,000 of taxes today and paying $1,000 of taxes a year from now, the taxpayer will always choose the later date. Assuming interest at a rate of 8%, the present value—the value today—of $1,000 due in one year is only $926. Put differently, the sum of $926 invested at 8% today will grow to $1,000 at the end of one year. If (because of accounting or other legal rules) the $1,000 tax is not due until a year from now, the taxpayer can meet that obligation by currently setting aside the sum of $926. But if the tax is due today, the full $1,000 will have to be surrendered. It follows that a year's delay is worth $74 ($1,000 – $926) to the taxpayer in cold hard cash. The government, of course, sees the matter in opposite terms: a year's delay "costs" the Treasury exactly the same amount. As suggested in Part A and elsewhere, the question of "pay now or pay later" is at the heart of many of the legal controversies that arise in the tax field, though this fact is not always apparent to the naked eye.[2]

(b)   Tax Rates

As far as individual taxpayers are concerned, the schedule of tax rates is *progressive,* or graduated, which simply means that as income increases an individual's tax liability also increases but at a greater rate. For the year 2018, the rate structure begins, in effect, with a zero-bracket—referred to as the *standard deduction*—of $24,000 for married couples, $18,000 for heads of households, and $12,000 for other single persons. All taxpayers are permitted to receive income up to these levels at a tax rate of zero.

Once the amount of the standard deduction is exceeded the positive rates take hold. For the year 2018, the tax schedule for married couples contains seven rate-brackets, to wit:

10% on taxable income up to $19,050;

12% on taxable income over $19,050 but not over $77,400;

22% on taxable income over $77,400 but not over $165,000;

---

[2]   The same point—that postponing her tax payments favors the taxpayer—can be made in another way. In the example above, if the $1,000 tax is not due for one year, the taxpayer (rather than the government) will earn the stipulated 8% return during that period. The taxpayer will then have 80 "extra" dollars of her own when the year is over. But if the $1,000 has to be paid to the Treasury immediately, the return on that money will belong to the government. Viewed as of the *end* of the year, therefore, there is $80 at stake. While the text suggests that the amount at stake is only $74, that is because the text is looking at the problem from the *beginning* of the year. Really, the $74 mentioned in the text and the $80 mentioned in this note are the same quantities. Thus, $74 is the present value (again, at 8%) of $80 due a year from now; $80 is just $74 one year later.

For convenience, an explanation of the concept of "present value," together with related Tables and a very brief "Exercise," is provided in the Appendix.

24% on taxable income over $165,000 but not over $315,000;

32% on taxable income over $315,000 but not over $400,000;

35% on taxable income over $400,000 but not over $600,000;

37% on taxable income over $600,000.

In tax terminology the applicable rate of tax at each bracket level is called the *marginal* rate of tax, while the rate that is applicable to the taxpayer's income as a whole is called the average or effective rate. A married couple with $180,000 of taxable income, for example, is subject to a rate of—

10% on the first $19,050	=	$ 1,905
12% on the next $58,350 ($77,400 minus $19,050)	=	$ 7,002
22% on the next $87,600 ($165,000 minus $77,400)	=	$ 19,272
24% on the last $15,000 ($180,000 minus $165,000)	=	$ 3,600
Total tax liability		$ 31,779

Although the couple's top marginal tax rate is 24%, their effective (average) rate on their taxable income is about 17.7% ($31,779 divided by $180,000). (If we take into account the fact that their standard deduction of $24,000 is the functional equivalent of the imposition of a zero tax rate on an additional $24,000 of income, their effective tax rate with respect to their total income is about 15.6% ($31,779 divided by $204,000)). Above the first bracket level, the effective rate is bound to be lower than the marginal rate on the taxpayer's last dollar of income, because the effective rate is simply a weighted average of the applicable marginal rates, which begin at 10% and rise to 24% only on the last $15,000 of the taxpayers' taxable income.

To illustrate the marginal-effective rate distinction still further, one occasionally hears someone say (usually of someone else): "X doesn't want to earn any more money this year because it will put her in a higher bracket." This statement may mean, simply, that the speaker thinks that X will not care to earn an additional $10,000 if that income will be taxed at a high marginal rate—say 35%. Since X would net only $6,500 after tax, she may prefer to substitute more leisure for that amount of additional spendable income. This could be a valid surmise, depending on X's personal preferences and how hard she would have to work to earn the $10,000. But if the quoted comment is supposed to signify that X will sustain an after-tax loss and actually be poorer in consequence of the additional earnings, then the speaker has obviously got his marginal and effective rates mixed up. Taken in this sense the comment could only be true if, by adding the $10,000 to her existing taxable income, the marginal tax rate applicable to the last $10,000 somehow became applicable to X's income overall. But it does not: the lower segments of X's income continue to be taxed at the same marginal rates as previously, *i.e.*, the first $19,050 at 10%, the next $58,350 at 12%, and so on. Hence, additional earnings will always involve *some* increase in a taxpayer's after-tax income as long as the highest marginal rate of tax is less than 100%.

There have been sharp debates in Congress and elsewhere about just how progressive the rate structure should be, but the fundamental idea of progressive marginal rates has not been seriously challenged in Congress in recent years. However, the merits of progressivity have been debated as a philosophical matter with more or less intensity for decades, generations, even centuries.[3] The federal income tax's closest brush with "proportionate taxation" (that is, taxation of all income at a single "flat" rate) occurred in the late 1980's; the Tax Reform Act of 1986 featured only two marginal tax rates, of 15% and 28% (or three marginal tax rates, if one counts the quasi-zero bracket created by the standard deduction).

Which is correct as a matter of social policy, a progressive rate-structure or a proportional rate-structure? President Reagan made his own view very clear on one occasion when, citing Biblical precedent, he asserted that "There can be no moral justification [for] the progressive tax."[4] President Clinton, on the other hand, though a Bible reader himself, insisted that a flat or proportional rate-structure unduly favors upper-income taxpayers and for that reason fails to meet a standard of tax equity or "fairness." Congress came close to supporting President Reagan's position in 1986, but then in 1993 moved in President Clinton's direction by imposing higher marginal rates—as high as 39.6%—on high-income taxpayers. Although there is ongoing political controversy over appropriate marginal tax rates at the top of the income distribution, the *principle*

---

[3]   Walter J. Blum and Harry Kalven, Jr., *The Uneasy Case for Progressive Taxation* (1953); Blum, *The Uneasy Case for Progressive Taxation in 1976*, in Campbell, ed., Income Redistribution (1977), p. 147. And see Bankman & Griffith, *Social Welfare and the Rate Structure: A New Look at Progressive Taxation*, 75 Cal.L.Rev. 1905 (1987).

[4]   "Proportionate taxation we would gladly accept on the theory that those better able to pay should remove some of the burden from those least able to pay. The Bible explains this in its instruction on tithing. We are told that we should give the Lord one tenth and if the Lord prospers us ten times as much, we should give ten times as much. But, under our progressive income tax, computing Caesar's share is a little different . . ." Reagan, *Encroaching Control: Keep Government Poor and Remain Free*, 27 Vital Speeches of the Day 677 (1961).

of progressivity in the tax rate-structure does not appear to be subject to serious political challenge at the moment.

While not strictly a matter of terminology, the inclusion in Code § 1(f) of an "indexation" provision can appropriately be mentioned here. An individual whose dollar income increases from one year to the next might be obliged to pay tax at a higher marginal rate (say 32% instead of 24%) on the increase, this being a natural consequence of rate progression. If, however, due to inflation the benefit of the increase is wiped out by a corresponding increase in the cost of living, the effect would be a heavier tax burden with no real improvement in the taxpayer's pre-tax economic position. In the bad old days before the enactment of § 1(f), this phenomenon was popularly (or unpopularly) known as "bracket creep." Wage and salary-earners were especially vulnerable. Even if a worker received a raise in wages, the raise was illusory if the prices of consumer goods rose in the same proportion. If her marginal tax rate also increased, the result was a decrease in the taxpayer's real disposable income.[5]

To put an end to bracket creep, Code § 1(f) now provides that the brackets used in the individual rate schedules shall be adjusted, or indexed, each year to reflect the percentage by which the Consumer Price Index, published by the Department of Labor, exceeds the CPI for the base year 1993. The same adjustment is to be made annually in the standard deduction amount. The Tax Cuts and Jobs Act of 2017, while retaining inflation adjustments, mandates the use of adjustments based on the so-called "chained" CPI, rather than the garden variety CPI. Unlike the standard CPI, the chained CPI reflects the possibility that consumers may respond to disproportionate price increases in some goods by shifting consumption to substitutes as to which there has been less inflation. If the price of butter, for example, goes up relative to the price of margarine, some consumers will switch to margarine rather than paying the new higher price for butter. This seemingly small and technical change is expected to reduce income tax inflation adjustments very significantly in the medium-to-long term.

A separate tax rate schedule is provided for corporations under § 11. Corporations are treated by the Code as taxpaying entities and are subject to a flat-rate tax of 21%. Taxable income is computed in much the same way for corporations as it is for individuals—roughly, gross income less business expenses—except, of course, that the

---

[5]   Even if inflation did not result in an increase in the top marginal tax rate applicable to a taxpayer's income, it could produce an increase in the taxpayer's effective (average) tax rate by causing a greater proportion of the taxpayer's income to be taxed at the taxpayer's top marginal rate.

personal expense deductions and standard deductions allowed to individuals do not apply.

A loose end. Section 1411, added to the Code by the Affordable Care Act of 2010, imposes a 3.8% tax on the net investment income of high-income individuals (in 2018, persons with adjusted gross incomes of more than $200,000 in the case of single taxpayers, or more than $250,000 in the case of joint returns). The revenue from the tax is earmarked for Medicare. The tax applies to interest, dividends, annuities, royalties, rents, and gains on the sale or other disposition of investment assets. Although the remainder of this book will generally refer to the 37% top rate on ordinary income and the 20% top rate on long-term capital gains, keep in mind that where § 1411 applies the combined top tax rate on ordinary investment income (*e.g.*, interest) is 40.8% and the combined top rate on capital gains is 23.8%.

The 3.8% tax on net investment income is new. By contrast, federal payroll taxes on wages have been around for many decades. An employee is subject to a payroll tax equal to 6.2% of her wages, up to a ceiling on taxable wages (in 2018) of $128,400. The employer is also taxed on those same wages, also at the rate of 6.2%. Revenue from both the employee and employer tax is dedicated to funding social security retirement payments. There are also payroll taxes to fund Medicare. These taxes are imposed on all wages; there is no wage ceiling for purposes of the Medicare taxes. Again, there are two identical rate (1.45%) taxes, one imposed on employees and one on employers. Finally, the Affordable Care Act recently added § 3101(b)(2), which imposes an additional 0.9% tax, applicable to wages in excess of $200,000 for a single taxpayer, or in excess of $250,000 in the case of a joint return. This tax is imposed only on the employee; there is no corresponding tax on the employer. Taking into account the 37% top income tax rate, the 1.45% basic Medicare tax, and the 0.9% additional Medicare tax, the top combined federal tax rate imposed on employees on their employment income is 39.35%. The combined top rate rises to 40.8% if we also consider the 1.45% tax imposed on the employer.

More than a loose end. Section 199A, added to the Code by the Tax Cuts and Jobs Act of 2017, generally provides a deduction equal to 20% of the "qualified business income" of a noncorporate taxpayer. For a taxpayer in the top (37%) rate bracket under § 1, § 199A produces an effective tax rate of 29.6% (that is, taxing 80% of income at 37% is the equivalent of taxing 100% of income at 29.6%). As with many other features of the 2017 legislation, § 199A is scheduled to terminate after 2025.

Although the deduction is available for most unincorporated businesses, it is never available to employees with respect to their employment income. Even for self-employed taxpayers, the deduction is not available if the business involves the performance of services in the fields of health, law, accounting, actuarial science, performing arts, consulting, athletics, financial services, brokerage services, or "any trade or business where the principal asset of such trade or business is the reputation or skill of one or more of its employees." The denial of the deduction for personal services businesses does not apply, however, in the case of a taxpayer with taxable income of $157,500 or less (single taxpayer) or $315,000 or less (joint return); the income limitations are based on the taxpayer's entire taxable income (not just the taxpayer's business income). The benefit of the lower-income rule is phased out as income rises above $157,500 (or $315,000), with the phase out complete at $207,500 (or $415,000).

Although unincorporated businesses other than personal services businesses are generally eligible for the deduction, they are subject to another rule that may cap their deduction at less than 20% of income. Under the cap rules, the otherwise allowable deduction is limited to the greater of (a) 50% of the wages paid by the business to employees, or (b) 25% of the wages paid by the business to employees, plus 2.5% of the original (unadjusted) basis of depreciable property used by the taxpayer in the business. Suppose, for example, a qualifying business has $1,000,000 of taxable income, pays $300,000 of wages, and uses depreciable assets with total original basis of $400,000. Absent the cap rules, the § 199A deduction would be $200,000. The first cap rule produces a ceiling of $150,000, and the second produces a ceiling of $175,000 ($75,000 plus $100,000). The allowable deduction is $175,000. Like the personal services rules, the cap rules do not apply to a taxpayer with taxable income below $157,500 ($315,000). The exemption is phased out as income rises above $157,500 ($315,000); the phase out is complete at $207,500 ($415,000).

The legislative history does not offer any rationale for § 199A, and it is certainly not self-evident that the owner of a qualifying business deserves to be taxed more lightly than the owner of an equal-income disqualified personal services business, or than an equal-income employee. The deduction limits based on percentages of wages paid suggest the deduction is intended as a reward for "jobs creators," but (as the American Bar Association pointed out to Congress, to no avail) law firms and other personal services businesses also create jobs. The best explanation for the provision is probably simply that, when Congress in 2017 reduced the corporate tax rate from 35% to 21%, owners of unincorporated businesses successfully demanded a parallel tax cut. Owners of personal services businesses, as well as the legions of employed taxpayers, apparently lacked the lobbying clout to insist on similar tax breaks for themselves.

Before the ink was dry on the 2017 tax legislation, the internet was awash in discussions of how disfavored taxpayers—employees and owners of services businesses—might attempt to transform themselves into owners of qualifying businesses.[6] Employees would abandon their employed status and become independent contractors. A law firm owning its own building might separate the law business from the real estate business; the law business could pay rent to the real estate business, and the real estate business could qualify for the benefits of § 199A. A law firm without a building of its own might try to play the same game with its intangible assets, including perhaps its "brand." An actor might develop a line of food products sold under his name and his visage, in the hope that the combined acting-and-food business would not be considered a personal services business. And so on.

There would be non-tax disadvantages to many of these strategies. For example, a professor transforming into an independent contractor would presumably have to give up tenure. There are also various tax law obstacles in the way of these plans. For example, there are detailed rules of long standing for distinguishing employees from independent contractors for tax purposes; if a person is an employee in substance, merely calling her an independent contractor will not make her one for tax purposes. It remains to be seen both how aggressively taxpayers will exploit these various strategies for shoehorning themselves into § 199A, and how aggressively (and successfully) the IRS will challenge the taxpayer efforts.

---

[6]　For one of the best discussions, see Avi-Yonah, et al., *The Games They Will Play: An Update on the Conference Committee Tax Bill* (revised December 22, 2017), available at ssrn.com.

Part A

INCOME

Code § 61, which contains the definition of "gross income," is the starting point for a study of the federal income tax. The section begins with a catch-all clause—"gross income means all income from whatever source derived"—and then proceeds to enumerate fifteen specific classes of receipts which are regarded as within the income definition. The enumeration is extensive; it picks up most or all of the common classes of income—salaries, wages, business profits, dividends, interest, rents and royalties—and includes as well a good many special kinds of benefits, such as annuities, income from discharge of indebtedness, and income in respect of a decedent. The intent is plain: to the extent that there might be doubt about one or another of the items enumerated, the desire of Congress to bring that item within the definition of income is made clear and unmistakable. But the enumeration is not designed to be exhaustive. The forms that commercial dealings can take in the modern world, and the labels that can be assigned to income from different sources, are simply too various for any listing to fully comprehend. Accordingly, the catch-all clause is expected to supplement the enumeration by including any non-enumerated items which can properly be defined as "income." In that way it plays an important, if subordinate, role in determining the scope of the provision.

Unavoidably, perhaps, the language employed by § 61 is somewhat tautological—". . . gross income means all income . . ."—and in the old days, at least, there was considerable preoccupation with the question of how much ground the catch-all clause was actually intended to cover. Was the quoted phrase—"all income . . ."—as sweeping, as embracing as it sounded, or were there certain inbuilt criteria which might actually operate to exclude some forms of enrichment from the tax base? In *Eisner v. Macomber*,[1] decided in 1920, the Supreme Court stated that "income may be defined as the gain derived from labor, from capital, or from both combined," a construction which could be taken to mean that *unless* the factor of labor or capital were present in a given case, the income definition would not encompass the item in question, and the income tax would not apply to it. One was therefore invited to speculate about the status under the law of such things as "give-away" prizes ($25,000 for catching the fish with the advertiser's identification tag on its tail[2]); awards for civic achievement (the Peace Prize—Nobel or Lenin);

---

[1]   252 U.S. 189 (1920).

[2]   *Simmons v. U.S.*, 308 F.2d 160 (4th Cir.1962).

"subsidies" such as scholarships and fellowships for deserving students; damages for breach of promise or alienation of affection; "found" property; and so on. Since these and various other kinds of receipts were arguably unrelated either to personal services or to capital investment (or both combined), might it not be said that they fell outside the concept of "income" which the Supreme Court had approved in *Macomber*? Or could it be asserted that "labor" or "capital" somehow inheres in every human activity? The *Macomber* definition apparently possessed metaphysical properties which made it difficult to apply in an absolute fashion, and hence most commentators contented themselves with the observation that close cases would have to be resolved on an individual basis.[3]

Happily, the Supreme Court in 1955 put an end to much, perhaps all, of the uncertainty which the *Macomber* decision had generated by discarding the labor-capital formulation in favor of a broader and simpler concept of "income." In *Commissioner v. Glenshaw Glass Co.*,[4] the taxpayers had received treble damage awards under the antitrust laws. Pointing out that two-thirds of the awards represented fines or penalties imposed on the wrongdoers for violating federal laws, the taxpayers argued that only the basic one-third portion which compensated for loss of profits could be treated as derived from labor or capital or both combined. Making no real attempt to bring the punitive damages within the *Macomber* definition, the Court nevertheless held that the awards were taxable in their entirety. "Here we have instances of undeniable accessions to wealth, clearly realized, and over which the taxpayers have complete dominion. The mere fact that the payments were extracted from the wrongdoers as punishment for unlawful conduct cannot detract from their character as taxable income to the recipients." Congress, the Court stated significantly, had applied "no limitations as to the source of taxable receipts, nor restrictive labels as to their nature." *Macomber*, it said, could not be regarded as the "touchstone" to all questions of gross income.

The Court thus resolved—more or less at a stroke—much of what had seemed troublesome and tantalizing about the term "income." With "source" declared irrelevant, the "touchstone" to all income questions becomes simple enrichment; all gains are taxable (at least if "clearly realized"), whether traceable to labor, to capital, or to mere good fortune. If punitive damages are within the scope of the income definition just because the recipient is made wealthier thereby, then so are prizes and awards (lucky or deserved); so are damages and subsidies of all sorts; and so are packets of cash found

---

[3]   Surrey and Warren, *The Income Tax Project of the American Law Institute,* 66 Harvard L.Rev. 761 (1953).

[4]   348 U.S. 426 (1955).

in the backs of taxicabs. Each represents an "accession to wealth," and that factor by itself, under *Glenshaw*, justifies inclusion in the tax base. The catch-all provision of § 61 is indeed as sweeping as it seems to be; the income tax is source-blind, and any measurable gain is within its reach.

The *Glenshaw* decision has survived the ensuing decades without material qualification, and it is altogether unlikely that the Court will ever return to a narrower view of the meaning of "income." It is therefore fair to ask at this point whether there is anything still left to debate under the heading "What is income?" The answer, of course, is: just about everything. Apart from the taxability of windfalls, punitive damages and similar trivia, the *Glenshaw* case resolves none of the real difficulties in the field, though it does, perhaps, help to sharpen the issues. The problems that survive the *Glenshaw* decision are, and in the nature of things always were, the critical ones from the standpoint of the structure of the tax law, and their solutions are not greatly advanced by the assertion that all realized gains are "income." This is not to say that a contrary decision in *Glenshaw* would not have been troublesome: if punitive damages had been held non-taxable even though they plainly enriched the recipient, Congress would presumably have had to extend the enumeration in § 61 to include such receipts and then might have had to resort to further enumeration if and when other unusual items obtained exemption in the courts. Although Congress is still obliged to explicitly exempt receipts it doesn't wish to cover, *e.g.*, college tuition scholarships (see Code § 117), this is done as a matter of conscious legislative design rather than chance judicial action. Our point, however, is that *Glenshaw* does not, and could not, reach the technical questions with which the law is chiefly concerned in taxing "income"; hence the decision, though important philosophically, has little direct effect on the learning job that lies ahead.

The structural or technical issues to be examined in this Part can very roughly be divided into three categories (implied by the *Glenshaw* opinion itself, as a matter of fact). Since income includes all "gains" that are "clearly realized" regardless of "source," the relevant questions would seem to be:

(a) What constitutes a "gain"? Has the taxpayer enjoyed the requisite "accession to wealth" by reason of some particular event, and if he has, in what amount? This question seems to have an economic ring to it rather than an abstract legal quality; it calls for a measurement of the taxpayer's personal wealth, or at least the change therein from one point in time to another—presumably the beginning and end of the calendar year. While that inquiry appears somewhat less problematic than the question of how to define "income," even so one anticipates disputes. And since income may be received in "kind" as well as in cash, there are likely to be valuation questions which will sometimes be difficult to answer.

(b)   When is income "clearly realized"? Conceding the presence of gain, is the benefit sufficiently "in hand" to be properly taxable? To be sure, the question can be answered intuitively in most cases. Gain from the sale of securities for cash is obviously "realized"; mere property appreciation almost equally obviously is not. But between these extremes are a good many ambiguous situations which require further analysis. As will be seen, gain and realization questions often seem to overlap or slide together—*Eisner v. Macomber* (5.02) is an example—and part of the effort to cope with each lies in keeping the two apart for discussion purposes.

(c)   Although "source" is irrelevant for purposes of § 61, this does not of course mean that Congress may not choose to make it relevant. In fact, the Code contains a large number of provisions which exclude particular kinds of receipts from the tax base—many more by this time than when the *Macomber* case was decided. In some instances Congress has acted simply to resolve doubts about gain or realization by excluding the item at issue or by providing fixed rules of measurement. But in many others, Congress has sought to effectuate a non-tax policy goal by affording an exemption based on source. As will be seen, the exclusion of particular kinds of receipts necessarily revives problems of definition. Suppose, for example, that "gifts" are specifically excluded from income (as they in fact are). Since there is plainly a realized gain to the recipient of a gift, we may have to decide in close cases whether a transfer of property was indeed a "gift," *i.e.*, as that term is defined for tax purposes.

The sections that follow all entail one or another of the three limiting categories just mentioned—gain, realization, and specific exclusion. But these categories are not exhausted in this Part. Both gain and realization questions crop up at many points: indeed, it is possible to assert that these issues are the predominant subject-matter of this book. Further, only a few, and not necessarily all the most important, of the Code's specific exclusions are treated here. But while the present Part is thus merely introductory, it should provide the reader with considerable perspective on a number of the detailed problems to be encountered later on.

1.   Non-Cash Benefits: Meals-and-Lodgings; Imputed Rents

1.01   General Comment

Many of the questions that arise about the scope of § 61 and the meaning of "income" seem to involve benefits "in kind," that is, receipts in a form other than conventional cash payments. These questions do not arise because of any basic doubt regarding the includability of non-cash receipts; it is perfectly clear that § 61 embraces cash and non-cash benefits alike. But non-cash items do often present valuation difficulties which are obviously not encountered when cash is received; moreover, there may be doubts about the application of the "realization" requirement in some instances, doubts which do not arise when property or services are exchanged for cash. Finally, the Code sometimes makes specific concessions for non-cash receipts—meals and lodgings (1.02) being one familiar example—or allows them to escape tax more or less by default—imputed rent (1.03) being a less familiar but considerably more important instance—while treating the cash equivalent as fully taxable.

In general, however, § 61 makes no distinction between cash and "kind" and it may be well to take the point in its affirmative application before going on to consider exceptions. As a first illustration, assume an employee-taxpayer receives a year-end bonus from his corporate employer consisting of 100 shares of the employer's stock. The stock has a traded value of $5 a share, or $500 in total, at the time it is issued in Year 1. Some months later, in Year 2, the employee sells the stock on the market for $6 a share, or $600. Two questions can be raised: first, how much, if anything, is includable in the employee's income in Year 1 by reason of the bonus? Second, how much gain should the employee report on the sale in Year 2?

The answer to the first question is straightforward once it is accepted that § 61 treats compensation in cash (salaries, wages, bonuses, fees) and compensation in kind alike. As there is no doubt about the market value of the employer's stock, the employee must include $500 in his Year 1 income just as if he had then received a cash bonus in the same amount.[5] To be painfully clear about the consequence, if the employee's applicable marginal rate of tax for Year 1 is 35%, he must pay a tax of $175 cash, even though the bonus itself is obviously not in cash form.

The second question—how much gain on later sale—takes its answer from the first. Since $500 out of the total of $600 realized was already taxed in Year 1, it is plain that no more than the balance of $100 should be taxed in Year 2. In computing taxable gain (or loss) from the sale of property, the Code, as might be expected, directs that the "amount realized" on the sale—$600 in our case—be reduced by the cost, or "basis," of the property sold. A taxpayer's cost for shares of stock or other property would normally equal his cash investment.

---

[5]   Regs. § 1.61–2(d). The discussion of *Commissioner v. Lo Bue, infra* at 19.01, is also relevant.

16

Here, however, the taxpayer actually paid nothing (except taxable services) for the stock received. But as a basis for the shares of zero would result in total taxable income of $1,100—$500 of compensation in Year 1, plus $600 of "gain" in Year 2—it is evident that a special concept of "cost" is required in order to prevent the first $500 from being counted twice. Accordingly, under a long-standing rule, property which was included in a taxpayer's income when received by him is treated as having a "cost" equal to its value at the date of receipt. Since the stock in our case was included in the employee's income at a value of $500 when received in Year 1, its basis in Year 2 for the purpose of computing gain (or loss) on sale is also $500. The additional income in Year 2 is therefore limited to $100.

This calculation, petty as it is, should nevertheless suggest that what is chiefly at stake from the standpoint of our employee-taxpayer is the timing, rather than the magnitude, of his taxable income. Thus, suppose the initial definitional question—whether a bonus in the form of stock is includable in "income"—were resolved in the negative, so that no portion of the stock's value was included in Year 1. In that event the taxpayer's basis for the shares would indeed be zero: the absence of a cash investment or a prior taxable receipt would have left the taxpayer with no basis, actual or constructive, to offset against the $600 of sale proceeds in Year 2. Hence the entire amount realized on the sale would be treated as gain. It follows that $600 is ultimately taxable under either view of the meaning of "income." Under the first, however, $500 is taxable in Year 1, $100 in Year 2; under the second, nothing is taxable in Year 1, but $600 is taxed in Year 2.

So why the fuss? Does the employee care, particularly, which way the matter is resolved? In fact he does; and intuition tells us that in most cases the employee will prefer the second set of outcomes to the first—that is, will prefer to postpone, rather than anticipate, the recognition of taxable income. But again, the question is why? One reason could be the effect of the progressive rate structure. Suppose, for example, that the stock bonus represents retirement pay; the employee is put to pasture at the end of Year 1, and as a result his income in Year 2 drops substantially. If his applicable marginal tax rate were expected to be lower in Year 2, the employee would be better off if the $500 bonus could be reported in the later period. Efforts by high-paid executives, and even by much lower-paid employees, to defer income to their golden years can sometimes be explained on this ground, at least in part.

But suppose that retirement is not in view for the employee in our example, and that his marginal tax rate is expected to be the same in both periods. Or, indeed, suppose that we had a completely flat or proportional income tax; that the rate schedule contained no progression whatever. Even then the taxpayer would prefer postponement to anticipation, and would seek to define "income" so as to shift the receipt in question from Year 1 to Year 2. The reason, of course, is that taxes are scheduled and paid on an annual basis—rather than once in a lifetime—and it is better to incur and pay any given dollar amount of taxes in later than in earlier years. An obligation to pay $175 in taxes immediately has a positive present value to the Treasury, and a negative present value to the taxpayer, of exactly $175. An obligation to pay $175 in taxes a year from now has a present value of $162.05 if we assume an 8% rate of interest; and only $156.28 if we assume a 12% interest rate. Accordingly, as long as funds can be invested at some positive rate of interest, taxpayers have a powerful incentive to defer as long as possible the surrender of their personal wealth to the Treasury. All taxpayers feel the same about this—savers and consumers alike—and it is not to any degree a function of progressive rates.

The point is an obvious one, we admit, but we choose to emphasize it here because it lies at the heart of so many of the technical and interpretative issues that arise in the tax law. Especially when the legal question is "What is taxable income?" or "What is a deductible expense?", the controversy often will involve the postponement or anticipation of tax obligations—nothing more or less. Admittedly, this generalization does not always apply, even in the areas just mentioned. As will be seen in connection with the taxability of meals-and-lodgings (1.02), for example, the income-definition question may sometimes entail the total forgiveness of tax rather than mere postponement. This will most often be true when the question is whether an item of current consumption—for example, meals-and-lodging or imputed rent—is to be included in income; if such items are not taxable in the year of consumption, they are generally never taxable. Outside of the current consumption category, however, most income and deduction controversies are about timing; they are now-or-later questions, rather than now-or-never questions. In any event, the student should be aided in classifying the subjects of "income," "realization," etc., by noticing when, and how often, what is at stake in a controversy over legal definitions is simply the taxpayer's desire to postpone the payment of tax and the Treasury's desire to accelerate it.

The point is important enough, we think, to justify one more illustration, which abstracts from a number of decided cases.[6] Assume again that the taxpayer is a well-paid corporate executive. His age today is 50, and he looks forward to retiring in 15 years. Although it has no systematic retirement program, the company is

---

[6]   See, *e.g.*, *U.S. v. Drescher*, 179 F.2d 863 (2d Cir.1950).

inspired to do something for this executive at least, and in order to fund his not-so-distant retirement it purchases an endowment policy[7] from an insurance company for a single lump-sum premium payment of $10,000. At a guaranteed rate of accumulation of roughly 8%, the premium payment will build up to $30,000 at the end of 15 years, at which time the executive will draw down the entire fund for use or investment during his retirement. Although the policy names the executive as beneficiary, it is issued to the company, which plans to hold the policy in its own safe until the executive reaches retirement age. The executive's rights are nonforfeitable—he gets $30,000 at age 65 even if he is fired or quits in the meanwhile—but he has no right to sell or borrow against the policy prior to age 65.

Is the $10,000 premium payment made by the company includable in the executive's gross income immediately, that is, in the year in which the policy is purchased? Or is it includable in his income only when he receives the maturity value in cash, at the end of 15 years? On the one hand, it can be argued that in view of the taxpayer's inability to realize current cash benefits through sale or pledge, the value of the policy to him in Year 1 is zero, or at least is indeterminate. To be sure, the bonus in the preceding example was taxed currently even though received in the form of stock, but there the stock could have been sold at once for cash, or pledged for a loan or traded for another security, and at all events was freely disposable by the employee from the date it was issued. Here, by contrast, the endowment policy is pretty well frozen until maturity. But, on the other hand, who doesn't feel better off, especially at age 50, when his employer buys him a sizeable retirement fund? The executive is surely wealthier with the endowment policy than without it, and what better measure of the economic benefit received than the cost of the policy itself? One suspects, moreover, that the executive may have proposed or consented to the policy purchase in lieu of receiving the same amount in straight salary; at the very least he himself chose to accept or continue an employment which entailed that special form of compensation.

The decided cases largely hold for the government in these circumstances and require immediate inclusion of the $10,000 premium payment in the employee's gross income (see 1.02, below). For the moment, however, our particular concern is not with arguments about the meaning of "income" under § 61. What we wish to focus on instead is the overall consequence in financial terms of the two competing views presented. What is at stake? Why is the

---

[7]   An endowment policy is a contract under which the obligor agrees to pay the policy-owner a lump-sum certain at the end of a stated number of years.

executive plainly better off if the definitional issue is resolved against current includability?

The answer can be given only if we settle another question first; namely, what happens when the endowment policy matures 15 years from now and the executive receives the face amount of $30,000 in cash? Plainly there is a "realization" at that point and just as plainly the "amount realized" is $30,000. The taxpayer's cost, or basis, for the claim which he then surrenders depends (as the stock-bonus case should suggest) on whether or not the earlier premium payment of $10,000 had already been included in gross income. Assuming it was included (that is, the government won the original litigation), the taxpayer's basis for the policy would be $10,000—the amount previously taxed to him—and the further gain recognized on maturity would be $20,000. Assuming the premium was not included in income (that is, the government lost the earlier case), the executive's basis would be zero, and the full amount of $30,000 would be taxable in the later period. Once again, therefore, as in the stock-bonus illustration, two sets of outcomes can be conceived of. Either $10,000 is taxed in the earlier year and $20,000 in the later year; or nothing is taxed in the earlier year and $30,000 in the later.

Now assume that the same marginal tax rate—say 35%—applies in both years so that the possible effects of progression and of legislated changes in the tax rate schedule are excluded. Assume also that the executive can invest his money at an after-tax rate of 8% throughout the relevant time period. The comparative impact of the pending legal determination—whether the $10,000 premium payment is, or is not, includable in the taxpayer's gross income in the current year—is simply the difference between a $3,500 tax payable now (.35 × $10,000) and the present value of a $3,500 tax payable in 15 years. Discounted at the same 8% rate, the present value of $3,500 due in 15 years is about $1,100, *i.e.*, $1,100 invested at 8% will grow to $3,500 by the end of a 15-year period. Hence, in terms of his current wealth status—how rich he is today—the controversy is worth $2,400 to the executive. This is the difference between the $3,500 tax which the government says is due now and the present value of the same tax—$1,100—if payment is deferred for 15 years. Although the dispute between taxpayer and Treasury appears to involve a tax of $3,500, in reality it is the $2,400 "difference" that they are fighting over.

As in the stock-bonus case, our point here is that the argument over income definition is essentially an argument about whether the tax should be paid sooner or be paid later, not about whether it should be paid at all. But the fact that the tax must be paid at some point obviously does not mean that the parties will be indifferent to when.

Although $2,400 seems a small amount to litigate,[8] in percentage terms the executive actually will have succeeded in reducing his tax burden by more than 68%—from $3,500 down to $1,100—if he can establish his right to the deferral. Once again, the Treasury sees the matter in opposite terms—tax-deferral means an absolute loss of revenue—and it is therefore never content (unless compelled by law) to simply "wait."

More is said about the tax treatment of endowment and other insurance contracts at 2.03, below.

1.02 Forced Saving and Forced Consumption— "Convenience of the Employer"

In the endowment policy case just given the executive was precluded from converting the endowment policy into present cash; neither sale nor pledge of the policy was permitted until retirement. If there was legal doubt about whether the $10,000 premium payment constituted "income" within the meaning of § 61, it was presumably because the taxpayer's freedom of choice had been restricted in the manner indicated. In effect, the executive was "forced" to save for his retirement, whether he wished to or not. Or so it could be argued. By contrast, most people are free—certainly one who receives a straight cash salary is free—to elect any mix of savings and consumption that appeals to him, within the limits of his own resources. This freedom may not rise to the level of a constitutional imperative, but it is certainly a common and desirable attribute of most people's economic lives. If it is constrained in some special way, then possibly he who suffers the constraint should be viewed as less well-off than others, both as a general proposition and for tax purposes.

The point can be illustrated with an example:

Assume an individual's life is limited to two time periods, Year 1 and Year 2. His financial resources consist of $100 cash, which he receives as income at the beginning of Year 1. He expects to earn nothing more for the rest of his "life," *i.e.*, nothing for the balance of Year 1 and nothing at all in Year 2. The individual is free to consume or save at his discretion; that is, he can consume the entire $100 in Year 1 and have nothing left for Year 2 if he chooses, or he can do just the opposite of that, or anything in-between. Finally, any amount which he does not choose to consume in Year 1 will be invested by him in a safe one-year bond at 8%.

Below is a diagram that pictures the full range of available choices. In effect, the individual can choose any pattern of current

---

[8]   The affluent reader should feel free, here and elsewhere in this book, to add as many zeroes as are required to make the problem seem important to him or her.

consumption-and-saving which falls on the diagonal line that connects the two axes. If he chooses to spend everything this year and save nothing for the next, he comes out at point X; if he does just the opposite, he comes out at point Y, since $100 saved and invested this year means that $108 will be available for spending next year. If he wants to spend half and save half, he should select point Z, in which event he would spend $50 this year and have $54 available next year. In any event, the decision is entirely his own, given his initial resources and the prevailing interest rate.

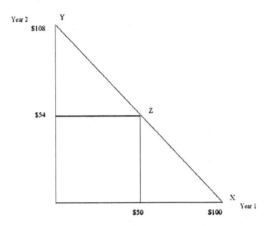

Suppose the executive in the endowment policy case actually desires to consume the entire $100 in Year 1, that is, to come out at point X without a thought for the morrow. An external power (say his employer) overrules him, however, and "compels" the executive to apportion his resources by investing $50 in an 8% bond, which is nonredeemable until the start of Year 2. However prudent this may seem to others, the result is out of accord with the executive's own preference, which is to spend everything at once. So query: should the full $100 of income be taxed in Year 1 even though the taxpayer has derived less than the full measure of personal satisfaction that he would otherwise enjoy? Or should his idiosyncratic nature somehow be taken into account? If so, can we really trust him to be honest about his feelings, and even if we can, what discount factor should the law apply for personal frustration?

Three possible solutions can be conceived of: (1) tax the executive on the full $100 despite the element of forced saving; (2) don't tax the $50 he is forced to save until Year 2 when the bond is cashed in because there is really no way to measure the impact of compulsion; or (3) reduce his $100 of income by some arbitrary figure—say 10%— in an effort to reach a plausible result.

As has been noted, the Code and the cases suggest that the full $100 would be taxed in Year 1. Presumably, all this talk of freedom and compulsion is viewed for what it is—nonsense. If the executive has taken a portion of his annual compensation in deferred retirement benefits, it is because he wants it that way; no other explanation is really credible. The Code does permit deferral of tax in the case of contributions to so-called qualified retirement plans which benefit a substantial proportion of the company's employees (not merely high-paid executives), but this is accomplished by a set of provisions designed specifically to prevent current taxability where the plan meets certain coverage requirements and related conditions.[9] Admittedly also, there is a good deal more that can be said about deferred compensation arrangements (see 11.01). Nevertheless, in the very simple illustration set out above, the result is likely to be the one that we have indicated, despite the apparent element of "forced saving."

In general, then, economic benefit is measured in objective terms for tax purposes; individual preferences, real or feigned, are treated as irrelevant. Yet there are exceptions to this rule, and perhaps the meals-and-lodgings exclusion in § 119 can best be understood as one such. At all events that section—and before its adoption many of the decided cases—excludes from income the value of meals and lodgings furnished to an employee by his employer, provided that the meals and lodgings are furnished on the employer's business premises and for the employer's "convenience." The situation envisaged is one in which the employee is compelled, or at least encouraged, by the exigencies of his job to eat his meals and/or sleep the night on the employer's premises instead of going home (or out to a restaurant, etc.) for the purpose of satisfying those basic wants. One thinks of the hardy lumberjack felling Sitka spruces in the Alaskan wilds, the merchant seaman rolling in his hammock, or the dedicated young intern on night call at his hospital, as probable candidates for the exclusion. Each is compelled to accept the accommodations which his employer provides, because the nature of the taxpayer's occupation excludes any feasible alternative.

But in fact the "convenience of the employer" rule has been extended well beyond hardship cases like these. In a celebrated decision,[10] the manager of a luxury hotel in Hawaii was permitted to exclude from income the value of a hotel suite which he and his wife occupied rent-free, as well as free meals furnished to them in the hotel dining room—altogether costing a regular hotel guest about $8,000 in 1934 (the equivalent of about $150,000 in 2018 dollars). It was established to the satisfaction of the court that the taxpayer's job required him to be present in the hotel, and "on the alert," at all times

---

9   Code § 401 *et seq.*

10   *Benaglia v. Commissioner,* 36 B.T.A. 838 (1937).

of the day and night. Since constant attention to duty was required, the taxpayer's living arrangement was found to have been dictated primarily by the employer's "convenience"; the benefit to the employee was incidental. Accordingly, the value of the meals and lodgings, his wife's along with his own, was not includable in the taxpayer's gross income under the predecessor of § 61. In 1954—seventeen years after the *Benaglia* decision—Congress confirmed the *Benaglia* result by enacting the § 119 exclusion for meals and lodging furnished on the employer's "business premises" and "for the convenience of the employer."[11]

In 2017 Congress enacted § 274(*o*), providing that an employer shall not be allowed a business expense deduction for the cost of any meals provided to employees and excludable by the employees under § 119. (The provision does not apply, however, to the employer's cost of providing housing excludable under § 119.) The effect is a kind of surrogate taxation, with the employer's taxable income overstated (by reason of the deduction denial) by the same amount that the employee's income is understated (by reason of § 119). Section 274(*o*) has a delayed effective date of 2026. In the meantime (from 2018 through 2025) § 274(n) permits the employer to deduct only 50% of the cost of providing meals excludable under § 119.

The emphasis in *Benaglia* and in § 119 on the *employer's* convenience has been questioned by many writers. Thus, why should the employer's motive in furnishing benefits to an employee have any bearing on the tax status of those benefits? An employer's goal is always to produce profits for itself, after all. It pays its employees cash salaries because it wishes to exploit their services for its own purposes; yet this element of "convenience," or advantage, to the employer obviously does not prevent the salaries from being taxable to the employees. Why should non-cash benefits be treated differently, especially when, as here, the benefit takes a form that relieves the recipient of living expenses which he would otherwise have to meet out of his (taxable) cash income? In effect, "the benefit to the employee is no less real because it is a byproduct of the employer's requirements."[12]

Perhaps, however, the "convenience-of-the-employer" rule is really a short-hand way of acknowledging the factor of restricted preference mentioned in connection with the endowment policy case above. In *Benaglia*, as in the endowment policy case, there is an

---

[11] The Supreme Court has held that § 119 applies only to meals received "in kind," but not to unrestricted cash allowances. Thus, a meal allowance paid to state troopers—which they could spend or not as they chose—was found to be "income" under § 61, and not excludable under § 119. *Commissioner v. Kowalski,* 434 U.S. 77 (1977).

[12] Bittker, *The Individual As Wage Earner,* 11 N.Y.U.Tax Inst. 1147 (1953).

element of personal compulsion which raises doubt about the value of the benefit to the recipient. Thus the hotel-manager must live on the hotel premises if he is to do his job (or at least the court in *Benaglia* so found). Yet it seems not unlikely that he would prefer to live more modestly if he were allowed to choose his own accommodations, and it is quite possible that he would elect to save some portion of the equivalent cash receipt. Indeed, his freedom is still further restricted: not only is the hotel-manager forced to consume when he might prefer to save, but he is forced to consume particular goods—hotel food and accommodations—instead of having the same free choice among commodities that is afforded to the rest of us. To be sure, it is difficult to imagine the taxpayer gagging on the dining-room fare or tossing restlessly all night in his canopied bed, but it just might be the case that hotel living grows wearisome over the long term (though, of course, what doesn't?) and that one presently comes to loathe it.[13]

The valuation problem implicit in the *Benaglia* case *might* be approached by asking how much, at a maximum, Mr. Benaglia would be willing to spend for the meals and accommodations furnished to him by his hotel employer. What is the most that he himself would pay for those accommodations as a matter of personal choice and apart from his employment, given that buying one thing necessarily entails giving up something else? Borrowing a term from economics, at what price would his "consumer surplus"—the difference between the market price of the commodity and his greater sense of well-being in acquiring that commodity—be exhausted? Maybe much less than $8,000—say only $3,000 or $4,000. If $4,000 is the most he would pay for the hotel accommodations, having a free choice about it, then perhaps *that* should be the measure of his includable gross income. In the well-known *Turner* case,[14] the taxpayer, whose annual income was a mere $4,536.16, won a name-that-tune prize consisting of four steamship tickets to Rio de Janeiro, which happened to be his wife's place of birth. The Turners and their two children used the tickets and had a lovely trip, but the question was how much should be included in the taxpayer's gross income as a consequence. The Commissioner insisted on $2,200, the retail value of the four steamship tickets. The taxpayer reported income of only $520. The Tax Court, more or less without explanation, found that the "correct" amount was $1,400. Apart from the obvious explanation—that the Court simply split the difference—the decision might be understood to reflect the Court's estimate of the ticket price at which Turner's consumer surplus would hit zero, meaning that any higher price

---

[13] See "Kleinwachter's conundrum" in Simons, *Personal Income Taxation* (1938) at p. 53.

[14] 13 TCM 462 (1954).

would generate a welfare loss as far as Turner was concerned. Given his modest income, $1,400 was as much as the steamship tickets were worth to him—that much, but not a penny more. Plausible? Not very, and the *Turner* decision itself is virtually unique.

The position of the IRS—overwhelmingly supported by the courts in post-*Turner* cases—is that if no exclusion provision (such as § 119) applies, in-kind benefits are taxable at their fair market value, rather than at the taxpayer's lower subjective valuation. The IRS and the courts are clearly right as a matter of policy; taxation on the basis of taxpayers' self-serving claims of low subjective values would be unworkable. But what if a taxpayer in the 35% bracket wins a nontransferable game-show prize with a fair market value of $10,000 and a subjective value of only $3,000? The $3,500 tax on the fair market value would be $500 more than the subjective value; the taxpayer would have to pay $3,500 to enjoy a prize worth only $3,000 to him. Moved by pity, the IRS has ruled that a taxpayer in this situation can avoid the tax by declining to accept the prize.[15] Should the same approach—either pay tax on the fair market value, or avoid the tax by refusing to accept the benefit—also apply to the "convenience of the employer" benefits currently excluded by § 119? Perhaps not, if one cannot renounce § 119-type benefits without also quitting one's job. Apparently Congress feels that a taxpayer should not be forced to choose between taxation at fair market value and a search for a new job, and that the only way to avoid putting a taxpayer to that choice—given the impracticality of subjective value taxation—is to exclude all "convenience of the employer" benefits from gross income. But is Congress right that the only choices are between taxation at fair market value and exclusion? Would it be better to split the difference, in an administrable sort of way, by providing that only (for example) 50% of the fair market value of "convenience of the employer" benefits are includable in gross income? As explained later (¶ 6.02), § 274(n) applies this sort of splitting-the-difference approach to the deductibility of business meals.

Whether all this solicitude for the victims of forced consumption should be taken seriously is, we concede, somewhat doubtful. Nevertheless, the meals-and-lodging exclusion does appear to reflect a willingness, on the part of Congress and the courts, to take account of the possibility that the taxpayer's rewards may be worth less to him than their market value, and to solve the measurement problem that results by valuing the benefit received at zero. That solution is the more striking because the controversy here is of the full forgiveness variety. If the value of meals and lodgings is not taxed

---

[15]   Rev. Rul. 57–374, 1957–2 C.B. 69.

currently, it will not be taxed at all; no subsequent opportunity to include the value of those benefits will arise. From both the taxpayer's and the government's standpoint, therefore, it is really now or never as far as includability is concerned. By contrast, as has been noted, the endowment policy case is in the sooner-or-later category: even if the premium paid by the employer were excluded from the employee's income currently, the proceeds of the policy would ultimately be taxed to the employee when the policy matured.

Quite apart from § 119 and the employer-convenience doctrine, for many years the Treasury, in an exercise of administrative discretion, generally did not attempt to tax employee fringe benefits which were relatively small in value and which were available to higher and lower paid employees alike, despite the absence of any Code provision excluding such benefits from gross income. Free parking or free use of a company gym were typical examples. Strictly speaking, such benefits would seem to constitute "income"; like meals and lodgings, they relieve taxpayers of expense which, if incurred directly, would usually be nondeductible. The administrative decision not to enforce taxation of these items was based on a sense that employees—especially lower-paid employees—would find it exceedingly burdensome to pay taxes in cash on income received in kind, as well as the burden to the Treasury of making the necessary individual assessments. This was an early example of an important phenomenon in the administration of the income tax—occasional decisions by the Treasury and the IRS not to enforce the dictates of the Code in particular areas. An important example is the IRS's announcement (still in effect) that it has no intention of enforcing the taxability of employee-retained frequent flier miles, even though the announcement implies (correctly) that such miles are taxable under the terms of the Code.[16] Because these deviations from the requirements of the Code are in a pro-taxpayer direction, the affected taxpayers are happy to accept the IRS's largesse. And because busybodies do not have standing in tax cases, offended third parties cannot compel the IRS to enforce the law. These administrative "customary deviations" from the Code, although often motivated by understandable concerns for conserving administrative resources and avoiding taxpayer rebellion, raise serious questions about the tax administrators' commitment to the rule of law.[17]

Concerned that the fringe benefit field had grown somewhat unruly, Congress in 1984 added § 132 to the Code, largely codifying what was understood to be existing Treasury practice. Under § 132, an employee's gross income does not include any fringe benefit that

---

[16]   I.R.S. Announcement 2002–18, 2002–10 I.R.B. 621.

[17]   Zelenak, *Custom and the Rule of Law in the Administration of the Income Tax*, 62 Duke L. J. 829 (2012).

constitutes (among other things) a "no-additional-cost service" (*e.g.*, free stand-by flights to airline employees), a "qualified employee discount" (sales of merchandise to store employees at cost), a "working condition fringe" (subscriptions to trade publications, security guard protection), a "de minimis fringe" (occasional supper-money, night-time taxi fare, company picnics, baseball tickets (but not a box for the season), etc.), or a "qualified transportation fringe" (free parking at work, transit passes).[18] The exclusions for "no additional-cost services" and "qualified employee discounts" apply to benefits received by highly-compensated employees only if the same benefits are available on the same terms to rank-and-file employees. The other exclusion categories, however, are not subject to non-discrimination rules. If (for example) an employer provides free parking at work to its executives, the executives can take advantage of § 132 despite the fact that the rest of the employer's work force must pay for parking. While § 132 describes the excludable fringes in considerable detail and effectively insulates such items from any change or extension of Treasury policy, it is equally clear that fringe benefits which do not qualify for exclusion are now includable in gross income (at fair market value) under § 61 unless specifically excluded by some other Code provision. Section 119 would be an example of the latter. Another (of much greater importance) would be § 106, which excludes employer-paid health insurance premiums and is further mentioned at 7.02, below.

The subject of meals and lodgings is considered again at 6.02 in connection with the deduction of "travel expenses" incurred in business. The two topics bear an obvious relationship since, apart from special circumstances, the cost of meals and lodgings is treated by the Code as a "personal, living or family expense" and cannot be deducted from the taxpayer's gross income. Note also that from the taxpayer's standpoint "deduction" and "exclusion" have the same net effect: a dollar excluded from gross income and a dollar deducted from gross income both result in a cash saving equal one dollar multiplied by the taxpayer's marginal tax rate; if the applicable rate is 35%, a dollar excluded and a dollar deducted both produce a saving of 35 cents. Should we therefore expect that the Code will *always* be symmetrical—that if a benefit is excluded when received in kind, it will also be deductible when acquired for cash? The answer—as the next subsection demonstrates—is no.

---

[18] However, § 274(a)(2), added to the Code in 2017, denies an employer any business expense deduction for the cost of providing a qualified transportation fringe benefit to an employee.

A loose end. Even school teachers sometimes get fringe benefits of a sort. In *Haverly v. U.S.,*[19] the taxpayer, a high school principal, received unsolicited textbooks from various publishers, sent in the hope that the taxpayer would adopt the books for classroom use. The taxpayer included nothing in his gross income when he received the books—after all, he hadn't asked for them. Later, however, instead of keeping them for himself, the taxpayer contributed the books to the school library, a qualified charity, and took a charitable deduction of $400, presumably the retail value of the books.

If unchallenged, the two steps together—first an exclusion, but then a deduction of the amount excluded—produce a result that is contrary to tax logic, *viz.,* if you exclude a receipt you can't also deduct it, or if you deduct a receipt you can't also exclude it, since either way you're getting twice the tax benefit to which you would otherwise be entitled. To put the point slightly differently, it makes no sense for the tax system to treat you as giving away something that the tax system never treated you as having received. To illustrate, assume the taxpayer has $400 of taxable salary income. He receives $400 worth of textbooks, which he excludes from gross income. He then deducts $400 for the gift to charity. The deduction offsets his $400 of salary income (the $400 worth of textbooks having already been excluded) and the taxpayer happily finds his taxable income reduced to zero. And all because of the unsolicited textbooks.

Assuming the latter outcome is untenable, there appear to be three ways of correcting it, all with the same result:

#1. Include the value of the books in gross income under § 61. The taxpayer would then have a "cost" for the books equal to the amount included—$400 in Haverly's case—just as if the taxpayer had purchased the books for cash. Having "paid" $400 for the books, a deduction for the subsequent gift to charity would be perfectly appropriate. The "rule" implied by this solution is a simple one: gross income includes any accession to wealth (textbooks as well as salary), whether in cash or in kind, and however derived.

#2. Exclude the books from gross income, but then deny any deduction for the gift to charity. The "rule" implied by this solution is that the charitable deduction shall be limited to the taxpayer's basis for the donated property. Having excluded the value of the books when he received them, the taxpayer would have no "cost" for tax purposes. His basis would be zero, so there would be nothing to deduct.

#3. Exclude the books from gross income and allow the deduction despite the prior exclusion, but treat the gift itself as a

---

[19]   513 F.2d 224 (7th Cir. 1975).

realization equal to the amount deducted. The "amount realized" would be $400. The taxpayer's basis is zero. Hence the gain recognized would be $400. The "rule" implied by this solution is that the deduction of a previously excluded item shall be regarded as a taxable transaction, just as if the excluded item had been sold for cash.

Of the three equivalent solutions, #3 may seem the most strained and artificial (and takes the longest to explain). As it turned out, however, solution #3 was the one the Commissioner argued for in the *Haverly* case. The problem with solution #2 was that the Code as then written[20] did not authorize limiting the charitable deduction to the taxpayer's basis but instead permitted a deduction for the full value of the donated property. And the problem with solution #1 was not lack of authority under § 61, but the hardship for school teachers receiving unsolicited textbooks and the dilemma facing publishers that have no better way to advertise their wares.

Actually, the Commissioner had at one point ruled that mere retention of unsolicited books (by a professional book reviewer) was sufficient to cause their value to be included in gross income. Having no doubt heard loud objections from affected parties, the Commissioner speedily issued a second ruling addressing only the situation of the taxpayer who donated the books to charity and claimed a charitable deduction. Haverly having done precisely that, the Commissioner insisted that he include $400 in his gross income. The Court, citing *Glenshaw Glass*, found that deducting the gift to charity was an exercise by the taxpayer of "complete dominion" over the property in question, and held for the Commissioner.

But wasn't the broader first ruling correct? Strictly speaking, unsolicited textbooks do have ascertainable value, and hence do constitute an "accession to wealth," even if the taxpayer just puts them on his bookshelf. That being so, why did the Commissioner withdraw the first ruling, thus sending the message (to anyone carefully following the saga) that the IRS would not assert taxability in the case of someone who just put his free books on the shelf? Can the Commissioner simply indicate that he does not intend to enforce some aspect of the tax laws? As noted earlier in connection with the Commissioner's pre-1984 treatment of miscellaneous fringe benefits, the Commissioner can and does send that message from time to time. (Even if some third party—say, a highly principled professor of tax law—is outraged by the Commissioner's failure to enforce § 61 in its full scope and majesty, he will not have standing to challenge that

---

[20]   Section 170(e)(1), which would presumably limit the taxpayer's deduction to his basis in the case of free product samples like the textbooks in *Haverly*, had not yet been added when the case arose.

failure in court. And the taxpayer benefitting from the Commissioner's failure will, of course, have no reason to object.) On reflection, the Commissioner must have decided that the administrative effort—identifying the textbook recipients (thousands of school-teachers), persuading them that the books were indeed "income," placing a value on the books, and then checking individual tax returns to be sure the correct amounts were reported—was not worth the auditing expense that such an effort would entail.

If, however, the taxpayer improperly sought a double tax benefit by deducting the excluded item, then, as matter of overriding principle, the Commissioner would insist on including the books in the taxpayer's gross income, presumably in the year for which the deduction was claimed.

1.03 Imputed Income

Another category of benefits "in kind" which are excluded from the coverage of § 61 is "imputed income"—that is, income derived from the use of "household durables" such as a personal residence, car or television, and income from the performance of services for one's own or one's family's benefit. The key to the exclusion is the absence of an exchange. Imputed rental income from property arises from the use of *your own* property, and imputed income from services arises from labor you perform *for yourself* (or for your family). Income from barter *exchanges*, by contrast, is within the scope of § 61. The income tax can thus be understood as a tax on market transactions and on the specialization of labor. A jack-of-all trades who satisfies all his needs by his own efforts owes no income tax.

The imputed income exclusion is much more important in dollar terms than, for example, the meals-and-lodgings exclusion just discussed, and it is therefore slightly astonishing to discover that it rests on no specific Code provision but simply "results" from a long-standing administrative practice of the Internal Revenue Service, which never has attempted to draw imputed income into the tax base. The Service's reasons, historically, may have included some doubt about the constitutionality of treating imputed income as "income," a concern about the valuation problems that would have to be surmounted if it were so treated, and perhaps a sense that the entire concept would be regarded by taxpayers as somewhat strange and theoretical. These reasons may seem less compelling today, but that is not to say that the Service, on its own motion, could now abruptly reverse its practice and require imputed income to be reported by individuals in their tax returns. Whatever its source or its wisdom, the exclusion is by this time of such great age and so deeply embedded in the tax system that it would take Congressional action, explicitly taxing such benefits in some form, to bring about a change.[21] Though not instantly apparent, the imputed income exclusion hooks up in important ways with other features of the tax law—the deduction for home-mortgage interest and for child-care expenses, to name two—and needs to be understood for its role as a building block if nothing else.

The concept of imputed income—and the scope of the exclusion—can be illustrated in two settings, the first involving income from property (the "household durables" mentioned above), the second involving income from services. We may, to begin with, compare two individual taxpayers, A and B, each with $100,000 cash. A invests his money in a house to be used as a personal residence for himself and his family. B buys an identical house but chooses to rent it out to a tenant while he himself lives in a rented apartment somewhere else. The annual rental value of A's house—the sum he would have to pay to a landlord if he himself were not the owner—is $10,000. B's tenant pays *him* $10,000 annually in rent and B pays *his* landlord the same amount. While A's *money* income is thus $10,000 less than B's, their economic incomes are obviously the same and so are their housing expenditures, although both income and expenditure are "imputed" in A's case but take the form of a cash receipt and a cash outlay in B's.[22] Assuming no other relevant differences exist, it seems well arguable that both should pay the same amount in taxes. If the Code's income definition permits A (as it does) to exclude the annual imputed rental value of his residence, then a considerable measure of interpersonal discrimination develops—or, at any rate, the tax law is seen to award a bonus to persons who, like A, prefer to own their own houses, and to impose a corresponding penalty on B-types who prefer to rent.

It follows that if we now desired to treat A and B equally—to achieve "horizontal equity" in the standard phrase—we could do so in one of two ways. Since exclusions and deductions have the same effect in respect to tax savings, we could either enlarge the definition of "income" to include imputed rent (thus requiring A to report $10,000) or else expand the list of personal deductions by permitting B to deduct the $10,000 rent on his apartment. If imputed rents were taxed, or if rental payments could be deducted, the two taxpayers would find themselves on an equal footing. To be sure, neither of these "reforms" is under serious consideration in Congress at

---

[21] For an account of how Congress and Treasury, in the early days of the federal income tax, came surprisingly close to including imputed income from owner-occupied housing in the base of the tax, see Zelenak, *Figuring Out the Tax: Congress, Treasury, and the Design of the Early Modern Income Tax* 205–225 (2018).

[22] Thuronyi, *The Concept of Income*, 46 Tax L. Rev. 45, 84 (1990).

present—the first would be fiercely resented by homeowners, while the second is too costly from the standpoint of the revenues.

As a practical matter, the real question in this field is whether to limit or deny interest deductions on home mortgages, a step that would bring homeowners (at least those with mortgages) and apartment renters much closer together. To understand the precise effect of this proposal requires a detailed comparison of home-owners, renters, and mortgage-payers; such a comparison is provided at 7.04 below.

Imputed income from personal services presents pretty much the same picture and can be mentioned more briefly. The illustration usually employed is that of the uncompensated labor of a full-time homemaking spouse-and-parent. The value of those services, though in some instances a significant fraction of the family's economic income, is obviously not treated as includable "income" under § 61. By contrast, two-earner couples using some of their earnings to pay for equivalent domestic help get no compensating deduction for the amounts expended. The child-care credit, mentioned at 6.01(a), below, represents an effort to modify this disparity, but its scope is limited and it does not purport to be a general solution of the problem.

Yet apart from the housework situation, and perhaps subsistence farming, it is difficult to conceive of any way in which the tax law could reach imputed service income, or any really persuasive reason why it should. Life is full of benefit-producing activities— shaving oneself, mowing one's own lawn, jogging around the block for exercise—which might, at a stretch, be converted into market purchases for cash. But presumably no one would seriously argue that § 61 should be broadened to include such imputations, or that the range of personal allowances should be expanded to permit deduction of their cash counterparts. It is inescapably true that a tax on "income" favors leisure over work—taking "leisure" to refer to all forms of self-rendered benefits, and "work" to mean the sale of one's services to others. But nothing can be done about this bias through modification of the income definition; it is a systematic "unneutrality" that simply cannot be avoided. By contrast, imputed income from property, such as imputed rents from owner-occupied housing, could fairly easily be included in the tax base if we desired to reach it. Hence, the unneutrality between owners and renters is one that we evidently prefer to tolerate and continue—to the extent, that is, that "we" are aware of it.

2. Recovery of Capital Investment

2.01 General Comment; Corporate Stock

Measurement of gain or loss on the sale of property—securities, real estate, etc.—is straightforward. The cost ("basis") of the property sold is first recovered out of the sale proceeds ("amount realized"). Any excess of amount realized over basis is regarded as "gain" and is included in gross income; any shortfall is regarded as "loss" and may be deducted from other income if the property is held for use in business or for investment. But while these rules are easily applied in most cases, there are some situations in which refinement is required, and in which a special cost-recovery "system" needs to be invented to fit the circumstances. It is surprising, indeed, how frequently tax controversies turn on just that issue, namely, which of two (or more) competing cost-recovery systems is appropriate in a particular case. In fact, a fair part of the Code itself is explicitly devoted to the seemingly routine task of *scheduling* the recoupment of invested capital. Once again, as in our endowment policy example, what is at stake in choosing a cost-recovery system is the *timing* of income and hence the anticipation or deferral of tax payments.

Broadly speaking, cost—or basis—recovery problems can be classified as involving (1) instances of partial or periodic dispositions of property, (2) dispositions of divided interests in the same property, (3) "transactions" in human capital, and (4) special concepts of basis aimed at avoiding over- or under-counting of income. This subsection and the next focus on partial or periodic dispositions; subsections 2.03 and 2.04 concentrate on human capital problems. Dispositions of divided interests are illustrated at 4.02 and elsewhere. An important special basis concept—that of adjusting the cost of property to reflect its previous inclusion in income—was mentioned at 1.01; another— the converse of the first—comes up at 3.02; yet a third—the basis of property acquired by gift—at 4.01. The problem of cost-recovery is pervasive.

Corporate stock. As a first and very simple case, assume that an investor buys 100 shares of stock for $5,000 with the expectation that an 8% dividend, or $400, will be paid annually. Of course, dividends may go up or down in the future and the value of the shares when he comes to sell them may be higher or lower than his cost. But let us allow ourselves a little foresight and assume that the taxpayer actually holds the stock for 15 years, that he does receive $400 in annual dividends, and that he finally sells the stock for slightly more than he bought it, say $5,100. How should the annual dividends be treated for tax purposes, and how much gain or loss should be recognized on final sale? Three possibilities can be considered:

(i)   Each annual dividend should be treated as a return of capital until the taxpayer has recovered his entire initial investment. Assuming dividends go along at the expected $400 level, nothing would be included in the taxpayer's income for the first 12½ years; thereafter all further dividends (a total of $1,000) would be included in full. When the stock was finally sold the entire sale price of $5,100 would also be includable in income because the taxpayer's cost would already have been returned to him (*i.e.*, his basis would have been reduced to zero) in the earlier years. In effect, recovery of capital would come *first* under this system and includable income would be deferred.

(ii)   Just the opposite. Annual dividends would be included in income in full (a total of $6,000). When the shares were finally sold, the sale proceeds would be credited against the taxpayer's entire original cost of $5,000, with only the gain of $100 then being recognized as income. Recovery of capital would come *last* under this system and includable income would be anticipated.

(iii) Something in-between. For example, allocate the $5,000 original cost to the future expected dividends by discounting each expected dividend to present value at the 8% rate. Assuming that dividend payments are to be made at 12-month intervals, the first payment would then have a present value at the date the stock was purchased of $370 ($400/1.08), the second $343 [$400/(1.08)^2], the third $318 [$400/(1.08^3)], and so on. In the first year, therefore, $370 would be treated as recovery of capital and $30 as taxable income; in the second and third years, respectively $343 and $318 would be recovery of capital while $57 and $82 would be income. This process would continue until the stock was sold, with each year's payment containing a larger income component than the one preceding it. On sale, the proceeds would be allocated to unrecovered cost—there would always be some—with the excess being recognized as gain.

Depending on one's criteria, there is perhaps something to be said for each of the above alternatives. System (i)—cost recovered first—seems to emphasize the risky character of an investment in securities. It implies that we ought to wait until it can be determined whether the taxpayer has actually made anything from the investment before imposing tax—a perfectly defensible idea from one standpoint. But on the other hand, *should* cost-recovery be a function of risk? If so, investors who buy relatively safe but low-yielding bonds will actually pay their taxes *later* than investors who buy risky but higher-yielding stocks and real estate. At a 5% yield cost-recovery will take 20 years, while at an 8% yield it will take only 12½—which is rather a curious outcome given the emphasis on risk.

System (iii), which looks kind of scientific, avoids the common fallacy of treating income and principal as if they were different things. The $5,000 initial investment, after all, is nothing more than the present value of the expected dividend stream of $400 a year. It is wrong to treat the two as if distinct, and therefore arguably right to allocate the cost of the dividend stream (*i.e.*, the principal) to each successive dividend, rather than only to the earlier ones or only to the final payoff. Once again, the idea is a defensible, if not a compelling, one. Against it (among other things) is the fact that it does require a "finding" as to the investor's anticipated dividend rate, which would frequently be difficult and conjectural.

System (ii)—cost recovered last—is the method which the tax law has adopted. Each annual dividend of $400 is taxed in full, without any adjustment to basis; the original investment is recovered only when the stock is sold. To be sure, the same aggregate amount of income is taxed to the investor under system (ii) as under (i) or (iii)—the totals, both of income ($6,100) and of cost-recovery ($5,000), are identical under all procedures. Under (ii), however, income, and hence tax obligations, are reflected early; under (i) and to a lesser extent (iii), they are deferred.

But why *should* the law choose system (ii) over the others, especially as the Treasury would realize about the same revenues under any system once it got rolling? The answer is that corporate stock is conventionally viewed as an asset of perpetual, or at least indefinite, economic life. The corporation itself, which operates a business of some kind, holds a portfolio of productive assets that depreciate over time and finally "obsolesce." Plant and equipment would be the best examples, but the same would be true of various intangibles such as patents and copyrights. The corporate entity, however, is self-renewing. Thus, management annually sets aside (whether actually or notionally) so much of the company's income as will be needed to fund the purchase of new productive assets when existing assets wear out and have to be replaced—a process that is expected to continue as long as operations remain profitable, that is, indefinitely. Annual dividends, then, represent the excess or residue of the corporation's income *after* making necessary additions to that replacement fund. As a result, the corporation's shares are assumed to retain their earning power from period to period, undiminished by dividend payments. Other things being equal (or static), stock worth $5,000 at the beginning of Year 1 will also be worth $5,000 at the beginning of Year 2, Year 3, etc. A shareholder's principal investment thus remains intact; his shares are, or are regarded as, a perpetuity rather than a wasting asset.

Even more simply, tax rules relating to cost-recovery generally follow ordinary accounting principles. Tax returns are quasi-accounting documents, after all, and the two systems have parallel goals in view, namely, to measure the results of completed activities on an annual basis. For tax (as well as accounting) purposes, the question that is central is: how much did it *cost* the taxpayer to earn the year's gross income? In the case of dividends on corporate stock, the answer, quite obviously, is nothing (other than the opportunity to invest in something else). This follows, once again, because corporate stock is an asset of perpetual life; though it may go up or down in value, it does not "waste" or wear away. The proper cost-recovery rule is therefore pretty much self-evident: an investment in corporate shares can be recovered no earlier than the day on which the shares are sold, for it is only then that their economic value terminates as far as the taxpayer is concerned.

For tax accounting purposes, land is also regarded as an asset of indefinite useful life, because it just lies there, indestructibly, and never completely wears out. The consequence, as with corporate stock, is that land investment is recoverable when the land is sold, not before. As will be seen, the cost of your professional skills (6.03(d)), tuition, books, etc., is not recoverable at all, not because your legal career is assumed to have perpetual life, but because its termination date is indeterminate!

A loose end. The investor above paid $5,000 for 100 shares of stock. Assuming he bought all his shares at one time, his basis per share would be $50. If he now sold 20 of those shares at a price of $60, or $1,200 in total, he would necessarily take the per share cost of $50 as his basis and report a gain of $200. No doubt he would prefer to treat the $1,200 sale price as a non-taxable reduction of his overall stock basis of $5,000, but as each share can be valued and sold independently of the others, the allocation of cost on a share-by-share basis is obviously appropriate. We would face a minor complication if the investor had bought one 50-share lot for $40 a share and a second 50-share lot for $60 a share, the question then being how to determine which lot the 20 shares sold were drawn from. If the taxpayer can satisfy the requirements of Reg. § 1.1012–1(c) for "adequate identification" of the shares sold, the taxpayer can treat the shares sold as coming from the high-basis lot. In the absence of "adequate identification," the same regulation resolves the basis recovery question (usually in the government's favor[23]) by treating the shares sold as coming from the earlier-acquired lot.

---

[23] Kluger v. Commissioner, 617 F.2d 323 (2d Cir. 1980).

The basis allocation problem was more difficult in the *Inaja Land Co.* case.[24] In *Inaja*, the taxpayer bought 1250 acres of riverfront land, together with related water rights, for $61,000 with a view to using the property as a private fishing club. A dozen years later, as part of a water project, the City of Los Angeles began diverting contaminated substances into the river upstream of the taxpayer's property, presumably killing all the fish and rendering the taxpayer's fishing club business worthless. Subsequently, with litigation threatened, the City settled by paying the taxpayer $50,000 for the grant of a perpetual right to continue diverting contamination into the river.

The taxpayer treated the $50,000 payment as a non-taxable recovery of basis. The Commissioner, contending that the payment represented compensation for loss of future business profits, insisted that the entire amount was subject to tax without offsetting basis. Holding for the taxpayer, the Tax Court found that the $50,000 had been paid for the sale of an easement—a right to use the taxpayer's property as a dump—that was essentially an interest in the property itself. As to basis, the Court held that it was impractical to allocate or apportion "cost" to the easement alone. The City's right to contaminate the river could not be isolated in the same convenient manner as a given number of acres or shares of stock, and hence any effort to allocate a set fraction of the taxpayer's cost to the easement was too conjectural to be accepted for tax purposes. The $50,000 would therefore be offset against the taxpayer's total property cost of $61,000, resulting in no present taxable gain and a reduction of basis from $61,000 to $11,000. If the remaining property were finally sold—at least if sold for more than $11,000—the taxpayer's gain could then be accounted for and taxed.

The *Inaja* case is generally criticized. The Tax Court might have developed a unit cost for the water rights by comparing the value of the property before and its value after the City's action and then allocating the overall cost of $61,000 on the same relative basis. Apparently, however, neither the government nor the taxpayer offered any evidence that would have enabled the Tax Court to perform such an allocation. Given the failure of proof by both parties on the basis allocation issue, the case should have been decided against the party with the burden of proof—the taxpayer.[25] The

---

[24]   9 T.C. 727 (1947).

[25]   Although § 7491 (a provision postdating *Inaja* by many years) now provides that the burden of *persuasion* in income tax litigation shifts to the government after the taxpayer "introduces credible evidence with respect to any [relevant] factual issue," the burden of *production*—that is, the burden of "introduc[ing] credible evidence"— always remains on the taxpayer. Because neither party in *Inaja* introduced credible evidence on the basis allocation issue, the burden-of-proof analysis of the case would be the same under § 7491 as under earlier law.

decision does illustrate a fairly common judicial reaction to the difficulty that arises when the recognition of taxable gain requires a valuation of non-marketable property rights. As in *Inaja*, the courts quite often duck the valuation problem by resorting to tax postponement, that is, by deferring recognition until the taxpayer's investment has been fully recovered and gain (or loss) can finally be determined. *Burnet v. Logan*, discussed at 14.03, below, is a famous example. The early treatment of annuities, next following, is another.

2.02 Annuities

Apart from recurring references to depreciation of buildings and equipment, we have yet to offer a case that fully illustrates a pro-rata (that is, a year-by-year) cost-recovery system. Annuities, discussed next, do provide such an illustration. Unlike land or corporate shares, annuities are investments of limited duration. The payout period is often measured by the annuitant's life, or perhaps the joint lives of spouses. At the same time, however, the number of payments actually to be received by the annuitant is uncertain—he may, or he may not, outlive his statistically determined life expectancy. How should the two factors—uncertainty of duration, but certainty of termination—be combined for purposes of determining the annuitant's annual income and the appropriate rate of cost-recovery? That, briefly, is the central problem considered in the subsection immediately following.

An annuity, generically speaking, is any sequence of equal payments made at equal time intervals, such as monthly rents, quarterly dividends, or semi-annual interest payments on a bond. In the present context, however, the term is to be taken to refer specifically to a retirement contract purchased from an insurance company which calls for equal periodic cash payments commencing at a certain date and continuing throughout the annuitant's lifetime. The annuitant pays a premium, or a series of premiums, to the company, which payment becomes the principal of the annuity very much like the principal of a loan. That investment earns interest in the hands of the company, and in return the company guarantees to make stated payments to the annuitant for life. The cost of the annuity—the premium—depends on the annuitant's life expectancy as derived from standard mortality tables. The annuitant may or may not outlive that term, of course, but the insurance company, which issues many such contracts, expects mortality gains and losses among annuitants to balance each other out. A particular annuitant thus gambles his longevity against that of the other annuitants, while the company serves as stake-holder for the group.

It is obvious that the payments made to the annuitant over the term of the contract must, from the company's point of view, come partly from the premium paid and partly from the earnings on that amount. From a tax standpoint, therefore, the question is the (by now) familiar one: how much of each annual payment should be treated as taxable interest-income, and how much as tax-free return of capital? And again—as the reader will anticipate with a groan— there are various scheduling alternatives that can be conceived of. We need not make our own listing this time, however, because the Code itself, having varied in its treatment of annuities over the years, has pretty well rung all the changes on our customary theme of sooner-or-later.

The Code history can be summarized quickly. In the early days the law did not tax annuity payments at all until the annuitant had received an aggregate amount equal to his entire investment in the contract—rather like the easement case discussed in section 2.01. As with installment transactions generally, the theory was that capital must be returned in full before there could be any income to be taxed by way of "profit." The result, of course, was to postpone the recognition of interest until the later years of the contract, or, in cases where the annuitant died prematurely, to avoid such recognition altogether.

In 1934, Congress altered the rules on annuities to require that a taxpayer receiving annual payments under an annuity contract include in annual income a fixed percentage—3%—of the cost of the annuity. The balance of each annual payment was regarded as return of capital until the annuitant's cost had been recovered. While this approach properly recognized that every payment includes an interest component, in the end it, too, proved unsatisfactory. In particular, where the premium paid in by the annuitant represented a large proportion of the value of the annuity at the time the payments began, the 3% rule generally overstated the income component and caused the rate of cost-recovery to be too slow. Thus, in a well-known case sustaining the constitutionality of the 3% rule,[26] an annuitant aged 45, with a life expectancy of 28 years, purchased for a premium of $100,000 a right to receive approximately $5,000 a year for life. Since under the 3% rule $3,000 a year was includable in income and only $2,000 was regarded as return of capital, the annuitant would have had to live 50 years from the date of purchase in order to recover his investment.

The 3% rule thus confronted some annuitants with well-nigh impossible longevity requirements, and it was replaced in 1954 by Code § 72, which contains the present treatment of annuities. The general purpose of § 72 is to impute the contractual rate of interest to the annuitant, instead of fixing a statutory rate which might turn

---

[26]   *Egtvedt v. U.S.*, 112 Ct.Cl. 80 (1948).

out to be excessive or inadequate. In the case just mentioned, for example, the annual cost-recovery factor would be determined by dividing the annuitant's investment in the contract ($100,000) by the aggregate of the payments to be received during his statistically anticipated lifetime (28 × $5,000 = $140,000). The result is an exclusion factor of 5/7ths ($100,000/$140,000), with the balance of each payment being includable in income. The annual payment of $5,000 would thus consist of about $3,570 (5/7 × $5,000) of capital and $1,430 of taxable income. An annuitant who lived to exactly his life expectancy would recoup his entire $100,000 investment tax-free and pay tax only on receipts in excess of that amount.

But suppose the annuitant died too early or lived too long. Are gains (from long life) or losses (from early demise) taken into account? Prior to the 1986 Act they were not; mortality gains and losses were simply disregarded by the Code. Thus long-lived annuitants continued to exclude a proportion of each annual payment from income even though their cost had already been recovered in full, while short-lived annuitants were denied a deductible loss. The Treasury, like an insurance company, came out about even on this, although individual annuitants obviously gained or lost at one another's expense. In effect, the basic gamble among annuitants was simply extended to include the tax consequences.[27]

Feeling, apparently, that the question of mortality gains and losses should be resolved in terms of individual taxpayers rather than annuitants as a group, Congress in 1986 amended § 72 so as to recognize such gains and losses for tax purposes. Under § 72(b), an annuitant who dies prematurely can deduct his unrecovered cost on his final tax return. An annuitant who survives his anticipated mortality date—and who, therefore, will have recovered his investment in full during life—must include in income the entire amount that he receives in subsequent years, *i.e.*, without exclusion. Strictly in terms of tax logic, the new system is more accurate than the old. Each annuitant is now allowed to recover no more and no less than the actual cost of her annuity, regardless of how long she happens to live. On the other hand, perhaps the previous system made more sense from a social policy perspective. Imagine the perplexity and dismay of an annuitant who, under current law, outlives his life expectancy and discovers the taxable income from his annuity has increased (because his basis recovery has ceased) even though the amount of his annuity payments has not.

Setting social policy concerns aside, does the current system make sense? Yes and no. While the income (interest) element is correctly determined by § 72 in overall terms, the scheduling of

----

27   See A.L.I. *Fed. Inc. Tax Stat.* (Feb. 1954) v. I., p. 252.

income and recovery of capital can still be questioned. As anyone knows who has ever paid off a home mortgage, interest always bulks very large in the early years (with repayment of principal correspondingly small), while the reverse relationship holds true of payments towards the end. Since the annuitant is in the position of a lender to the insurance company, just as the bank is a lender to the home-buyer, a more accurate view of the apportionment between income and principal would result in higher tax payments (more income) in the earlier years than in the later. Suppose, for example, that an annuitant's life expectancy is only three years (to keep the illustration brief). He purchases an annuity for $50,000 with interest at 5%, which entitles him to equal annual payments of $18,360.43 starting in Year 1. The resulting schedule of receipts—viewed apart from § 72—would look like this:

Period	(1) Outstanding principal at beginning of period	(2) Payment	(3) Interest due at end of period [5% of (1)]	(4) Principal repaid at end of period [(2)–(3)]
1	$50,000.00	$18,360.43	$2,500.00	$15,860.43
2	34,139.57	18,360.43	1,706.98	16,653.45
3	17,486.12	18,360.43	874.31	17,486.12
Total		$55,081.29	$5,081.29	$50,000.00

In effect, the annuitant's income for the first year is $2,500, for the second year $1,706.98, and for the third $874.31. Under § 72, however, the annuitant's cost of $50,000 is recoverable on a level basis—$16,666.67 a year—so that his includable income is $1,693.76 in each of the three years. The result is that income of about $807 is deferred from the first year to the third (and about $13 from the second year to the third). Even though the illustration involves a time-span of just three years, the "value" of the deferral (positive to the taxpayer, negative to the Treasury) is quite considerable in percentage terms. Thus, the tax on $807 is $282 at a 35% rate. Since payment is deferred for two years, the annuitant can meet his obligation by setting aside (whether actually or mentally) only $242 at the end of Year 1 (assuming, as usual, an 8% interest rate). The "saving"—$40—is equivalent to a 5-point reduction in the applicable tax-rate. This saving measures the benefit to the taxpayer (cost to the Treasury) of allowing the annuitant to recover his investment at a level rate instead of on an ascending basis as column (4) of the above schedule would require.

While all of this is slightly tiresome, it may help (a) to remind the reader about the effect of income-deferral, discussed at 1.01 above, and (b) to prepare the reader for our discussion of depreciation at 6.08, where the same sort of analysis will be proposed.

2.03 Life Insurance

Everyone would agree, we suppose, that the purpose of buying life insurance is to provide funds to replace the earning capacity of the insured in the event that he dies during his working life. If family savings were large enough to maintain accustomed living standards without the insured's earnings, as they might be in the case of a very wealthy family, then presumably insurance would be unnecessary and the amounts otherwise expended on annual premiums could be devoted to other uses. That, of course, is not the general case, and as a result most people consider insurance to be an important element of family finance. But insurance—in the pure sense of protection against early death—is obviously not a substitute for savings. Once the breadwinner reaches retirement age and his earnings from employment come to an end, pure insurance protection ceases to be useful. The source of family income has then got to be some form of savings—accumulated cash or securities, pension benefits funded by one's employer, social security, and so on. Family financial planning thus normally entails a two-fold obligation: insurance protection in case death occurs prior to retirement, and a savings plan to meet post-retirement needs and for bequests.

It happens that life insurance can (and perhaps for most insurance buyers still does) help to accomplish both objectives. In the case of ordinary whole-life or endowment insurance policies, the insured's annual premium partly goes to buy pure protection against premature death—the so-called *term* feature of the insurance contract—and partly also to build up the cash value of the policy itself—the contract's *savings* feature. If the death of the insured occurs very early on, the policy proceeds payable to his beneficiary will consist almost entirely of pure insurance; if very late, almost entirely of savings plus accumulated interest; if in the middle, some of each. One can, of course, buy protection alone in the form of term insurance, and a good many people do just that. But since term insurance returns nothing if the insured survives the expiration of the term, presumably the family will be obliged to do its saving in some other way.

To illustrate the financial elements involved, suppose a man age 40 buys a 25-year endowment insurance policy with a face value of $100,000 at an annual premium of $3,500. The company promises to pay the face of the policy to the named beneficiary if the insured dies within 25 years, or to pay the face of the policy to the insured himself at the end of 25 years if he survives. Suppose the insured dies at the end of 15 years and his beneficiary collects the $100,000 face amount. The following is the allocation of proceeds between pure insurance and savings-plus-interest, as well as a calculation of the insured's mortality "gain":

1.	Total premiums paid ($3,500 × 15)		$52,500
2.	Actuarial cost of term insurance		18,000
3.	Cash value (terminal reserve):		
	Cash reserve fund (1–2)	34,500	
	Interest at 4%	<u>8,000</u>	42,500
4.	Proceeds allocable to term insurance ($100,000 – 42,500)		57,500
5.	Net mortality gain (4–2)		<u>39,500</u>

To summarize, the $100,000 of insurance proceeds consists of three elements: (1) $34,500 of paid-in-cash reserves, (2) $8,000 of accumulated interest, and (3) $57,500 of pure insurance of which $39,500 represents the excess over allocable term insurance premiums of $18,000.

Are any or all of these elements subject to income tax? The answer is no. Code § 101(a) provides a blanket exclusion for insurance proceeds payable by reason of death, so that the entire face amount of $100,000 is received tax free by the insured's designated beneficiary. Does the exclusion make sense—in tax terms, that is, and apart from considerations of personal bereavement and the like? Insofar as the cash reserve fund of $34,500 is concerned, it pretty clearly does. That fund, paid in by the insured, is the simple equivalent of a bank account which is left by will to the decedent's heir, and if one accepts that gifts and bequests are properly (or at least plausibly, see 4.01) excluded from the recipient's income, exclusion here is consistent and proper as well. But the other two components of the policy proceeds—term insurance and accumulated interest—appear to be within the reach of § 61, and their exclusion is open to question.

Thus the policy-holder in our illustration realized a mortality gain of $39,500; in effect, the insured and his family have "won" their gamble with the mortality tables, as compared with other policy-owners who survive the 25-year term. As noted, the term feature of the policy serves to replace the future earnings that are lost by reason of the insured's premature death. While the family is thus made whole financially, and there is a recovery of human capital in cash form, it should not be overlooked that the future earnings themselves would have been subject to tax as wages, salary, etc., had the decedent lived to realize them. Policy-owners who do survive are, of course, taxed on their earnings in the usual way; so that as between longer-and shorter-lived individuals, or as between earned income and mortality gains, the tax law favors the latter against the former.

Or does it? If the law were to aim at equal treatment of all policy-owners, shorter-and longer-lived alike, it presumably would require that the proceeds of term insurance be included in the income of the beneficiary, but at the same time permit *all* term-insurance buyers to deduct their allocable premiums as costs incurred for the protection of taxable income. Decedents (or their beneficiaries) would then be taxed on their net mortality gains; survivors would be taxed on their net earnings. This alternative treatment—of deductions for term insurance premiums and taxation of term insurance proceeds—sounds very different from the actual rules of nondeductibility of premiums and exclusion of proceeds. In fact, however, the two systems will produce equivalent results if (1) the same tax rate applies for purposes of the premium deduction and the proceeds inclusion under the alternative treatment, and (2) taxpayers take the applicable tax regime into account in selecting the nominal amount of their insurance coverage. Suppose that, under the current tax rules, a taxpayer in the 20% bracket would choose to buy $100,000 of term insurance at a premium cost of $1,000. Because there are no tax consequences to either the premium payment or the receipt of policy proceeds, his after-tax premium cost is the same as his pre-tax cost ($1,000), and the after-tax proceeds (if any) will be the same as the pre-tax proceeds ($100,000). Under the alternative set of tax rules, he could replicate these results by paying a $1,250 premium (at an after-tax cost of $1,000, taking into account the $250 tax savings from the $1,250 deduction) for coverage of $125,000 (which translates to after-tax coverage of $100,000, taking into account the $25,000 tax on the proceeds).[28] But what if the tax rate applicable to policy proceeds is higher than the tax rate against which premium deductions are taken? Suppose, for example, the taxpayer is currently in the 20% bracket, but that the policy proceeds—because of their large amount—would be taxed in the 35% bracket. This would make no difference, of course, under current law. The taxpayer would still pay $1,000 (nondeductible) for $100,000 of coverage (nontaxable). Under the alternative system, however, if the taxpayer pays a $1,250 premium (at an after-tax cost of $1,000), and the pre-tax policy proceeds are $125,000, the after-tax proceeds will be only $81,250 ($125,000 reduced by tax of $43,750). It is only because of the

---

[28] This is an example of the equivalency, under a single ("flat") tax rate structure, of a wage tax (exemplified by the current tax treatment of term life insurance) and a consumption tax (exemplified by the alternative system). For an explanation of this equivalency, see the "Note" at p. 493, "Income Tax, Consumption Tax, Flat Tax."

possibility that different tax rates may apply to the premiums and to the proceeds that there is any real difference between the no-tax-consequences regime of current law and the deduction-and-inclusion alternative.

The exclusion of the $8,000 of accumulated interest on the cash reserves raises still more serious questions of tax policy because its realization has nothing particularly to do with the "forced" element of premature death, family bereavement and so on. Cash value, including interest, can be realized through surrender of the policy at any time prior to maturity, and as such is fully available to the decedent throughout his lifetime. Here the most striking comparison is between insurance owners and investors in other kinds of interest-bearing debt, such as bonds or savings accounts. The latter are taxed year-by-year as interest accrues, whether the annual accruals are withdrawn or left to compound. Taxability extends even to the purchaser of bonds issued at a discount, where no annual cash payments are made at all and "interest" is represented by the yearly increase in the value of the bond itself.[29] To be sure, most people who buy insurance do not regard the annual increase in the policy's cash value as in the category of currently available funds, though no doubt some do. But this element of "attitude" and voluntary forbearance hardly seems an adequate basis for the exclusion of very large amounts of interest income. Yet no better reason—other, of course, than a Congressional desire to shield insurance buyers from tax—can easily be proposed.

Moving to the survivors' side again, what about those policy owners who outlive the 25-year period and who then receive the face amount of the policy as a straight refund of savings plus interest? Is there tax symmetry at this point as between longer- and shorter-lived policy-holders? Section 72(e)(1) requires that the proceeds of a matured policy be included in income, but only to the extent that such proceeds exceed the *total* of the premiums paid by the insured. In our illustrative case, therefore, the $100,000 of proceeds would be offset by $87,500 of premiums ($3,500 × 25), and $12,500 would be includable in the policy-owner's income. Once again, survivors are treated less generously than decedents in the sense that interest accumulations may finally be subject to tax, though the tax is still deferred until the policy proceeds are drawn down, usually at maturity. On the other hand—adding one anomaly to another—the $12,500 figure may well fall short of the total interest that has accrued, because the premiums, which are allowed to be credited against the amount received, partly went to pay the cost of the term feature of the policy. By contrast, if the insured had purchased term

---

[29]   § 1272, discussed at 17.04(b), below.

insurance separately, none of the premiums paid would offset his return from other forms of savings, because insurance premiums are a nondeductible personal expense.

The exclusionary system is thus something of a tangle, though its main component (the exclusion of proceeds paid on death) is plain enough and there is a heavy flavor of condolence about the whole affair. As noted, the Code distinguishes between decedents and survivors by permitting the former to exclude all accumulated interest plus mortality gains. More generally, the law, by allowing interest on cash reserves to accumulate tax-free, substantially "prefers" insurance to most other forms of savings, and we can therefore add life insurance to homeownership as a source of tax-favored investment income.[30]

2.04 Damage Awards

(a) Personal Injury

One way to view the exclusion of insurance proceeds under § 101(a) is to say that the exclusion serves as a proxy or substitute for a system of depreciating human capital. As will be seen (6.03(d)), the Code does not permit the costs of professional training or skills-acquisition to be deducted, either currently or over the individual's career life in the form of an annual depreciation allowance. In addition, all sorts of work-connected expenses—commuting, restaurant lunches, a new suit—are disallowed as "personal," although in many instances such costs are incurred solely because of the demands made by the taxpayer's job. As against these disallowances, however, the Code does afford certain compensating tax benefits which relate to retirement, death and disability, and which in some measure take the place of an earned-income allowance or of "personal" depreciation. Thus, income which is dedicated to the taxpayer's retirement—contributions to qualified employee pension

---

[30] The term "tax preference" is often used to describe statutory (or administrative) rules that exclude certain types of income from the tax base by reference to their source. As noted, interest on municipal bonds, interest accumulations on insurance policies, imputed rents from home-ownership—these and various other kinds of benefits, though within the meaning of "income", are specifically exempted from tax (in whole or in part) for reasons of national policy.

Many have argued that tax preferences are inequitable because they favor some taxpayers over others; also, that preferences are inefficient—cost too much—in carrying out the goals that Congress has in view. See Surrey, *Pathways to Tax Reform* (1973); compare Bittker, *A "Comprehensive Tax Base" as a Goal of Income Tax Reform*, 80 Harv.L.Rev. 925 (1967); and see Graetz, *Legal Transitions: The Case of Retroactivity in Income Tax Revision*, 126 U.Pa.L.Rev. 47 (1977). While broad issues of this sort are scanted in the present volume, in a "Note" at p. 485 we do try to answer one question that students often ask about tax preferences, namely: if tax preferences are so good, why doesn't *everybody* buy tax-preferred assets? The "Note" explains why tax preferences are largely taken over by upper-bracket taxpayers and considers also whether there is anything left of a preference once the market gets through with it.

plans, for example—is often permitted to be deferred until retirement occurs and actual payouts begin. As has been seen, death benefits— chiefly term insurance or its equivalent—which replace the decedent's future earnings, are usually excluded from income entirely. These tax concessions can hardly be described as a systematic effort to deal with the problems of retirement and death— there are anomalies in every direction—but the range of items covered is so considerable that the absence of a thoroughly articulated scheme of tax relief may not matter very much in the end.

The economic consequences of personal injury bear an obvious resemblance to those which result from premature death, and it will not surprise the reader to learn that damage awards (from individual tortfeasors or through worker's compensation) are excluded from the recipient's gross income under Code § 104(a). Although such awards obviously serve among other things to replace lost earnings, and although such earnings would otherwise be taxable when received (indeed, *are* taxable to one who receives them in the normal course of his employment), the analogy to term insurance is easily drawn and the two exclusionary provisions, § 101(a) and § 104(a), are consistent in their premises and goals.

Section 104(a)(2) specifically excludes "any damages (other than punitive damages) received ... on account of personal physical injuries or physical sickness." In addition to lost earnings, the major elements of actual damages in physical injury tort cases are medical expenses and pain-and-suffering. The exclusion applies to all three types of actual damages. The policy justification for the exclusion of medical expense damages is straightforward. Medical expenses are deductible under § 213 (7.02(a)), and the exclusion serves in lieu of an inclusion followed by an offsetting medical expense deduction. In keeping with this policy rationale, § 104(a) provides that the exclusion does not apply to damages on account of medical expenses incurred and deducted by the taxpayer in an earlier year. The policy justification for the exclusion of pain-and-suffering damages is a bit more complicated. Pain-and-suffering damages are a sort of forced sale of the taxpayer's good health (or freedom from pain). Under ordinary circumstances, a taxpayer has no cost basis in her good health. But for § 104(a)(2), then, the entire proceeds of the forced sale would seem to be includable in gross income, with no reduction for recovery of basis. While this treatment could be justified in terms of cold tax logic, it seems harsh, considering that (1) the tort victim didn't *want* to convert her good health to cash, and (2) most people are never forced to convert their good health to cash and consequently never have to pay tax on the value of their good health. To create tax parity between those who are forced to sell their good health and those who are not, § 104(a)(2) excludes pain-and-suffering damages from gross income. What about someone who *consents*, in return for cash compensation, to an injury of a sort that would be covered by § 104(a)(2) if caused by a tortfeasor—someone who, for example, sells (illegally) a kidney? Because the compensation for the consented-to injury does not qualify as "damages," § 104(a)(2) does not apply. Assuming (as will almost surely be the case) the taxpayer can establish no basis in his kidney, the entire amount he receives will be includable in gross income. The congressional solicitude is limited to those who *involuntarily* sell their good health.[31]

The word "physical" was added to § 104(a)(2) in 1996 in order to resolve a prior ambiguity about the scope of the exclusion, one that generated a long and turgid series of litigated cases. The section previously referred merely to "personal injuries" without being limited to injuries of a physical nature. The Commissioner took the position that damages for non-physical injuries, such as defamation, malicious prosecution and, more recently, deprivation of civil rights under federal or state statutes, fell outside of the exclusion and were to be treated as taxable or non-taxable depending on whether they did or did not constitute "gross income" under § 61. By and large, the courts were unsympathetic to the government's view and generally held that damages for non-physical injury resulting from the commission of a tort were excludable under § 104(a)(2) as then written.[32] Apparently concerned that the exclusion was in danger of being pushed too far—*e.g.*, downsized employees seeking to exclude their severance pay as damages for "emotional distress"—Congress amended the section to provide that the exclusion shall be limited to damages received on account of physical injury or illness only.

The excludability of punitive damages has also been litigated. An earlier amendment made it clear that punitive damages for non-physical injury—a TV star awarded punitive damages for a lurid tabloid story—were not within the exclusion, but the status of punitive damages for physical injury was uncertain. In the 1996 *O'Gilvie* case,[33] the Supreme Court made it clear that punitive damages, designed to punish the offender rather than compensate the victim, are includable in income no matter what the nature of the taxpayer's injury, and the subsection now confirms or codifies that holding.

---

[31]   *Perez v. Commissioner*, 144 T.C. 51 (2015) (taxpayer who voluntarily sold some of her ova to infertile couples could not exclude the payments she received as "damages" under § 104(a)(2)).

[32]   *Threlkeld v. Commissioner*, 87 T.C. 1294, *aff'd*, 848 F.2d 81 (6th Cir. 1988) (excluding damages for malicious prosecution). But see *Commissioner v. Schleier*, 515 U.S. 323 (1995) (holding § 104(a)(2) did not apply to damages received under the Age Discrimination in Employment Act).

[33]   *O'Gilvie v. U.S.*, 519 U.S. 79 (1996).

(b)   Commercial Damages

Damage recoveries obviously arise out of involuntary transactions—a forced taking rather than an intended realization—and, as stated, it is not surprising that the Code should supply relief to the victim in some form. The latter observation is partly borne out even in the case of damage to tangible property, such as buildings or equipment. If the taxpayer's recovery (usually insurance proceeds) for damage done to his property just equals his basis in the property, then of course no gain results. If the amount recovered exceeds the property's basis, both quantities being readily ascertainable, the excess is taxable just as it would be if realized through sale. Still, the occasion for realization is imposed on the taxpayer, not chosen, and it seems unfair to require him to pay tax currently on the appreciation of business assets which he did not intend to dispose of, particularly if the cash received as damages or insurance is promptly put back into new assets of equivalent function. Accordingly, if a taxpayer, within a specified time period, reinvests the proceeds of an "involuntary conversion" in business property of a similar character, Code § 1033 allows him to exclude the gain that would otherwise be recognized. As the intention is merely to postpone such recognition—rather than, as in the case of personal physical injury, to forgive the tax entirely—the section requires the taxpayer to carry over the basis of the old property to the newly acquired property, regardless of the latter's actual cash cost.

Ironically in view of this concern for forced realizations, the leading case in the field of commercial damage awards—*Raytheon Production Corp. v. Commissioner*[34]—is one in which the proceeds qualified neither for exclusion under § 104 (since a corporate taxpayer was involved) nor, apparently, for the postponement relief afforded by § 1033. The taxpayer, a manufacturer of radio tubes, had received an award of damages in an antitrust suit which arguably represented compensation for the destruction of business "goodwill"—that is, profitable relations with potential customers. The award was held to be fully taxable. Section 1033 would apparently have been inapplicable (actually, the section had not yet been enacted) because no similar or like property could readily be acquired—apart, perhaps, from the purchase of another company in the same field of activity.

These results, which otherwise look rather stern, may perhaps be explained on the ground that the costs of generating the taxpayer's goodwill had already been deducted by it in earlier years. Such costs would have consisted chiefly of the company's annual outlays for advertising, public relations and sales promotion, as well as research

---

[34]   144 F.2d 110 (1st Cir. 1944).

and development.[35] Assuming that those outlays were treated as currently deductible expenses, Raytheon in effect would already have offset the costs incurred in building up its goodwill against ordinary taxable business income. Its basis for the goodwill said to have been damaged therefore quite properly was zero, for if the costs of acquiring the asset had previously been deducted, a double benefit would result if the same costs were to be included in basis when the asset was sold or "converted." By contrast, outlays by individuals to acquire professional skills through education and training are generally disallowed as "personal." If this disallowance of training expenses helps to explain why the Code does not tax damages for loss of an individual's earning capacity, then the earlier deductibility of the advertising and related expenses may also serve to explain why the court in *Raytheon* reached the opposite result.

Perhaps the unavailability of § 1033 relief has a related justification. To be sure, the company would be required to take the entire antitrust recovery into current income without an apparent opportunity for deferral. But if it subsequently determined to reacquire the goodwill lost—as § 1033 assumes—this would be done, again, through advertising and sales promotion. Such expenses being deductible when incurred, one would expect that expenditures for restoration of the company's goodwill would offset income equal to the damage award within a relatively brief period of time. The overall effect would then differ little from the pattern of relief afforded by the section itself.

———

A loose end. Suppose an individual taxpayer, injured in an auto accident, accepts a transfer of Blackacre from the tortfeasor in lieu of cash damages. Blackacre has a value of $20,000 at the date of transfer, and is later sold by the taxpayer for $25,000. How much gain is taxed on the sale, *i.e.*, what is the taxpayer's basis for Blackacre? The taxpayer has invested no money of his own in the property; nor, by reason of § 104(a), was the property included in his gross income. His basis, nevertheless, presumably is $20,000 and only $5,000 is recognized as gain. The reason: § 104(a) is not a postponement but a forgiveness provision, and a zero basis would mean that the damage award of $20,000 would ultimately be taxed, contrary to the Code's intention. Congress might have limited the tax-relief for personal injury awards to deferral, as it did in the case of property damage under § 1033, by requiring the recipient of cash damages to purchase an annuity or the like. But in fact it went further and forgave the tax on personal injury awards entirely.

---

[35] See *infra*, 6.03(b).

3. Increase in Net Worth—Cancellation of Indebtedness

3.01 General Comment

Borrowing money does not create income to the borrower or loss to the lender since each party has the same net worth before and after the loan transaction. The lender exchanges cash for the borrower's promise to pay interest and principal at fixed dates, and the borrower receives cash but issues his "bond." When repayment of principal occurs at maturity—everything else being equal—the transaction is simply reversed, cash replaces obligation, and again there is no element of taxable income or allowable loss.[36]

The pattern is thus a simple one. Nevertheless, loan transactions have generated a number of interpretative problems—largely on the borrower's side—which have seemed important enough in some instances to merit review by the Supreme Court. A few of these are briefly detailed in the paragraphs immediately following. Yet another problem—cancellation of indebtedness income—is reserved for 3.02.

(a) Effect of Inflation

In *Bowers v. Kerbaugh-Empire Co.*,[37] the taxpayer had borrowed money on its subsidiary's behalf which was repayable in German marks. When the time came to repay, the mark had declined in value so that the dollar-cost of paying off the loan was less than the dollar-value of the loan at the time the funds were borrowed. The government contended that the difference was taxable income. Although the Supreme Court held for the taxpayer on the ground that the subsidiary's unsuccessful business operations had actually produced an overall loss for its parent, the Court apparently accepted that a gain resulting from foreign currency inflation will generally qualify as "income" within the meaning of § 61.

The latter conclusion is, of course, exactly what one would expect—banks and others who speculate in foreign exchange, like speculators in any other kind of "security," are plainly taxable on their gains and can deduct their losses. Such gains and losses, however, reflect changes in the purchasing power of the dollar relative to the purchasing power of other currencies, and this enables us to ask more generally how gains and losses attributable to dollar inflation (or dollar deflation) are treated under the tax law. The question is especially relevant to debtors and creditors in a period of

---

[36] Interest paid on the loan is of course includable in the lender's income and (subject to a variety of limitations; see 6.06) deductible by the borrower.

[37] 271 U.S. 170 (1926).

rapid inflation. Unless actual inflation is fully anticipated in the interest rate, debts repaid in inflated dollars may obviously entail a gain of some sort to the debtor and a corresponding loss to the creditor. Are such gains and losses normally reflected in income under § 61, that is, apart from dealings in foreign exchange?

To illustrate the inflation problem, suppose that D borrows $1,000 from C to be repaid one year later. D promptly invests the $1,000 in a tangible asset, say land. Assume that an inflation of 12% occurs during the ensuing 12-month period, so that at the time the loan matures the sum of $1,120 would be required to restore to C the same real purchasing power that he parted with when the loan was made. Assume also that owing to the inflation D's land has appreciated to a value of $1,120 by the same date, though of course the value of the property in real terms is entirely unchanged.

Suppose, as one alternative, that D elects to refinance his obligation at the end of the year by borrowing $1,000 from a second lender and using that sum to pay off his debt to C. Has D made a gain? The answer is clearly affirmative: his equity in the land, which was zero at the time the property was purchased, is now $120. But does he have taxable income? The reader's intuition, we would guess, is that he does not.

As a second alternative, suppose that instead of merely refinancing, D sells the property outright for $1,120 cash, pays C $1,000 in satisfaction of the debt, and retains the balance of $120 for himself. Once again, D has made $120. This time, however, the reader's probable intuition is that the gain will be includable in D's gross income.

In both cases, as it happens, the intuition is correct. Curiously, however, it is not D's economic income that is ever taxed in either case. D's real gain is traceable solely to the loan repayment. Inflation enables D to repay $1,120-worth of borrowed funds (*i.e.*, the $1,000 of borrowed year-one dollars, which equate to $1,120 in year-two dollars) using only $1,000 (of year-two dollars). The effect is the same as if there had been no inflation but the face amount of C's claim had been reduced by $120. Yet that transaction, taken by itself, is tax-free as the refinancing example shows. By contrast, the taxable gain in the second example is traceable solely to the sale of the property for cash, although in real terms the property is worth no more when sold than when D purchased it a year earlier. We must conclude, then, that only the *number* of dollars counts for tax purposes, while the presence or absence of actual (*i.e.*, inflation-adjusted) gain is disregarded. The loan-repayment in our example generates real income to D but no dollar increment; the property sale produces a dollar increment but no income in real terms; yet the latter is taxed and the former is not.

We are not suggesting that anything can easily be done to resolve this dilemma. The required adjustments, though not hard to conceptualize in our simple case, would entail considerable complexity if brought to bear on all transactions and on all taxpayers.[38] Still, the problem is a serious one: a tax mechanism which measures gains and losses in nominal dollars operates poorly during periods of sharp inflation, and the effect is especially visible in the case of borrowers, lenders and property-owners generally.

At the least, the example just discussed should serve as background for the issues considered in 3.02. As will be seen, discharge of indebtedness may indeed result in taxable income where the *number* of dollars paid to the creditor is actually fewer than the number borrowed. The borrower's gain—as in *Kerbaugh-Empire*—can then be measured conveniently as a dollar increment. Yet, as suggested, the much larger instance of debt-cancellation income—which occurs when loans are nominally repaid in full, but with inflated dollars—escapes tax entirely, owing to the failure of the tax system to adjust for changes in the general price level.

The astute reader may recall that this book's "Introduction" described how § 1(f) of the Code indexes the various tax rate schedules for inflation, in order to prevent "bracket creep." Yet the preceding discussion claims that the federal income tax is *not* indexed for inflation. So which is it—is the income tax inflation-indexed, or is it not? It is and it isn't. In the absence of indexing, inflation would have two types of effects on the income tax; current law adjusts for one type of effect but not the other. The *tax rate* schedule is indexed for inflation, thus preventing inflation from pushing taxpayers into higher rate brackets. But the various provisions defining the *tax base* are not indexed for inflation, with the result that taxable income (based on nominal dollars) may differ significantly from true economic income (based on inflation-adjusted dollars).

(b) Discharge by Third Parties

The *Old Colony Trust* case[39]—also decided by the Supreme Court in the early days—presents a very different kind of question, but happily a simpler one. In *Old Colony*, the taxpayer, president of a major corporation, received a cash salary of nearly $1 million in 1918. His employer further agreed to pay all federal income taxes incurred by the taxpayer in order to ensure that the million-dollar

---

[38] See Shuldiner, *Indexing the Tax Code*, 48 Tax L.Rev. 537 (1993). And see, Note, *Inflation and the Federal Income Tax*, 82 Yale L.J. 716 (1973).

[39] *Old Colony Trust Co. v. Commissioner*, 279 U.S. 716 (1929).

salary would be the taxpayer's *net* compensation after tax. As a result the corporation paid federal income tax in 1919 of about $700,000 on the taxpayer's behalf. (Tax rates were very high in 1918 because of World War I; the top marginal rate that year was 77 percent.) The question before the Court was whether the latter amount should be included in the taxpayer's gross income as additional salary. Reasoning that the tax was paid by the employer in consideration of the services rendered to it by the taxpayer, the Court held that the $700,000 tax-payment represented "income" within the predecessor of § 61. Hence, though paid directly to the Treasury, the amount was taxable to the employee as if first received by him in cash.

The result in *Old Colony* is not surprising, at least not today. It is obvious that a taxpayer is enriched if his obligations—whether to the government or to private creditors—are discharged by a third party, and it is not even necessary at this late date to argue that the discharge is equivalent to a cash receipt. All that is needed to attract § 61 is enrichment and "realization." Both being present in the *Old Colony* case on almost any theory, the fact that the transaction took place in an employment context and was intended as additional compensation to the employee plainly justifies the taxable result.

Still, there is the teasing point that under the Court's holding the government collected more in taxes than it would have collected if the employee had paid the first layer of tax himself. In the latter event the total tax would have been $700,000; as it turned out the total tax was $700,000 *plus* the additional tax on that $700,000— perhaps another $500,000—for an aggregate tax which exceeded the employee's basic compensation of $1 million. So isn't the Treasury getting too much? Shouldn't the tax-collector be content with the basic $700,000, whether paid by the taxpayer personally or by his employer?

One way of seeing why the government's position was correct in *Old Colony* is to consider its relationship to Code § 275, which specifically disallows any deduction for *federal* income taxes. (By contrast, § 164 authorizes a limited deduction for *state and local* income taxes.) Perhaps surprisingly, nothing of substance is at stake in the choice between the no-deduction rule of § 275 and an opposite rule allowing a deduction for federal income taxes. Suppose Congress has decided that a person with a pre-tax salary of $1 million should pay income tax of $200,000. It can achieve the desired result either by (1) the combination of the no-deduction rule of § 275 and a flat tax rate of 20 percent, or (2) the combination of the opposite rule and a flat tax rate of 25 percent. In the former case, the $200,000 tax is 20 percent of $1 million; in the latter case, the $200,000 tax is 25 percent of $800,000 (*i.e.*, $1 million less a $200,000 federal income tax deduction). The point generalizes. For any flat-rate income tax *without* a federal income tax deduction, there is a higher-rate income tax *with* a federal income tax deduction that produces identical results. Given the lack of any real stakes in the choice between § 275 and its opposite (assuming appropriate adjustments in tax rates in response to that choice), Congress very reasonably opted for the simpler no-deduction rule. This avoids the headache-inducing circularity of the opposite rule, under which one's taxable income would depend on one's tax liability, and one's tax liability would depend on one's taxable income. Because of § 275, the federal income tax features a *tax-inclusive* tax base—*i.e.,* amounts paid or payable as income tax are included in the tax base. By contrast, under a *tax-exclusive* tax system—of which retail sales taxes are the most familiar example—the amount of the tax is not included in the tax base. As a little contemplation of income taxes and retail sales taxes may suggest, some types of taxes seem naturally to lend themselves to tax-inclusive bases, while other types are most easily designed with tax-exclusive bases. To repeat, nothing of substance is at stake in the choice between the two sorts of tax bases, as long as the tax rate is adjusted to reflect the choice made.

In any event, § 275 in effect contemplates that federal income taxes are to be paid out of the taxpayer's after-tax income. To illustrate, suppose that an individual earns $1,000 in Year 1 on which a tax of 30%, or $300, is due and payable on April 15 of Year 2. Suppose the taxpayer's earnings in Year 2 are $1,500, out of which he pays the prior year's tax of $300. Since federal income tax is not a deductible expense, his taxable income for Year 2 is unaffected by the tax payment and is equal to his full earnings of $1,500. His tax for Year 2, at the same 30% rate, is therefore $450, as compared with only $360 (.30 × ($1,500 − $300)) if Year 1's income tax were allowed as a deduction.

May the taxpayer in our example avoid the higher tax result by accepting a salary of only $1,200 in Year 2 and arranging for his employer to pay the prior year's income tax directly to the government? If so, the no-deduction rule (in § 275) and the exclusion rule (inferred from § 61) would be inconsistent with one another. To be sure, such inconsistency can be found in other areas of the tax law—*e.g.,* the exclusion of imputed income from personal residences but the non-deductibility of apartment rents. Here, however, the consequence would be to render all federal income taxes deductible by employees through the medium of readily arranged direct-payment schemes. This would be especially attractive for higher bracket taxpayers, and the disallowance feature of § 275 would then effectively be repealed. As Congress could hardly have intended that result, the Court's *Old Colony* decision, reasonable in any event, merely spared Congress the task of amending § 61 so as to expressly include in gross income federal income taxes paid on behalf of employees.

The point just made—that the payment (or reimbursement) of non-deductible federal income taxes is taxable to an employee—can also be seen at work (backhandedly, to be sure) in *Clark v. Commissioner*,[40] a venerable Board of Tax Appeals decision. In *Clark*, the taxpayer had retained "experienced tax counsel" to prepare his and his wife's federal income tax returns for the year 1932. Apparently having misunderstood the operation of certain Code provisions, counsel prepared and filed a joint return for the spouses, whereas separate returns for husband and wife would have legitimately saved the taxpayer some $20,000 in taxes. Acknowledging his error, counsel in 1934 reimbursed the taxpayer for the taxes he needn't have paid. The Board, rejecting the Commissioner's effort to apply *Old Colony*, held that the reimbursement was not includable in the taxpayer's gross income, because "It was, in fact, compensation for a loss which impaired petitioner's capital."

The *Clark* case was rightly decided, we think, and right also in stressing the taxpayer's loss of "capital." Just because federal income taxes are *not* deductible and *do* have to be paid out of after-tax income, the recovery of taxes improperly assessed should not result in additional taxable income. Thus, an ordinary refund by the Treasury of taxes that have been over-withheld from an employee's paycheck is obviously not income to the employee. *Clark* didn't involve a refund as such—his tax liability was properly determined once the taxpayer had mistakenly been led to file a joint return—but the circumstances seem close enough to justify equivalent treatment.

(c)   When Is a Loan Not a Loan?

Since "loans" are not currently taxable to the borrower, it may be important in a given case to decide whether a purported loan deserves that characterization or really should be treated as something else. Suppose, for example, that the sole shareholder and chief executive of a small corporation "borrows" a substantial sum of money from the company. The loan is represented by a demand note, but as the company is entirely controlled by the borrower, any demand for repayment is obviously within his sole discretion. Is the "loan" a loan, or is it in reality a taxable dividend? At bottom, the problem arises because the law accepts the notion that stockholders and their wholly-owned corporations can actually engage in arm's length dealings with one another—sales of property, salary for

---

40   40 B.T.A. 333 (1939), discussed in Zelenak, *The Taxation of Tax Indemnity Payments: Recovery of Capital and the Contours of Gross Income*, 46 Tax L.Rev. 381 (1991).

services, loans, etc.—even though it is evident that the two parties are really a unit and are not at all at arm's length. Having indulged the fiction, however, it becomes necessary to take it seriously and insist that the arm's-length standard be observed. In consequence, there is a continuing and burdensome duty to scrutinize transactions between stockholders and corporations in order to determine whether the self-serving characterization adopted by the taxpayers should be respected or rejected. In many instances the Code itself takes a hand (see § 302, for example). But in others (including the loan-dividend issue) the matter is left to be thrashed out through tedious argument between taxpayer and revenue agent on the occasion of an audit. As a matter of practice, if the amount borrowed is large relative to the stockholder's individual resources, and if the loan remains outstanding for an extended period of time, the Service is likely to insist that it is really a dividend and includable in the recipient's income. To avoid this consequence stockholders will usually pay such loans down from time to time—perhaps through short-term bank borrowing at the year-end—or will try to keep the total "debt" within limits which they believe will be viewed as reasonable.

On another front, what about "loans" which only become loans as a consequence of subsequent events? In *U.S. v. Lewis*,[41] the taxpayer received a commission from his employer in Year 1. In Year 3 it was found that the commission had been erroneously computed and the taxpayer was obliged to repay a portion of it to the employer. Was the Year 1 receipt "income," or could the taxpayer insist that it was really a loan in view of what took place in Year 3? Finding that the commission had initially been received by the taxpayer under a "claim of right," the Supreme Court held the entire amount includable in Year 1 and refused to permit a retroactive adjustment despite the repayment. While the repayment was presumably deductible as a business expense in Year 3, it is possible that the taxpayer's marginal tax rate was lower at that time than in the earlier year, so that the deduction failed to make him entirely whole. On the other hand, one obviously cannot allow a taxpayer to exclude salary, commissions, etc., merely because his right to retain the item is disputed and may someday be denied. The solution, quite obviously, lies not in narrowing the income definition, but in modifying the annual accounting concept under which each year's financial events are treated as discrete. As indicated at 10.02, the Code has moved substantially in the latter direction since *Lewis* was decided, so that the potential harshness of the outcome is now considerably abated.

---

[41]   340 U.S. 590 (1951).

As a final example of the problems in this area, what about
robbers? If money is embezzled, extorted, or stolen at the point of a
gun, does the criminal have taxable income within the meaning of
§ 61? Or can it be argued that as the "taxpayer" has a legal obligation
to repay his victim in the event that he is apprehended, the initial
taking should be treated as a mere loan? Having considered the
matter on no fewer than two prior occasions, the Supreme Court
finally concluded in *James v. U.S.*[42] that a plausible distinction could
be drawn between theft and legitimate borrowing and held that
stolen money was fully taxable in the year obtained.

Bernard Madoff, the proprietor of a gigantic Ponzi scheme, was
convicted in 2009 of defrauding his investors out of billions of dollars.
Don't those billions have to be included in his gross income under the
James decision? If so, the clever fellow would owe the largest tax
deficiency in the nation's history, in addition to his other distinctions.
In lieu of discussion, the reader may pursue an ample literature on
this engaging if slightly idiotic topic.[43]

(d) Mortgages

Yet another range of issues affecting borrowers (on which the
Supreme Court has also spoken) concerns the treatment of mortgage
indebtedness. If a taxpayer purchases real estate in part with
borrowed funds, issuing a mortgage as security for the loan, does his
basis for the property include the borrowed money or only the cash
that he draws from his own resources? If he borrows against
appreciated property but without personal liability for the debt, is the
borrowing merely a loan or is it a realization and hence a taxable
gain? These and related questions, which truly are of wide
importance, are considered in Part E, below.

3.02 Cancellation of Indebtedness

The Supreme Court has held that the retirement of outstanding
indebtedness at less than its face amount results in taxable income
to the debtor. Congress specifically confirmed that outcome in
§ 61(a)(12), which states that "gross income means . . . Income from
discharge of indebtedness." As shown below, however, Congress also
evidently considered the general rule to be too severe in some cases
and in § 108 supplied relief provisions to cushion its impact.

---

[42]   366 U.S. 213 (1961). The earlier cases are *Rutkin v. U.S.,* 343 U.S. 130 (1952),
and *Commissioner v. Wilcox,* 327 U.S. 404 (1946).

[43]   See, *e.g.,* Bittker, *Taxing Income from Unlawful Activities,* 25 Case
W.Res.L.Rev. 130 (1974).

(a) Cancellation of Business Debt

In *U.S. v. Kirby Lumber Co.*,[44] the taxpayer-corporation in 1923 issued more than $12 million of its own bonds in exchange for property equal to their par value. Later in the same year, the bonds having obviously declined in the market, the taxpayer repurchased $1,100,000 par value of the bonds for $138,000 less than par. The Supreme Court sustained the government in treating the latter amount as taxable income. "As a result of its dealings," said Justice Holmes, "[the taxpayer] made available $138,000 [of] assets previously offset by the obligation of bonds now extinct." Accordingly, there was a realized "accession to income, if we take words in their plain popular meaning. . . ."

Although the facts in *Kirby* are not fully developed, it seems reasonable to assume that the company was able to repurchase its bonds at a discount because of a general rise in the market rate of interest. The Court stated specifically (though without supporting data) that "there was no shrinkage of assets" at the company level. Evidently, the Court (a) perceived that there had been an addition to the taxpayer's balance sheet Net Worth as a result of trading cash for bonds of greater face amount, and (b) believed that the taxpayer's "available" assets had increased in an equal measure. In the Court's view, the act of issuing bonds at one date and buying them in at a discount when the rise in interest rates had driven down their value belonged to the category of canny investment—on the "short" side of the market, so to speak. The resulting gain was taxable like any other profit derived from speculative activity.

The decision in *Kirby* is certainly correct, but the rationale—that additional assets thereby became "available" to the taxpayer—is a trifle obscure. Could the taxpayer have avoided inclusion by showing that its net worth had been reduced by losses or by a decline in the value of other property? By and large, § 61 is not subject to a "balance-sheet improvement" test: a worker's wages are includable in *gross* income even if for separate reasons his year-end net worth has shrunk. Such shrinkage may (or may not) be taken into account in determining his final "taxable income" figure, but a finding of "gross income" normally depends on the *particular* transaction at issue, not on the taxpayer's overall financial condition. Should the *Kirby* situation be regarded differently?

Perhaps a better or at least a broader way to approach the entire subject of debt-cancellation is to remind oneself that borrowed funds are not includable in the borrower's income to start with. If a taxpayer borrows $1 million and issues its bond to the lender in the

---

[44] 284 U.S. 1 (1931).

same principal amount, the cash received is not regarded as income because the bond is viewed as offsetting the cash-receipt. Yet despite the exclusion of the borrowed funds from income, the expenditure of those funds by a borrower who is a business taxpayer results in a business expense deduction or an increase in the basis of the taxpayer's depreciable assets. If the funds are used to pay wages or to purchase inventory, the borrowed funds will be deductible currently because such outlays are treated as current business expenses. If the funds are used to buy machinery, the deductions will take the form of either immediate deductions under § 168(k) or § 179, or annual depreciation allowances over the tax life of the equipment.[45] In any event, the expenditure of the borrowed funds will sooner or later produce a tax benefit, while the borrowing itself is tax-free.

Of course, the Treasury normally is made whole when the loan is repaid. The repayment of the bond principal is *not* deductible and therefore has to be made out of after-tax income—the prior exclusion is balanced by a later *non*-deduction, so to speak. In effect, the taxpayer is allowed both (a) to exclude the amount borrowed, and (b) to deduct the outlay of the borrowed funds. This, however, assumes that he will (c) subsequently repay the amount borrowed out of his income after tax.

If, as matters turn out, the taxpayer is *not* obliged to repay the full amount of his loan—not do (c), in effect—then, to prevent an undercounting of his taxable income, he should be asked to give up an equivalent portion of the benefit that resulted from combining the exclusion and deduction under (a) and (b). He can't have it all *three* ways. Having somehow contrived to reduce his repayment obligation, he must now either go back and include a portion of the borrowed funds in income (give up (a)), or else accept a disallowance of his prior tax benefits (give up (b)). It doesn't much matter which of these two earlier events is constructively reversed, provided that the debt-cancellation is seen to require a reversal of one or the other.

While it might, therefore, be more accurate to tax a portion of the earlier borrowing or to disallow a portion of the prior deductions, the Court in *Kirby* lacked a statutory basis for making any such refined adjustments. It did the next best thing, however, by requiring the cancelled debt to be included in current income. Notice, though, that the Court did not justify the result in *Kirby* along the lines suggested here—*i.e.*, as a means of correcting the earlier exclusion of the loan proceeds from gross income, once it becomes clear that the assumption of eventual repayment (on which the earlier exclusion had been premised) was mistaken. Instead, the Court relied on a

---

[45]   See *infra*, 6.10(a), for the details.

balance sheet analysis, under which income results because the taxpayer's Net Worth increases when the amount of debt cancelled exceeds the amount paid by the taxpayer to the creditor. The choice between these two rationales for the taxation of debt cancellation income usually makes no difference, because the same income inclusion would be required under either rationale. On occasion, however, the choice between the two rationales (call them mistake-correction and balance-sheet) is crucial to the tax result—as will be explained below, in the discussion of cancellations of nonbusiness debts.

While there may have been no shrinkage of assets in *Kirby*, in later cases, especially those arising during the 1930's, debt-cancellation was very commonly a consequence of the debtor's financial weakness and in effect represented a kind of voluntary, or *de facto*, composition with creditors. (Of course, debt-cancellation resulting from the debtor's financial weakness became common again during the lead up to and in the aftermath of the 2008 financial crisis.) In these cases, the fall in value of the taxpayer's outstanding indebtedness stemmed not from a general rise in interest rates, but from a decline in the taxpayer's own credit-worthiness, which led investors to attach a higher degree of risk to its securities than when those securities were originally issued. If the taxpayer then took steps to reduce the danger of default by repurchasing its debt at a discount, should the "saving" be treated as a taxable gain? The Supreme Court supplied an affirmative answer in *Commissioner v. Jacobson*.[46] By repurchasing his bonds at a discount, said the Court, the taxpayer, though in straitened financial condition, improved his net worth by the difference between the face amount of the bonds and the price he paid for them. The taxpayer's gains were comparable (the Court thought) to those he would have realized had he bought a third party's bonds at a discount and later resold them at face value.

Technically defensible, the outcome in *Jacobson* is nevertheless somewhat unappetizing, and it is understandable that Congress should have responded to the plight of debtors in these circumstances by enacting § 108, which, as amended, provides that debt-cancellation income shall be excluded from a taxpayer's gross income if the taxpayer is insolvent or the debt discharge occurs in a formal bankruptcy proceeding. As a corollary, the taxpayer must reduce certain "favorable" tax attributes—chiefly net-operating loss carryforwards (see 10.01)—in the same amount so as to prevent a double benefit.[47]

---

[46]   336 U.S. 28 (1949).

[47]   Reacting to a slump in real estate values, the 1993 Act added § 108(c), which extends the exclusion to the cancellation of mortgage debt on business real estate, provided that an election is made under § 1017 to reduce the basis of such (or similar

It may be worthwhile, finally, to note that prior to the 1986 Act relief under § 108 was made available not only to debtors in distress (like the taxpayer in *Jacobson*), but also to *Kirby*-type taxpayers who might be in perfectly healthy condition and simply benefitting from a general rise in market rates of interest. While perhaps not very significant in earlier times, the latter phenomenon took on large proportions in the early 1980's, a period in which interest rates went sharply up and, as a corollary, bond prices went sharply down. Offered an opportunity to improve their balance sheets, many publicly-held companies reacted by repurchasing their own outstanding debt at market prices well below face value, in that way generating debt-cancellation income in large amounts. Such income was reported as such to shareholders and for accounting purposes, but for tax purposes it would usually be excluded under § 108.

Presumably feeling that statutory relief was inappropriate in these circumstances, Congress in 1986 amended § 108 so as to confine exclusion to debtors that are insolvent or in formal bankruptcy. As a result, solvent debtors—again, typically, public companies that repurchase their outstanding bonds at a discount— are now required to recognize debt-cancellation income currently, that is, in the year the cancelling transaction takes place.

(b) Cancellation of Personal (Nonbusiness) Debt

The discussion above is in terms of a business taxpayer—a corporation, say—which in most cases would have acquired depreciable property with the funds it had borrowed and, as stated, would be entitled to an annual deduction for depreciation. At the risk of some confusion, we should add that the mistake-correction rationale described above also supports the inclusion of debt-cancellation income where the borrowing is personal and the borrowed funds are expended on non-deductible consumption. Unlike business expenses, consumption expenditures are supposed to be made out of *after*-tax income. Since the borrowing itself is not taxed, however, the related consumption is actually being purchased out of *pre*-tax resources. Once again, the apparent tax benefit disappears when the consumer's loan is repaid, provided that the repayment is in full. But if a portion of the debt is cancelled for some reason, then to that extent, in retrospect at least, the earlier borrowing should be included in income.

In some situations, however, the cancelled debt will not be associated with borrowed funds which financed untaxed consumption. Suppose, for example, an uninsured motorist drives

---

depreciable) property in the same amount. Since deductible depreciation will be lower, taxable income in future years will be increased. The effect, therefore, is to postpone or defer the excluded income to later periods.

negligently on a personal errand and injures a pedestrian. The pedestrian obtains a $100,000 judgment against the motorist, but the motorist makes it so difficult for the pedestrian to collect that the pedestrian finally accepts a payment of $80,000 and abandons his claim to the other $20,000. Does the motorist have debt cancellation income? Under the mistake-correction theory, he does not. He did not receive any tax-free consumption when the debt was created, so there is no need for a mistake-correcting adjustment when a portion of the debt is cancelled. Under the balance-sheet theory, in contrast, he does have debt cancellation income; his net worth increases by $20,000 when liabilities decrease by $100,000 while assets decrease by only $80,000. Our view is that mistake-correction should be the sole theory of debt-cancellation income, with the result that the $20,000 debt cancellation should not be taxed to the negligent motorist. Rather remarkably, however, nearly nine decades after *Kirby* the courts still have not clearly decided between the two theories of debt cancellation income, and the tax result in the case of the negligent motorist remains uncertain.

The relationship between personal consumption and debt cancellation was fairly dramatically tested in the *Zarin* case,[48] which involved the settlement of a very large gambling debt between the taxpayer, a compulsive craps-shooter, and an all too accommodating Atlantic City casino. Using chips supplied to him on credit by the casino, and playing day and night, the taxpayer rolled up a debt of nearly $3.5 million (having previously lost and paid $2.5 million out of his own pocket). The casino finally demanded payment and, when the taxpayer failed to pay (actually, he issued checks that bounced), brought suit in State court. The taxpayer's defense was that the debt was legally unenforceable because the casino had been found by the New Jersey Casino Control Commission to have violated State law limitations on the permissible extension of credit to any single patron. Ultimately, the parties settled the matter for a payment by the taxpayer of $500,000. Ever alert, the Commissioner (of Internal Revenue) thereupon asserted that the taxpayer had realized, and must include, cancellation of indebtedness income in the amount of $3 million.

A closely divided Tax Court held for the Commissioner chiefly on the ground that the chips supplied on credit represented a true loan, one that the taxpayer expected to repay and would have had to repay if he had won at the craps-table instead of losing. Settling the debt for less than face amount produced taxable income, therefore, under § 61(a)(12). Symmetry or consistency required such a result, the court thought, even though the casino's claim might in fact be

---

[48]   *Zarin v. Commissioner*, 916 F.2d 110 (3d Cir. 1990).

unenforceable. If it were otherwise—that is, if unenforceability meant that there had really been no debt at all—then the receipt of the chips should have been treated as income in the first instance, since plainly the casino did not intend to make the taxpayer a gift. The taxpayer obviously regarded himself as a borrower throughout, however, so that his failure to repay the debt in full must have a taxable consequence.

The dissenters (in one way or another) simply would not or could not accept the proposition that a man who has lost $3.5 million gambling somehow winds up with $3 million of taxable income because the "house" agrees to settle for $500,000. In the words of one dissenter, "the concept that the petitioner received his money's worth from the enjoyment of using the chips (thus equating the pleasure of gambling with increase in wealth) produces the incongruous result that the more a gambler loses, the greater his pleasure and the larger the increase in his wealth." Yet another dissenter indignantly observed that the majority decision was "tantamount to taxing the petitioner on his losses."

On appeal, the Third Circuit reversed (2–1), holding, among other things, that the element of unenforceability created doubt about the *amount* of the taxpayer's liability to the casino as well as the fact of liability itself. In effect, the dispute about liability necessarily subsumed a dispute about just how much the taxpayer owed, the casino claiming $3.5 million and the taxpayer holding out for $0. The $500,000 settlement meant that the parties had resolved their disagreement through the customary process of give-and-take, but it did not mean that the taxpayer had *acknowledged* a debt of $3.5 million and then obtained the cancellation of a part. Until the parties settled their dispute by accepting the $500,000 figure, there was no agreed-upon indebtedness to be cancelled.

Only a grouch would object to the outcome in *Zarin* and perhaps one way to rationalize the decision would be to make the convenient surmise that the taxpayer never really expected the casino to demand the full face amount of the borrowed chips unless he came out winners. The settlement could be taken as an indication that the casino itself anticipated that there would be some renegotiation of losses beyond a certain point, with the lawsuit merely being a way of opposing the taxpayer's effort to get away scot-free. What is affecting about the taxpayer's position, of course, is the fact that his debt was the product of a rather pitiable mental state, which the casino did not hesitate to exploit. On the other hand, the law obviously cannot assess consumption benefits on an individual basis or depart from the general rule that benefit is measured by market price. Thus, while most unaddicted people would agree that the consumption benefits realized by an addict are negative if viewed objectively, presumably a "sick gambler" exception to the *Kirby Lumber* rule would be unworkable as an administrative matter. In the end, therefore, it might be simplest if the Service read the *Zarin* decision to mean that the settlement of *any* sizeable gambling debt implies or presumes a prior informal understanding between the parties. As evidenced by the settlement itself, the implied understanding is that large players who are also heavy losers may ultimately be entitled to a volume discount.[49]

A loose end. Section 108(a)(1)(E), added to the Code in 2007, was a response to the dramatic drop in home prices that began in the middle of the last decade. The provision was enacted as a temporary measure, and as of this writing does not apply in years after 2017. It would not be at all surprising, however, if Congress eventually extends its application, possibly with retroactive effect. For the years in which it applies, the provision generally allows a homeowner to exclude from gross income cancellation of "acquisition indebtedness" on the homeowner's primary residence, as long as the cancellation is on account of either a decline in the value of the home or the homeowner's perilous financial condition. Although the provision requires a taxpayer taking advantage of the exclusion to reduce his basis in the home by the amount excluded, in most cases the basis reduction will not adversely affect the taxpayer (because (1) the taxpayer has not disposed of the home, (2) the taxpayer has disposed of the home but does not realize a gain even after the basis reduction, or (3) the taxpayer realizes a gain on the disposition but is able to exclude the gain under § 121 (15.02)).

4. Gifts and Bequests

Code § 102(a) excludes gifts and bequests from the gross income of the donee or heir. Presumably such benefits could be reached under the broad approach to "income" taken by the Supreme Court in the *Glenshaw Glass* case, and one could even imagine a *de minimis* exemption for birthday gifts and the like that would help to make sense of the matter administratively. But as things now stand it is only the capital transfer levies—the federal gift and estate taxes— that are applicable to "donated estates." In effect, gross income does not include intra-family divisions of wealth, whether during the donor's life or at his death.

Consider, for example, a gift of $100,000 cash from Grandmother (GM) to adult Granddaughter (GD). What justifies not taxing GD on the $100,000 when it will buy just as much as any other $100,000, and when $100,000 from most other sources (salary, for example)

---

[49] For a somewhat different rationale in support of the no-tax result in *Zarin*, see Zelenak, *Cancellation-of-Indebtedness Income and Transactional Accounting*, 29 Va. Tax Rev. 277, 319–25 (2009).

would be taxable to GD? The standard explanation is based on the understanding of income as the opportunity to consume. A taxpayer with $1 of income has the opportunity to engage in a dollar's-worth of consumption, either now or in the future. A taxpayer's dollar's-worth of consumption opportunity should be reflected in an inclusion of $1 in the taxpayer's income tax base. From this understanding follows the three-part rationale for not taxing GD on her $100,000 gift from GM: (1) each consumption opportunity should be taxed once and only once, (2) the $100,000 cash represents only one $100,000 consumption opportunity, which GM has transferred to GD, and (3) GM has already paid tax on the $100,000. Thus, to tax GD on the gift would be to double-tax a single consumption opportunity. In effect, GM has already paid the tax on GD's behalf. There are plausible objections to this explanation. For example, one might believe that GM *does* consume the gifted $100,000—perhaps in the form of extra attention and affection from GD, or perhaps merely as a warm glow from giving. In that case, there are two consumptions and there should be two taxes, one on GM and a second on GD. Or one might accept the premise that there should be only one tax, but contend that the tax should be imposed on the taxpayer who ends up with the consumption opportunity rather than on the earner. Under this view, the gift should serve to shift the tax liability on the $100,000 from GM to GD—which could be done by allowing GM to claim a $100,000 deduction and taxing GD on $100,000. Of course, large gifts generally flow from higher-bracket taxpayers to lower-bracket taxpayers, so this deduction-plus-inclusion approach would mean taxpayers could use gifts to shift income from higher-bracket to lower-bracket family members, at considerable cost to the Treasury. Apparently viewing double taxation of gifts (*i.e.,* taxing the $100,000 as income to GD without allowing a deduction to GM) as too harsh and income-shifting via gifts as too lenient, Congress settled on the single-tax-on-the-donor approach embodied in § 102.

Three kinds of structural or interpretative issues remain. First: what should be done about a gift of property which has appreciated or declined in value relative to the donor's cost? Who bears the tax on the appreciation, and who deducts the loss? Second: how should we handle gifts of divided interests in the same property, that is, gifts in trust with income to A and remainder to B? Third: what about "gifts" that take place in a commercial setting? What class of recipients is the exclusion really designed to protect?

4.01 Gains and Losses—Realization by Whom?

Gifts or bequests of *cash* present a single straightforward issue, to wit, shall the gift or bequest be included in the income of the donee or heir? As indicated, § 102(a) excludes the receipt and in effect permits family wealth to be transferred from older to younger, or richer to poorer, or dead to living, without the imposition of an income tax on the grateful recipient. But suppose the gift or bequest is "in kind"—say shares of stock. And suppose the property has appreciated in the transferor's hands so that its value at the time of the transfer is above the transferor's original cost. Should the transferor (donor or decedent) be taxed on the transfer as if it were a sale? Or should the previously unrealized appreciation remain unrealized until the shares are actually sold for cash, and then be taxed to the transferee (the donee or heir)? Not one but *two* candidates for taxability emerge on the scene. Since presumably it would be improper to tax both transferor and transferee on the same element of property appreciation, and perhaps equally improper to tax neither, the obvious task is to choose between them. Although the stock appreciation "accrued" while the shares were held by the transferor, the sale-for-cash, when made, will be effected by the transferee. Which of these events should be regarded as the vital link to taxability?

The pattern of gift and bequest—older-to-younger, richer-to-poorer—plainly suggests that transferors on the whole may be subject to higher marginal tax rates than transferees. In making the choice referred to above, therefore, the impact of the progressive rate structure is fully implicated. If gifts and bequests can be used to shift unrealized gains from higher- to lower-bracket individuals within the family, then taxpayers who own appreciated property can minimize the effect of the progressive rates at their own discretion. *Inter vivos* gifts, in particular, would become a major element in family tax-planning. If gifts and bequests are treated as "realizations," on the other hand, their value is obviously reduced from the standpoint of personal tax-saving. To be sure, owners of appreciated property can still decide for themselves whether to retain their property or to sell it for cash and incur a tax, but the further discretion to determine *who* should be taxed on the appreciation would be denied.

For reasons that will become apparent, the Code treatment of capital transfers in kind can best be understood if gifts are discussed separately from bequests. And as respects gifts, it will also help to talk separately about transfers of appreciated, and transfers of depreciated, property. As usual, our explanation is by example. We should add that the theme briefly sounded in this subsection—that of income-shifting among family members—attains symphonic proportions in Part C, below.

(a) Lifetime Gifts

Code § 1015(a) provides that for the purpose of determining *gain* on the sale of property acquired by gift, the donee's basis is the same as the basis of the property in the hands of the donor. For the purpose of determining *loss* (other than in the case of a donee-spouse), the donee's basis is the donor's basis or the market value of the property at the date of the gift, whichever is lower. The reason for establishing different basis rules to measure gains and losses will appear when we consider gifts of property whose value has *declined* in the donor's hands. But for the moment, confining ourselves to gifts of *appreciated* property, it is apparent that the main effect of § 1015(a) is to carry over the donor's basis to the donee. Section 1015(a) thus makes the donee responsible for any appreciation in value that took place while the property was held by the donor, as well as any further change in value between the date of gift and the date of final sale.

Adapting the illustration used by the Supreme Court in *Taft v. Bowers*,[50] assume that the donor's original cost for certain shares of stock was $1,000. Assume further that the shares were worth $2,000 at the date of gift; and that the donee finally sells the shares for (i) $5,000, or (ii) $1,750, or (iii) $600. As the donee's basis under § 1015(a) is the same as the donor's—$1,000—the respective outcomes are: (i) gain of $4,000, (ii) gain of $750, and (iii) loss of $400[51]—the gain or loss in each case being taxable or allowable to the donee. The donee steps into the donor's shoes for the purpose of computing gains and losses, and all the results are the same in dollar amount as if the donor had retained the shares and sold them for his own account.

In *Taft v. Bowers*, the taxpayer, a donee of appreciated property, argued that § 1015(a) should be struck down as unconstitutional on the ground that it ultimately required donees to treat gifts as taxable income by limiting their basis to the donor's cost. While the Court sustained the provision as "appropriate to a general scheme of lawful taxation," the taxpayer's description of the *consequence* of § 1015(a) was nevertheless perfectly correct. The section does in fact restrict the scope of the gift exclusion by denying the donee a basis for the property equal to its value at the date the gift is received. Section 102(a) thus *permanently* excludes from the donee's income no more than the original cost of the property. The pre-gift appreciation factor—from $1,000 to $2,000 in the above example—is merely deferred, and is ultimately taxed to the donee if the property retains its value.

But despite this analysis, the decision in *Taft v. Bowers* must be regarded as favorable to taxpayers of wealth. Had the case gone the other   way—had   the   donee   succeeded   in   establishing   her

---

[50]   278 U.S. 470 (1929).

[51]   In case (iii), the entire decline in value occurred after the date of gift. Since the value of the shares at the date of gift exceeded the donor's basis, that basis ($1,000) is still carried over to the donee.

constitutional right to a basis of $2,000—the government would obviously have had to press the courts or the Congress to adopt a concept of "realization by gift." The Treasury could not have tolerated for long a system in which property appreciation was periodically obliterated for tax purposes through back-and-forth transfers among family members. Its response to an adverse decision in the *Taft* case, therefore, would have had to be an insistence that the donor himself be regarded as the "taxable person," and that gifts of appreciated property be treated as equivalent to sales for cash. In effect, the issue in *Taft v. Bowers* was not whether to tax pre-gift appreciation at all, but whether to tax it to donors or donees—Congress, with the Court's approval, opting for the latter.

As suggested, the choice of the donee as the "taxable person" particularly benefits families with substantial property, if we assume that donors (parents and grandparents) are generally in higher tax brackets than donees (children, grandchildren, etc.). In addition, of course, no tax is payable until the property is finally sold. Put another way, the effect of § 1015(a) and the *Taft* decision is really to permit taxpayers to decide for themselves just *who* shall be the recipient of taxable income in the light of their own tax situations. If the donee's tax rate is lower than the donor's, the property can be transferred in kind and then sold by the donee at a lower tax cost than the donor would incur. If the donor's tax rate is lower than the donee's, the property can be sold in advance of the gift and the cash proceeds transferred net of tax. Taxpayers are free to adopt whichever procedure will minimize the impact of the rate structure on family income, and in that sense can decree their own tax obligations.

Can a donor also give away his *losses* if that seems advantageous? Suppose the donor owns property with a basis higher than its current value and the donee is a well-paid executive whose tax bracket exceeds the donor's or who happens to have realized exceptionally large gains in a particular year. At this point the Code becomes exceedingly moralistic, not to say draconian, in its effort to prevent taxes from being minimized. As indicated, § 1015(a) provides that for purposes of calculating loss on the sale of property acquired by gift, the donee's basis is the *lower* of cost or market at the date the gift is made. Suppose that the donor's original cost for certain stock was $2,000 but the stock was worth only $1,000 at the date of gift. For purposes of computing loss on subsequent sale, the donee would have to use the lower market value of $1,000. Assuming the donee finally sells the stock for (i) $750, (ii) $1,600, or (iii) $2,250, his recognized gain or loss is as follows:

Sale Price	Basis under § 1015	Recognized Gain (or Loss)
$ 750	$1,000	($250)
$1,600	$1,000/$2,000	–0–
$2,250	$2,000	$250

In case (i) the donee's allowable loss is limited to $250 because his basis is the market value of the stock at date of gift, $1,000. In case (ii) using the basis for determining loss would produce a gain (of $600) and using the basis for determining gain would produce a loss (of $400). For tax purposes, then, case (ii) produces neither loss nor gain. In case (iii) the basis for determining loss is irrelevant, but the sale price of $2,250 exceeds the gain basis by $250.

Cases (i) and (ii) show that built-in losses (in contrast to built-in gains) *cannot* be shifted from donor to donee. The donee simply cannot take advantage, by way of loss recognition, of any decline in value which occurred prior to the gift. Just *why* the Code should be tougher on losses than on gains is not completely obvious, however, since the tax-saving on a dollar of gain which is shifted from a high- to a low-bracket taxpayer is precisely the same as that to be had on a dollar of loss shifted in the opposite direction.

What happens to the unrecognized losses in cases (i) and (ii), *i.e.,* $1,000 and $400 respectively? Answer: they are never allowed to *anyone*—a curious result, to be sure, but one which few taxpayers are likely to experience in view of the ready salability of most kinds of property. Where the property consists of marketable securities, for example, the donor obviously is free to sell and give away the cash proceeds, thus realizing his loss in advance of the gift and avoiding the penalty of a permanent disallowance.

As indicated at 5.04, the lower-of-cost-or-market rule was eliminated by the 1984 Act where the donee is (or was) the donor's spouse. In the latter case, the donee's basis is now the same as the donor's for purposes of calculating gain and loss alike.

(b) *Bequests*

The treatment of bequests differs from the treatment of gifts in one major (some would say horrendous) respect. Although there is no realization of gain or loss by a decedent, under § 1014 the basis of all property acquired by inheritance becomes its fair market value at the date of the decedent's death. Thus, appreciation and depreciation in value are both wiped out by death, and the decedent's heirs are obliged to recognize only those changes in property value that take place subsequently. If an investor buys property for $1,000 for example, and the property is worth $1,500 at his death, the investor's heirs will take it over at a stepped-up basis of $1,500 and the $500 of appreciation will be eliminated for tax purposes. By obvious contrast, under § 1015 a lifetime gift of the same property would leave the donees with a basis of $1,000 and hence with $500 of potentially taxable gain. While property that has declined in value takes a stepped-*down* basis at death, it may be assumed that older people will often act to realize their potential losses at least to the extent of currently realized gains, so that the penalty feature of § 1014 is no doubt far less painful in aggregate than the bonus feature is pleasuresome.

No convincing rationale for the death-basis rule has ever been suggested,[52] but it seems apparent that there is a connection in the congressional mind between the federal estate tax and the stepped-up (or stepped-down) basis rule of § 1014. To be sure, the estate tax applies only to very large estates because of the large estate tax exemption amount ($11.2 million in 2018). Also, generally speaking, there is no estate tax on property received by inheritance from a spouse. But actual payment of estate tax is irrelevant for this purpose. Basis is adjusted at death whether or not the estate in question is large enough to be taxable; the mere fact that the estate is within the estate tax exemption does not deprive the heirs of the basis adjustment under § 1014. As has been observed,[53] "less aggregate wealth incurs estate and gift tax than escapes gain under the income tax." More generally, the income tax and the estate tax really have little to do with each other; the income tax is a tax on annual accretions to wealth and pays the cost of government, while the estate tax is an excise tax on inheritances and is intended, at least in part, to prevent large accumulations from passing down the generations in dynastic fashion. But even so, and whether rational or not, one senses that the estate tax may be seen or felt as a form of "realization at death," with the rule of § 1014 in some sense being a response to that perception. The benefit conferred thereby on families of wealth is, of course, very considerable.

4.02   Divided Interests—Gifts in Trust

Assume that an individual dies owning corporate securities with a basis and value of $100,000. Under the decedent's will, the securities are to be held by a bank as trustee for the benefit of the decedent's wife and son. The wife is to get the "income" from the securities, estimated to be $8,000 a year, for life. At her death the

---

[52]   Zelenak, *Taxing Gains at Death*, 46 Vand. L. Rev. 361 (1993). For the early history of the death basis rule (albeit a history lacking a convincing rationale), see Zelenak, *Figuring Out the Tax: Congress, Treasury, and the Design of the Early Modern Income Tax* 83–96 (2018).

[53]   Dodge, *What's Wrong with Carryover Basis Under H. R. 8*, 91 Tax Notes 961, 962 (2001).

trust is to terminate and the corpus—the securities or whatever other property the trustee then holds—is to be transferred to the son absolutely. The wife's age is 70 at the date of the decedent's death and she has a life-expectancy of 15 years; the son's age doesn't matter for our purposes.

How does § 102(a) apply in these circumstances? If the decedent had left his securities outright to a single individual—say the son— the legatee would obviously be entitled to exclude no more than the value of the securities—$100,000—as a "bequest or inheritance." Income *from* the property in the form of dividends or interest would of course be taxable to the son as owner of the securities, just as it was taxable to the decedent during his lifetime. The exclusion for gifts and bequests applies to the value of the securities at the time of their receipt, but not to the income which they subsequently generate.

Is the outcome any different if the beneficial interest in the property is divided between two individuals, as in the example above? In *Irwin v. Gavit*,[54] the Supreme Court held, in effect, that § 102(a) applies only to the corpus of a trust. The taxpayer had been left an income interest in a testamentary trust for a period of 15 years, with remainder to his daughter. Arguing that the income which he received annually from the trust was "property" acquired by bequest, the taxpayer sought to exclude such amounts from his gross income under the literal language of § 102(a). The Supreme Court held for the government. Stressing what Justice Holmes regarded as the commonly understood distinction between principal and income, the Court held that the annual payments were fully includable in the taxpayer's income. The Code provision excluding gifts and bequests, said Holmes, "assumes the gift of a corpus and contrasts it with the income arising from it, but was not intended to exempt income properly so-called. . . ." Two dissenting Justices, evidently out of touch with common understanding, argued that since the taxpayer's interest in the trust was in fact a "gift by will—a bequest," the payments received by him literally qualified for the exclusion.

Although somewhat oracular, the *Gavit* opinion is plainly correct in its main conclusion. If both corpus *and* income were exempt from tax under § 102(a), the exclusion for gifts and bequests would be greater when divided interests were created than when the entire property was given to one person. Using our example again, a victory for the taxpayer in *Gavit* might have meant that not only the $100,000 of securities ultimately received by the son, but also the $8,000 of annual income paid to the wife, would qualify for exclusion. Assuming the wife lived out her 15-year expectancy, the total amount

---

[54]   268 U.S. 161 (1925).

excluded would then be $220,000—$100,000 principal plus $120,000 (15 × $8,000) of income—a result which Congress could not possibly have intended unless it meant to encourage all testators and donors to create split interests in their property. The holding in *Gavit*, now codified in § 102(b)(2), makes it clear that only the principal of a gift or bequest is excludable from the income of the donee or heir.

There is, however, another feature to the *Gavit* decision—one that deserves the reader's careful attention. In holding that trust income cannot be excluded by a life-tenant or other income beneficiary, the Court in effect decided not merely how much should be taxed, but *to whom*. The dissenting Justices, after all, were literally correct when they pointed out that the income-beneficiary, as well as the remainderman, had received an "inheritance" from the decedent; there were two heirs under the decedent's will, not merely one. Conceding, as the majority in *Gavit* held, that the income of the trust was not exempt under § 102(a), why should it necessarily follow that all such income must be taxed to one of the decedent's heirs and none to the other? Why not treat the income as divided in some way between the life tenant and the remainderman? And correspondingly, why not allow each to get some benefit from the § 102 exclusion? *Gavit* implies that the exclusion goes to the remainderman alone (perhaps because in common understanding it is he who owns the corpus), while the life-tenant gets all the taxable income. This conclusion, however, is at least debatable and, as will be seen, the "system" thus approved is not the only one that can be conceived of.

The point can be made clear, we hope, by returning to our example. Again, assume two beneficial interests in the trust property, life-estate and remainder. The life-tenant's interest is a "wasting asset"; it terminates at the wife's death, which is expected as a statistical matter to occur in 15 years—though, of course, it may occur sooner than that or later. We can place a present value on the life tenancy by discounting the expected 15 annual payments of $8,000 at, say, 8%. The amount so determined—about $68,000— represents the wife's "share" of the total bequest at the time the trust is created. As there is no more than $100,000 of property in total, the present value of the remainder interest is necessarily worth the balance of $32,000. With each year that passes the present value of the life estate decreases, because one less payment can be expected before the widow's statistical life expectancy is reached. For the same reason the present worth of the remainder goes up; the remainderman is one year closer to obtaining full possession of the entire property.

These actuarial verities suggest that instead of taxing all the trust income to the life-tenant, as required by *Gavit*, we could, in the alternative, treat the life-tenant as if she owned an *annuity*. Her "investment" would be equal to the present value of the life-estate at the decedent's death—that is, $68,000—and this amount would be recovered ratably over the period of her life-expectancy. Indeed, had the decedent simply left his wife the $68,000 in cash, she could presumably have purchased an $8,000 life annuity for that very sum. With a 15-year life-expectancy, she would then anticipate payments totaling $120,000 (15 × $8,000). Under the formula applicable to annuities (see 2.02), she would treat 68/120ths of each annual payment—$4,533—as recovery of capital, and the balance, $3,467, as taxable income. The total cost-recovery over the period of her life expectancy would, of course, equal $68,000, the present value of the life estate at the commencement of the trust.

What about the remainderman under this approach? As noted, the decline in the value of the life estate which results from the passage of time is necessarily mirrored by a growth in the value of the remainder interest. In fact, assuming that the value of the trust principal remains constant, the value of the remainder will increase from $32,000 to $100,000 over the 15-year period. Using the same straight-line method as was allowed to the life tenant, the remainderman would therefore be required to report annual income of $4,533, the yearly increase in the value of the remainder. Since he would receive no actual cash distribution, however, the remainderman would be entitled to add the amount taxed to the basis of his remainder interest, so that if the life tenant were to die at the end of 15 years, the remainderman's basis for the corpus received on termination of the trust would be $100,000.

In effect, under the above approach, the remainderman is treated as if he had purchased a 15-year endowment policy for $32,000 cash. It might, indeed, be argued that as the interest-accumulation on an endowment contract issued by an insurance company is not taxed until the policy matures (see 2.03, above), the same element of deferral should be allowed when the policy is "issued" by a private individual, that is, the decedent. If this view were accepted, the average remainderman would still be taxed on an aggregate income of $68,000, but not until the termination of the trust.

The "system" just described divides the exclusion afforded by § 102(a) *between* the life-tenant ($68,000) and the remainderman ($32,000). By contrast, the *Gavit* decision (as the Treasury regulations indicate[55]) allocates the entire exclusion to the remainderman as if he alone were the recipient of the "bequest." Thus, the life tenant is annually taxed on the full $8,000 of trust

---

[55] Reg. § 1.1014–5.

"income"—no portion of her annual distribution is excludable as recovery of basis.[56] The remainderman, on the other hand, is taxed on *nothing* during the term of the trust. Although the remainder interest grows in value from year to year, that growth is excluded from the remainderman's income under § 102(a). When the trust terminates, the remainderman's basis for the trust property, which he then receives from the trustee, will be the same as the trustee's basis for the property—$100,000 in our example. In effect, the son's basis for his remainder interest goes up from $32,000 to $100,000 over the term of the trust, until, on termination, that basis equals the basis of the property in the hands of the trustee. This adjustment assures that the remainderman will get the full benefit of the bequest exclusion just as if the property had been left to him outright instead of being placed in trust. Thus, if the son sells the property for cash after the trust has terminated, he will recognize no gain on such sale unless the property has appreciated in value since the date of the decedent's death. Once again, the effect of all this is to tax the trust income to the life-tenant alone, and to allocate the entire exclusion to the remainderman.

In summary, if the trust lasts exactly 15 years, the overall taxable income, overall excludable bequest, and basis on termination under each of the two "systems" would be as follows:

	Gavit System		"Annuity" System	
	Income beneficiary	Remainder-man	Income beneficiary	Remainder-man
Total taxable income	$ 120,000	–0–	$ 52,000	$ 68,000
Total excludable bequest	–0–	$ 100,000	68,000	32,000
Basis on termination		100,000		100,000

The choice between these two approaches to the taxation of divided interests thus essentially is a question of who shall bear the tax on current trust income. The annuity system (rather like the dissent in *Gavit* itself) stresses the fact that there are two bequests involved, and in effect allocates the exclusion, and hence the income, between them. The *Gavit* approach in a sense disregards the two-bequest factor, allocating the entire exclusion to the remainderman and all the income to the life tenant.

---

[56]   Code § 273.

On the side of the *Gavit* approach—which otherwise seems slightly inferior on theoretical grounds—is a considerable element of practicality and convenience. The life tenant does, after all, receive the annual cash flows of the trust, and everything else being equal, one can argue that tax-payment obligations ought to be associated with cash inflows if no serious distortion results. It is true that the imposition of tax does not generally depend upon the receipt of cash by taxpayers; but where two candidates for taxation appear, one of whom receives cash while the other receives implicit income only, the choice problem is probably best resolved by taxing the former and excusing the latter. The so-called annuity system, moreover, requires the imputation of a suitable discount rate. This can be done fairly confidently in the case of a fixed-income security like a bond, but where the trust property consists of stock, real estate or other assets whose expected yield is uncertain, the selection of a discount rate often would be difficult and controversial.

At all events, the taxing system adopted in *Gavit* is the foundation for a much more elaborate superstructure of rules governing the taxation of trusts and trust beneficiaries.[57] Apart from a very brief mention in Section 9, below, those rules, which are exceedingly technical, are omitted from this volume. At bottom, however, their purpose, like the Court's in *Gavit*, is chiefly to determine who gets the gift (or bequest) exclusion, and who is stuck with the taxable income, when more than one or even two plausible candidates are in the running and available for either role.

Problems relating to divided interests in the same property are a recurring nuisance in the tax law, as will be seen at many points. The *Gavit* discussion, as well as some of the remarks made at 2.01 in connection with the taxation of dividends, should help to introduce certain mechanical elements—chiefly discounting and compounding—which are common to all.

4.03 Commercial Gifts

The term "gift" is not defined in § 102(a). While the context—"gift, bequest, devise or inheritance"—strongly suggests that the exclusion is aimed at intra-family transfers of wealth, generosity is not solely a function of family relationship, and one may have friends, household servants, employees, even business associates, towards whom one feels a generous impulse now and then. In any event, motives are sometimes mixed. An employer may feel both a business and a personal obligation to a retiring employee, and a gift of the traditional gold watch, along with the employer's check for $10,000, may partly be explained in business terms but partly also as an

---

[57] Code § 641 *et seq.*

expression of personal affection. Must the employee treat the check (putting to one side the miserable watch) as a taxable bonus, or can it be excluded from income under § 102(a)? What standards or guidelines should the law apply in distinguishing "gifts" from compensation?

The Supreme Court has indicated that the term "gift" in § 102(a) is largely to be defined by reference to the motives of the payor.[58] If the payment, though voluntary, is "in return for services rendered," or proceeds from "the constraining force of any moral or legal duty," or anticipates a "benefit" to the payor, then it is taxable to the payee even if characterized as a "gift" by the payor. On the other hand, if the payment proceeds from a "detached and disinterested generosity," if it is made "out of affection, respect . . . or like impulses," then it is an excludable gift even though the relationship between payor and payee has previously been in a business context. Apparently feeling that further efforts at formal definition would be useless, the Court in the *Duberstein* case[59] stated that "primary weight in this area must be given to the conclusions of the trier of fact," that is, the trial judge or the jury, whose task is evidently to determine in each case, mainly on the basis of the parties' self-serving testimony, whether the payor acted out of affection and respect or constraint and obligation. The government's effort to promote specific rules aimed at distinguishing transfers of property made for "personal" reasons from those made for "business" reasons was rejected as overly mechanical. Instead, the Court held that each case must be approached individually and that in ascertaining the payor's motives resort should be had to the "fact-finding tribunal's experience with the mainsprings of human conduct."

Presumably, the Court realized that it was inviting a wide variety of results among the decided cases in the field of commercial gifts; in any event, the cases generally show a lack of coherence. Thus, although the "retiring employee" cases have usually been found to involve taxable income, triers of fact have sometimes been led to regard what surely looks like severance pay as an excludable gift. In the *Stanton* case[60] for example, the taxpayer, president of the real-estate investment subsidiary of Trinity Church in New York, was awarded a "gratuity" of $20,000 (over $290,000 in 2018 dollars) on his resignation after many years of service. It was explained by a church official that the taxpayer "had a pleasing personality . . . did a splendid piece of work . . . was liked by all the members of the Vestry personally." Finding nothing but "good will, esteem and

---

[58] See, *e.g.*, *Robertson v. U.S.*, 343 U.S. 711 (1952); *Bogardus v. Commissioner*, 302 U.S. 34 (1937).

[59] *Commissioner v. Duberstein*, 363 U.S. 278 (1960).

[60] *Stanton v. U.S.*, 186 F.Supp. 393 (E.D.N.Y.1960).

kindliness" in the minds of the Vestrymen, the trial court held the payment to be excludable from income under the Supreme Court's motivation test.

The "gifts-to-widows" cases show even greater diversity. A corporation, typically closely-held, makes payments to the widow of a deceased executive, usually by continuing the decedent's salary for a year or two.[61] In some instances the decedent, and through him his widow or estate, is actually the company's controlling stockholder. Emphasizing the absence of legal obligation to the widow or economic benefit to the corporation, some courts have held the payments to be exempt; others, stressing the value of the decedent's prior services to the company, have found the payments to be taxable income. No systematic basis can be suggested for distinguishing the tax winners in these cases from the tax losers. In the end, it is simply a matter of divergent perceptions about "the mainsprings of human conduct" on the part of the triers of fact.

Must there be such diversity of result? Or could a standard be proposed which would lead to a larger measure of uniformity among the cases? If no such standard exists, because motivation (even under the government's personal-or-business test) inevitably depends on the fact-finder's subjective impression of the parties' sincerity, could we at least find ways of limiting the occasions for controversy and dispute? To be sure, the Supreme Court's emphasis on the fact-finder's role pretty well assures that the Court itself will never again review the question of how "gift" should be defined for income tax purposes. But is there also some means of reducing the burden on the trial courts and administrators who meet the problem on a day-to-day basis?

Code § 274(b), added in 1962, has undoubtedly accomplished a good deal in this direction by imposing tax symmetry on the payee and the payor (other than employees and employers; see below). The section prohibits the deduction as business expenses of gifts to individuals (in excess of $25), and thus makes clear—as the decided cases had not previously done—that payments treated as exempt gifts to payees cannot also be deducted by payors.[62] The payor can defend its business expense deduction by claiming that its motivation for the transfer was compensation for services or an anticipated benefit to itself, rather than "detached and disinterested generosity." Given the Supreme Court's focus in its § 102 analysis on the transferor's intent, however, the payor's claimed business motivation

---

[61]   *E.g., Poyner v. Commissioner*, 301 F.2d 287 (4th Cir. 1962).

[62]   Compare *Carter's Estate v. Commissioner*, 453 F.2d 61 (2d Cir. 1971), holding a payment to an employee's widow excludable under § 102(a), with *Bank of Palm Beach & Trust Co. v. U.S.*, 476 F.2d 1343 (Ct.Cl. 1973), allowing the employer to deduct the same payment as a "business" gift. The cases arose prior to § 274(b).

will undermine—probably fatally—any attempt by the payee to claim the payment is a tax-free gift. If the payor wishes, instead, to support the payee's "gift" characterization by asserting a gift-type motivation for the payment, it will have to forgo a deduction for the amount paid, and in effect make the payment out of after-tax income. Thus, Congress is content if at least one party pays the tax, whether it is the payee (through inclusion) or the payor (through disallowance).[63] Although payor and payee still can adopt contrary characterizations of the same item, the contradiction between the payor's stated motive in making the payment and the payee's attempt to label it a gift should render the payee's position untenable in most (and perhaps all) such instances.

In 1986 Congress decided to go beyond tax symmetry and to deny the "gift" characterization entirely in the case of employee-payees. Accordingly, § 102(c) now provides that no exclusion shall be allowed for amounts paid by an employer to an employee (other than gifts regarded as *de minimis* under § 132, *e.g.*, birthday and holiday gifts of property—not cash—of modest value). Of the cases mentioned above, *Stanton* would appear to be most clearly affected by the newer provision. The taxpayer having been an employee of the payor, the $20,000 cash "gratuity" paid to him on his resignation would no longer qualify for exclusion even though the employer's motives were found to be wholly generous and disinterested.[64] Payments to employees are simply placed outside the "gift" category as far as the payee is concerned, nondeductibility by the payor being irrelevant.

In a sense, § 102(c) confirms or supports the result reached by the Supreme Court in the *Old Colony* case, discussed at 3.01. There the employer's effort (unsuccessful) was to compensate a valued executive *net* of the executive's income tax by paying that tax directly. A similar effort was made in *Stanton* (successfully as it turned out) by characterizing the retirement bonus as a "gift." In ruling out the latter characterization, § 102(c) in effect bars employers from assuming their employees' tax burdens by forgoing otherwise allowable deductions. In *Stanton*, of course, the employer, a church, was presumably exempt from tax, so that a forgone deduction would have cost it nothing in any case.

---

[63]   Strictly speaking, of course, Congress should be indifferent as to which party pays the tax only if the two parties have the same marginal tax rate, which will often not be the case.

[64]   Would it make a difference if the employer waited until the employment relationship had ended before making the payment? Read literally, § 102(c) covers only payments to "employees"; it says nothing about payments to *former* employees. It seems likely, however, that the IRS and the courts would interpret the provision as covering any payment arising out of an employment relationship, even if the relationship had ended before the payment was made.

A loose end. A standard restaurant tip of 15 percent or 20 percent is clearly not an excludable gift. Despite the absence of a legal requirement to tip, diners leave tips "in return for services rendered" and from "the constraining force of [a] moral . . . duty." The IRS's problem with respect to tips is not whether tips are includable in gross income (they clearly are), but collecting the tax. An IRS study estimated that taxpayers reported only about 16 percent of their tip income in 1981. In response to this information, Congress enacted § 6053 in 1982. Under this provision, if the employees of a "large food and beverage establishment" do not voluntarily report to the restaurant (and to the IRS) tips totaling at least 8 percent of the restaurant's gross receipts from food and beverage sales, then the restaurant must allocate the shortfall among its employees and report the allocation to the IRS on the employees' W-2 forms (information returns). If a restaurant's customers actually tip at an average rate of 16 percent, § 6053 will be effective in enforcing taxation of half—but only half—of the tips.

5. The Realization Requirement—*Macomber*, *Bruun*, and the Divorce Cases

5.01 General Comment

The realization requirement has such a varied application in the income tax field that it cannot be summarized or canvassed in a single section and is best taught on the pervasive method. Still, some sort of general introduction should be attempted, and this is done here, as it is in many of the casebooks, by briefly examining certain of the acknowledged classics in the field, namely, *Eisner v. Macomber*, *Helvering v. Bruun*, *Cottage Saving*, and the *Davis* and *Farid-Es-Sultaneh* cases. Another group of realization problems, largely associated with real estate transactions, appears in Part E.

It is important to remind oneself at the outset that realization is strictly an administrative rule and not a constitutional, much less an economic, requirement of "income." Early cases, like *Macomber*, do give support to the idea that the Constitution limits "income" to realized gains, but at present most tax commentators would be likely to feel that the Congressional taxing power is not seriously restricted by such an implied requirement, and that Congress is free to treat gains and losses as "realized" pretty much whenever it chooses. As was suggested at 4.01(b), Congress could surely tax property appreciation at gift or at death if it desired to do so, and while a gift or bequest can be regarded as a realization event through semantic manipulation, it is difficult to suppose at this late date that the constitutionality of taxing such appreciation would depend on whether gifts and bequests could be forced into the mold of "realization."

Assuming, moreover, that "income" refers to the annual increase in one's disposable wealth, then, from an economic standpoint, a stockowner whose unsold shares have appreciated in value by $1,000 over the course of a year has just as much "income" as a stockowner who receives $1,000 in dividends or a speculator who sells his shares and realizes $1,000 of trading profits. The latter two, of course, are taxed currently, while the former, owing to the realization requirement, is permitted to treat his gain as exempt from tax until he disposes of his appreciated shares. Yet the increase in disposable wealth is identical for each, though reflected in cash in the latter cases and in kind in the former. To be sure, stock that has gone up one year may go down the next and finally be sold for no more than the original purchase price. But the same is true for the trader who sells his stock at year-end and reinvests the gain in other shares which subsequently decline, or of the dividend-recipient whose company sustains an operating loss in the period following. We may indeed wish to do something about fluctuating income through the adoption of an averaging device of some sort (see 10.01); but the possibility that income will fluctuate from year to year, or that gains *may* be succeeded by losses, can hardly be taken to show that the taxpayer has not been enriched when the value of his property appreciates. "If all business ventures were initiated and completed within the fiscal period, the realization criterion would lead to no serious confusion. But, in a world where ventures often have neither beginning nor end within the lives of interested parties, it is hard to argue that one may grow richer indefinitely without increasing one's income."[65]

Yet all this argumentation should not be taken to mean that an overall change in the realization requirement is contemplated or even desirable. Our tax system does not reach mere changes in property value, and apart from recurring proposals to treat gifts and bequests as realization events, few commentators would suggest that the realization requirement should be materially altered. The difficulty of making annual property appraisals may be the chief reason for this attitude of acceptance; the absence of ready cash to pay the tax on property appreciation and the consequent "forced liquidation" of assets to meet tax obligations is another. To be sure, neither reason is especially compelling where readily marketable property (*e.g.*, listed securities) is concerned; nor, as has been seen, does the law shrink from taxing compensation even when received in kind. Still,

---

[65] Simons, *op. cit.* note 12, p. 82. For discussion (extensive), see Shaviro, *An Efficiency Analysis of Realization and Recognition Rules under the Federal Income Tax*, 48 Tax L.Rev. 1 (1992); Strnad, *Periodicity and Accretion Taxation: Norms and Implementation*, 99 Yale L.J. 1817 (1990); Fellows, *A Comprehensive Attack on Tax Deferral*, 88 Mich.L.Rev. 722 (1990); Shakow, *Taxation Without Realization: A Proposal for Accrual Taxation*, 134 U.Pa.L.Rev. 1111 (1986).

the justifications for a realization requirement seem reasonably strong to most observers, and as stated, no overall change is imminent. Our main purpose here, in any case, is not to question realization as a policy matter; rather, the object is to stress that because the realization requirement exists, the income tax is a tax on *transactions* instead of being a tax on income in the economic sense. Dividends, interest and rents, gains on sales of property, salaries, wages and fees—all these are taxable because they occur through the medium of an "exchange." Property appreciation, though undoubtedly an enrichment to the property owner, is exempt from tax precisely because the transactional aspect is thought to be lacking. As noted earlier (1.03), the absence of an exchange is also the key to the exclusion from gross income of imputed rental income and imputed income from services performed for oneself.

The materials that follow should help to illustrate the scope of the realization requirement. They should also confirm (as the reader perhaps already suspects) that its application in close cases is fairly arbitrary. In that respect, as in others, realization bears a resemblance to the problem of cost-recovery considered in Section 2. Once again, what is chiefly at stake from the taxpayer's standpoint is the anticipation or deferral of tax payments—that is, the timing of taxable income. An investor who sells appreciated property for cash pays a tax on the appreciation currently and can reinvest only the after-tax proceeds. An investor who retains his appreciated property—or who can somehow dispose of it without triggering a "realization"—pays no tax and therefore has more available for reinvestment. Although unrealized appreciation may be taxed in the future if the property is sold, the postponement can be of considerable value to the property-owner, as has been seen, and it is often worth his while to litigate when the application of the realization rule is in doubt. In addition, there is always the possibility that the angel of § 1014 (4.01(b)) will fly over the property before it is sold, in which case the basis will be increased to fair market value and the appreciation will never be taxed.

5.02 Stock Dividends

In *Eisner v. Macomber*[66] the Supreme Court was required to decide whether a common stock dividend could constitutionally be taxed as "income" to the shareholder-recipients. The taxpayer owned 2,200 shares of Standard Oil common stock. Standard Oil declared a 50% stock dividend and the taxpayer received 1,100 additional shares of which about $20,000 in par value represented earnings accumulated by the company since the effective date of the original income tax law. The statute then applicable expressly included stock

---

[66] 252 U.S. 189 (1920).

dividends in income, in effect taxing such dividends in much the same way as dividends in cash.

In a lengthy opinion by Justice Pitney—matched by an interminable dissent from Justice Brandeis—the Supreme Court held that stock dividends could not be treated as income within the meaning of the Sixteenth Amendment:

> We are clear that not only does a stock dividend really take nothing from the property of the corporation and add nothing to that of the shareholder, but that the antecedent accumulation of profits evidenced thereby, while indicating that the shareholder is the richer because of an increase of his capital, at the same time shows he has not realized or received any income in the transaction.

The Brandeis dissent—based more on concepts of corporate finance than taxation—argued in effect that a stock dividend is really a two-step affair consisting of (i) a cash distribution, followed by (ii) a purchase of additional shares through the exercise of stock subscription rights. Looked at in that way, stock dividends are actually the equivalent of cash dividends and are therefore properly taxable. There was also a very brief dissent from Justice Holmes, who observed, "I cannot doubt that most people not lawyers would suppose when they voted for [the Sixteenth Amendment] that they put a question like the present to rest."

Congress responded to the *Macomber* decision by amending the statute to exempt stock dividends from tax, and the same exemption (with exceptions not relevant for us) appears in § 305(a) of the present Code.

The constitutional issues raised by *Eisner v. Macomber* are explored briefly in the "loose end" at the end of this section. For the moment, however, our focus is not on the Constitution, but on the relationship between the holding in *Macomber* and the overall treatment of corporations and shareholders under the Internal Revenue Code. In effect, *Macomber* held that the tax law applies differently depending on whether a dividend is received in stock or in cash. Is this distinction a sound one, given the structural design of the Code in this area, or does it create an inconsistency which ought to be regretted? Viewed apart from the Constitution, and viewed also as if Congress had never legislated on the subject of stock dividends but had left the matter entirely to common law development, which of the two positions taken in *Macomber*, Pitney's or Brandeis', seems best to accord with the acknowledged elements of the taxing scheme? In short, is the outcome good or bad, wise or foolish?

A description of the tax treatment of corporations and shareholders should begin with Code § 11, which imposes a separate tax on corporate earnings at a flat rate of 21%. Taxable income is determined for corporations in pretty much the same way as it is for individuals, but the separate 21% corporate income tax applies without regard to whether the individual shareholders who "own" the company would pay tax at a different rate (or rates) if the corporate income were charged to them directly. The corporate tax is imposed on corporations as entities; it does not purport to be a proxy or substitute for the tax that would otherwise be payable by the individual security-owners.

This distinction between a corporation and its owners is reflected in the fact that a second-level tax is imposed on the corporation's shareholders when corporate earnings are distributed as dividends. The dividend (if in cash) is includable in the shareholder's gross income in full, and is taxed at the shareholder's rate for long-term capital gain (usually 15% or 20%). But although taxable to the shareholder, the dividend distribution is *not* deductible by the corporation. Dividends are not regarded as business expenses and cannot be deducted in computing corporate taxable income. As a result, corporate income is taxed *once* at the entity level when received by the company itself; when (or if) the company's after-tax earnings are distributed to the shareholders as dividends, a *second* tax is imposed on the shareholders themselves.

Of course most corporations do not distribute all of their after-tax earnings as dividends—indeed, closely-held corporations usually distribute little or none. Typically, a corporation will retain some (often the greater part) of its annual earnings to finance the replacement or expansion of its plant and equipment, to pay for research and development, or to make new investments. Everything else being equal, the amount retained by the company and reinvested in productive assets will be reflected directly in the value of the company's shares. Undistributed earnings are obviously not lost to the shareholders; rather, they show up as unrealized stock appreciation which in some measure reflects the increase in tangible and other assets held by the firm. From a tax standpoint, however, the important point is that retained earnings are not taxed to the shareholders *until* they are actually distributed as dividends. No "constructive" dividend is imputed to the shareholders; the only tax imposed is at the corporate level as long as earnings are kept back by the corporation for use in its business. To be sure, unrealized stock appreciation will ultimately be converted into taxable gain when the stock is sold for cash. But, as noted, that event may be deferred for many years—perhaps for a lifetime, in which case § 1014 will convert the deferral to a permanent exclusion—and in the meanwhile a shareholder whose stock appreciates from year to year enjoys an increase in his personal wealth without increasing his income subject to tax.

The contrast between the tax treatment of corporate earnings distributed as dividends and undistributed corporate earnings reflected in increased share value creates a need to draw a clear dividing line between dividends and retentions. Investors, as well as the Treasury, have an interest in clarity at this point since individual investment choices will be guided in part by the tax consequences of the distribution policies which particular corporations adopt and make known to the public. Many investors prefer large annual dividends and a regular flow of cash despite the tax disadvantage; others prefer the opposite pattern. What is important, obviously, is that the investor have some idea in advance of just what sort of tax-and-distribution package he is buying.

Unfortunately, the dividing line between dividends and non-dividends cannot be drawn in the same way as the line between income and non-income: that is, one cannot say that dividends entail gain or enrichment while non-dividends do not. A shareholder who owns stock worth $110 *prior* to the payment of a $10 dividend is no richer *after* the dividend is paid when the stock (ex-dividend) drops to $100. The investor's personal net worth remains $110, whether represented by stock alone or stock plus cash. In *Macomber*, Justice Pitney stressed that the stock dividend added nothing to the interests of the shareholders, that the shareholders were no richer after the additional shares had been received than they were before. He was, of course, correct. The trouble is that exactly the same observation can be made about cash dividends—they, too, leave the shareholder no richer after than before. Essentially, therefore, the question in *Macomber* was not whether the shareholder had gain in an economic sense, but whether in legal or accounting terms the stock dividend was to be regarded as a taxable event.

Stripped of its constitutional element, the issue in *Eisner v. Macomber* in the end comes down to a "battle of similarities." Is a stock dividend (as the majority held) "more like" a situation in which a corporation simply accumulates its earnings and makes no distribution at all? Or is it (as Brandeis thought) "more like" the receipt of a cash dividend which is followed by a reinvestment of the cash received in additional shares? So limited, it seems apparent that Pitney had the better of the debate. Overall, the aim of the tax law is to impose a tax on "dividends" when assets representing corporate earnings are transferred to the shareholders. Stock dividends, however, merely give the shareholders additional pieces of paper to represent the same equitable interest; they do not transfer assets or create new priorities among the security-holders. The total value of the common shares, though now spread out over a larger number of units, is left unchanged from its previous level. In effect, nothing of substance has occurred. Justice Brandeis' effort to construct, or read in, a cash distribution was strained and unconvincing. The plain fact is that Mrs. Macomber did not receive, and could not have obtained, a cash payment from Standard Oil. Had she wished to substitute cash in an amount equivalent to the value of the stock dividend, she would have had to sell the dividend shares to other investors. No other cash source was made available. The Brandeis analysis would have had more force if Standard Oil had announced itself willing to pay a dividend in stock or cash at the shareholder's election, or if shareholders had been given an option to redeem their dividend shares (that is, to cash them in) immediately after the distribution. But no such option or election was afforded. In purely mechanical terms, therefore, the Brandeis view was unpersuasive. The majority was right: a stock dividend more closely resembles a simple accumulation of earnings than it does a cash dividend or even an optional dividend of cash-or-stock.

As noted, Code § 305 adopts the *Macomber* decision by excluding common stock dividends from the shareholder's gross income. Section 307 provides as a corollary that the shareholder's basis for the dividend shares is a proportionate part of the cost of the original lot. To illustrate, suppose A owns 100 shares of General Motors at a cost of $49.50 a share, or $4,950. GM now declares a 10% stock dividend and distributes 10 additional shares to A, which he promptly sells on the market for $50 a share, or $500. Under § 307, A's basis for his GM stock becomes $45 a share ($4,950/110). The 10 dividend shares thus take a basis of $450, and when sold for $500, a capital gain of $50 results. By contrast, if the Brandeis view of stock dividends had prevailed, the shareholder would have $500 of income. The dividend would be taxed in full rather than being offset by a portion of the shareholder's original cost, and it would be taxed immediately rather than when the shares were finally sold. Given this set of consequences, stock dividends, like smallpox, would by now have become a thing of the past.

A final note may be useful, at least to some readers. In addition to corporations, there are also two traditional *non*-corporate forms of doing business; namely, partnerships and sole proprietorships. (The limited liability company (LLC), a relatively recent innovation, is generally treated as a partnership for tax purposes.) A large law firm would be organized as a partnership. The corner shoe-repair shop might be a sole proprietorship. Partnerships and proprietorships (and LLCs taxed as partnerships) are not subject to an entity-level tax as corporations are, but instead are treated simply as accounting entities whose net income (or loss) is included directly in the gross income of the partners or proprietor.

To illustrate, assume Smith & Jones, a law firm with 50 partners, has gross fees of $60 million this year and expenses (salaries, rent, etc.) of $40 million. S & J's net income, obviously $20 million, is reported on a partnership information return but is not taxed to the partnership as an entity. Rather, the $20 million of partnership net income is included in the gross income of the 50 happy partners in accordance with their relative percentage interests in the partnership. If some of them have income from other sources—dividends, interest—gross income includes such other income as well.

Although S & J's net income is $20 million for the year, it is likely that the firm's management committee will decide to pay out to the partners somewhat less than the full amount, say only $19 million, and hold back $1 million as a reserve for future expansion costs or possible emergencies or whatever. The partners must nevertheless include the full $20 million in their individual gross incomes. The $1 million hold-back is taxed just as if distributed and becomes a contribution by each partner to his partnership capital account—in effect, an investment in the partnership. If a partner withdraws from the partnership or retires at some point, he presumably gets back whatever amount is then in his capital account with no further tax to pay.

Same for proprietorships. The shoe repair shop calculates its net income—sales less expenses—on the proprietor's Schedule C ("Profit or Loss from Business"), which is attached to his individual tax return for the year. That amount is included in the proprietor's gross income, whether actually withdrawn or left in the business, together with his income from other sources, if any.

Since partnerships and proprietorships are free of the two-level tax that afflicts corporations and shareholders, why would anybody choose to do business in corporate form? Big companies with tens or hundreds of thousands of shareholders really cannot do otherwise—the New York Stock Exchange lists corporate stock, not partnership interests—and in any event Code § 7704 provides that a publicly-traded partnership is taxed as a corporation. But what about smaller companies whose ownership is limited to just a few individuals, maybe even just one? The answer is given—or, rather, the question is discussed—at 9.03(b), below. At the risk of spoiling the suspense, one point made in the later discussion is worth previewing here. If a closely-held corporation satisfies the statutory definition of a "small business corporation," its shareholders can elect out of the double-tax regime ordinarily applicable to corporations, with the result that the single-tax regime of Subchapter S (Code § 1361 *et seq.*) applies. The

Subchapter S rules are broadly similar to the partnership tax rules; the S corporation itself pays no tax, but S corporation shareholders are taxed on their proportionate shares of the corporation's income, whether or not the income is distributed.

———————

A loose end. How did Justice Pitney conclude, in *Macomber*, that the tax on stock dividends was unconstitutional? The answer is a bit complicated. The Constitution provides (in both art. I, § 2, cl. 3, and art. I, § 9, cl. 4), that any federal "direct" tax must be apportioned among the states in accordance with their populations. The Constitution does not, however, enumerate or define direct taxes. Only two types of taxes—head (capitation) taxes imposed at a flat dollar amount on the privilege of having a head, and *ad valorem* real property taxes—were clearly within the original understanding of direct taxes. When Congress enacted a low-rate income tax in 1894, without (of course) making any attempt to apportion the tax among the states in accordance with their populations, taxpayers quickly challenged it as an unconstitutional unapportioned direct tax. One year later, in *Pollock v. Farmer's Loan & Trust Co.*,[67] the Supreme Court struck down the tax. The Court broadly (and dubiously) interpreted the direct tax category to include not only *ad valorem* property taxes (on both real and personal property), but also taxes on the income from property (both real and personal). Strictly speaking, *Pollock* did not rule out all forms of federal income taxation; either an apportioned income tax or an unapportioned tax limited to labor income would have been permissible. Congress had no interest, however, in a tax of either sort.

In 1913 the Sixteenth Amendment was ratified, in direct—albeit delayed—response to *Pollock*. It reversed the result in *Pollock* by providing, "The Congress shall have power to lay and collect taxes on incomes, from whatever source derived, without apportionment among the several states, and without regard to any census or enumeration." Enactment of the modern income tax followed quickly upon the heels of the ratification of the Amendment. Why was the congressional attempt to tax stock dividends still unconstitutional—according to the *Macomber* majority—even after the ratification of the Sixteenth Amendment? The Court reasoned that a tax on a stock dividend (i) was not a tax on "income" within the meaning of the Sixteenth Amendment, (ii) was a "direct" tax within the meaning of the original Constitution, and (iii) was therefore invalid for lack of apportionment.

———————

[67]   158 U.S. 601 (1895).

If the Supreme Court had persisted in its narrow interpretation of "income" in the Amendment, the Constitution would have imposed serious constraints on the ability of Congress to expand the base of the income tax. Although the Court has never explicitly overruled *Macomber*, in a number of later opinions it has described the realization requirement as "founded on administrative convenience"[68]—quite a comedown for what started out as a rule of constitutional law. In the decades following *Macomber*, Congress has enacted several specialized provisions which the *Macomber* court would almost certainly have considered unconstitutional taxes on unrealized appreciation. For example, § 475 requires securities dealers to include annually in their gross income any increase in the value of securities held as inventory. Despite the seeming impermissibility of such a tax under the *Macomber* analysis, the constitutionality of § 475 (and other similar provisions) is not in serious doubt.

The meaning of "income" in the Sixteenth Amendment returned briefly as a hot topic in 2006, when the Court of Appeals for the District of Columbia concluded, in *Murphy v. I.R.S.*,[69] that taxation of damages relating to nonphysical personal injuries (*e.g.,* from intentional infliction of emotional distress) was unconstitutional because such damages were not income. The opinion was subjected to withering criticism in the blogosphere from tax and constitutional law experts. Upon reconsideration,[70] the court decided that a tax on damages for nonphysical injuries was not a direct tax (within the meaning of the original Constitution). As a result, the tax was valid without apportionment, regardless of whether it qualified as a tax on income.

It is possible, of course, for the Internal Revenue Code to violate some general constitutional requirement, rather than a tax-specific requirement. In practice, however, it hardly ever happens. A rare exception is *Moritz v. Commissioner*,[71] in which the Tenth Circuit struck down, as a violation of equal protection, a provision allowing never-married women—but not never-married men—a deduction for dependent care expenses. Mr. Moritz was represented by the team of Ruth Bader Ginsburg and her husband (and prominent tax attorney) Martin Ginsburg. Although any number of facially-neutral provisions of the income tax may have disparate impacts on men and women, or on taxpayers of different races or ethnicities, the Internal Revenue Code is now free (to the best of our knowledge) of the sort of explicit

---

[68]   *Cottage Savings Assn. v. Commissioner,* 499 U.S. 554 (1991), quoting *Helvering v. Horst,* 311 U.S. 112, 116 (1940).

[69]   460 F.3d 79 (D.C. Cir. 2006).

[70]   493 F.3d 170 (D.C. Cir. 2007).

[71]   469 F.2d 466 (10th Cir. 1972), *cert. denied,* 412 U.S. 906 (1973).

discrimination struck down in *Moritz*. The last instance of explicit discrimination was the tax definition of marriage—on which depends many tax results, mostly favorable to married couples but sometimes unfavorable—as being limited to a relationship between a man and a woman. That final instance was eliminated by the Supreme Court's 2013 decision in *United States v. Windsor*,[72] holding that the definition of "marriage" in the Defense of Marriage Act—as limited to a union between a man and a woman—violated the Due Process Clause of the Fifth Amendment.

Another loose end. In *Macomber*, Justice Pitney observed that common stock dividends "take nothing from the property of the corporation. . . ." In other words, the absence of significant effect at the shareholder level is mirrored by an absence of significant corporate-level effect. To illustrate, assume that X Corporation has the following balance sheet *prior* to the declaration of any dividend:

Assets		Liabilities and Net Worth	
Cash	$ 3,000,000	Common stock (1,000,000	
Other current assets	7,000,000	shares at $10 par)	$10,000,000
Fixed assets	10,000,000	Retained earnings	10,000,000
	$20,000,000		$20,000,000

Assume that at the year-end X Corporation declares, and promptly pays, (i) a dividend of $1,000,000 in *cash*; or (ii) a dividend of $1,000,000 face amount of its own newly issued *bonds*; or (iii) a 5% common *stock* dividend with a value of $1,000,000. Its balance sheet after each alternative form of distribution would look like this:

---

[72]   570 U.S. 12 (2013).

(i) Cash Dividend

Assets		Liabilities and Net Worth	
Cash	$ 2,000,000	Common stock (1,000,000	
Other current assets	7,000,000	shares at $10 par)	$10,000,000
Fixed assets	10,000,000	Retained earnings	9,000,000
	$19,000,000		$19,000,000

(ii) Bond Dividend

Assets		Liabilities and Net Worth	
Cash	$ 3,000,000	Bonds	$ 1,000,000
Other current assets	7,000,000	Common stock (1,000,000 shares at $10 par)	10,000,000
Fixed assets	10,000,000	Retained earnings	9,000,000
	$20,000,000		$20,000,000

(iii) Stock Dividend

Assets		Liabilities and Net Worth	
Cash	$ 3,000,000	Common stock (1,050,000	
Other current assets	7,000,000	shares at $10 par)	$10,500,000
		Capital surplus	500,000
Fixed assets	10,000,000	Retained earnings	9,000,000
	$20,000,000		$20,000,000

The cash dividend produces a contraction *both* in total assets and in Net Worth—and in any case is known to be taxable. The bond dividend is more difficult to categorize; indeed it, rather than the stock dividend, is really the hard case. Total assets are unchanged, but Net Worth is reduced through a shift of $1,000,000 of Retained Earnings to the Bond account. The shareholders still hold nothing more than "pieces of paper," however, and it seems well arguable that without a severance or disinvestment of corporate assets the distribution should be viewed as non-taxable. On the other hand, the shareholders are now elevated to a creditor status to the extent of $1,000,000. The bond-capital is insulated, to a degree, from the ups and downs of the operating business; the bonds represent a right to withdraw corporate assets on maturity; and interest payments are deductible by the corporation (dividends are not). While the correct treatment is by no means self-evident as an original matter and *Macomber* could certainly be cited in support of a tax-free outcome, the Supreme Court in *Bazley v. Commissioner*[73] held that bond distributions are taxable to the stockholders in the amount of their fair market value at the distribution date. Hence bonds and cash are

---

[73]   331 U.S. 737 (1947).

treated alike for this purpose, with the result that bond dividends are now extremely rare.

Coming finally to the stock dividend alternative, it appears that the only balance sheet changes are an increase in the number of shares outstanding and an obligatory transfer from the Retained Earnings account to the Capital Surplus and Common Stock accounts to reflect the value of the newly issued shares. No reduction in the corporation's total assets occurs, because no assets have been distributed. Even more important in view of *Bazley*, there is no contraction of corporate Net Worth, which includes the Common Stock as well as the Capital and Retained Earnings accounts. Whereas the cash or the bond dividend reduces the overall value of the common stock by $1,000,000, the stock dividend leaves the total value of the common shares unchanged and, as stated, merely spreads that value over a larger number of shares. To be sure, the increase in number of shares outstanding is a change of some sort, yet the alteration is of a nominal character when regarded in objective terms.

5.03 Leasehold Termination—*Helvering v. Bruun*

Helvering v. Bruun,[74] another old-timer in the realization field, furnishes a brisk little exercise in tax mechanics. Reducing the main elements to a hypothetical, suppose a taxpayer purchases a tract of vacant land and promptly leases it to a manufacturing concern for 20 years. The lease calls for annual rental payments which are relatively low by market standards, but it also requires that the lessee promptly construct a factory building on the land at a cost of not less than $1,000,000. The building is to become the property of the lessor on termination of the lease and thus apparently constitutes a form of rent-in-kind. Assume that the new building (which is immediately put up by the lessee and costs exactly $1 million) has a useful life of 25 years—5 years longer than the lease itself—and is expected to have a depreciated value of $200,000 at the time the lease expires.

Conceding that the annual cash rentals are income to the lessor, what about the value of the leasehold improvement, which is to vest in the lessor absolutely at the end of 20 years? Does the factory building represent an "accession" to the taxpayer's wealth? If it does, is it "clearly realized"? And if it is, just when does such realization occur?

An inspection of the *Bruun* opinion indicates that no fewer than *four* possible answers can be given to these questions. The first three all assume that the factory building is taxable as additional "rent" to the lessor at some point, but they diverge as to the proper time of

---

[74]   309 U.S. 461 (1940).

inclusion. In effect, these three alternatives reflect the various positions which the Treasury took prior to the *Bruun* decision in an effort to develop a "rule" that would satisfy the courts. The fourth alternative—that argued unsuccessfully by the taxpayer in *Bruun*—apparently assumes that the factory building is not to be viewed as rent (or at least as *realized* rent) at *any* point during the term of the leasehold. In summary, the alternatives are:

#1. *Prepaid rent.* Treat the anticipated value of the factory as includable rent in the year in which the building is erected—Year 1—but discount that anticipated value for the 20-year duration of the lease. If the building is expected to be worth $200,000 at the end of 20 years, the present discounted value of that figure, using an 8% discount rate, is about $50,000. Since this $50,000 of additional rent would be treated as realized in Year 1, perhaps the "transaction" would be regarded as closed at that point and nothing further would be realized when the lease came to an end. The lessor's basis for the building on termination of the lease would then be $50,000—equal to the amount previously included—and his depreciation allowance for the remaining 5 years of the building's useful life would be $10,000 a year, computed on the straight-line method.

#2. *Prorated rent.* Treat the anticipated value of the factory as rent, but instead of including the discounted value in Year 1, spread the full $200,000 over the term of the lease. Thus the lessor would realize and be taxed on $10,000 a year throughout the 20-year term.[75] On expiration of the lease the taxpayer's basis for the building would be $200,000, and his deductible depreciation for the next 5 years would be $40,000 annually.

#3. *Postpaid rent.* Treat the factory as taxable rent, but include nothing until Year 20 when the lease expires and the building becomes the property of the lessor. Assuming actual value equals anticipated value at that date, the effect would be to tax $200,000 on termination of the lease. As with alternative #2, the lessor's basis for the building then would become $200,000, and his subsequent depreciation allowance would be $40,000 a year.

#4. *No rent at all.* Treat the building as unrealized property appreciation and do not tax its value as "rent" at any time. With nothing included in income, the lessor's basis for the building on termination of the lease would obviously be zero, and he would get no depreciation allowance during the 5-year period that followed.

Alternatives #1 and #2—the prepaid and prorated rent alternatives—both require a prediction as to what the value of the factory building will be 20 years into the future. But, as Yogi Berra

---

[75] An economically accurate spreading of the $200,000 over the 20 years would allocate smaller amounts to the early years and larger amounts to the later years, but that detail can be set aside for present purposes.

is reputed to have said, "It's tough to make predictions, especially about the future." Being a tangible asset, the building may or may not be worth $200,000 when the lease expires, and any current estimates of future value are likely to vary over a fairly wide range. While this does not mean that an appraisal is impossible (long-lived assets are bought and sold every day), it does suggest that the risks of making an incorrect prediction are considerable. As already observed (see, *e.g.*, the easement example at 2.01), where uncertainty about valuation exists, the tax law often finds *deferral* to be a convenient and expedient way of coping with the problem. It is not surprising, therefore, that the Treasury's earliest Regulations in this area supported alternative #3, the postpaid rent alternative. Those Regulations held that the value of leasehold improvements was income to the lessor, but only on termination of the lease, that is, in Year 20 in the above illustration. Since termination was the event that caused the realization, "value" for this purpose meant the actual, rather than the expected, value of the improvements at the end of the lease. If, for example, the factory building were worth as much as $300,000 when the lease expired, the taxpayer's includable rent would be that larger figure. His basis for the purpose of computing depreciation thereafter would also be $300,000.

Eminently practical, and ultimately approved by *Bruun* itself, alternative #3 was initially rejected by the courts. Indeed, the pre-*Bruun* cases held that no taxable realization occurred either when the leasehold improvements were installed *or* when the improvements vested in the lessee on expiration of the lease. The factory building, it was reasoned, could not be severed and disposed of separately from the land, was not "portable and detachable" unless torn down and scrapped. While there might be gain to the lessor in economic terms, since the land and building were physically "merged" such gain must be treated as unrealized until the entire property was sold for cash. *Macomber* was said to support this approach—essentially alternative #4—because it, too, stressed the need for a severance of "profit" from underlying "capital" as a condition of taxability.

In the *Bruun* case, the taxpayer-lessor acquired title to certain leasehold improvements through forfeiture of the lease for nonpayment of rent. Impliedly rejecting these earlier court decisions, the Supreme Court held that the value of the improvements was realized by the taxpayer in the year in which the forfeiture occurred.[76] The improvements, the Court observed, were received by the taxpayer "as a result of a business transaction," namely, the leasing of the taxpayer's land. It was not necessary to the recognition

---

[76] Under the actual facts of *Bruun*, the term of the lease exceeded the useful life of the improvements. Accordingly, the Court's choice was apparently limited to inclusion at the time of the forfeiture or no inclusion at all.

of gain that the improvements be severable from the land; all that had to be shown was that the taxpayer had acquired valuable assets from his lessee in exchange for the use of his property. The medium of exchange—whether cash or kind, and whether separately disposable or "affixed"—was immaterial as far as the realization criterion was concerned. In effect, the improvements represented rent, or rather a payment in lieu of rent, which was taxable to the landlord regardless of the form in which it was received.

Although acceptable as an interpretation of the realization requirement, the outcome in *Bruun* in some respects is rather harsh. It seems likely, for example, that the taxpayer's underlying land—which, of course, also reverted to his possession on forfeiture of the lease—had declined in value over the term of the lease for the very same reason (the Depression of the thirties) that had caused the lessee to default on his rental obligation. If the lessor had shown that the fall in land value relative to his original cost was equal to, or greater than, the value of the leasehold improvements, could he have offset his economic loss against that rental income? The answer, most probably, is no. A mere decline in the value of the land, resulting from a drop in the real estate market, would be treated as unrealized property depreciation (*Macomber* would indeed be applicable as to that element), and hence that decline could not be used to offset the realized value of the leasehold improvements. This interplay between the realization rules is unfortunate from the lessor's standpoint, even unfair. But, in a sense, it can't be helped. As already noted, the realization requirement turns the income tax into a tax on transactions rather than a tax on economic gains and losses, with consequences that can sometimes be distressing to the taxpayer as well as beneficial.

In the end, Congress disapproved the result in *Bruun* and eliminated the "realization" by adding § 109 and § 1019 to the Code. Section 109 excludes from a lessor's income the value of leasehold improvements realized on termination of a lease.[77] As a corollary, § 1019 denies the lessor a basis for the property so excluded. In effect, nothing is required to be taken into income when the lease terminates, but no depreciation is allowed thereafter. Under *Bruun*, as stated, if the factory building is worth $200,000 on the termination date, then that amount is included by the lessor in his income and becomes the "tax-paid" basis for the property. With the building having a remaining useful life of 5 years, the lessor would deduct

---

[77] Under Reg. § 1.109–1(a) the exclusion does not apply to improvements whose value is intended to be in lieu of current rents. Taken literally, this exception would seem to undermine the deferral treatment apparently authorized by §§ 109 and 1019 and to revive something like the prepaid rent alternative described above. However, it has rarely been applied.

$40,000 a year as depreciation. Under §§ 109 and 1019, nothing would be includable at termination, but there would be no tax-paid basis for depreciation during the ensuing 5-year period. Sections 109 and 1019 precisely embody the result sought unsuccessfully by the taxpayer in *Bruun*—alternative #4 in effect—which goes to show that there is more than one forum in which taxpayers can dispute their tax obligations.

The choice between the *Bruun* "solution" and that of §§ 109 and 1019 involves nothing more than the *timing* of the lessor's tax payments. Under either, the deductible depreciation allowance precisely offsets the amount (if any) previously included in the lessor's income. But timing choices are important. From the taxpayer's standpoint, the present statutory treatment offers maximum deferral of income, and it is therefore preferable to any of the alternatives.

A loose end. The above comment about "deferral of income" can be made a bit more specific with an illustration. This time, however, we can limit the comparison to alternatives #3 and #4, that is, to a comparison between the *Bruun* "solution" and the statutory relief provisions. Once again, assume that the value of the factory building is $200,000 when the lease terminates in Year 20. Assume further that the building will generate rent of $50,000 a year for the remaining 5-year period. Under *Bruun*, as stated, the lessor-taxpayer has $200,000 of income in year 20; his basis for the building is $200,000; and his deductible depreciation is $40,000 a year. His net rental income in Years 21–25 is therefore $10,000 a year ($50,000 − $40,000). Under §§ 109 and 1019, by contrast, the taxpayer has zero income in Year 20, a zero basis for the building, and zero annual depreciation. Hence, annual rental income is $50,000 in Years 21–25. Finally, assume that the taxpayer pays tax at a rate of 35% in all affected periods.

For convenience, let's treat Year 20 as Year 0 and Years 21–25 as Years 1–5. The question to be answered is: What is the *present value* of the taxpayer's income tax obligations in Year 0 under each of the two tax regimes?

Under *Bruun*

		(1)	(2)	(3)
		Taxable Income	Tax Due	Present Value of (2) at 8%
Year:	0	$200,000	$70,000	$70,000
	1	$ 10,000	$ 3,500	$ 3,241
	2	$ 10,000	$ 3,500	$ 3,000
	3	$ 10,000	$ 3,500	$ 2,779
	4	$ 10,000	$ 3,500	$ 2,573
	5	$ 10,000	$ 3,500	$ 2,383
Totals		$250,000	$87,500	$83,976

Under §§ 109 and 1019

		(1)	(2)	(3)
		Taxable Income	Tax Due	Present Value of (2) at 8%
Year:	0	$ 0	$ 0	$ 0
	1	$ 50,000	$17,500	$16,205
	2	$ 50,000	$17,500	$14,997
	3	$ 50,000	$17,500	$13,895
	4	$ 50,000	$17,500	$12,862
	5	$ 50,000	$17,500	$11,917
Totals		$250,000	$87,500	$69,876

Total income ($250,000) and total tax due ($87,500) are the same under both regimes, but the present value of the taxpayer's income tax obligation is $83,976 under *Bruun* and only $69,876 under the statutory relief provisions. The reason for the difference, of course, is that under *Bruun* $200,000 of income is included in Year 0 and $70,000 of taxes must be paid in Year 0, while under the statutory provisions such income and such taxes are deferred to later periods. As already amply noted (see 1.01), the present value of a dollar of tax that is payable in a later year is always less than a dollar of tax that has to be paid in the current year. The difference between the two is $14,100 in our illustration, assuming a discount rate of about 8%.

Did Congress intend to create a tax *saving* for people in Bruun's circumstances? Probably not. The aim of §§ 109 and 1019 was to relieve lessors—suddenly confronted with large tax obligations—of the need to raise cash, and do it in a hurry, at a time (the 1930's) when the real estate market was scraping bottom. What was not understood, perhaps, was that the means chosen—permitting current income to be deferred to later periods—also had the effect of reducing the lessor's tax obligation absolutely.

5.04 Marital Property Settlements—*Davis* and *Farid-Es-Sultaneh*

A taxpayer who transfers appreciated property in satisfaction of a debt obviously realizes a taxable gain just as if the property had been sold for cash. To illustrate, suppose an individual agrees to buy a car from a dealer for $10,000, but instead of paying cash he somehow persuades the dealer to accept 100 shares of X stock, a listed security. The stock has a market value exactly equal to the purchase price of the car—$10,000—but has a basis in the car-buyer's hands of $3,000. It is clear that the swap results in a realization to both parties; the buyer realizes $10,000 and has a $7,000 gain; the dealer also realizes $10,000 and has a profit represented by his mark-up on the car. Gain and profit having thus been recognized on both sides of the transaction, each party thereafter holds the property acquired from the other at a basis equal to its fair market value on the date of the exchange—again, $10,000.

But suppose the car buyer's dollar obligation to the dealer is disputed. The car actually lists for $10,200 but the buyer asserts that one of the dealer's salesmen told him he could have it for only $9,800. After much wrangling the buyer agrees to transfer and the dealer agrees to accept the X stock worth $10,000 in full satisfaction of the claim. Should the tax outcome be any different merely because the parties contested the amount of the buyer's debt, neither conceding that the other's calculation was correct? Obviously not: the fact that the buyer's obligation was unliquidated, in the sense that it was open to dispute, has no bearing either on the existence of a realization event or on the "amount realized" by the parties pursuant to their settlement. Again the buyer recognizes a gain of $7,000, the dealer is taxed on his profit, and each party holds the property received at a basis of $10,000.

The question raised by the *Davis* and *Farid-Es-Sultaneh* cases was whether these simple conclusions should apply in a family setting in the same way as in a commercial context—the gift problem turned upside-down, so to speak. If a husband transfers appreciated property to his wife in consideration for her release of marital property rights (*e.g.*, dower or statutory right of intestate succession), should that "transaction" be regarded as a taxable exchange? By painful analogy, the wife's status *could* be equated with that of the dealer in the illustration above, the husband's with that of the buyer. The marital property settlement would, of course, be viewed as equivalent to the settlement of the unliquidated claim. But *should* the marital relationship be viewed in these cold-hearted terms?

In *Farid-Es-Sultaneh v. Commissioner*[78] the taxpayer-wife (ex-wife by the time of the sale in question) sold certain shares of stock which she had previously received from her husband-to-be (later her husband, and still later her ex-husband) pursuant to an antenuptial agreement. Under that agreement the taxpayer, in consideration for the shares, had surrendered all marital property rights in the husband's estate. The stock had a basis in the husband's hands of 15 cents a share, but a fair market value of $10 a share when transferred to the taxpayer. The Commissioner contended that the taxpayer's basis in the shares was the same as her husband's—15 cents— because the shares had been received by her as a gift. The court held, however, that the transfer was not a gift for income tax purposes but an exchange of valuable property interests—stock for marital property rights. As a result, it found the taxpayer's basis for the shares to be $10—their fair market value at the date transferred— and reduced her taxable gain accordingly. In effect, the wife's status was treated as identical with that of the auto-*dealer* in the illustration above, whose basis for the stock received from the buyer in exchange for the car was also equal to its fair market value.

In *U.S. v. Davis,*[79] which involved a property settlement incident to divorce rather than marriage, the husband's side of the transaction was at issue. Pursuant to an agreement reached by the parties after a lengthy dispute, the taxpayer transferred appreciated securities to his wife in consideration for the surrender of her marital property claims. Consistent with the *Farid* approach, the Supreme Court found that the transfer was not a gift (nor a mere division of property belonging to the marital partnership as might be true in a community property state), and held that the taxpayer had realized a taxable gain on the exchange. The husband and the car-*buyer* in the illustration were thus also put on a par, each realizing a taxable gain by reason of the transfer.

The *Davis* and *Farid* decisions are undoubtedly defensible in terms of the realization criterion: in general, transfers of property in satisfaction of contract obligations, fixed or disputed, are taxable events, with the amount realized being measured by the value of the property transferred. But as against the larger Code policy embodied in the gift exclusion—§ 102 and its corollary, § 1015—the cases seem misguided, or at least doubtful, in result. If property transfers between spouses are "gifts" when they take place during marriage (with the result that the basis of the property in the transferor's

---

[78]   160 F.2d 812 (2d Cir. 1947).

[79]   370 U.S. 65 (1962).

hands carries over to the transferee), it is difficult to see why transfers which are prompted by the formation of the marital unit should be treated differently. And if transfers from deceased husbands to surviving widows are viewed as *non*-realization events (see 4.01) even though the marital relationship thus comes to an end, it is hard to see why a realization should be deemed to occur when the marriage is terminated through divorce. The presence of a contract obligation, though it otherwise justifies a finding of taxable event, seems insufficient on the whole to remove pre-marital and (much more important) post-marital property arrangements from the ambit of the gift provisions. Quite obviously, family wealth is being divided between husband and wife in both instances, and it is this circumstance—rather than the presence of "consideration" in *Farid* or of arm's-length dealing in *Davis*—that ought to govern the tax outcome.

Having heard criticism of the *Davis/Farid* rule for many years, Congress in the 1984 Act finally overcame those decisions by adding § 1041 to the Code. Section 1041 provides that a transfer of property between spouses, or between former spouses where the transfer is incident to divorce, shall be treated as a "gift" for income tax purposes. Overruling *Davis*, § 1041(a) provides that no gain or loss shall be recognized by the transferor-spouse; as a corollary, § 1041(b) provides that the basis of the transferred property in the hands of the transferee-spouse shall be the same as it was for the transferor. The lower-of-cost-or-market exception—which, under § 1015, limits the basis of a donee for the purpose of determining *loss* on subsequent sale—is made inapplicable; in effect, the basis of gifts between spouses is now governed by § 1041 exclusively. In the *Farid* case itself, somewhat oddly, the stock transfer actually took place before the marriage—indeed, while the taxpayer's husband-to-be was married to somebody else. Hence, the taxpayer would not have qualified as a "spouse" under § 1041 at the time of the transfer. More commonly, we suppose, a property transfer pursuant to an antenuptial agreement would be contingent on and would follow the marriage ceremony, so that the transferee would in fact be a "spouse" as defined.

The legislative changes just described were regarded by most tax specialists as overdue and welcome. Larger issues to one side, the *Davis/Farid* rule had been a complicating factor in divorce settlements and resulted also in better treatment for residents of community property states (the Service having held that *Davis* did not apply to an equal division of community property) than for residents of common law jurisdictions. From the standpoint of the Treasury itself, moreover, the *Davis/Farid* rule added considerably to the burdens of enforcement in this area. Thus, transferor-spouses sometimes seemed not to know about *Davis,* or to find it counter-intuitive (or at least inconvenient), and hence often omitted to report their taxable gains when appreciated property was transferred. By contrast, transferee-spouses, well aware of *Farid,* almost invariably computed gain or loss on the subsequent sale of such property by using a basis equal to the fair market value of the property at the time it was received. The Treasury thus ran the risk that gain would be reported by neither spouse, unless it was prepared to audit every substantial property settlement.

5.05 *Cottage Savings* and the Realization Threshold

As the cases discussed in this Section might suggest, the Code contains no general rule or explicit set of criteria that enables us, with confidence, to determine just when a realization has taken place for tax purposes. True, § 1001(a) indicates that a "sale or other disposition" of an asset is a realization event, but (i) the meaning of those terms (especially "disposition") are somewhat fuzzy around the edges, and (ii) § 1001(a) does not purport to be the *only* realization provision in the Code. We would ordinarily say that there is a "realization" when one property is exchanged for another—an exchange being, of course, a "disposition" of the asset relinquished in the exchange. In a sense, however, that statement begs the question, because we may still be obliged, in a close case, to decide whether what has happened does in fact constitute an "exchange". In the *Cottage Savings*[80] case, the taxpayer, a savings bank, held a portfolio of residential mortgage loans with a face value of $6.9 million. Mortgage interest rates having risen sharply (the year was 1980), the market value of the taxpayer's mortgage portfolio had dropped to $4.5 million. Eager to realize a deductible loss of $2.4 million, the taxpayer swapped its beneficial interest in the portfolio for an equivalent interest in a residential mortgage portfolio held by another savings bank (actually several others) in the same locale. To avoid disturbing or confusing individual mortgagors, each bank continued to receive monthly payments from its own original borrowers and would then remit the amounts received to the other. The Federal Home Loan Bank Board (or FHLBB, pronounced, we suppose, "flub") which then had supervisory authority over savings banks, ruled that the parties to the swap were not required to record their losses for regulatory purposes. FHLBB's ruling was crucial to the mortgage swap plan, because taking the losses into account for regulatory purposes would have put many of the banks at risk of being shut down by FHLBB. By issuing its ruling FHLBB took upon itself the role of tax strategist for the industry it regulated; its admitted objective was to enable the banks to generate losses for tax purposes without also generating

---

[80] *Cottage Savings Ass'n v. Commissioner,* 499 U.S. 554 (1991).

losses for regulatory accounting purposes. One imagines that the IRS was not pleased that another federal agency appeared to be siding with taxpayers against the IRS.

The taxpayer's loss having been disregarded for regulatory purposes, the Commissioner insisted that it should similarly, and for analogous reasons, be disallowed for tax purposes. Losses are recognized only when realized, and a realization occurs only when the properties exchanged are "materially different" from one another. Here, far from being "different," the underlying mortgage portfolios were virtually identical in economic substance, from which it followed (in the Commissioner's view) that the purported exchange should be viewed as a non-event.

Reversing the court of appeals, the Supreme Court held for the taxpayer and allowed the loss as claimed. The Court agreed that "material difference" is the applicable test of realization under Code § 1001(a), but it did not agree that that test had been flunked merely because the properties exchanged were economic substitutes or equivalents. While the test for FHLBB regulatory purposes might indeed be one of economic substance, for tax purposes the test was more formalistic. As the mortgages exchanged were secured by different homes and involved different mortgage-borrowers, the banks on either side emerged with "legally distinct entitlements" which were "not identical." More important, the swap itself sufficed to meet the administrative aims that underlie the realization requirement. The transaction was an arms-length deal between unrelated parties. As such, it "put both Cottage Savings and the Commissioner in a position to determine the change in the value of Cottage Savings' mortgages relative to their tax bases" and thus to reckon up gain or loss under § 1001(a).

After *Cottage Savings,* are there any exchanges that would *not* be treated as dispositions—and thus as realization events—under § 1001(a)? Yes; an exchange of identical assets would not qualify as a realization event. If a taxpayer holds General Motors stock with a high basis and a low value, and exchanges her stock for identical shares, there would be no realization even under the "hair-trigger" approach of *Cottage Savings.* But what if, instead of *exchanging* shares, the taxpayer *sold* her GM shares for cash, and immediately used the cash to purchase identical replacement shares? The cash sale would indeed qualify as a *realization* event under § 1001(a), but (as we shall see in the introduction to Section 15) a special *nonrecognition* rule would nevertheless apply to prevent the taxpayer from taking the loss into account for tax purposes.

The *Cottage Savings* decision, and in particular the Court's emphasis on realization as an administrative requirement, seems quite correct on the whole, but of course it does—yet again—make evident the capricious role that realization plays in the tax field. Thus, if the realization requirement can be met at a very low threshold, as the decision implies, then "realization" virtually becomes elective with the taxpayer, which presumably accounts for the Commissioner's determined opposition in the *Cottage Savings* case itself. If mortgage interest rates had gone down in 1980 and the value of its mortgage portfolio had risen, the bank would simply have retained the portfolio and avoided any current gain recognition. With a loss on hand, it chose to swap and trigger a realization. The result is to expose the Treasury to something of a whipsaw and, conversely, to award the savings-bank industry a tax benefit that Congress probably did not intend.

The problem of elective or voluntary realization is not confined to savings banks, of course, but arises in connection with investment activity of all sorts. A stock-market investor is likely to find at the end of the year that some of his stocks have appreciated (relative to his cost) while others have declined. Since gain or loss is realized and recognized only if a security is actually sold, the investor would be prompted to sell the losers and retain the winners if, as in *Cottage Savings*, the realized losses could be deducted from gross income without restriction. To prevent this, the Code permits the investor to offset so-called capital losses *only* against his realized capital gains (with any unused losses allowed to be carried forward to subsequent years). Except in very limited amount, capital losses cannot be offset against salary or business profits or, indeed, against income from any source other than realized capital gains. Investment losses are thus confined by the Code to a separate schedule and in that way kept isolated from other kinds of taxable income.

While the whipsaw danger illustrated by the *Cottage Savings* case is by this means eliminated in most instances, the statutory machinery that has had to be fabricated in order to deal with the problem is fairly awesome, as will be seen at 16.03. Once again, the realization requirement deserves the credit, or the blame, for much Code detail and complexity.

There is more on realization at 13.03 et seq.

5.06 Deferral and Exemption: Individual Retirement Accounts

The advantage to the individual taxpayer of deferring income—illustrated at 1.01 in connection with the "endowment policy" case, at 2.02 in connection with annuities, and at 5.03 in connection with § 109 and the *Bruun* decision—has been a topical theme in this Part. Also mentioned have been those special but important instances in which the Code operates to exempt from tax the income from certain types of capital investment. Interest on insurance contracts (2.03) is one example of an income exemption; imputed rents from owner-occupied housing (1.03) is another; municipal bond interest (see p. 1) is yet another. Though not obvious at a glance, it turns out that there is a link between these two tax phenomena. More than a link, indeed, there is an identity: generally speaking, "deferral" and "exemption" produce equivalent results.

This can be seen, we hope, if we compare three kinds of Individual Retirement Accounts (IRAs), of which the first entails the "deferral" of *current* income, the second the "exemption" of *future income*, and the third neither of the above. The purpose at this point is merely to outline the structure of these several IRA devices as a way of illustrating the equivalence of deferral and exemption. For that reason we ignore all but the basic statutory details.

Under Code § 219, individual taxpayers who are not covered by a qualified employee benefit plan (and lower-income taxpayers even if they are so covered) can contribute up to $5,500 (in 2018) of their annual earnings to an IRA and deduct such contributions from gross income. IRA investment earnings are tax-exempt until the taxpayer makes withdrawals from the IRA account, which he is required to begin doing at a stated retirement age. When withdrawn, the entire amount taken out of the IRA account—annual contributions plus investment earnings—is included in the taxpayer's gross income.

Call this IRA #1.

With a view to increasing the domestic savings rate, long deemed a lagging feature of our economy, the Taxpayer Relief Act of 1997 made available a new type of IRA called a "Roth IRA," thus memorializing forever the name of the late Senator William V. Roth, Jr. of Delaware, then Chairman of the Senate Finance Committee. Under § 408A, no current deduction is allowed for annual contributions, but the taxpayer is permitted on retirement to withdraw the entire account tax-free, that is, without including the amount withdrawn in gross income. As with the old-style IRA, interim investment earnings are tax-exempt.

Meaning no disrespect to Sen. Roth, let's call this savings device IRA #2.

Yet a third arrangement, available even to qualified plan participants—call it IRA #3 and see § 408(*o*)—allows neither a current deduction nor a tax-free withdrawal on retirement, although (as with IRAs #1 and #2) interim earnings are tax-exempt.

By way of illustration, assume a taxpayer in the (hypothetical) 30% tax bracket makes a single contribution to his IRA in year 0 and withdraws the entire fund at the end of 10 years. The taxpayer has

$5,000 of pre-tax earnings which he will use in year 0 to (i) pay any tax due in year 0 on those earnings, and (ii) make an IRA contribution of the remainder. In the case of IRA #1, no tax is due in year 0 because of the IRA deduction, so the taxpayer can invest the entire $5,000 in the IRA. In the cases of IRA #2 and IRA #3, the lack of a deduction for the contribution means the taxpayer will have to pay $1,500 tax in year 0, and thus will be able to invest only $3,500 in the IRA. Assuming a 7% rate of return on IRA investments, the fund would roughly double by the end of year 10. Outcomes:

	After-tax Contribution to IRA	Taxes due in Years 1–9	Amount of IRA in Year 10	Taxes due in Year 10	Amount received after tax in Year 10
IRA #1: Deductible now, but includable later	$5,000	0	$10,000	$3,000	$7,000
IRA #2: Not deductible now, but not includable later	$3,500	0	$7,000	0	$7,000
IRA #3: Not deductible now, and includable later	$3,500	0	$7,000	$1,050	$5,950

Since IRA #3 allows no deduction when the IRA account is created, but then also taxes the increase in value when the account is withdrawn, it is not a shock to discover that the net to the taxpayer is less than in the case of IRA #1 or IRA #2, each of which forbears from imposing tax at one point in time or at the other. What might seem slightly surprising, however, is the fact that IRAs #1 and #2 produce the *same* net result even though the two appear to operate quite differently, with IRA #1 permitting a full deduction in year 0 but taxing the entire withdrawal in year 10 and IRA #2 doing just the opposite. Why should this be so? Why is it that IRA #1 and IRA #2 come out exactly the same despite the apparent difference between the two sets of operative rules?

Answer:

As to IRA #1, the government and the taxpayer "own," respectively, a 30% and a 70% share in the account from the beginning. Both shares increase in value over the 10-year period. The government's claim is fully satisfied when it receives its 30% share, which has grown from $1,500 to $3,000, in year 10. The value of the taxpayer's 70% share has by then grown from $3,500 to $7,000, which growth represents the investment income earned on the taxpayer's share over the 10-year period. But since the government, having received its own 30% share, makes no further claim, such investment income is entirely tax-free.

As to IRA #2, the government actually takes its 30% share—$1,500—in year 0. That satisfies the government's claim, however, and it takes nothing further when the account is withdrawn. While the original value of the taxpayer's share, $3,500, increases to $7,000 by year 10, such increase is never taxed. As with IRA #1, therefore, the income earned on the taxpayer's net investment is finally received by him tax-free.

As to IRA #3, the government likewise takes its 30% share, $1,500, at the beginning. The value of the taxpayer's 70% share increases from $3,500 to $7,000 just as above, but this time the government also takes 30% of that increase—$1,050—in year 10. As a result, the taxpayer is left with only $5,950 when the account is withdrawn.

The "insight" thus achieved is that IRAs #1 and #2, though superficially different, produce an equivalent result, to wit: both eliminate the taxpayer's investment income from the tax base. In effect, current deduction equals subsequent exclusion, assuming the taxpayer's marginal rate is the same at both points in time. Perhaps the simplest way to understand this point is mathematically. If the tax rate is 30% in both of the relevant years, then the formula for the taxpayer's after-tax amount in year 10 under IRA #1 is: $\$5,000 \times 2 \times (1 - .3) = \$7,000$; the formula for the taxpayer's after-tax amount in year 10 under IRA #2 is: $\$5,000 \times (1 - .3) \times 2 = \$7,000$. (The multiplication by 2 represents the doubling of the investment over the 10-year period.) In each case, the same three numbers are being multiplied; only the order of the numbers differs. Given the commutative property of multiplication, the order in which the numbers are multiplied does not affect their product.

Does this illustration mean that a taxpayer eligible to invest under either the IRA #1 regime (a "traditional" or "regular" IRA) or under the IRA #2 regime (a Roth IRA) should be indifferent between the two? Not necessarily, for two reasons. First, in many cases the taxpayer's marginal tax rate is likely to be different in the year of withdrawal from the taxpayer's rate in the year of investment. If the taxpayer anticipates a different tax rate in the later year, he should (all else being equal) opt for the IRA type that imposes tax in the lower rate year—*i.e.*, a traditional IRA if he thinks the rate will be lower in the later year, and a Roth IRA if he thinks the rate will be higher in the later year. Second, although the statutory ceiling on IRA contributions ($5,500 in 2018) is nominally the same for both types of IRAs, any given dollar amount invested in a Roth IRA is effectively a larger investment than the same dollar amount invested in a regular IRA, because the Roth IRA investment is made with after-tax dollars. This phenomenon can be seen in our example, in which $3,500 invested in a Roth IRA is the functional equivalent of $5,000 invested in a traditional IRA. It follows that $5,000 in a Roth IRA is the equivalent of $7,143 in a traditional IRA (if the relevant tax rate is 30%).[81] The difference, however, is that the law allows a taxpayer to put $5,000 into a Roth IRA in a single year, but it does not allow a taxpayer to put $7,143 into a traditional IRA. The moral is that a taxpayer who wants to make the largest possible IRA investment should put his money in a Roth IRA, rather than in a traditional IRA.

The comparison of the three IRA types also has more far-reaching implications, which are explored in a Note at the end of this book.[82] Instead of taxing income, a tax system might have a consumption base (as with a retail sales tax or a value-added tax) or a wage base (as with a payroll tax). Although traditional and Roth IRAs are both creatures of the current "income" tax, in fact the traditional IRA (IRA #1) is based on consumption tax principles, and the Roth IRA (IRA #2) is based on wage tax principles. Only IRA #3 is really consistent with *income* taxation. Thus, a comparison of the three IRA types can provide insights into the more general policy choice among income, consumption, and wages as tax bases. The interested reader can find the explanations behind these assertions in the aforementioned Note.

Congress in recent years has frequently resorted to the tax-free savings-account device as a way of supporting objectives considered important to middle- and upper-income taxpayers. In addition to the individual retirement accounts described above, taxpayers are now permitted to establish tax-exempt savings accounts for medical and educational purposes, among others. Without describing those plans in any detail, it can be seen (as we hope the foregoing discussion makes clear) that the effect is to eliminate investment income from the tax base by permitting taxpayers to deduct their annual contributions to such accounts, as in IRA #1 above, or to withdraw the account tax-free, as in IRA #2.

---

[81] $3,500/$5,000 = $5,000/$7,143.

[82]   Note, *Income Tax, Consumption Tax, Flat Tax,* p. 493.

Gross Income—Questions and Answers

Question 1: Emma is a third-year associate at Jones & Smith, a large law firm in New York City. As an inducement to join the firm, Jones & Smith promised Emma (and all its other new associates) that it would provide free legal services when, or if, an associate should decide to purchase a condominium or coop apartment in the City. Normally, J & S charges a fee of $10,000 for representing an apartment buyer. This year Emma decided to buy a condominium and was represented by Charles, a senior associate in the J & S real estate department, who carried the legal work through to completion. As promised, the firm charged Emma nothing for Charles' services. What are the tax consequences to Emma?

Answer: Certainly Emma has enjoyed an economic benefit by reason of Charles' legal work, and certainly the benefit was due to Emma's being employed by J & S. The question, then, is whether § 132(a), which covers a variety of so-called employee fringe benefits, allows Emma to exclude the $10,000 (or any part of it) from her gross income.

From Emma's standpoint, the best result—complete exclusion— would be achieved if she could bring Charles' legal work within § 132(a)(1) ("no additional cost service"), (a)(3) ("working condition fringe"), or (a)(4) ("de minimis fringe"). Subsection (a)(2), which excludes "qualified employee discounts," is subject to a percentage limitation and is therefore less favorable to Emma.

A "no additional cost service" is defined by § 132(b)(2) as a service with respect to which the employer (J & S) incurs "no substantial additional cost (including forgone revenue)" in providing such service to the employee. As suggested earlier, an empty seat on an airplane would be a good example. In the present case, unless Charles is seriously under-employed and spends his days watching the clock, the case for "no substantial additional cost" will be hard to establish. The firm could have generated revenue if Charles had spent his time working for the firm's paying clients; Charles is not an empty airline seat. Rule it out.

A "working condition fringe" is defined by § 132(d) as a service the cost of which would be deductible by Emma as a business expense if paid by her directly. Fairly obviously, the cost of a personal residence, along with related legal expense, does not qualify as a "business expense" and is not deductible by a homebuyer. Easily ruled out.

A "de minimis fringe" is defined by § 132(d) as a service whose value is "so small" that accounting for it is impracticable. $10,000? Not "so small" to Emma, and in any case large enough for J & S to think the service worth offering as an inducement to prospective employees. In all likelihood, not applicable.

Finally, a "qualified employee discount" is defined by § 132(c)(1)(B) as a discount on services regularly offered to customers (clients) by the taxpayer's employer. No doubt this covers Charles' services to Emma. However, the exclusion is limited to 20% of the price that a customer would normally be charged. Further, § 132(j) allows the exclusion only if the discount is offered to employees on a non-discriminatory basis, not just to the highly paid. Assuming either (a) that Emma, though well paid, is not among the "highly compensated," or (b) that Emma is "highly compensated" but the firm offers the same fringe benefit to its non-highly-compensated employees, then Charles' legal work on her behalf should fit comfortably within this subsection. But the excludable amount will be limited to 20%, or $2,000.

Question 2: Lafcadio, a baseball fan, happened to be sitting in the third row of the rightfield bleachers when Barry Bonds hit his record-making 73rd home run. The ball plopped into Lafcadio's lap. He promptly had the ball autographed and dated by Bonds himself in order to assure its authenticity. Having been identified in the newspapers as the lucky fan who caught the famous ball, Lafcadio at once received purchase offers from collectors of baseball memorabilia, of which the highest was $1,000,000 cash. Tempted, but feeling that Bonds' record would never be broken and that the value of the ball would go much higher in the future, Lafcadio declined to sell, and the ball, carefully wrapped in tissue paper, now rests securely in Lafcadio's safe-deposit box.

Should Lafcadio include the value of the ball—presumably $1,000,000—in his gross income?

Answer: Lafcadio has certainly experienced an increase in his personal net worth, so that the "threshold" for taxability has been crossed. But that, by itself, is not enough to answer the question, since, as we all know, there needs to be a "realization" as well.

You could view the matter as if Lafcadio had won a taxable lottery prize. If Lafcadio had won $1,000,000 in cash, the prize would of course be taxable, and § 61 generally makes no distinction between benefits realized in cash and benefits realized in kind. Lafcadio is perfectly free to sell the ball—nothing restrains him except his own investment judgment. Hence (arguably), the value of the ball should be included in gross income.

On the other hand, isn't it also true that when you buy a ticket to a ball game for (say) $50, a small portion of the purchase price is paid for the opportunity to catch or otherwise grab a souvenir baseball, whether a foul ball or, less often, a home run? The fact that so many fans, young and old, come to the ballpark carrying baseball gloves is clear proof of that observation—not to mention the wild scramble that takes place every time a ball is hit into the stands. What you get for your ticket price, then, is (a) the fun of watching the game and rooting for your team and (b) the delicious expectation that you may wind up with a souvenir baseball. The game itself may be exciting and memorable or it may be a total bore; you may be fortunate and get a souvenir ball or you may not. Both (a) and (b) are among the consumption benefits that you hope to realize and for which you have paid a considerable sum, *i.e.*, $50. But whether you do or you don't realize those benefits is of no interest to the tax system. Consumption benefits are not taxable even when the benefits turn out to be worth much more to the consumer than the price he has paid; nor, of course, can he deduct anything if the game turns out to be a dud. Hence (arguably), Lafcadio should include nothing in income until he gives up his "consumption benefit" and sells the ball for cash.

Could the same argument be made if Bonds' home run ball went over the stadium wall, and Lafcadio, strolling to a dentist's appointment (or perhaps innocently kayaking in McCovey Cove), just happened to pick it up? Tougher case, we think, because there appears to be no "consumer benefit" defense. Reg. Sec. 1.61–14(a), which is of long standing, would apparently treat the ball as taxable "treasure trove," just as if Lafcadio had found a diamond ring or a bundle of cash.

In the *Cesarini*[83] case, the taxpayers bought a battered old piano at an auction sale for $15. The piano was used by their daughter for piano lessons. Whether the good child made much progress we don't know, but years later, while cleaning the piano, the taxpayers found $4,467 (more than $35,000 in 2018 dollars) in cash tucked in behind a C-sharp minor chord in the lowest register. Citing the treasure trove Regulation, the Court held that the money was includable in the Cesarinis' gross income under the "from whatever source derived" language of § 61(a)—as against the taxpayer's contention that the money was excludable as a "gift" from heaven under § 102(a). It is worth noting, however, that no reported case has ever considered the application of the treasure trove regulation to any sort of treasure trove other than U.S. currency—a fact that strongly suggests that the IRS does not, in practice, assert the application of the regulation to found property other than cash. In terms of both valuation and liquidity concerns, there is much to be said in favor of waiting until the taxpayer disposes of in-kind treasure trove to impose the tax, and

---

[83]   *Cesarini v. U.S.*, 296 F.Supp. 3 (N.D. Ohio 1969).

perhaps that is what the IRS is actually doing—despite the continued on-the-books presence of the treasure trove regulation.[84]

Question 3(A): Diggory makes a gift of stock to his daughter, Eustacia. The stock cost Diggory $20,000, but at the date of the gift it is worth only $15,000. Eustacia later sells the stock for (a) $22,000, (b) $13,000, or (c) $18,000. How much gain or loss does Eustacia recognize under each alternative?

Answers:

(a) Gain of $2,000. Section 1015(a) provides in general that a donee's basis for property acquired by gift shall be the same as it would be in the hands of the donor. Accordingly, Eustacia's basis is $20,000 and her gain is $2,000.

(b) Loss of $2,000. The same subsection provides that if the basis of the property in the donor's hands is greater than its market value at the time of gift, then, for purposes of determining loss, the donee's basis shall be the market value. Accordingly, Eustacia's basis for determining loss is $15,000 and her loss is $2,000.

(c) No gain or loss. Once again, Eustacia's basis in the property is the same as Diggory's basis, $20,000, except that for purposes of determining loss Eustacia's basis is the lower market value, or $15,000. The $20,000 gain basis means that Eustacia will realize a gain only if she sells the property for more than $20,000, and the $15,000 loss basis means that she will realize a loss only if she sells the property for less than $15,000. Since the property was sold for $18,000, Eustacia has neither gain nor loss on the sale.

Question 3(B): Suppose Eustacia received the stock from her employer as a bonus and hence had gross income equal to the value of the stock when received, *i.e.*, $15,000. Assuming the same alternatives as above, how much gain or loss would Eustacia recognize on sale?

Answers:

(a) Gain of $7,000. Although she has paid nothing for the property, inclusion in income is treated as a "cost" under 1012—just as if Eustacia had purchased the stock for $15,000—in order to prevent the same income from being counted twice. Accordingly, her basis is $15,000 and her gain is $7,000.

(b) Loss of $2,000. Once again, having included the property in gross income, Eustacia has a "cost" basis of $15,000 for the purpose of determining loss as well as gain.

---

[84] For more (too much?) on this topic, see Zelenak & McMahon, *Taxing Baseballs and Other Found Property*, 84 Tax Notes 1299 (1999).

(c)   Gain of $3,000.

Question 4: Andrew was injured in an auto accident and sued the other driver for $10,000. The other driver's insurance company offered to settle Andrew's claim for $2,000, but Andrew rejected that offer. Pierre, Andrew's tailor, has presented Andrew with a bill for making three new suits in the amount of $3,000. Unable to pay, Andrew persuades Pierre to accept an assignment of his damage claim in full satisfaction of Pierre's bill. Ultimately, and to everyone's surprise, the insurance company agrees to settle Andrew's damage claim for $9,000 and pays that amount over to Pierre as assignee.

What are the tax consequences of these events to Andrew and Pierre?

Answer: For openers, Pierre presumably has gross income of $3,000 under § 61(a), equal to the amount of his bill for personal services. He could argue that the value of the assigned claim was indeterminate or even that he valued it at no more than the $2,000 that the insurance company was then offering. However, since he accepted the claim in "full satisfaction," the probability is that the claim will be taken to be equal in value to the bill itself. The *Farid-Es-Sultaneh* and *Davis* cases are relevant, though in both cases the consideration for release of the spouse's (or near-spouse's) claim was publicly traded stock whose market value was readily determinable.

What about Andrew? Section 104(a)(2) excludes from gross income "the amount of any damages . . . received . . . on account of physical injury. . . ." It doesn't say "received from the tortfeasor," but that seems pretty obvious because it is only the tortfeasor (or his insurer) who would be obligated to pay "damages." What Andrew got from Pierre—satisfaction of a tailoring bill—certainly doesn't qualify as "damages," so perhaps Andrew has to recognize a $3,000 gain on the sale of his claim. On the other hand, § 104(a)(2) could (perhaps should) be read to extend to cases in which the damage claim is assigned at a discount by an accident victim who cannot wait for his claim to be satisfied by a slow-moving and unsympathetic insurance company. The assignee, Pierre, would then be seen simply as a conduit between Andrew and the insurer.

Back to Pierre, who finally got $9,000 from the insurance company. It looks like Pierre's bonanza—$6,000, assuming he included $3,000 as payment for his tailoring services—should be includable in Pierre's gross income, either because it is an undeniable "accession to wealth" under the *Glenshaw Glass* case or because Pierre has on this occasion turned himself into a profitable finance company, needles and thread notwithstanding. On the other hand, the settlement amount is certainly "damages . . . received . . . on account of personal injury . . . ," though of course the injury was

Andrew's not Pierre's. Pierre might argue that one (like himself) who buys a personal injury claim at a discount does so in the expectation that his tax position will be the same as that of the accident victim, who would of course be entitled to exclude such damages if received directly. Otherwise, says Pierre, the discounted figure paid to somebody in Andrew's position would have to be reduced by the expected tax on the assignee, and needy accident victims would, in effect, be deprived of the full benefit of the § 104(a)(2) exclusion. Well, it's an argument.

Question 5: The Potter National Bank does not pay interest on depositor's checking accounts. It does, however, provide free banking services—unlimited free ATM access, and unlimited free checking—for any month in which a depositor maintains a minimum checking account balance of $5,000. George Bailey faithfully maintains a $5,000 minimum balance and makes extensive use of the free banking services. Are there any federal income tax consequences for George?

Answer: In theory, George should include in his gross income the value of the free banking services. This is not imputed income. Imputed income exists only in the absence of an exchange. Here, there clearly is an exchange—George gives the Bank the use of his money, and in return the bank gives him banking services. The banking services are a sort of in-kind interest income—albeit a rather strange sort, since the value of services does not depend on the amount of money on deposit as long as the $5,000 minimum is satisfied, and since George can control the value of the services he receives by deciding how often to use the ATM and how many checks to write. In practice, the IRS does not attempt to collect tax on the value of such services, and banks certainly do not issue 1099s reporting the value of such services. This is a de facto administrative exclusion, which persists despite the absence of any statutory foundation.

Question 6: Toonces is a very bad driver—so bad that he cannot buy liability insurance. He drives anyway, and negligently injures a bicyclist while driving on a personal errand. The injured bicyclist sues Toonces, and obtains a judgment for $200,000. Although Toonces has assets well in excess of the amount of the judgment, he makes it as difficult as possible for his victim to collect his damages. Finally, the frustrated victim offers to give up the right to collect $50,000 of the judgment, if Toonces will pay the other $150,000. If Toonces accepts the victim's offer, will he have $50,000 of debt-cancellation income?

Answer: We don't think he should, but some courts would probably disagree. The problem produces different results depending on whether one subscribes to the balance-sheet theory of debt-cancellation income, or to the mistake-correction theory. Under the balance-sheet theory, Toonces eliminates $200,000 debt at a cost of only $150,000. Because his balance sheet improves by $50,000, he has $50,000 of debt-cancellation income. Under the mistake-correction theory, by contrast, he would have no income. According to the mistake-correction theory, debt-cancellation income results only when the incurring of the debt produced a tax benefit for the taxpayer (typically, the receipt of tax-free loan proceeds), based on the assumption that the taxpayer would eventually pay off the debt. Here, Toonces received no favorable tax treatment when the debt was incurred, so there is no need for a mistake-correcting income inclusion when a portion of the debt is canceled. Although our view is that the mistake-correction theory should be the *only* theory of debt-cancellation income,[85] the law remains unsettled.

Question 7: A customer at a Waffle House restaurant (not an upscale chain) leaves his waitress a credit card tip of $1,000. The customer and the waitress did not know one another, the waitress provided only the usual services accompanying a $10 dinner, and the customer offered no explanation of his motivation for leaving so generous a tip. Can the waitress legitimately omit the $1,000 from her tax return for the year of the tip, on the grounds that it was a gift rather than compensation for services?

Answer: We wouldn't have the nerve to make up this problem. The story is true. It had its fifteen minutes of fame in the national media because Waffle House initially insisted on refunding the $1,000 to the customer, before seeing the error of its ways and allowing the waitress to keep the tip.[86] An ordinary tip of 15% or 20% ($1.50 or $2 in this case) is clearly taxable under the standard endorsed by the Supreme Court in *Duberstein*. Despite the absence of any legal obligation to tip, the ordinary tip is "in return for services rendered," and proceeds from "the constraining force of [a] moral . . . duty." But the 10,000 percent tip in this problem is different in kind, not merely in degree. We are forced to speculate as to the key issue under the *Duberstein* analysis—the motive of the tipping customer— but the best guess is that the customer was motivated by something along the lines of "detached and disinterested generosity." If so the result is a gift excludable under § 102.

Question 8: Gaggle, Inc., a very large and very profitable Silicon Valley corporation, located on a large suburban "campus," provides free gourmet meals—breakfast, lunch, and dinner—for all its

---

[85] Zelenak, *Cancellation-of-Indebtedness Income and Transactional Accounting*, 29 Va. Tax Rev. 277 (2009).

[86] "Waffle House Apologizes for Taking Waitress' $1,000 Tip," *News & Observer* (Raleigh, N.C.), June 10, 2014.

employees who choose to partake. An employee who takes full advantage of Gaggle's generosity could easily consume $10,000 worth of food in a year. Gaggle currently does not keep track of the consumption of individual employees, and does not report any income relating to the free meals on the Forms W-2 of any of its employees. Rather, it takes the position that all the meals qualify for exclusion from gross income under § 119. Assess the merits of Gaggle's position.

Answer: We didn't exactly make up this one either. According to media reports, Google, Facebook, Yahoo, and similar tech corporations behave very much like fictional Gaggle.[87] Under § 119, excludable meals must be furnished "on the business premises of the employer" and "for the convenience of the employer." The first requirement is clearly satisfied here. According to the regulations, meals will be considered to have been provided for the convenience of the employer if "the employee could not otherwise secure proper meals within a reasonable meal period. For example, meals may qualify . . . when there are insufficient eating facilities in the vicinity of the employer's premises."[88] This provides a colorable basis for the exclusion of lunches, at least in the case of tech corporations with "campuses" so large that the nearest restaurants and fast food joints are ten miles away.[89] It does not, however, seem to provide any basis for the exclusion of breakfast at the beginning of the workday, or of dinner at the end. It would have been just as convenient for the employer if the employees had eaten those meals at home. Again according to media reports, after years of paying little attention to this issue, the IRS has recently become more interested in asserting the taxability of these meals.[90]

In 2017 Congress intervened with a statutory amendment. Section 274(*o*)—which has a very delayed effective date of 2026— provides that an employer cannot deduct as a business expense the cost of providing any meals excludable by employees under § 119. This does not affect the tax treatment of the employees themselves, but it will have the effect of taxing the employer as a surrogate for its employees (albeit only at the relatively low corporate rate of 21%). In

---

[87]   Mark Maremont, "Silicon Valley's Mouthwatering Tax Break," *Wall Street Journal*, April 7, 2013.

[88]   Reg. § 1.119–1(a)(2)(ii)(c).

[89]   Of course, if it weren't for Gaggle's own free gourmet cafeteria, Gaggle would have no trouble persuading any number of restaurants to establish outposts on Gaggle's premises, thereby solving the remoteness problem. It is also a bit puzzling that the writers of the quoted passage from the regulations seem to have been unfamiliar with the concept of the bag lunch.

[90]   Mark Maremont, "Silicon Valley Cafeterias Whet Appetite of IRS," *Wall Street Journal*, September 1, 2014.

the meantime—from 2018 through 2025—§ 274(n)(2) permits the employer to deduct only 50% of such expenses.

Question 9: Upon Ronald's return to work after having suffered a heart attack, two of his coworkers incessantly harangued him, until finally he suffered a second a heart attack as a result. Ronald sued his employer and his two coworkers for the tort of intentional infliction of emotional distress (IIED), and eventually settled the case for $350,000. The settlement agreement did not allocate the $350,000 among Ronald's several damage claims. Rather, it merely characterized the settlement amount "as noneconomic damages and not as wages or other income." Assuming that the entire settlement proceeds are on account of Ronald's claim for actual (non-punitive) damages relating to the tort of IIED, that $175,000 of the $350,000 is for claims relating specifically to the heart attack, and that no portion of the $350,000 is for the cost of medical care, how much (if any) may Ronald exclude from gross income under § 104(a)(2)?

Answer: The problem is closely based on the 2010 Tax Court case of *Parkinson v. Commissioner*.[91] The result turns on the interpretation of the 1996 amendments to § 104(a)(2), which limited the exclusion to damages on account of "physical" injuries and sickness, and which specifically provided that "emotional distress shall not be treated as a physical injury or physical sickness" (except for damages for medical care attributable to emotional distress). The Conference Report on the 1996 legislation stated that "the term emotional distress includes symptoms (*e.g.*, insomnia, headaches, stomach disorders) which may result from emotional distress." Taking its cue from the 1996 amendments and the legislative history, in *Parkinson* the IRS argued that Mr. Parkinson's heart attack was analogous to a headache or stomach disorder—a mere symptom of emotional distress—and thus did not qualify as a physical injury. Although there is a certain cold logic to the IRS's position, the Tax Court was of the commonsense view that a heart attack is certainly a physical injury, regardless of what brought it on: "It would seem self-evident that a heart attack and its physical aftereffects constitute physical injury or sickness rather than mere subjective sensations or symptoms of emotional distress." Pulling a rabbit out of its hat, the Tax Court decided that half of the settlement (which had not been allocated by the parties to the tort suit) was on account of the heart attack and therefore excludable, and half was on account of nonphysical injuries and therefore taxable.

---

[91]   *Parkinson v. Commissioner*, TC Memo. 2010–142.

Part B

DEDUCTIONS

Are deductions necessary? Couldn't we simply have a tax on *gross* income and in that way dispense with the niggling subject of deductions altogether? The answer, unfortunately (or perhaps fortunately), is no. Reducing gross income to a net figure by subtracting the taxpayer's expenses is an unavoidable step unless the income tax is to be turned into a kind of sales or excise tax on transactions by volume. Our income tax system is premised on the idea that enrichment is the best measure of the taxpayer's ability to bear the costs of government. While gross income may give some indication of the taxpayer's income status, it would obviously be arbitrary and in many instances highly unfair to accept that figure as final. A lawyer who receives $300,000 in fees this year may, or may not, derive an economic benefit from her professional activities; it all depends on how much she had to spend in the process. Office rent, library costs, employees' wages, outlays for travel and entertainment of clients—these and many other expenses will have been incurred in generating the fees received. Whether the lawyer made or lost money, and in either event how much, cannot be known until her costs are counted and subtracted from her receipts. Without quibbling about whether Congress *could* tax the gross figure if it wished to do so, there can certainly be no doubt that the *net* figure is the only suitable measure of the taxpayer's "income" properly so-called.

The importance of taxing net, rather than gross, income might lead one to expect that the definition of "deductible expense" would be as broad and sweeping as the definition of includable income. If § 61(a) defines gross income to mean "all income," then perhaps the corollary should be to define taxable income as gross income less "all expenses." But plainly this approach would go too far. The income tax is aimed at the taxpayer's net accession to wealth, and it is obvious that unless the latter figure is automatically to be reduced to zero in every case—that is, receipts less all expenditures—a distinction must be drawn between business outlays, on the one hand, and expenditures that represent personal consumption on the other. Business expenses—the costs incurred by the taxpayer in earning gross income—are nondiscretionary in the sense that the income is conditioned on the outlay. Personal expenditures reflect the disposition which the taxpayer elects to make of the wealth that she has earned. Business expenses must necessarily be deductible if the income tax is to be imposed on "income"; for the same reason, personal expenditures should be disallowed.

117

In contrast to the all-embracing definition of gross income in § 61, therefore, the Code's definition of deductible expense, though broad, is limited to those costs which are associated with the taxpayer's business or investment activities. Sections 162(a) and 212 allow deduction for *all* the ordinary expenses incurred in business or other profit-seeking pursuits, thereby achieving that generality of application which is required if the income tax is to be a tax on *net* income. On the other hand, the connection with business or profit-seeking is equally stressed: nothing is deductible unless it represents a cost incurred in earning gross income. Section 262 makes the same point doubly clear by expressly disallowing all "personal, living, or family expenses."

While the line between business and personal expense is of the essence in all this, the fact is that Congress itself has chosen to cross that line fairly freely by allowing deductions for a variety of items which are plainly personal in nature. Doctor's bills, gifts to charity, interest on home mortgages, residential property taxes—these and certain other expenses, concededly personal, are expressly permitted to be deducted (subject to various limitations) by the taxpayer in computing her taxable income. Quite obviously, the question raised thereby is why there should be *any* allowance for personal expense. What special reasons can be given for excepting the enumerated items from the general rule?

The discussion in this Part is divided into two sections. Section 6 takes up business expenses in general, with emphasis on the limitations which the Code and the courts have imposed on the scope of § 162(a). Section 7 reviews the personal expense deductions and their apparent, or at least asserted, justifications.

6. Business Expenses

As indicated above, Code § 162(a) authorizes the deduction of "all the ordinary and necessary expenses incurred during the taxable year in carrying on any trade or business." Together with a few other provisions of a more specific nature—chiefly, § 163 relating to interest and §§ 167 and 168 relating to depreciation—the quoted language constitutes virtually the entire statutory framework for the deduction of business expenses.

Given the breadth and generality of § 162(a), it is customary to analyze the provision by reference to its limitations and boundaries, by showing what is outside its scope, rather than by attempting to enumerate all the various expense items that do qualify for deduction. Taking this approach, the principal limitations on the scope of the section are usually said to involve the following issues:

(1)　Whether or not the particular expense was "ordinary and necessary";

(2)　Whether the expenditure was a current expense or a capital investment; and

(3)　Whether the expense was incurred in business or for personal reasons.

Apart from certain specific items which entail special criteria, almost all of the cases that students are asked to consider can be assigned to one or another of these three categories.

Although they emerge from a different perspective, the questions presented by the deduction cases often have a good deal in common with the gross income problems that were discussed in Part A. Exclusions and deductions from gross income would generally be expected to run together when the same items are involved, because the question in either event is essentially as to the composition of taxable income. While this expectation is sometimes disappointed, the theoretical issues will at least be similar and familiar. In addition, the concern about timing which received such emphasis in Part A is equally important in the present context. Quite frequently—especially when the question is one of current expense versus capital expenditure—the controversy between taxpayer and Treasury ultimately concerns the acceleration or postponement of tax payments. Just as the taxpayers in Part A preferred to include an item in income later rather than sooner, so the taxpayers in this Part prefer the immediate deduction of an expense to the deferral of that deduction. The reason for this preference has already been explained; our purpose here is merely to point out that even though the focus now is on deductions from, rather than inclusions in, gross income, the stakes are often much the same.

The distinction between personal expenses and business expenses presents what may be the hardest classification problem in the entire tax field. One is almost compelled to proceed by rote rather than by attempting to articulate general principles. The reason for the difficulty, we suppose, is that the notion of a sharp division between pleasure-seeking and profit-seeking is alien to human psychology and essentially unrealistic. Everybody combines work with pleasure to some degree; no one is able to separate and quantify the two elements at every point, nor even always to state which objective is predominant. But the tax law cannot embrace this comfortable commonplace; it *must* proceed as if individual behavior were divisible into two parts, because the concept of net (taxable) income depends directly on the idea that one's business and one's personal life can be distinguished. The problem, then, is how to draw a dividing line that is equitable and meaningful—one, moreover, that can be administered without resort to truth serum. If X, a corporate executive who pays tax at a rate of 35%, spends $10,000 on a trip to Europe, and if the cost can be reduced to $6,500 by asserting that the purpose of the trip was to investigate prospective markets for her employer, the temptation for X not merely to claim but to believe that she had a business goal in view is well-nigh irresistible. And of course she really may have. The dilemma, at all events, is evident.

What follows is a partial listing of items whose status as a personal or business expense has been disputed by taxpayers and the government. We have already admitted that classification is difficult in this field, but perhaps—and very tentatively—one might suggest that the *potentially* allowable expenses can be divided into two groups. The first includes those outlays which represent the special cost of being an employed person. Child-care and commuting costs presumably belong to this category; perhaps there are other members, such as higher clothing expense. In general, though with exceptions, expenses of this sort are treated as personal and are disallowed under § 262. The second and more troublesome class includes expenditures which reflect a departure from the taxpayer's everyday pattern of employment, but which also appear to afford a considerable measure of strictly personal gratification. Travel and entertainment are the prime examples here. In this area the law follows a winding course, allowing some items, disallowing others (wholly or partly), and occasionally attempting to make an allocation between "business" and "personal" elements based on what appear to be objective factors.

6.01 Everyday Expenses of Employment

(a) Childcare and Housekeeping

In *Smith v. Commissioner*,[1] the Board of Tax Appeals (the predecessor of the Tax Court) denied a deduction for babysitting expenses. The taxpayers, a married couple, argued that since Mrs. Smith would have been unable to leave her child and take a paying job "but for" the services of a babysitter (Mr. Smith also being employed), the latter's fee should be regarded as a necessary business expense. Observing that childcare was one of the basic functions of family living, the Board reasoned that if the babysitter's fee were allowed because essential to the taxpayer's employment, then by extension all consumption expenditures—food, shelter, clothing, recreation—which enable taxpayers to carry on the day's activities must become deductible as well. "Yet these," said the Board, "are the very essence of those 'personal' expenses the deductibility of which is expressly denied."

---

[1]   40 B.T.A. 1038 (1939).

Male chauvinism? Perhaps not—but still not wholly satisfying as to rationale. While it is true that one must have food and shelter in order to work, it is also true that one must eat and live somewhere even if one doesn't work. Expenses which are common to everyone, employed and non-employed, are clearly not deductible. But what has that "rule" got to do with the Smiths' babysitting fees? We can assume that the taxpayers were honest in asserting that those fees would not have been incurred had Mrs. Smith remained a homemaker; the Smiths were apparently not in a position to hire a maid merely to provide Mrs. Smith with more leisure. Accordingly, childcare services were simply *not* among the family's basic consumption expenditures if we take an *unemployed* Mrs. Smith as our starting point. The disputed childcare expense was plainly an additional cash outlay that would have been avoided had Mrs. Smith remained unemployed, and in this sense it was clearly an expense of her employment. Why, then, should it not have been allowed?

The issue in *Smith* can be made more general. If we compare A, who has $100,000 of income from employment, with B, who has $100,000 of dividends, it is easy to predict that A's cost of living will be higher than B's (everything else being equal) and that the difference will be traceable directly to A's status as an employed person. Quite obviously, it is costlier to go to work than to stay at home. Commuting to and from the job, for example, entails substantial expense. If you live in New York City and travel roundtrip on the subway every day, the annual cost now runs to more than $1,400; if you come in from Scarsdale, the figure is very much higher. People who are not employed are free of regular commuting expense; if they ride the subway, it must be because they want to. Other kinds of expenses which fall more heavily on working people would include restaurant lunches (more costly than eating at home), business clothing (more costly than informal dress), and housekeeping services (more costly than keeping house yourself). In brief, there is a cost-of-living differential which results from carrying on an employment, and the amount is certainly not insignificant in most cases.

The question presented by the *Smith* case, broadly speaking, was whether this differential (or any part of it) should be allowed as a business expense. The answer—that it should not—was undoubtedly correct, although not (as the Board maintained) because all the personal expenses of every employed person would otherwise become deductible. The *additional* expenses of earning a living—as compared with the basic expense of just living—can presumably be identified in many instances and, as stated, the babysitter's fee in *Smith* was pretty clearly of that class. The real justification for the disallowance of these additional expenses is simply congressional intent, which was surely clear by the time the *Smith* case was decided. In effect, the tax law *never* has been interpreted to contemplate a deduction for the everyday expenses of being employed.

Whether such expenses *should* be deductible under a theoretically pure ("ideal") income tax is a bit of a conundrum. Under an ideal income tax, all business expenses would be deductible, and all personal expenses would not. Business expenses would be those caused by the taxpayer's profit-motivated activities, and personal expenses would be those caused by the taxpayer's personal (non-business) life. The problem, of course, is that the classic work-related expenses of child care and commuting are jointly caused by one's business activities and one's personal life. Take away either the child or the job and the child care expenses disappear. Take away either one's home or one's workplace and the need to commute between the two disappears. If the home caused half the commuting expense and the workplace caused the other half, then the tax law could—simply enough—allow a deduction for half of the expense. In fact, however, the home is a necessary (but not sufficient) cause of *all* the commuting expenses, and the same is true of the workplace. It is not obvious how the ideal income tax should treat such jointly-caused expenses. In the actual income tax, of course, commuting and child care are both non-deductible. The underlying principle seems to be: if one can imagine a different taxpayer, with the same job but a different personal life, who would not incur the expense—because she sleeps on a couch in the office in one case, and because she has no children in the other—then the expense is not deductible.

Although there is still no deduction for child care expenses, the current income tax does provide two limited tax benefits for working parents with childcare expenses. Section 21 (described below, at 7.07(b)) allows a rather modest credit against tax for childcare expenses; for most working parents the maximum credit is $1,200 if they have two or more young children, or $600 if they have a single child. And if a taxpayer's employer offers a "dependent care assistance program" (DCAP), § 129 allows a taxpayer to exclude from gross income up to $5,000 of employer reimbursement of the taxpayer's child care expenses.[2] A $5,000 exclusion is the equivalent, of course, of inclusion of $5,000 in gross income followed by an offsetting deduction of the same amount.

Apart from the childcare credit and the DCAP exclusion—which are often far less valuable to taxpayers than an unlimited deduction for childcare expenses would be—there are very few tax benefits (by

---

[2]   Sections 21 and 129 are coordinated to prevent a taxpayer from obtaining tax benefits under both provisions for the same expenses.

way of deduction, exclusion, or credit) for work-related expenses.[3] If every family included exactly one working person, and every working person incurred the same amount of non-deductible work-related expenses (for commuting, work clothes, and so on), the non-deductibility of such expenses would make no difference; the result would be the same as if the expenses were deductible, but tax rates were correspondingly raised across-the-board. In fact, however, there are tremendous differences among households in their levels of non-deductible work-related expenses. Some households have one employed member, some have two, and some (especially older households) have none. And even between two households with the same number of employed persons, some have much higher levels of necessary (but nevertheless non-deductible) work-related expenses than others. There is a strong argument, then, that the current system overtaxes (a) two-earner households relative to one-earner households, (b) young and middle-aged adults relative to retirees, and (c) persons with high-work related expenses (for example, unavoidably long and costly commutes) relative to those with low work-related expenses. Perhaps these are inequities we must simply learn to live with. A deduction for commuting and other work-related expenses would complicate individual tax returns enormously (and undoubtedly lead to cheating by more than a few taxpayers) if the deduction was based on actual expenses. On the other hand, it would be simple enough to allow employed persons some sort of formula-based deduction—determined with reference to the amount of their employment income, rather than according to their actual employment-related expenses. Such a deduction could achieve only rough justice, but it might well be fairer than the current system.[4]

(b) Nice Clothes

In the well-known *Pevsner* case,[5] the taxpayer, sales manager of an elegant ladies shop specializing in expensive Yves St. Laurent-brand merchandise, sought to deduct as a business expense the cost of YSL clothing and accessories purchased by her from the shop itself at a store discount. The shop *required* its personnel to wear YSL apparel during the working day so that customers could admire the outfits and see how great they looked on all the sales people, including Ms. Pevsner. In effect, said Ms. Pevsner, she served both as a saleslady and a model. Just why the shop didn't supply the clothes for free and take them back at the end of the week or the end of the season was not explained, but in any case the Commissioner

---

[3] A rare exception is the § 132(f) exclusion for free parking at work (up to $260 per month in 2018).

[4] For a proposal for a formula-based deduction for work-related expenses, see Zelenak, *The Income Tax and the Costs of Earning a Living,* 56 Tax L. Rev. 29 (2002).

[5] *Pevsner v. Commissioner,* 628 F.2d 467 (5th Cir. 1980).

actually *stipulated* (a) that the taxpayer was required by her employer to buy the YSL clothes and wear them while at work, and (b) that she *never* wore those clothes away from work but simply hung them in her closet when the working day was done. It was conceded that the taxpayer's "lifestyle" was modest and inconspicuous and did not rise to a social level at which YSL merchandise would be appropriate, even occasionally. Nevertheless, insisting that the clothes were adaptable for general use, and noting that the taxpayer was not prohibited from wearing them outside the shop, the Commissioner disallowed the deduction under § 262 on the ground that the taxpayer's expenditure, some $1,600 for the year, was a "personal" expense.

Reversing the Tax Court, which held for the taxpayer, the Court of Appeals approved the Commissioner's position and sustained the disallowance. As a matter of "administrative necessity," said the court, the Commissioner was justified in using an "objective" test to determine whether clothing expense was business-related or personal. As the clothes in question were adaptable to general wear, the expense must be regarded as personal even though the taxpayer might not, or would not, have bought such expensive items if otherwise employed. Presumably the floodgates would open wide if taxpayers could deduct clothing expense on the ground that the "nice clothes" they were expected to wear during the working day were never worn at other times, and if those clothes cost more than the taxpayer would normally spend given his or her customary lifestyle. Suppose, said the court, that another salesperson at Ms. Pevsner's shop, having made the same expenditure for the same reason, was found to live at a "socio-economic level" at which YSL clothes were commonly worn by all the ladies all the time. If a "subjective" test of allowability were used, then humble Ms. Pevsner could deduct her outlay while her prosperous co-worker could not. "This result," the Court asserted, "is not consonant with a reasonable interpretation of Section 162 and 262."[6]

True, perhaps, but why deny the deduction to either of them? Once it is conceded that wearing YSL-brand dresses was a job requirement and not just a personal preference, the case for deductibility—not only for Ms. Pevsner but for her hypothetical co-worker—seems pretty strong. If we look back to the famous *Benaglia* decision (1.02), the element of personal benefit, far more prominent there than here, turned out to be a failing argument from the

---

[6]   Even if Mrs. Pevsner had persuaded the Court of Appeals that the cost of her clothes was a legitimate business expense, the cost would have been an unreimbursed employee business expense, subject to the restrictions of § 67 on the deductibility of miscellaneous itemized deductions (discussed at 7.05), and thus not deductible at all in 2018 through 2025.

Commissioner's standpoint as against a finding that the meals and lodging had been furnished to the taxpayer for "the convenience of the employer" rather than as additional compensation. Whether, as a subjective matter, the taxpayer in *Benaglia* could or couldn't afford to live in a resort hotel along with the other affluent guests, and whether he did or didn't like hotel living, was never an issue. Benaglia made the case for exclusion under § 61 by persuading the Board of Tax Appeals that he *had* to live in the hotel in order properly to perform his duties as manager. There was personal benefit, but not personal choice. Why shouldn't Ms. Pevsner and her co-worker, both of whom would be wearing their employer's dresses because the employer insisted on it as a condition of their employment, also get help from the "convenience" doctrine even if (as one supposes) the elegant outfits were a pleasure to wear? To be sure, *Pevsner* involves a deduction from gross income while *Benaglia* involved an exclusion. The relevant legal issue, however, is the same.

The *Pevsner* and *Benaglia* decisions appear to be inconsistent at some deep level. If we believe Ms. Pevsner's story—namely, that the YSL clothes had to be worn as a means of promoting sales—then, if *Benaglia* is our guide, the $1,600 outlay should have been allowed as a business expense without regard to the question of incidental personal benefit. In general, clothing, like meals and lodging, is a personal expense. But surely a distinction can be made between the clothes you choose to wear to the office (nice as they are) and the store merchandise that Ms. Pevsner said she was obliged to wear and model every day. That, presumably, was Ms. Pevsner's answer to the floodgates argument. The Tax Court accepted it, and the tax at stake was peanuts. Why did the Commissioner bother to appeal?

In the end, we suspect that the Commissioner's principal interest in litigating the *Pevsner* case had little to do with the silly proposition that modest Ms. Pevsner and her high-living hypothetical colleague might otherwise have to be treated differently under §§ 162 and 262. Rather, or more probably, his aim was to avoid the need to make case-by-case determinations based on the presence or absence of "convenience of the employer." The Commissioner's experience with the employer convenience doctrine in respect to meals-and-lodgings had been a long and painful one, resulting ultimately in a weak statutory solution, § 119, which provoked still more litigation, including an appeal to the Supreme Court.[7] Ms. Pevsner's claim, if allowed on the basis of her own self-serving testimony, would or might have led to something similar for clothing expense once taxpayers learned that the convenience doctrine had currency in that area as well. The goal in the *Pevsner* litigation, we believe, was to

---

[7]   Commissioner v. Kowalski, supra at 1.02.

gain approval for an "objective" test that would enable the Commissioner to avoid repeating that costly experience. The Commissioner's "stipulations" gave Ms. Pevsner an opportunity to present as strong a case for convenience of the employer as could possibly be made. For the same reason, the Commissioner's victory in the Court of Appeals creates as strong a contrary precedent as the government could ask for.

As matters now stand, the Service will allow a business expense deduction for the cost of job-related "uniforms" that really can't be worn for any other purpose. But as to clothing of general wear the reaction is almost certain to be disallowance on "objective" grounds, alleged convenience of the employer notwithstanding. A taxpayer in Mrs. Pevsner's position today would, however, enjoy one small tax consolation. If an employee of a clothing boutique purchases clothing from her employer at an employee's discount, the discount is excludable from income under § 132(a)(2) (discussed at 1.02) if it satisfies the criteria for a "qualified employee discount."

(c) Commuting to Work

Some of what has been said about the *Smith* and *Pevsner* cases may also help to explain the Supreme Court's approach to "travel" costs in *Commissioner v. Flowers.*[8] Although it has long been established that daily commuting expense is personal and not deductible, § 162(a)(2) specifically allows the deduction of "traveling expenses (including amounts expended for meals and lodging ...) while away from home in the pursuit of a trade or business." The term "traveling expenses" is a term of art in the income tax; it refers both to transportation costs and to the ordinary living expenses— "meals and lodging"—which are incurred by a taxpayer in connection with a business trip.[9] But since transportation and restaurant meals (less commonly special lodging) are part of almost every employed person's daily expense, there is an obvious need to define the status of business travel rather narrowly.

In *Flowers,* the taxpayer, a lawyer, lived and practiced law in Jackson, Mississippi. He presently accepted the position of general counsel with a railroad whose main office was in Mobile, Alabama, more than 200 miles from Jackson. As he was unwilling to move to Mobile, the railroad allowed the taxpayer to do most of his work in Jackson, but required him, at fairly frequent intervals, to perform services in Mobile as well. The taxpayer sought to deduct the cost of meals and lodgings during his visits to Mobile on the ground that

[8]   326 U.S. 465 (1946).

[9]   Although § 162(a)(2), standing alone, would seem to support a deduction for the entire cost of meals eaten on a business trip, § 274(n) (discussed at 6.02) provides that only half the cost of business travel meals is deductible.

these costs were travel expenses incurred while away from home. The Internal Revenue Service, opposing the deduction, contended that the word "home" in § 162(a)(2) must be understood to refer to the taxpayer's place of business rather than the location of his family residence. In this view, the taxpayer's "home" was Mobile, not Jackson, so that in effect the cost of traveling to and living in Mobile was not a business expense within the meaning of the statute.

The Supreme Court, although declining to decide upon the meaning of "home" in this context, sustained the disallowance on the ground that the expense in question had been incurred by the taxpayer for his own convenience rather than for business reasons. The Court stated that the appropriate test of deductibility was whether the travel had been motivated by the "exigencies of business" or by considerations of personal preference. Because Flowers could have chosen to live in Mobile, thereby avoiding the need for travel, the expenses were found to be self-imposed and "personal"—of which the best evidence was the railroad's willingness to allow Flowers to live and work in Jackson *only* "on condition that he pay his [own] traveling expenses between Jackson and Mobile and pay his [own] living expenses in both places."

Actually, the *Flowers* case may be a bit closer than Justice Murphy's opinion makes it appear. It would not be unusual, after all, for the railroad to maintain executive offices in two different locations; and since some of the railroad's litigation took place in or around Jackson, with whose courts and local bar Flowers had long acquaintance, a case could surely be made (at least a window-dressing case) that Jackson was a suitable place to locate the office of general counsel. That Flowers also preferred to live in Jackson would merely be an advantage in recruiting him for that position. But, though not much discussed in the opinion, the factor mentioned above—that Flowers' employment contract expressly denied him reimbursement for his Mobile expenses—should by itself have been fatal to his deduction claim. Why, after all, would an employee incur *unreimbursed* expenses in the course of his employment other than for strictly personal reasons? If the railroad directed Flowers to attend a business meeting in, say, Atlanta, his travel expense would be reimbursed without question and excluded or deducted from his gross income.[10] But traveling from Jackson to Mobile was obviously regarded by the parties as unrelated to Flowers' employment—the contract made that perfectly clear.

---

[10] The distinction between reimbursed and unreimbursed employee business expenses is further discussed at 7.06, below.

Like the *Smith* decision, the opinion in *Flowers* makes more out of the confusing element of causation than may really be necessary.[11] It would have been enough, we think, to have identified the taxpayer's expenses as commuting costs and to have disallowed them on the straightforward basis that commuting expenses, while certainly a matter of business exigency, have never been deductible. Again, such costs are part (perhaps the main part) of the living-cost differential mentioned above. The fact that Flowers had a long commute was indeed a matter of personal choice—commuting costs obviously vary depending on whether an individual prefers to live in the city or in the suburbs. Yet it was not the absence of a business nexus that justified the outcome in *Flowers,* since even the minimum cost of commuting is disallowed by § 262. Although the bus or subway fares which the city-dweller pays each day to go to work are an unavoidable expense of her employment, the implied statutory purpose is to deny them. The *Flowers* decision is quite properly a finding that the same disallowance applies to long-distance commuting, even when that entails additional living costs. Though awkward semantically, the Service's interpretation of "home" as synonymous with principal place of business is really a way of asserting that the ordinary expenses of the working day are to be treated as personal. One's "day" begins at work as far as the tax law is concerned.

Section 162(a)(2) has occasioned a sizeable quantity of litigation over the years as taxpayers and the Treasury have struggled to identify the dividing line between commuting and business travel. Two recurring issues can be mentioned by way of illustration. First, what constitutes being *"away* from home" for the purposes of the statute? Suppose a salesman who lives and works in New York City spends a day visiting customers in Connecticut. He gets an early start, and eats breakfast in Bridgeport, lunch in New Haven and dinner in Hartford. He then drives all the way home to New York, briefly greets his wife and stumbles into bed. Can the salesman deduct the cost of his restaurant meals as a "travel expense"? In *U.S. v. Correll,*[12] the Supreme Court upheld the Commissioner in denying a deduction in these circumstances and approved the Commissioner's interpretation of "away" as meaning away *overnight.* In effect, had the salesman elected to spend the night in Hartford, the preceding day's meals and the night's lodging would have been deductible. Any sense in this? Perhaps not, although the reader is hereby challenged to come up with something better. Essentially, the question raised by *Correll* is whether taxpayers who sometimes put in long hours and

[11] See Klein, *Income Taxation and Commuting Expenses: Tax Policy and the Need for Nonsimplistic Analysis of "Simple" Problems,* 54 Cornell L.Rev. 871 (1969).
[12] 389 U.S. 299 (1967).

cover many miles during the working day should be treated more favorably than those who punch a clock and are wholly sedentary. The general answer is no,[13] and the overnight rule is simply a device for making the necessary distinction between everyday living expenses on the one hand, and on the other, "travel."

The overnight rule ties into a second important interpretative issue. If the salesman is not regarded as away from home unless he spends the night in Hartford, what should be his status if his employer sends him to Hartford for a six-month period to open a new branch office? At this point we need to look at the question of away-ness from the opposite end. Could it now be argued that the taxpayer has actually shifted his home from City A to City B, that he is not so much a traveler from New York as a resident of Hartford? Another rule-of-thumb is called for, it appears, but this time one that distinguishes between permanent removals and temporary absences from the original place of employment. The Service has conceded that the cost of meals and lodgings incurred during a period of temporary reassignment are deductible, and Congress has decreed (in the flush language at the end of § 162(a)) that the duration of "temporary" employment may not exceed one year. The one-year time limit is necessarily arbitrary, and one's intuition is that it tends to err on the generous side. At all events, before 2018 the rule was especially beneficial to an otherwise neglected group of taxpayers, namely, college professors. As far as § 162(a) is concerned, a professor who spends an academic year as a visiting instructor at another institution can deduct as travel expense all of her reasonable living expenses for that period.[14] Sadly, however, recently-enacted § 67(g) (discussed at 7.05) provides that unreimbursed employee business expenses—including our visiting professor's travel expenses—are not deductible at all in 2018 through 2025. If our professor is confident Congress will not extend the application of § 67(g) beyond 2025, perhaps she should plan her next visiting professor gig for 2026. Alternatively (as explained in the "loose end" at the end of 7.05), if our professor can persuade her temporary employer to pay her rent in the city of her temporary employment (either directly or through a

---

[13]　Fortunately for law firm associates working late, the Service has never attempted to tax reimbursed "supper money," O.D. 514, 2 C.B. 90 (1920), and the Committee Reports accompanying § 132—see 1.02, above—expressly state that "occasional" supper money is to be excluded from income as a *de minimis* fringe.

[14]　What about the professor's husband, who assists (or at least encourages) the professor in her research during the visiting year? Prior to 1993, it might have been asserted that the husband's "travel expenses" should be deductible as well. Under amended § 274(m), however, such deductions are disallowed unless the spouse is the taxpayer's employee and performs services that are more than incidental. So much for the husband's meal expenses. On the other hand, the entire cost of the rented housing may still be deductible, on the theory that the professor would have rented the same housing if she had not been accompanied by her husband. Under a marginal cost analysis, then, none of the housing expense should be allocated to the husband.

reimbursement arrangement), in consideration of an appropriate reduction in her cash salary, she can exclude that rent payment from her gross income—the practical equivalent of inclusion and an offsetting deduction—even in 2018 through 2025.

If one looks to the policies underlying the rule,[15] rather than to the rule itself, allowing the professor to treat her visiting professor gig as just a long business trip was always dubious. The deduction for the cost of meals eaten on business trips—actually, for half the cost, taking § 274(n) into account—is based on the notion that it costs more to eat restaurant meals than to eat in one's kitchen. The visiting professor, however, can rent a house or apartment, shop at a supermarket, cook in a kitchen, and eat no more expensively than at her permanent home. The deduction for the cost of lodging occupied during a business trip is based on the assumption that the cost is duplicative, because the business traveler must continue to pay the rent or the mortgage at home even though she is not using her residence during the trip. But the visiting professor may be able to avoid duplicative housing expenses—for example, if she rents her permanent residence, and is able to sublet it for an amount equal to the rent due under her lease. The morals are (1) that rules sometimes diverge from the policies motivating the rules, (2) in this case, the divergence was to the considerable benefit of visiting professors, and (3) even when an unduly generous tax rule seems well established, there is always the risk that Congress will eventually bestir itself to repeal the tax break.

Perhaps the final twist in all this relates to the status of *real* traveling salesmen, those luckless individuals who spend all of their working time on the road, living in hotels and eating in restaurants, strangers wherever they go.[16] May such a person deduct his travel expenses? While pure transportation costs must certainly be allowed—airfares from city to city, for example—the cost of meals and lodgings has been denied in these circumstances on the simple basis that the traveling salesman has no home to be "away" from.[17] It could be argued, not unreasonably, that "away from home" simply means "not at home," in which case the statutory language would support deductions for homeless traveling salesmen. However, neither the courts nor the IRS have read the statute that way. As a matter of policy, perhaps the homeless salesman should be allowed to deduct half the cost of his meals (because the 50% deduction for meals is premised on restaurant meals being more expensive than

[15] The policies underlying the deductions for business meals and lodging are considered in more detail at 6.02.

[16] For an outstanding—albeit fictional—example, see the Del Griffith character played by John Candy in *Planes, Trains and Automobiles* (1987).

[17] *Rosenspan v. U.S.*, 438 F.2d 905 (2d Cir. 1971).

home cooking), but should not be allowed to deduct the cost of motel rooms (because the lodging deduction is premised on the existence of duplicative shelter expenses, which the homeless salesman does not have). But that would require treating him as "away from home" for purposes of meals but not for purposes of lodging, and the statutory language provides no support for such a bifurcation.

(d)　Litigation Expense

U.S. v. Gilmore[18]—which arose under § 212 rather than § 162— also raises a problem of "causation" which bears some resemblance to that presented in *Flowers* and *Smith*. In *Gilmore* the taxpayer had incurred substantial legal fees in litigating a hotly contested divorce. A major portion of the fees was attributable to defending against his wife's claim to ownership of a controlling interest in the family business. Had the wife succeeded, the taxpayer's principal source of livelihood—his salary as chief executive—might have been threatened or lost. Accordingly, the taxpayer sought to deduct a part of his legal fees as an expense incurred for the "conservation . . . of property held for the production of income." Following its earlier decision in *Lykes v. U.S.*,[19] the Supreme Court sustained the Commissioner in disallowing the deduction as a "family" expense under § 262. The Court reasoned that the deductibility of legal fees depends upon the origin of the litigated claim rather than upon the potential consequence of success or failure to the taxpayer's income status. Since the origin of the present litigation was to be found in the taxpayer's marital difficulties, no deduction was allowable.

While the outcome in *Gilmore* is generally viewed as satisfactory, the argument from cause-and-effect is, as usual, slightly circular. To be sure, there would have been no litigation without the divorce; but without the property ownership the taxpayer's legal fees would have been appreciably smaller. Just why the divorce rather than the property interest must logically be viewed as *the* "source" of the added legal expense is not completely obvious. But perhaps the result in *Gilmore* can be explained more simply by pointing out that the costs of rearranging titles within a family group—costs which fall at random on the large class of persons owning valuable assets—have always been regarded as a personal expense of property ownership. Legal fees incurred in preparing a will are viewed as personal from the standpoint of a testator; likewise, the costs of collecting a legacy— for example, fees incurred in a will contest—are treated by the Regulations as nondeductible from the standpoint of the legatee.[20] Of course a property settlement that is incident to a contested divorce is

---

[18]　372 U.S. 39 (1963).

[19]　343 U.S. 118 (1952).

[20]　Reg. § 1.212.

likely to be much more expensive than a simple will, and Congress might have chosen, as it has for extraordinary medical expenses, to allow such costs as a deductible personal expense. But since it has not done so, the Court in *Gilmore* correctly perceived that it had no warrant to differentiate between divorce settlements and other kinds of intrafamily property dispositions.

A loose end. The working wife and mother may have been (in the Board's phrase) a "new phenomenon" in 1939 when the *Smith* case was decided, but she is obviously anything but unusual today. What *is* new, or at least newer, is the phenomenon of working spouses who also *live* separately—actually occupy separate residences—because their jobs are centered in different localities. The customary economies of a combined household have to be sacrificed under these circumstances and the cost-of-living differential noticed in connection with the *Smith* case is increased substantially. Does the Code, and in particular the travel expense deduction as interpreted in *Flowers,* provide relief?

In *Hantzis,*[21] the taxpayer, a second-year student at Harvard Law School, took a ten-week summer job with a firm in New York City. The taxpayer's husband held a full-time teaching position in Boston, where the couple maintained their regular family residence. To carry out her summer clerkship, the taxpayer rented a small apartment in New York and for the most part, apparently, ate her meals in restaurants. Asserting that she had been "away from home [*i.e.,* Boston] in the pursuit of a trade or business" for the summer months, she sought to deduct the apartment rent, meals, and cost of transportation between Boston and New York (roughly equal in total to all her summer earnings) as travel expense under § 162(a)(2).

The Court of Appeals, reversing the Tax Court, upheld the Commissioner's disallowance on the ground (in effect) that Ms. Hantzis had no business-home in Boston to be "away" from. Ms. Hantzis' summer work in New York might be regarded as a trade or business, but if so that was the only one she had, because being a student, even a student in professional school, does not constitute a trade or business for tax purposes. Hence, while Ms. Hantzis plainly maintained two homes during the summer months, the home in Boston was maintained as a matter of personal choice rather than business necessity. It followed that her transportation and added living costs in New York were not deductible as "travel expense." Mr. Hantzis, to be sure, had a full-time professional commitment that made it necessary for *him* to maintain a residence in Boston; but,

---

[21] *Hantzis v. Commissioner,* 638 F.2d 248 (1st Cir. 1981).

though taxed as a couple, each of the spouses (in the court's view) "must independently satisfy the requirement that deductions taken for travel expenses incurred in the pursuit of a trade or business arise while he or she is away from home."

Apart from the not very surprising conclusion that going to law school is not a "trade or business" (see 6.03, below), the *Hantzis* case merely confirms the holding in *Flowers* that long-distance commuting—even when combined with meals and lodging expense—does not qualify as "travel." Like *Smith* in an earlier era, the decision also makes clear that two-career families create no special exception to the general disallowance of employee business expenses. It is true, after all, that the Hantzises were *obliged* to maintain two separate residences in order to generate a given level of household income, and for that reason they obviously had less discretionary income after meeting essential housing costs than either a single-earner household or a two-earner household with a single residence. The taxpayer hoped to mitigate the resulting disadvantage by converting § 162(a) into a limited two-career family allowance. As in *Smith*, however, the court was presumably correct in regarding the larger purpose of the Code as contrary.

Hantzis does not mean, however, that no law student can ever treat a summer clerkship as a business trip. The key to successfully distinguishing *Hantzis* is the existence of a *business* reason for maintaining a residence in the city in which one attends law school. Suppose a part-time night law student with a full-time day job takes a three-month leave from the day job in order to do a summer clerkship in a distant city. The distinction from *Hantzis* is clear, and the hypothetical student should qualify for a deduction under § 162(a)(2). In 2018 through 2025, however, the hypothetical student will get no deduction because of § 67(g) (discussed at 7.05), which disallows all deductions for unreimbursed employee business expenses in those years. What if our student is a full-time law student, whose only employment-related connection with the city in which she attends law school is a 10-hour per week, $10 dollar per hour, job in the law school library (and the year is either before 2018 or after 2025)? She can certainly argue this is enough to distinguish her case from that of Ms. Hantzis, but it is unlikely either the IRS or the courts would accept the argument.

6.02 Business or Pleasure—Travel and Entertainment

If it isn't pressed too hard, a distinction can usefully be made between the issues raised in the preceding section and those presented here. The question in *Smith*, *Pevsner* and *Flowers* was whether the business-related expenses of the working day can be deducted under § 162 (they cannot); the question here, by contrast, is whether an expense which is concededly deductible *if* it is a business expense is in fact what it is claimed to be. The trip to Europe mentioned earlier represents a deductible expense if the executive's purpose is to drum up export business for her company, but it is not deductible if her purpose is vacationing. Quite obviously, there is a danger that taxpayers whose jobs may sometimes justify travel and entertainment will be tempted to classify as business expense what is actually pure consumption, while those of us who lack such opportunities are compelled to buy our pleasures out of after-tax income. Code amendments over the past few decades have imposed limitations on travel and entertainment expenses—culminating in 2017 with a blanket disallowance of deductions for expenses relating to "an activity which is of a type generally considered to constitute entertainment, amusement, or recreation."

The character of the problem—trivial yet difficult—is illustrated by the Supreme Court's decision in the *Rudolph* case.[22] In *Rudolph,* a Dallas insurance company sponsored a "convention" in New York City for insurance agents who had achieved sales above a certain level. Wives were included and all expenses were reimbursed by the company. The Court sustained the Commissioner both in refusing to permit the taxpayer to exclude the reimbursement and in denying him a deduction for the expense. Although the taxpayer argued that he was constrained to attend the convention out of loyalty to his employer, the Court noted that only one morning of the 3-day convention period was taken up with business meetings and concluded that the entire arrangement was a bonus in the form of a paid vacation. Dissenting, Justice Douglas pointed out that the Commissioner had previously consented to the deduction of convention expenses for many other categories of professionals— clergy, lawyers, teachers, etc.—and demanded to know why insurance agents should be singled out for disallowance. Confused at some points and absurdly gullible at others, the dissent nevertheless reflects a certain basic truth about conventions generally: they are often just an opportunity for frolic. If clergy may frolic deductibly, then why not insurance salesmen? The presence of wives (it was said) was to keep the frolic within proper bounds. Taken seriously,[23] Douglas' dissent is really an objection—not altogether without reason—to the *ad hoc* quality of administration in this area.

---

[22] *Rudolph v. U.S.*, 370 U.S. 269 (1962).

[23] Not easy to do, we admit. The dissenting opinion is characterized as "utterly reckless" in Wolfman et al., *The Behavior of Justice Douglas in Federal Tax Cases*, 122 U.Pa.L.Rev. 235, 272 (1973). The dissent is especially notable for its suggestion that a weekend in Manhattan should not be viewed as a pleasure trip: "If we are in the field of judicial notice, I would think that some might conclude that the weekend in New York City was a chore and that those who went sacrificed valuable time that might better have been spent on the farm, in the woods, or along the seashore."

As has been noted, § 162(a)(2) permits deduction of the cost of meals and lodging as well as transportation, so that if a taxpayer makes a business trip (overnight, yet temporary), not only her air or railroad fare but her hotel and restaurant expenses are allowable. The deductibility of transportation is perhaps self-explanatory—the business traveler must get to her destination and then return to her regular place of employment—but the deduction of meals and lodging, which are clearly personal expenses in any other context, requires brief explanation. As to lodging, a twofold justification for the deduction can be offered. First, the purely personal satisfaction which a taxpayer derives from living in a hotel room is likely to be less than its cost when the travel is occasioned by business rather than pleasure. One must have shelter, of course, but where her travel is solely a function of business need, it is not unreasonable to assume that the taxpayer would not incur the same expense for personal enjoyment. Second, and relatedly, the hotel expense usually duplicates the cost of maintaining the taxpayer's regular household at home and in that respect can be viewed as an added financial burden. As to food, the element of duplication is obviously lacking— the traveler can't eat one meal in two places at the same time—and hence the justification for the deduction is somewhat weaker. The explanation must reside, therefore, in the notion that a restaurant meal is a "constrained" expenditure, that it involves more expense than the taxpayer would otherwise incur, and so on. Once again, the concept is that the taxpayer's personal satisfaction in being "forced" to eat out may be less than the cost of the meal itself. At an early point the Service took the position that the deduction for restaurant meals should be limited to the excess over what the taxpayer would have spent on food at home. But while logical, this approach proved difficult to administer and was ultimately abandoned. Expenditures which are "lavish and extravagant" may still be disallowed under a 1962 amendment, but lacking a specific dollar limitation it is unlikely that this restriction has had significant effect in practice.

Entertainment expenses—the alleged cost of currying favor with customers and business associates—present related problems. Suppose A, a Wall Street lawyer, takes B, a valued client, to lunch. No travel is involved—both live in New York City. Over lunch the two diners discuss a range of topics, including business, politics and religion. They eat well—the bill is $100—and part from each other with a feeling that their relationship has been cemented. Is the cost of the lunch deductible by A as "business entertainment"? If so, then especially under the higher tax rates that applied before the 1986 Act, the martinis, quiche and paupiettes de boeuf were a bargain. Assuming that A was in the 50% tax bracket, the after-tax cost of *both* lunches would be only $50. By contrast, if A had eaten alone (which in any case she dislikes), her own non-deductible meal would have cost her the same amount. Hence from one standpoint B's companionship actually produced a free lunch. The same banal scenario could be extended to attendance at nightclubs, theaters, sporting events and so on, as well as the use of luxury facilities such as yachts and country clubs.

Prior to 1962 (when § 274 was added to the Code) the feasting just described was probably fully deductible provided that A's expenditure could be shown to have *some* element of business purpose. While some cases required that the business purpose outweigh any other purpose for the activity in question, other cases seem to have settled for a good deal less. In the famous African safari case,[24] for example, the owner of a local dairy company sought to deduct the expenses which he and his wife had incurred on a big game hunt. Although hunting was a life-long family hobby, the taxpayer contended (with loyal support from his advertising manager) that he had obtained valuable goodwill for the dairy business by showing films of the safari to local groups, displaying his trophies—heads and things—in a "museum" at the plant, and inviting customers to dine on the remains. The Tax Court actually bought this argument and allowed the safari costs to be deducted in full as an advertising expense. The taxpayers "admittedly enjoyed hunting, but enjoyment of one's work does not make that work a mere personal hobby. . . . There is evidence that this trip represented hard work on the part of the taxpayers, undertaken for the benefit of the Dairy, rather than a frolic of their own. . . ." Thus "evidence" of a business *connection,* though not proof of a predominant business *purpose,* appears to have sufficed.

Two other features of the pre-1962 treatment should be noted, the first reflected in the *Sutter* case,[25] the second in the much-abused *Cohan* decision.[26] In *Sutter,* the question for decision was whether an individual should be permitted to deduct the expenses of his *own* entertainment if incurred in the company of customers or clients. The taxpayer, a physician engaged in industrial medicine, claimed deductions for the cost of attending business luncheons and entertaining clients aboard his cabin cruiser. The Tax Court held that the cost of self-entertainment, even though incurred in a business setting, was not deductible unless the expense could be shown to be "different from or in excess of" that which the taxpayer would have incurred for his own gratification. The qualification established by the Court resembles the one which formerly applied to the excess cost of restaurant meals purchased while on travel status, and as with the

---

[24] *Sanitary Farms Dairy, Inc. v. Commissioner,* 25 T.C. 463 (1955).

[25] *Sutter v. Commissioner,* 21 T.C. 170 (1953).

[26] *Cohan v. Commissioner,* 39 F.2d 540 (2d Cir. 1930).

earlier limitation the difficulty of segregating "excess" entertainment costs made the *Sutter* rule virtually impossible for the Service to administer. As a result, with the exception of "abuse" cases—an effort by lawyer A to deduct *all* his lunches on the theory that every luncheon companion is a prospective client or business associate[27]—the Service in practice disregarded *Sutter* and allowed the expenses of self-entertainment to be deducted in full.

The *Cohan* decision furnished the administrative framework for the policing of "T & E" expenditures prior to 1962. In *Cohan* the Board of Tax Appeals, having found that the famous showman had spent substantial sums on travel and entertainment, some portion of which was undeniably business-related, nevertheless disallowed his claimed deduction in full on the ground that the amount claimed was unsupported by vouchers or bookkeeping entries. On appeal, the Board's decision was remanded by the Second Circuit, which held (in an opinion by Learned Hand) that "absolute certainty in such matters is usually impossible and is not necessary." The court believed, rather surprisingly, that Cohan "probably could not have" kept an account of his entertainment expenditures. T & E expenses can be estimated if documentary proof is lacking, and hence "the Board should make as close an approximation as it can, bearing heavily if it chooses upon the taxpayer whose inexactitude is of his own making." The *Cohan* case was decided in 1930; tax rates were low and the practice of business entertaining probably not widespread. Both conditions reversed themselves in the ensuing decades, and by 1962, when Congress finally took a hand, the *Cohan* rule reportedly had become a leading source of controversy between taxpayers and IRS agents on field audits. In effect, the *Cohan* rule had degenerated into a form of gamesmanship, with a good many taxpayers deliberately overstating their unsubstantiated T & E expenditures in the expectation that a given percentage would in any event be disallowed on audit. From a national perspective, the problem with this practice was that most returns necessarily escaped audit altogether, so that the overstated amount was usually allowed in full by default. *Cohan* thus represented an invitation to tax cheating through the exaggeration of entertainment expenses, a practice which could be rationalized on the ground that all taxpayers of a certain class engaged in it. What is puzzling, at least in hindsight, is how Hand could have failed to foresee this consequence when he led the Second Circuit in authorizing a rule of "approximation."

"The slogan—'It's deductible'—should pass from our scene," sloganized President Kennedy in his Tax Message of 1961, and later

---

[27]   *Moss v. Commissioner,* 758 F.2d 211 (7th Cir. 1985).

Presidents—notably Carter, Reagan and Clinton—have also stressed the need to eliminate or restrict the deduction for expense-account spending. Congress responded rather weakly to Kennedy's plea for legislative change in this area, but in 1962 it did add § 274, which overruled the *Cohan* case among other things. Thus, § 274(d) required that the taxpayer maintain "adequate records" of time, place, amount and business purpose in order to support a claim for entertainment expense deductions; the right to approximate (and to do so after the fact) had been withdrawn. More generally, § 274(a) allowed deduction of entertainment expenses only if the outlay was "directly related" to the taxpayer's business or preceded or followed a "bona fide business discussion." While the latter requirements presumably strengthened the Service's hand in challenging doubtful items, the relevant evidence was obviously within the taxpayer's control and one generally assumes that the *kinds* of expenditures—restaurant meals, tickets to sports events—that were deductible prior to the addition of § 274 continued to be deductible after its enactment.

President Reagan launched a new attack on the entertainment expense deduction in his "Tax Proposals" of 1985, and this time Congress reacted by imposing a flat percentage disallowance on all outlays falling into the entertainment category, business meals included. Under § 274(n), added in 1986 and amended in 1993, only 50% of amounts expended on business meals and business entertainment could be taken as an expense deduction, the remaining 50% being disallowed.

Finally (at least for now), the Tax Cuts and Jobs Act of 2017 amended § 274(a)(1)(A) generally to prohibit any deduction for the cost of business "entertainment, amusement, or recreation." It took over half a century, but in 2017 Congress finally enacted something close to the treatment of business entertainment expenses that President Kennedy had proposed in 1961. Thus, no deduction is now allowed for the costs of entertaining business associates at sporting events, the theater, or fancy restaurants. The 2017 amendment does not, however, affect the deductibility of the costs of meals consumed while away from home on a business trip, which continue to be deductible subject to the 50% disallowance rule of § 274(n).

Business travel meals that are reimbursed by an individual's employer are fully deductible (really, excludable) by the employee, but the employer itself is then made subject to the 50/50 restriction. This can be understood as a form of surrogate taxation; the employee is undertaxed (by not being required to pay tax on the personal half of the cost of his meal), but the employer is correspondingly overtaxed (by not being allowed to deduct the entire cost of the meal, none of which was consumed by the employer itself), and the correct total amount of tax is paid (but only if the employer and the employee are in the same tax bracket).

We might add, finally, that the general idea of disallowing business entertainment expenses effectively puts that class of outlays in the same category as the "commercial gifts" discussed at 4.03, above. If (as in the *Duberstein* case) Lawyer A had made a gift of some sort to Client B—say a case of the best champagne—the cost would *not* be deductible by A unless B were willing (which is unlikely) to include the item in income. Business entertainment now gets the same treatment. B includes nothing, but A's expense is disallowed. In that respect, as with commercial gifts, there is tax symmetry: A bears the tax on B's benefit. The same, in a sense, is true of the entertainment A buys for herself. Theoretically, A (the lawyer) *should* be allowed to deduct the theater ticket if the outlay really has a business purpose; but it is also well arguable that A (the theater-goer) should be required to include the same amount in income as a consumption benefit. Putting the expense and the benefit together obviously produces a wash; in effect, the "correct" outcome is reached by including nothing but allowing no deduction.[28]

A loose end. Section 274(a)(3), which was added to the Code in 1993, disallows all deductions for dues paid to "any club organized for business, pleasure, recreation, or other social purpose." This rule makes good sense with respect to the typical golf or tennis club; the personal consumption element seems large enough to justify a blanket disallowance. But what about airlines "clubs," the sole purpose of which seems to be to allow the harried traveler to rest between connecting flights, untroubled by *hoi polloi* milling about in the remainder of the airport. No one would think these glorified lobbies were clubs, but for the airlines' decision to call them clubs as a marketing device. Given that taxation is supposed to be about substance rather than form, surely § 274(a)(3) does not apply to airlines clubs? Actually, according to the applicable Regulation, it does.[29] In issuing the Regulation, Treasury indicated it was constrained by the legislative history of § 274(a)(3), which specifically indicated that airlines clubs were indeed clubs for purposes of the disallowance rule.

We have it on good authority (we wouldn't know from personal experience) that a traveler who purchases a first-class ticket from an airline is entitled to use that airline's club facilities during the trip.

---

[28] Halperin, *Business Deduction for Personal Living Expenses: A Uniform Approach to an Unsolved Problem*, 122 U.Pa.L.Rev. 859 (1974).

[29] Reg. § 1.274–2(a)(2)(iii)(a).

In effect, some portion of the price of the first-class ticket is for the use of the club facilities. Nothing in the Code denies a business traveler a full deduction for the cost of first-class airfare. Notice the surprising tax results. A frugal business traveler, who flies coach and purchases a "membership" in an airline's club is not permitted to deduct any portion of the club dues. But a more extravagant business traveler, who always flies first-class, and who receives club privileges as part of the first-class package, is allowed to deduct his airfares in their entirety. There are two morals. First, the rules for distinguishing business from personal expenses are often arbitrary. (We've mentioned this arbitrariness before, but the airline's club dues situation is an especially striking example.) Second, always fly first-class.

Another loose end. § 280A, added to the Code in 1976, quite sharply circumscribed the deductibility of so-called home office expenses—maintenance, utilities, depreciation/rent—by providing (in part) that such expenses shall be allowed only if the space that is supposed to qualify as an office is "exclusively used on a regular basis" as the taxpayer's "principal place of business." The aim, presumably, was to prevent professionals and others who make occasional business use of their homes—a lawyer, for example, who finds it more convenient to do some paperwork in her den on weekends than go downtown to her office—from converting residential expenses into business expenses through self-favoring exaggeration. On the other hand, taxpayers who really do devote a portion of their homes to an exclusive business use—a commercial artist, say, who does all her work in a studio set aside for that purpose—would qualify under the Section and obviously should.

But what about those taxpayers for whom an "office" as such is really only incidental to the work they do—typically, we suppose, an independent professional whose services are performed where the services are needed rather than seated at a desk? In the *Soliman* case,[30] the taxpayer, an anesthesiologist, sought to deduct expenses incurred in maintaining a home office in which he did his professional reading, kept his billing records and performed certain other routine administrative tasks—none of which, of course, involved anesthetizing patients. Reversing the court below, the Supreme Court upheld the Commissioner's disallowance on the ground that the home office did not qualify as the taxpayer's "principal place of business" within the meaning of § 280A. Though he had no other office, it was clear that the doctor's administrative chores were far less important than his hands-on work in the operating room, and clear also that he spent much more professional time in the hospital

---

[30] *Commissioner v. Soliman,* 506 U.S. 168 (1993).

than anywhere else. Since office tasks were less important and involved less time than hospital work, the office could not be viewed as the taxpayer's "principal" business location for purposes of the Code provision.

Finding the outcome in *Soliman* overly restrictive (and perhaps aware that more and more voters are engaged in doing business from home), Congress in 1997 overruled that decision by enlarging the definition of "principal place of business" to include a home office used by the taxpayer for "administrative or management activities," provided that the taxpayer has no other "fixed location" that he uses for the same purpose. Pretty clearly, Dr. Soliman's home office expenses—$1,200 for the year in question—would now be deductible, as will the expenses of other small service providers who operate out of their homes and who perform services at the homes and offices of their customers.

The five-year revenue cost of this seemingly modest Code amendment was estimated to be $2.4 billion, obviously indicating that large numbers of taxpayers, probably in the hundreds of thousands, were likely to be affected. Loosening up the definition of "principal place of business" is also likely to present the Service with fairly serious audit problems, because the amendment really constitutes an open invitation to self-employed taxpayers to take a home office deduction in *some* amount, even when the taxpayer's home office activities are distinctly minor, if not imaginary. The accompanying Committee Report virtually engraves the invitation by confirming that even those taxpayers who maintain a fixed office elsewhere—doctors, lawyers—may take an additional deduction for home office expenses if they do a substantial part of their paperwork at home rather than at the fixed office location. To be sure, § 280A continues to require that the alleged home office be used "exclusively" for business. Even so, it is not hard to predict that many a cozy den will now be found to qualify as an "office."

A further element can be mentioned. Dr. Soliman's services as an anesthesiologist were of course performed at a hospital, which necessarily entailed his traveling every day from home to hospital and back again, presumably by car or taxi. He claimed a deduction for such daily transportation expenses—some $3,600 for the year— but that claim was no more successful than his claim for home office expenses. As indicated above, the cost of the daily commute from home to one's principal place of business, a cost incurred by almost every working person, is and always has been treated as a nondeductible personal expense. That is true even though the taxpayer's principal workplace changes at frequent intervals because his services are performed on-site—a self-employed electrician, for example, who works on one project and then another, spending a week or so at each before moving on to the next, or Dr. Soliman himself, who performed services at several different hospitals in his community. The taxpayer is treated no differently because his local job-site is shifting and temporary than he would be if he commuted every day to a single fixed location.

On the other hand, a taxpayer who, *during* the working day, travels from his principal place of business to another business location—the same electrician traveling *between* two ongoing projects, or Dr. Soliman going from hospital X in the morning to hospital Y in the afternoon—*can* deduct the associated transportation costs under § 162(a), because that category of travel is not regarded as regular home-to-work commuting. With this distinction in mind, the Service in a 1994 Ruling (Rev. Rul. 94–47) held that a deduction is allowed for transportation expenses incurred by a taxpayer in traveling between his home office and another local work site *provided* that the home office actually qualifies as the taxpayer's "principal place of business" under § 280A. The Ruling was of course issued before the 1997 amendment to § 280A, and in speaking of a taxpayer's home office as his principal place of business the Ruling obviously had reference to the narrow statutory definition of "principal place of business" that was approved by the Court in *Soliman.* However, the same rationale continues to be applicable under amended § 280A, as the IRS confirmed in a 1999 Ruling (Rev. Rul. 99–7). Thus, transportation expenses between a qualified home office—as liberally redefined—and any other local work location are now deductible.

Trivial? Not really. As noted, the good Doctor's transportation expenses—home to hospital and back—were three times greater than his home office expenses.

6.03 Capital Expenditures

Section 263 (with help from § 263A) disallows deductions for the cost of acquiring property, the useful life of which extends substantially beyond the close of the taxable year. Land and buildings, machinery and equipment, patents and trademarks, are major types of assets that continue in use for more or less extended periods of time. Since the cost of such properties represents a present payment by the taxpayer for economic benefits that will accrue to her in the future, the tax law requires that the expenditures be "capitalized" rather than deducted as a current expense. This of course does not mean that the taxpayer will never be allowed to recover such expenditures. Section 167 (discussed at 6.08 below) authorizes an annual allowance for the exhaustion or wear and tear of capital assets, so that in the case of plant, equipment or other productive assets with limited useful lives the construction or acquisition cost will be recovered on a year-by-year basis through the medium of depreciation or amortization deductions. The cost of non-depreciable assets—land is an example—is also recoverable, but as such property is assumed to be of perpetual or at least indefinite useful life the recovery is postponed until the property is sold.

Whether a given outlay should be treated as an "expense" under § 162 or a capital expenditure under § 263 thus usually boils down to a question of timing. If the outlay in question is an expense, it is deductible at once and reduces the taxable income of the current year. If the outlay is a capital expenditure, it is deductible over a period of years; in the case of tangible property the number of years in the "recovery period" is specified by § 168. If the outlay is a capital expenditure but the property acquired is of indefinite useful life, then the outlay is recoverable only as an offset against the proceeds of final sale.

While the classification of an outlay as an expense or a capital expenditure is normally clear, there are, inevitably, instances in which the proper treatment is in doubt. Four such problem areas are discussed below: (a) the distinction between "repairs" and "alterations"; (b) the treatment of business intangibles; (c) the distinction between "lease" and "purchase"; and (d) the treatment of education expenses. At stake in categories (a)–(c) is simply the acceleration or postponement of tax payments—deduction now or deduction later. In category (d) the issue is a sharper one in a sense, because a finding of "capital expenditure" is equivalent to a permanent disallowance. In all four situations, of course, it is in the taxpayer's interest to treat doubtful items as deductible expenses and in the Treasury's "interest" to treat such items as capital expenditures.

(a) Repairs or Alterations

In addition to the original acquisition cost of plant, machinery and the like, which generally has to be capitalized, the Regulations require that subsequent expenditures that alter the property's capacity or function, or that extend its useful life, be capitalized as well. Thus, the addition of three stories to an existing office building would obviously be a capital expenditure. Similarly, amounts spent to restore worn-out plant or equipment to its original condition— rebuilding an old building, for example—would be treated as "making good the [depreciation] for which an allowance is or has been made" and would also have to be capitalized.

By contrast, amounts spent for "repairs" are permitted to be deducted as a current expense under § 162(a). This is true even though the repair itself would usually have an economic value to the taxpayer that extends beyond the current taxable year. Suppose a machine part breaks for some reason and has to be replaced. Although the new part (if it doesn't break) is expected to last as long as the machine itself, it presumably qualifies as a "repair" and is therefore deductible under § 162. But why should that be so? If the general rule is that an expenditure for property having an extended useful life must be capitalized, why should the cost of the new machine part be treated as a current expense merely because it has the status of a repair? Why not simply add the outlay to the basis of the machine and then recover the taxpayer's total investment through depreciation over the balance of the machine's useful life?

The somewhat long-winded answer is that there is (or ought to be) a certain parallelism between the deduction for repairs under § 162(a) and the deduction for business casualties under § 165(a). A machine that breaks down because a vital part malfunctions can be said to have sustained a kind of accidental impairment that *resembles* a casualty in the sense that it results in a sudden loss in the value of the machine itself and is more or less unexpected. If the taxpayer's equipment were damaged by a true casualty—fire, let's say—the resulting loss (unless covered by insurance) would be deductible *as* a casualty,[31] while subsequent outlays for repair would be capitalized and added back to basis. Thus, if a machine with a value and adjusted basis of $10,000 sustains $2,000 of fire damage, the casualty loss is fully deductible and the basis of the machine is reduced to $8,000. If the taxpayer then spends $2,000 to repair the machine, the outlay is nondeductible (the casualty loss having been deducted already, and Reg. § 1.161–1 providing that "[d]ouble deductions are not permitted") but is added back to basis, which is restored to $10,000. An equivalent loss attributable to a malfunction results in no deductible loss and no reduction of basis. If, however, the taxpayer repairs the machine at the same $2,000 cost, a current deduction *is* permitted for the repair expenditure and the overall tax effects are just the same. The taxpayer's $2,000 economic loss is recognized in both cases—in the former, by treating the casualty itself as the realization of a deductible loss, in the latter, by accepting the repair expenditure as a proxy measure of the loss caused by the malfunction.[32]

In larger terms, the point to be made is that the casualty or the malfunction simply serves to precipitate the loss in value that will in any case take place over time as the taxpayer's equipment is used up in production. Thus, the taxpayer in the above example is entitled to

---

[31]   A decline in the value of property damaged in a true casualty (in the words of the statute, "a fire, storm, shipwreck, or other [similar] casualty") is treated as a realized loss even if the taxpayer has not sold or otherwise disposed of the property.

[32]   Johnson, *Soft Money Investing Under the Income Tax*, 1989 U.Ill.L.Rev. 1019, 1089 (1989).

recover her adjusted basis of $10,000 in future taxable years through annual allowances for depreciation. Casualty or malfunction causes an instant loss in value; depreciation is anticipated, in effect, and to the extent thereof is allowed to be deducted all at once.

In 2013 the Treasury issued final Regulations elaborating—at *much* greater length than the prior Regulations—on the distinction between deductible "repairs," on the one hand, and, on the other hand, "betterments," "restorations," and "adaptations," the cost of which must be capitalized.[33] In general, the new Regulations constitute a sort of restatement of the income tax law of repairs—a summarizing and tidying up of decades of cases and rulings distinguishing deductible repairs from non-deductible improvements.

According to the new Regulations, an expenditure is for a non-deductible "betterment" (rather than for a deductible "repair") if it is "reasonably expected to materially increase the productivity, efficiency, strength, quality, or output of the unit of property."[34] Under this standard, everything would be a "betterment" rather than a "repair," if the comparison were between the damaged condition of the property just before it is fixed and its condition after it has been fixed. But the Regulations make clear that that is not the appropriate comparison. Instead, the proper comparison is between the condition of the property immediately *before* the damage necessitating the fix, and the property's condition as fixed. As long as an asset's post-fix condition is not an improvement over its pre-damage condition, the fix will generally qualify as a deductible repair.[35]

One question that has proved especially troublesome in the repair field is how to classify relatively large-scale outlays of which the aim is not merely to correct a malfunction or replace a worn-out part, but to adapt the equipment in the light of changed or newly discovered conditions that otherwise compromise its usefulness. The equipment has operated satisfactorily to date within its own mechanical limits. Now, however, owing to a change in surrounding circumstances, the taxpayer finds that it simply won't do its accustomed job unless it is modified or augmented in some respect. The taxpayer accordingly makes a sizeable expenditure that alters or adds to the equipment in a material way. Yet the taxpayer's only aim is to maintain existing operations; she expects no increase in future revenues. Should the outlay be treated as a capital investment or as a mere repair?

---

[33]   Reg. § 1.162–4(a); Reg. § 1.263(a)–3.

[34]   Reg. § 1.263((a)–3(j)(1)(iii).

[35]   Reg. § 1.263(a)–3(j)(2)(iv)(C).

In the well-known *Mt. Morris Drive-In* case,[36] the taxpayer acquired a tract of farm land for the purpose of building an outdoor movie theater. Covering vegetation was cleared from the property in order to build ramps for automobiles, and as a result of this removal of ground-cover the drainage of rainwater onto a neighboring farm increased substantially. Threatened with suit by the adjoining landowner, the taxpayer at a cost of $8,000 installed a drainage system which carried the excess rainfall to a public drain. The original acquisition of the farmland took place in 1947; the drainage system was added in 1950, although the lawsuit was threatened some two years earlier. The drainage system itself, quite obviously, had a useful life that extended well beyond the current taxable year.

On these facts, a majority of the Tax Court held that the outlay was a capital expenditure and rejected the taxpayer's effort to deduct it as a current expense. The majority found that the need for a drainage system had been obvious and foreseeable at the time the original construction work was undertaken. Accordingly, the taxpayer's initial capital investment was "incomplete" until the drainage system was added to the property; the outlay was part of the basic cost of the drive-in theatre, just as gutters and drains would be part of the basic cost of a house. In a brief concurring opinion, Judge Raum asserted that capital expenditure treatment was proper *whether or not* the need for a drainage system could have been foreseen in 1947, and whether the outlay was contemporaneous with the original construction or took place at a subsequent time. Finally, a dissent argued that since the drainage facility "did not improve, better, extend, increase, or prolong the useful life of the property," the outlay ought to be allowed as an ordinary and necessary business expense. Though somewhat cryptic on this point, the dissenting judges apparently thought that the need for a drainage system arose *after* completion of the original theater construction and was attributable to events that could not have been anticipated. The 2013 Regulations endorse the Tax Court majority's view that the cost of fixing defects that "arose during the production of the unit of property" must be capitalized.[37]

The *Mt. Morris* decision can be contrasted with that in *Midland Empire Packing Co. v. Commissioner*,[38] in which the question was whether the cost of lining basement walls with concrete to prevent oil seepage created by a neighboring refinery should be treated as a deductible repair or as a capital expenditure—*Mt. Morris* from the perspective of the drainee, as it were. The walls of the basement, which had been used for 25 years for the storage of meat and hides,

---

[36]   *Mt. Morris Drive-In Theatre Co. v. Commissioner,* 25 T.C. 272 (1955).

[37]   Reg. § 1.263(a)–3(j)(1)(i).

[38]   14 T.C. 635 (1950).

had proved entirely satisfactory until the refinery went up, at which point the said seepage began and the taxpayer was told by federal inspectors that it had to line the walls or shut down its plant altogether. The Tax Court held, this time unanimously, that the expenditure for wall-lining, nearly $5,000, was "essentially a repair" and hence deductible as a current business expense. The 2013 Regulations also endorse the result in *Midland Empire*, by not requiring capitalization of an expenditure "to correct damage to a unit of property that occurred during the taxpayer's use of the unit of property."[39]

Can the two decisions, *Midland Empire* and *Mt. Morris,* be reconciled? One senses that the installation of drainage equipment in *Mt. Morris* represented an addition to the taxpayer's plant rather than a mere replacement, while the concrete lining in *Midland Empire* could be viewed as responsive to an event somewhat resembling a natural disaster—seepage if not flooding. Hence, perhaps current expense treatment was more plausible in the latter case than in the former. On the other hand, as noted, the basement walls in *Midland Empire* were already 25 years old, which may mean that the storage facility had been fully depreciated at the time the outlay in question was made. If so, the facility would have had an adjusted basis in the taxpayer's hands of zero and its useful life would be over (*i.e.,* for tax purposes). As suggested earlier, the repair deduction is apparently to be explained on the ground that it takes the place of depreciation otherwise allowable to the taxpayer in future periods. Accepting that proposition, it should follow that one cannot "repair" a fully depreciated asset. Or so it would seem. The IRS, however, permits taxpayer to claim deductions for costs of repairing fully-depreciated property. In Rev. Rul. 2001–4,[40] for example, the IRS ruled that an airline could deduct as a repair the entire $2 million (!) it spent in 2000 on a "heavy maintenance" visit on a plane, despite the facts that (1) the § 168 cost recovery period for commercial airliners is seven years and (2) the airline had acquired the plane in 1984.[41]

(b) Business Intangibles and Advertising

The general requirement that the cost of long-lived assets be capitalized applies not only to tangible property such as plant and equipment, but also to intangible assets from which the taxpayer expects to realize economic benefits in future years. Here, however,

---

[39]   Reg. § 1.263(a)–3(j)(2)(iv)(C).

[40]   2001–1 C.B. 295.

[41]   The result in the Ruling does not appear to have been changed by the 2013 Regulations. See Reg. § 1.263(a)–3(j)(2)(iv)(B) (not requiring capitalization of the cost of "correct[ing] the effects of normal wear and tear").

there may be some difficulty in identifying the "asset" to which the expenditure relates. Suppose, for example, that a business taxpayer spends money developing manuals and videos for the purpose of training employees to handle certain complex office machinery. The outlay obviously improves current work performance, but it is also true that (1) the manuals and videos will be of substantial value in training new employees in the future, and (2) employees trained on the manual this year will continue to use their training in future years. How should the expenditure be treated? Is it deductible as a current expense or should it be capitalized in whole or part? If capitalized, can it be amortized over the period of its "useful life," and how would that period be determined?

Prior to the Supreme Court's decision in the *INDOPCO* case,[42] the rule or "principle" thought to govern this elusive question was the following. If the intangible business expenditure created a "separate and distinct asset," or if it could be linked to a tangible asset of some sort, then the expenditure had to be capitalized and recovered either through amortization if it had a determinable useful life or, if not, on final sale of the business itself as an offset against the sale price. *But* if no such "separate and distinct asset" was created by the expenditure, then the outlay could be deducted as a current expense rather than being capitalized. The cost of training materials in the illustration above would presumably be deductible as a current business expense under this rule, because training expenditures, while obviously expected to improve employee work performance in the future, created no "separate and distinct asset" that could be entered on the company's balance sheet.

So stated, the "rule" was wobbly and uncertain, and practitioners, as might be expected, would invariably resolve doubts about particular expenditures in favor of current deductibility. In the much-discussed *INDOPCO* case, INDOPCO, a publicly-held company, incurred investment banker's fees and related costs in connection with a friendly acquisition of INDOPCO by another corporation.[43] Pointing out that no separate and distinct asset had been created to which such outlays could be allocated, the taxpayer sought to deduct rather than capitalize the fees (which ran into the millions) as a current expense. The Supreme Court held for the Commissioner. "Although the mere presence of an incidental future benefit . . . may not warrant capitalization, a taxpayer's realization

---

[42]   *INDOPCO v. Commissioner*, 503 U.S. 79 (1992). The case is discussed in Bankman, *The Story of INDOPCO: What Went Wrong in the Capitalization v. Deduction Debate?*, in *Tax Stories* 183 (Caron ed., 2003).

[43]   Law students may be chagrined to learn that INDOPCO paid the investment banking firm of Morgan Stanley a fee of $2.2 million, while paying the Debevoise law firm a paltry $490,000.

of benefits beyond the year in which the expenditure is incurred is undeniably important . . ." Here, quite obviously, the transaction— that is, the acquisition—produced "significant benefits" that would be realized by the taxpayer in future years. It followed that the fees could not be deducted currently but had to be capitalized under § 263.

The "future benefits" rationale adopted in *INDOPCO* is quite broad and would seem to give the Commissioner considerable latitude in determining whether intangible asset outlays are or are not to be classified as capital expenditures. Environmental cleanup costs of all sorts could readily be brought within the *INDOPCO* rationale, one would think; other examples, as suggested, might be employee recruitment and training expenses, plant-closing costs, perhaps even bonuses paid to encourage early retirement. The big question—one that greatly exercised the tax bar and fairly consumed the professional literature for a time—was just how aggressive the Commissioner might decide to be in applying the *INDOPCO* future-benefits test. Would she now require capitalization for a wide variety of intangible business expenditures which, before *INDOPCO*, had routinely been deducted as current expense under § 162(a)? Or would she leave what many considered "well enough" alone? There was fear and loathing among practitioners and a lot of organized pressure on the Commissioner to act with due restraint or, better yet, not to act at all.

In the end, and after more than a decade of study, the Treasury largely abandoned the *INDOPCO* future-benefits test on the ground that it lacked the certainty and clarity necessary for "sound administration," and instead proceeded to issue rulings and Regulations which in substance restored the "separate and distinct asset" standard that prevailed in pre-*INDOPCO* years. Going back to the example above, the Service in Rev.Rul. 96–62[44] held that "[a]mounts paid or incurred for training, including the costs of trainers and routine updates of training materials, are generally deductible as business expenses under [§ 162] even though they may have some future benefit." And in yet another eagerly awaited ruling, the Service held that severance payments made to employees in connection with downsizing are deductible as current expense even though such payments "may produce some future benefits, such as reducing operating costs and increasing operating efficiencies." The extensive final *INDOPCO* Regulations (or, more accurately, anti-*INDOPCO* Regulations), promulgated in 2003, are likewise largely favorable to current deductibility in fact situations where a rigorous application of the future-benefits standard might have prompted a

---

[44]   1996–2 C.B. 9.

contrary outcome.[45] In the 2003 Regulations the IRS largely
abandoned its 1992 Supreme Court victory in *INDOPCO*; one might
even say that the IRS effectively overruled the Supreme Court.
Strangely enough, the IRS generally has *de facto* power to overrule
IRS-favorable Supreme Court decisions. Taxpayers benefitting from
the IRS's abandonment of a Supreme Court victory will have no
reason to object, and any objecting third parties will generally lack
standing to challenge the IRS's *volte-face.*

Whatever its scope, the *INDOPCO* decision has not altered the
long-standing treatment of one major category of intangible
expenditure that may exceed all others in size and importance,
namely, advertising.[46] From a very early date, and presumably now
with implied congressional approval, amounts spent by business
taxpayers for the purpose of stimulating sales of their products or
services through advertising and sales promotion have been treated
as trade or business expenses under § 162(a) and allowed to be
deducted currently. As a theoretical matter, it might be argued that
the annual cost of promoting brand X should somehow be divided
between current sales, a deductible expense, and future sales
activity, a capital expenditure. In practical terms, however, such an
allocation would be difficult and perhaps impossible to carry out in
other than an arbitrary fashion. As a result, the Service, with rare
exceptions, permits advertising and related outlays to be deducted
currently and makes no effort to identify a separate capital
expenditure component. For the usual reason—namely, that
deduction now is preferable to deduction later—the effect is generally
favorable from the taxpayer's standpoint.

The discussion above concerns self-developed or self-generated
intangibles—that is, intangibles created by the taxpayer through its
own direct expenditures. A somewhat different set of considerations
applies where intangible assets, including goodwill, are acquired by
the taxpayer on the purchase of an entire business—that is, where
the taxpayer buys intangible assets as part of the acquisition of
another firm. This topic, which has been the subject of important
legislation, is taken up at 6.11, below.

(c)   Lease or Purchase

In *Starr's Estate,*[47] the taxpayer acquired an automatic
sprinkling system under a 5-year lease for an annual rental of $1,240.
The lease was renewable for another five years at virtually no cost,

---

[45]   Regs. §§ 1.263(a)–4 and 1.263(a)–5.

[46]   Rev. Rul. 92–80, 1992–2 C.B. 57 ("The *INDOPCO* decision does not affect the
treatment of advertising costs as business expenses which are generally deductible
under section 162 of the Code").

[47]   *Starr's Estate v. Commissioner,* 274 F.2d 294 (9th Cir.1959).

and while no further provision was made for additional rental periods, the court found that because of the individualized nature of the equipment the lessor-manufacturer would not reclaim it once the first 5-year term had been completed. The taxpayer sought to deduct the annual rental payments as ordinary business expenses, but the Commissioner disallowed the deductions on the ground that the purported lease was really an installment purchase which must be capitalized. The Court of Appeals sustained the Commissioner. Stressing that the manufacturer had retained no significant residual interest in the property, the court held that the arrangement amounted to a conditional "sale" for federal tax purposes, even though formal title had not passed to the "buyer," and even though the contract was a "lease" under local law.

Although the Commissioner had sought to capitalize the entire amount paid by the taxpayer—a total of $6,200—the court in *Starr's Estate* quite properly observed that as the payments were made in installments over a 5-year term, some portion of each payment must be regarded as implicit interest. Since the lump-sum purchase price of the same equipment was known to be $4,960, the court suggested that the difference—$1,240—be allowed as a deduction over 5 years at the rate of $248 a year. The sprinkler system itself was found to have a useful life of 23 years, so that the taxpayer presumably would be entitled to a yearly depreciation allowance of about $216 as well. His total annual deduction would thus be $464 during the 5-year payment period, and $216 thereafter, as opposed to $1,240 for each of the first 5 years if the "lease" had been recognized as such. The court also intimated that the entire matter was rather piddling. Once depreciation and interest had been allowed, it said, "the attack on many of the 'leases' may not be worth while in terms of revenue."

In a sense the latter observation is the most interesting feature of the court's opinion. *Was* the litigation "worth while" from the Treasury's standpoint? If we assume a 50% tax rate (as it then was) in all relevant periods, the "tax value" in a given year of deducting $1,240 as rent was obviously $620. The present value of $620 a year for 5 years discounted at a rate of (say) 5% is about $2,700. By contrast, the tax benefit of deducting $464 as depreciation and interest was $232, and of deducting $216 as depreciation alone, $108. The present value of $232 for 5 years and $108 for 18 years thereafter turns out to be about $2,000. Hence the controversy was worth roughly $700 ($2,700 minus $2,000) on a present basis. While that amount seems rather small in absolute terms, it would have reduced the after-tax cost of the sprinkler system by some 14%. Moreover, the transaction in *Starr's Estate* was not an isolated phenomenon; if the arrangement had gone unchallenged, then presumably many other installment sales of long-lived and higher-priced equipment would have been converted into "leases" for tax purposes.

Yet even when this is said, what *real* difference does it make to the government whether equipment transactions are treated as sales or leases? It is true that Starr's deductions as a "lessee" exceeded the depreciation which he would have been allowed as an "owner" during the years in question. But on the other side of the transaction, the manufacturer—who is also a taxpayer, of course—would (or should) have been required to report the payments as rental income. Instead of deducting its manufacturing costs over the same 5-year period (as was permitted in the case of an installment seller), the manufacturer as "lessor" and legal owner of the equipment would have had to depreciate the sprinkler system over its much longer useful life. What the "lessee" gained by anticipating deductions, the "lessor" would lose by delay. Hence the Treasury would appear to be a mere stakeholder; the lessee's tax saving would be offset by the lessor's sacrifice, and the reduction in purchase price referred to in the preceding paragraph would really be borne by the manufacturer of the equipment.

So shouldn't the Treasury be content in all such cases? Why contest the parties' effort to characterize the transaction as a "lease" when the advantage to one taxpayer is compensated for by a disadvantage to the other? The answer is that *if* the benefit and sacrifice were *always* mutually offsetting, the Treasury might well be inclined to leave the matter to the parties and accept whatever characterization they adopted. Indeed, in that event the parties themselves might just as well bargain directly about the purchase price of the equipment instead of fooling around with tax arrangements. If, for example, Starr and the sprinkler manufacturer were *both* 50% taxpayers, then they achieved nothing by labeling the transaction as a "lease" that could not have been accomplished as well by knocking 14% off the price of the sprinkler system.[48]

The difficulty with adopting this view, of course, is that in many cases either there is a difference in applicable marginal tax rates between the parties to a transaction or one party has positive taxable income while the other does not. As a result, the accelerated deductions may be of greater tax value to one taxpayer than to the other. Where such differences in individual tax circumstances exist,

---

[48]　Unless they reported the transaction inconsistently, which is precisely what they did. According to 30 T.C. at 863–64, the sprinkler manufacturer devised the "lease" as a means of stimulating sales to deduction-hungry customers. The manufacturer itself, however, reported its profit from the transaction in the same manner as the profit from an installment sale. The cost-saving "offered" by the manufacturer was thus entirely at the Treasury's expense, or would have been apart from the litigation.

the taxpayers, if free to characterize the transaction as a "sale" or "lease" entirely at will, would choose whichever label minimized their *combined* tax burden, and then on some basis would divide the tax saving between them. In all such cases the government would be the loser—indeed, the only loser—and would bear the entire burden of the adjustment. The Treasury's authority to insist that leases or sales shall be recognized as such only if *federally* established criteria are satisfied operates as a check on this process and limits the freedom of taxpayers to allocate and schedule deductions for their own benefit. In a sense, then, the real issue in *Starr's Estate* was whether the Treasury possessed such authority. The determination that it did is the chief significance of the decision.

There is more to be said about the lease-purchase distinction, especially in connection with the larger subject of depreciation. Accordingly, the topic is raised again, and discussed in a more contemporary setting, at 6.10(b), below.

(d) Education

Roughly stated, the cost of education or training is deductible as a current expense if the aim of the expenditure is to maintain or improve skills used by the taxpayer in an existing trade or business, or if the education is required by the taxpayer's employer as a condition of continued employment. The expense of a refresher course or a keeping-up-with-current-developments course is thus deductible as a sort of intellectual repair. A practicing lawyer, for example, was allowed to deduct as an expense the cost of attending the annual N.Y.U. Federal Tax Institute—a week-long presentation of entirely forgettable papers on current tax questions—because the "education" there received enabled him "to keep sharp the tools" that he used in his practice. The Service had argued that the outlay should be disallowed as a personal expense, thereby threatening the Institute with virtual extinction.[49]

A deduction for the cost of acquiring *new* skills—by rough analogy to the status of betterments as distinguished from repairs— is usually denied unless the taxpayer can show that her intent is merely to enhance the skills that she already possesses. A teacher who goes to summer school in order to qualify for a higher civil service classification may deduct her costs on a showing that she is seeking to advance within her existing profession. But an accountant who goes to law school, allegedly to improve her performance as an accountant, is denied deduction by the present Regulations on the ground that the educational expense qualifies her for a new trade or business, whether she intends to enter that business or not. In most

---

[49] *Coughlin v. Commissioner*, 203 F.2d 307 (2d Cir.1953). And see Reg. § 1.162–5(b).

cases, therefore, the cost of acquiring an education which leads to a degree—J.D., M.D., Ph.D.—is not deductible; presumably the same is true of other vocational training expenses—learning to be a computer operator, auto mechanic, and so on. On the other hand, the Tax Court has recognized that possession of an M.B.A. qualifies one to do nothing that one could not do without the degree, with the result that the costs of obtaining an M.B.A. are deductible if acquiring the M.B.A. either (1) maintains or improves skills used by the taxpayer in his current employment, or (2) is required by his employer as a condition of keeping his job.[50]

The cost of a professional education is said by the Regulations to represent an "inseparable aggregate of personal and capital expenditures." Actually, of course, the "personal" component in attending law or medical school is pretty small for most people; nonexistent for some. While the cost of going to college can perhaps be viewed differently, professional and vocational training is almost entirely business-related and unquestionably represents a capital expenditure. Nevertheless, the tax law does not recognize a right to recover the investment in professional training through annual depreciation or amortization deductions. The reason usually given for the denial is that capital investments may be depreciated or amortized only if they have an ascertainable useful life, and since one cannot be sure just how long an individual's training will serve as a productive resource—she may never practice law or she may still be wobbling into court at ninety—the cost cannot be amortized. On the other hand, it has been argued that human life being the finite thing it is, the individual's statistical life-expectancy, perhaps even her career-expectancy, is just as reliable and accurate a measure of the useful life of a professional education as an appraiser's estimate of the life of a building. Indeed, buildings seem to go on forever; lawyers plainly don't. "It is true that an asset with an indefinite life may not be amortized, but it does not follow that the life of an asset must be definitely predictable in order that it be definite or finite."[51]

The argument for permitting professional education costs to be amortized has undeniable force. Its defect—if it can be called that— is that it contains no intrinsic means of distinguishing between professional or vocational school expenses and the costs of general education. Apparently, it remains true that a college degree promises a higher income for the recipient than she would otherwise attain, and perhaps the same can be said of prep school or even private grade

---

[50] *Allemeier v. Commissioner*, 90 T.C.M. 197 (2005). From 2018 through 2025, however, all unreimbursed employee business expenses are disallowed by § 67(g) (discussed at 7.05).

[51] Wolfman, *The Cost of Education and the Federal Income Tax*, 42 F.R.D. 535 (1966).

school. While Congress could no doubt draw a defensible line between general and specialized or between lower and higher education, the same task would be exceedingly difficult if attempted through administrative rulemaking or a process of case-by-case judicial development. In effect, the denial of training expenses is of such long standing that a reversal of policy—rather like taxing imputed rents or permitting a deduction for commuting costs—would now require congressional action to establish the relevant criteria.

In fact, Congress did act in 1997 to create tax benefits for educational outlays at the college level. While no change was made in the "business or personal expense" classifications just discussed, a variety of tax credits and other tax incentives aimed at encouraging post-secondary education were added by the Taxpayer Relief Act of 1997, chiefly for the benefit of middle-income families. These new Code features are briefly described at 7.09, below.

6.04 "Ordinary and Necessary"

To be deductible under § 162(a) an expenditure must not only be incurred in "carrying on a trade or business," but also qualify as "ordinary and necessary." Just what this further limitation means has never been entirely clear, although the quoted phrase has appeared in the statute virtually from its inception. The leading case on the subject is *Welch v. Helvering,*[52] decided by the Supreme Court in 1933. Unfortunately, Justice Cardozo's opinion contains so much soggy philosophy that its main thesis is difficult to locate. As a result, the case itself has been a source of some confusion. Most commentators today, we think, would view the decision as chiefly involving the distinction between current expense and capital expenditure, and in fairness it is that issue which the opinion seems to emphasize.

The taxpayer in *Welch* had been an executive of a corporation that went bankrupt in the grain business. Having decided to establish a similar business on his own, the taxpayer paid off the bankrupt company's debts in an effort to establish his own financial credit and regain his status and reputation with customers of his former firm. The Supreme Court sustained the Commissioner in denying deduction for the payments on the ground that the expenditures were not "ordinary" within the meaning of § 162(a), even though they might have been "necessary" for the buildup of the new business.

Perhaps without really intending to, the Court used the word "ordinary" to express two quite different limitations on the scope of § 162(a), of which the first seems largely unwarranted. Initially

---

[52]   290 U.S. 111 (1933).

taking the term to mean customary or typical, the Court found that the taxpayer's action in repaying the bankrupt's debts was "in a high degree extraordinary." "Men do at times pay the debts of others without legal obligation ... but they do not do so ordinarily. ..." Until such conduct should become the business norm, therefore, it must be viewed as falling outside the statute. No evidence was cited to support a finding that the voluntary repayment of debts discharged in bankruptcy was altogether novel, and indeed one reads the fact-recital with a feeling that the taxpayer's action was entirely sensible from a business standpoint. Even if it *were* unprecedented, it is difficult to think of any reason why the tax law should bar deduction on that ground alone. Once one is satisfied that the expenditure was in fact designed to generate business income—a point conceded in *Welch*—the object of the statute would appear to have been met. Section 162(a) aims at reducing the gross income derived from business by related expenses. If the expenditure was dictated by the taxpayer's business judgment, it ought to be deductible even if also found to be unusual "in a high degree."

In any event, this aspect of the *Welch* opinion has had no more than a limited application in later cases, and the Treasury has not regarded itself as authorized thereby to create normative classifications for business outlays.

Justice Cardozo applied the term "ordinary" in another sense in *Welch,* and by and large it is this second meaning which has received the greater emphasis in subsequent decisions. In effect, the Court found that in paying off the old creditors of his former firm the taxpayer really was engaged in making an outlay that belonged to the category of capital expenditure. The debt repayments were designed to restore the taxpayer's credit and to reestablish his reputation with other firms. Hence they could reasonably be regarded as the purchase price of customer goodwill, a capital asset. "Ordinary" business expenses, by contrast, were those which belonged to the category of deductible current expense. Used in the sense of "everyday" or "recurring," the term merely served as a shorthand way of distinguishing between capital expenditures and current items. To be sure, § 263 accomplishes the very same end, just as § 262 expressly disallows expenditures that are personal; hence, as has often been observed, the "ordinary and necessary" restriction seems at best to be excess statutory baggage.

Actually, the decision in *Welch*—treating the payments to the old company's creditors as capital expenditures—seems a bit harsh, even if technically correct. The Court's opinion doesn't tell us who those creditors were, but one assumes that they were suppliers whose unpaid invoices led finally to the old company's bankruptcy. Had the old company avoided bankruptcy and paid its creditors in due course—or even after long delay—those payments would presumably have been "ordinary and necessary" and would have been deductible as current expense. Perhaps the same would have been true if the old company had emerged from bankruptcy as a continuing entity and had then chosen to forgo the benefit of the bankruptcy discharge and pay its creditors what it owed them. In a general (though not a technical) sense that is exactly what happened, since the Welches were the sole owners of both the old and the new company and continued to do business in the same way as before. On this view, the effect of the bankruptcy was to convert what would have been a deductible current expense into a non-deductible capital expenditure, a result that seems debatable, or at least unfortunate. The result in *Welch* is also in tension with the tax treatment of advertising. If Welch had attempted to create goodwill for his new venture by advertising that he was an honest fellow, the cost of that advertising would have been deductible (as discussed at 6.03(b)). Why should the tax system treat Welch any differently when he pursues the same goal through different means?

Caught up in its own phrase-making, the Court gave little attention to the business context before it. From the taxpayer's standpoint the result was particularly painful. Self-created "goodwill" is regarded by the tax law as a capital asset of indeterminate useful life, one that lacks a predictable or ascertainable expiration date. As a consequence, its cost cannot be recovered through annual deductions for depreciation or amortization. Instead such cost would be recoverable only when the business was finally sold or liquidated. In *Welch*, however, even this distant expectation of a tax benefit was placed in doubt. Although the debt repayments seem to have related exclusively to the taxpayer's professional interest, the Court also saw a personal element in the matter, as if the money had been spent to meet a moral as much as a business obligation. Viewed in this way—that is, as involving an "inseparable aggregate" of personal and professional expenditures—it is by no means clear that any form of cost recovery would ever be allowed.

The late great country singer Conway Twitty (real name of Harold L. Jenkins) was the protagonist of a Tax Court case with echoes of *Welch*.[53] Twitty had persuaded some of his friends, including Merle Haggard, to invest in Twitty Burger, Inc., which operated a chain of fast food restaurants. The restaurant menus featured Twitty's visage, a message from Twitty, and a picture of a "Twitty bird" (a small yellow bird strumming a guitar). Inexplicably,

---

[53]　*Jenkins v. Commissioner*, 47 T.C.M. 238 (1983).

the corporation failed.⁵⁴ Rather than letting his friends lose their investments, Twitty repaid them out of his personal assets, claiming a business expense deduction for the payments. As with Welch, Twitty made the payments despite the absence of any legal obligation. Citing *Welch*, the IRS argued that it was "very nice" of Twitty to reimburse the investors, but that he did so for purely personal reasons. The Tax Court ruled for Twitty on the grounds that a failure to reimburse the investors could have hurt his reputation with his fans—and thus his ability to sell records and concert tickets. The IRS apparently did not press a second argument for denying Twitty a deduction—that his payments, even if business-motivated, were capital rather than current outlays, because they were aimed at protecting his long-term income-producing capacity rather than his current-year record and ticket sales. If the IRS had made that argument, Twitty might have succeeded in distinguishing *Welch* on the grounds that Twitty was merely maintaining or repairing (6.03(a)) his slightly-damaged reputation as a country musician of integrity, whereas Welch was rebuilding from scratch his more-or-less demolished business reputation.

A loose end. Business expenses have sometimes been disallowed under a so-called "public policy" exception where deductibility of the expenses would frustrate a well-defined state or national policy. Thus, fines paid by a trucking company for deliberately overloading its trucks were disallowed by the Supreme Court in *Tank Truck Rentals, Inc. v. Commissioner*.⁵⁵ The Court reasoned that the state law would be frustrated if the fines were allowed as business expense, because the deduction would take the sting out of the penalty. Congress codified the result in *Tank Truck* in 1969 by enacting § 162(f), which in its current form denies a deduction "for any amount paid or incurred (whether by suit, agreement, or otherwise) to, or at the direction of, a government or governmental entity in relation to the violation of any law."

Illegal or "improper" payments are also occasionally held to be non-deductible under the public policy exception (or on the ground that they aren't "necessary"), although the Supreme Court has permitted deduction for wages and rents paid by an illegal bookmaking business.⁵⁶ The state law defined the wage and rental

---

⁵⁴ The chain's signature entree was the "Twitty Burger," consisting of a bun, ground sirloin, a pineapple ring, graham cracker crumbs, shortening, two slices of bacon, and mayonnaise. Perhaps the coronary arteries of the chain's clientele could not handle long-term exposure to the Twitty Burger.

⁵⁵ 356 U.S. 30 (1958).

⁵⁶ *Commissioner v. Sullivan*, 356 U.S. 27 (1958).

payments themselves as illegal, but the Court apparently thought it more important to avoid imposing tax on the gross receipts of the business. Code § 162(c), also enacted in 1969, now specifically denies deduction for certain illegal bribes and kickbacks (and even for *legal* bribes and kickbacks under Medicare and Medicaid). The section does not stop at the water's edge, because it disallows payments made to foreign government officials which "would be unlawful under the laws of the United States if such laws were applicable to such payment and to such official." Other public policy-based disallowance provisions include: § 162(e), which prohibits deductions for several types of lobbying and political expenditures; § 162(q) (a 2017 innovation), which denies a deduction for "any settlement or payment related to sexual harassment or sexual abuse if such settlement or payment is subject to a nondisclosure agreement"; and § 280E, which denies all deductions for expenses relating to "trafficking in controlled substances."

Notice something unusual about these public policy-based deduction-denial provisions. When the rules defining taxable income deviate from true economic income, the deviation is ordinarily in a downward direction—that is, exclusions of various economic benefits from gross income and deductions for various personal expenditures result in an income tax base considerably smaller than economic income. The usual pattern is reversed, however, in the case of public policy-based disallowances of deductions for what are—from an economic perspective—genuine business expenses. For example, a taxpayer denied a deduction for "ordinary and necessary" fines incurred in the course of its business operations will thereby be taxed on more than its actual net income.

6.05 Reasonable Compensation

Section 162(a)(1) provides that the taxpayer's business expenses shall include a "reasonable allowance" for salaries and other compensation. Since payments to employees for services rendered would plainly qualify as business expenses without specific mention, it is generally assumed that the quoted phrase is intended as a limitation on the amount allowable; in effect, no deduction is permitted for salaries which *exceed* a "reasonable" amount. Even so, the purpose of the subsection is not intuitively obvious. Why isn't every salary reasonable by definition? Apart from possible imprudence (for which it oughtn't to be penalized anyway), why would an employer ever pay more to obtain its employees' services than market conditions "reasonably" require?

The answer can be seen in two contexts. In both, the issue of reasonable compensation arises only because payor and payee are related parties—either as corporation and shareholder or as members of the same family—so that the "overpayment" actually entails no economic loss to the employer. With infrequent exceptions—the *Patton* case, discussed below, is one—the reasonable-salary rule has been used by the Service not as general authority to impose wage ceilings, but as a means of preventing income-shifting between related taxpayers whose economic interests are essentially identical.

As explained (5.02), under the present tax system corporate income is exposed to an extra measure of taxation. Corporate earnings are taxed first to the corporation itself at the rate set forth in § 11 (at the moment, a flat rate of 21%). When, or if, the corporation distributes the amount that is left to its shareholders as a dividend, the shareholders are required to include the dividend in gross income and, in effect, are taxed again. To be sure, the corporation is not *compelled* to distribute its after-tax earnings. It may elect to retain such earnings for use in its business, and in that event only the corporate-level tax is applicable. If it does make a dividend distribution, however, or is found to have done so, then a tax is imposed at both the corporate and the shareholder levels.

Since 2003, dividends have generally been taxed at the rates applicable to long-term capital gains (currently 15% or 20% for most dividend-receiving taxpayers). The effect is to make the problem about to be described less urgent than formerly, though it is not without some significance even now.

Apart from any "reasonableness" limitation, salary payments made by a corporation to its employees are of course deductible, and that is true even if the employee is also the corporation's major or even its only shareholder. That said, the somewhat volatile role of "salary"—particularly in the case of closely-held corporations—can easily be surmised. Suppose Smith is the sole shareholder and also the chief executive of X Corporation, which pays tax at a rate of 21%. Let's focus on a particular $100,000 chunk of X's income. After paying tax of $21,000, X distributes $79,000 to Smith as a dividend. The dividend tax—20% of $79,000—is $15,800. The corporate and dividend tax together total $36,800, which reflects a combined tax rate of 36.8%.[57] The net to Smith ($100,000 − $36,800) is $63,200. Suppose Smith would then make a gift of the $63,200, to support her ne'er-do-well and otherwise impecunious adult child. By contrast, what happens if Smith puts her child on the corporate payroll, and has the corporation pay the child a "salary" of $100,000 for doing very

---

[57]   If the corporate tax rate is 21% and the dividend tax rate is 20%, why is the combined tax burden only 36.8%, rather than 41% (*i.e.*, 21% plus 20%)? The answer, of course, is that the second tax—the 20% tax on the dividend—is imposed not on the entire $100,000, but only on the $79,000 remaining after the imposition of the first tax.

little or nothing of value. If the salary characterization succeeds for tax purposes, X will pay no tax on the $100,000 (after taking the salary deduction into account), and the child's income tax on the "salary" could be as low (in 2018) as $8,739 (if the child is married, and neither the child nor the child's spouse has any other income). The total tax is about $28,000 less under the second approach— again, if it works—than under the first. The beauty of it all, of course, is that the choice between "salary" and "dividend" lies entirely with Smith—the corporation is obviously her creature and does her bidding. From a purely business standpoint, moreover, it makes no difference whether corporate assets are conveyed as salary or as a dividend except, of course, as the choice of labels may succeed in minimizing taxes.

It is at this point that the Commissioner is likely to assert that the purported $100,000 salary exceeds a "reasonable" wage for the services of Smith's child, and must be disallowed as excessive under § 162(a)(1). This disallowance would not, of course, mean that the $100,000 receipt was any the less a distribution as far as Smith is concerned. In effect, the bonus would be recharacterized as a *dividend* to Smith (includable as income by Smith in her capacity as shareholder, but not deductible by X Corporation), followed by a gift from Smith to her child. It must be conceded, however, that as a result of the lowering of the corporate tax rate to 21% (in 2017) and the taxation of dividends at the favorable rates applicable to long-term capital gains (introduced in 2003), there is less to be gained now than ever before from attempts to convert nondeductible dividends to deductible salaries. In fact, if the purported salary were paid to Smith herself (rather than to her child), and if Smith were in the 37% top bracket, the burden of the single tax of 37% would actually be slightly *higher* than the combined 36.8% burden of the corporate tax and the shareholder dividend tax.

The test for what is a "reasonable allowance for salaries" has always been somewhat shaky and intuitive, with the courts struggling to isolate relevant "factors" such as evidence of salary levels in similar firms, the scarcity of qualified employees, the special demands of the employer's business, and so on. More recently, the appellate courts have moved to a more sophisticated (sounding) test which attempts to compare the taxpayer's challenged salary with the net return to the company's shareholders after that salary has been paid. Was the salary justified from the standpoint of the shareholders as independent investors? If so, the deduction would be allowed even though high by conventional standards.

In the *Exacto Spring* case,[58] for example, the taxpayer-corporation paid Heitz, its chief executive (founder, research director, marketer, salesman and almost everything else), a salary of $1 million. Heitz owned 55% of the taxpayer's stock, 45% being owned by outside investors. The Commissioner insisted that $400,000 was a "reasonable" salary and sought to add $600,000 back to the company's taxable income. Holding in part for the Commissioner and in part for the taxpayer, the Tax Court in effect split the difference by finding that a salary of $700,000 (but not $1 million) was "reasonable" and therefore added $300,000 back to the company's taxable income. On appeal, the Seventh Circuit reversed and directed judgment for the taxpayer. The Tax Court's approach, which consisted of weighing and juggling a half-dozen elusive and ill-defined "factors", was analytically inadequate, said the Court. Instead, the single appropriate test under § 162(a)(1) was what Judge Posner called an "indirect market test," *viz.*, whether "Heitz's compensation was consistent with Exacto's investors earning a reasonable return" on their capital investment. Based on expert testimony, and given the risks of the business, an independent investor in Exacto Spring would reasonably expect a 13% return. He would of course be "overjoyed" if he did still better. For the year in question, as it turned out, investors in Exacto achieved a return of more than 20% even after deducting Heitz' million-dollar salary from net operating income. It followed that the salary itself was well within "reasonable" limits and should have been allowed in full.[59]

Smith's effort to convert dividends into compensation—and the Commissioner's response—has a good deal in common with the shareholder-loan device described at 3.01. There the shareholder's aim was to withdraw funds from the corporation for her personal use, but at the same time to avoid the *individual*-level tax by characterizing the withdrawal as a borrowing. Since borrowed funds are not included in the borrower's income, a "loan" of $100,000, though not deductible by the corporate lender, results in no additional tax at the individual level. Here, by contrast, the effort is to avoid the *corporate*-level tax by withdrawing funds in the form of "salary." In both situations, the Treasury's aim is to defend the two-level tax system by insisting that the withdrawal, objectively viewed, is neither a loan nor a salary payment but a dividend.

Section 162(a)(1) has occasionally (though infrequently) been applied to disallow salary payments to *unrelated* individuals on the ground that the amount paid was simply too large to be regarded as

---

[58] *Exacto Spring Corp. v. Commissioner*, 196 F.3d 833 (7th Cir. 1999).

[59] The Court also thought it useful, in passing, to suggest (1) that federal judges are underpaid, at least when compared to Mr. Heitz, and (2) that double taxation of corporate income is a lousy idea.

"reasonable." In *Patton v. Commissioner,*[60] for example, the taxpayers, father and son, operated a small machine shop in the form of a partnership. For a number of years they employed a bookkeeper—one Kirk, the possessor of a grammar school education and two years of commercial training in high school—at an annual salary of less than $2,000. In 1941 General Motors began sending the partnership very sizeable quantities of work; and immediately thereafter the taxpayers contracted with Kirk to pay him an annual salary equal to 10% of the partnership's net sales. Under this agreement Kirk received, and the partnership deducted, $46,000 (around $670,000 in 2018 dollars) for the year 1943. The Commissioner determined that $13,000 represented reasonable compensation for Kirk's services as bookkeeper and disallowed the balance as excessive. Kirk was not related to the Pattons, and it was not suggested that the payment had been intended as a gift.

A majority of the Court of Appeals sustained the Commissioner's action on the ground that persons of similar training doing similar work for other firms were paid far less than $46,000 a year. Kirk's responsibilities obviously did not justify a salary of that size, and the mere fact that the parties themselves may have regarded the arrangement as reasonable was not binding on the government. In effect, the Commissioner was free to apply his own salary standard, presumably on the basis of objective market data. A dissent argued that the contract between Kirk and the partnership was "bona fide" even if improvident from the company's standpoint. Although the salary turned out to be "too high," that was "no business or concern of the Government." The decisive question was whether the parties had intended the payment as salary, and since no contrary showing was made, the amount paid should have been allowed in full.

The dissenting opinion is, of course, perfectly correct as a matter of tax policy. No reason whatever can be advanced for disallowing salary payments to employees, provided they really are salary payments and not dividends or gifts in disguise. Further, the disallowance in *Patton* can be objected to on the ground that it actually led to a double tax on the company's earnings, though without the customary justification of a corporate-shareholder relationship. Thus the salary disallowance increased the partnership's net income and hence the taxable income of the two partners. At the same time Kirk himself remained taxable on the full amount received. The Commissioner did not assert that the $46,000 was anything *other* than salary—the disallowance was based solely on reasonableness of amount—and Kirk had no apparent obligation to repay the alleged excess to the partnership. Accordingly, the

---

[60]   168 F.2d 28 (6th Cir. 1948).

disallowed portion—some $33,000—was taxed both to the payors *and* to the payee at the high wartime rates which then prevailed, a result that can only be characterized as punitive.[61]

Could there be more to the *Patton* saga than meets the eye? It is striking that the Patton Company entered into the contingent pay arrangement with Kirk *after* it had been assured of the GM business, and at a time when a very large increase in company income could easily be foreseen. But why would the partners ever have done *that?* The reported record of the trial in the Tax Court shows that Kirk received his salary in cash but that he neither deposited it in a bank account nor used it to purchase investments or other property. Queried as to where the money had actually gone, Kirk testified that he had simply "kept it at home,"[62] presumably in a cookie jar. While the latter assertion was never disproved, one senses that the government may have suspected, or perhaps even have been convinced, that the cash in question (net of Kirk's personal tax) had ultimately found its way back into the hands of the Pattons themselves. The excess compensation claim may thus have been a way of taxing the company profits to the persons whom the government regarded as the real payees.

As will be seen below, there is another side to the reasonable compensation problem. If the payment of excessive compensation presents dangers from the standpoint of the Treasury, especially as between related parties, what about arrangements involving the contrary pattern? In our initial illustration, suppose that Smith elects to take *no* salary from the corporation in a given year. She has substantial income from other sources and her own marginal tax rate (say, the top individual rate of 37%) is higher than the corporation's 21% rate, so that overall taxes can be minimized if the customary salary payment is simply omitted. In effect, there is income-shifting in the opposite direction, *i.e.*, from an individual to her controlled corporation. Although § 162(a)(1) could be read to *require* the payment of a reasonable salary, the fact is that it has not been so construed. On the whole, income-shifting between shareholders and corporation by means of *under*-compensation for services is tolerated by the tax law. The explanation (to the extent there is one) for what thus appears to be an asymmetrical application of the reasonable salary standard is given at 9.03, along with a description of the special and contrasting rules that govern family partnerships.

---

[61] As noted, the Commissioner has rarely used the reasonableness limitation as authority to review arm's-length salary arrangements, and indeed the Regulations confirm that contingent payment contracts made "pursuant to a free bargain" will generally not be challenged even though the amounts paid thereunder turn out to be unusually large. Reg. § 1.162–7(a)(2).

[62] 6 T.C.M. 482, 486 (1947).

* * *

A loose end. Reacting to a steady stream of adverse publicity about the astronomic salaries paid to American corporate executives (especially as compared with the relatively modest compensation levels of their German and Japanese counterparts), Congress in 1993 added § 162(m), which denies deduction for salaries in excess of $1 million where the employer-payor is a publicly-held corporation and the payee is the corporation's CEO, CFO, or one of the corporation's three highest paid executives (other than the CEO and CFO). Before a 2017 statutory amendment, an exception was made, and deduction was allowed, if the excess salary was based "on the attainment of one or more performance goals," such as an increase in the corporation's earnings or share price. In practice, the pre-2017 version of § 162(m) resulted in neither disallowance of deductions for significant amounts of executive compensation nor reduced levels of executive compensation. Instead, corporations simply made sure that all compensation paid to top executives in excess of $1 million was incentive-based (and thus eligible for the exception for compensation tied to "performance goals").[63] The 2017 amendment repealed the exception for performance-based compensation, thus for the first time giving § 162(m) some real bite.

Since deductions for executive salaries in excess of $1 million (whether fixed or performance-based) are now disallowed, such excess payments (if made at all) will have to be made out of the payor's after-tax income. The effect from the corporation's standpoint would then be equivalent to the distribution of a dividend. Dividends, though taxable to the recipient, are not deductible by the distributing corporation. In a closely-held setting, as noted above, the "reasonable salary" limitation of § 162(a)(1) is intended to achieve the same effect: salary payments found to be unreasonable in amount remain taxable to the payee, but deduction is denied to the payor-corporation and the purported salary is added back to corporate taxable income. There is of course a major difference between the closely-held and the publicly-held situation. In a closely-held case, the excess salary recipient is invariably the corporation's principal shareholder. As such, she is obviously indifferent (apart from taxes) to whether the cash she receives is paid to her as a deductible salary payment or as a nondeductible dividend—she gets it all in any event. What she does care about, and all she cares about, is how the legal characterization—salary or dividend—affects the tax bills of the corporation and of herself. By contrast, the executive of a publicly-held corporation is a "mere" employee (certainly not a controlling

---

[63]   Schizer, Executive Compensation and Hedging: The Fragile Legal Foundation of Incentive Compatibility, 100 Colum. L. Rev. 440 (2000).

shareholder) and would therefore get no benefit if the excess salary amount were simply added to the corporation's annual dividend and distributed to shareholders generally. Put otherwise, the executives and the shareholders of a publicly-held corporation are two different sets of people—executives don't get dividends and shareholders don't get salaries—so that the customary rationale for disallowance is lacking.

Many, of course, have argued that the formal structure of the modern public corporation hides a deeper reality. Although its shareholders have legal power over corporate management, the publicly-held corporation is said by some to be an entity that is essentially within the domination and control of self-perpetuating managers—managers who are practically, if not legally, independent of the company's shareholders and therefore free to put their personal income goals ahead of the interests of the ostensible owners. In effect, the salaries received by inside managers (not just annual pay, but also bonuses, stock options and pensions) are said to include a kind of "rent" or status-income that reflects the entrenched power of incumbent office-holders who cannot easily be dislodged. If one accepts this analysis (some do, some don't), then, as a matter of tax policy it can be argued that inside managers hold a kind of super-equity and that excess salary payments (defined as payments over $1 million) may be characterized as quasi-dividends. It would follow, again as a matter of tax policy, that such payments ought not to reduce the corporate tax base any more than conventional dividends do, and that disallowance is for that reason justified.[64]

6.06 Interest

Speaking generally, § 163(a) allows a deduction for interest paid or accrued during the taxable year. Thus, interest expense incurred by a corporation, say, on funds borrowed to finance current operating expenses (a short-term bank loan, typically) or to build a manufacturing facility (perhaps a long-term loan from an insurance company or even a public bond issue) generally qualifies for deduction on the same basis as any other recurring outlay. The same is true (special limitations aside) for an individual investor who pays interest to her broker on funds borrowed to buy securities on margin or to a bank on a real estate mortgage loan. In either case, the borrower hopes and expects to generate gross income by putting the borrowed funds to work in its (or her) business or investment activities. Interest paid to the lender obviously subtracts from the borrower's profits—may even reduce such profits to a negative

---

[64] Zelinsky, *The Tax Policy Case for Denying Deductibility to Excessive Executive Compensation,* 58 Tax Notes 1123 (1993).

figure—so that deductibility fully accords with the goal of the system, which is to impose a tax on net income.

To be sure, there can be problems even in this context. Although § 163(a) states that interest is deductible when "paid," *prepaid* interest—interest paid in advance—presumably has to be capitalized. Similarly, under § 263A, interest incurred by a builder on a short-term construction loan—even though payable currently— must be added to the cost of the completed structure and recovered over the structure's entire useful life. This, however, merely shows that interest, like any other business outlay, is subject to the capital expenditure limitation described at 6.03, of which the object is to match gross income from a particular source with its associated costs.

In certain situations, nevertheless, the Code disallows the interest deduction by specific provision. The courts, on occasion, have done the same even without specific statutory authority. The reason for such disallowance is both general and important, and needs to be understood as background for the major legislative changes made by the 1986 Act (described at 13.02), and by the 2017 Act (described below). The discussion that follows attempts to clarify this moderately complex feature.

Though by no means unrelated to the material in this section, the subject of *personal* interest—interest on home loans, auto loans, credit cards, etc.—is taken up separately at 7.04.

(a)   *"Tax Arbitrage" and Special Disallowances*

Despite its apparent similarity to other kinds of expenditures, interest—the cost of "hiring" capital funds for business, investment or personal use—turns out to be one of the most volatile elements in the entire Code structure, an observation that is attested to by the sheer number of Code provisions addressed to the question of when or in what amount interest must be included in income, excluded, deducted, capitalized, disallowed, and so on. Some of these topics are discussed elsewhere in this volume—bond discount, a species of "hidden" interest, is considered at 17.04, for example—but it may be useful here to emphasize one particular problem that makes the interest deduction an especially sensitive Code topic. Actually, it is not so much the deduction itself that causes the problem alluded to as it is the presence in our law of so many categories of exempt or partially exempt income which may be *combined* with deductible interest in the hands of a single taxpayer. This, in turn, creates a dangerous and unstable condition for which the Code—at its own peril, so to speak—simply must provide a remedy.

The point can be made very easily by asking how high-income taxpayers would behave if the Code *lacked* present § 265(a)(2), which disallows the deduction of interest on indebtedness incurred to purchase municipal bonds paying interest qualifying for tax exemption under § 103. Absent § 265(a)(2), a 35%-bracket taxpayer would be well-advised to borrow money in order to buy tax-exempt municipals even if the interest she had to pay on her loan was greater than the interest she expected to receive on her bond investment. Thus, suppose the taxpayer buys $1,000,000 of municipal bonds yielding 8%, or $80,000 a year, tax-free. To finance the investment she borrows $1,000,000 from a lender (pledging the bonds) at an interest cost of 10%, or $100,000 a year. Is she crazy? Not if the loan interest is deductible. Apart from taxes, the investment results in a loss of $20,000 a year; but when we observe that the $80,000 inflow is tax-exempt while the $100,000 outflow is deductible (§ 265(a)(2) aside), the result is a *positive* annual return of $15,000, *i.e.*, the $35,000 tax saving (35% of $100,000) less the net interest cost of $20,000. This, moreover, although the taxpayer hasn't put a penny of her own money into the deal. And why stop at $1,000,000?

All of this looks pretty much like tax-avoidance—sophisticated tax-avoidance, if you like—which, if unimpeded, could have serious consequences for the income tax. Especially during recent periods when tax rates were higher and the rate structure was more sharply progressive, but even under the rate structure we have today, one would expect upper-income taxpayers to resort very freely to arrangements of the sort described. The taxpayer's *taxable* income would be reduced to a minimum thereby, though her *after-tax* income would actually be increased. Nothing, perhaps, could have so damaging an impact on the morale of *other* taxpayers (once they came to understand what was happening) than the realization that higher-bracket people had been provided with an easy means of subverting the system.

As indicated, Code § 265(a)(2), which goes back many years, largely blocks our illustrative device by denying deduction of interest on funds borrowed to "purchase or carry" municipal bonds, although the government's practical difficulties in proving a "purchase or carry" nexus between borrowings and bonds may limit the effectiveness of the disallowance in some cases. Even if § 265(a)(2) is wholly effective, however, the important fact remains that municipal bonds are not the only source of exempt or partially exempt income. Others, equally prominent, have already been mentioned. Insurance (see 2.03) is one; although interest on ordinary savings accounts is taxable whether or not withdrawn by the depositor, the "inside" interest build-up under a life-insurance policy or annuity contract is generally exempt. Depreciation on plant and equipment is another; while business income is of course generally taxable, the effect of rapid depreciation allowances—ACRS (6.10)—is to create a partial exemption through the medium of income-deferral. A third example, here based on the common-law realization requirement, is investment in appreciating securities (5.01). An increase in the value of a stock investment is taxed to the investor only if she happens to sell the stock during the taxable year; no tax is imposed if she doesn't sell, even though the year's unrealized appreciation plainly represents an "accession to wealth" in economic terms. Finally, as observed (1.03), the purchase of household durables—homes, cars, washing machines—generates imputed income equal to the annual rental value of the property, though of course no effort is made to include such amounts under § 61.

In each of these (and other) situations, the asset yielding exempt income can be, and often is, purchased by borrowing the purchase price. In each, therefore, the opportunity exists for achieving a "tax arbitrage" effect—taking in exempt income with one hand and paying out deductible interest with the other—of the sort illustrated by the municipal bond example. As already emphasized, the consequences, from the standpoint of both revenues and taxpayer morale, may be serious. Hence, the question of how to cope and what to do becomes a critical issue in tax policy.[65] Two obvious legislative alternatives arise. The simplest (simplest to conceive of, that is) would be to eliminate the income exemptions that represent the first leg of the arbitrage device. If municipal bond interest, insurance policy build-up, unrealized stock appreciation and imputed income were made taxable, and if rapid depreciation were converted into economic depreciation, all by Code amendment, the risk of structural damage in these areas would disappear. No objection could be raised against an investment program or a course of dealing that combined *taxable* income with deductible interest, the latter then simply being an appropriately recognized cost of earning the former. But if such legislative action is unfeasible, whether for practical or political reasons, the danger of tax avoidance has presumably got to be met by dealing with the other leg of the device—that is, by denying or restricting the deductibility of interest on amounts borrowed to finance the purchase of the exempt-source asset. What is needed, in the end, is tax-symmetry: if income is exempt, then the related financing cost should be non-deductible; equating the deduction side with the income side—treating *both* as "non-existent" for tax purposes—effectively removes the arbitrage effect referred to above, at least as far as loan-financed investors are concerned.

Congress has slowly—very slowly—reacted to the exemption-deduction problem just described by imposing restrictions in specific

---

[65] See Warren, *Accelerated Capital Recovery, Debt, and Tax Arbitrage*, 38 The Tax Lawyer 549 (1985). And see Shakow, *Confronting the Problem of Tax Arbitrage*, 43 Tax L.Rev. (1987).

areas of known abuse. Code § 265(a)(2), mentioned above, is one such. Another, as will be seen in the subsection immediately following, is § 264(a)(2)—added to the Code in 1954—which disallows interest on debt incurred to purchase a single-premium insurance or annuity contract. Still another (a 1969 enactment) can be found in § 163(d), which limits the deduction of "investment interest" in any taxable year to an amount not in excess of the taxpayer's investment income (*e.g.*, dividends and interest), with disallowed amounts being carried forward to subsequent periods. The aim of the latter provision, obviously, is to prevent taxpayers from combining a *present* interest deduction with *deferred* property appreciation by borrowing to purchase growth stocks or other investments that produce little current income and may ultimately generate capital gains taxable at a lower rate.

In the 1986 Act, Congress further undertook to limit tax arbitrage by restricting the deductibility of interest and other expenses attributable to real estate tax shelters. The 1986 provisions—chiefly § 469—are important, even vital, to the integrity of the income tax, but they do add detail and complexity to a statute already famous for those attributes. Such complexity could have been avoided, perhaps, if the first leg of the arbitrage device—exempt-source income, here in the form of over-rapid depreciation—had been the focus of reform, but that is a lot to ask of a legislative process exposed to pressure from many quarters. As might be expected, therefore, it is the second element—the deduction leg—on which the 1986 changes concentrate. These changes and related matters are taken up in some detail at 13.01 and 13.02. Our hope here is that the comments made above will have helped to set the stage for later discussion.

Until 2017, business interest—*i.e.*, interest paid on money borrowed for use in an active business—was not subject to any large-scale limitations on its deductibility. That has now changed, however, with the enactment of § 163(j). The new provision generally limits the deduction for business interest to 30% of the taxpayer's "adjusted taxable income" (defined, for 2018 through 2022, as taxable income computed without regard to business interest expense, depreciation and amortization—*i.e.*, what is known in corporate finance circles as EBITDA).[66] Among the several statutory exceptions to § 163(j), the most significant is that it does not apply to any taxpayer with average annual gross receipts of $25 million or less.

---

[66]   For 2023 and later years, "adjusted taxable income" is to be computed taking depreciation and amortization into account; this will greatly reduce adjusted taxable income for many taxpayers, thus reducing the 30% ceiling and increasing the impact of § 163(j).

Although the legislative history does not indicate the rationale for the new limitation, Congress likely enacted it out of concern about the tax arbitrage opportunities that would result from the combination of the unlimited deductibility of business interest expense and the immediate deduction of the entire cost of most tangible personal property under the 2017 Act's version of § 168(k) (described at 6.10(a)). Immediate expensing under § 168(k) is roughly equivalent to tax exemption for the income produced by the expensed asset (as explained at 6.10(a)), so an unlimited business interest deduction combined with full expensing under § 168(k) would have been a recipe for tax arbitrage on a dramatic scale. However, the operation of the new ceiling on deductible business interest does not depend on the extent to which a particular taxpayer has taken advantage of § 168(k) (and other expensing provisions with similar effects), so the 30% ceiling will be overly restrictive for some taxpayers and insufficiently restrictive for others.

(b) Sham Transactions

The seductive appeal of tax arbitrage has led, on occasion, to the framing of transactions that have virtually no economic substance but apparently fall within the literal terms of § 163(a). On the whole, though not invariably, the courts have been able to block the sought-for arbitrage effect by resorting to "general legal principles." The Supreme Court's decision in *Knetsch v. U.S.*[67]—a case which arose in a year prior to, but which was decided after, the enactment of § 264(a)(2)—is an example.

Simplifying somewhat, in *Knetsch* the taxpayer bought a 2½% annuity contract from an insurance company for $4,004,000, of which only $4,000 was paid in cash while $4,000,000 was "borrowed" from the company on a 3½% non-recourse note. Of course, borrowing at 3½% in order to invest at 2½% is a recipe for a guaranteed annual pre-tax loss equal to 1% of the amount borrowed and invested. A wise man once defined tax shelters as "deals done by very smart people that, absent tax considerations, would be very stupid."[68] So Knetsch's transaction must have been a tax shelter. What hoped-for alchemy was to turn Knetsch's pre-tax loss into an after-tax profit? Read on.

Under the terms of the contract, the annuity would return $90,000 a month (*if* all indebtedness was paid up) commencing when Knetsch reached the age of 90. The interest due on the $4,000,000 note—$140,000—was paid by Knetsch in advance. Under the "Table of Cash and Loan Values" which was attached to the annuity

---

[67] 364 U.S. 361 (1960). See Blum, *Knetsch v. United States: A Pronouncement on Tax Avoidance,* 1961 Sup. Ct. Rev. 135.

[68] Graetz, *100 Million Unnecessary Returns: A Fresh Start for the U.S. Tax System,* 112 Yale L.J. 261, 278 (2002).

contract, the cash value of the annuity would increase to $4,100,000 at the end of the first year, with a similar increase in each succeeding year. Knetsch was permitted to "borrow" this increase of $100,000 as well—again on a non-recourse note—to meet the interest charge on the $4,000,000 premium loan, so that his actual out-of-pocket interest payment was only about $40,000. Knetsch also prepaid $3,500 of interest on the second note.

As a result of all this paperwork, Knetsch actually parted with some $47,500 in cash. Total "interest payments," however, if recognized as such, were $143,500. Assuming Knetsch was in the 50% bracket (his actual marginal tax rate—the year was 1953—was nearly 80%), the interest deduction, if allowed, would have resulted in a tax saving of $71,750 (.50 × $143,500). The net benefit to Knetsch for a single year (he repeated this procedure the following year) would have been the difference between the tax saved ($71,750) and the cash laid out ($47,500), or $24,250, which was not a bad day's work. As noted, the annual interest build-up in the cash value of an annuity is not currently taxable, and Knetsch (or his advisor) apparently expected that such build-up would be treated as a low-taxed capital gain when the annuity finally matured.

Finding that the transaction lacked a business purpose, the Supreme Court disallowed the interest deduction in full. Since the interest payable on the notes—3½%—exceeded that receivable under the annuity—2½%—the arrangement was plainly pointless apart from the expected tax saving. The taxpayer took no real risk because his debt was in the form of a non-recourse note which could not be enforced against his personal assets. And the insurance company took only the very remote risk that interest rates might someday fall below 2½%, thereby making it profitable for Knetsch to repay the amounts that he had "borrowed." The statute, said the Court in effect, was not set up to cover make-believe transactions. It was evident that no one would have done the deal that Knetsch did other than for tax reasons; hence § 163 did not apply. The Court was disturbed neither by the fact that § 264(a)(2) was inapplicable to the year in question, nor by any negative implication arising from its subsequent enactment.

Although it succeeded as a defense against tax avoidance in *Knetsch*, the doctrine of "business purpose" (or "economic substance" or "non-tax motive") is in some respects a frail and uncertain instrument. As suggested, the annuity deal in *Knetsch* could conceivably—*conceivably*—have produced an economic advantage for the annuitant. Entitled to a 2½% return on his "investment," Knetsch would actually make money at the insurance company's expense if market interest rates ever fell below 2½%, in which event Knetsch could borrow the annual premium at a lower interest cost than the rate of return promised to him by the company. No one, of course, expected that such a thing would ever happen. But it could. However remote, there was a *possibility* that Knetsch might profit from the deal, and presumably it is not the business of the Commissioner to question the taxpayer's investment judgment as long as the contractual relationship that has been established by the parties is "real" under local law. The Commissioner is then left to argue that a transaction should be disregarded for tax purposes (even though it *could* be profitable and does have legal status) if the taxpayer's principal purpose is tax-avoidance. The difficulty with that position is that there are, after all, a great many transactions that are undertaken solely with a view to minimizing taxes—buying tax-free municipal bonds instead of higher-yielding corporate securities, selling stock at the close of one year rather than the start of another in order to accelerate the recognition of a loss, and so on. These actions might not be taken without the expectation of a tax benefit, and yet no one would argue that they should be disregarded solely for that reason. Nor does it suffice to say, for example, that the exemption of municipal bond interest is specifically authorized by the Code. So is the deduction of interest on indebtedness; yet the Court in *Knetsch* held that the absence of an independent business purpose was disqualifying under § 163. Just *why* business purpose is a condition that taxpayers must satisfy in some instances but not in others is a question that the Court majority made no attempt to answer.

If the Supreme Court had ruled in Knetsch's favor, Congress could still have shut down *Knetsch*-type tax shelters, prospectively, through the enactment of targeted legislation. In fact, Congress did exactly that by enacting previously-mentioned § 264(a)(2)—after the facts of *Knetsch* had occurred but before the Supreme Court's consideration of the case. Two other provisions enacted in the years following *Knetsch* would also be sufficient to defeat *Knetsch*-type shelters today. Section 163(d) denies a deduction for investment interest expense in excess of investment income, and § 72(e)(4)(A) treats borrowing against appreciation in an annuity policy as a taxable event. Given the demonstrated ability of Congress to legislate against particular shelter types, what purpose is served by the sort of *judicial* tax shelter policing employed by the Supreme Court in *Knetsch*? The answer (which may be obvious to some readers) is that attacking tax shelters only with prospective legislation would always leave the government one step behind taxpayers and their tax shelter advisers. When Congress finally got around to shutting down a shelter of one type, taxpayers would simply move on to a new variety of tax shelter, which would produce the desired results until Congress legislated against it, at which point taxpayers would move on again, and so on. As long as Congress is unwilling or unable to enact targeted anti-shelter legislation with retroactive effect, only judicial invalidation of shelters—using the business-purpose doctrine featured in *Knetsch* or one of several kindred anti-abuse doctrines—can solve the government's always-one-step-behind problem.

The clash between tax-avoidance and business purpose has bedeviled the income tax throughout its history, and the *Knetsch* decision was by no means the last word on the subject. Indeed, the loan-back annuity transaction in *Knetsch* is primitive compared to some of the complex avoidance transactions that confront the Commissioner today. Recent developments in this area—including the 2010 codification of the so-called economic substance doctrine in § 7701(o)—are described in some detail in *Note: Tax Shelters and Economic Substance* at p. 495, below.

———————

A loose end. Returning to the vexed subject of "tax arbitrage" (and risking a tiny bit of complexity), we might point out that § 265(a)(2) makes a distinction, in effect, between personal service income and income from investment.

As stated, § 265(a)(2) bars the taxpayer from deducting interest on amounts borrowed to purchase tax-exempt municipal bonds. The aim is to prevent taxpayers from combining exempt income with deductible interest expense to shelter income from other taxable sources. But, of course, Congress did not intend to eliminate the municipal bond exemption; its intent was merely to deny an interest deduction to borrowers. Investors who draw on their *own* resources to purchase municipal bonds are obviously unaffected. Thus, suppose a 35%-bracket taxpayer owns a $100,000 *taxable* corporate bond yielding 10% or $10,000 a year. Everything else being equal, he can sell his taxable bond and purchase an exempt municipal bond yielding 8% or only $8,000 a year. Assume the two bonds are otherwise alike in quality. Why would he give up 10% for 8%? Simple answer: to increase his after-tax return on investment. The taxable bond leaves him with $6,500 after tax, the municipal with $8,000 after tax, so it is plainly in the taxpayer's interest to make the switch. The concept of "implicit taxes" may be helpful here. Because of market forces, a taxpayer purchasing an asset producing tax-favored income will generally have to accept a lower pre-tax rate of return than on a comparable asset producing fully-taxable income. That reduced pre-tax rate of return is sometimes referred to as an implicit tax. In the above example, in which taxable bonds pay 10% and municipal bonds pay 8%, the implicit tax rate is 20%; in other words, the 8% tax-free interest rate is the equivalent of receiving a 10% pre-tax rate of interest and paying tax on that interest at 20%. As long as the implicit tax rate—20% in our example—is lower than the taxpayer's explicit marginal tax rate—35% in the same example— the taxpayer should prefer the tax-exempt investment to the taxable alternative.

And Congress intends that the high-bracket taxpayer with money of his own to invest should be attracted to municipal bonds. The purpose of the municipal bond exemption is to subsidize state and local borrowing costs by allowing states and cities to raise money from the public at a reduced rate of interest. The effect, however, is to give the self-financed investor the very same "arbitrage" benefit that § 265(a)(2) denies to those who, lacking such investable resources, would have to borrow to buy municipals and would then deduct the interest paid to the lender from their salaries and other personal service income. Like the would-be arbitrager in the main text, the self-financed investor trades a 6.5% for an 8% after-tax return with no increase in risk, but he achieves that result by "borrowing" from himself.

It follows that § 265(a)(2) chiefly operates to prevent the conversion of personal service income into exempt municipal bond interest, but of course does nothing to stop an investor from converting *taxable* investment income into *exempt* investment income by selling a taxable bond and buying a municipal. In practical terms, this means that the municipal bond exemption under § 103 is available only to those who can self-finance.

Is this distinction tenable or should § 265(a)(2) be repealed? What would happen to the market for municipal bonds if it were repealed? Who would gain, who would lose? If interested, please see Note, *What is the True Value of a Tax Preference?* (p. 481), where these questions are examined further.

6.07 Losses

Section 165(a) authorizes a deduction for any loss "sustained" (*i.e.,* realized) during a taxable year which is not compensated for by insurance or otherwise. In the case of individual taxpayers (taxpayers other than corporations), § 165(c) limits the deduction to losses incurred in a trade or business or in connection with "any transaction entered into for profit," and to losses resulting from "casualty" or theft. Apart from casualty losses (discussed at 7.02 below), the aim of § 165(c) is to carry out the customary distinction between costs (here, losses) which relate to a taxpayer's business or investment activities and are therefore properly deductible in determining her taxable income for the year, and costs which are personal and hence properly disallowed. The distinction is essentially the same as that discussed at 6.01 in connection with business or personal expenses. Here, however, the problems of classification are somewhat easier to cope with. "Losses" typically result from dispositions of *property,* and as compared with ambiguous expense items (such as travel) the status of property is normally clear. A hundred shares of General Motors stock is plainly an investment asset; the family automobile is just as clearly personal. As shown below, interpretative problems of a recurring nature do exist—chiefly in connection with sales of personal residences—but it is fair to say that these are minor on the whole.

The disallowance of losses from sales of personal property deserves a brief explanatory comment. With the exception of casualty losses attributable to a federal disaster, the tax law treats any realized decline in the value of "household durables" as personal. If a taxpayer buys a car for $20,000, devotes it to family use for a year and then sells it to a used-car dealer for $18,000, the $2,000 "loss" is assumed to represent a personal consumption expenditure of the same character as food, clothing or recreation. A taxpayer who spent $2,000 leasing a car for personal use would be entitled to no deduction for that expense, and there is no reason why the taxpayer buying a car for $20,000 and selling it for $18,000 should be treated more favorably than the lessee. Once again, unless taxable income is to be reduced to zero, the taxpayer's expenditures for personal living must be disallowed. This is true whether the expenditure is for current items—food, recreation, or rental of personal-use property— or reflects the annual decline in the value of capital goods, such as a home or car. To be sure, the used-car market may have fluctuated (upward or downward) between the time of purchase and the time of resale, so that the $2,000 "loss" may actually be greater or smaller than the amount of depreciation originally anticipated. But while the tax law could (and perhaps should; see 15.02) take separate account of market changes by distinguishing between expected and actual depreciation, the plain fact is that it does not. Logically or otherwise, the law regards the decline in value as wholly attributable to personal use and allows no portion of the loss.

In the case of owner-occupied housing, in contrast with personal-use vehicles, taxpayers' actual motives are typically mixed. Of course a homeowner buys a house in order to live in it, but she probably also hopes and reasonably expects to make a profit on the eventual sale of the house. Is the profit motive sufficient to justify treating a loss on the sale of an owner-occupied home as deductible, in whole or in part? Rightly or wrongly, the income tax treats the homeowner no differently from the car owner. The home is considered a non-business asset in its entirety, and any loss on its sale is a nondeductible personal loss.

In *Gevirtz v. Commissioner,*[69] however, the taxpayer had evidence of profit-seeking beyond that of the ordinary homeowner. The taxpayer had purchased a tract of land for the purpose of constructing an apartment building, but then, finding that other apartment houses were going up in the same area, changed her mind and built a large personal residence which she herself occupied for a period of some five years. At the end of that period the taxpayer vacated the residence, and having made unsuccessful efforts to sell or rent it, finally surrendered the property to the mortgagees who had financed its acquisition. Contending that her original profit motive in buying the land had continued throughout her occupancy (the residence, she said, could have been broken up into separate apartments), the taxpayer sought to deduct her investment in the property as a loss. The Court of Appeals found that the taxpayer had abandoned her original commercial purpose when she built and occupied the residence, and sustained the Commissioner in treating the loss as personal. An individual's motives may sometimes be mixed, the court observed, but here it was apparent that profit-seeking had ceased to be the taxpayer's dominant interest once the residence was built, and that business goals were "only on the edge" of her mind thereafter.

Actually, of course, Judge Frank hadn't the faintest idea of what was on Mrs. Gevirtz' mind at any given moment. For all he knew she never thought of anything *but* profit during the years in question. Yet even if the "motive" evidence had been more favorable to the taxpayer, the court's decision in all likelihood would have been the same. Suppose, for example, that Mrs. Gevirtz had been able to demonstrate—by reference to correspondence with real estate brokers or even prospective tenants—that she had continued throughout the years in question to make active plans to exploit the property commercially. If such evidence were strong and believable, would the loss have been allowed? One suspects a negative answer; in effect, evidence of business purpose *never* could have been strong enough to overcome the factor of *personal occupancy* unless the latter had been extremely brief in duration. The decline in value for which a deductible loss was claimed occurred while the taxpayer was living in the residence. As a result, it simply had to be treated as a personal consumption cost. To allow a "loss" on the ground that the taxpayer's profit motive had continued to be central would be to invite all taxpayers to attempt to treat personal assets as investment property by claiming that their personal use was only incidental or subordinate. The burden on the Treasury of sorting out the true from the false in every case would then become considerable. It is obviously simpler, and presumably also consistent with Congressional intent,

---

[69]   123 F.2d 707 (2d Cir. 1941).

to view personal occupancy or personal use as *absolutely* inconsistent with the presence of a profit motive. Hence, even if Mrs. Gevirtz's original business purpose had remained active and visible throughout, the factor of personal occupancy would almost certainly have "convinced" the court that profit-seeking had become a secondary goal.

Weir v. Commissioner,[70] which can be contrasted with *Gevirtz,* may help to support the point just made. In *Weir* the taxpayer bought shares in a corporation which owned an apartment building in which he himself was a tenant. His aim in becoming a stockholder—as shown by the fact that he sold the stock when he decided to move from the building—was to have a voice in the building's management, presumably to help assure that the accommodations remained to his liking. The Court of Appeals held that the loss incurred on the stock sale was deductible under § 165(c)(2). Since dividends on the stock would constitute "profit," the statutory requirement was met despite the taxpayer's obvious personal motive in acquiring the shares. The taxpayer's capital was being "used to produce taxable income," and that being so he was entitled to his deduction without "a hectic and ridiculous search for non-profit motives." In effect, although § 165(c)(2) appears to refer to the taxpayer's state of mind ("transaction entered into *for* profit"), both *Weir* and *Gevirtz* reflect a judicial interest in avoiding the use of subjective factors in distinguishing between personal property and business or investment assets. If the property in question generates receipts which are includable in the taxpayer's gross income, as in *Weir,* then any loss incurred will almost certainly be deductible; if the property is devoted to personal consumption, as in *Gevirtz,* the loss will almost certainly be denied.

Somewhat more typical than situations in which the taxpayer's "motives" are mixed are cases in which property—usually residential—is alleged to have been converted by the taxpayer from an admittedly personal to an arguably commercial use. Suppose a homeowner decides to sell her residence and move to an apartment. The residence was purchased for $500,000, but the best offer the taxpayer can get today is $400,000. Convinced that the market will improve if she waits, the taxpayer decides to rent the house on a month-to-month basis until a better price can be had. Two years later she regretfully sells the residence for only $350,000. Is the owner's "loss" deductible under § 165(c)(2)? The answer depends upon whether a "conversion" from personal to commercial property has taken place, with the cases generally holding that an actual renting, at least if moderately continuous and prolonged, will be accepted as

---

[70]   109 F.2d 996 (3d Cir. 1940).

proof of the requisite change in character. Unsuccessful efforts to rent apparently will not suffice—the property does not shed its "personal" character until it actually produces includable gross income.

While the distinction between an actual and an attempted renting seems artificial (no such distinction would be made had the property never been devoted to personal use), the *amount* of deductible loss that is at stake will often be small. The Regulations prescribe that the basis for computing loss on the sale of a converted residence cannot exceed the property's original cost, or its value at the time of conversion, whichever is *lower*.[71] In the example above, therefore, assuming an actual renting occurred immediately, the homeowner's basis for computing loss on sale would be only $400,000, reduced by depreciation allowable during the two-year rental period. The $100,000 difference between her original cost ($500,000) and the value of the house at the conversion date ($400,000) would still be disallowed as "personal."

A loose end. Section 165(b) provides that the basis for determining loss under § 165(a) shall be the adjusted basis provided by § 1011 for determining loss from the sale or other disposition of property. To get a deduction, therefore, the taxpayer must establish that she *has* a basis for the property disposed of. Suppose a lawyer is entitled to a fee of $1,000 for work performed for a client. The client doesn't pay, goes bankrupt. Can the lawyer deduct the $1,000 that she has lost? Assuming she uses the cash method of accounting and has not yet taken the fee into gross income, the answer is: no. Generally, "basis" requires either a cash investment or a prior inclusion in income. A claim to *untaxed* wages, salaries or fees has a basis of zero, and hence there is nothing to deduct under § 165(b) even though the claim proves uncollectible. This rule obviously makes sense; if you never had something for tax purposes, you can't lose it for tax purposes. (For the same reason—absence of "basis"— the claim could not be deducted as a "bad debt" under § 166, discussed next.)

6.08 Bad Debts

In the case of both corporations and individuals, debts which become worthless during the taxable year are deductible from gross income under § 166. If the debt is a "business" debt—as it would always be in the case of a corporation—it may be deducted when it becomes wholly worthless, or it may be deducted when partially worthless. In the case of an individual taxpayer, deduction is also

---

[71]   Reg. § 1.165–9(b)(2).

permitted for "nonbusiness" debts—whether incurred in connection with a profit-seeking activity or in a personal setting such as a loan to a relative—but such debts must have become wholly worthless, because a deduction for partial worthlessness is not allowed. In addition, under § 166(d) the loss sustained on the worthlessness of a nonbusiness debt is treated as a short-term capital loss, and is therefore available only as an offset against capital gains plus $3,000 of ordinary income per year (see 16.03).

The distinction in § 166 between business and nonbusiness debts requires that a line be drawn between those activities of the individual taxpayer which constitute a "trade or business" and those of her pursuits which, although clearly of a profit-seeking nature, solely involve the management or conservation of investment capital. The necessity for making this often difficult distinction is avoided elsewhere in the deduction sections of the Code, with an apparent gain in simplicity of administration, by permitting similar treatment for "trade or business" activity and for profit-seeking activity of a nonbusiness character (*e.g.,* the management of investments). Thus, as respects losses, § 165(c) allows deduction both of losses incurred in a trade or business and of losses incurred in any profit-seeking transaction, though not connected with a trade or business. In either case, the characterization of the loss as ordinary or capital depends on the nature of the asset disposed of. Similarly, §§ 162 and 212 permit the deduction of ordinary and necessary expenses whether incurred by the taxpayer in her trade or business or in the management of investments, though here the business-investment distinction is relevant for purposes of the adjusted gross income computation and the limitation imposed by § 67 on "miscellaneous itemized deductions" (see 7.06 and 7.05, respectively).

The distinction between business and nonbusiness bad debts is most clearly felt where the taxpayer is the sole or principal stockholder of a corporation, is active in its affairs, and has made loans to the corporation in the form of advances on open account.[72] In *Whipple v. Commissioner*,[73] for example, the taxpayer, an active businessman who had promoted a number of corporate ventures, made sizeable loans to a particular corporation of which he was the major stockholder and chief executive. The corporation was unsuccessful, and on liquidation its assets proved insufficient to repay the taxpayer's loans in full. Contending that his work as corporate manager and promoter constituted an independent "trade or business," the taxpayer sought to deduct the unpaid balance of the

---

[72]   Debt represented by a "security"—a bond or debenture—specifically is given capital loss treatment when worthlessness occurs. Code § 165(g). Mere "advances" do not create a "security," however.

[73]   373 U.S. 193 (1963).

loans as a business bad debt. Disapproving a number of lower court decisions which had been favorable to taxpayer-promoters, the Supreme Court held that the loans were nonbusiness debts and hence could only be utilized as capital losses offsettable against capital gains. The Court found, in effect, that entrepreneurial activity— devoting one's energies to the promotion and management of corporate enterprises—was not of itself a "trade or business." The taxpayer's aim was to generate dividends and capital gains for himself by producing business income for his corporations. While the corporations were obviously in "business," the individual was not. Dividends and capital gains, said the Court, are "distinctive to the process of investing," and "investing is not a trade or business."

By placing loans to controlled corporations in the nonbusiness category, the *Whipple* decision in effect produces symmetrical tax treatment of promoters' gains and losses. To see why this is so, suppose an individual finances a new corporate venture by investing $50,100 cash, of which $50,000 is in the form of a loan to the company and $100 is for the company's common shares. Assume the business succeeds and the company is finally sold for $80,000. Since debt is "senior" to equity, the proceeds of sale would first be allocated $50,000 to repayment of the loan, and then the balance of $30,000 to the promoter's stock. The promoter realizes no gain on the debt repayment because the debt is simply paid off at face amount. The entire promotional gain—$29,900—would therefore be attributable to the shares, and as corporate stock is a capital asset, the gain would be taxed as capital gain. Now suppose that the enterprise is unsuccessful and is sold for only $20,000. Once again, the proceeds of sale would first be allocated to the debt of $50,000, so that a bad debt loss of $30,000 would result (together with a stock loss of $100). If the bad debt were treated as a "business" bad debt, then virtually the entire promotional loss would become a deduction from ordinary income. Promoter's gains would thus always be treated as capital gains, while promoter's losses would be treated as ordinary.

But presumably such unbalanced treatment of gains and losses from the same activity would be improper. Whipple himself, as the Court's opinion relates, had had a number of "winners" to go along with the "loser" for which the business bad debt deduction was claimed, and it could well be said of him, as of any promoter, that his losing promotions were a "cost" of his successful ventures. Since § 166 distinguishes between "business" and "nonbusiness" debts, rather than between capital and noncapital assets, a symmetrical result could be achieved only if promoters' loans were placed in the nonbusiness category. Although "nonbusiness" classification seems somewhat strained in this context, the *Whipple* decision ultimately reflects a finding that Congress did not intend to afford a special benefit to entrepreneurial activity by permitting the "profits" thereof to be treated as capital gain while allowing the "costs" to be deducted from ordinary income.

6.09 Depreciation—General Background

Though not the sort of topic that lawyers love, the depreciation allowance has grown so important over the past couple of decades that a somewhat lengthy discussion of it appears unavoidable. The Economic Recovery Tax Act of 1981, enacted at the start of President Reagan's first term, made significant changes in this field which, though somewhat modified since, obviously need to be summarized. But the present depreciation rules will not mean very much to readers unless some general accounting and economic background is provided first. Accordingly, the subject of depreciation is here dealt with in two jumps: background and historical elements are discussed in this Section, while the current rules and related matters are left to 6.10 and 6.11.

(a) Eligible Property

Code § 167—which still supplies the basic authorization—takes account of the progressive exhaustion of plant, equipment and other long-lived business and investment property by allowing an annual deduction for depreciation. Generally (and apart from the special procedures introduced by the 1981 Act), the cost of the property, less salvage value, is recovered on a year-by-year basis over the period during which the property is expected to be economically useful to the taxpayer. To illustrate, suppose a company buys a machine for $4,500. The company expects to use the machine in its business for five years and then sell it as "scrap" for $500. Using the straight-line method of depreciation (other methods can also be devised, as shown at (d), below), the taxpayer would deduct $800 a year over the five-year term, a total of $4,000. Since a portion of the cost of the machine is thus converted into a deductible expense each year, the taxpayer's basis for the machine, initially $4,500, also must be reduced by $800 a year. At the end of the first year, therefore, basis would be $3,700, at the end of the second year $2,900, and at the end of the fifth year, $500. If the machine is finally sold to a junk dealer for its anticipated salvage value of $500, no gain or loss results from the sale; if for more or less than $500, a gain or loss is recognized accordingly. In effect, the taxpayer's original expenditure of $4,500 is "returned" to it through a combination of (a) depreciation deductions during the property's useful life, (b) the amount realized as salvage, and (c) taxable gain or deductible loss on the final disposition of the asset.

The depreciation allowance is available both for business property—plant and equipment—and for investment property such as an apartment house or an office building. It extends to intangible assets—patents, copyrights, leases—as well as tangibles, though as respects intangibles the deduction is usually referred to as "amortization" rather than "depreciation." Property is depreciable (or amortizable) for purposes of § 167 if its useful life is definite and predictable, as it would be in the case of buildings and machines which wear out over a determinable period of time; it is not depreciable if the property's useful life is perpetual or indefinite, land being the chief example.[74]

(b)   Limitation to Cost

The depreciation allowance is limited in total to the taxpayer's basis, or cost, for his property.[75] Cost is generally equal to cash investment, though as has been seen the concept of basis is subject to a good many special rules and formulations. Since depreciable property is often acquired in part with borrowed money—a mortgage loan to buy a building, for example—it is obviously important to decide whether basis for depreciation purposes includes the borrowing or is restricted to the amount drawn from the taxpayer's own resources. This question is considered in some detail at 13.01, below, but for the present the short answer is that "cost" includes borrowed funds as well as equity investment.

"Cost" in the present context refers to *historical* cost, not the cost of replacing the property in the future when it wears out. The depreciation allowance, both for tax and for accounting purposes, is designed to offset the taxpayer's *original* investment against the gross income received in subsequent years, and in that way to limit the taxpayer's net taxable income to the excess of revenues over related expenses. It does *not* purport to measure the amount that would have to be set aside each year to fund the cost of replacement; nor, of course, being a mere bookkeeping entry, is it designed actually to generate such a fund.

One consequence of this distinction is that taxpayers who own depreciable assets during a period of inflation are likely to suffer what amounts to an increase in their tax burdens without enjoying an equivalent increase in their "real" incomes. Thus, a company which before an inflationary price increase has annual income of $1,200 and depreciation deductions of $800 has taxable income of $400. At a 21% tax rate, its tax liability is $84, which represents 7% of its gross income. If prices suddenly double because of inflation, the

---

[74]   Prior to 1993, acquired intangibles such as "goodwill" would have been another example. As explained at 6.11, however, Code § 197 now affords such assets a fixed period of amortization.

[75]   The limitation to cost does not apply in the case of certain mineral properties, to which special rules—beyond the scope of this discussion—may be applicable.

company's gross income becomes $2,400 but its depreciation allowance remains $800. It then has taxable income of $1,600 (*four* times the pre-inflation amount) and pays a tax of $336, which is 14% of gross income. Since the doubling of prices means that there is no *real* increase in the company's gross income, it can be argued that the depreciation allowance should also be doubled so that the company's taxable income and its resulting tax may continue to be the same percentage of gross income as previously. But while the argument has undeniable force, the effect of inflation is not limited to owners of depreciable property, and any effort to adjust for inflation—presumably through basis indexation—should properly be extended to all property owners, certainly including lenders and other recipients of fixed incomes. As suggested at 3.01, however, no such general reform is now in view (though often discussed), and there appears to be no good reason why owners of depreciable assets should be singled out for special consideration. The point must simply be conceded that the tax law works poorly during periods of sharp inflation. As explained a bit later (6.10), current law allows taxpayers to recover the cost of depreciable assets considerably more quickly than would be allowed under a system designed to measure actual economic depreciation. This generosity is sometimes defended on the grounds that it compensates for the lack of an inflation adjustment to the amounts deductible under the depreciation rules. The idea is that deducting too little too quickly might have the same economic effect as deducting the right amount more slowly. Only by sheer coincidence, however, would the two wrongs combine to make a right.

(c) *Useful Lives*

Estimating an asset's useful life—how long it is likely to be in service in the taxpayer's business—is obviously of considerable importance. Too brief an estimate of useful life will result in tax deferral, too long an estimate in tax anticipation. If, for example, a machine costing $4,000 net of salvage has an *actual* service life of 10 years, the proper straight-line deduction is $400 a year. If the estimate of useful service life is only half that term, however, the deduction taken annually in the first 5 years of use will be $800 and in the last 5 years zero, with the result that the tax on $2,000 of taxable income will be deferred from the earlier 5-year period to the later. While the taxes postponed are ultimately recouped by the Treasury, the taxpayer (for reasons already amply noted) gains a tangible benefit from the deferral of his tax obligations. To be sure, the opposite consequence arises if the estimate of useful life is longer than the period of actual use. If a machine has an actual service life of only 5 years and the estimate is 10, then depreciation which should have been allowed during the earlier period will be postponed until the asset is retired; taxable income will have been anticipated and taxes paid "too soon."

As will be seen, the Code in 1981 pretty well abandoned the notion that depreciation should be spread out over an asset's *true* useful life and now permits business taxpayers to depreciate their property over periods that are (and are expected to be) much shorter than the periods of actual service. In enacting the Accelerated Cost Recovery System (ACRS) described at 6.10, Congress' stated aim was to stimulate investment in plant and equipment, and with this overriding goal in view it simply discarded accuracy of measurement as an objective for the tax law to pursue. Actually, as the next few paragraphs show, the idea of manipulating the depreciation allowance in order to influence private investment decisions was not a new one in 1981. While the 1981 enactment went much further than any of its predecessors, the same concept has been promoted by economic policymakers, and in one form or another accepted by Congress, for more than sixty years. This has been so, moreover, whether control of Congress and the Treasury was in the hands of liberals or of conservatives during any particular era.

(d) Permissible Methods

As just implied, there are really two different approaches that can be taken to the question of what constitutes a "proper" depreciation allowance. One approach is concerned with the effect of the allowance on the measurement of taxable income. From this standpoint, the adequacy of the allowance is tested by the accuracy of the income measurement that results. The question is: what system of depreciation generates a "true" picture of the taxpayer's income experience for the taxable year? The second approach involves the use of the depreciation allowance as a method of encouraging (or, perhaps, retarding) investment in depreciable assets. Here the adequacy of the allowance depends on whether it influences businesses to expand (or contract) the level of their outlays for such property in accordance with the aims of government economic policy. Accurate income measurement, surely the aim of "pure" tax policy, is more or less consciously subordinated to fiscal objectives, employment goals, and so on.

Most would agree, we think, that at least since the enactment of the 1954 Code, the depreciation allowance has largely been shaped by the second approach and has reflected a congressional policy of encouraging growth and expansion. Prior to 1954 taxpayers were generally required to use the relatively conservative straight-line method of depreciation in apportioning the cost of depreciable property over its useful life. The 1954 Code, however, liberalized the rules relating to apportionment by authorizing taxpayers to elect an "accelerated" method of depreciation—*e.g.*, the declining balance method at twice the straight-line rate[76]—for new tangible property having an extended useful life. These accelerated methods, like the straight-line method, spread recovery of the taxpayer's investment over the entire service life of the asset. But unlike the straight-line method, which results in equal annual deductions throughout an asset's useful life, the newer methods concentrated larger deductions in the earlier years of the asset's life and thus effected a speedier return of the greater part of the taxpayer's cost.

It is easy to see why the availability of accelerated depreciation methods would be expected to spur investment in depreciable property. Consider again a machine that costs $4,000, has a useful life of 5 years, and can be expected to generate gross income of $1,200 a year (net of maintenance expenses). Should a businessman, whose income is taxed, say, at a combined state and federal rate of 40%, buy the thing or not? The answer depends on whether the present value of the expected after-tax revenues generated by the machine exceeds, or falls short of, the required investment of $4,000. If the present value of expected after-tax revenues exceeds the required investment, then of course he *should* acquire the machine because the effect is to replace cash with tangible property of greater worth. If the contrary is true, the investment should be rejected.

Assume that the taxpayer is able to raise money from banks or other investors at an after-tax cost of 10%. Since that is what he has to pay for investment capital, it is logical to use the same 10% rate of discount in determining the present value of the income stream which he expects to receive. The following are the relevant calculations, comparing (a) the straight-line method with (b) the double declining balance method of depreciation:

---

[76] Under this method (sometimes referred to as "double declining balance"), the first step is to determine the percentage of cost that would be deductible each year under the straight-line method. For 5-year property, for example, that would be 20%. The next step is to double that percentage—here, to 40%. Each year, then, the taxpayer claims a deduction equal to 40% of its *remaining* basis. For a 5-year asset with an original basis of $1,000, the deduction (assuming (1) a full year of depreciation is allowed for the year the asset is placed in service, and (2) no salvage value) is $400 in the first year, $240 (40% of $600) in the second year, and $144 (40% of $360) in the third year. Of course, continued application of this approach would never result in recovery of the taxpayer's entire original basis. Accordingly, the system switches to straight-line recovery of the remaining basis over the remaining recovery period in the year in which that produces a larger deduction than continued application of the double declining balance method. Here, that would mean a deduction of $108 (50% of $216) in the fourth year, and another $108 deduction in the fifth year.

(a) Straight-Line

	(1)	(2)	(3)	(4)	(5)	(6)
					Net Cash Flow	Present Value of (5) at
Year	Gross Income	Deprecia-tion	Taxable Income	Tax Payable	(1)–(4)	10%
1	$1,200	$ 800	$ 400	$160	$1,040	$ 945
2	1,200	800	400	160	1,040	859
3	1,200	800	400	160	1,040	781
4	1,200	800	400	160	1,040	710
5	$1,200	800	400	160	1,040	645
Totals	$6,000	$4,000	$2,000	$800	$5,200	$3,940

(b) Declining-Balance

	(1)	(2)	(3)	(4)	(5)	(6)
					Net Cash Flow	Present Value of (5) at
Year	Gross Income	Deprecia-tion	Taxable Income	Tax Payable	(1)–(4)	10%
1	$1,200	$1,600	($400)*	($160)**	$1,360	$1,236
2	1,200	960	240	96	1,104	912
3	1,200	576	624	250	950	713
4	1,200	432	768	307	893	610
5	$1,200	432	768	307	893	553
Totals	$6,000	$4,000	$2,000	$800	$5,200	$4,024

* Loss offsettable against other income

** Amount refunded

With one exception, the column *totals* are the same under both depreciation methods. The critical exception is column (6)—"present value of net cash flows"—which totals $4,024 under the declining-balance method, but only $3,940 under the straight-line method. The reason for the difference is that under the declining-balance method net cash flows are larger in the early years and smaller in the later years (yearly tax payments necessarily follow a converse pattern), while under the straight-line method net cash flows (and tax payments) are level throughout the five-year period. Because the discounted value of near-term receipts is greater than that of distant ones, the present value of the sum of the net cash flows is greater under the declining-balance method than under the straight-line method, even though the total dollar amount received over the five-year period is the same for both.

The important point, at all events, is that the investment in the machine has a *positive* net present value of $24 ($4,024 – $4,000) if the declining balance method of depreciation is used, but a *negative* net present value of $60 ($4,000 – $3,940) if the taxpayer is restricted to the straight-line method. Quite obviously, therefore, the taxpayer should buy the machine if, but only if, the declining-balance method of depreciation is available. Hence Congress can directly influence taxpayers' investment decisions by permitting (or denying) the use of the accelerated cost-recovery procedure.

But now suppose we alter our approach to the depreciation allowance and emphasize income measurement instead of investment incentives. Suppose that the "economic policy" approach is abandoned or renounced at this point and that Congress decides to require all taxpayers to use the depreciation method which results in a "true" measure of annual taxable income. Which of the methods just discussed (if either) would be appropriate? Since the declining-balance method has been described as "accelerated", does this imply that the straight-line method is "correct" in the sense that it produces a more accurate measure of the change in the taxpayer's wealth-status between the beginning and the end of the taxable year?

Presumably the purpose of tax or accounting depreciation (putting fiscal policy aims aside) is to reflect the *annual loss in value* of the taxpayer's depreciable assets that results from their use in the taxpayer's business. The question which the depreciation allowance *ought* to answer is: how much less are such assets worth at the end of the year than they were at the beginning? The taxpayer's "true" annual income, then, is his gross income less the sum of (a) his current expenses plus (b) the decline for the year in the economic value of his capital equipment.

In our illustration above, the $4,000 machine is expected to generate gross income (after current maintenance expenses) of $1,200 a year for 5 years. The implied before-tax rate of return on the taxpayer's investment is about 15%; that is, $1,200 a year for 5 years discounted at a rate of 15% equals $4,000. If we apply this discount rate to each expected payment in turn, the schedule of present values looks roughly like this:

Year:	1	2	3	4	5	Totals
Expected receipt	$1,200	$1,200	$1,200	$1,200	$1,200	$6,000
Present value	$1,045	$ 905	$ 790	$ 687	$ 573	$4,000

The present value of all five payments must of course add up to $4,000, the original cost of the equipment.

How does this schedule look after the first year of use has passed? The second, the third, etc.? As each year of useful life expires the expected stream of payments becomes shorter and the present value of the sum of all remaining payments necessarily declines. There is just that much less to anticipate in the way of future returns. The taxpayer's economic loss from the year's operations—his annual cost—is measured by the decline in the present value of anticipated receipts which takes place between the beginning and the end of the taxable year. In effect, the difference between the value of the future income stream on January 1 and its value on January 1 of the following year represents the cost of using the machine for the year in question. If the object of the depreciation allowance is to reduce gross income by the true cost of operations, then the annual allowance should be no more or less than that amount.

Here is a schedule of the yearly decline in the present value of the taxpayer's investment:

	Present Value of Investment	Present Value of Remaining Payments					Annual Loss in Present Value
		1	2	3	4	5	
Start of Year 1	$4,000	$1,045	905	790	687	573	
End of Year 1	3,427		1,045	905	790	687	$573
End of Year 2	2,740			1,045	905	790	687
End of Year 3	1,950				1,045	905	790
End of Year 4	1,045					1,045	905
End of Year 5	–0–						1,045
						Total:	$4,000

The last column shows the true measure of economic cost from year to year and indicates that the correct apportionment method is one which *starts low and rises:* $573 in Year 1, then $687, $790, $905, and finally $1,045 in Year 5. The resulting schedule of taxable income, of course, is the inverse: $627 of taxable income in Year 1, $513 in Year 2, $410 in Year 3, $295 in Year 4 and finally $155 in Year 5. Income is thus *higher* in the earlier years than in the later.

This corrected depreciation method—sometimes called "sinking-fund" depreciation—looks peculiar and unfamiliar at first glance. Really, however, it is nothing more than the ordinary and conventional method by which a bank amortizes the principal amount of a mortgage loan. As stated elsewhere (2.02), anyone who has ever paid off a home mortgage knows that principal payments are small in the early years and large in the later ones, with interest (income to the lender) being correspondingly greater in the beginning and smaller at the end. The machine owner above occupies essentially the same status as a mortgage-lender: both invest their capital in the expectation of a future periodic return. Hence if the depreciation allowance were designed to produce an accurate measure of taxable income, the same cost-recovery procedure would seem to be appropriate for each.

It must be admitted, on the other hand, that the sinking-fund depreciation method is a great deal easier to apply in the case of mortgages, leases and other property whose future yield is fixed by contract than it is for tangible assets like machines. The income from a mortgage or a lease can be determined without engaging in predictions and projections that depend entirely on future events. By contrast, the cash-flow to be derived from the operation of a tangible asset is not a fixed quantity and would have to be estimated. Since such estimates are very hard to make, it is understandable why the sinking-fund method has never been used for machinery, equipment and other tangibles. The above analysis unrealistically assumes a machine that remains as good as new for five years—without decreasing output or increasing maintenance requirements—and then suddenly turns to dust (like the "wonderful one-hoss shay" of Oliver Wendell Holmes (Senior), which "went to pieces all at once . . . and nothing first, just as bubbles do when they burst"). If the analysis were redone using more realistic assumptions about decreasing productivity and increasing maintenance requirements, the proper depreciation method would be less decelerated than sinking fund, or possibly even straight-line or accelerated. The larger point, however, as stated, is that economic depreciation is simply a function of expected cash flows.[77] Once again, "true" depreciation is the difference between the present value of expected cash flows at the start of the taxable period and the present value of expected cash flows at the end of such taxable period. Where, as in our example, expected cash flows are level from period to period, the sinking-fund method is the *only* proper method of apportioning the taxpayer's capital investment in accordance with the economic cost of use. By contrast, even the straight-line method of depreciation turns out to be accelerated.

A loose end. Bored with this topic? Try a slight digression:

---

[77] Samuelson, *Tax Deductibility of Economic Depreciation to Insure Invariant Valuations,* 72 J. of Pol. Econ. 604 (1964).

Students sometimes ask whether depreciation (under whatever method) is supposed to create a fund for the replacement of tangible assets when their useful lives are over. As stated above, and as we hope the following discussion[78] will make clear, the answer, perhaps unexpectedly, is No.

For tax and accounting purposes, "net income" (or "taxable income") means gross income less all allowable expenses. Assuming Corporation X owns long-lived tangible assets such as buildings and equipment, those expenses would of course include an annual depreciation allowance. If X owns a truck that cost $50,000, and the truck has a useful life of 10 years, then (on a simple straight-line basis and ignoring salvage value) X would deduct $5,000 a year as depreciation. So, if X had income of $105,000 this year *before* taking the depreciation allowance, its income net of depreciation will be $100,000. That's obvious.

But is it also true that X "needs" to set aside $5,000 a year for 10 years to replace the truck at the end of its 10-year useful life? Assume (for the sake of simplicity) that a new truck can be expected to cost exactly the same $50,000 10 years from now. Assume also that X's business activities customarily generate a 10% return. Depreciation can be thought of as capital that has been disinvested from the depreciable asset (the truck) and left at risk generally in the operation of the business. If X (actually or notionally) invests $5,000 a year at 10% for 10 years, the fund will grow to nearly $80,000 by the end of the 10-year period, which is much more than the expected cost of a new truck. The reason, of course, is that $5,000 allocated every year to a replacement fund would grow at a compound rate of 10% if the business should succeed in earning 10% as expected. The effect is just the same as if X put $5,000 into a 10% savings account every year, left the interest to compound at a 10% rate, and then withdrew the entire amount after 10 full years had passed. As stated, the savings account, together with accumulated interest, would by then have grown to the sum of nearly $80,000.

What is needed is not $50,000 in *total* charges over 10 years, but charges which, compounded at the expected 10% rate of return, will grow to a total of $50,000 in that time.

Actually, the amount that X needs to set aside annually in order to generate a fund of $50,000 at the end of the 10-year period is about $3,135 (as a glance at the relevant compound interest table tells us). In effect, a set-aside or disinvestment of $3,135 each year for 10 years

---

[78] The following is loosely adapted from Blum and Katz, *Depreciation and Enterprise Valuation*, 32 U. Chi. L. Rev. 236 (1965).

at a compounding rate of 10% will accumulate to exactly $50,000, the expected replacement cost of X's worn-out equipment.

In a nutshell, the reason for the difference is that "replacement" is a cost that will be incurred in the future. By contrast, depreciation is simply an accounting procedure by which a capital expenditure made in the past is converted into current expense over the useful life of the asset acquired. Both numbers are "correct" but each has a purpose that is different from the other's.

6.10 ACRS and Leveraged Leases

(a) ACRS

As indicated at 6.09, the permission to use accelerated depreciation methods—double declining balance, for example, in place of the slower straight-line method—has the effect of increasing after-tax returns to the owners of depreciable property. Investments that might otherwise have been unprofitable are transformed into profitable ones, and businesses are thus encouraged to replace and expand their existing stock of capital goods. It should be stressed (and of course we already have) that the increase in after-tax returns is here accomplished not through an outright tax exemption (as in the case of municipal bond interest, for example), but by the slightly subtler device of allowing business taxpayers to defer their *current* income tax liabilities to later periods. But though it goes by another name, tax deferral is really no different from tax reduction or exemption—the effect would be the same if the income from depreciable property were taxed at lower rates than those that normally apply, or if all or a portion of such income were exempted from tax entirely.

This can be seen in a fairly dramatic way if we carry the accelerated cost-recovery idea to its extreme and allow expenditures for machinery and equipment to be deducted all at once, as if they were current expenses. This is, in fact, permitted by § 168(k), for most machinery and equipment (but not buildings) placed in service after September 27, 2017, and before 2023. For these assets, Congress has ditched the "capital expenditure-depreciation allowance" concept altogether and simply permitted taxpayers to "expense" their outlays for long-lived property under § 162(a). What is the impact on the taxpayer's tax liability, at least as it relates to income from the property in question?

The answer, as has been shown,[79] is that the income from the property effectively becomes exempt from tax—exactly as if an

---

[79] Brown, *Business-Income Taxation and Investment Incentives*, in Income, Employment and Public Policy 300 (1948). And *see* discussion at 5.06 above.

explicit exemption, rather than a "mere" accelerated deduction procedure, had been enacted. To illustrate, suppose a taxpayer is prepared to invest $4,000 in a machine that will generate revenues of $6,000 (150% of cash investment) in one or more future years. The investor's *pre-tax* profit, $2,000, thus represents a 50% return on his investment. Assume (as above) that the investor is taxed at a rate of 40%. If the $4,000 outlay is not deductible until the $6,000 of revenues are received, the investor's *after-tax* return will be 30%. Thus, the pre-tax profit of $2,000 is reduced by a tax of 40%, or $800. After-tax profit is then $1,200, which represents a 30% return on the taxpayer's investment of $4,000. Since the pre-tax rate of return is 50%, and since tax is imposed at a rate of 40%, the 30% after-tax return (60% of 50%) is exactly what one would expect.

But now suppose that the taxpayer placed the machinery in service in 2018, when the temporary rule of § 168(k) provides that outlays for machinery are fully deductible when made. Since the taxpayer was willing to invest $4,000 with no immediate deduction, she would have been willing to invest $6,667 once a full deduction was allowed. The $6,667 deduction would offset other income taxable at a 40% rate, and hence the machine would cost the taxpayer only 60% of $6,667, or $4,000 net of the tax saving. The future revenues to be expected would then be $10,000 (150% of cash investment, as before), but this sum would be taxed in full when received because the taxpayer's original investment would already have been deducted and her basis for the asset would be zero. The taxpayer would therefore have taxable income of $10,000 on which she would pay a tax of $4,000 – 40% of $10,000—and her net realization would be $6,000. Since she originally invested $4,000 in the machine ($6,667 before tax but only $4,000 after the benefit of full deduction), her after-tax profit would be $6,000 – $4,000, or $2,000. This, of course, represents a 50% return (rather than merely 30%) and, hence, it is as if the income on the originally contemplated investment had been exempted from tax entirely.[80] Stated axiomatically, immediate deduction combined with nominal taxation of investment returns produces results equivalent to no deduction combined with full exemption of investment returns, if the applicable tax rate is assumed to be constant for all affected periods.

The 1981 Tax Act, which added § 168 to the Code, did not go all the way to full and immediate deduction for capital expenditures. It did, however, move quite substantially in that direction by substituting sharply abbreviated depreciation schedules for the "useful life" limitation that had governed the depreciation allowance

---

[80]   Under the income-exemption alternative, the taxpayer would have bought a $4,000 machine (no deduction being allowed, either up-front or later, for the purchase price), and the machine would have generated tax-free revenues of $6,000.

in the past. Under earlier practice, the depreciation allowance was spread out over the period during which the property was expected to have continuing economic value in the taxpayer's business. Since estimates rather than certainties were involved, determination of the useful life of physical assets was for many years a major source of controversy in individual cases. In the 1960's, and again in the early 70's, the Treasury and Congress adopted standardized useful-life tables for broad classes of property in an effort to minimize such disputes. The result of this was to shorten applicable depreciation schedules in many instances, but at least in theory the service life of the asset and the period over which depreciation was allowable were still intended to bear a proximate relationship.

Code § 168—which contains the so-called Accelerated Cost Recovery System—largely discards the concept of actual service life and instead frankly treats the depreciation allowance as a means of subsidizing capital investments. Under ACRS, the cost of an asset is recoverable over a predetermined period that is, and is intended to be, significantly shorter than the useful life of the asset or the period during which the asset is expected to be used in the taxpayer's business. Thus, most tangible personal property (machinery and equipment) is now depreciable over periods of 5 to 10 years (in years in which § 168(k) expensing does not apply), even though actual service lives are typically a good deal longer. Real property— previously depreciable over periods ranging up to 60 years—is now assigned a recovery period of 27.5 years in the case of residential buildings and 39 years for other business structures. Generally, the double declining balance method is to be used in computing the annual depreciation allowance for personal property and the straight-line method for real property. Finally, the salvage value limitation is eliminated and the full cost of the property is allowed to be recovered over the relevant term.

As stated, the cost-recovery periods established under § 168 are substantially shorter than the true useful lives of most kinds of business equipment—automobiles, for example, are placed in the 5-year class, although the anticipated service life of a car is said to be 7 or 8 years. The result (as usual) is that the effective rate of tax on income from investment in plant and machinery is much lower than the statutory rate; put differently, it is as if a portion of such income were tax-exempt.

In addition to § 168(k), § 179 provides another route to immediate deduction of the cost of machinery and equipment, for smaller businesses. Unlike § 168(k), § 179 is a permanent provision. For 2018 and later years, the maximum amount deductible under § 179 is $1 million. The $1 million ceiling is reduced by one dollar for every dollar by which the taxpayer's cost of § 179 property purchased during the year exceeds $2.5 million. Thus, no deduction is allowed under § 179 to a taxpayer paying $3.5 million or more during the year for machinery and equipment.

Although the provisions allowing immediate expensing of some or all of the costs of long-lived business assets are inconsistent with income tax norms, full expensing of the costs of such assets would be theoretically proper under a consumption tax—as explained in a Note at the end of this book.[81] This suggests a different way of viewing the expensing provisions. Instead of understanding them as deviations from an income tax (in the interests of subsidizing investments in business machinery and equipment), they can be viewed as either a compromise between an income tax and a consumption tax base (in the case of partial expensing provisions) or as the adoption—for limited purposes—of a consumption tax base (in the case of full expensing provisions).

(b)   Leveraged Leases and the Transfer of Tax Benefits

As suggested, quick-depreciation rules generate very substantial benefits for corporations and other taxpayers whose businesses call for large-scale capital investment. On the other hand, since ACRS is a tax-*reduction* mechanism, it is obviously only those taxpayers that actually *have* taxable income, and hence do owe taxes, that will welcome the relief. Unprofitable companies may have equally urgent capital investment requirements, but as they currently operate at a loss, accelerated cost-recovery affords them no benefit, at least for the time being.

To cope with this "problem," tax lawyers long ago invented a legal device by which, in effect, unprofitable companies may simply *transfer* their excess depreciation deductions to profitable companies that can use them. The device in question—generally known as a "leveraged lease"—is nothing more or less than an updated version of the arrangement that was at issue in *Starr's Estate* (see 6.03(c)). To see how it works, suppose L decides to purchase certain heavy equipment for $10 million. L has massive net operating loss (NOL) carryforwards (§ 172) from large tax losses in earlier years; the NOL carryforwards can be used to offset L's income in this and future years, with the result that L is *de facto* a tax exempt organization for the foreseeable future.[82] Assuming the equipment is five-year property (and that § 168(k) expensing does not apply), allowable

---

[81]   Note, *Income Tax, Consumption Tax, Flat Tax,* p. 493.

[82]   For 2018 and later years, the allowable NOL carryforward for any given year may not exceed 80% of the taxpayer's pre-NOL taxable income for the year. As a result, having large NOL carryforwards no longer makes a taxpayer *fully* tax-exempt for the foreseeable future. For ease of exposition, the example in the text disregards that detail.

depreciation under ACRS would be $2 million in the year of purchase (even if purchase is at the year-end), $3.2 million in the second year, $1.92 million in the third year, $1.152 in the fourth and fifth years, and $.576 in the sixth.[83] Because of its *de facto* tax exempt status, L has no use for those deductions. Accordingly, matters are arranged so that P, a profitable company, will formally purchase and own the equipment but will then at once lease it to L for a period that represents a substantial proportion of the equipment's economic life, which is well in excess of the five-year ACRS period. P will have borrowed (hence the term "leveraged") the greater part of its purchase price, say $8 million, from a bank or other lender on the security of the equipment itself. The balance of the purchase price— $2 million—will be drawn by P from its own resources, and it is this $2 million of "equity" that represents P's actual investment in the deal.

In order to repay its $8 million indebtedness, P will turn over L's annual rental payments to the lender, which will apply them to interest and principal. The amount of such rentals will suffice—but usually just suffice—to amortize P's $8 million indebtedness (plus interest) over the term of the lease. Sometimes there will be a little left over for P to put in its own pocket after annual debt service is accounted for, but such excess is likely to be small. In effect, L's rental obligation is pegged at or near a level that will just satisfy the debt requirements; P itself can expect little or nothing in the way of an annual return on its $2 million investment.

So what does P get by laying out $2 million in cash for equipment that it has never seen? Obvious answer: chiefly the ACRS deductions described above—plus any net rents, plus whatever residual value the equipment may possess at the end of the lease. On the minus side, P will have to include in income the $8 million of rents allocable to the repayment of debt principal; while the annual interest paid by P to the lender is deductible, payments on principal are not. Since, however, much the greater part of such rents will be "received" by P and taxed in later years than those in which the ACRS deductions are taken, P will enjoy the usual benefit of income deferral. Deductions are anticipated, in effect, while income is deferred.

The net present value of all of these factors (but most especially the deferral benefit) will exceed P's initial cash outlay and will afford P a better return on its $2 million than P could get by investing the same funds in its own business or in other projects of equivalent risk.

---

[83]   Code § 168(b)(1) and (d). The allowance is smaller in the first year than in the second year because of the "half-year convention," which permits only six-months'- worth of depreciation deductions for the first year. The deduction for the final year is also for only six-months'-worth of depreciation.

This will be true even though, as noted, P is likely to receive little or no cash or other property of value until the lease expires (if then).

As to L, the benefit of the arrangement is also clear. Without P's participation, L would presumably have had to borrow (or otherwise obtain), and repay with interest, the full equipment purchase price of $10 million. Now, however, L needs to "borrow" only $8 million.[84] The remaining $2 million will have been supplied by P virtually interest-free—that is, largely in exchange for L's ACRS deductions, which L could not have used anyway.

As usual, the Treasury will be the only loser in all this; in effect, the leveraged lease is just a roundabout way of cashing in L's unused tax benefits. Indeed, it might be simpler (certainly cheaper: no legal fees or brokerage commissions) if the Code permitted L to obtain the tax value of its unused deductions *directly* from the Treasury as a cash refund (*i.e.*, of the taxes L *would* have saved if it *had* had any taxable income to apply the deductions against). At the other extreme, the Code could conceivably (at least in the case of long-term leases) restrict the availability of ACRS to the actual *user* of the equipment—here L—and thus deny those benefits to P, a mere lessor.

But in fact the Code follows neither course. As matters stand, L can effectively sell its tax entitlements to P, provided only that the legal arrangement between them constitutes a "lease" rather than a loan or (as in *Starr's Estate*) a conditional sales contract. Federal standards—among others, that the expected residual value and remaining useful life of the equipment be more than minimal, so that P will really "own" something when the lease is over—are determinative in this regard. The fact that P and L *call* their arrangement a "lease" does not make it one for tax purposes.[85] Aided by skilled counsel and an accommodating appraiser, however, the parties usually find the applicable requirements not difficult to meet.

And why stop with old-fashioned equipment leasing? How about the entire sewer system of the city of Hamburg? Hamburg, a fine old Hanseatic town in northern Germany, desperately needs an infusion of cash in order to maintain city services. Under the terms of a so-called SILO deal—sale-in, lease-out—P purchases Hamburg's reeking sewers for $X million (payable in installments) but promptly leases those sewers back to the city on a long-term basis. Hamburg

---

[84]   L's rental payments under the lease are designed to be sufficient to enable P to cover the debt service on its $8 million loan. Thus, L's lease obligations are the economic equivalent of the obligations associated with borrowing $8 million.

[85]   See, *e.g.*, *Rice's Toyota World, Inc. v. Commissioner*, 752 F.2d 89 (4th Cir. 1985). But see *Frank Lyon Co. v. U.S.*, 435 U.S. 561 (1978), in which the Supreme Court approved a leasing transaction that entailed a transfer of tax benefits and little else. The decision is criticized in Wolfman, *The Supreme Court in the Lyon's Den: A Failure of Judicial Process*, 66 Cornell L.Rev. 1075 (1981).

keeps a percentage of the purchase price, maybe 10%, and puts the rest in a trust to guarantee the rental payments. P, which borrowed the $X million from a bank, uses the rents to meet its loan obligation, and then of course takes an annual depreciation allowance on Hamburg's sewer system, which it now owns. As usual, the relevant calculations leave P with a substantial tax benefit even after Hamburg takes its cut. Hamburg, needless to say, does not pay U.S. income taxes.

Brilliant or scandalous—which? The government successfully attacked SILO as a sham transaction. In *AWG Leasing Trust v. U.S.*,[86] the court held for the government, finding that the SILO "deal was an attempt to create an appearance of a sale but without any real economic substance"—"a pure abusive tax shelter," in the words of another court. In 2004 Congress enacted § 470 to eliminate the benefit of SILOs involving municipalities, foreign governments and other tax-exempt "seller-lessees." Despite the enactment of the statutory "fix," as explained earlier (6.06) the application of the sham transaction doctrine to pre-§ 470 cases is important because the new provision operates only prospectively.

A loose end. In the much-debated *Simon* case,[87] the taxpayer, a violinist employed by the New York Philharmonic Orchestra, purchased a Tourte bow—Tourte being a 19th-century French bow-maker and his bows among the best ever made—for the rather astonishing price of $30,000. The taxpayer used the bow day-in day-out for his orchestra performances and presumably played the better for it. Tourte bows are made of wood (scarce Pernambuco wood, we are told), and are therefore perishable; but unlike trucks, machinery and other tangible business property, the bows that M. Tourte fabricated do not lose their value with use or with time. Quite the contrary: rare as they are, Tourte bows, like Stradivarius violins, have a substantial "collector's value" and are almost certain to appreciate over the years as fewer and fewer become available for purchase.

Asserting that his bow was "property used in the trade or business" under Code § 167(a), the taxpayer took annual depreciation deductions in accordance with the schedule for 5-year property then provided by § 168. The Commissioner, following a long-standing practice with respect to rare and appreciating musical instruments

---

[86]   592 F.Supp.2d 953 (N.D. Ohio 2008). See also *Altria Group, Inc. v. United States*, 658 F.3d 276 (2d Cir. 2011) (same result on similar facts).

[87]   *Simon v. Commissioner*, 103 T.C. 247 (1994), *aff'd*, 68 F.3d 41 (2d Cir. 1995), *nonacq.* 1996–2 C.B. 1.

(and presumably other "functional" antiques), disallowed the deductions on the ground that the Tourte bow was a non-depreciable asset.

The issue presented in *Simon* appears to have given the Tax Court fits, but in the end the court held for the taxpayer. The Tourte bow, said the majority, was in fact subject to "exhaustion, wear and tear" of a "substantial" nature and hence must be deemed to be a wasting asset having a limited useful life. In enacting § 168 and the ACRS rules, Congress specifically intended to minimize the importance of *actual* useful lives—so frequently the subject of past disputes—by establishing statutory recovery periods for various classes of depreciable property. Once found to be depreciable, the Tourte bow did indeed belong to the statutory class of five-year property under § 168, even though actual useful life would obviously be much longer. Five judges dissented on the ground that the useful life of the bow should be regarded as indefinite or at least unascertainable. A Tourte bow, being a "work of art," could be expected to rise in value over time rather than decline. It followed that the bow, although a tangible asset, should *not* be regarded as subject to "exhaustion, wear and tear" and, accordingly, must be treated as non-depreciable property.

Judge Gerber, dissenting separately, called for an allocation of the $30,000 purchase price. The Tourte bow, he observed, had a dual function in the taxpayer's hands, being both professional equipment and a collectible. To the extent the purchase price was allocable to the collectible feature, the property was non-depreciable; to the extent allocable to the equipment function—but only to that extent—depreciation should be allowed. Under the majority's view, warned Gerber, "Taxpayers will be able to depreciate items with current business utility and intrinsic collector's value and, after 3 or 5 years, have the tax benefit of the entire cost. . . . The process may be duplicated over and over, providing substantial writeoffs with the cost borne by the public fisc." Judge Gerber's allocation theory has a certain appeal, yet it does appear to divide the Tourte bow into two discrete physical units, which is hard to envision. A bow is a unitary object, after all, and it is difficult (as another dissenter stressed) to say that it can wear out for one purpose but not the other. Either it wears out or it doesn't wear out, but not both.

The taxpayer's victory in the Tax Court was affirmed by the Second Circuit, although only by a two-to-one vote.[88] Essentially the same issue—this time involving an antique viol rather than a bow—

---

[88]   68 F.3d 41 (2d Cir. 1995).

was presented to the Tax Court in the same year by the *Liddle* case.[89] The Tax Court also decided *Liddle* in the taxpayers' favor, and the Third Circuit unanimously affirmed. The Commissioner indicated her "nonacquiescence" with the results in *Simon* and *Liddle*, which means taxpayers residing outside of the Second and Third Circuits who claim deductions under similar circumstances can expect (if audited) to have their deductions challenged by the IRS.

Even within the Second and Third Circuits, *Simon* and *Liddle* do not change the long-established rule that depreciation deductions are not available for antiques and art objects *not* subject to wear and tear—for example, paintings (or antique musical instruments) on display in the lobby of a fancy hotel. What is the ACRS status of an oriental carpet in the lobby of an upscale law firm? In the Second and Third Circuits, it is probably depreciable if it is on the floor and is regularly walked on (even if experts have assured the firm that the carpet can survive centuries of footsteps), but not if it is hanging on the wall.

Another loose end. Suppose a taxpayer owns a piece of heavy construction equipment (a crane, for example). Suppose also that the equipment cost the taxpayer $100,000, and that § 168 provides that equipment of this sort is to be depreciated over a twenty-year period, using the straight-line method (the § 168 details are just for illustrative purposes). Does it follow, then, that if the taxpayer uses the equipment in its business for all of the current year the taxpayer is entitled to a deduction of $5,000 under § 168? Not necessarily. Suppose the taxpayer is in the business of producing and selling electric power, and that it uses the equipment (in the current year) solely in connection with the construction of a new electricity-generating facility. In *Commissioner v. Idaho Power*[90] (on which this hypothetical is loosely based), the Supreme Court ruled that a taxpayer in this situation is required to add the current year's depreciation allowance on the equipment to its basis in the new facility, rather than currently deducting the depreciation on the equipment. Suppose § 168 provides that the new facility is depreciable on the straight-line method over a fifty-year period. In that case, the $5,000 depreciation on the equipment would be deducted—as part of the cost of the facility—at the rate of $100 per year for fifty years, beginning with the year the taxpayer places the facility in service.

---

[89]   *Liddle v. Commissioner,* 103 T.C. 285 (1994), *aff'd,* 65 F.3d 329 (3d Cir. 1995), *nonacq.* 1996–2 C.B. 2.

[90]   418 U.S. 1 (1974).

Students often find the result in *Idaho Power* to be counterintuitive, but the Court's analysis is clearly correct. Depreciation on one long-lived business asset can be part of the cost of constructing another long-lived business asset, and in that situation the depreciation must be capitalized to the new asset—in effect, transferred from the basis of the construct*ing* asset to the basis of the construct*ed* asset—rather than being currently deducted. The result in *Idaho Power* is now codified and extended by the so-called uniform capitalization (unicap) rules of § 263A.

Of course, when a depreciable asset is used to produce current income rather than to produce another long-lived asset, the amount calculated as the cost recovery allowance under § 168 is currently deductible. For example, if the taxpayer had used the heavy equipment to make repairs on existing facilities, rather than to construct a new facility, the current year's § 168 allowance for the equipment would have been currently deductible.

6.11 Purchased Intangibles; Code § 197

Suppose X Corporation buys the entire business of Y Corporation for a purchase price of $5 million, of which $3 million represents the value of tangible property—plant and equipment— and $2 million represents the value of Y's "goodwill," that is, the excess of the value of the business as a going concern over the separate value of its tangible assets. The $2 million goodwill value reflects a number of special elements, including Y's well-established customer base and its reputation for reliability and prompt customer service. Having paid $5 million for the business as a whole, X wants to know what its basis will be in the several Y assets for the purpose of calculating annual depreciation under Code § 167.

Prior to 1993 the answer would be $3 million, the cost of the acquired tangibles. Plant and equipment are of course depreciable, and X is plainly entitled to recover its basis in those assets through annual depreciation allowances in the usual manner. To be sure, X also has a basis of $2 million for the goodwill. But goodwill, like land or corporate stock, has traditionally been regarded as an asset of indefinite useful life and, as such, deemed non-amortizable. Cost recovery would therefore be postponed until the goodwill itself was disposed of, presumably through a sale of the acquired business to yet another purchaser. In that event—but only then—X would be entitled to offset its unrecovered investment against the sale proceeds.

Faced with this painful limitation (again, prior to 1993), taxpayers in X's position often attempted to separate out and identify some particular intangible—customer-lists and supply contracts were the usual candidates—for which a finite or determinable useful life could be established. The Commissioner generally opposed that effort, and disputes were frequent. In the *Newark Morning Ledger* case,[91] the Supreme Court permitted a corporation that purchased a chain of newspapers to amortize that portion—some $68 million—of the total purchase price that was allocable to "paid subscribers." Using expert testimony, the taxpayer was able to show the approximate rate—14 years for one paper, 23 for another—at which existing subscriptions could be expected to lapse, whether because the subscriber died, moved away or simply failed to renew. Dissenting, Justice Souter argued in effect that customer patronage was within the "settled meaning" of "goodwill"; hence, under rules of long standing, annual amortization was impermissible even if the taxpayer's self-serving statistical projections were accepted as valid.

Section 197, enacted in 1993, supersedes the *Newark Morning Ledger* decision and has put an end to most controversies between taxpayers and the government over the treatment of purchased intangibles. Under § 197, the cost of most intangibles acquired in connection with the purchase of a business—but most particularly goodwill or going-concern value—is recovered on a straight-line basis over a fifteen-year period. The list of intangible assets to which the provision applies is a long one and includes (besides goodwill) franchises, trademarks, know-how, customer lists, covenants not to compete, and more. The fifteen-year term is admittedly arbitrary. In some instances—for example, non-compete agreements with terms of less than fifteen years—§ 197 actually lengthens the period of amortization for which the intangible would otherwise qualify. The statutory approach is generally known as "rough justice," with accuracy being sacrificed for convenience and simplicity.

As stated, § 197 puts to rest an issue that has been the source of frequent dispute and for that reason alone is welcome. From the standpoint of "tax theory," on the other hand, the idea of permitting purchased goodwill to be amortized can be questioned. Put very simply, while the tangible assets purchased by X (in the hypothetical above) will in fact wear out and be used up over a period of years, the goodwill acquired by X from Y should not. Thus, X will certainly take steps to maintain the value of the acquired goodwill by spending money on advertising, sales promotion, customer relations, etc., just as Y did when the business belonged to it. Under settled practice (see 6.03(b)), those outlays, although made for the purpose of maintaining or enhancing the value of a capital asset, are themselves treated as currently deductible business expenses. In combination, then, the taxpayer is permitted both (1) to amortize a capital asset that is presumed (by § 197) to have a limited useful life, but then also (2) to

---

[91] *Newark Morning Ledger Co. v. U.S.*, 507 U.S. 546 (1993).

deduct as a current expense the annual cost of "rebuilding" that asset in order to prevent its useful life from ever coming to an end. As our earlier discussion of "repairs" should suggest, (1) and (2) are essentially in conflict. If goodwill is permitted to be amortized, then advertising should be treated as a capital expenditure. If advertising is treated as a current expense, then goodwill should be regarded as a non-amortizable perpetuity. Allowing both annual amortization *and* current expense deductions amounts to doubling-up.

The latter point can be illustrated by a hypothetical based on the *Newark Morning Ledger* case. Suppose $1.5 million of the purchase price of a newspaper is properly allocable to the paper's subscriber list. Suppose also that if the purchasing taxpayer did nothing to replace departing subscribers, the list would decline in value at the rate of $100,000 per year, thus becoming worthless at the end of fifteen years (precisely as § 197 would have it). But the taxpayer spends $100,000 each year on advertising to attract new subscribers, with the result that the number of subscribers—and thus the value of the list—never changes. At the end of fifteen years, the taxpayer will have spent $3.0 million on the subscription list ($1.5 million at the outset, and $100,000 each year for fifteen years thereafter), and the list will be worth (as always) $1.5 million. By the end of the fifteen years, then, the taxpayer should have been allowed deductions totaling $1.5 million, and should have a $1.5 million basis in the list. The theoretically correct way to reach that result would involve treating the advertising costs as capital expenditures rather than as current deductions, and allowing amortization deductions for the list. In a two-wrongs-making-a-right sort of way, however, pre-§ 197 rules produced the correct bottom-line tax treatment by allowing current deductions for advertising expenses and not allowing amortization of the cost of the list. With the combination of deductible advertising and § 197, however, the result under current law at the end of the fifteen years will be total deductions of $3 million (half as advertising expenses and half under § 197) and a zero basis in the list.

7. Personal Expense Deductions

7.01 General Comment

Much of the discussion in Section 6 was directed at the distinction between business and personal expenditures. Though sometimes difficult to formulate, that distinction is vital to the concept of a tax on "income". Personal consumption expenses must obviously be treated as non-deductible on the whole; if they were allowed, the individual tax base could be eliminated through expenditures on personal living items and the notion of a tax on economic gain would have been abandoned. Yet despite this general approach, the Code does permit deductions for a variety of expenses which are clearly personal in character. Medical expenses, casualty losses (but only if related to a federally-declared disaster), contributions to charity, interest on home-mortgage loans, and state and local income and property taxes are the most important examples of personal expenses which are allowable (subject to significant limitations) in computing individual taxable income. Since these allowances represent departures from the concept of economic gain as the relevant tax base, it is reasonable to ask what justifies or explains their presence in the tax law. That question is the more urgent because deductions of any kind necessarily generate larger tax benefits for high- than for low-bracket taxpayers, and in that respect detract from the progressivity of the income tax.

From the standpoint of their purpose or effect, the personal expense deductions allowed to individuals can be divided into three categories. The first includes involuntary and unexpected outlays which are large enough to exhaust a significant proportion of a taxpayer's annual income. Extraordinary medical expenses are an obvious example; a taxpayer who is hit with large medical bills for herself or for a member of her family is plainly less well off than a taxpayer with equal income whose family is healthy, and a tax law that failed to recognize her loss in taxpaying capacity would appear harsh. The same can be said of casualty losses involving personal property, such as a car or a home. A taxpayer whose house has been damaged by a hurricane suffers a reduction in personal wealth (unless she is reimbursed by insurance) which many would agree should entitle her to be differentiated from taxpayers who have escaped disaster.

The second category of personal expense deductions includes outlays which Congress wishes to encourage and subsidize. A clear example is the deduction for contributions to charity. Unlike medical expenses, charitable contributions are voluntary and represent the donor's personal choice among all of his various consumption alternatives. By permitting this "good", but not others, to be paid for in pre-tax dollars, the Code obviously intends to make charitable giving less expensive from the standpoint of donors. If a donor decides how much to give to charity based on the after-tax cost of giving, the donor acts as a conduit for the delivery of a subsidy from the federal government to the charity. Suppose, for example, a donor in the (hypothetical) 25% bracket would give $900 to a particular charity in the absence of a deduction for charitable contributions. Given the existence of the deduction, however, the donor can give the charity $1,200 at an after-tax cost of $900 (because the $1,200 deduction produces a tax saving of $300). If the donor accordingly increases his pre-tax contribution from $900 to $1,200, the effect is to transfer $300 from the government (in the form of lost tax revenue) to the charity (in the form of an increased contribution), with the donor acting as the middleman. This can be understood as a matching-grant subsidy, under which the government gives $1 to the taxpayer's favorite charity for every $3 (after-tax) given by the taxpayer. The higher the taxpayer's marginal tax rate, the more generous the matching grant formula becomes. While some critics have argued that private philanthropy should not be supported indirectly out of public funds, it seems probable that most people regard the activities of charities as socially desirable and would oppose withdrawal of the deduction.

Yet another, and a very important, example of a "subsidy" is the deduction permitted to homeowners for mortgage interest and local property taxes. Homeowners are favored by the tax law relative to apartment renters, both because the imputed income from homeownership is excluded from gross income (see 1.03) and because a portion of the owner's expenses are allowable as deductions (see 7.04). Apartment rents, of course, are non-deductible. The effect, quite obviously, is to encourage homeownership over tenancy by extending a substantial tax preference to those who choose to buy instead of rent.

The third category of personal expense deductions includes state and local taxes. Prior to 2017 legislation, taxpayers who itemized their deductions (rather than claiming the standard deduction) were permitted to deduct unlimited amounts of state and local real and personal property taxes, and income taxes—and were given the option to deduct unlimited amounts of state and local sales taxes in lieu of income taxes. (Both before and after the 2017 legislation, however, state and local taxes were not deductible for purposes of the alternative minimum tax (discussed at 7.10).) The Tax Cuts and Jobs Act of 2017 very controversially imposed a $10,000 ceiling on the total amount of state and local taxes (of all deductible types) that a taxpayer may deduct on a return.[92] Notice the strange contrast between (a) the $10,000 ceiling on deductible state and local taxes, which denies deductions to taxpayers who pay unusually large amounts of state and local taxes, and (b) the percentage-of-adjusted-gross-income floor of § 213 (10% or 7.5%, depending on the year), which allows deductions *only* to taxpayers with unusually large medical expenses.[93]

As of this writing, state legislatures in a number of "blue" states are considering various plans for end-runs around the $10,000 ceiling, by converting large portions of their state income taxes to either charitable deductions or payroll taxes imposed on (and

---

[92]   The provision can produce large marriage penalties; two unmarried taxpayers can deduct up to $20,000 between them, whereas a married couple is limited to $10,000.

[93]   The medical expense deduction is discussed at 7.02(a).

deductible by) employers. It remains to be seen what the states will actually do, and how Congress, the Treasury, the IRS, and the courts will respond. The next few years should be interesting.

Is the $10,000 ceiling justified from a disinterested policy perspective? We leave it to the reader to answer that question, but here are two points to consider in mulling it over. First, from the perspective of a theoretically pure "ideal" income tax, there is a strong argument that dollars one pays as state tax should not be deductible to the extent one receives services from the state in return for taxes paid, and should be deductible to the extent the state redistributes one's tax payments to others.[94] Second, the state and local tax deduction (to the extent it still exists) can plausibly be understood as a federal subsidy to state and local governments using taxpayers as conduits, under an analysis similar to the one offered above regarding the deduction for charitable contributions. The idea is that residents of a state are willing to accept higher state tax burdens given the deductibility of state taxes than the burdens they would tolerate absent deductibility. As noted earlier (3.01), federal income taxes are not deductible in any event.[95]

Critics of the personal expense deductions have argued over the years that the existing allowances are too generous, particularly in subsidizing voluntary outlays like charitable gifts and home-mortgage interest. Also, as stated, it has been objected that their impact is anti-progressive: the value of a deduction depends on the taxpayer's marginal tax rate; hence, high-bracket taxpayers enjoy the largest benefit per dollar of outlay for any allowable personal expense.[96] Partly in response to criticism of this sort, Congress in 1990 adopted an overall (yet selective) limitation on personal expense deductions, which purports to cut back slightly on the deductible amount for upper-income individuals. For technical reasons (the details of which we will spare the reader) the practical effect of § 68 is almost always to act as a disguised increase in a taxpayer's marginal tax rate, rather than to reduce the tax benefit derived from a taxpayer's marginal deductible expenditures. Under § 68, the itemized deductions otherwise allowable to a taxpayer are reduced by 3% of the excess of the taxpayer's adjusted gross income over an inflation-adjusted threshold amount (in 2017, $313,800 for a married couple filing a joint return, and $261,500 for a single taxpayer). Medical expenses and casualty losses, both being subject to

---

[94] For more on this issue, see "Another loose end" at the end of this section.

[95] Section 275.

[96] Pechman, *Federal Tax Policy* (1983) p. 91. Compare Andrews, *Personal Deductions in an Ideal Income Tax*, 86 Harv.L.Rev. 309 (1972), and Turnier, *Personal Deductions and Tax Reform: The High Road and the Low Road*, 31 Villanova L.Rev. 1703 (1986). And see Griffith, *Theories of Personal Deductions in the Income Tax*, 40 Hastings L.J. 343 (1989).

independent percentage limitations (see 7.02) and both being in the category of non-voluntary outlays, are exempt from reduction under § 68; also exempt is "investment interest," which really represents a cost of earning taxable income.[97] Section 68 does not apply in 2018 through 2025, but as of now it is scheduled to reappear in 2026.

Some other tax-favored personal expenses have already been mentioned or are mentioned later on. Thus, the credit for child-care expenses was briefly described at 6.01, and the allowance for personal bad debts at 6.08. The present section is limited to medical expenses and disaster losses, charitable contributions, home-mortgage interest and local property taxes. A few further remarks are made about the "standard deduction," and the concept of "adjusted gross income." The section concludes with a comment on the "earned income tax credit."

A loose end. This is as good a place as any to mention the concept of tax expenditures and the tax expenditure budget. Treasury Assistant Secretary of Tax Policy Stanley Surrey first propounded the tax expenditure concept in a 1967 speech. According to Surrey, the federal income tax features "a system of tax expenditures under which Governmental financial assistance programs are carried out through special tax provisions rather than through direct Government expenditures. This second system is grafted onto the structure of the income tax proper; it has no basic relation to that structure and is not necessary to its operation."[98]

The concept of tax expenditures is a bit fuzzy around the edges, because tax expenditures are to be defined by reference to a theoretically pure income tax, and there is room for argument about how to define the reference tax. Still, in most cases it is clear enough what is—and is not—a tax expenditure. The various personal deductions—especially the deductions for charitable contributions, home-mortgage interest, and state and local taxes—are prominent examples of tax expenditures. Of course, provisions designed to subsidize particular business activities—ACRS (6.10) being an obvious example—are also within the scope of the tax expenditure concept.

---

[97]   Discussed at 6.06, above.

[98]   Surrey, excerpts from remarks before the Money Marketeers on *The U.S. Income Tax System: The Need for a Full Accounting*, Nov. 15, 1967, in U.S. Department of Treasury, Annual Report of the Secretary of the Treasury on the State of the Finances for the Fiscal Year Ended June 30, 1968 (1969), at 322.

After returning to Harvard Law School, Surrey elaborated on the tax expenditure concept in a book published in 1973.[99] In 1974, largely in response to Surrey's advocacy, Congress enacted legislation requiring both the Congressional Budget Office (CBO) and the executive branch to prepare annual tax expenditure budget analyses. They have done so ever since, with the CBO relying on the staff of the Joint Committee on Taxation for production of its analyses, and with Treasury taking responsibility for the executive branch's analyses.

The revenue losses from the more significant tax expenditure items are truly impressive. For example, the Joint Committee on Taxation estimated the 2017 individual income tax revenue loss from the home-mortgage interest deduction at $63.6 billion, the revenue loss from the charitable deduction at $56.9 billion, and the revenue loss from the state and local tax deduction at $69.3 billion.[100] However, all these amounts should be significantly smaller in 2018 and later years, as a result of various aspects of the 2017 tax legislation—including new limitations on the deductibility of home mortgage interest and state and local taxes, major increases in standard deduction amounts, and reductions in marginal tax rates.

In Surrey's view, to identify a provision as a tax expenditure was to stigmatize it. His hope was that focusing congressional attention on tax expenditures by means of mandated annual reports would lead Congress to conclude that many tax expenditures were indefensible and should either be repealed outright or replaced with better-designed direct spending programs. Although Surrey succeeded in institutionalizing the tax expenditure budget exercise, a perusal of today's Internal Revenue Code will confirm that he did not succeed in his ultimate goal of removing most tax expenditures from the Code.

Another loose end. State and local governments supply a wide variety of "public" goods and services to their residents—schools, roads, parks, etc.—most or all of which fall into the category of personal consumption benefits. The overall cost of such goods and services is of course paid by the residents themselves in the form of state and local taxes. Is it consistent or inconsistent as a matter of "tax theory" to allow those taxes to be deducted? Ordinary consumption expenditures—"personal, living, or family expenses"— are not deductible if the good or service is purchased from a private source. Should the rule be different because the "seller" is a state or local government?

---

[99] Surrey, Pathways to Tax Reform (1973).

[100] Staff of the Joint Committee on Taxation, *Estimates of Federal Tax Expenditures for Fiscal Years 2016–2020* (JCX–3–17, January 30, 2017).

The answer may depend on whether you think (on the whole) that the individual taxpayer derives benefits from state and local government equivalent in value to the tax she pays. If so—if taxes paid and goods and services received are roughly equal—then perhaps *disallowance* is justified, as it would be if the taxpayer bought the same goods and services at the same price from a private supplier. On the other hand, if you think taxes paid and benefits received are unrelated or at least unequal, perhaps deductibility is proper. An individual who pays more in taxes than she realizes in benefits is thereby subsidizing the benefits received by others. In effect, the taxpayer is giving up a portion of her income for the use of somebody else—not voluntarily, of course, but as a forced exaction.

Since it is difficult to compare one individual taxpayer with another *within* a state or locality, the issue, so stated, is hard to resolve. By contrast, comparing the residents of one state with the residents of another state on a *group* basis is easier. Tax levels obviously differ from state to state, some higher, some lower. It can be argued that federal deductibility favors individuals living in high-tax as compared with low-tax states, because the former enjoy greater public service benefits than the latter. Allowing state taxes to be deducted permits residents of high-tax states to "buy" their public service benefits—better schools, better roads, better parks—with pre-tax dollars and in that way shifts a part of the cost to residents of low-tax states whose public service benefits are smaller. But choice of residence is a matter of personal preference: if you decide to locate in a high-tax state because you wish to enjoy superior amenities, then the tax you pay is the tax you have *chosen* to pay; nobody made you live and pay taxes in one place rather than another.

Arguing along these lines prior to the 1986 Code revision, the Treasury itself urged Congress to eliminate the deduction for state and local taxes. Opposition was terrific, however, and in the end the disallowance proposal was abandoned. Perhaps Congress was right—or at least not wholly wrong—to reject the disallowance proposal. The analysis in the preceding paragraph assumed that the taxes imposed on residents of high tax states were used to provide various public service amenities to the same residents paying the taxes. If, instead, most of the taxes imposed on the more affluent residents were used for redistributive purposes—that is, to provide benefits to less affluent residents—the case for deductibility would be strengthened considerably.

In any event, the introduction of the $10,000 ceiling in 2017 can be understood as a belated and partial adoption of Treasury's proposal from the 1980's. The nondeductibility of state and local taxes under the alternative minimum tax (AMT, discussed at 7.10) is also a significant step in the direction of the Treasury proposal.

7.02 Medical Expenses, Health Insurance, and Casualty Losses

As noted above, the medical expense and casualty loss deductions serve similar purposes: the refinement of a taxpayer's net income base by excluding from it large and unanticipated outlays or losses that impair the individual's ability to meet her tax obligations. While the general intent is reasonably clear, there are, as usual, problems of classification and definition which test the scope or coverage of the provisions.

(a) Medical Expense

Code § 213(a) allows a deduction for all medical and dental expenses paid by the taxpayer (and not reimbursed by insurance) for herself, her spouse and dependents. Included are payments made during the year for diagnosis and treatment, prescription drugs (but not medicine-cabinet items like aspirins and bandages), and medical equipment, hospital care, and health and accident insurance. Under a 1990 amendment, the cost of elective cosmetic surgery—*e.g.*, face-lifts—is no longer deductible.

Section 213(a) limits the medical expense deduction to the amount which exceeds 10% (7.5%, in 2017 and 2018) of the taxpayer's "adjusted gross income" (roughly, gross income less trade or business expenses) for the year. An individual with $100,000 of adjusted gross income is thus denied deduction for the first $10,000 of the year's medical costs. The purpose of the limitation is, of course, to distinguish between recurring expenses which can be planned for in the family budget—annual check-ups, periodic visits to the dentist—and extraordinary outlays which impose a large and unexpected burden on the family's resources.

Since expenditures "prescribed" for sick people—a vacation in Florida; an air-conditioning unit—also frequently are made by healthy people as well, there are, inevitably, controversies over whether a particular outlay really constitutes an expenditure for medical care. In *Ochs v. Commissioner*,[101] for example, the taxpayer's wife, having had a serious throat operation, was advised by a doctor that her recovery would be impaired unless she was separated from her two young children, who caused her "nervousness and irritation." Accordingly, the children were sent off to boarding school. The taxpayer sought to deduct the school expense as an expenditure for medical care made necessary by his wife's condition.

Over a heart-rending dissent by Judge Frank, the Second Circuit denied the deduction on the ground that the outlay in question was a

---

[101] 195 F.2d 692 (2d Cir. 1952).

personal family expense within § 262 rather than a medical expense under § 213. In effect, the court distinguished between the direct costs of medical treatment, obviously deductible, and the increase in family living expenses which inevitably results from the illness of a parent, especially a full-time homemaker. As noted previously (1.03), while the imputed value of self-rendered household services is traditionally excluded from gross income, no equivalent deduction is allowed to those who prefer to pay for such services in cash and spend their free time doing other things. The question in *Ochs,* ultimately, was whether a deduction should be permitted when the family is *compelled* to purchase housekeeping services because of the homemaker's illness and inability to do housework, rather than from mere personal preference. It seems evident, even then, that Congress did not intend § 213 to have so large and indefinite a reach. The section speaks primarily of "medical care" and does not refer to other increased costs of illness. Hence the court was undoubtedly right, or at least consistent with congressional intent, in disallowing the children's boarding school expense.

In a widely publicized 2010 case, a divided Tax Court, sitting *en banc*, allowed a medical expense deduction for hormone therapy and male-to-female sex reassignment surgery.[102] The Court determined that the taxpayer's diagnosed condition of gender identity disorder qualified as a disease for purposes of § 213(d)(1)(A) (which defines a medical expense as an amount paid "for the diagnosis, cure, mitigation, treatment, or prevention of disease"), and that the hormone therapy and surgery qualified as treatments for the disease. The Court also held, however, that the costs of breast augmentation surgery were not deductible by reason of § 213(d)(9), which generally denies a deduction for "cosmetic surgery or other similar procedures."

Between the percentage-of-AGI floor on the medical expense deduction and the availability of the deduction only to taxpayers who itemize rather than claiming the standard deduction (7.06), most taxpayers are unable to claim deductions for most of their medical expenses. The tax laws provide two opportunities, however, for "end runs" around the limitations of § 213. First, § 223 allows a taxpayer to claim a deduction—without the application of a percentage-of-AGI floor and regardless of whether the taxpayer claims the standard deduction—for amounts contributed to a health savings account (HSA). To be eligible to make an HSA contribution, the taxpayer must be covered by a high deductible health plan (HDHP). In 2018, HSA contributions are deductible up to $3,450 (in the case of a taxpayer with self-only HDHP coverage) or $6,900 (in the case of a taxpayer with family HDHP coverage). Amounts in the HSA may

---

[102] *O'Donnabhain v. Commissioner,* 134 T.C. 34 (2010), *acq.* 2011–47 I.R.B.

then be used to pay medical expenses not covered by the HDHP. Second, a taxpayer employed by an employer offering a cafeteria plan (§ 125) may elect, late in one year, to have his cash salary reduced in the following year, with the employer contributing the amount of the salary reduction to a health flexible spending arrangement (health FSA) for the employee's benefit. In the following year, the employee can draw on his health FSA to pay for medical expenses not covered by insurance. The amounts contributed by the employer to the health FSA are excluded from the employee's gross income. It is not easy, as a policy matter, to reconcile the HSA and health FSA provisions with the otherwise-applicable limitations of § 213. One might reasonably conclude that Congress should either repeal the § 213 limitations or repeal the HSA and health FSA provisions.

Section 213(d) includes medical insurance within the definition of "medical care," so that premiums paid on a health insurance policy are deductible in the same way as direct medical expenses. Much more important is the fact that § 106 excludes health insurance premiums paid by an employer from the employee's *gross* income, in that way benefitting employees (by far the greater number) who do not find it worthwhile to itemize their personal expenses or who, if they did, would be subject to the 10% floor limitation. The legislative aim, obviously, is to encourage employers and employees to allocate to health insurance premiums a portion of what the employee would otherwise receive as taxable cash wages. The § 106 exclusion is actually a tax concession of huge proportions; in total dollar terms, it is the largest single exclusion allowed to individual taxpayers in the entire Code. The Joint Committee on Taxation estimated the 2017 revenue loss from § 106 at $164.7 billion and the revenue loss from § 213 at a relatively paltry $10.1 billion.[103] In the grand perspective, then, the exclusion is by far the more important provision. On the other hand, the deduction probably generates more interpretive controversies and more work for lawyers, and hence receives more attention in most books written for law students (including this book).

A loose end. Prior to 2010, policy analysts had long complained about a gap in federal subsidies for health insurance. Very low-income individuals and families were eligible for Medicaid, and most middle-middle and upper-middle income taxpayers received employer-provided health insurance and thus benefited from the § 106 exclusion. Lower-middle income taxpayers, however, were ineligible for Medicaid and often did not receive health insurance through their jobs (and so did not have anything to exclude under § 106). In theory they could buy their own health insurance and claim

---

[103] Staff of the Joint Committee on Taxation, *Estimates of Federal Tax Expenditures for Fiscal Years 2014–2018* (JCX–3–17, January 30, 2017).

a deduction under § 213, but in practice few could afford expensive non-group coverage. The 2010 health care legislation responded to these complaints by (among other things) enacting new § 36B, creating a "premium assistance credit" designed to cover much of the cost of health insurance for persons with incomes between 100% and 400% of the federal poverty level (with the generosity of the credit inversely related to income). The credit is refundable, which means that if the credit amount exceeds the claimant's pre-credit federal income tax liability, the claimant is nevertheless entitled to the full credit amount. The provision became effective in 2014, and survived several almost-successful repeal efforts in 2017.

(b) Casualty Losses

Section 165(c)(3) allows a deduction for unreimbursed casualty losses resulting from casualty, even though the property lost or damaged is of a personal character. In 2018 through 2025, however, a casualty loss is deductible only if it is attributable to a federally-declared disaster. It is not obviously fair to distinguish between a taxpayer "lucky" enough to have her home destroyed by a major hurricane and the doubly unlucky taxpayer whose home burns down in a single-fire, but such is the effect of the federal disaster requirement. Under § 165(h), personal casualty losses are allowed only to the extent that they exceed, in aggregate, 10% of adjusted gross income. In addition, deduction is denied for the first $100 of each casualty. No deduction is allowed for casualty insurance premiums, presumably because such premiums represent a cost of earning tax-free imputed income through personal use of the insured property.

The measure of the allowable casualty loss is simply the difference between the value of the property before and after the casualty, but not in excess of the taxpayer's adjusted basis in the property. If a residence which was purchased for $500,000 and has a value of only $400,000 is totally destroyed by a hurricane, the deductible loss is limited to $400,000. If the residence was worth $600,000 before the fire, the deduction is limited to the taxpayer's basis of $500,000. In the first case the decline in value from $500,000 to $400,000 is treated as a personal expense resulting from "use" (see 15.02). In the second case, the rise in value from $500,000 to $600,000 represents unrealized and untaxed property appreciation, and hence is not included in the taxpayer's cost.

7.03 Charitable Contributions

With exceptions to be noted, § 170(a) allows a deduction for contributions to charity up to a limit of 50% (up to 60% in the case of *cash* contributions made in 2018 through 2025) a taxpayer's adjusted gross income. Contributions are deductible only if made to an organization—educational, religious, scientific, etc.—which the statute describes as an eligible donee. Gifts to designated individuals are not deductible even if funneled through a charitable organization; and no deduction is allowed to the extent that the donor receives something of value, such as a raffle ticket or admission to an entertainment event, in return for her contribution. The 50% limitation appears generous from one standpoint, in that it allows free-handed donors to cut their taxable incomes in half (and, given progressive marginal rates, to reduce their tax liabilities by considerably more than 50%). From another standpoint, the presence of an upper limit shows that Congress was unwilling to permit the very rich to reduce their taxes to zero by turning over their entire incomes to charity and living out of savings.

Deduction is allowed under § 170(a) whether the taxpayer makes her contribution in money or in "property". Where the property has appreciated in the taxpayer's hands, a double benefit is allowed in most cases because the full value of the property (not merely its cost) is deductible, while the appreciation is *not* regarded as realized by virtue of the gift. To illustrate, suppose a taxpayer purchased certain shares of stock some years ago for $5,000. The stock is now worth $25,000 and the taxpayer, as it happens, is eager to donate $25,000 to her favorite charity. The taxpayer will be allowed to claim a $25,000 deduction, despite the fact that she has never included in income the $20,000 of appreciation. This violates the fundamental tax principle that deductions and losses should be limited to basis. If the tax system has never treated the taxpayer as having received the $20,000 appreciation, it cannot logically treat the taxpayer as losing (or donating) the appreciation. In a well-ordered tax system, the taxpayer would be allowed to claim a $25,000 deduction only if the donation was treated as a realization event triggering taxation of the $20,000 appreciation. (Notice, by the way, that taxation of the $20,000 gain coupled with allowance of a charitable deduction for the $20,000 would still be quite taxpayer-favorable if the gain is taxed at the 20% long-term capital gain rate and the deduction is allowed against ordinary income in the 37% bracket.) It seems that the rule allowing a deduction for unrealized appreciation in donated property developed early in the history of the income tax, as a simple conceptual error.[104] By the time the error was widely recognized as a violation of tax logic, however, it had developed a constituency among charitable organizations and their wealthy donors.

---

[104] The early history of this issue is surprisingly convoluted. For the details, see Chapter 4 of Zelenak, *Figuring Out the Tax: Congress, Treasury, and the Design of the Early Modern Income Tax* (2018).

In 1969 Congress modified the treatment of appreciated property under § 170, but as far as conventional gifts of appreciated securities are concerned the modification consists only of imposing a 30% limitation on the amount that can be deducted instead of the higher 50% limit. The effect of the restriction is not likely to be serious for most donors—especially as a five-year carryover of excess contributions is permitted—and it remains a standard item of promotion for charities (universities and art museums especially) to stress the tax benefits that result from making appreciated gifts in kind. On the other hand, in the case of property-gifts which entail even more serious tax avoidance potential—where a sale of the property would result in ordinary income (inventory, for example) or short-term capital gain—Congress acted more firmly by restricting the donor's deduction to the property's cost and disallowing the appreciation.[105] The deduction is also limited to basis in the case of contributions of tangible personal property (art, for example) if the use of the property by the charity is "unrelated to the purpose or function constituting the basis for its [tax] exemption."

Contributions of a taxpayer's services to a charity are closely analogous to contributions of appreciated property. In both cases, tax logic dictates that no deduction should be allowed for donations of amounts never taken into income. In the case of services, unlike the case of appreciated property, the law is consistent with the logic. Reg. § 1.170A–1(g) denies the service contributor any deduction for the value of her services. This makes perfect sense, of course, given that the contributor is not required to include in income the value of those services.

As noted above, no charitable deduction is allowed to the extent of any value received by the taxpayer from the charity in return for the taxpayer's contribution. Thus, if a taxpayer receives a $10 tote bag as a thank-you for making a $100 contribution to her local public radio station, her deduction is only $90. More significantly, even though most colleges and universities are eligible to receive tax-deductible contributions, amounts paid to them as tuition are not deductible as charitable contributions to any extent.

The § 170 quid-pro-quo rule was invoked by the Supreme Court in the 1989 *Hernandez* case.[106] The majority upheld the Service's disallowance of charitable deductions claimed by Scientologists for the fees they paid the Church of Scientology for religious services known as "auditing" and "training". In a strong dissent, Justice

---

[105] Compare the *Haverly* decision, discussed at 1.02, above. Code § 170(e)(1) now embodies our "solution #2" (in effect) by limiting the taxpayer's deduction to his cost—in *Haverly*, zero—where gain on a sale of the contributed property would not have qualified as long-term capital gain.

[106] *Hernandez v. Commissioner*, 490 U.S. 680 (1989).

O'Connor noted that the IRS routinely set aside quid-pro-quo principles when the benefits received by the payor were purely religious in nature. In a 1970 Revenue Ruling,[107] for example, the Service held that pew rents were fully deductible, despite the fact that they entitled the payor to occupy a particular pew during religious services. Justice O'Connor argued that the First Amendment did not permit the IRS to apply quid-pro-quo analysis to Scientologists, while not applying it to similarly-situated adherents of other faiths.

Four years later, as part of a comprehensive settlement of the many then-pending disputes between the IRS and the Church of Scientology, the IRS announced that it was abandoning the position it had successfully asserted before the Supreme Court in *Hernandez*.[108] Like Protestants paying pew rents, Catholics paying to have Masses said for special intentions, and Jews paying for tickets to High Holy Days services, Scientologists can now deduct the amounts they pay for "auditing". The *Hernandez* story illustrates that the IRS has the *de facto* power to overrule the Supreme Court, by giving up a victory it won in litigation before the Court.

7.04 Home Mortgage Interest

Before the 1986 Code revision, interest on personal borrowings of every kind was fully deductible by taxpayers who chose to itemize their personal expenses. Thus, interest on residential mortgages, on installment purchases of cars and home appliances, on vacation loans, credit cards and charge accounts—all such payments were allowable (to itemizers) under § 163(a), a section that made no distinction between borrowing for business and for personal reasons. Just *why* that distinction was lacking—it is of course central to the aim of § 162 and other deductible expense provisions—has never been very clear. As noted at 6.05, an interest deduction is plainly justified when the amounts borrowed are used to generate taxable income, but when the borrowing is used to finance current consumption (such as a vacation, or simply everyday living expenses) or the acquisition of consumer durables (such as a car or home) producing only nontaxable imputed income, the allowance of interest expense is arguably anomalous.

Largely for the latter reason, apparently, though with one major exception, the 1986 Act added § 163(h), which disallows deductions for "personal interest." Consumers' financing costs—even including interest on federal tax deficiencies—are now, like other consumer outlays, required to be paid out of after-tax income.

---

[107] Rev. Rul. 70–47, 1970–1 C.B. 49.

[108] Rev. Rul. 93–73, 1993–2 C.B. 75.

The big exception (without which passage of the Act would have been unlikely) is for interest on home mortgages. Generally, under § 163(h) home mortgage interest continues to be allowable as an itemized expense deduction. As amended in 2017, the statute permits the deduction of interest on only "acquisition indebtedness"—that is, debt incurred in order to purchase, construct, or improve a qualifying residence of the taxpayer. Interest on up to $750,000 (the amount is *not* subject to adjustment for inflation) of acquisition indebtedness is deductible.[109] Deduction for home mortgage interest is allowable not only with respect to the taxpayer's principal residence, but also with respect to one so-called second residence. In effect, Congress was induced to give vacation homes preferred status, a decision that instantly (and successfully) raised a claim from boat owners that nothing in the term "residence" excludes a home at sea. The regulations make clear that a qualified residence need not be real property; yachts, trailers, and motorhomes can all qualify.[110]

Home mortgage interest, when added to residential property taxes, bulks large among all the itemized deductions. As noted at 7.06, personal expenses are worth itemizing only to the extent that the total of such expenses exceeds (in 2018) $24,000 on joint returns or $12,000 for single persons. Presumably, however, most middle-income taxpayers do not regularly incur deductible expenses in excess of the $24,000 (or $12,000) figure apart from expenses that are residence-related. Hence, if home mortgage interest and property taxes were not allowed, relatively few would find it worthwhile to itemize at all. Homeowners as a group (a very large group, to be sure) are thus the principal beneficiaries of the whole expense-itemization scheme. However, in the aftermath of the 2017 legislation—taking into account the increase in the standard deduction amounts, the decrease in the dollar cap on home acquisition indebtedness, and the $10,000 ceiling on the deductibility of state and local taxes—it is expected that less than 10% of taxpayers will itemize their deductions in 2018 and later years. Thus, even most homeowners will not benefit from the newly-revised version of the expense-itemization scheme.

Is it "equitable" and consistent with the net income concept to permit homeowner-mortgagors to deduct their mortgage interest? The answer (unfortunately) is yes-and-no; it all depends on with whom the mortgagor is being compared. If the comparison is with a homeowner who owns her residence free and clear, the interest deduction allowed to the mortgagor is equitable. The free-and-clear

---

[109] Prior to the 2017 legislation, the ceiling on acquisition indebtedness was $1 million. A transition rule retains the $1 million ceiling for debt incurred on or before December 15, 2017.

[110] Reg. § 1.163–10T(p)(3)(ii).

owner earns imputed income on her investment which is regarded, by fixed tradition (1.03), as exempt from tax. The mortgagor's interest deduction simply puts her on an equal footing. But if the comparison is with an apartment-dweller or other tenant who rents her home, then the interest deduction gives the mortgagor a clear advantage. The reason, obviously, is that the tenant gets no deduction for her cash rental payments, because these are treated as a nondeductible personal expense.[111] As noted previously, the basic inconsistency in the law arises from the fact that the imputed rental value of owner-occupancy is not taxable, while cash rental payments are not deductible. Mortgage interest is in a sort of swing position between the two: allowing the interest as a deduction creates equity in one direction but not the other; disallowing it would have the same effect, but the directions would be reversed.

To illustrate all this, compare four representative individuals: Outright Owner, Old Mortgagor, Young Mortgagor, and Tenant. Each of the first three buys a home for $200,000. Tenant rents a home of the same value.

Outright Owner buys her home for cash—no mortgage.

Old Mortgagor has bonds worth $200,000 that yield $12,000 a year in taxable interest. She could sell those securities but she doesn't want to, and instead prefers to buy her home with a mortgage loan of $200,000.

Young Mortgagor has no savings to speak of, so she, too, takes out a $200,000 mortgage loan and expects to pay her mortgage interest out of her salary income.

Finally, Tenant, like Young Mortgagor, has no savings and expects to use her salary to pay her rent.

The homes belonging to Outright Owner, Old Mortgagor and Young Mortgagor all yield gross imputed rent of $16,000 a year. Annual depreciation, not deductible, is $4,000, so the net imputed rent is $12,000. For both Old Mortgagor and Young Mortgagor the annual mortgage payment is $16,000, of which $12,000 is deductible interest and $4,000 is principal, which is not deductible. Finally, T's apartment rent, not deductible, is $16,000 a year.

The four taxpayers all pay tax at a (hypothetical) marginal rate of 30%.

---

[111] It is possible, however, that tax benefits conferred on the renter's landlord—most notably, ACRS deductions and deferral of tax on unrealized appreciation in the rental unit—may be, to some extent, passed on to the renter in the form of lower rents.

Here is how they compare:

		Out-right	Old Mort	Young Mort	Ten't
1.	Gross imputed rent from occupancy	$16,000	$16,000	$16,000	$16,000
2.	Less:				
a.	Depreciation/principal	4,000	4,000	4,000	
b.	Rental payment	_____	_____	_____	16,000
3.	Net imputed rent (1 minus 2)	12,000	12,000	12,000	–0–
4.	Taxable income:				
a.	Net imputed rent	–0–	–0–	–0–	–0–
b.	Interest		12,000		
c.	Wages			12,000	12,000
d.	Less: mortgage interest	_____	(12,000)	(12,000)	_____
		–0–	–0–	–0–	12,000
5.	After-tax yield on $200,000 investment	$12,000	$12,000		
6.	After-tax wages			$12,000	$ 8,400

The effect of § 163 in these circumstances is to place the two Mortgagors in the same favorable position as Outright Owner, while leaving Tenant to absorb a 30% tax on her wages. It is easy enough to argue that Tenant is treated inequitably as compared with the other three, and that the "solution" is to require both Outright Owner and the two Mortgagors to include their "net imputed rent" in income. But if this step is ruled out, whether for administrative or political reasons, the proper treatment of the two Mortgagors becomes uncertain. The latter, obviously, could argue that to disallow their mortgage interest deductions would place them at a disadvantage relative to Outright Owner, and that this would be unfair. But it is equally true that allowing the interest deductions gives the Mortgagors an advantage over Tenant, which is unfair to Tenant. In any case, if the Code *were* amended to disallow the deduction of mortgage interest, Old Mortgagor (but not Young; see below) could sell her bonds and pay her mortgage down to zero so as to obtain the same benefit from the imputed income exclusion as is now received by Outright Owner. In reality, then, it is the net imputed rent exclusion, rather than the interest deduction, that is responsible for the lack of tax equity in this area.

One further comparison might be noticed. Although one doesn't usually think of home ownership in such terms, the fact is that both Old and Young Mortgagor are enjoying a "tax arbitrage" as described at page 169, above. Imputed rent is excluded from gross income, while home mortgage interest is deducted by taxpayers who itemize. Precisely that combination—exclusion of incoming and deduction of outgoing—constitutes a classical tax arbitrage which, in any other context, urgently requires a Code remedy. Usually, the remedy takes the form of disallowing the interest deduction leg of the arbitrage device. That is true under § 265(a)(2), for example, in the case of interest paid on funds borrowed to buy tax-exempt municipal bonds. But no such limitation is imposed on home mortgage interest (subject to the several restrictions described above). The reason, of course, is that homeownership is at the heart of the American Dream, at least as Congress dreams it. Also, a taxpayer can only occupy one home at a time and thus can generate only so much exempt imputed income. Municipal bond interest is obviously available in virtually unlimited amounts.

The American Dream rationale can be extended to illustrate one more structural point, again by comparing home mortgages with municipal bond financing. As observed at page 174, § 265(a)(2) makes a distinction, in effect, between investment income and personal service income. The disallowance of interest deductions under § 265(a)(2) obviously affects those taxpayers who would have to borrow to buy municipal bonds—presumably wage and salary earners—but has no effect on investors who can self-finance by selling taxable securities and reinvesting in municipals. The aim, apparently, is to prevent the exemption for municipal bond interest from being used, through borrowing, to offset personal service income. With this in mind, we can compare Old Mortgagor and Young Mortgagor. Old M, as noted, could achieve the same preferred tax position as Outright Owner by selling her taxable bonds and paying off her mortgage. Even if the home mortgage interest deduction were disallowed, therefore, Old M could easily obtain the benefit of the imputed income exclusion, just as an investor can obtain the benefit of the municipal bond exemption by switching from taxable securities to municipals.

The same would not be true for Young M, who owns no securities and has to finance her home-purchase by using salary income to meet her mortgage interest obligation. Happily for Young M, however, the Code contains nothing equivalent to § 265(a)(2) in the home mortgage area. Putting it differently, the "tax arbitrage" mentioned above extends to personal service income in Young M's case, with the consequence that homeownership is made easier for younger taxpayers.

* * *

Having scattered our discussion of this topic, it may help to note that "interest"—at least those interest expenses most likely to be encountered by taxpayers generally—is now subject to a *fourfold* classification under the Code:

(1) Interest incurred in the conduct of an active trade or business. For example, a company (proprietorship or partnership) borrows money from a bank to finance its operating expenses. Interest costs of this kind are generally deductible from gross income like any other business expense (subject to the new limitations imposed by § 163(j), described at 6.06(a)).

(2) Investment interest. For example, an individual maintains a margin account with her broker and borrows money to finance her securities investments. As indicated at 6.06(a), § 163(d) limits the deduction of investment interest in any taxable year to an amount not in excess of the taxpayer's investment income, with disallowed amounts being carried forward to later years. Also as indicated, interest on debt incurred to finance certain tax-exempt investments—*e.g.*, municipal bonds—remains nondeductible.

(3) Interest taken into account in determining a taxpayer's income or loss from what the Code oxymoronically refers to as a "passive activity." For example, a limited partnership borrows funds to finance the purchase of depreciable real estate. For the reasons given at 13.02, § 469 restricts the deduction of losses attributable to passive activities to the income *from* such passive activities, and thus bars the taxpayer from reducing taxable income derived from other sources.

(4) Consumer interest: disallowed by § 163(h) except for interest on home acquisition indebtedness.

From the standpoint of deductibility, therefore, the "best" kind of interest is generally active business interest, allowable subject to the least onerous restrictions. Second, perhaps, is home acquisition indebtedness interest, allowable subject to the $750,000 ceiling on qualifying indebtedness, provided that the taxpayer itemizes deductions rather than claiming the standard deduction. More or less tied for third would be investment interest and passive activity interest: both are allowable, but both are restricted to offsetting income from related sources only. Dead last is non-residential consumer interest, which is not allowable at all.

Because of the different deductibility rules for different types of interest, there is a need for rules explaining how particular dollars of interest expense are to be assigned to the various categories. Generally speaking, the Regulations adopt a tracing approach, under which interest is assigned to a category based on how the taxpayer used the loan proceeds to which the interest relates.[112] Given the fungibility of money, this tracing rule provides significant tax planning opportunities. Suppose you have just graduated from law school, and you plan to begin practicing as a solo practitioner. You want to buy office furniture and equipment costing $50,000, and you also want to buy a new car (for personal use) costing $50,000. You can make one purchase with your own money, but you will have to borrow the $50,000 for the other purchase. Does it make any tax difference what you buy with your own money and what you buy with the borrowed money? It certainly does. If you use the borrowed money to buy the office furniture and equipment, the interest will be fully deductible active business interest. But if you use the borrowed money to buy the car, the interest will be non-deductible personal interest.

7.05 Miscellaneous Deductions

For historical reasons of no great importance, the Code distinguishes (in the case of individual taxpayers) between "trade or business" expenses, allowable under § 162(a), and expenses incurred in managing investment property such as a securities portfolio. The latter are deductible under § 212 provided they meet the usual criteria of "ordinary and necessary," current rather than capital expenditure, and so on. As these are the same criteria that apply to trade or business expenses, one might suppose that investment-related outlays would simply be netted off against investment income—in effect, be deducted from gross income to reach *adjusted* gross income—in the same way that business expenses are netted off against business income. Not so. Presumably in order to minimize recordkeeping and simplify returns for taxpayers electing the standard deduction, § 62(a) requires that most investment-related expenses (as well as unreimbursed employee business expenses) be deducted from adjusted gross income in the same manner as allowable *personal* expenses. The result is that "miscellaneous deductions" of the sort described are never of any benefit to those taxpayers (over 90% of all taxpayers, under current law) who claim the standard deduction.

For itemizing taxpayers, however, the "miscellaneous deduction" category long served as a handy repository for all kinds of expenditures, some of them only doubtfully qualifying for deduction

---

[112] Reg. § 1.163–8T.

in the first place. One familiar example would be subscriptions to newspapers and periodicals. Is a subscription to the *New York Times* or *Wall Street Journal* deductible under § 212 because it helps keep the subscriber abreast of political and economic news that affects her investment planning? Presumably not, but the subscriber is likely in many cases to resolve the doubt (or rather *her* doubt) in favor of deduction anyway. Hypotheticals in the fields of education and travel may also come to mind—for example, a law professor traveling on his own dime to the annual law school convention, which is generally held in some city attractive to tourists. In effect, the "miscellaneous deduction" category may stimulate the itemizing taxpayer to find *something* that belongs there—"errors of law" in this connection are perhaps not uncommon—with the consequence that the Service's auditing burdens are increased.

To reduce those burdens, the 1986 Act added § 67, which provides that "miscellaneous itemized deductions" shall be allowed only to the extent that the sum of all such deductions exceeds 2% of the taxpayer's adjusted gross income. Deduction of small-scale outlays—subscriptions, unreimbursed employee business expenses (typically for allegedly business-related travel), safe-deposit rentals, tax-return preparers' fees—was thus effectively eliminated for most individuals.

As if that were not bad enough (from the perspective of taxpayers who would like to claim miscellaneous itemized deductions), 2017 legislation has made § 67 even more draconian. In 2018 through 2025, miscellaneous itemized deductions are not deductible to any extent under any circumstances. At least in the case of unreimbursed employee business expenses, complete nondeductibility finds support in the commonsense notion that, if the expense were really necessary for the employee to do his job, the employer would have footed the bill. The 2%-of-AGI floor is scheduled to reappear in 2026, although it will not be surprising if Congress decides to extend the complete disallowance rule.

A reader of § 67 will find it is written in a counterintuitive—even backwards—sort of way. Instead of listing the itemized deduction types which *are* miscellaneous itemized deductions, it lists the types which are *not*. Thus, the inclusion in the § 67 list of deductions for (among other things) home mortgage interest, state and local taxes, and charitable contributions, means those deductions are *not* subject to the strictures of § 67.

––––––––––

A loose end. We should clarify that *employee* business expenses are treated very differently under Code § 62 depending on whether such expenses are reimbursed by the taxpayer's employer or paid by the taxpayer himself without reimbursement. In the usual case, an employee who incurs expenses in the course of his employment will be reimbursed by the employer on whose behalf the expenses were incurred. Thus, a law firm associate travels to another city to see a client. Hotel, meal, and transportation expenses are likely to be charged directly to the firm or, if paid by the associate, reimbursed on presentation of the relevant credit card receipts. Rarely would an employee incur unreimbursed employment expenses, although it may happen under special circumstances.

Code § 62(a) provides (in a somewhat confusing way) that employee business expenses are allowable in determining adjusted gross income only if such expenses are reimbursed "under a reimbursement or other expense allowance arrangement with [the taxpayer's] employer." If reimbursed, as they usually would be, employee business expenses are treated as "above-the-line" expenses and are deductible from gross income. To make life easier for individual employees, the Regulations[113] permit the taxpayer-employee to exclude the reimbursements from his gross income (rather than including and then deducting a long list of expense items), provided that the employee has properly accounted for his expenses to his employer. The law firm associate above can simply disregard his reimbursed travel expenses in making out his own tax return. The law firm itself, of course, or the client if the expense is passed on as a "disbursement," would treat the associate's reimbursed travel as a deductible business expense under § 162(a). By contrast, if an employee business expense is unreimbursed, it can be deducted by the taxpayer-employee only as a miscellaneous itemized deduction—meaning it cannot be deducted at all, in 2018 through 2025.

7.06 Standard Deduction and Adjusted Gross Income

As a result of 2017 legislation, over 90% of all individual taxpayers are expected to take the standard deduction in lieu of itemizing their allowable personal expenses. (In earlier years, roughly two-thirds of individual taxpayers claimed the standard deduction.) Introduced in 1944 as a means of reducing the need for individual recordkeeping, the standard deduction has increased in amount over the years and in 2018 stands at $24,000 for married couples, $18,000 for unmarried heads of households, and $12,000 for other single persons (with all dollar amounts to be adjusted for inflation in later years). Thus, all married taxpayers who elect the standard deduction are, in effect, taxed at a rate of zero on their first $24,000 of income. Taxpayers who incur allowable personal expenses

---

[113] Reg. § 1.62–2(c)(4).

in excess of the standard deduction amount will still want and be entitled to itemize such expenses and deduct them from adjusted gross income, but, of course, as a practical matter it is only the excess over the standard deduction that generates a tax benefit.

The term "adjusted gross income," as defined in § 62, means the taxpayer's gross income less her deductions of the types listed in § 62. These listed ("above-the-line") deductions are primarily for trade or business expenses (other than unreimbursed employee business expenses), but also include (among other things) deductions for contributions to individual retirement accounts (IRAs) and interest on education loans. Adjusted gross income serves as the base-point for determining certain of the personal expense deductions—in particular, those that are phased out for higher-income taxpayers, and those that are allowable only to the extent they exceed a certain percentage of income. If these restrictions were calculated by reference to *gross* income, the results would frequently be illogical or unfair. For example, a businessperson with $400,000 of gross income and $300,000 of business expenses would be allowed to deduct her medical expenses only to the extent that they exceeded $40,000 (10% of $400,000), whereas a taxpayer with a salary of $100,000 could deduct all such expenses in excess of $10,000. But as each taxpayer has the same $100,000 of net income after business expenses, it is plain that the 10% floor should also be the same for both.

In effect, then, adjusted gross income represents the taxpayer's gross income from all sources, reduced by the business expenses described in Section 6, and by certain other favored deductions. The standard deduction or, alternatively, the itemized deductions described in this Section, are then subtracted from adjusted gross income in order to reach "taxable income" under § 63. The latter, of course, is the figure to which the rate schedule is finally applied in arriving at the individual's tax liability for the year.

For nearly the entire history of the federal income tax, a taxpayer was entitled to claim a personal exemption (in effect, a deduction) for herself, her spouse, and each of her dependents (as defined in §§ 151 and 152). The amount of the exemption was adjusted annually for inflation; in 2017 the amount was $4,050. Personal exemptions were generally understood as serving a dual purpose. First, in combination with the standard deduction, personal exemptions served to exempt from tax persons with incomes at or below the poverty level; personal exemptions adjusted the tax-free poverty level based on family size. Second, personal exemptions also adjusted tax liabilities for differences in family size at income levels well above poverty. Suppose, for example, that one married couple with $100,000 income had no children, while another couple with the same income had four children. One might conclude that the childless couple had greater ability to pay tax than the couple with four children, and thus should have a somewhat higher tax liability. By allowing the former couple only two exemptions, while allowing the latter couple six exemptions, the personal exemption rules produced that result.

Legislation enacted in 2017, however, provides that the personal exemption amount is zero (a rather strange, or perhaps lawyerly, way of expressing the unavailability of exemptions) in 2018 through 2025. As consolation for the loss of their exemptions, taxpayers received two new benefits—a near-doubling of the standard deduction (for married couples, for example, from $12,700 in 2017 to $24,000 in 2018), and (as described in 7.07 immediately below) a doubling of the child tax credit from $1,000 to $2,000. The increases in the standard deduction amounts, combined with the denial of personal exemptions, can be understood as a folding of the personal exemptions into the standard deduction. Notice, however, that many taxpayers will be disadvantaged (relative to prior law) by that approach, even if the amount of the new standard deduction equals or exceeds the sum of the old standard deduction and their old personal exemptions. Imagine, for example, a married couple with potential itemized deductions of $23,000. Under current law, they will claim a $24,000 standard deduction and will get no tax benefit from their potential itemized deductions. If the law instead entitled them to, say, a $12,000 standard deduction and two exemptions of $4,000 each (adding up to only $20,000), they could claim $23,000 of itemized deductions *and* two personal exemptions of $4,000 each, resulting in total deductions of $31,000–$7,000 more than under the actual law.

———

A loose end. Before 1983, under a long-standing administrative practice (which reflected congressional intent), Social Security benefits were wholly excluded from the recipient's gross income no matter how much income (dividends, rents, etc.) he or she received from other sources. This was true even though only half of the contributions paid in during the recipient's working life had come out of his or her own after-tax income—the other half having been paid in by his or her employer but never taxed to the individual worker. Concluding that this arrangement was too generous to higher-income retirees, Congress adopted § 86, which may require inclusion in gross income of as much as 85% of the benefits received annually if the recipient's income exceeds $44,000 (in the case of married couples) or $34,000 (for single persons).

7.07   The Child Tax Credit and Dependent Care Credit

(a)   Child Tax Credit

The much-proclaimed child tax credit, supported by President Clinton and by congressional leaders of both parties, entered the law in 1997, and was doubled in amount in 2017. At its simplest, § 24 allows a credit against tax for each child under the age of 17 at the close of the taxable year. (The seventeenth birthday is a rather strange cut-off date for the credit; the typical 17-year-old has not yet graduated from high school, and is not becoming less expensive to support as he grows older.) The credit amount is $2,000 times the number of the taxpayer's "qualifying children." The credit begins to phase out when the taxpayer's adjusted gross income reaches the "threshold amount" of $400,000 for married couples, or $200,000 for single parents. Under § 24(b), the allowable credit is reduced by $50 for each $1,000 of adjusted gross income above the threshold amount. For a couple with more than one child, the phase-outs of the several credits operate consecutively, rather than concurrently. (The statutory language itself is hopelessly ambiguous on the issue of concurrent versus consecutive phase-outs, but the IRS has adopted the relatively taxpayer-favorable consecutive phase-out interpretation.) For a married couple with one qualifying child, the credit would be phased out completely once adjusted gross income reached $440,000; for a couple with two children, the phase-out would be complete once adjusted gross income reached $480,000. In both cases, the phase-out functions as a hidden increase of five percentage points in the taxpayers' effective marginal tax rate, over the entire range of the phase-out. If a taxpayer's child is older than 17 but still qualifies as a dependent (for example, a full-time student younger than 24), there is a $500 credit in lieu of the $2,000 credit for younger children.

Following a liberal-vs.-conservative debate about the proper role of the child tax credit—whether a subsidy for low-income families (lib.) or merely a tax-reduction measure (cons.)—Congress compromised by making the credit partially refundable, in that way providing a limited benefit to parents whose pre-credit income tax for the year is less than the credit amount or who owe no income tax at all. Under § 24(d), the credit is refundable to the extent of 15% of the amount by which earned income exceeds $2,500. If, for example, a married couple with one child had earned income of $15,000, their regular tax would be zero after subtracting the standard deduction. The couple would then be entitled to a refund of $1,875—the lesser of (i) the usual $2,000 credit amount for one child, or (ii) 15% of $12,500 ($15,000 minus $2,500). Now suppose the same parents had earned income of $15,834. Their regular tax would still be zero but the refundable credit would go up to a full $2,000—15% of $13,334 ($15,834 minus $2,500). The refund amount actually increases (up to $2,000) as the parents earn more. In effect, § 24(d) produces a *negative* marginal tax rate, under which the government gives the parents a larger transfer payment as their income increases (over a limited range). (For the right to an additional refund under the Earned Income Tax Credit—which, as it happens, features negative marginal tax rates over some income ranges and positive rates over others—see 7.08, below.)

(b) Dependent Care Credit

The Board of Tax Appeals' decision in the *Smith* case (6.01(a)) made it clear at an early point that child care expenses are not deductible as business expenses under § 162(a) even when incurred— in *Smith* by a working wife and mother—as a necessary cost of taking a job outside the home. Along with the other customary expenses of the working day—commuting, restaurant lunches, etc.—child care costs continue to be treated as "personal" and non-deductible even though very plainly an added charge on family income, especially in the case of two-earner families and single parents. Since 1954, however, the Code has permitted working couples and single parents with dependent children to take a limited nonrefundable credit against tax for child care and housekeeping expenses. Under § 21, subject to the phase-down rule below, an individual who pays child care expenses enabling him or her to be employed may take a credit against tax of 35% on $3,000 of such expenses annually if there is one qualifying child, or on $6,000 of such expenses if there are two or more qualifying children. The maximum credit is thus $1,050 if there is one child, $2,100 if two or more. The $3,000 and $6,000 ceilings on credit-generating expenses are not indexed for inflation, and Congress has increased the ceilings only once (and modestly) since the 1970's. If the ceilings of the 1970's had been indexed for inflation, today they would be roughly five times their current amounts.

The 35% credit rate is reduced by one percentage point for each $2,000 (or fraction thereof) of adjusted gross income above $15,000, but cannot be reduced below 20%. So, a taxpayer with two dependent children, adjusted gross income of $45,000, and child care expenses of $8,000 would be entitled to a credit of $1,200; that is, $6,000, the maximum amount of employment-related expenses permitted to be taken into account, times 20%, the credit percentage as reduced by the taxpayer's adjusted gross income in excess of $15,000.[114]

---

[114] As noted earlier (6.01(a)), § 129 provides an alternate route to a tax benefit— in the case of § 129, an exclusion—for amounts spent on child care, but only if the taxpayer-parent's employer offers a dependent care assistance program (DCAP).

7.08 EITC

Previously fairly modest in its aims and revenue cost, the Earned Income Tax Credit (EITC) was greatly expanded in 1993 and now plays a major role in our national anti-poverty system. Simply put, EITC is an earnings subsidy for low-wage working families. Other more traditional family anti-poverty programs—of which Temporary Assistance to Needy Families (TANF) and the Supplemental Nutrition Assistance Program (SNAP) are the most significant—provide benefits to people who qualify for assistance on the basis of "need" and who might be unemployed and have no earnings whatever. By contrast, EITC ("pro-work, pro-family") is a program that benefits working people only. In effect, the subsidy is directed at, and largely confined to, low-wage people who hold jobs and earn taxable income, and who also have parental responsibilities.

The subsidy provided for by Code § 32 is in the maximum amount of $6,444 (in 2018), and it is treated as a "payment" of income taxes by the taxpayer. If the credit exceeds the taxpayer's positive tax liability, the excess becomes a tax "refund" for the year. The credit amount varies based on both the amount of the claimant's income and the number of "qualifying children." For a married couple with two children, for example, the subsidy rises with wages up to earned income of $14,320, at the rate of 40 cents of credit for each dollar of earned income. The maximum credit amount (for parents with two children) of $5,728 is reached at the $14,320 earnings level. The credit amount then remains constant for earnings up to $24,400, but is reduced as earnings go higher (the credit amount is decreased by 21.06 cents for every dollar of income above $24,400), finally falling to zero at an earnings level of $51,598. Thus, if the couple had wages of $14,320 in 2018, their positive tax liability (after the standard deduction) would be zero and their EITC refund would be the full amount of $5,728. They would also be entitled to a refundable child tax credit of $1,773—that is, 15% of the excess of $14,320 over $2,500. If the same couple had wages of $25,000, their regular tax liability would still be $100 and the credit would be phased down to $5,602. They would also be entitled to a refundable child tax credit of $3,375, so they would owe zero tax for the year and would receive a total refund of $8,887 ($5,602 EITC, plus $3,375 child tax credit, minus $100 pre-credit tax liability).

The calculations required to compute the amounts of the EITC and the refundable child tax credit are likely to be beyond the skill of ordinary taxpayers, so that those affected no doubt require paid professional assistance—or at least the assistance of return preparation software—in preparing their annual tax returns.

Experts apparently disagree about whether, as a matter of social policy, it is or is not a good idea to tie work and government assistance together. That issue we leave to them. From our narrower standpoint what is notable is the particular use to which Congress now puts the federal tax system.[115] The income tax is a mechanism that is aimed at collecting revenues. EITC is a device that is designed to do just the opposite, that is, to push out transfer payments. Joining the two together (other considerations to one side) is therefore slightly ingenious. In effect, we have a large-scale public assistance program that relies upon the same legal rules and calculations that apply generally to the taxpaying middle class—a program, moreover, that is to be administered by the Internal Revenue Service rather than by a government welfare bureaucracy. Because it is part of the tax system, EITC enables low-income taxpayers to make their benefit claims not by showing "need" but by the simple act of filing annual income tax returns. Benefits, as shown, then take the form of tax "refunds" rather than welfare checks. The expectation, or the hope, is that EITC will be cheaper to administer than a traditional welfare program and also less demeaning to its beneficiaries.

7.09 Education Incentives

One of the chief aims of the Tax Relief Act of 1997 was to provide incentives for post-secondary education by subsidizing college tuition costs, largely through the medium of credits against tax. This, of course, has nothing to do with "tax policy" as such. As in so many other areas, it simply represents a willingness to use the tax law as a means of carrying out a national program that Congress deems worthy of support. The task of administering the program falls to the Internal Revenue Service, which assumes the burden of preparing the relevant forms and instructional materials, writing appropriate Regulations, issuing revenue rulings when requested, and auditing and verifying the claims for credit or deduction that will appear on millions of tax returns. There is nothing new in this. To a considerable extent, the length and complexity of our tax law, as well as the alleged "intrusiveness" of the IRS, are the natural consequence of Congress' decision to piggyback a wide variety of programs for social and economic betterment onto the tax system instead of administering those programs through direct cash subsidies. The education incentive scheme established by the 1997 Act is one example of this familiar legislative practice, but there are many others.

The principal elements of the education incentive program appear in § 25A and consist of two credits against tax, the Hope

---

[115] Alstott, *EITC and the Oversimplified Case for Tax-Based Welfare Reform,* 108 Harv.L.Rev. 533 (1995).

Scholarship credit (confusingly referred to in the Code as both the "Hope Scholarship credit" and the "American Opportunity Tax credit") and the Lifetime Learning credit. The two credits are allowed to the taxpayer who pays the bills—the student herself, the student's spouse, or the student's parents if the student is a dependent. The Hope Scholarship and Lifetime Learning credits are primarily for the benefit of middle-income families. Accordingly, the Hope Scholarship credit phases out ratably between $160,000 and $180,000 of adjusted gross income for married couples and between $80,000 and $90,000 for single taxpayers. The Lifetime Learning credit phases out ratably between (in 2018) $114,000 and $134,000 of AGI for married couples and between $57,000 and $67,000 for single taxpayers.

The Hope Scholarship credit allows the taxpayer to take a credit of 100% for the first $2,000 and 25% for the next $2,000 of tuition and related expenses (including course materials, but not meals and lodgings) for the first four years of college—a maximum credit of $2,500 a year. The credit is allowed on a per student basis, that is, for each eligible student in the family. Forty percent of the credit is refundable; the remaining 60% is not.

The nonrefundable Lifetime Learning credit is 20% of tuition and fees up to $10,000—a maximum credit, therefore, of $2,000 annually. The credit is available on a per taxpayer rather than a per student basis, meaning that a taxpayer can take only a single Lifetime Learning credit each year even though he may be paying bills in that year for more than one eligible student. It is unclear whether a married couple paying $20,000 of tuition can claim a Lifetime Learning Credit for 20% of only $10,000, or whether they can claim a credit for 20% of the entire $20,000. The relevant statutory provision (§ 25A(c)(1)) says the ceiling is $10,000 *per taxpayer,* and it is well established that spouses filing a joint return generally count as two taxpayers.[116] On the other hand, the legislative history indicates the joint return ceiling on credit-eligible expenses is $10,000,[117] and IRS Form 8863 (which has no status as legal authority) follows the legislative history. Unlike the Hope Scholarship credit, the Lifetime Learning credit can be claimed for an unlimited number of taxable years and is available for graduate as well as undergraduate tuition and fees. An eligible student must be enrolled on at least a half-time basis or be taking classes for the purpose of acquiring or improving job skills.

A taxpayer cannot claim both the Hope Scholarship and the Lifetime Learning credit for the same student in the same year—an election has to be made to take one or the other. However, if the

---

[116] See, e.g., Reg. § 1.151–1(b).

[117] HR Rep. No. 220, 105th Cong., 1st Sess., 345 (1997).

student has run through her Hope Scholarship credit eligibility by completing the first four years of college, the Lifetime Learning credit is still available with respect to her tuition and fees for subsequent years, graduate school included. In addition, the taxpayer-payor—a parent, say—can elect the Hope Scholarship credit for one child and take the Lifetime Learning credit for other children who are beyond the four-year level. Thus, Betty is in law school, Billy is a fifth-year undergraduate, and little Bobby is a frosh, all being supported by their long-suffering and self-depriving parents. Provided they are within the phaseout limits, the parental taxpayers can take a $2,500 Hope Scholarship credit for Bobby's tuition and a $2,000 Lifetime Learning credit for Betty and Billy assuming the combined tuition expenses of the latter two are at least $10,000. (If the combined tuition expenses of the latter two are at least $20,000, and the statutory ambiguity discussed above is resolved in the parents' favor, they can claim a $4,000 Lifetime Learning Credit.) Once Bobby is beyond the first four years of college, only the single annual Lifetime Learning credit remains available even if Billy and Betty are by that time deep into graduate or professional school.

The 2001 Act added § 222, providing a further tax-saving option. The provision expired at the end of 2017. It has been extended before, however, and it will be no surprise if Congress extends it again. The following discussion (which uses the present tense for convenience) describes the expired (but likely to be revived) provision. Parents who incur "qualified higher education expenses" for their offspring can deduct (not credit) up to $4,000 a year from gross income for tuition and related costs. The deduction is from gross income—that is, above-the-line—and is therefore available even if the taxpayers do not itemize their personal expenses. Although a taxpayer may not claim the § 222 deduction and a Hope Scholarship or Lifetime Learning credit for the *same* student in the same year, the devoted parents above would apparently enjoy a minor tax bonanza. Having wisely had their three bright children close together, they can deduct $4,000 for law student Betty's tuition and related expenses under § 222, take the $2,000 Lifetime Learning credit for fifth-year undergraduate Billy, and take the $2,500 Hope Scholarship credit for first-year Bobby, all in a single taxable year.

The § 222 deduction is not fully available to married taxpayers whose adjusted gross income exceeds $130,000 or to single taxpayers whose AGI exceeds $65,000. The term "qualified higher education expenses" has the same meaning here as it does under § 25A, so that taxpayers can take the § 222 deduction without establishing a relationship to a "trade or business," as would be required for deductibility under § 162.

A tax benefit for taxpayers anticipating future education expenses is provided by the so-called Coverdell education savings account (§ 530, named in honor of a deceased member of Congress), now expanded to include elementary and secondary school expenses, whether incurred in public, private or religious schools. Subject to certain income phase-out limitations, farsighted parents are permitted to contribute up to $2,000 annually to a tax-favored investment account set up to fund the beneficiary's future tuition, books, and room and board expense. Annual contributions are not deductible but earnings on the account, including future distributions for qualified education expenses, are tax-exempt.[118] Not many young families can actually save $2,000 a year, of course, much less pay private school tuition, but for those happy few who can afford to send their kids to private prep or elementary school, a Coverdell ESA may help to defray the cost. If a distribution from a Coverdell ESA is used to pay the beneficiary's college expenses, the taxpayer-student must choose between (i) excluding the distribution from gross income and claiming no credit under § 25A for expenses covered by the distribution, or (ii) including the distribution in gross income and claiming a § 25A credit for expenses covered by the distribution.

Finally, although personal interest (other than home mortgage interest) continues to be nondeductible, a limited exception is made for qualified student loan interest. Under § 221, and again subject to income phase-outs, borrowers may deduct from gross income interest of $2,500 annually on loans used to pay education expenses of the taxpayer, his spouse or dependents. As indicated, the permitted deduction is from *gross* income, which reflects the probability that recent graduates may not yet be homeowners or itemizers and therefore would need an above-the-line deduction to get any practical benefit.

On a separate front, the rules relating to cancellation of indebtedness income (3.02) in connection with education loans produce results that law school graduates, at least a few, will welcome. Some universities, and many law schools, sponsor student loan programs under which a loan may be forgiven or partly forgiven if, following graduation, the borrower takes a public service job that pays less than a job with a regular commercial employer. Section 108(f) excludes from gross income the forgiveness of student loans made by a governmental entity or by a tax-exempt charity (including a university), if the borrower is committed to working for a certain period of time under the direction of an exempt organization or a

---

[118] Code Sec. 529 extends similar tax benefits to a qualified tuition program sponsored by a state or by a private college or university, and (as amended in 2017) applies to savings for K-through-12 education, as well as savings for higher education. See IRS Pub.970.

governmental unit in an occupation or an area of "unmet needs." An indebted law school graduate working for a legal assistance office or for legal aid can therefore claim the exclusion if and when the law school forgives the debt.

By our count, the tax-subsidized education provisions described above are at least six in number, all together creating what some might regard as a considerable pile of Code clutter. The aim, obviously, is to expand educational opportunities for our splendid youth. Our guess, however, is that the effect will be less than advertised. Families that are willing to pay $X to send their sons and daughters to Columbia University or Duke University (to choose two examples totally at random) without tax breaks will no doubt be willing to spend the same $X *net* of tax breaks, that is, after taking the tax breaks into account. The "payee" understands this very well, we imagine, which suggests that the Hope Scholarship credit, the Lifetime Learning credit, the Coverdell ESA, and the deduction for interest on education loans, are all likely, at least in part, to be absorbed by tuition increases—in the end (one hopes) resulting in a bit more income for deserving school teachers, especially of the post-secondary variety.

7.10 The Alternative Minimum Tax

By this point the reader probably needs no reminding that the income tax features a good many preferences and exceptions of importance. As stated much earlier, some tax preferences—the non-inclusion of unrealized property appreciation, say—simply represent inbuilt limitations of the system itself about which relatively little could be done even by the most reform-minded legislator. Others, however, such as accelerated depreciation (so labored over at 6.09 and 6.10), the municipal bond interest exclusion, or the deduction for residential mortgage interest, plainly reflect a congressional decision to subsidize particular categories of business, investment and even personal activity. As amply explained, quick depreciation rules are intended to encourage the purchase of plant and equipment, exemption for municipal bond interest is intended to reduce state and local borrowing costs, mortgage interest deductions are intended to encourage homeownership, and so on and on. Whether it is wise or foolish to use the federal tax system as a subsidy device has been debated for decades, but on the whole Congress appears to accept the idea that the tax system may properly be used to further non-tax objectives. Indeed, on some occasions—the adoption of ACRS in 1981 is a famous instance—it has shown itself willing to narrow the tax base in ruthless and dramatic fashion in order to promote other national goals.

In 1969 the Secretary of the Treasury provoked national outrage when he announced that 155 persons with adjusted gross incomes of $200,000 or more had paid no 1966 income tax as a result of their extensive use of various tax preferences. Congress could have responded to the public outrage in several ways. It might have explained to the nation that tax preferences further various important non-tax policy goals, and that taxpayers purchasing tax-favored assets pay significant "implicit taxes" in the form of lower pre-tax rates of return—all leading to the (debatable) conclusion that there is nothing wrong with a few high-income individuals paying no income tax because they have responded enthusiastically to the Code's investment incentive provisions. Or Congress might have treated the Secretary's report as a wake-up call, and responded by eliminating or scaling back many of the subsidies embedded in the Code. Instead of adopting either of these approaches, however, Congress enacted the predecessor of today's alternative minimum tax (AMT), for the purpose of ensuring that taxpayers with high economic incomes would generally be required to pay at least some income tax.

The base of the AMT is "alternative minimum taxable income" (AMTI), the definition of which disallows many of the exclusion and deduction subsidies featured in the taxable income base of the regular tax. The AMTI definition does allow, however, a high exemption (in effect, a zero rate bracket); in 2018 the exemption amount is $109,400 for a married couple and $70,300 for a single taxpayer. A taxpayer with regular tax preferences disallowed for purposes of the AMT may have AMTI considerably greater than his regular taxable income, even after subtraction of the AMT exemption amount. AMTI is then subjected to a semi-flat tax, with rates of 26% and 28%, to produce a "tentative minimum tax." For many higher-income taxpayers, AMTI will be greater than regular taxable income, but the AMT rates will be lower than regular tax rates (compare the 28% top AMT rate with the 37% top regular tax rate). Because these two differences work in opposite directions, the tentative minimum tax may be lower or higher than the taxpayer's regular tax, depending on which difference predominates. If a taxpayer's tentative minimum tax is lower than his regular tax, the AMT has no effect. If the tentative minimum tax is higher than his regular tax, however, the taxpayer must pay (i) his regular tax, and (ii) the AMT, defined as the amount by which the tentative minimum tax exceeds the regular tax. The practical effect is the same, of course, as simply requiring the taxpayer to pay the higher of his regular tax or tentative minimum tax.

For several decades, the AMT worked more-or-less as intended, in that it applied almost exclusively to very high-income taxpayers taking extensive advantage of various investment preferences under the regular tax. In the last decade or two, however, the profile of the typical AMT taxpayer has changed dramatically, with the merely affluent being at greater AMT risk than the truly wealthy. In 2017, for example, the AMT applied to 29.4% of taxpayers with incomes between $200,000 and $500,000, and to 62.9% of taxpayers with incomes between $500,000 and $1 million, but to only 19.9% taxpayers with incomes of $1 million or more.[119] This democratization of the AMT (the AMT also applied, in 2017, to 1.9% of taxpayers with incomes between $100,000 and $200,000) has several explanations.

The relatively low rate of applicability of the tax to the truly rich is explained largely by two factors. First, several important tax breaks formerly allowed to high-income taxpayers for purposes of the regular tax are now disallowed across-the-board, and thus no longer create differences between AMTI and regular taxable income. The disallowance of passive losses by § 469 (13.02(b)) is probably the single most important example. Second, the two most important tax preferences for investment income in the current Code—the preferential tax rates on long-term capital gains and on corporate dividends—are *not* disallowed for purposes of the AMT.

The high impact of the AMT in 2017 on merely affluent taxpayers with six-figure (but not seven-figure) incomes is largely explained by two other factors. First, several of the most important AMT preference items in the 2017 income tax were classic middle-class deductions, rather than tax breaks for the wealthy. Most significantly, personal exemptions and deductions for state and local taxes were (and are) completely disallowed for purposes of the AMT. Thus, having a large number of children and living in a high-tax state were major risk factors for the AMT. The AMT disallowance of these middle-class tax deductions is less significant in 2018 and later years—not because the AMT treatment of these items has changed (it has not), but because the regular tax treatment has changed (with the personal exemption amount set at zero (as described at 7.06) and the deduction for state and local taxes capped at $10,000 (7.01)). Second, the so-called Bush tax cuts of 2001 and 2003 significantly reduced regular tax liabilities, without making corresponding reductions in the AMT. Reducing the regular tax while leaving the AMT unchanged makes the tentative minimum tax higher than the regular tax for a larger number of taxpayers. Taking into account both the complexity of the AMT and its unintended impact on merely affluent taxpayers claiming tax benefits no more exotic than state and local tax deductions, most tax policy analysts favor either the repeal of the AMT or its complete overhaul. In fact, however,

---

[119] Tax Policy Center, *Briefing Book* (2018), available at www.taxpolicycenter. org/briefing-book/who-pays-amt.

Congress has made no major revisions to the AMT (although in 2012 Congress indexed the AMT for inflation, and in 2017 Congress significantly increased the exemption amounts). The reason, of course, is budget constraint. No one believes that the AMT, in its present form, is a good tax, but so far Congress has been unwilling to accept the revenue loss that would accompany its repeal.

It must be said, too, that no one is marching in the streets in protest of the AMT, despite the complexity and illogic of the tax. The AMT makes tax planning difficult or impossible for many taxpayers, because they are uncertain whether they are subject to the AMT. Without knowing whether one is subject to the AMT, one does not know one's true marginal tax rate, nor can one be sure whether or not (for example) property tax on a home one is considering purchasing would be deductible. More generally, the AMT plays a major role in turning the tax system into a "black box," which produces tax liabilities by a process incomprehensible to most taxpayers. From a civics perspective, there is a strong argument that taxation without comprehension is as inimical to democracy as taxation without representation. Why, then, are there no protests in the street? The most powerful trigger for protests would be the agony taxpayers would endure if they had to do their AMT calculations with paper, pencil, and calculator. Today, however, almost all returns are prepared (either by paid preparers or by taxpayers themselves) with the aid of software programs, and AMT number-crunching—no matter how difficult for a human being—is no challenge for a software program. In short, we blame TurboTax for the absence of a popular uprising against the AMT.

A loose end. In the *Banaitis* case (consolidated by the Supreme Court with the *Banks* case),[120] the taxpayer, having entered into a contingent fee arrangement with his attorney, sued his former employer (a bank) for firing him for refusing to breach his fiduciary duty to customers. The defendant settled the case in 1995 for a little less than $9 million, of which a bit less than $4 million was paid directly to the attorney, the taxpayer receiving the balance of slightly less than $5 million. Banaitis included the amount paid to him—call it $5 million—in his gross income on his 1995 tax return,[121] but he

------

[120]   543 U.S. 426 (2005).

[121]   Although the facts of the case arose prior to the 1996 amendments to § 104(a)(2) (2.04(a)), under the current version of § 104(a)(2) it would be clear that Banaitis's damages were not on account of a *physical* personal injury, and thus would not be within the scope of the gross income exclusion.

did not include in his gross income the amount—call it $4 million—paid directly to his attorney.

The Commissioner insisted that the entire settlement—call it $9 million—be included in gross income, and that the attorney's fee of $4 million be treated as a "miscellaneous itemized deduction" under § 67. If so treated, the deduction would have been subject to the 2%-of-AGI floor of the pre-2018 version of § 67 (reducing the deduction by about $180,000). Far more important from the taxpayer's standpoint, "miscellaneous itemized deductions" were (and are) nondeductible for AMT purposes. Hence, the entire damage award—unreduced by the attorney's fee—would be subject to the 28% AMT. The result of all this would have been a tax liability, everything included, of about $2.5 million. The damage award of $9 million would therefore have been reduced by the contingent fee of $4 million plus income tax of $2.5 million, leaving the taxpayer with only $2.5 million to call his own. In the absence of the AMT, the regular tax on $5 million would have been only about $2 million (on the simplifying assumption that the 1995 top rate of 39.6% applied to the entire $5 million of taxable income). Thus, the AMT disallowance of the attorney's fee deduction made a difference of about $500,000 in Banaitis's tax bill.

The Supreme Court unanimously held for the Commissioner. The Court rejected the taxpayer's "partnership" argument—that the taxpayer and his attorney should be viewed as engaged in a joint venture, of which the attorney's distributive share was $4,000,000. The Court placed reliance on the income attribution cases—*Eubank, Horst, Earl* (8.01 et seq.)—and concluded that "a contingent fee agreement should be viewed as an anticipatory assignment to the attorney of a portion of the client's income from any litigation recovery." An even closer analogue, perhaps, would be the *Old Colony* case (3.01), in which the federal income tax paid by his employer on the taxpayer's behalf was held to be includable in the taxpayer's gross income. In essence, the taxpayer in *Old Colony* made a similar argument—that the federal income tax belonged to the Treasury and was never "his" to begin with—but equally without success.

Persuaded that the *Banks-Banaitis* result was harsh, Congress in 2004 amended § 62 to permit attorney's fees paid in connection with lawsuits involving discrimination to be treated as "above the line" expenses and therefore (i) deductible from gross income for regular tax purposes, and (ii) not subject to disallowance under the AMT. However, the 2004 amendment is limited to attorney's fees paid in connection with claims of "unlawful discrimination" (as specially defined). Presumably, the Court's holding in *Banks-Banaitis* would still apply to fees paid in other types of nonphysical personal injury cases—*e.g.*, defamation—where the damage award is taxable. The result today would be even harsher than under prior law, because of the complete nondeductibility of miscellaneous itemized deductions under the regular tax in 2018 through 2025.

Questions and Answers: Deductions

Question 1: Donald, an experienced real estate developer, wants to build a large apartment complex on the west side of Gotham City. Donald owns 50 acres of west-side property. At present the area is zoned for business use only, so Donald needs a zoning variance from the Gotham Community Planning Board that will permit him to build a residential structure on his land. After much negotiation the Board states that it will give Donald the variance he requires, provided that Donald agrees to contribute six of his 50 acres to the City to be used as a playground for schoolchildren living nearby. Donald accepts the Board's condition and promptly deeds the requested acreage to the City. Donald's basis for the six contributed acres is $10x. The fair market value of those six acres is $75x.

Noting that Gotham City qualifies as a "governmental unit" within the meaning of Code Section 170(b)(1)(v), Donald asks you for assurance that the arrangement just described will be treated as a deductible gift to charity. Will it?

Answer: Probably not. Donald's property transfer is obviously in exchange for the zoning variance—a valuable business benefit—rather than being a gift to charity from which the giver derives no more than personal satisfaction. The Regulations and the decided cases make it clear that a transfer of property to charity for which the transferor receives a consideration is deductible only to the extent that the fair market value of the property transferred exceeds the value of the consideration received.[122] Since the exchange in question was preceded by "much negotiation," Donald would have difficulty showing that he gave up more than he got.

But if it's not a gift to charity, what is it? Logically, it appears that Donald "exchanged" his appreciated land for a valuable legal right pursuant to a bargain with the City of Gotham, in which event Donald might actually have to recognize a taxable gain of $75x – $10x = $65x. *U.S. v. Davis* (6.03), in which the Supreme Court held that taxable gain was realized on an exchange of appreciated securities for the release of marital property rights, would apparently support that result. However, it does not appear that the Commissioner has ever insisted on so treating a transaction of this sort. More likely, while being denied a charitable contribution deduction, Donald would be required to add his $10x basis to the construction cost of the

---

[122] Regs. §§ 1.170A–(1)(h)(1) and 1.170A–(13)(f)(5). See also *Ottawa Silica Co. v. U.S.*, 699 F.2d 1124 (Fed. Cir. 1983). This Q & A devised with the aid (though not necessarily the approval) of Prof. Martin J. McMahon, Jr.

new apartment buildings and recover it over the "useful life" period prescribed for residential rental property under § 168(c). A somewhat gloomier alternative is that the $10x would have to be added to the basis of the remaining 44 acres of land, in which event, presumably, the $10x would be recoverable only when the property was sold.

Question 2: Under a special Code provision, breeders of ostriches (large, nasty-tempered, flightless birds) are allowed to report the profit realized on the sale of their animals as long-term capital gain.[123] The initial cost of breeding an ostrich is $5,000, and the breeder can usually get $15,000 for the creature at the end of four years when the ostrich is an adult. Having treated the initial breeding cost as a non-deductible capital expenditure, and being taxed on his $10,000 profit as long-term capital gain, a breeder with a long-term capital gain rate of 15% pays a tax of only $1,500 when he sells the ostrich. The Treasury, which thinks that ostriches should be treated as "inventory" or "stock in trade" in the hands of a breeder, has urged Congress to change the law and treat the gain on ostrich sales as ordinary business income, taxable at ordinary income rates up to 37%. As a concession to the ostrich lobby, the Treasury has stated that if this change is made, it will allow breeders to deduct the $5,000 breeding cost as a current business expense.[124]

How should ostrich breeders feel about the Treasury's proposal?

Answer: Thrilled and delighted. Suppose a particular breeder faces a long-term capital gain rate of 15% and an ordinary income rate of 35%. Under present law, the breeder invests $5,000 per ostrich, realizes $15,000 before tax, reports a $10,000 capital gain, pays a $1,500 capital gain tax, and nets $13,500 after tax. Under the Treasury proposal, which would allow the breeder to deduct (rather than capitalize) his breeding cost, the breeder should be willing to invest $7,692, thereby increasing the size of his flock (for sticklers, pride) proportionately. Why? Because deducting $7,692 from income otherwise taxable at a 35% rate leaves him with a net after-tax investment of $5,000, the same amount that he was willing to invest when the outlay had to be capitalized. Assuming (as above) that the price of an ostrich triples over a four-year period, his investment will increase in value to 3 × $7,692, or $23,076. Having fully deducted his initial cost, his basis for the herd is zero and the entire $23,076 realized on sale is taxable as ordinary income at the 35% rate. His tax is $8,076. What he nets, therefore, is $23,076 − $8,076 = $15,000! In effect, the tax on his profit has been completely eliminated. Whereas under present law the breeder is taxed at a rate of 15% and nets only $13,500 because ostrich profits are treated as taxable

---

[123] There is, of course, no such provision.
[124] Treasury, of course, has made no such proposal.

capital gain, under the Treasury proposal he nets the full $15,000 even though his profits are treated as ordinary income and taxed at a rate of 35%.

As explained at p. 105, the reason for this happy result is that "expensing" a capital investment is equivalent to full exemption of the yield on that investment. The Treasury might just as well propose that the breeder's profits be exempt from tax entirely, as if ostriches were municipal bonds.

Question 3: The Reliable Construction Company is in the business of constructing office buildings. One of its projects last year was the construction of a building to serve as its own headquarters. Reliable used a particular bulldozer on its own office building project all of last year. Reliable's original cost of the bulldozer was $100,000, and last year was the bulldozer's second cost-recovery year. Assuming the bulldozer is five-year property for purposes of § 168, and that no portion of the cost of the bulldozer was deducted under either § 168(k) or § 179, what is the amount of Reliable's § 168 deduction for the bulldozer for last year?

Answer: Zero. This is a trick question. Using the half-year convention for the year in which the bulldozer was placed in service, and using the double-declining balance method of accelerated depreciation, 32% of the cost of a five-year asset (here, $32,000) is recovered in the second recovery year. Rev. Proc. 87–57, 1987–2 C.B. 687. The impediment to deduction here is *Idaho Power*, and the codification of *Idaho Power* principles by § 263A. Instead of deducting $32,000, Reliable will subtract the $32,000 from the basis of the bulldozer, only to add it to the basis of the building. When Reliable places the building in service, it will recover the $32,000 along with the rest of its basis in the building, using the straight-line method over 39 years (*i.e.,* at the rate of about $820 per year).

Question 4: Terry and Jordan, an unmarried couple, together purchased an expensive house (as joint tenants) for use as their residence. They financed most of the purchase price with a $1.5 million home mortgage loan, on which they were jointly and severally liable. On their tax returns for their first year of owning the home, Terry and Jordan each claimed a deduction for interest on $750,000 of the $1.5 million of loan principal. Were they entitled to do so, or are their interest deductions limited by §§ 163(h)(3)(B)(ii) and (C)(ii)?

Answer: The basic rule is that interest on up to $750,000 borrowed to purchase a home may be deducted.[125] The wrinkle here is that the statute is unclear as to how this limitation applies in the case of unmarried co-owners of a residence. According to

---

[125]   Rev. Rul. 2010–25, 2010–44 I.R.B. 571.

§ 163(h)(3)(B)(ii), "The aggregate amount treated as acquisition indebtedness for any period shall not exceed $750,000." The difficulty is that the provision does not indicate whether the ceiling applies on a per-taxpayer or a per-residence basis. If the limitation is per-taxpayer, then Terry and Jordan are each entitled to deduct interest on $750,000 of principal. If the limitation is per-residence, then *together* they are entitled to deduct interest on only $750,000 of principal (presumably $375,000 each). In the 2012 *Sophy* case,[126] the Tax Court adopted the Service's position that the ceilings apply on a per-residence basis, rather than on a per-taxpayer basis. The Ninth Circuit, however, ruled in the taxpayers' favor, reversing the Tax Court.[127] The Ninth Circuit's interpretation produces much more favorable treatment under § 163(h)(3) for unmarried co-owners than for married owners (who cannot deduct home mortgage interest on more than $750,000 of principal, whether filing jointly or separately).

Question: The Vapor Shoppe, Inc., sells medical marijuana to customers entitled to purchase medical marijuana under the law of the state in which it is located. Although its activities are perfectly legal under state law, those activities are nevertheless in violation of federal law (under which marijuana remains a "controlled substance"). Last year the Vapor Shoppe had gross receipts (all from sales of marijuana) of $3.3 million, costs of goods sold (marijuana purchased from wholesale suppliers) of $2.3 million, and business expenses (wages, rent, utilities, etc.) of $150,000. What was the Vapor Shoppe's taxable income for last year?

Answer: Section 280E disallows all deductions for amounts paid or incurred in connection with trafficking in controlled substances. This disallowance provision is, of course, founded on public policy concerns. The effect is to punish drug traffickers by taxing them on more than their actual net income. The IRS's position, with which the Tax Court concurs,[128] is that § 280E applies to marijuana businesses even if they are legal under state law. (This is equally true whether state law permits only medical marijuana sales, or also permits sales for recreational use.) At first glance, then, it would seem that the Vapor Shoppe is not entitled to deduct either its costs of goods sold or its business expenses, with the result that its taxable income is $3.3 million—the same as its gross receipts. However, the Regulations under § 61 provide that costs of goods sold are deductible from gross receipts in calculating gross income, rather than deductible from gross income in calculating taxable income.[129] Because of this

---

[126] *Sophy v. Commissioner*, 138 T.C. 204 (2012).

[127] *Voss v. Commissioner*, 796 F.3d 1051 (9th Cir. 2015).

[128] *Californians Helping to Alleviate Medical Problems, Inc. v. Commissioner*, 128 T.C. 173 (2007); *Olive v. Commissioner*, 139 T.C. 19 (2012).

[129] Reg. § 1.61–3(a).

treatment of gross receipts, Congress was concerned that denial of a deduction for costs of goods sold might result in an unconstitutional unapportioned direct tax (5.02, first "loose end"). More precisely, the concern was that a tax on gross receipts (without a deduction for costs of goods sold) might be a direct tax and might not be an income tax— and so not within the sweep of the Sixteenth Amendment's authorization of an unapportioned income tax. Reflecting that constitutional concern, the legislative history of 280E indicates that the provision does not disallow deductions for costs of goods sold, and the IRS and the Tax Court have followed the legislative history. Accordingly, the Vapor Shoppe's gross income is $1 million ($3.3 million gross receipts less $2.3 million costs of goods sold), and its taxable income is also $1 million (because of the § 280E disallowance of the $150,000 of business expenses). The dollar amounts in this problem are rounded versions of the facts of one of the Tax Court medical marijuana cases (*Olive*). With numbers such as these—costs of goods sold more than fifteen times as great as business expenses— the § 280E disallowance of business expenses is almost trivial compared to the allowances of costs of goods sold. Whether this ratio of costs of goods sold to expenses is typical for traffickers in controlled substances, we really couldn't say.

Question 6: Amber has not cut her hair for years; it is currently four feet long. She has decided to have her hair cut short, and to donate the hair to a charity that makes wigs for cancer patients undergoing chemotherapy. She has done some research on eBay, and has discovered that the fair market value of four feet of hair like hers is about $1,000. If she gives the hair to charity, how much (if anything) can she properly claim as a charitable deduction? (If it matters, human hair grows at the rate of six inches per year.)

Answer: Her basis in her hair is zero. (Presumably, shampoo and conditioner are to be treated as costs of maintaining the hair, rather than as costs of acquiring or improving the hair allocable to basis.) Under § 170(e)(1)(A), she may claim a deduction for the unrealized appreciation in her hair only if the $1,000 of gain would have been long-term capital gain if she had sold the hair instead of donating it. The remainder of the analysis requires some anticipation of the capital gains material discussed later (in Part F). Is the hair a capital asset? Section 1221 provides that an asset is a capital asset unless it is within one of the statutory exceptions to capital asset status. No exception seems to apply to the hair on one's head, so the hair should qualify as a capital asset. For the gain on a hypothetical sale to be long-term, § 1222(3) provides that the taxpayer must have held the asset for more than one year. If Amber cut off and donated all her hair, it would seem that the last six inches (*i.e.*, the six inches closest to her scalp) would not have satisfied the holding period requirement for long-term gain. Thus she would get a deduction for the fair market value of 3.5 feet of her hair, but no deduction for the value of the other six inches. She could decide not to cut off and donate the last six inches, without decreasing the amount of her charitable deduction. If it seems bizarre that tax results might depend on the rate of growth of human hair—and it *should* seem bizarre—that is no stranger than the court's reasoning in the case most nearly on point. In *Lary v. United States*,[130] the court denied the taxpayer a deduction for donating his blood to the Red Cross, on the grounds that the four-month life of the average red blood cell was insufficient to satisfy the holding period for long-term capital gain.

---

[130]   *Lary v. United States*, 787 F.2d 1538 (11th Cir. 1986).

Part C

ATTRIBUTION OF INCOME

Although a taxpayer may regard her immediate family—her husband and minor children, say—as an economic unit from the standpoint of resources and expenditures, with a few important exceptions the federal income tax treats each member of the family as a separate taxable person.[1] This separate-taxable-person treatment means, for example, that if a child has earned income in his own right (for example, from work as an actor or from—to invoke ancient history—delivering newspapers), the income is taxed to the child himself. The tax law does not lump the child's income together with his parents', even though parents and children are obviously members of a single household. The same is true of other family "entities", such as family trusts and family corporations. Such entities, natural or otherwise, are generally viewed as separate taxpayers, each with its own independent status under the tax law.[2]

At the same time, of course, the federal income tax structure is progressive: as an individual receives additional income, his tax also goes up but at a greater rate of increase. This is so because additional segments of income may be taxed at higher marginal rates than their predecessors. It follows that a family whose income is taxed to one member only—say the father—would usually pay a higher overall tax than a family whose income is divided evenly among all the members of the group. For example, if a married couple with three children has taxable income this year (2018) of $200,000, the tax (on a joint return) is about $26,000. But if the same income can somehow be reported on four returns (the joint return plus one each for the three children) at the rate of $50,000 for each return, the overall tax on the family will be about $16,000, and a tax-saving of roughly $10,000 will have been achieved.

Potential savings of this size operate as an inducement to the taxpayer to find some means of shifting taxable income to the lower-bracket children. If part of the taxpayer's income derived from property, for many decades a simple tax reduction strategy was to

---

[1]   The two most significant exceptions to the separate-taxable-person treatment of family members? First, the so-called kiddie tax (9.02) generally taxes *unearned* (*i.e.*, investment) income of children at their parents' marginal tax rate (although for 2018 through 2025 the kiddie tax rates are determined by reference to the income tax rates applicable to trusts, rather than by reference to the actual tax rates of the child's parents). Second, in many (but not all) respects a husband and wife electing to file a joint return (9.04) are treated as a single taxpayer.

[2]   There is a significant exception here as well. Income of a so-called grantor trust (9.01) is taxed to the grantor, rather than to the trust.

transfer that property to the children by outright gift. Thus, if a father gave a hundred shares of stock to his daughter, the periodic dividends which the daughter received thereafter would be taxed to her as owner of the property. Moreover, under the rule of *Taft v. Bowers* (4.01), any unrealized appreciation in the value of the stock also would be treated as belonging to the child, even though such appreciation occurred before the gift was made. This strategy still works with respect to gifts of income-producing property to non-dependent *adult* children of the taxpayer (or, for that matter, to friends and relations of the taxpayer other than the taxpayer's children), but the so-called kiddie tax (9.02)—added to the Code in 1986—now defeats this strategy in the case of gifts to minor children and dependent adult children. Technically, the kiddie tax does not change the rule that income from property is taxed to the owner of the property, but it taxes the child on that income at the marginal tax rate of the child's parents (or, in 2018 through 2025, under the unfavorable tax rate schedule applicable to trusts), thus eliminating the income-shifting benefits of gifts to minor children and dependent adult children.

What about those whose income is derived from personal efforts rather than property ownership? If the tax on dividends, interest and rents can be shifted by outright gifts of the underlying property (in situations to which the kiddie tax does not apply), what about wages, salaries and fees? One cannot give away one's skills very easily, yet there is something disturbing in the conclusion that income-shifting is a device available to property owners alone. Can the tax on fruits of personal services be shifted? If not, what justifies or at least explains the apparent discrimination? And even with respect to property owners, there may be questions of a troublesome nature when the gift is other than a simple outright transfer of all substantial rights. Suppose, for example, that the owner of income-producing property transfers it to another family member (with respect to whom the kiddie tax does not apply) but retains a right to revoke the transfer and take the property back whenever he chooses. Will the property be regarded as belonging to the transferee for tax purposes, or will the transferor's revocation right be considered the equivalent of continued ownership? The law must decide how far the property owner should have to go in the direction of an outright transfer to assure that the income from a gift of property will be taxed to someone other than himself. Here, as in the case of gifts of personal service income, there appear to be *two* candidates for taxability, each with a significant link to the income in question. And as no legal basis exists for apportioning the income between them, it is evidently necessary for the law to choose one candidate to the exclusion of the other. The question, of course, is which.

The development of legal principles governing choice of taxable person was largely left to judicial construction during the early days of the income tax. Between 1930 and 1940 the Supreme Court decided a substantial number of cases involving income attribution, largely under the authority of what is now § 61. These early cases generally favored the government (with certain significant exceptions). While their results were "correct" in the sense that any other set of outcomes would have put taxpayers in a position to render the progressive rate structure a virtual nullity, the Court's use of § 61 for this purpose was, shall we say, creative. The section defines gross income but actually says nothing directly about *to whom* the income belongs. Yet the alternative to judicial rulemaking (at least until Congress should act) would have been to allow taxpayers to make the choice of taxable person *for themselves,* and thus to minimize their tax burdens more or less at will.

The discussion that follows is divided into two sections. Section 8 digests the early cases and shows how the Supreme Court formulated "common law" attribution principles under the general authority of § 61. These decisions became the basis for subsequent legislative action, particularly in the fields of trusts and family partnerships. Although partly displaced by specific Code provisions, the early decisions continue to have application in many situations not expressly covered by statute, and for this reason they are part of the basic professional vocabulary of every tax specialist. Section 9 considers some of the statutory rules on income attribution: 9.01 takes up the subject of gifts in trust, now largely dealt with by detailed Code provisions; 9.02 describes the kiddie tax; 9.03 examines family business associations, especially family partnerships. Brief reference to another statutory "solution"—the split-income joint-return procedure which is available to husbands and wives—is made in the subsection immediately following, with further details at 9.04, while the Code treatment of alimony (drastically changed by 2017 legislation) is described at 9.05.

8. The Early Cases

8.01 Gifts of Personal Service Income; *Lucas v. Earl*; *Poe v. Seaborn*

(a) Redirected Salary

In *Lucas v. Earl*,[3] the taxpayer, a lawyer, entered into a contract with his wife in 1901, 12 years before the enactment of the modern federal income tax. Unless the taxpayer was amazingly prescient, federal income tax avoidance was not the motivation for the contract.

---

[3]   281 U.S. 111 (1930).

The contract provided that the future income earned by either spouse would be treated as belonging equally to both. In 1920 and 1921—after the enactment of the income tax but long before the enactment of the present joint-return procedure for husbands and wives—the taxpayer earned salary and fees, presumably in substantial amounts, of which one-half was paid over to his wife pursuant to the contract. The question presented was whether the taxpayer should be required to include in his gross income the entire amount of the salary and fees, or only the one-half portion that he retained. Stressing that the income-splitting agreement was valid and binding under state law, the taxpayer argued that the aim of the Code was to tax income only if beneficially received. Since his wife possessed the absolute right to receive and enjoy one-half of the income under the contract, the taxpayer urged that that share must be regarded as "hers" within the meaning of § 61, and that only the half retained could be treated as "his."

Assuming Mr. and Mrs. Earl pooled their economic resources, why did it matter to them whether Mr. or Mrs. Earl was taxed on Mrs. Earl's one-half share? It mattered not because they cared who was required to write the check to the government for the tax on her share (they surely did not care), but rather because of the difference in the marginal tax rates of the spouses. If Mrs. Earl's share was taxed to her, and assuming she had no other income, it would be taxed at the low rates prevailing at the bottom of the tax rate schedule. But if Mrs. Earl's share was taxed to Mr. Earl, it would be (metaphorically speaking) stacked on top of his one-half share of his earned income (on which he was indisputably the taxpayer), and thus taxed at the higher marginal rates prevailing farther up the tax rate schedule.

Speaking through Justice Holmes, the Supreme Court held that the "anticipatory" assignment of yet-to-be-earned wages is ineffective under the federal income tax to shift income to the assignee, whatever its effect as a matter of ordinary contract law. Without denying the validity of the contract and the wife's legal claim to one-half the income, the Court held that the intent of the statute was to "tax salaries to those who earned them"—in this case, of course, the husband. This statutory purpose could not be "escaped" through the medium of "anticipatory arrangements ... however skillfully devised." Regardless of the parties' motives—that is, even if they had no intent to avoid taxes (as they almost certainly did not, at least at the outset)—"the fruits" of the taxpayer's labor could not be "attributed to a different tree from that on which they grew." In effect, it was the exercise of the taxpayer's income-producing skills, rather than the actual receipt of the pay envelope by the donee, which must be considered as determinative.

The *Earl* decision thus limits the candidates for taxability in personal service cases to one. Mr. Earl was denied the freedom to make his *own* choice of taxable person; rather, that choice was made for him through the imposition of a rule of attribution which ties service-income to the person who earns it. By contrast, income in the form of property appreciation may, under § 1015(a) and the holding in *Taft v. Bowers* (4.01), be shifted from donor to donee at the taxpayer's sole discretion. Thus the owner of appreciated property may decide for himself whether to sell the property and include the gain in his own income, or give it away and shift the gain to the donee's lower marginal tax rate (assuming, that is, that the kiddie tax does not apply). The taxpayer in *Earl* sought a similar discretion as to personal earnings by arguing that beneficial receipt should be regarded as the sole criterion of taxability. Had the Court agreed, the result would have been to permit a taxpayer to make his own decision as to whether he, or someone else, should be taxed on his ordinary employment income. Since other family members will often confront lower marginal rates than the taxpayer himself, in many cases the taxpayer would simply designate such others to receive, and pay the tax on, a portion of his annual earnings.

This suggests, of course, that it was not so much fruits-and-trees—that ghastly metaphor—which concerned the Court in *Earl* as it was the prospect of a wholesale "escape" from the progressive rate schedule. The issue, after all, was *who* should be taxed—Mr. or Mrs.—on the one-half share of salary and fees, not whether such income should be taxed at all or be taxed to the parties twice. If the government had lost in its effort to attribute the income to Mr. Earl, then surely Mrs. Earl would have had to include the amounts in her income for the years in question; having won, the government must then concede that the receipts were excludable by Mrs. Earl as gifts under § 102(a) since it was clear that the assignment was gratuitous. Accordingly, the government's only interest in the matter was to prevent the taxpayer from effectively reducing the applicable rate of tax by splitting his salary income with his wife. Not merely spouses, of course, but minor children and perhaps other family dependents could have been made parties to contracts like the Earls', thus allowing one person's earned income multiple runs through the lower ranges of the tax rate schedule. Since the great bulk of family income comes from personal services, a government defeat in *Earl* would have seriously damaged the entire concept of graduated rates. While it may be true that taxpayers are free to reduce their taxes by legal means—"everybody does so, rich or poor; and all do right . . ."[4]—still nothing could have been less consistent with congressional intent than Earl's attempt to deflate the rate structure. Hence the

---

[4]   L. Hand, J., in *Commissioner v. Newman*, 159 F.2d 848, 850–51 (2d Cir.1947).

government's victory in *Earl* was really inevitable, whether Earl the man be viewed as fruit or tree. It is worth noting here that the treatment of gifts as non-deductible by donors and as tax-free to donees, rather than as deductible by donors and taxable to donees (a road-not-taken discussed in the introduction to Section 4), is a necessary backstop to the policy decision reflected in *Earl*. If the gift rule were otherwise—if gifts were deductible by donors and taxable to donees—gifts of earned income (after the income had been earned) could be used to accomplish the same income-shifting goals that under *Earl* could not be achieved by anticipatory assignments of income.

Having succeeded so well in the *Earl* case (the Court's decision was unanimous), the government might reasonably have expected an equally favorable outcome in *Poe v. Seaborn*,[5] a case decided only a few weeks later and raising issues of a similar character. In *Seaborn,* the taxpayer and his wife were residents of the State of Washington, under whose community property laws the income of either spouse, whether from property or from services, was treated as belonging equally to the other. At the same time the state law gave the husband legal power to manage and dispose of the community's assets in any way he chose, "short of committing a fraud on his wife's rights." For the year 1927 Seaborn and his wife each filed a separate return reporting one-half of the family income, which comprised Seaborn's salary, plus interest, dividends and gains from the sale of real estate. Despite *Lucas v. Earl,* the Court held that the local law was effective for federal tax purposes and sustained the taxpayer in reporting only half of the salary and property income on his return. The Court pointed out that in *Earl* the salary income would have belonged to the husband alone in the absence of the contract entered into with his wife. Here, by contrast, "the earnings are never the property of the husband, but that of the community," owing to the operation of the state law.

Considerations of legal title, which in *Earl* were described as "attenuated subtleties," thus proved determinative in *Seaborn.* The decision presumably reflected the Court's reluctance to allow local property institutions of long-standing to be subordinated to the federal tax law, especially as Congress must have been aware of the community property laws at the time the federal income tax first was enacted. In addition, the element of tax avoidance, with which the Court was surely concerned in *Earl* (despite the absence of a tax-avoidance motive for the Earls' own contract), was less urgent in *Seaborn* for at least two reasons. In the first place, the splitting of income was accomplished by operation of law rather than through

---

[5]   282 U.S. 101 (1930).

voluntary contract, and hence was confined to residents of the small handful of community property states. Taxpayers could emigrate from common law to community property jurisdictions in an effort to obtain split-income benefits, but it was unlikely that the tax saving would be great enough to induce many to undertake the pains of relocation. Second, the scope of the income-splitting permitted under *Seaborn* was limited to husband and wife; the "community" to which the income belonged did not include minor children or other dependents. Hence *Seaborn* authorized *doubling* the width of the tax brackets, but no more.

Yet even when these differences are noted, the plain fact is that *Seaborn* injected an element of geographical discrimination into the taxation of family income—most especially personal service income. In the aftermath of the Supreme Court's decisions in *Earl* and *Seaborn,* the tax on any given dollar amount of earnings of a husband with a homemaking wife would be considerably higher if the couple resided in a common-law marital property state, than if they lived in a community property state. From the standpoint of national tax policy, such discrimination was highly undesirable. Despite the Court's concern for local property law systems, *Seaborn* prompted a number of common-law states to adopt, or prepare to adopt, the law of community property as a means of extending the federal tax benefits of *Seaborn* to their citizens. The effort was not always successful. In *Commissioner v. Harmon,*[6] the Court ruled that a husband's earnings continued to be taxable to him despite the adoption of a community property law by the state of Oklahoma. As the state's community system was elective rather than mandatory, the income-splitting was found to result from the taxpayer's voluntary action in electing to have the community rules apply; thus *Earl* rather than *Seaborn* was held to be controlling.

Against this background of tax-induced changes in state marital property laws, Congress in 1948 acted to equalize the status of married couples living in common law and in community property states. The Code was amended to authorize *all* married couples to aggregate their income and deductions on a joint return, and to pay tax under a rate schedule with brackets twice as wide as the brackets for unmarried taxpayers. Thus, a married couple would pay a tax equal to twice what a single person would pay on one-half of their combined taxable income. The effect was virtually the same as if all the states in the Union had adopted the community property system at one stroke, although *federal* enactment of the income-splitting joint return "meant that the political credit for reducing taxes was

---

6　　323 U.S. 44 (1944).

concentrated on Congress rather than dispersed among the state legislatures."[7]

Joint returns are considered in more detail at 9.04. It suffices here to note simply that the consequence of the 1948 legislation was to eliminate the discriminatory effect of the *Earl-Seaborn* pair of cases, and to place all married couples on a parity as far as income-splitting is concerned.[8]

(b) Services in Kind

The *Earl* case involved an effort by the taxpayer to reduce his taxes by redirecting fees earned from a third party (Earl's clients or employer) to his wife. *Earl* blocked this attempt by requiring that earned income be attributed to the person who performs the services, even though the cash itself is paid over to an assignee. But suppose a taxpayer makes a gift of personal service income "in kind." For example, suppose the taxpayer performs services of a commercial nature for another member of his family and refuses to accept compensation for his work. A father might manage his child's securities, or an adult daughter manage an apartment building belonging to her elderly parents—in each case, of course, without charging a fee for the services performed. The effect, quite obviously, is to increase the net income of the "donee" and to reduce that of the taxpayer-donor. Since there is thus, potentially, a shift of personal service income between related individuals, does *Earl* require that the cash value of the taxpayer's services be included in his own income (and excluded or deducted from that of the donee)?

The answer really cannot be delivered in a single breath. In general, however, the *Earl* doctrine has *not* been extended to uncompensated services, even though the effect of such arrangements may be to transfer earned income from higher to lower-bracket family members. The reason, quite simply, is sheer impossibility; the *Earl* doctrine would become unbearably burdensome if it were stretched to cover every instance in which one family member performed uncompensated services for another. The services imagined earlier—managing the child's securities or the parents' apartment building—though not without value, are likely to be relatively modest, to be carried out separately from the performer's full-time occupation, and in any case would be viewed by the parties as a function of ordinary familial obligation. It is virtually inconceivable that the *Earl* decision was intended to authorize the government to attach a cash value to every gratuitous intra-family

---

[7] Bittker, *Federal Income Taxation and the Family,* 27 Stanford L.Rev. 1389 (1975).

[8] See Surrey, *Federal Taxation of the Family—The Revenue Act of 1948,* 61 Harv.L.Rev. 1097 (1948).

service, and equally unlikely that the government would wish to exercise such an authority if it existed.

It is probably fair to say, then, that taxpayers may perform uncompensated services for other family members without fear of income attribution under *Earl*. And this conclusion probably holds true even if the services are much more than modest—as where the father undertakes to manage a corporation or a partnership business which is owned by his children. This does not mean that Mr. Earl, the lawyer, could have shifted half his income to his wife by purporting to be her employee—that is, by contracting to work for a fixed wage or a percentage of receipts. Since Mrs. Earl presumably had nothing to contribute to the "firm", the employment undoubtedly would have been disregarded as a sham and all of the income taxed to Mr. Earl on the ground that no true employment relationship had been created. But if Mrs. Earl contributed vital services—if she, too, were a lawyer, for example—or if the business required substantial capital which Mrs. Earl supplied, then, as stated, the principles of income-attribution apparently would not prevent Mr. Earl from minimizing the family's taxes by accepting less than full compensation for his services.

The distinction between "redirected income," "sham employment," and "services in kind" has given the Service difficulty in cases where the beneficiary of the uncompensated service is a charity. As noted at 7.03, contributions to charity of money or other property are deductible by the giver. Under § 170(b), however, the amount deductible in any taxable year may not exceed 50% (or 60%, in the case of cash contributions) of the donor's adjusted gross income. Although the Regulations under § 170 state that "[n]o deduction is allowable . . . for a contribution of services,"[9] in effect a charitable deduction for uncompensated personal services is "allowed" in unlimited amount—not through explicit deduction, to be sure, but by permitting the "volunteer" to exclude the value of the services rendered from his gross income. Charity work, whether in the form of direct assistance (a doctor working without pay for a clinic, say) or of fund-raising activities, is obviously widespread, yet no one has ever supposed that such efforts result in anything but excludable imputed income to the individual. This implied exclusion is not subject to the percentage limitation which applies to the deduction for gifts of money or other property; in effect, the value of the services is not taken into the volunteer's income in the first place.

In several published rulings, the Service has tried to distinguish for this purpose between redirected fees, which it regards as

---

[9]   Reg. § 1.170A–1(g).

contributions of property, and services in kind. In Rev. Rul. 71,[10] the Service held that the percentage limitation of § 170(b) would apply where an entertainer arranged with his sponsor or employer to pay his performance fee directly to his favorite charity. Where, however, the charity itself sponsored the performance or entertainment, the fact that the entertainer contributed his services free of charge would not result in taxable income to him. In effect, therefore, no limitation would be imposed on the amount he could exclude. Whether in a given case the charity was in fact the entertainer's employer *pro tem,* or was merely the beneficiary of income earned from third parties, was a question of "substance," "good faith," and "reality"—whatever those terms might mean.

The charitable-donee problem is only one example of the difficulty the Service has had over the years in coping with, and limiting, the implied exclusion for services-in-kind. Another important instance can be seen in the long drawn-out struggle over the tax status of family partnerships. The latter topic (which was finally dealt with by specific legislation) is taken up at 9.03, below.

8.02 Assignment of Deferred Income: *Helvering v. Eubank*

In *Earl,* as has been seen, the taxpayer made an assignment of salary and fees for legal services to be rendered in the future. The assignee's receipt was thus dependent on the assignor's willingness to go on working. If the assignor at any time decided to retire, take a vacation or otherwise substitute leisure for income-producing effort, the assignee's right to receive cash payments would obviously come to a halt. In this sense the gift of income in *Earl* was revocable by action (or inaction) of the assignor and remained subject to his control both as to time of realization and as to magnitude. To be sure, the Holmes opinion makes nothing of this circumstance, stressing instead the simple connection between taxability and personal effort. Still, it could be argued that a different result might have been reached in *Earl* if the taxpayer had assigned to his wife a claim derived from services *already completed.* In the latter event the assigned claim would have had a value in the assignee's hands which was independent of the assignor's future efforts; it would be "property" like cash or securities, and hence, perhaps, like them assignable.

In *Helvering v. Eubank,*[11] the taxpayer on the termination of his insurance agency assigned to a family trust his right to receive renewal commissions which he had earned through the sale of

---

[10]   1953–1 C.B. 18. *See also* G.C.M. 27026, 1951–2 C.B. 7.
[11]   311 U.S. 122 (1940).

insurance policies in earlier years. Since the taxpayer was on the cash method of accounting, the commissions would not be taxed to him until actually received in cash. The commissions were subsequently collected by the trustee and held for the benefit of other family members. The question presented was whether the commissions, when received, were includable in the taxpayer's income despite the assignment, or were taxable to the assignee. The court of appeals held that the assignment was effective to shift the income to the latter. It conceded that an individual could not "escape taxation upon his compensation in the year in which he earns it." That, presumably, was the rule of the *Earl* case. "But when a taxpayer who makes his income tax return on a cash basis assigns a right to money payable in the future for work already performed . . . he transfers a property right, and the money, when received by the assignee, is not income taxable to the assignor."

On appeal, the Supreme Court reversed. In a brief opinion, the Court held that a mere power to collect the commissions, which was all the assignee had received from the assignor, was insufficient to shift the income to the assignee for tax purposes. Accordingly, the renewal commissions were taxable to the assignor himself in the year received by the assignee. The Court did not suggest that the assignment by itself produced income to the taxpayer—that would be a rule of realization rather than one of mere attribution. It refused, however, to agree that personal service income, which for some reason (*e.g.*, the taxpayer's accounting method) is not includable in the year in which the services are rendered, thereby becomes "property" which can be shifted to another taxpayer by gratuitous assignment. Although Justice Stone's opinion is somewhat cryptic, the Court apparently felt that the donee was merely a passive repository whose relationship to the income was too weak to support a claim of ownership.

Taken together, the *Earl* and *Eubank* cases bar the assignment (for tax purposes, that is) of most kinds of conventional compensation rights. Thus a typical executive pay package would include (i) a current annual salary, plus (ii) a promise of further payments for a period of years following the executive's retirement. *Earl* makes clear that the current salary element will be taxed to the executive in full despite a prior agreement with his employer to pay a portion of it to other family members. *Eubank* makes equally clear that the executive will be taxed on the retirement benefits, when paid, even though the right to receive those benefits is assigned to another in advance of payment, and even though inclusion is deferred by reason of the taxpayer's accounting method or other applicable rules of realization.

Despite their considerable impact in the personal compensation field, there is a closely related area—that of self-created property rights—in which the rules of *Earl* and *Eubank* simply don't work. Suppose a well-known artist paints a landscape, puts a frame around it, and gives it to his son. The painting is worth, say, $10,000 at the date of the gift. The donee is tempted to sell the painting at once—there are plenty of bidders—but on reflection decides to hold the canvas for a while in the hope of a better price. It turns out that the decision was a wise one: the art market improves substantially, and the painting is finally sold by the son for $25,000. If we assume a zero basis for the painting, then there is $25,000 of income which plainly has to be taxed to someone. But to whom—the artistic father or the shrewdly calculating son? If we concentrate solely on the connection between taxability and personal effort, a theoretically correct answer can easily be given. Since $10,000 is traceable to the father's work as an artist and $15,000 to the son's shrewd calculation, the $25,000 of income should be attributed in precisely the same proportion, *i.e.,* $10,000 to the father, and $15,000 to the son. Each would thus recognize his own particular contribution to the total and the *Eubank* rule would be given a properly refined application.

The difficulty with this solution is that income-attribution rules are nearly always applied on an all-or-nothing basis. Apportionment (which would necessitate a hindsight valuation of the painting at the date of the gift) is not authorized by the statute and has never been attempted by the courts, while the only logical alternative—to treat the gift itself as a taxable event—is contrary to the present understanding of the realization requirement. Only one of the two candidates for taxability can be chosen, and under the decided cases it will evidently be the son. As compared with the donee in *Eubank* the son obviously has more than a mere "power to collect." He owns the painting, may decide when or whether to dispose of it, and negotiates the price and terms of sale. These elements of personal discretion are sufficiently material to cause the son to be treated as the source of the income. It follows that self-created property rights—which would also include patents and copyrights—are effectively assignable for tax purposes despite the element of personal services on the part of the assignor.

Taking the matter a short step further, suppose an author or inventor transfers his copyright or patent to a publisher or manufacturer under a royalty arrangement and then assigns the royalty contract to a donee. Since the donee thereby acquires no more than a "power to collect," one would tend to suppose that the royalties, when paid, would be taxable to the donor. To be sure, an assignment of the copyright or patent itself would be effective for tax purposes—the donee, like the son with the painting, is free to exercise his own discretion with respect to the disposition of the property (selling or retaining the movie rights in a book, exploiting an invention directly or selling it for a lump sum, and so on). But where the copyright or patent has already been disposed of by the donor, it seems reasonable to expect the *Eubank* case to be controlling. The courts, however, have held that because a prior assignment of the copyright or patent would suffice to shift the taxable income to the donee, a subsequent gift of the royalty contract must be treated similarly.[12] In extended form the reasoning is that (1) a copyright or patent is effectively assignable because it is "property" rather than a mere personal service claim; (2) a royalty contract derived from the transfer of a copyright or patent is therefore also "property"; and hence (3) *Eubank* does not apply. What has happened, of course, is that the problem of apportioning taxable income which led to the exception for self-created rights in the first place has been transformed into a shorthand distinction between "property" and "services." So altered, the exception has been applied to cases in which there is really *no* apportionment problem whatever—cases, that is, in which the donee has no discretion and contributes nothing to the production of the income that is finally realized.

For a taxpayer to take advantage of the rule permitting income-shifting by gifts of self-created property, the property must be of a sort generally treated as property—and bought and sold as such—for non-tax purposes. Paintings, copyrights, and patents obviously satisfy this standard. But suppose a lawyer hired to draft a complicated contract for a client gives the contract to her adult daughter, and the daughter sells the contract to the client. Because drafted-to-order contracts are not generally treated as property for non-tax purposes, the hoped-for income-shifting will not be achieved. This will be treated as an ineffectual attempt to shift income from services, rather than as a successful shifting of income from self-created property.

8.03 Gifts of Income from Property—*Horst, Blair* and *Schaffner*

(a) The Horst *Case*

Assume that a taxpayer—call him F for father—purchases a $1,000 5% coupon bond on January 1. The bond matures in twenty years and interest is payable annually. Suppose that F at once detaches and gives to S, his adult son, the first year's coupon, which entitles S to collect $50 in cash on December 31. At a discount rate of 5%, the value of S's coupon at the date of the gift is $47.60. Since bond

---

[12] *Heim v. Fitzpatrick,* 262 F.2d 887 (2d Cir.1959). Compare *Strauss v. Commissioner,* 168 F.2d 441 (2d Cir.1948), involving an unsuccessful attempt to assign contingent deferred compensation rights and presumably controlled by *Eubank.*

and coupon together are worth $1,000, the present value of F's bond (coupon detached) is necessarily $952.40. When it matures, on December 31, the coupon will of course be worth $50. By the same date F's bond plus the remaining coupons will have recovered in value to $1,000. Thus—

	Value of coupon/bond on Jan. 1	Value of coupon/ bond on Dec. 31	Increase in owner's net worth	Cash Received
S	$ 47.60	$ 50	$ 2.40	$50
F	952.40	1,000	47.60	–0–

In these circumstances, how much should F and S include in their respective gross incomes for the taxable year?

Not one, not two, but three possible answers can be given:

Answer 1: Follow the cash flow. Since S receives $50 in cash on Dec. 31, while F receives nothing, tax the entire interest payment to S. To be sure, F has enjoyed an increase in net worth during the taxable year of $47.60, but as this increase is not in the form of cash, there might be hardship in imposing on F an obligation to pay the tax. By contrast, S has funds in hand with which to meet that obligation. As noted in discussing the *Gavit* case (see 4.02), where two candidates for taxability appear, one with cash and the other without, there is a certain practical wisdom in choosing the former to bear the tax burden.

Answer 2: Disregard the gift of the coupon entirely. The coupon is nothing more than a right to collect $50 on Dec. 31; and since F could as well have collected the payment himself and then transferred the cash to S by gift, tax F on $50, and S on nothing. Under this approach F is treated as the constructive owner of the coupon throughout the taxable year. The $50 of interest received by S is attributed to F, even though the latter received no cash whatever.

Answer 3: Follow the net worth increase. Since S's net worth increases by $2.40 during the taxable year, while F's net worth increases by $47.60, tax the $50 of interest to S and F in the same proportions. This, surely, would be the actual result if, instead of a detached coupon worth $47.60, F had given S a 5% savings account containing $47.60 in cash, and at the same time had deposited $952.40 in a savings account of his own. S would then earn and be taxed on interest of $2.40 over the year, while F would earn and be taxed on $47.60. Arguably, the tax outcomes should be alike whether F chooses to invest in bonds paying 5% interest or in savings accounts of equivalent yield.

Each of the three answers is plausible. Which is best depends on one's criteria:

Answer 1—tax S on $50, F on 0—finds support in the Supreme Court's decision in *Irwin v. Gavit,* the facts of which are in many respects similar to those of our hypothetical (see 4.02). The issue in *Gavit* was whether the annual income of a testamentary trust should be attributed to the income beneficiary, to whom it was distributed, or be excluded as a gift or inheritance. By likely implication, if the income beneficiary were *not* taxed on all the current trust income, then the amount excluded would have to be taxed to the remainderman of the trust. The latter step could be justified on the ground that the value of the remainder interest increases with the passage of time, much as does the value of F's bond in our illustration. Faced, in effect, with two candidates for taxability, the Court in *Gavit* chose the income beneficiary rather than the remainderman, presumably because the former received the actual cash distribution from the trust.

Returning to our bond-and-coupon hypothetical, one can easily view S as the income beneficiary (though for one year only), F as the remainderman, the coupon as the annual income, and the bond as the corpus of a "trust". If the *Gavit* precedent were regarded as controlling, the result, of course, would be $50 of taxable income to S and zero to F—which is just what the taxpayer in *Horst* contended.

Answer 2—tax F on $50, S on 0—is the one which the Supreme Court actually gave in *Helvering v. Horst.*[13] In a lengthy opinion by Justice Stone, the Court held that the current interest payments on the taxpayer's bonds were includable in the taxpayer's income despite his annual gifts of the coupons to his son. In effect, the Court taxed F, the "remainderman," on the income from the property, and by implication viewed S, who actually collected the income at the year-end, as the recipient of an excludable gift. The result in *Horst* was thus exactly opposite to the outcome in *Gavit,* but the Supreme Court's opinion is of little help in understanding why. Justice Stone's opinion is largely and murkily preoccupied with the question of realization. The Court struggles—without much success—to find a rationale in the notion that because the donor obtained personal satisfaction from the act of giving, the gifts themselves should be regarded as a realization of taxable income. Yet it is plain that the Court did not intend to alter the settled rule that a gift of appreciated property does not result in a realization by the donor, so that the still unanswered question is why the transfer of a bond-coupon should be treated differently.

---

[13]   311 U.S. 112 (1940).

Confusing verbiage aside, it has long been obvious that the critical element in the *Horst* case was not the gift of the annual coupons but the donor's continued retention of the bond. This can easily be seen if we ask whether the result in *Horst,* or in our illustration, would be the same if F, having given the first coupon to S, then promptly gave the bond itself with the remaining coupons to his daughter (D). Since F was taxed on the interest received by S when F was the owner of the bond, should we now expect that D will take F's place and be taxed in the same way because *she* has become the bond owner? Unless *Horst* was meant to overrule *Gavit,* which is nowhere indicated, the answer is clearly no. The tax pattern established by the earlier decision would now take hold: S, the "income beneficiary," would be taxed on the interest represented by the bond coupon, while D, the "remainderman," would be entitled to the gift exclusion and would be taxed on nothing. Both of the candidates for taxability are donees in this version, and the choice between them falls on S. Since in *Horst* the outcome is reversed, one deduces that it is the presence of F, the donor, as a candidate for taxability that makes the vital difference. Whereas in *Gavit* the donor is out of the picture, in *Horst* he is obviously very much in it, and indeed the arrangement is one which he himself has created.

But why should it matter whether the part of "remainderman" is played by a donee or by the donor himself? The answer is that by holding on to the bond and the remaining coupons, the donor retains the power to direct and redirect the flow of property income at frequent intervals, and thus in effect to reduce the applicable tax rate to a minimum. In our illustration, as in the *Horst* case, the donor gave away the coupon for a single year only. Once that year had ended, he would of course be free to keep the next year's interest payment for himself, or to assign it to the same donee again, or to choose another donee if he wished. The same range of choices would be available in each succeeding year, so that the donor would effectively have reserved a power to redistribute the income annually among all the members of his family, including himself. In making this yearly choice, one would expect the donor to assign the income to the possessor of the lowest marginal rate of tax, everything else being equal. It is true that F could *always* shift the future interest income to a donee of his own selection by giving away the entire bond. That step, however, would permanently vest the income in the new owner, and in the course of time the donee might well move into a tax bracket no lower than the donor's. But if the choice of donee is permitted to be made on an annual basis, then each year presents the donor with a fresh opportunity to assess the impact of the rate structure on the several members of his family and to make the choice that minimizes the family's tax obligations.

The *Horst* decision blocked the device just mentioned by treating short-term gifts of income as ineffective for tax purposes. The power to redistribute property income at brief intervals, if retained by the donor, was treated as equivalent to the ownership of the income itself. Realization—at least in the ordinary understanding of that term—was not especially relevant; the bond interest when received by S was taxable to F just as if the latter had actually received it at the year-end. Essentially, the tax-shifting effort failed in *Horst* because the donor's control over the flow of income was so substantial that his prior ownership was viewed as continuing despite the gift. As in *Earl*, the taxpayer was denied the right to make his own choice of taxable person. The choice was made for him, so to speak, through the medium of a rule which attributed the income to the donor as long as he retained ownership of the underlying property.

Answer 3—tax F on $47.60, S on $2.40—is apparently now the result in our hypothetical involving the gift of an interest coupon by a donor retaining the bond itself. In analogous situations not involving debt instruments—for example, a father giving a son the right to collect rents on an apartment building owned by the father, or to receive dividends on stock owned by the father—*Horst* (*i.e.,* Answer 2) is still the law. However, § 1286 (enacted in 1982) mandates the bifurcation-of-income approach of Answer 3 when a taxpayer owning a debt instrument makes a gift of the right to receive one or more interest payments while retaining the debt instrument itself. Although this rule permits a limited amount of income-shifting, the result is far from a tax bonanza; it only replicates the result that could have been obtained by F's giving S a savings account of $47.60 and depositing $952.40 in a savings account for himself.

(b) Blair *and* Schaffner

The *Horst* case involved what is commonly referred to as a gift of a carved-out interest—a part of the taxpayer's property is carved out and transferred to the donee, but the remaining part is retained by the donor. As already suggested, the significance of this factor is that it leaves the donor free to make temporary and periodic allocations of taxable income. The progressive rate structure is obviously vulnerable to such practices, but the *Horst* decision (or § 1286, when it applies) furnishes the Treasury with a powerful means of defense.

The importance of "carving-out" in the field of income-attribution can be seen by comparing the Supreme Court's decisions in *Blair v. Commissioner*[14] and *Harrison v. Schaffner*.[15] Both *Blair* and *Schaffner* involved assignments of rights to trust income, yet the taxpayer succeeded in *Blair* but failed in *Schaffner*. The reason, presumably, is that the element of carving out was absent in the former case and present in the latter.

In *Blair* the life-tenant of a testamentary trust assigned to his children specified dollar interests in the income of the trust. Although the donor retained the unassigned portion of the trust income for himself, the donees' interests were to continue for the duration of the life estate and were thus coterminous with the donor's. The Service contended that the gifts were only of a "right to receive . . . income" and hence should be taxed to the donor. The Court, however, held the *donees* taxable. In *Schaffner,* the income beneficiary of a trust also assigned to her children specified dollar amounts of trust income, but here the amounts assigned were to be paid out of the income of the trust for the following year. Thereafter, and for all subsequent years, the trust income would again be paid to the donor. This time the Court held the *donor* taxable, despite the taxpayer's contention that the gifts were of "property" and hence taxable to the donees.

Both *Blair* and *Schaffner* are generally assumed to be correct and likewise mutually consistent. The assignment in *Blair* was of a permanent interest in the donor's property—once given away the donees' fractional interests could never revest in the donor because the gifts were to last as long as the life estate itself. The donor's power to control the income stream represented by his life estate was to that extent terminated and could never be revived. Essentially, the gifts in *Blair* resembled the transfer by a stockholder of a portion of his shares, or the transfer by a building owner of an undivided interest in his real estate; in either such event, the dividends or the rents from the property transferred would undoubtedly be taxable to the donee. To be sure, the life estate was itself a right to taxable income. Yet the life estate was all the property the donor had, and as the fractional interests were assigned without reversion the assignment was entitled to the same effect as the assignment of any other property.

In *Schaffner,* by contrast, the taxpayer transferred one out of a series of income payments—very much as if the stockholder or the real estate owner gave away one year's dividends or one year's rents. As in *Horst,* the transferor was free to dispose of the subsequent payments in any way he chose, designating other recipients from time to time or retaining such payments for himself. No permanent addition was made to the donee's taxable income: the donor could reassess his tax position at the end of the year and make a new

---

[14]   300 U.S. 5 (1937).
[15]   312 U.S. 579 (1941).

judgment in the light of foreseeable circumstances. The gift was thus a temporary income allocation, a carving-out, and it is precisely this which the *Horst* decision condemns.

A loose end. The *Schaffner* case involved a "wasting asset"—an asset of limited duration whose value is zero at the end of its useful life—and for this reason presents a somewhat weaker case for attribution than *Horst* itself. Suppose a taxpayer buys a ten-year lease for $50,000 under which he is to receive ten annual payments of $7,500. Using the straight-line method of amortization, the first and each succeeding payment will include $2,500 of income plus $5,000 of return of capital. Suppose the taxpayer gives the *first* of the series of payments to his son. The son will receive not only $2,500 of income (otherwise taxable to the donor) but $5,000 of the donor's invested capital. As far as the $5,000 of capital is concerned, it is lost to the donor and can never again be used by him to generate disposable income. Whereas in *Horst* the bond owner's principal was restored once the coupon-year had passed, here the opportunity to redirect the yield on a portion of the donor's capital has been terminated. Hence, perhaps the gift should be regarded as a transfer of "underlying property" rather than of a mere right to income. In effect, however, the *Schaffner* case rejects this argument, because it extends the prohibition against "carving-out" to wasting as well as non-wasting assets, or, rather, ignores the difference between the two.

Suppose, in the same hypothetical, that after nine years have passed the lease owner gives the *last* of the ten rental payments to his son. Although the effect seems exactly the same from every standpoint, there is no carving-out and the gift would most likely be effective for tax purposes. Once the first nine payments have been received, the tenth payment is "all the property the donor has." The fatal element of a reversion is lacking.

8.04 Gifts in Trust—*Corliss, Wells* and *Clifford*

The trust device is exceedingly useful from the standpoint of a donor of property who wishes to retain elements of control over the disposition of his gift. As compared with a transfer of property to an individual donee, a gift in trust enables the grantor to determine the beneficial ownership of the property over more than one generation by providing for life estates with remainders to descendants. In addition, the distribution of trust assets, whether income or corpus, can be flexibly arranged by authorizing the trustee to make payments in varying proportions to any member of a class—say the grantor's children—or even to retain and accumulate the trust income in a given year if that seems preferable. The grantor, moreover, may reserve a right to receive or apply the income for his own benefit, or to recover the corpus on termination of an income interest granted to another, or even, as in *Corliss v. Bowers,*[16] to revoke the trust and restore the trust property to his personal ownership. Finally—again as compared with a gift to an individual—the creator of a trust is able to appoint the manager of the property by designating a person of responsibility and skill in the handling of investments—a bank, a lawyer, a friend, even himself—to serve as trustee. These elements of flexibility and discretion are difficult or impossible to create when property is simply given outright to an individual donee—there really are no viable legal means of limiting a donee's right to deal with the property as he himself sees fit when the gift is in outright form.

Yet the very flexibility of the trust device means that lines must be drawn between gifts in trust that are effective for tax purposes because they sufficiently resemble outright gifts to be treated in the same way, and gifts in trust that are ineffective because the grantor's interest continues to predominate. Thus, how far must the grantor go in the direction of a complete surrender of his personal authority over the trust property before trust income will be treated as belonging to the beneficiaries? Put otherwise, what rights and interests may the grantor retain without continuing to be regarded as the substantial owner of the property transferred? This issue obviously arises only with respect to lifetime or *inter vivos* trusts. While testamentary trusts also present choice of taxable person questions (see 4.02), the candidates for taxability are necessarily restricted to the living beneficiaries and do not include the grantor-decedent.

The Supreme Court's early decisions in the field of lifetime trusts can be treated more briefly than the cases discussed in the preceding subsections because gifts in trust are now governed entirely by specific statutory provisions. Indeed, Congress showed an inclination at a very early point to resolve trust attribution problems by legislative enactment, and as the dissent in *Helvering v. Clifford*[17] shows it was possible even then to argue with some force that Congress intended "trusts and estates" to be wholly free from the judicial rule-making process that had been applied to individuals under the authority of § 61. The Court majority rejected this limitation in *Clifford,* but when Congress in 1954 adopted the detailed statutory coverage referred to above it expressly provided that the new Code sections should have exclusive application. Hence, unlike *Earl, Horst* and *Blair,* which continue to be governing authorities in the area of gifts to individuals, the cases discussed next

---

[16]   281 U.S. 376 (1930).
[17]   309 U.S. 331 (1940).

should be read chiefly as background for the present-day statutory treatment of gifts in trust described at 9.01, below.

The Revenue Act of 1924 contained two statutory provisions relating to the attribution of trust income to trust grantors. The first—now embodied in Code § 676(a)—provided that a grantor would be taxed on trust income if he retained a power, exercisable alone or with a nonbeneficiary of the trust, to revest the trust corpus in himself. The second—the forerunner of present § 677(a)(3)—provided for the taxation of the grantor where the trust income could, in the discretion of any person, be distributed to the grantor or accumulated for his benefit, or applied to the payment of premiums of insurance on the grantor's life. In *Corliss v. Bowers,* the taxpayer had created a revocable trust for the benefit of his wife and children. Sustaining the constitutionality of the first of the two provisions mentioned above, the Supreme Court held that the grantor's power to revoke the trust and thus to stop payment to the income beneficiary was equivalent to actual ownership of the trust property. With reference to taxation, said the Court,

> [I]f a man disposes of a fund in such a way that another is allowed to enjoy the income which it is in the power of the first to appropriate it does not matter whether the permission is given by assent or by failure to express dissent. The income that is subject to a man's unfettered command and that he is free to enjoy at his own option may be taxed to him as income, whether he sees fit to enjoy it or not.

In *Burnet v. Wells,*[18] the taxpayer had transferred to an irrevocable trust certain property the income from which was to be used to pay the premiums for an insurance policy on the grantor's life. On the grantor's death the policy proceeds were to be collected by the trustee (who also presumably owned the policy) and invested for the benefit of the grantor's daughter. Conceding that it applied by its terms, the taxpayer argued that the second of the two 1924 amendments was unconstitutional insofar as it taxed a grantor on trust income applied to the payment of insurance premiums because it thereby sought to tax one who (quoting the dissent) "retained no vestige of title to, interest in, or control over the property transferred to the trustee." Once again the Supreme Court held for the government, although only by a vote of 5–4. An insured person, it found, is under an obligation—moral if not legal—to continue to pay the premiums on his life insurance, and Congress therefore could reasonably determine that the use of trust income for that purpose conveyed a taxable benefit to the grantor:

---

[18]   289 U.S. 670 (1933).

> Even if not a duty, it [insurance] is a common item in the family budget, kept up very often at cost of painful sacrifice. . . . It will be a vain effort at persuasion to argue to the average man that a trust created by a father to pay premiums of life insurance for the use of sons and daughters is not a benefit to the one who will have to pay the premiums if the policies are not to lapse.

The dissenting Justices argued fervently that the grantor had actually severed all connection with the trust property and that the statutory amendment was unconstitutional because it sought to tax "the income of A [the trustee or the beneficiary] as the income of B [the grantor]."

Viewed in hindsight, neither *Corliss* nor *Wells* involved an especially startling expansion of the ordinary concept of "income". As respects revocable trusts, the grantor could be taxed because he had control of the trust, and therefore of its earnings, even though the income was actually received by the beneficiary. The income was his if he wanted it; the beneficiary had nothing that could not be taken back by the grantor at will. The element of "unfettered command," at least when exercisable by the grantor in his own favor, was sufficient to support a taxable link between the grantor and the trust. Insurance trusts obviously present a harder case, but as a grantor is clearly taxable if trust income is used to meet his legal support obligations—his children's medical bills, for example—it also seems reasonable for Congress to have regarded life insurance premiums as belonging in the same category. Presumably the grantor was willing to maintain the premiums out of his own funds originally, and the trust was simply an irrevocable commitment of income to the same purpose.

Although *Corliss* and *Wells* were thus decided on the basis of specific statutory provisions, the Supreme Court's decision in *Helvering v. Clifford* shows that the Court continued to believe that its own authority under § 61 had not been preempted by congressional action in the trust field. In *Clifford,* the grantor created a trust for the benefit of his wife. The trust was to terminate at the end of five years and the corpus was then to be paid over to the grantor himself as remainderman. The grantor also appointed himself to be the sole trustee with broad management powers and with a power to distribute the trust income to his wife or to accumulate it for her benefit. In fact, the trust income was annually distributed to the grantor's wife. Although the trust arrangement was plainly not within either of the two subsections mentioned above, the Court held that the grantor was the owner of the trust for purposes of § 61 and hence taxable on the trust income. "[T]he short duration of the trust, the fact that the wife was the beneficiary, and the retention of control over the corpus by the [taxpayer]" all led "irresistibly" to that conclusion. According to the Court,

> We have at best a temporary reallocation of income within an intimate family group. Since the income remains in the family and since the husband retains control over the investment, he has rather complete assurance that the trust will not effect any substantial change in his economic position. . . . [W]hen the benefits flowing to him directly through the wife are added to the legal rights he retained, the aggregate may be said to be a fair equivalent of what he previously had. . . .

Justice Douglas' opinion stressed the point that "no one fact is normally decisive" in determining whether the grantor or the beneficiary should be treated as the "owner" of the trust. As in *Horst* the short-term nature of the beneficiary's income interest was surely a major factor in the outcome—it is as if the bond-owner had detached five annual coupons while retaining the bond—but the Court was plainly unwilling to isolate that circumstance and state that it, by itself, was either necessary or sufficient. The same, of course, was true of the other significant elements which linked the corpus to the grantor—the grantor's power to accumulate or distribute the trust income at his discretion, his broad powers of management, and the fact that the trust income was to go to the grantor's wife. The Court's approach was to aggregate these factors, thus avoiding the need to give precise weight to any particular criterion. Most commentators, perhaps, would have guessed that the short-term feature was critical and indeed was *both* necessary and sufficient. But no one could be certain. The power to accumulate—to "compel" the beneficiary to save the trust income during the five-year term—was an important element of control; perhaps it, too, could be regarded as equivalent to ownership. Management powers seemed somewhat less significant, and trusts for the benefit of one's wife were reasonably common; yet when these factors were joined together the totality might suffice to meet the Court's conception of continued ownership. Once again, the "aggregative" approach placed the matter in substantial doubt.

Some commentators applauded, while others condemned, the *Clifford* decision for its vagueness and elasticity. The Treasury responded to *Clifford* by issuing detailed regulations in which the significance of various possible factors was weighed and sorted out in an effort to provide reasonable guidelines for taxpayers and their advisors. The Regulations emphasized individual elements of the trust arrangement—duration of the trust, extent of the grantor's control, power to manage in his own interest—rather than the balancing of factors which the Court had seemed to approve, and the lower courts were by no means always friendly to the government's position. The scope of the *Clifford* decision being uncertain, it became evident in time that a statutory solution was required. As noted above, Congress in 1954 provided that solution in the form of a set of detailed Code provisions[19] which effectively put an end to "judicial balancing" in this field.

While the *Clifford* case was thus superseded by congressional action, it remains true that the present statutory treatment owes much of its inspiration to that decision, and the case itself, along with *Earl* and *Horst,* is something of a high point in the history of the Supreme Court's confrontation with the problem of income attribution.

8.05 Summary of Attribution Principles

The income-attribution cases are really simpler than they look. On the whole, the Supreme Court's opinions in this field are over-long and confusing—*Horst, Clifford, Blair* could all have been handled much more briefly, especially the first-named. *Eubank,* on the other hand, is really too brief and cryptic, and at all events should have drawn its precedent from the *Earl* decision rather than claiming to be indistinguishable from *Horst. Earl* itself, finally, might have been a better opinion if Holmes had omitted the fruit-and-tree metaphor, both for literary and for conceptual reasons.[20] The problem throughout, perhaps, was how the Court could aid in developing a set of anti-tax avoidance rules—how it could act to give protection to the graduated rate structure—without directly admitting that it was engaged in judicial lawmaking. Operating under a limited mandate, the Court sought to safeguard the rates by manipulating the legal concepts of "income," "property," and "ownership" instead of making bald utterances about tax-avoidance. But the quoted terms are inherently confusing and indefinite; they can be used to mean almost anything. In a sense, therefore, in summarizing the attribution rules, it is better and simpler to stress the *results* of the decided cases than to linger over the reasoning.

Taking this approach, the decisional law of income attribution can be restated as follows:

(1) *Personal service income* is taxable to the person who does the work, no matter whom he designates to receive the pay envelope. This is true whether the services are to be rendered in the future, as

---

[19] Section 671 *et seq.*

[20] The *Earl* opinion has been described as "late vintage Holmes, magisterial in tone, studded with quotable phrases, and devoid of analysis." Bittker, *Federal Income Taxation and the Family,* 27 Stanford L.Rev. 1389, 1401 (1975).

in *Earl*, or have already been completed at the time the designation is made, as in *Eubank*. But there are exceptions:

(a) Uncompensated services—services in kind—are apparently allowed to be excluded from the taxpayer's income in most cases. The general rule of *Earl* is not applied here and the value of the uncompensated service is treated in the same way as imputed income. As will be seen at 9.02, however, this exclusion is in turn reversed where the taxpayer is a member of a family partnership, though not where he is an employee of a family corporation.

(b) Patents, copyrights, works of art, and the like are free of the general rule even though plainly a product of personal efforts. The statute does not provide for the apportionment of income between donor and donee, and as both parties may reasonably claim to have made a contribution to the income ultimately realized on disposition of the asset, the general rule gives way to considerations of feasibility and permits the donee to report all the income as his own.

(2) Gifts of *income-producing property,* as in *Blair,* are effective to shift the future income to the donee for tax purposes. Here, too, there are exceptions:

(a) The donor remains taxable if he has a right to take the property back, as in *Corliss,* or to use the income for himself or to meet his own obligations, as in *Wells.*

(b) The donor remains taxable if he has a right to alter the identity of—that is, to redesignate—the donee in his own discretion. A short-term gift of property, as in *Clifford,* or a gift consisting of a limited number of income payments drawn from a larger series, as in *Horst* and *Schaffner,* is ineffective to relieve the donor of tax.

(c) Somewhat indefinitely—*Clifford*—the reservation by a donor of powers to manage and dispose of trust property may be treated as equivalent to continued ownership. As stated, the scope of this exception and the meaning of continued "ownership" are now reflected with reasonable clarity in a group of specific statutory provisions which supersede the *Clifford* decision.

Even as oversimplified, the above rules suggest that property—stocks, bonds, real estate—is treated more favorably under the tax law than personal services. While he was barred from assigning a single coupon only, the father in *Horst* was obviously free, if he wished, to shift the interest income to his son by giving away the entire bond. Apart from the restriction on short-term transfers and the like, and outside the application of the kiddie tax, income from investments can readily be divided among the members of a family by making gifts (including gifts in trust) of the underlying property itself. No equivalent division is possible with respect to service income. With minor exceptions there appears to be no way to assign the fruits of personal effort; wage and salary earners are simply stuck with the progressive rates. To be sure, there is a difference in administrability. While it is easy enough to link wages to wage-earners, any effort to reallocate property income to donors would run into near-hopeless problems of tracing and identification. But this in itself hardly answers the basic criticism.

There may, however, be another way of looking at the whole question. It could be said that what the law does in this field is simply to prohibit the shifting of *pre-tax* income, while allowing the transfer of savings. Thus, suppose a lawyer earns fees of $100,000 and pays tax at a rate of 35%. *Earl* makes it impossible for the lawyer to give the fees away before paying his income tax of $35,000. Once the tax is paid, however, and the lawyer meets his own living expenses, he is free to do what he likes with the amount that is left. The sense one has of discrimination against earned income as opposed to income from property may ease a bit if we reflect that "property" is simply the taxpayer's earned income *after tax*. There is a tendency to think of personal service income and "property" as always belonging to two different and distinct individuals or to two different *classes* of individuals. Not so, of course, and perhaps one gets a different feeling about the problem of discrimination and favoritism if the legal rules are put this way: A taxpayer who derives income through personal efforts must pay the tax thereon; he can, however, give his savings to his kids.

There is yet another plausible answer to the criticism that the income-attribution rules treat income from property more favorably than income from services. The rules for both types of income might be reconciled as being two applications, in different circumstances, of the same principle—that income should be taxed to the person with the strongest ongoing connection with the source of the income. In the case of income from property, a property owner can sever his connection with the source of the income by making an outright gift of the income-producing property; the tax law accordingly allows him to shift the tax burden on post-gift income to the donee, who now has the strongest connection with the income source. In the case of personal services income, however, the source of the income is the "human capital" of the service provider himself. Because it is not possible for the service provider to sever his connection with himself—to alienate himself from his own human capital—the service provider always has the closest connection with the source of his earned income, and thus is always the taxpayer with respect to that income.

9. Statutory Treatment of Income Attribution

9.01 Grantor Trusts

The present statutory treatment of trusts (and estates) can be viewed in two parts. The first—contained in Subparts A-D of Subchapter J—pertains to ordinary or conventional trusts in which the grantor retains no significant interest and the trust income is taxed to the named beneficiaries or the trustee. All testamentary trusts necessarily fall into this class; so do most *inter vivos* trusts, because there is little point (in most circumstances) in creating a lifetime trust if the income from the trust property continues to be taxed to the grantor. Although trusts are treated as independent taxable entities by the Code (taxable under a separate rate schedule), it is not the intention thereby to increase the taxes of those who use the trust device. In computing its annual taxable income, therefore, the trust is permitted to take a *special deduction* for distributions made to its beneficiaries. This means that the beneficiaries and not the trust are taxed on the income distributed during the year; the trust serves merely as a "conduit" through which taxable income flows into the hands of the individual recipients.

The trust itself is taxed only if the trustee accumulates the trust income in a given year instead of distributing it. Since 1986, § 1(e) has provided a highly compressed tax rate schedule for trusts. In 2018, for example, the 37% rate applies to all taxable income of a trust in excess of $12,500. With all substantial amounts of undistributed trust income (of a non-grantor trust) taxed at the top individual rate, accumulation trusts are no longer attractive as devices for shifting income to lower tax brackets.

The second element of the statutory scheme appears in Subpart E of Subchapter J. It is concerned exclusively with so-called grantor trusts, and represents the legislative solution to the problems created by *Clifford*. Only *inter vivos* trusts are affected, quite obviously, since the aim of the Code at this point is to prevent living grantors from avoiding tax by shifting income to other family members while still retaining an interest in or a power over the property placed in trust. Where that interest or power is considered to be substantial, the Code in effect ignores the separate existence of the trust and treats the grantor as if he continued to own the property directly. As noted earlier, the intention of Congress was to overcome the uncertainties of the *Clifford* case through specific legislation and to place the entire question of grantor trusts outside the scope of judicial construction under § 61(a). Accordingly, § 671 provides that the statutory rules described below are exclusive with respect to whether trust income is taxable to a grantor "solely on the grounds of his dominion or control over the trust." This element of exclusivity does not, however, supersede or preempt other standing rules of income attribution such as those approved in the *Earl* and *Horst* cases. Thus, an attempted assignment of personal service income to a trust, though not alluded to in Subpart E, would still be ineffective as an income-shifting device because "dominion or control over the trust" is not the basis of the assignor's liability under those circumstances. But when the issue is of the *Clifford* variety—*i.e.,* whether the grantor's interest in the trust is so substantial as to be the equivalent of continued ownership—the specific statutory provisions are given exclusive application.

From the standpoint of a trust grantor, the *Clifford* rules operate to set the minimum conditions for income-shifting. As suggested above, there is little reason to create a lifetime trust that *offends* the statutory limitations: if trust income continued to be taxed to the grantor because he had retained an interest in or power over the trust property, then the grantor might as well have kept the property in his own hands to start with—why bother with a trust at all? By the same token, there is no compelling reason for the grantor to give up a greater interest in the trust property than the Code specifically demands. Having surrendered whatever rights he must in order to shift income to the lower-bracket beneficiary, the grantor can if he wishes (and presumably would) reserve to himself all the remaining elements of ownership. Thus the main object in creating a lifetime trust—often the only object—is to reduce the family tax burden. To achieve that end the grantor would usually do as much as, but also as little as, the statutory rules—now to be summarized—require.

Before delving into the details of the grantor trust provisions, we must acknowledge that these rules are not nearly as important today as they were before the enactment of (i) the compressed § 1(e) tax rate schedule for accumulated trust income and (ii) the kiddie tax of § 1(g) (9.02). Avoiding grantor trust status is no victory (and may even be a defeat, depending on the grantor's own marginal tax rate) if the trust income is accumulated and taxed at 37% under § 1(e). Avoiding grantor trust status is also no victory if the trust income is distributed and taxed to a child, if the kiddie tax applies and imposes a tax rate of 37%. As a general rule, avoiding grantor trust status now results in shifting of investment income to a lower-bracket taxpayer only if (i) the trust income is currently distributed rather than accumulated, and (ii) the income is distributed to an adult beneficiary who is not subject to the kiddie tax. It is doubtful whether the grantor trust rules described below would have been so elaborate if the compressed tax rate schedule for trusts and the kiddie tax had existed when the grantor trust rules were enacted. The lessened significance of the grantor trust rules has not, however, inspired Congress to simplify them.

(a) Reversionary Interests

Code § 673 picks up the principal feature of the *Clifford* case by providing that a grantor is treated as the owner of the trust property whenever he (or his spouse) retains a reversionary interest in income or corpus having a value in excess of 5% of the trust property. Assuming an 8% interest rate, the 5% rule means that a retained reversion cannot take effect for nearly 40 years if grantor trust status is to be avoided. Assuming a 6% interest rate, even a reversion taking effect in 51 years would be too valuable to avoid grantor trust status. Quite obviously, therefore, a near-complete divestiture of interest on the part of the grantor is required. The 5% rule applies, moreover, whether the reversion takes effect after a term of years or on the death of an income beneficiary (other than the death of a child during minority), so that a trust to pay the income to an aged parent for life, remainder to the grantor, will always be treated as a grantor trust.

(b) Income for Grantor's Benefit

Code § 677(a)—the constitutionality of which was upheld in *Burnet v. Wells*—treats the grantor as the "owner" if the trust income is or may be distributed to or accumulated for the benefit of the grantor or his spouse, or applied to the payment of premiums on an insurance policy on the grantor's life. The grantor is taxed under these circumstances where the power to dispose of trust income resides in the grantor himself, in a nonadverse party, or in both, provided that the approval of an adverse party is not required. The term "adverse party" is defined as one having an economic interest in the trust that would be adversely affected by the exercise of the power.

In *Helvering v. Stuart*[21] the Supreme Court held under the predecessor of § 677(a) that the income of a trust which could be used for the support and maintenance of the grantor's minor children was taxable to the grantor whether used for that purpose or not. Section 677(b) was enacted as a response to the *Stuart* decision. It provides that the grantor is not taxed merely because the trust income *may* be applied to the support of his dependents; the grantor is taxed, however, to the extent the income *is* so applied.

---

[21]   317 U.S. 154 (1942).

(c)   Revocability and Powers to Control Enjoyment

Sections 676(a) and 674(a) tax the grantor where he (or a non-adverse party) retains substantial powers of disposition over the income or corpus of the trust. The former section is simply the current version of the revocable trust provision which was approved in *Corliss v. Bowers*—a grantor who retains power to revoke the trust is treated as the owner of the trust property. Both sections are coordinated with the 5% rule of § 673; the grantor is not taxed currently if the retained power cannot affect the trust for a period such that the grantor would not be treated as the owner if the power were a reversionary interest.

Section 674 is of considerable importance insofar as the details of trust draftsmanship are concerned, and it is also here that the most difficult and debatable legislative judgments were made by Congress. The section begins in subsection (a) by treating the grantor as the owner of the trust if the beneficial enjoyment of corpus or income is subject to a power of disposition exercisable by anyone other than an adverse party, but then goes on in subsections (b)–(d) to list the exceptions which actually define the scope of the general rule. The exceptions are of two sorts—those which apply regardless of whom the grantor appoints to serve as trustee, and those which apply where the trustee is "independent," *i.e.,* neither the grantor himself nor anyone related or subordinate to the grantor. If the grantor wishes to serve as trustee himself or to appoint a related or subordinate party, the powers permitted to be granted to the trustee without causing the grantor to be taxed are the limited discretionary powers described in subsection (b); if the grantor appoints an independent trustee, the much broader powers described in subsection (c) will be permitted. The choice is thus "essentially between giving the trustee the grantor really prefers limited discretionary powers and giving a trustee selected from a restricted list broader discretionary powers."[22]

Among the more important powers which the grantor himself may exercise as trustee under § 674(b) are the power to invade corpus for a current income beneficiary if chargeable to that beneficiary's share, and the power to accumulate income for a current income beneficiary provided the accumulations are ultimately payable to the beneficiary himself or his estate or appointees. In effect the grantor may retain a power either to advance or to postpone the beneficiary's receipt of income or corpus, such power to be exercisable in the grantor's sole discretion or in the discretion of any person he selects. A trust for the benefit of the grantor's child, with powers in the

---

[22] Westfall, *Trust Grantors and Section 674: Adventures in Income Tax Avoidance*, 60 Colum.L.Rev. 326 (1960).

trustee to invade corpus or accumulate income for the child's benefit, is thus not regarded as "owned" by the grantor even if he appoints himself the trustee.

If the grantor is willing to appoint an "independent trustee"— which may include not only a corporate fiduciary (a bank or trust company) but the grantor's lawyer or accountant—§ 674(c) permits him (without adverse tax consequences) to create what is called a spray trust. Not only can the trust corpus be advanced or the income accumulated, but the trustee is free to decide which person among a class of beneficiaries (*e.g.,* the grantor's children) will actually receive the income or corpus from time to time and in what proportions.

The permission to choose among beneficiaries in § 674(c) obviously enables the trustee to do precisely what was condemned in the *Horst* case, namely, to allocate the trust income to the lowest marginal ratepayer or to distribute it in a manner which equalizes the taxable income of the beneficiaries. Moreover, the "independence" from grantor influence which is presumed to reside in the bosom of the grantor's banker, lawyer or accountant may be more apparent than real in many cases. As compared with an outright gift, where the property income is permanently vested in an identifiable donee, § 674(c) allows the grantor to end his own tax liability without making a definite choice of the person to whom the property income will be attributed thereafter. Hence if we assume that outright gifts represent the basic model of permissible tax-shifting, § 674(c) is something of a departure in the direction of more discretion and more liberal treatment for property owners and their families.

(d) Persons Other than Grantor Treated as Owner

Section 678(a), which embodies prior case law,[23] provides that a person other than the grantor will be treated as the owner of a trust if such person has sole power to vest the corpus or income in himself, whether or not exercised. Like the other statutory provisions in this area, § 678(a) displaces § 61(a) and has exclusive application. However, it is narrower in scope than the sections which provide for taxing grantors. A trust created by the taxpayer's father, say, which empowers the taxpayer to distribute trust income to his wife or to accumulate it for the benefit of his children would not be treated as owned by the taxpayer since he lacks the power to obtain the income for himself directly. The same arrangement, if created by the taxpayer himself with property acquired from his father by gift or inheritance, would run afoul of § 677(a), so that in effect the parties are rewarded for their foresight.

---

[23]   *Mallinckrodt v. Nunan,* 146 F.2d 1 (8th Cir.1945).

A loose end. The use of interest-free demand loans (instead of revocable gifts) to shift income from high-bracket to low-bracket family members was reportedly much resorted to prior to the enactment in 1984 of § 7872. While the device itself seems rather transparent, the general view appeared to be that such arrangements had no income tax consequences for either borrower or lender. A parent, for example, faced with tuition and related costs of $40,000 a year for his 24 year-old law-student child, might lend the child $400,000 on a non-interest bearing note. Although theoretically free to do otherwise, the well-behaving child would invest the funds in a 10% U.S. Treasury bond, pay his own college expenses, and then hand the bond over to his parent in repayment of the loan on graduation day. While the bond interest would be taxed annually to the child (who would presumably have little other income), the parent in effect would have succeeded in excluding from his own gross income the otherwise nondeductible cost of the child's law school education.[24]

The 1984 provision—subject to a *de minimis* exception and other conditions—deals with family loans by imputing an interest payment from child to parent and then treating the interest actually forgone as a gift-back from parent to child. Thus, the child would first include the Treasury bond interest in his gross income and then deduct an imputed interest payment to the parent. The parent would include the imputed interest in *his* gross income and would then be deemed to have returned that sum to the child as a nondeductible gift. The result, quite obviously, is the same as it would be if the parent had purchased the bond for himself, received the interest, and then made a gift to the child of the latter amount.

Code § 7872 applies as well to interest-free loans between corporations and shareholders. In the corporate-shareholder context, however, the imputation concept is designed to assure that the Treasury bond interest will be taxed at *both* levels—as it would be if the corporation simply bought the bond itself and then distributed the bond interest to the shareholder as a dividend. Accordingly, if we substitute corporation for parent and shareholder for child in the above illustration, the results under § 7872 are (1) inclusion of the Treasury bond interest in the shareholder's gross income followed by

---

[24] Prior to being shut down by § 7872 in 1984, this income-shifting technique was probably used more often to finance undergraduate educations than to finance graduate and professional educations. Even apart from § 7872, however, under current law the technique would not work for undergraduate education because the kiddie tax (9.02) would apply. If our hypothetical law student is at least 24, the kiddie tax would not apply, and the technique described in the text would still succeed but for § 7872.

the deduction of an imputed interest payment to the corporation, (2) inclusion of the imputed interest payment in the corporation's gross income, and (3) payment of an imputed dividend to the shareholder by the corporation equal to the interest actually forgone. The imputed dividend, though taxable to the shareholder, is not deductible by the corporation. When the dust has settled, therefore, one finds that an amount equal to the bond interest will have been taxed once at the corporate level and again to the shareholder, which is just what our double-tax system requires.

9.02 Unearned Income of Minors (and Some Young Adults)—The Kiddie Tax

As already generally observed, the problem of income attribution arises, essentially, because the Code treats the taxpayer and each member of his family as a separate taxable person. Except for spouses, who normally file jointly, each family member calculates his or her own taxable income based on the rules of attribution described above, computes tax, and files his or her own individual tax return. The attribution rules are designed to prohibit the assignment of personal service income and to limit an assignor's discretion in the case of property gifts, but the tax law does not attempt to deal with family income-splitting by redefining the taxable unit. The notion that parents and children might be viewed as a single taxpayer, however plausible, is not one that has ever been seriously considered by Congress, perhaps because the question of when a child ceases to be a "child" and becomes an independent adult with a separate household is really one of fact rather than legal definition.

Without departing from this principle of separate taxability, § 1(g) takes a significant step towards family unity. Under § 1(g), the net unearned income (dividends, interest, etc.) of a child who is under 18 is taxed to the child as if included in his parents' income (in years before 2018 or after 2025), or under the compressed § 1(e) rate schedule applicable to trusts (in 2018 through 2025). The provision also applies to the unearned income of an adult child, if the child's earned income does not exceed one-half of the amount of the child's support for the taxable year, and either (i) the child is younger than 19, or (ii) the child is younger than 24 and is a full-time student. In essence, the provision applies if the parents can claim the child as a dependent. When § 1(g) applies, the child's net unearned income is still taxed to the child (unless the parents elect to include the income on their own return), but it is taxed at the parents' marginal tax rate, or under the trust rate schedule (depending on the year). The aim, quite obviously, is to prevent high-bracket parents from shifting income into the hands of low-bracket children through gifts of securities and other investment property—gifts which, under a normal application of the income-attribution rules, would achieve precisely that result. The provision applies, however, without regard to the source of the child's income-producing property. If a child's income-producing property was a gift from doting grandparents or a rich aunt, the income is nevertheless taxed at the parents' marginal tax rate (or under the trust rate schedule), not the marginal tax rate of the grandparents or aunt. By way of *de minimis* exclusion, the term "*net* unearned income" means unearned income less the sum of $1,050 plus the greater of (1) expenses actually incurred in producing such income or (2) $1,050 of the standard deduction. Generally, therefore, the first $2,100 of unearned income is free of the kiddie tax rules.[25] The child's "earned" income—newspaper routes, TV sitcom roles—is still taxed to the child independently.

As indicated, § 1(g) operates—has effect—in all cases where the income from property transferred by gift is taxable to the *donee* under the customary income-attribution rules. A typical instance would be a *non*-grantor trust—for example, a trust to pay the annual income to a named beneficiary, with the grantor having no reversionary interest and retaining no discretionary powers with respect to income or corpus. Under prior law, the trust income would "belong" to the beneficiary, whatever his age, and would be taxed at the beneficiary's marginal rate. Under § 1(g), while such income is still taxed to the beneficiary, the tax that is payable is determined by reference to his parents' marginal rate, or to the trust rate schedule (again, depending on the year). This is true, as noted, whether the grantor of the trust is the beneficiary's parent or someone else, and would be true even if the trust were testamentary rather than *inter vivos*.

Final question: Why didn't Congress simply tax the child's unearned income directly to the parents by including such income in the parents' return?[26] The answer—fairly obvious, we suppose—is that the parents do not have legal access to the child's income to pay the tax, and could conceivably find their own resources insufficient for that purpose. Hence, the income is taxed to the child, which makes the child's assets available for tax payment. Of course, in all family income-shifting situations the family members are much more concerned about the rate at which the income is taxed, than about who is required to write the check to the government. Thus, the fact that § 1(g) does not actually impose a tax liability on the parents is of scant consolation to families subject to the provision.

---

[25]   The dollar amounts are subject to inflation adjustments; the amounts in the text are for 2018.

[26]   Under § 1(g)(7), the parents may elect to include the child's income in their own return, but are not required to do so.

9.03 Family Business Associations

(a) Partnerships

As suggested at 7.01(b), the Supreme Court experienced considerable difficulty in the early days in applying the principles of *Clifford* and *Earl* to family partnerships. The issues were reviewed by the Court on two separate occasions—first in *Commissioner v. Tower*,[27] then again in *Commissioner v. Culbertson*[28]—and in neither instance could the Court generate an opinion which was sufficiently clear and definite to settle recurring controversies between taxpayers and the government. In the end, Congress legislated a set of operating rules for family partnerships by enacting § 704(e). These rules have worked reasonably satisfactorily over the years; family partnership taxation is no longer the raging problem it used to be. Even so, it may be worthwhile to see just why it was that the Supreme Court found the general question of income attribution so hard to handle in the family business context—why, that is, the customary attribution rules that had been formulated by the Court in other situations proved not to be self-executing here

Suppose a taxpayer owns and operates a business—say a cattle ranch, as in the *Culbertson* case—in which capital (livestock, grazing land), as well as the taxpayer's personal services, are both income-producing factors. The taxpayer has heretofore operated the ranch as a sole proprietorship, but he now decides to reconstitute the business as a partnership by assigning to each of his three children a 25% interest in the capital and income of the enterprise. Father and children execute a partnership agreement under which each is to receive one-quarter of the net income annually as well as one quarter of the partnership capital in the event of sale or dissolution. The father retains the right to manage the ranch, including the right to decide what proportion of the partnership profits is to be distributed each year and what proportion is to be retained and reinvested in additional tangible assets.

Since the father will continue as manager, he is of course entitled to a salary for his labors. But that, too, ultimately, is within his discretion. Quite obviously, any salary that he does take will, like wages paid to other employees, reduce the partnership's net income and hence be reflected in lower income-shares for the partners (*i.e.,* himself and the children). If for some reason he chooses to forgo his salary in a given year, then, equally obviously, partnership net income and individual shares will be increased. Thus, if the salary forgone is $100,000, each partner will enjoy a $25,000 increase in his

---

[27]   327 U.S. 280 (1946).

[28]   337 U.S. 733 (1949).

or her partnership share; in effect, the father "recoups" one-quarter, but gives up three-quarters, of the compensation he could have claimed.

It is important to note that partnerships, unlike corporations, are *not* treated as separate taxable entities. Partnership net income is determined in roughly the usual way—by deducting business expenses from gross income. The net figure is then included in the gross income of the individual partners—whether or not actually distributed—in accordance with their agreement, which is 25% each in our example.

Prior to the enactment of § 704(e), the Internal Revenue Service sought in cases like the above to treat *all* of the partnership income as taxable to the donor-partner under the attribution principles established in *Clifford* and *Earl*. Initially, at least, the Supreme Court was receptive to the government's approach. In the *Tower* case, the Court appeared to hold that family partnerships would not be recognized for tax purposes unless the donee-partner contributed either (a) "vital services" or (b) "original capital" to the firm. If the donee performed no service, as was frequently true, and if the donee's capital interest had been acquired by gift from the taxpayer, then the partnership would be ignored. In *Culbertson,* however, the Court implied that the foregoing was too narrow an interpretation of its earlier decisions, and asserted that what really counted in determining whether a family partnership should enjoy recognition was whether the parties had a "bona fide intent" to form a partnership. If "the partners joined together in good faith to conduct a business, having agreed that the services or capital to be contributed presently by each is of such value to the partnership that the contributor should participate in the distribution of profits, that is sufficient. . . ." While this declaration was apparently intended to liberalize the treatment of family partnerships, the Court did not make clear what it regarded as the criteria of "good faith" for this purpose; moreover, the presence of four concurring opinions raised doubt about the finality of the Court's position. At all events, the *Culbertson* decision reportedly had little practical effect in advancing the resolution of disputes in this field, and the tax status of family partnerships continued to be litigated until Congress finally legislated a solution.

In hindsight, one surmises that there were two reasons for the Court's inability to establish settled rules of income attribution for family partnerships. The first—essentially reflecting uncertainty about the effect of the *Clifford* case—arose from the fact that partnerships, being operating businesses, necessarily involved a commingling of assets belonging to the donee *and* the donor. In exercising his management powers over the partnership business, the donor might be expected to make decisions about his own share of partnership income, and hence also about the donee's, which reflected the outlook of an executive-entrepreneur rather than a conventional fiduciary. In particular, he might decide to retain and reinvest all the annual partnership profits in excess of his salary, so that the donee-partner would receive absolutely nothing until the donor finally decided to sell the business, or retired or died. Viewed from one standpoint, therefore, although the gift of a partnership interest was in a formal sense "complete", the donor's status as managing partner would enable him to deprive the donee of independent ownership and control as long as the donor, acting in his own interest, chose to keep the partnership alive. Whether this fell within the ban of *Clifford,* or was to be treated as an effective transfer under *Blair,* was, perhaps, a matter for doubt in the absence of a specific statutory rule.

The second uncertainty—possibly even more important than the first—concerned the application of the *Earl* decision. As stated previously, while *Earl* prohibited the assignment of personal service income in the form of salaries or fees earned from third parties, the same prohibition apparently did not apply to uncompensated services—that is, to transfers of personal service income in kind. But while the traditional exclusion for intra-family services was appropriate, or inevitable, in the case of incidental management assistance—a father managing his child's securities—it might well appear to go too far in cases where the uncompensated labor represented the taxpayer's full-time occupation. The difficulty, however, was that *Earl* itself contained no intrinsic means of distinguishing between major and minor transfers of service income, or between full-time professional activity and mere family favors. Lacking a basis for making that distinction, the Court perhaps felt that it could not authorize an extension of *Earl* to family partnerships without at the same time committing itself to the absurd proposition that all intra-family services were taxable to the performer.

The "bona fide" requirement of *Culbertson* may be understood as a rough effort to cope with the difficulties just mentioned. The insistence upon a contribution by the donee-partner of capital or services as a condition of "good faith" was, seemingly, an attempt to apply the philosophy of *Clifford* and *Earl* with a broadsword by converting the entire question into one of "intent". But this approach proved inadequate. Not only was the meaning of good faith unclear, but the broadsword treatment made it difficult to separate effective gifts of property from ineffective gifts of services, although that distinction otherwise prevailed throughout the income-attribution field.

Congress responded to the confusion by enacting what is now § 704(e), which preempts the prior case law. Briefly described, § 704(e) permits gifts of partnership interests to be treated as complete for tax purposes despite the retention of substantial management powers by the donor. The donor's motive in making the gift no longer has significance. From the taxpayer's standpoint, therefore, the *Clifford* question has been favorably resolved. At the same time, however, § 704(e) prevents "deflection" of personal service income to the donee by requiring an allowance of reasonable compensation for the donor's services. The *Earl* doctrine is thus applied to uncompensated services, but the application is limited to family partnerships and does not intrude on the traditional exclusion described above. The overall effect is to treat gifts of partnership interests like gifts of any other property. The property element is capable of transfer, very much like stock or real estate, while the service element is subjected to a rule of attribution. While the latter feature might have been expected to generate a good many disputes about the value of the donor-partner's services, in fact there has been relatively little litigation under § 704(e) to date, and it seems clear that the Service no longer views the problem as especially serious.

(b)   Corporations

§ 704(e) is, we think, about the only place in the Code where Congress has required that employees not be *underpaid* for tax purposes. Section 162(a) limits the business-expense allowance for salaries and wages to a "reasonable" amount, but that provision, as has been seen (6.05), is generally understood to bar the deduction by an employer of payments that are excessive. It has rarely been interpreted to require the imputation of *additional* salary where the employee's compensation is too low by market standards. Since the ranching business in *Culbertson* could as easily have been carried on in corporate form—with Culbertson giving his children stock in a corporation instead of interests in a partnership—why didn't Congress extend the rule of § 704(e) to family corporations as well as family partnerships? As matters stand now (and have always stood), the only defense the Treasury has against income shifting through the medium of under-compensated or uncompensated services by a corporate employee is the general rule regarding personal service income laid down in *Lucas v. Earl*. As already noted, however, the courts apparently do not read the *Earl* case as extending to services "in kind," and the result is that under present law Culbertson almost certainly could avoid personal tax on his services by incorporating the ranch and refusing to accept a salary for his work.

The justification, or at least the explanation, for this outcome is slightly complex and not especially satisfying. As noted earlier, corporate income is subject to a two-level tax. It is taxed once at the corporate level when realized, and then again at the shareholder level when distributed as a dividend (net of the corporate tax). Thus, if Culbertson—now chief executive of the family corporation— chooses to forgo all or a part of his annual salary with a view to increasing the returns to the other family stockholders, the salary forgone will be taxed both to the corporation and to the stockholders (himself, perhaps, included) when the net amount is paid out in dividends. Depending on rates, the overall tax bite may still be less than if the same amount were paid to Culbertson in salary and then transferred to the donee by gift, but it is likely to be greater (just because of the double tax) than it would be if the family partnership device were used. Possibly, then, the omission of anything equivalent to § 704(e) in the family corporation area can be explained on the ground that there is simply less tax avoidance to worry about.

Probably, though the real explanation for the omission lies in a congressional policy to aid the growth and expansion of small businesses, at least if carried on in corporate form. In earlier historical periods, the topmost individual rate of tax was very much higher than the corporate tax rate. During the 1960's and 1970's, for example, the highest corporate rate was 52%, while the highest individual rate was 70% (actually 90% (!) at the time the *Culbertson* case was decided). In the absence of a statutory equivalent of § 704(e), Culbertson could arrange to have the business income taxed at the lower prevailing corporate rate by simply electing to reinvest that income in additional corporate assets instead of drawing it out as salary. Stated differently, if Culbertson decided to use a portion of what would otherwise be his "savings"—the excess of his "true" salary over whatever he needed for living expenses—to expand his ranch by purchasing more land or more livestock, the tax law permitted him to do so at what was then a bargain rate of tax. Quite obviously, the benefit was available only if the company retained its income for expansion instead of paying it out as dividends. The retained income might still be subject to a shareholder tax some day—if the stock were later sold at a gain, for example—but that day could be very distant and might not even dawn within the lifetime of existing stockholders.

All of this suggests that from the standpoint of small businesses, the separate corporate tax has been a conscious subsidy device. Congress has really *expected* small corporations to be used as tax-deferral mechanisms; the absence of a corporate version of § 704(e) reflects a legislative intention to assist their growth by permitting the stockowner-entrepreneur to shift personal income to the company. Although the dramatic difference described above between the top corporate tax rate and the top individual tax rate diminished over time (in 2017, for example, there was only a 4.6 percentage point difference between the top corporate rate of 35% and the top individual rate of 39.6%), the Tax Cuts and Jobs Act of 2017 has reintroduced major tax favoritism for retained corporate earnings, with a corporate tax rate (21%) 16 percentage points lower than the top individual rate (37%). Even in situations where business income earned by a partnership or sole proprietorship would be eligible for the 20% deduction of § 199A (described in this book's Introduction), resulting in an effective top rate of 29.6%, there is still an 8.6 percentage point advantage to operating in corporate form, in the case of retained earnings—including retained earnings resulting from a controlling shareholder declining to be paid a salary for his work for the corporation.

Section 704(e) shows that Congress does not intend quite the same benefit to be available to family partnerships. While income derived from partnership *capital* can be shifted to family donees and accumulated at their lower marginal rates, income derived from the donor's personal *services* cannot. The reason for the limitation, perhaps, is that since partnerships and partners are not subject to a double tax on business earnings, the donee-partners' lower rates would apply whether the salary income forgone by the donor were reinvested in additional business assets or simply withdrawn by the partners for their personal use. The purpose of the "subsidy"— expansion of the enterprise—could not be assured, therefore. Moreover, individual donees would often be taxable at even lower rates than those that apply to corporate income, and perhaps the latter concession is as far as Congress wished to go.

The whole scheme is absurdly clumsy, and complicated far beyond the above description.[29] Our object here, however, is merely to explain why personal service income can be shifted in a corporate setting more or less without question, when so much judicial and legislative effort has been directed at preventing the same kind of shifting in the case of family partnerships.

9.04 Joint Returns: Taxation of Married and Single Persons

From a tax standpoint, as explained at 8.01, the Supreme Court's decision in *Poe v. Seaborn* created a geographical distinction between community property and common law jurisdictions by permitting married couples living in community property states to split their family income, including earned income, and thus, in effect, double the width of the rate brackets. The enactment of joint-return legislation in 1948 eliminated that distinction by permitting

---

[29] See Bittker and Eustice, *Federal Income Taxation of Corporations and Shareholders* (7th ed., 2000) Ch. 1.

all married couples, wherever they resided, to treat the family income as if earned equally by each spouse. Under the original joint-return procedure, tax liability was determined by (a) computing a tax on one-half of the couple's taxable income, and then (b) doubling the tax so computed. As a result, the marginal tax rate applicable to a married couple was the same as that of a single person with only half as much income. If a married couple had $100,000 of taxable income, the marginal tax rate on the last dollar would be the same as the marginal rate for a single person with taxable income of only $50,000, and the average tax rate on their total income would be the same as the average tax rate for a single person with taxable income of $50,000.

Given a sharply progressive rate structure, however, this income-splitting procedure necessarily meant that single persons paid substantially higher taxes than married couples at the *same* income levels. Two married couples each with $100,000 of income would pay the same tax whether they lived in Washington State or New York. But a single person who also earned $100,000 would pay much more than either for the obvious reason that the single taxpayer would be subject to the rates applicable to $100,000 of taxable income while the married taxpayers would be subject to the rates applicable to $50,000 of taxable income. At high income levels single taxpayers wound up paying fully 50 percent more in tax than married taxpayers with the same income. Some degree of difference between married and single taxpayers could no doubt be justified— the same $100,000 income stream supports *two* people in the case of a married couple—but in 1969 Congress decided that the disparity was too large and took steps to reduce it by establishing separate rate schedules for married and unmarried taxpayers in § 1(a) and § 1(c), respectively. The effect was not to eliminate the disparity between single persons and married couples filing jointly, but to restructure the relationship so that the tax on a single person would not exceed 120 percent of the tax on a married couple with the same taxable income. This had no substantive effect on married taxpayers (whose tax liabilities were unchanged), but for single taxpayers the effect was to lower the rates generally, with the principal beneficiaries being individuals in the middle and upper brackets where the disparity had been the greatest.

The relationship between the tax status of married persons and the tax status of single persons actually makes a lot of trouble for the income tax.[30] One would prefer that the tax law be "neutral" in its effect on the decision to marry or not to marry, but the fact is that it

---

[30] See Zelenak, *Marriage and the Income Tax*, 67 S. Cal. L. Rev. 339 (1994); Gann, *Abandoning Marital Status as a Factor in Allocating Income Tax Burdens*, 59 Texas L. Rev. 1 (1980).

is not. Marriage, as such, entails a tax "bonus" in many instances but also entails a tax "penalty" in many others, both being a function of the progressive rate-structure. The "bonus" element is straightforward. Assuming that A has positive taxable income while B has none, the tax due on A's earnings under § 1(c) when A is single will obviously be greater than the tax due under § 1(a) after A and B have become a married couple, the "bonus" being the difference between the two.

By contrast, where husband and wife—call them C and D—are both employed and each has earnings that are not greatly different from the other's, the effect of combining the spouses' taxable income may be to *increase* their overall tax liability relative to what that liability would have been had they remained single. The 1969 legislation reduced the disparity between married and single individuals at the same income level, but in doing so it created a "penalty" for married couples whose income is earned by the spouses in roughly equal proportions.

To illustrate all this, imagine a hypothetical two-rate income tax (it turns out that all the interesting issues with respect to the relative tax treatment of married couples and single persons can be modeled using just two tax rates). Our two-rate system features the same basic relationship between the tax rate schedule for married couples and the tax rate schedule for single taxpayers as the 1969 legislation, in that the lower bracket for married couples is wider than the lower bracket for single taxpayers but less than twice as wide. Let's suppose that married couples are taxed at the rate of 10% on their first $70,000 of income, and at 20% on all additional income; single persons at taxed at 10% on their first $50,000 of income, and at 20% on all income above $50,000.

Marriage Bonus [+]/Marriage Penalty [–] Under Hypothetical Rate Structure

Taxpayers	Taxable Income	Combined Tax	Effect of Marriage
A, B single	$100,000; 0	$15,000 + 0 = $15,000	
AB married	$100,000	$13,000	+ $2,000
C, D single	$50,000; $50,000	$5,000 x 2 = $10,000	
CD married	$100,000	$13,000	– $3,000

As suggested, both the marriage bonus, +$2,000, and the marriage penalty, -$3,000, are undesirable phenomena if we believe that the tax law should be strictly neutral as far as choice of marital status is concerned. Unfortunately, no *general* solution to the problem exists as long as the Code (a) maintains a progressive rate structure *and* (b) requires that married couples with the same total income—whether earned by one spouse alone or by the two spouses equally—pay the same amount of tax. Given these two constraints—progressive marginal rates and equal taxation of married couples with equal marital income—complete tax neutrality simply cannot be achieved. To see this, consider two possible solutions to the bonus/penalty problem in the hypothetical:

Solution #1: Return to the 1948 system and make the joint-return 10% bracket twice as wide as the 10% bracket for single taxpayers—in other words, have the joint-return 10% bracket apply to the first $100,000 of taxable income. The married couples would then owe $10,000 each. The penalty on CD would be eliminated, but A's bonus would be increased to $5,000 (*i.e.*, $15,000, the tax on A single, minus $10,000 = $5,000). So the "neutrality" objective fails.

Solution #2: Require all husbands and wives to file separate returns—in effect, give up the present joint-return procedure. The penalty on C and D would be eliminated, but AB married would then pay tax of $15,000, the tax on A single, while CD married would pay tax of only $10,000, thus violating constraint (b), which requires married couples with the same total income to pay the same tax. There is no way out of this unless we reduce the tax on A single to $10,000. Then, however, A single, with an income of $100,000, would be taxed at the same marginal rate as C or D single, each with an income of only $50,000, and progression would be abandoned, thus violating constraint (a).

Despite these inherent contradictions, current law mitigates the marriage penalty by adopting a limited version of Solution #1. The standard deduction for married couples is twice that allowed to single taxpayers ($12,000 for singles, $24,000 for married couples, in 2018). In addition, the 10%, 12%, 22%, 24%, and 32% rate brackets applicable to joint-return filers are twice the width of the corresponding rate brackets for singles. Towards the top end of the income distribution, however, two-income married couples can still be subject to substantial marriage penalties; the 37% bracket begins at $500,000 (in 2018) for unmarried taxpayers, and at the only slightly higher level of $600,000 for married couples. There are also features of the Code outside of the rate structure that produce very significant marriage penalties. Consider the following three examples. (1) The EITC rules (7.08) result in large marriage penalties for some lower-income two-earner couples. (2) The $10,000 ceiling on the deductibility of state and local taxes (7.01), introduced by the Tax Cuts and Jobs Act of 2017, is the same for single taxpayers and for married couples. Thus two unmarried taxpayers could deduct up to $20,000 of state and local taxes between them, while a married couple would be limited to a $10,000 deduction. It is unclear why the 2017 Congress decided to penalize marriage in this respect, while at the same time it was making the tax rate structure of § 1 more favorable to marriage. (3) Another non-rate-schedule marriage penalty, relating to the ceiling on the deductibility of home mortgage interest, is described in the answer to Question 4 at the end of Part B.

Before the Supreme Court's 2013 landmark decision in *United States v. Windsor*,[31] the IRS interpreted § 3 of the Defense of Marriage Act (DOMA) as prohibiting it from recognizing same-sex marriages for federal tax purposes. A same-sex couple, although validly married under state law, was not treated as married under the federal income tax—and so could neither enjoy an income tax marriage bonus nor suffer a tax marriage penalty. After *Windsor* declared § 3 of DOMA to be unconstitutional as a violation of the guarantee of equal protection, the IRS quickly issued a Ruling providing guidance as to how the IRS intended to implement *Windsor*.[32] In addition to making the basic point that the IRS would now recognize same-sex marriages for federal tax purposes, the Ruling also indicated that the IRS would "recognize the validity of a same-sex marriage that was valid in the state where it was entered into, regardless of the married couple's place of domicile."

A loose end. The marriage penalty phenomenon has been widely publicized, and is clearly politically salient. (Legislation enacted in 2003, for example, was aimed at reducing or eliminating marriage penalties for moderate-income couples, and 2017 legislation provided additional marriage penalty relief higher up the income distribution.) Another phenomenon of joint returns—call it the stacking effect— has received much less attention. Suppose a couple has one child, a toddler. The husband is firmly committed to his job, and the wife is trying to decide between full-time homemaking and paid employment. Working as a full-time homemaker, the wife produces tax-free imputed income (1.03). If she takes a paying job, she will replace that tax-free income with taxable wages. Moreover, with the limited exception of the child care credit (7.07(a)), the couple will not be entitled to any tax benefits for the costs of replacing her homemaking services and for the extra costs (commuting, clothes, etc.) of being employed. So far this has nothing in particular to do with joint returns; all the above would be true even if married couples always filed separate returns. But consider the rate at which the

---

[31]   *United States v. Windsor*, 133 S.Ct. 2675 (2013).
[32]   Rev. Rul. 2013–17, 2013–38 I.R.B. 201.

wife's wages will be taxed. Under a separate return system, her wages would be taxed at the low rates prevailing at the bottom of the tax rate schedule. On their joint return, however, her income will be stacked on top of her husband's income (which has, in effect, used up the lower rate brackets), so that even her first dollars of earned income will be taxed at relatively high rates. Of course, nothing in the Code says that the husband's income gets the benefit of the lower rates and the wife's income is taxed at the higher rates, but if the couple takes the husband's job as a given and consider the wife's employment as the open question—in other words, if the wife's income is at the margin in their decision-making—then the stacking effect will come into play. The stacking effect may be sufficient to cause the wife to decide to remain a full-time homemaker, rather than accepting paid employment.

Although the stacking effect and the marriage penalty are both joint-return phenomena, they are *not* just two ways of describing the same thing. The stacking effect analysis takes as givens (i) the existence of the marriage, and (ii) the husband's earned income, and treats as "up for grabs" the wife's choice between homemaking and paid employment. In contrast, marriage penalty analysis takes as givens (i) the amount (if any) of one person's earned income, and (ii) the amount (if any) of the other person's earned income, and treats as "up for grabs" the decision to marry or remain single. Another way of seeing the difference between the two phenomena is to note that a 1948-type system (with brackets twice as wide for married couples as for single taxpayers) would produce no marriage penalties, but would nevertheless produce stacking effects.

Another loose end. Section 1(d) allows married couples to file separate returns, subject to a tax rate schedule set forth in that subsection. Why doesn't this solve the marriage penalty problem? Can't a couple that would be subject to a marriage penalty if they filed a joint return avoid the penalty by the simple expedient of filing two returns under § 1(d)? Sadly, they cannot. Section 1(d) features a particularly unfavorable tax rate schedule, with brackets only half the width of the joint-return brackets. As far as the tax rate schedules are concerned, filing two returns under § 1(d) would never produce a lower combined tax liability than filing a joint return, and would sometimes produce a considerably higher combined tax bill.[33] Why,

---

[33] In a few cases, however, filing separate returns might produce a tax savings from a reduction in the combined taxable income of the spouses. If one spouse has significant expenses subject to a percentage-of-AGI floor (such as medical expenses), filing a separate return can reduce the amount of the deduction disallowed by the floor, because only the AGI of the spouse with the expenses will be shown on that spouse's separate return. Even when this would be true, in some cases the tax savings from the larger deduction would be more than offset by the tax cost of the unfavorable § 1(d) rate schedule.

then, do some couples elect to file separate returns? In most cases, it is because one spouse does not trust the other, and is unwilling to accept the joint-and-several liability for tax on the other's income that would result from filing a joint return.

9.05 Alimony and Separate Maintenance

Prior to 1942, alimony payments made by a husband to his ex-wife were neither taxable to the wife nor deductible by the husband. No statutory authorization existed for a deduction (plainly, such payments were not business expenses), and the wife's receipt was held not to be "income" within the meaning of § 61. Sections 71(a) and 215(a), which reversed this pattern, were chiefly intended to afford relief to husbands who, on occasion, found that their tax equaled or even exceeded the income that was left after making alimony payments. Section 71(a) provided (notice the past tense; more on that below) that alimony and separate maintenance should, in general, be included in the gross income of the payee spouse; § 215(a) allowed a corresponding deduction to the payor spouse for payments includable by the payee. Of course, the income-shifting benefits from playing the alimony tax game were self-limiting. If alimony payments were large enough, they would equalize the marginal tax rates of payor and payee. Any additional alimony payments, after marginal rates had been equalized, would produce no net tax savings, and might even produce a net tax increase.

The income-shifting alimony tax regime had its share—perhaps more than its share—of complexities, the details of which we have spared the reader in the preceding description. The regime was also vulnerable to the critique that it was inconsistent with the rule of *Lucas v. Earl* (8.01), under which earned income is supposed to be taxed to the earner rather than to the person with the beneficial enjoyment of the income. In the Tax Cuts and Jobs Act of 2017, Congress—perhaps influenced by the above-mentioned concerns—repealed the income-shifting rules for alimony, with the repeal effective in 2019. Thus, in 2019 and later years, alimony is generally neither deductible by the payor nor taxable to the payee. Although it could be argued that alimony would be included in the gross income of the payee even in the absence of § 71, given the broad sweep of the § 61 definition of gross income, the 2017 legislative history indicates that alimony received is to be free of tax under the new regime. Transition rules preserve the old income-shifting alimony tax rules in the case of payments made pursuant to divorce instruments executed before 2019.

As noted at 5.04, above, property settlements in a divorce that involve a transfer of appreciated property from one spouse to the other are now treated as non-taxable under Code § 1041.

Attribution of Income—Questions and Answers

Question 1: Dorothea, age 50, is the life-tenant of a trust created by her deceased father. The trust generates income of $20,000 a year. Dorothea doesn't need the income at present, so she assigns to her adult son, Ladislaw, by gift, the right to receive all the trust income for the next five years. Ladislaw, a medical student, has large credit card debts which he is desperate to pay off. Accordingly, he sells his five-year income interest to a local investor for $65,000 cash, paid in a single lump sum.

What are the tax consequences of these events to Dorothea and Ladislaw (and the local investor)?

Answer: Dorothea is taxed on $65,000 of ordinary income, Ladislaw on zero. Having assigned her interest in the trust income for only five years, it is obvious that Dorothea has retained a valuable reversion in the life estate. While Code § 673(a) does not apply directly, the 5% rule in that provision is a fair indication that Congress considers the retention of a reversionary interest having more than minimal value as equivalent to continued ownership of the assigned property by the donor. In any case, it seems quite clear that the same result is reached under the Supreme Court's decision in *Helvering v. Horst*. The *Blair* case is obviously distinguishable even though it did involve the gift of a fractional interest in a life estate, because the gift in *Blair* was for the full duration of the life estate itself and the donor did not retain a reversion.

Since the trust income would be taxable to Dorothea if Ladislaw received it year-by-year, the same should be true of the lump-sum that Ladislaw realized by selling his interest in advance. Under the rule of *Irwin v. Gavit* (4.02) and Code § 273, Dorothea's basis for her life estate is zero. Accordingly, the full amount of $65,000 would be includable in her gross income. Put differently, if Dorothea herself had sold a five-year income interest for $65,000, the result would be full inclusion of the amount received. Since the gift to Ladislaw is treated as "incomplete" for tax purposes, the outcome is the same.

With the $65,000 taxed to Dorothea, Ladislaw, the donee, is treated as receiving the $65,000 as a non-taxable gift.

The local investor would be entitled to amortize the cost of his five-year income right, a wasting asset. Assuming he is allowed to use straight-line amortization (as is permitted to annuitants by § 72), rather than the economically accurate and less generous sinking fund method (6.09(d)), then he would be entitled to deductions at the rate of $65,000/5 years = $13,000 a year. He would report $20,000 − $13,000 = $7,000 a year as taxable interest income. Income to be reported by the parties is thus $65,000 (Dorothea) plus 0 (Ladislaw) plus 5 x $7,000 = $35,000 (local investor), a total of $100,000, which is equal to the income of the trust over the 5-year term.

Question 2: Tom, an amateur cook, is famous among gourmets for inventing five delicious dishes using fresh horsemeat (stew, fricassee, kebab, etc.). Nobody knows Tom's secret recipes. Tired of cooking, Tom writes the recipes down and gives them to his daughter, Sophia, who puts them away in a desk drawer. Some time later, Tom receives a phone call from a cookbook publisher who offers him $5,000 for the horsemeat recipes. Tom explains that the recipes are now in Sophia's hands. The publisher makes the same offer to Sophia, who accepts.

Who is taxable on the $5,000, Tom or Sophia?

Answer: Self-created property—a painting, a copyrighted musical composition—is generally considered to be "property" rather than "services" (despite the absence of any capital investment) and therefore free of the rule of *Lucas v. Earl*. A gift of such property is effective to shift income from the property to the donee. Tom's horsemeat recipes would fall into the "property" category if they appeared in a copyrighted cookbook, and might do so even if regarded merely as "secret processes" or "trade secrets." If so, the $5,000 would be taxable to Sophia, the donee.

On the other hand, though tired of cooking, Tom presumably had not forgotten the horsemeat recipes and hence was capable of telling the publisher exactly how to make the wonderful stew, fricassee, etc. It follows that Tom could have accepted the publisher's offer and earned the $5,000 for himself. Unlike the gift of a painting or a copyrighted composition, the recipes in this sense remained within Tom's control. Had he wished to divulge his secrets (and unless you think Sophia would then have had a cause of action against him), he could easily have reduced the value of Sophia's interest in the recipes to zero. Taking this view of the matter, the $5,000 would seem to be taxable to Tom, the donor, because he retained the power to revoke the gift or, putting it differently, because he never really surrendered the recipes and simply "designated" Sophia to receive the sale proceeds.

Question 3: Mr. and Mrs. Smith, a very affluent two-earner married couple, have roughly equal salaries of about $500,000 each. Out of idle curiosity, they ask their accountant to calculate how much more or less income tax they pay as a married couple than the combined tax they would pay as two single persons. When the accountant tells them that they pay more than $10,000 of tax marriage penalty every year (attributable partly to the tax rate structure of § 1, and partly to the marriage penalty produced by the $10,000 cap on the deduction for state and local taxes), they decide to do something about it. Doing their own legal research with the assistance of the internet, they discover Code § 7703(a)(1), which provides that "the determination of whether an individual is married shall be made as of the close of the taxable year." This gives them the brilliant idea of avoiding the marriage penalty while remaining married (the vast majority of the time), by getting divorced in the last week of every year and remarried in the first week of the next year. Because they are not sure that the courts of their home state would be willing to grant them annual divorces under these circumstances, their plan is to obtain the divorces while on vacation in an accommodating foreign jurisdiction. If they go through with this plan, and if the foreign divorces are recognized by their state of domicile, will the plan have the desired tax effect?

Answer: Probably not. It is clear that the Smiths could permanently avoid the marriage penalty by getting divorced and staying divorced—even if they continued to live together as a couple. The quick remarriage, however, brings into play the judge-made sham transaction and step transaction doctrines. The IRS could argue with some force that a divorce followed a week later by a planned remarriage should be disregarded as a sham, or that the two offsetting steps—divorce and remarriage—should be collapsed into a mere continuation of the marriage. On the other hand, if the foreign divorce was valid under the law of their home state, then the divorce would have had real consequences if one of the Smiths had died during the week they were divorced. Perhaps that should be enough to save the divorce from sham status. The facts of the problem are inspired by *Boyter v. Commissioner*,[34] in which the Fourth Circuit held that the sham transaction doctrine was potentially applicable to the Boyters, and remanded to the lower court for a determination of whether the Boyters' divorce was, in fact, a sham. There is no reported case on remand.

Question 4: As explained in the text (9.04), it is simply not possible to design a tax system which simultaneously features (1) progressive marginal rates, (2) marriage neutrality (*i.e.*, neither marriage bonuses nor penalties), and (3) couples neutrality (*i.e.*, equal tax on equal-income married couples, regardless of how the income is divided between the spouses in each marriage). But consider a tax-and-transfer system which combines an income tax imposed at a flat rate of, say, 20%, and a "demogrant"—a universal cash grant of, say, $10,000 per person per year, and which treats the individual (rather than the married couple) as the taxable unit. If the demogrant is thought of as part of the tax system, then the system features progressive *average* tax rates, despite its lack of progressive

---

[34] *Boyter v. Commissioner*, 668 F.2d 1382 (4th Cir. 1981).

marginal rates. A person with income of $50,000 pays zero net tax ($10,000 tax minus $10,000 demogrant), for an average rate of zero. A person with income of $100,000 pays $10,000 net tax ($20,000 tax minus $10,000 demogrant), for an average rate of 10%. At $200,000 income, the net tax is $30,000 ($40,000 minus $10,000), and the average rate is 15%. As income increases, the average rate approaches—but never quite reaches—20%. The system obviously features marriage neutrality (no bonuses or penalties), because all taxes and demogrants are determined without reference to marital status. Finally, the system features couples neutrality. Any married couple with combined income of $X will have a net tax liability of $X(20%) − 2($10,000), regardless of how the $X of income is divided between the spouses. Should Congress enact this elegant solution to the income tax marriage trilemma?

Answer: Does the flat-tax-plus-demogrant appeal to your policy preferences, apart from its cutting of the Gordian knot of the marriage tax trilemma? If so, then the elegant solution to the marriage tax trilemma provides an additional reason to urge this reform. But the proposal will not be attractive to everyone. Liberals may not be satisfied with a system under which the flat marginal tax rate imposed on everyone serves as a ceiling on the average tax rate imposed on the wealthiest taxpayers. And conservatives may not like the idea of $10,000 annual cash handouts to everyone, whether deserving or undeserving. If one strongly objects to either a 20% tax rate ceiling or a $10,000 demogrant, then the nifty solution to the marriage tax trilemma is not reason enough to enact the proposal.

Question 5: Last year Otis "Bad" Blake, a popular country singer, performed two concerts for charity. One of the concerts was part of his twenty-city nationwide tour, for which operators of the various venues paid Blake a fee of $200,000 per concert. Blake simply announced that he would donate his fee from his Atlanta concert to the Red Cross. The other concert was an annual benefit concert presented (with a different headliner every year) by a cancer research charity. The charity did all the work of putting together and promoting the concert; Blake had only to show up and sing. Blake, of course, waived his usual concert fee. What are the tax consequences to Blake of these two concerts?

Answer: The problem concerns the distinction between "redirected income" and "services in kind." In the case of the Atlanta concert, the redirected fee is includible in Blake's gross income. He should be entitled to claim an offsetting deduction for his contribution of the fee to charity, but if he is very generous (in ways not mentioned in the problem) his deduction may be limited by the percentage-of-adjusted-gross-income ceiling on charitable deductions imposed by § 170(b). In the case of the cancer charity concert, however, Blake does not have to include in gross income the value of his donated services. Although he is not entitled to claim a charitable deduction for the value of his services,[35] the effect of the non-inclusion is the equivalent of inclusion and an offsetting deduction—with the quasi-deduction not being subject to the various limitations imposed on charitable deductions under § 170.

---

[35] Reg. § 1.170A–1(g).

Part D

TAX ACCOUNTING

Code § 446(a) provides that "taxable income shall be computed under the method of accounting on the basis of which the taxpayer regularly computes his income in keeping his books." This provision reflects the general approach of tax accounting. It indicates, as might be expected, the Tax Accounting at tax accounting largely depends upon and accepts the principles of ordinary commercial accounting. There are, however, some important differences, and by and large it is the areas of divergence, rather than the similarities between the two systems, which are taken up in this brief Part. In some instances these differences are the product of administrative and other policy considerations peculiarly relevant to taxation; in others (the tax treatment of prepaid income would be an example; see 12.02) they appear merely to be the result of doubtful reasoning on the part of the courts and the Internal Revenue Service.

Although extensive, freedom to choose a method of accounting is not unlimited. Section 446(b) broadly authorizes the Commissioner to reject, or at least contest, the taxpayer's accounting practice if that practice does not "clearly reflect income." Much of the litigation described in Sections 11 and 12 entails an application of that standard. In general, the courts have tended to regard the subject of accounting as "administrative", and have shown a considerable willingness to follow the Commissioner's lead on close questions. This, in turn, has prompted Congress, from time to time, to adopt provisions aimed at relieving particular hardship situations. Overall, this pattern of judicial caution and congressional liberalization has led to a steady, but also a painfully slow, improvement in the applicable rules.

In a sense, the precise timing of revenues and expenses is more important for tax-accounting purposes than it is for general accounting purposes. Allocation of borderline items to one period rather than another in the company's financial statements can, if necessary, be explained to investors and other interested persons by means of footnotes to the income statement or the balance sheet. When the accounting decision is one that has to be reflected on an income tax return, however, the stake is an increase or reduction in the taxpayer's actual cash tax obligations, with mere explanation being secondary. Accordingly, the conflicts are likely to be sharper in a tax setting, particularly when there has been a rise or decline in rate-levels as between two taxable years, or when an individual taxpayer, by reason of a change in her income, faces higher marginal rates in one taxable period than in another.

This Part is divided into three sections. Section 10 deals with the annual accounting requirement—the requirement that income be determined and reported at fixed intervals of a year. Sections 11 and 12 describe the principal accounting methods used by individual and business taxpayers, namely, the cash and the accrual methods of accounting. The effort, as usual, is to concentrate on the questions that have occasioned controversy, and to emphasize major elements of the tax accounting system rather than details.

10. Annual Accounting

10.01   Loss Carryovers—*Burnet v. Sanford & Brooks*

Code § 441 provides, in effect, that the taxpayer's taxable income shall be computed on the basis of her "annual accounting period." For almost all individuals the annual accounting period is simply the calendar year; corporations and other business taxpayers frequently use fiscal years—say July 1 to June 30—which may conform to the normal cycle of their manufacturing or marketing activities. In either case the taxpayer's income is determined and reported at 12-month intervals, and tax is assessed and paid on the basis of events occurring between the beginning and the end of each such period. While the taxpayer's true income cannot really be ascertained until the taxpayer's economic existence is over, it is obvious that no functioning tax system could afford to wait for its collections until the end of an individual's lifetime or until the termination of a business enterprise. Income and taxes must be reported and paid periodically, and the 12-month unit is familiar to almost every taxpayer. But even so, there is something artificial about this attempt to cut the flow of economic activity into segments for the purpose of making annual tax payments, and distortions—sometimes serious distortions— necessarily result.

Roughly speaking, the history of the annual accounting requirement is one of literal enforcement by the courts, followed in a few important instances by the enactment of specific relief legislation. Compared, for example, with the innovative role it played in the field of income attribution (Part C), the Supreme Court has been notably cautious and conservative in its approach to accounting problems. (Put differently, the Court mainly followed the government's lead in both areas.) Mindful that the Treasury was required to process and audit millions of tax returns annually, the Court in its early decisions was plainly reluctant to apply the income definition under § 61 in ways that might complicate the needs of practical tax administration. As a result, the somewhat delicate task of balancing more equity against heavier administrative burdens was largely, and wisely, left to Congress and the Treasury.

In *Burnet v. Sanford & Brooks Co.*[1] the taxpayer had entered into a dredging contract with the United States, but ultimately abandoned the undertaking and sued the government for breach of warranty. Between 1913 and 1916 the taxpayer incurred expenses of $176,000 in excess of the payments received under the contract. In 1920, as a result of the lawsuit, the taxpayer recovered the excess expenses of $176,000, plus $16,000 of interest conceded to be taxable. The taxpayer apparently had other sources of revenue during the periods affected because it reported a positive net income for the year 1914. For 1913, 1915 and 1916, however, it reported net losses from business operations after deducting the expenses just mentioned.

The question presented was whether the award received in 1920 was includable in the taxpayer's gross income for that year. The taxpayer argued that as the dredging contract had produced no profit whatever, the amount received in 1920 could not be "income" within the meaning of the 16th Amendment. Since, however, the requirement of annual accounting could not simply be dismissed, the taxpayer proposed three alternative mechanisms by which its prior losses could be given proper recognition: (i) allow the operating losses sustained in 1913–15–16 to be carried forward as an offset against the award received in 1920; or (ii) treat the dredging contract as a unitary transaction, with the excess expenses being added back to the income of the earlier years and the award being excluded from that of the later;[2] or (iii) treat the earlier outlays as capital expenditures (or as "loans" to the government) which could later be charged off against the award. Each of these devices, in the taxpayer's view, would succeed in recognizing the absence of gain under the contract, and would do so without detracting from the integrity of the annual accounting requirement.

Reversing the court of appeals, the Supreme Court sustained the Commissioner in treating the award as fully taxable in 1920. The Court held that each accounting period must be regarded as a discrete unit for tax purposes, and found that "income" under the Constitution could properly be understood to refer to accessions taking place solely within the taxable year. Annual accounting, said the Court, was a familiar practice prior to the adoption of the 16th Amendment; the Amendment did not require Congress to adopt a

---

[1]　　282 U.S. 359 (1931).

[2]　　An election to report on the completed-contract method of accounting actually was available to the taxpayer, if made in advance. No doubt assuming that its expenses would be offset annually by adequate progress payments from the government, the taxpayer did not make the election. In effect, the taxpayer was asking the Supreme Court to allow it to make the election on a hindsight basis.

system of transactional rather than periodic reporting, even if the former were deemed practicable. The Court did not indicate whether a line would have to be drawn at *some* point—suppose, *e.g.,* that Congress attempted to impose an accounting period of a month or a week or a day. It was plain, however, that an annual time-unit posed no such problem.

The reason the Court gave for rejecting the taxpayer's plea for some sort of transactional accounting—rather than strict annual accounting—was beside the point, in terms of the taxpayer's situation. The Court stated that the income tax would be unworkable if a taxpayer could "postpone[e] the assessment of the tax until the end of a lifetime, or for some other indefinite period, to ascertain more precisely whether the final outcome of the period, or of a given transaction, will be a gain or a loss." This is an excellent reason for not allowing events in later years to affect tax liabilities for earlier years, and in fact that is very much the general rule. Subject to a small number of narrow statutory exceptions,[3] nothing that happens after the close of a taxable year can alter a taxpayer's tax liability for that year. But Sanford & Brooks was not asking the Court to keep its 1920 tax liability open pending post-1920 developments. Rather, the taxpayer was simply asking to be allowed to *look back* from 1920 to earlier years in determining the tax consequences of receipts in 1920. Looking back does not conflict with the need for finality so eloquently expressed by the Court (because we can look back *right now*), and in fact the tax law routinely looks to events of earlier years to determine the tax consequences of events of later years—with the subtraction of an earlier year's basis from a current year's amount realized being only the most prominent example. In short, the Court could have decided in the taxpayer's favor without having done violence to the sanctity of the annual accounting period, because that sanctity prohibits only looking forward from the current year, not looking back.

In the end, Congress mitigated the effect of the annual accounting rule (though not quite soon enough to help Sanford & Brooks) by adopting the net operating loss carryover provisions of § 172. Under that section, as amended in 2017, losses incurred in business can be carried forward to offset income in any number of later years (until, of course, the losses have been fully utilized), subject to the constraint that the allowable NOL for any year may not exceed 80% of the taxpayer's pre-NOL income. Companies

---

[3]   For example, § 1033 allows a taxpayer to avoid recognizing gain on the involuntary conversion of appreciated property if he replaces the converted property with similar property during the two years following the year in which the conversion occurs. For another example, § 219(f)(3) allows a taxpayer to deduct an IRA contribution on his return for (say) 2018 if he makes the contribution in the first three-and-one-half months of 2019.

experiencing fluctuating profits and losses are thus treated roughly the same in overall terms as companies with a flat income stream.

Alternating profit and loss years are more likely to occur in the case of corporate than individual taxpayers. Most individuals derive their incomes from personal services, so that "losses"—in the sense of an excess of business expenses over personal earnings—are unlikely to arise even if the individual is unemployed. The Code does not generally permit a carryover of unused personal expenses or standard deductions. On the other hand, individuals may suffer hardship under the annual accounting requirement solely by reason of the progressive rate structure. An author, for example, who receives sizeable royalties in the year in which her best-selling novel is published may have earned little or nothing in earlier years when the book was being written. While the progressive tax concept assumes a higher marginal tax rate on higher levels of income, plainly there would be inequity if those whose incomes fluctuate widely were required to pay much heavier taxes than those who earn at a steady pace. Prior to 1986, the individual rate structure was fairly steeply progressive, and the Code, accordingly, extended relief to taxpayers with fluctuating income by means of a four-year averaging device. Under former §§ 1301–1305, if a taxpayer's income in the current year exceeded 140% of her average income for the preceding 3 years, the excess was taxed as if it had been earned in equal installments over the 4-year span. The marginal tax-rate applicable to the excess income, then, became the rate that would have applied had such income been spread out evenly over the four years instead of being "bunched" into a single taxable period.

However reasonable in concept, the averaging rules proved rather complex in operation, especially where the taxpayer's marital status changed during the affected period. Also, it was not clear that the eligibility requirements always succeeded in confining the benefits of averaging to taxpayers with fluctuating income as intended. Thus, the beneficiaries of income-averaging sometimes turned out to be taxpayers who had enjoyed a sudden but *sustained* increase in earnings, such as students entering upon their "real" careers following graduation. Critics of the averaging provisions also pointed out that the rules dealt with only one inequitable situation, that is, a series of low-income years followed by a high income year. Nothing was done for taxpayers experiencing a sharp *decline* in income following a period of high earnings (*e.g.*, out-of-work executives), although such taxpayers similarly presented an appealing case for relief.

Instead of improving it, the 1986 Act simply eliminated the individual income-averaging system by repealing the relevant Code sections. That decision has the merit of simplicity, and with the reduction in tax-rates (relative to pre-1986 rates) and the adoption of a less steeply progressive rate structure, the need for an averaging system has obviously declined. Income fluctuations are less likely to produce marginal rate differences; and when they do occur, such differences are likely to be less severe than formerly. The "author" mentioned above may still pay higher taxes than a salary-earner whose income is relatively stable, but Congress evidently deemed the disparity too small (and infrequent) to justify a complex statutory remedy.

Under current law, the most dramatic differences between taxpayers with fluctuating incomes and those with steady incomes occur at the lower end of the income distribution. Imagine two taxpayers, each a single parent with one child. A earns $22,000 in each of two years, while B earns nothing in the first year (as a result of involuntary unemployment) and $44,000 in the second. If the income tax were based on biannual accounting, A and B would have identical tax results over the two-year period. Under our annual accounting system, however, B fares much more poorly than A. One problem for B is that she is entitled to only one year's-worth of standard deduction; her standard deduction for the no-income year is simply wasted. A, by contrast, has enough income to use her standard deduction in both years. The biggest problem for B, however, concerns the EITC (7.08). Because the EITC is calculated as a percentage of earned income, B is entitled to no EITC in her no-income year. And because the EITC is phased out as income rises above the phase-out threshold, B is also entitled to no EITC in her $44,000-income year (under 2018 EITC parameters). In sharp contrast, A is close to the "sweet spot" for the EITC; in each year her EITC will be a bit under $3,000. Finally, B is entitled to no child tax credit in her no-income year, while the partial refundability rules for the child tax credit (7.07(a)) will permit A to claim the full $2,000 credit in both years. The difference in the two-year tax consequences for A and B are dramatic in terms of absolute dollars and even more dramatic in percentage-of-income terms. Special income-averaging rules for low-income taxpayers could make a tremendous difference to B,[4] but Congress has not shown any great interest in that approach.

10.02   Claim of Right

Section 172 provides a considerable measure of averaging to offset the harsh effect of the annual accounting system. It does not, however, purport to cope with the somewhat narrower class of problems which are usually referred to as "transactional." The

---

[4]   Batchelder, *Taxing the Poor: Income Averaging Reconsidered,* 40 Harv. J. on Legis. 395 (2003).

Supreme Court's decision in *North American Oil Consolidated v. Burnet*[5] provides the background. In *North American,* the company, upon the entry of a lower court decree in 1917, received income from the operation of certain oil properties whose ownership had previously been disputed. The income had been earned in 1916 but was paid over to a receiver until the dispute should be resolved. The lower court decree was appealed, and finally affirmed in 1922. Since its marginal tax rates apparently were lower in both in 1916 and in 1922 than in 1917, the taxpayer argued that the income should be taxed either in 1916 when it was earned or in 1922 when the taxpayer's right to the funds was finally established. But the Supreme Court sustained the Commissioner in treating 1917 as the proper year for inclusion. In 1916, the taxpayer had nothing more than a disputed claim. In 1917, however, it actually received the cash income, which it then held under a "claim of right" and without restriction as to use. Accordingly, the income properly became taxable in that year, even though its ultimate ownership continued to be disputed, and even though the taxpayer might still have been "adjudged liable to restore its equivalent" in 1922. In effect, current inclusion was required where the taxpayer (a) received the funds in question, (b) treated them as its own, and (c) conceded no offsetting obligation. While *borrowed* money is not taxable owing to the borrower's obligation to repay (3.01), the fact that a receipt is subject to dispute or other contingencies which extend beyond the taxable year does not create a similar basis for exclusion.

The *North American* decision can best be explained and defended on practical grounds. Although it might be fairer to wait until contingencies affecting the receipt are resolved, the Treasury has a plausible interest in immediate taxation. Postponement creates the risk that the taxpayer might become insolvent before the tax is paid. In addition, the task of deciding when income has attained an appropriate level of "certainty" would be administratively burdensome. Although the last appeal from the lower court decree was exhausted in 1922, North American might still have feared a legal attack on some collateral ground which it could have cited as reason for a further delay in reporting the income. Quite obviously, actual receipt of the disputed funds is an event that is easier to identify than the final resolution of a controversy.

But while the claim of right doctrine makes practical sense, it does create a possibility of hardship in those cases in which the contingencies are finally resolved *against* the taxpayer and the disputed income has to be surrendered to another claimant. In *U.S.*

---

[5]   286 U.S. 417 (1932).

v. Lewis,[6] the taxpayer-employee received a bonus of $22,000 in 1944 which he reported as income for that year. In 1946, pursuant to a state court judgment that the bonus had been computed improperly, he returned $11,000 to his employer. Claiming that the excess bonus had been received under a mistake of fact, the taxpayer sought to reopen his 1944 return and recompute his tax for that year by excluding the excess amount. The Supreme Court, however, relying on the *North American* decision, held that the full bonus was taxable in 1944 under the claim of right doctrine. Claim of right, said the Court, was a rule of finality which was deeply rooted in the tax system, and no exception could be permitted merely because the taxpayer was "mistaken as to the validity of his claim."

Actually, the claim of right doctrine need not have been invoked at all in the *Lewis* case. The taxpayer's right to the bonus was not disputed in 1944, so that inclusion of the income in that year was not in doubt and, indeed, was never contested by the taxpayer. What the taxpayer sought was not postponement (as in *North American*), but an opportunity to treat the earlier receipt and the later repayment as a single, unified transaction for tax purposes. While the government conceded that the repayment of the excess bonus would be deductible in 1946, it is evident that the taxpayer's applicable tax-rate was higher in 1944 (a war year, of course) when the bonus was received. Hence the tax saved in the later period would be less than the tax paid on the prior inclusion. The taxpayer argued, in effect, that his tax liability for 1944 should be reduced to take account of the subsequent loss. In the absence of specific legislative authorization, however, the Court refused to apply a transactional approach in taxing the bonus income, and held, instead, that the receipt and the repayment must be reflected in separate taxable years.

Different time directions are at issue in *Sanford & Brooks*, on the one hand, and in *Lewis* on the other. In *Sanford & Brooks*, the taxpayer wanted the tax treatment of events in a later year to be determined by reference to events in an earlier year. As explained earlier, and despite the Court's rejection of the taxpayer's argument in *Sanford & Brooks*, such looking-back does not interfere with the administrative need for tax finality and is not inconsistent with fundamental income tax principles (in fact, the offsetting of basis against amount realized works in precisely this manner). In *Lewis*, however, the taxpayer wanted his tax results *in 1944* to be altered by events occurring *in 1946*. Judicial acceptance of Lewis's argument would indeed have interfered with the perceived need for finality of tax results; no one could have been certain, at the end of 1944, of

---

6   340 U.S. 590 (1951).

Lewis's ultimate 1944 tax liability. Accordingly, the Court's rejection of Lewis's argument was entirely reasonable.

In 1954, Congress reacted to the hardship evident in *Lewis* and similar cases by adding § 1341 to the Code. Briefly, if an item was included in income in a taxable year because of the claim of right doctrine, and if in a later year it is established that the taxpayer did not have an unrestricted right to the item, so that a deduction exceeding $3,000 is allowable, the tax for the later year will be whichever of the following is the lesser: (a) the tax in the later year computed with the deduction, or (b) the tax in the later year without the deduction, but reduced by the amount by which the tax in the earlier year would have been decreased if the item in question had been excluded from the earlier year's income. When § 1341 applies, taxpayers never lose and often win. If a taxpayer's marginal tax rate was higher in the earlier inclusion year than in the later repayment year, the taxpayer chooses option (b) and obtains a tax reduction in the later year equal to the tax cost of the inclusion in the earlier year (thus not losing).[7] If the taxpayer's marginal tax rate was lower in the earlier year than in the later year, the taxpayer chooses option (a), with the result that the taxpayer obtains a deduction in the later year that is more beneficial than the inclusion in the earlier year was costly (thus winning).

Notice that § 1341 leaves the basic claim of right doctrine intact; the *North American* rule is still applicable for the purpose of determining *when* unsettled income is required to be included for tax purposes. The section reverses the outcome in *Lewis,* however, by authorizing a reduction in the earlier year's tax (in effect) where an item included in one taxable period becomes deductible in another.

Despite being carefully drafted, § 1341 has unexpectedly generated litigation as to its intended scope. To see why, please return to the "excess compensation" issue discussed at 6.05, above. The Commissioner, finding that the salary paid by X Corporation to Mr. Smith, the corporation's sole stockholder and chief executive, was "excessive" under § 162(a)(1), disallowed the "excess" as a business expense and required that it be added back to the corporation's taxable income and treated as a nondeductible dividend. Mr. Smith remains taxable on the entire amount received,[8] but, as stated, the amount found to be excessive is now regarded as a dividend rather

---

[7]   In one respect option (b) is less favorable than a taxpayer victory in *Lewis* would have been. If Lewis had prevailed in his case, he would have been entitled to interest on his overpayment of tax in 1944. By contrast, no interest is allowed to taxpayers electing option (b) under § 1341.

[8]   However, as a dividend the payment will be taxed at the preferential rate (generally 15% or 20%) applicable to long-term capital gains, rather than at the ordinary income rates (as high as 37%) applicable to salaries.

than a salary payment. The Commissioner's purpose, obviously, is to prevent avoidance of the customary double-tax regime, a regime that applies—even in the case of smaller, closely-held corporations—when after-tax corporate earnings are distributed to shareholders as dividends. What the Commissioner wants is (i) a tax at the corporate level on the excess salary payment and then (ii) a dividend tax on the same amount at the shareholder level.

But now suppose that X Corp., foreseeing the Commissioner's excess salary claim, adopts a resolution requiring any salary payment that is disallowed and found to be excessive to be returned to the Corporation by the employee (Smith) to whom it has been paid. Smith dutifully returns the excess amount. The Corporation surrenders the deduction, to be sure, but what about Smith? Claiming that § 1341 applies, Smith takes a credit against tax for the tax he paid in the year the salary payment was received or, if greater, the tax benefit of a current deduction. The result, if § 1341 does apply, is to return X Corp. and Smith to the tax position they would have been in had the excess salary device never been attempted.[9] Putting it differently, X and Smith had nothing to lose by attempting to avoid the double tax through payment of the excess salary, provided that the shareholder-level dividend tax can be eliminated under § 1341 if the attempt fails. They'll do the same thing next year, we suppose, hoping to escape an audit. While the Commissioner will have succeeded in preventing avoidance of tax (this time) by disallowing the corporate-level deduction, there is nothing to prevent or discourage Smith from trying again if § 1341 is available.

Presumably with this dilemma in mind, the government in the *Van Cleave*[10] case argued that § 1341 should apply only if the excess salary payment was subject to a claim by the payor at the time the original salary payment was made—if it merely *"appeared* that the taxpayer had an unrestricted right" to such payment—but *not* if the taxpayer actually did have such an unrestricted right and the duty to return the payment arose solely as a consequence of an event taking place in a subsequent year. In *Van Cleave,* as in the case of Mr. Smith, it is obvious that no duty to return the excess salary would arise in the absence of a later-year audit of the corporation's tax return, despite Van Cleave's foresight in having his corporation adopt the give-back resolution referred to above. Hence § 1341, in the government's view, was inapplicable. If inapplicable, Smith would have a taxable dividend in the earlier year of payment and then,

---

[9]   Actually, Smith will be in an even *better* position than if the device had never been attempted, if (i) his marginal tax rate in the later year is higher than his marginal tax rate in the earlier year, and (ii) he elects to claim a deduction in the later year rather than a credit for the tax paid in the earlier year.

[10]   718 F.2d 193 (6th Cir. 1983).

presumably, a non-deductible contribution to corporate capital in the give-back year.

The Court in *Van Cleave* was not persuaded. Holding for the taxpayer, the Court found that the purpose of § 1341 was to provide "transactional" relief even when the duty to repay was solely the result of a subsequent event.

A loose end. What about the *character* of the repayment, a question not answered by § 1341. In the *Arrowsmith* case,[11] the individual taxpayers properly reported long-term capital gains on the liquidation of their wholly-owned corporation—capital gain then as now being taxed at a substantially lower rate than "ordinary" income. Several years later a judgment was rendered against the corporation, which the taxpayers paid as transferees of the corporation's assets. Since the payment did not entail the "sale or exchange of a capital asset" but merely the satisfaction of a liability, the taxpayers sought to treat the payment as a business loss deductible from ordinary income. The Supreme Court sustained the Commissioner in treating the payment as a capital loss on the ground that paying the corporation's debt was part of the original liquidation rather than a separate event, even though the payment was made in a subsequent taxable year.

A somewhat similar question has arisen with respect to the recapture of short-swing profits under § 16(b) of the Securities Exchange Act of 1934. Under § 16(b), a corporate "insider" who makes a gain on the purchase and sale (or sale and purchase) of the corporation's stock within a period of six months is required to surrender the gain by repaying the same amount to the corporation itself. The statutory purpose, obviously, is to deter insiders from taking advantage of breaking news, good or bad, before it breaks. Following *Arrowsmith* and reversing the Tax Court, the appellate courts have held that as the taxpayer's initial gain would be a capital gain, at least in economic terms, the subsequent recapture must be treated as a capital loss rather than an ordinary business expense.[12]

10.03 The Tax Benefit Rule

What about the converse of the *Lewis* pattern? Suppose a taxpayer (Lewis's employer, say) properly deducts an outlay in one year and then in a later year reclaims and recovers the same amount? Under the so-called tax benefit rule—largely a judicial creation but one of long-standing—the subsequent recovery is included in the

---

[11] *Arrowsmith v. Commissioner*, 344 U.S. 6 (1952).

[12] E.g., *Cummings v. Commissioner*, 506 F.2d 449 (2d Cir. 1974).

taxpayer's income, provided that the earlier deduction produced a tax saving in the prior period. Stated somewhat technically, if the deduction of an item offsets taxable income, then the item itself (the claim against Lewis) takes a basis in the taxpayer's hands of zero. When it is "exchanged" for cash, the taxpayer realizes reportable gain equal to the amount received. As in the mirror-image claim of right situation, the recovery of an amount deducted in an earlier year does not result in any change to the taxpayer's tax bill for the earlier year. The general rule that events in later years do not affect tax results for earlier years applies in both the claim of right and tax benefit contexts. Instead, the required tax adjustment—for the repayment or recovery, as the case may be—is made in the later year.

Some odd applications of the tax benefit rule have arisen. In *Alice Phelan Sullivan Corp. v. U.S.,*[13] the taxpayer in 1939 and 1940 contributed two parcels of real estate to charity and deducted the value of the contributions from its income. The gifts were conditioned on the property's being used for religious or educational purposes. In 1957, the donee decided not to use the gifts and returned the properties to the taxpayer. The Court of Claims sustained the Commissioner in requiring the taxpayer to include the properties in its income for 1957 at a value equal to the amounts deducted as charitable contributions in the earlier years. While the return to a taxpayer of her own property—*e.g.,* the repayment of a loan—normally does not produce taxable income, "the principle is well engrained in our tax law that the return or recovery of property that was once the subject of an income tax deduction must be treated as income in the year of its recovery."

As with the *Lewis* decision (*i.e.,* before the enactment of § 1341), the *Sullivan* case stops short of adopting a complete transactional solution to the problem of prior deduction and subsequent inclusion. Tax rates in 1939–40 when the real estate was contributed to charity were well below the rates that prevailed in 1957 when the property was recovered, so that from the taxpayer's standpoint the overall "transaction" produced a net tax increase. The same consequence would occur, of course, if the taxpayer's applicable bracket rate changed from one year to the other even though the rate schedule itself remained constant. In an earlier decision involving similar facts[14] the Court of Claims had applied the tax benefit rule to require the taxpayer merely to repay the taxes previously saved—in effect, employing a kind of common-law version of § 1341. But in *Sullivan* the court reversed this aspect of its prior decision on the ground that statutory authority for it was lacking.

---

[13] 180 Ct.Cl. 659, 381 F.2d 399 (1967).
[14] *Perry v. U.S.,* 142 Ct.Cl. 7, 160 F.Supp. 270 (1958).

Under § 111, if a deduction produced *no* tax benefit when taken, then the subsequent recovery of the item deducted will be excluded from the taxpayer's income in the later year. By far the most common application of this rule is with respect to state income tax refunds. If a taxpayer claims state income taxes among his itemized deductions in one year, and receives a refund of some portion of those state income taxes in a later year, the refund will be taxable in the later year under the tax benefit rule. But if the taxpayer claims the standard deduction in the year in which he paid the state income taxes, then a state income tax refund in a later year will be excluded under § 111. Aside from the relief provided by § 111 in the extreme case of an earlier deduction producing no tax benefit whatsoever, Congress has provided no relief from the rigors of the tax benefit rule analogous to the relief provided by § 1341 from the rigors of the claim of right doctrine. If a taxpayer deducts an item in a year in which his marginal tax rate is 10%, and recovers it in a later year when his marginal tax rate is 35%, that is just too bad for the taxpayer; the tax in the later year is imposed at 35%. Given the close analogy between the claim of right situation and the tax benefit rule situation, there is no good reason for the congressional decision to treat the two situations so differently. Either § 1341 is too generous, or § 111 (by reason of its narrow scope) is not generous enough.

Although the "recovery" concept stressed in *Sullivan* is indeed familiar and engrained, the Service, with support from the Supreme Court, has applied the tax benefit rule in broader terms than the word "recovery" suggests. In *Bliss Dairy*,[15] the taxpayer-corporation had purchased cattle feed for use in its operations and deducted the full cost of the feed in the year of purchase. The company was liquidated in the following taxable year and among the assets distributed to its shareholders was a substantial portion of the feed just mentioned. Code § 336 (since amended) then provided that a corporation shall recognize no gain on distributing its assets in liquidation even though the property distributed has a basis in the corporation's hands that is lower than the value of such property at the distribution date. Since Bliss had already deducted its cost, the basis of the unused cattle feed was zero; its value was about $60,000.

Sustaining the government, the Court held that the value of the unused feed should be included in the corporation's income and reported on its final return despite the non-recognition rule of § 336. In taking an expense deduction for the cattle feed, the taxpayer in a sense warranted that the feed would be used, or consumed, in its business; such use, in turn, would one day generate gross income to match the earlier deduction. By liquidating, as it were, in mid-

---

[15]   Decided together with *Hillsboro National Bank v. Commissioner,* 460 U.S. 370 (1983).

stream, the taxpayer had obviously eliminated the latter feature of the transaction; no matching income would ever materialize, because the cattle feed had been withdrawn from the taxpayer's business. While the expense deduction might have been proper when taken, subsequent events—the liquidation—proved "fundamentally inconsistent" with its original justification. Accordingly, the cost of the cattle feed must be restored to the company's income—added back to profits—and the prior tax benefit surrendered.

Though a bit of a tangle, Justice O'Connor's opinion in *Bliss* reaches a reasonable and expectable result.[16] The decision confirms that the tax benefit rule goes beyond the limited "recovery" situation dealt with in *Sullivan* and operates as a kind of recapture or reconciliation principle as well.

11. The Cash Method

As noted earlier, the cash receipts and disbursements method of accounting is used by almost all individual wage and salary earners. It is used, also, by a good many personal service companies and other small and medium-sized enterprises.[17] Compared with the accrual method of accounting, which often requires that income and expense items be recognized prior to (or after) their receipt or payment, the cash method has the merit of simplicity. The recognition of income and expense is governed by the chronology of cash receipt and disbursement; revenues and expenditures are recognized at the time cash is received or paid out regardless of when the claims or obligations actually arose. The result, among other things, is that bookkeeping and accounting duties are minimized; indeed, for most cash method taxpayers, all "accounting" is done in the family checkbook.

Perhaps the main interpretative problem that has arisen in connection with the cash method is the treatment of deferred compensation. If an executive receives, in addition to a cash salary, a promise from her employer to make further payments after the executive retires, is the value of that promise currently includable in the executive's income along with the salary, or can it be deferred until actual payment takes place? *Cash* method seems to imply deferral, but perhaps the employer's promise (like the endowment policy at 1.02) should be regarded as the *equivalent* of cash and hence

---

[16] *See* White, *An Essay on the Conceptual Foundations of the Tax Benefit Rule,* 82 Mich.L.Rev. 485 (1984).

[17] Section 448(a) expressly prohibits use of the cash method by larger corporations and certain other entities. However, corporations and partnerships with average annual gross receipts of $25 million or less are permitted to use the cash method by §§ 448(b) and (c).

be taxed currently at its discounted value. This and related issues are examined in the subsection next following.

A converse problem is considered at 11.02. If expenses are normally recognized by cash method taxpayers at the time actual outlays are made, what should be the treatment of expenses that are paid in advance, say a three-year fire insurance premium? May a taxpayer accelerate her expense deductions by making prepayments? Or does the capital expenditure rule restrict the operation of the cash method and require the taxpayer to amortize the insurance premium over the three-year period? As with the deferred compensation problem, the question here is how to reconcile the premise which underlies the cash method—that net income for the taxable year shall be determined by reference to receipts and disbursements—with the broad statutory requirement that the taxpayer's accounting method shall "clearly reflect" his annual income.

11.01 Constructive Receipt and Cash Equivalency

The Treasury, in Regulations of long standing, has made it clear that in determining gross income under the cash method, a taxpayer may not look solely to the *cash* that she has realized, nor even solely to her *actual* receipts. "Generally, under the cash method . . ., all items which constitute gross income (whether in the form of cash, property, or services) are to be included for the taxable year in which actually or constructively received." Reg. § 1.446–1(c)(1). Two enlargements are thus implied: receipt may be constructive as well as actual; and includable income may take other forms than cash. Neither extension is surprising, yet both tend to blur the simple concept of cash method accounting.

(a) Constructive Receipt

Briefly stated, the constructive receipt doctrine prescribes that a taxpayer may not postpone taxation of income that is available to her merely by failing to exercise her power to collect it. An employee whose year-end wages have been made available cannot avoid inclusion by waiting until the next year to pick up her pay envelope; a lawyer cannot return her client's check with a request to pay the fee in a later period. Once the receipt is earned and within the taxpayer's control, it is includable despite her efforts to delay it. Any other rule would put wage and fee earners in a position to defer their income more or less at will and thereby achieve a kind of homemade averaging outside the specific limits of the statute.

The constructive receipt doctrine is a "rule of law" for determining when income is taxable, which means that taxpayers, as well as the Commissioner, may invoke it. In *Hyland v.*

Commissioner,[18] the taxpayer was the chief executive and controlling stockholder of a personal service corporation. He performed services for the corporation in 1942 but received no actual cash salary in that year. Although the company's board of directors had approved a salary allocable to 1942 of about $35,000, the amount was not actually paid until 1943. While the taxpayer's original return for 1942 did not include the salary item, in an *amended* return filed some years later, he did report the $35,000 as 1942 income and excluded it from income for 1943. We may assume that the taxpayer's applicable tax rate turned out to be lower in 1942 than in 1943.

The taxpayer argued that in view of his control of the corporation, and in view also of the board's resolution, the salary was constructively received by him in 1942. He stressed that he could have reduced the salary to possession in that year simply by causing the corporation to issue a check. The Court of Appeals, nevertheless, sustained the Commissioner in taxing the salary in 1943. It held that the constructive receipt doctrine would not be applied merely because the taxpayer, as controlling stockholder, could have directed the company's treasurer to make the salary payment. That argument, said the Court, would prove too much, for it would mean that in every close corporation the corporate earnings would be "constructively received" by persons having the power to compel their distribution. But as corporations and shareholders are assumed to be separate taxable persons, mere power or control could not be taken as equivalent to the exercise thereof. Not the power to cause the board to act, therefore, but an actual crediting or setting aside of the funds in question would be necessary to support inclusion.

In a sense, of course, the position urged by the taxpayer in *Hyland* was one that most taxpayers would oppose, because it threatened a privilege long regarded by the owner-managers of closely held corporations as their birthright (as noted at 9.03(b)). Thus, under present law a shareholder-executive in a small company may entirely or partially forgo her annual salary. The amount forgone will then be taxed to the corporation; it will not be "imputed" to the individual merely because her services would reasonably entitle her to take down an equivalent amount. In the alternative, the executive may draw her full salary (thereby generating a corporate deduction and eliminating the corporate tax on her salary), pay the individual tax, and then reinvest the money in the corporate business by lending it back or buying additional stock. In short, the owner-manager may elect, annually, to pay tax *either* at the corporate rate *or* at her individual rate on that portion of her salary (actual or

---

[18]　175 F.2d 422 (2d Cir. 1949).

constructive) which she desires to leave in the company's hands for use in the business.

Quite obviously, had the "constructive receipt" argument succeeded in *Hyland,* there would at least have been a danger that the Commissioner would take the resulting "rule of law" as authority to *require* owner-managers to include a reasonable salary in their gross incomes under all circumstances. But such an authority would be contrary to the accepted (if unstated) legislative scheme just described and would represent a departure from existing practice. The Commissioner has plainly recognized the intent of Congress in this respect: although the *Hyland* opinion left open the possibility that the *government* "might successfully invoke the doctrine of constructive receipt against the sole stockholder of a one-man corporation," with rare exceptions the Commissioner has not attempted, under either the constructive receipt doctrine or the income-attribution rules, to impute taxable salaries to controlling shareholders.

(b) Deferred Compensation

A major distinction between the cash and the accrual method of accounting arises in connection with the treatment of accounts receivable. Amounts due from clients, customers, or employers are not included in a cash method taxpayer's income until actually received in cash; by contrast, accrual method taxpayers normally report such items when the services are completed or the merchandise is shipped and the amount due has been billed or invoiced. Suppose, for example, that a salesperson earns commissions for goods sold during the current year, but the commissions are actually paid in the following year. If the salesperson is on the cash method, the commissions will be includable in the later period even though they were fully earned in the first year and their amount was undisputed. If the salesperson used the accrual method, the commissions would be taxed in the earlier period even though actual payment was made subsequently. Assume in either case that the commissions are paid by the taxpayer's employer in due course—that is, early in the second year. Then, as between the two, the cash method salesperson enjoys the relatively modest advantage of a one-year deferral of tax. This results because the cash method excuses the taxpayer from currently reporting items which happen to be outstanding at the close of the taxable year, and also incidentally allows the taxpayer to associate her cash inflows with her tax payment obligations.

The illustration just given assumes that the delay in payment of the salesperson's commissions is merely a year-end phenomenon and not a conscious effort to reduce taxes. But suppose the deferral has been carefully prearranged between the salesperson and her employer, and suppose also that the period of delay is much longer than a single year. Anticipating that her marginal tax rate will be lower after her retirement, the salesperson and her employer enter into a deferred compensation agreement which provides that a portion of the salesperson's annual earnings will be withheld by the employer and paid out in installments after the salesperson reaches retirement age. Perhaps the agreement even provides for imputed interest on the amounts withheld, as if the funds were deposited in a savings account for the salesperson's benefit. If this arrangement succeeds from a tax standpoint—that is, if inclusion is deferred until actual payments begin—the salesperson will have postponed her taxes for a substantial period, and will have obtained the further advantage of the lower post-retirement rates. In effect, the cash method of accounting, the chief aim of which is to simplify the taxpayer's bookkeeping, will thus have been converted into an *ad hoc* tax-deferral and tax-rate-averaging device.

The Commissioner has attacked deferred compensation arrangements under both a constructive receipt and an economic benefit theory. His success, however, has been limited. In *Commissioner v. Oates*,[19] for example, the taxpayer, an insurance agent, was entitled on the termination of his agency to receive renewal commissions as they were earned over the succeeding nine-year period. The commissions were expected to be relatively high for the first few years, and then to decrease owing to the lapse of policies and other factors, finally reaching a low point by the end of the nine-year term. Prior to the commencement of payments and before any amounts were actually due, the taxpayer and his employer entered into a new agreement which provided that the renewal commissions would be paid in fixed monthly installments over a fifteen-year period at the rate of $1,000 a month. While the commissions earned by the taxpayer during the first year of the contract were nearly $50,000, he received and reported only the lesser amount to which the revised agreement entitled him.

Holding that neither the constructive receipt nor the economic benefit theory applied, the court of appeals rejected the Commissioner's effort to tax annually the full amount of the commissions earned. As to constructive receipt, the court found that doctrine applicable only to compensation *already* due and payable. While the taxpayer could not turn his back on income which was actually tendered to him, this did not mean that he was barred from arranging for the deferral of compensation in *advance* of the time it was earned. As to "economic benefit," the court rejected the argument

---

[19]   207 F.2d 711 (7th Cir. 1953).

that each year's earned commissions were effectively realized by the taxpayer, and then applied to the purchase of the $1,000-a-month annuity. Finding that the amended contract "was in the nature of a novation" rather than an exchange, the court held that only the actual cash payments received by the taxpayer could be treated as "realized" in any taxable year.

The *Oates* decision can be contrasted with the so-called "endowment policy case" mentioned at 1.02, above. There it was stated that an employee would be taxed *currently* on the value of an annuity or endowment policy purchased *from* an insurance company *by* the taxpayer's employer, the policy to be turned over to the taxpayer at the date of his retirement. In *Oates,* the taxpayer also received a promise of future payments in the form of an annuity issued by an insurance company, but, as it happened, the insurance company itself was the taxpayer's employer. The *Oates* decision shows that the unconditional promise of the *employer,* even though itself a sound insurance company, to pay compensation in the future will not give rise to a constructive receipt or a taxable economic benefit to a cash method employee. But if the employer substitutes for its own promise either a fund outside its control or the unconditional obligation of a third party, that act does give rise to current income for the reason that the fund or the obligation is regarded as the equivalent of cash.

Having largely failed in its effort to treat deferred compensation arrangements as currently taxable, the Service in a 1960 ruling conceded the major elements of the controversy, and held, in effect, that conventional, unfunded deferred compensation agreements would be given their intended effect for tax purposes. In Rev. Rul. 60–31,[20] an executive was employed under an agreement which provided for an annual salary plus deferred compensation, the latter to be paid after termination of the executive's employment. The deferred payment obligation was annually credited on the employer's books and, once credited, was nonforfeitable. The Service ruled that the executive would be taxable only when he received the deferred amounts, because a "mere promise to pay, not represented by notes or secured in any way, is not regarded as a receipt of income within the intendment of the cash receipts and disbursements method."

No Code provision explicitly provides for the tax deferral permitted by Rev. Rul. 60–31. Rather, the deferral results from the Ruling's interpretation of the doctrine of constructive receipt. There are, however, Code provisions explicitly establishing two basic types of tax-deferred retirement savings. As explained earlier (5.06), taxpayers can deduct contributions to Individual Retirement

---

[20]   1960–1 C.B. 174.

Accounts (IRAs), subject to restrictions on eligibility and ceilings on tax-deductible amounts. Employees can also save for retirement, on a tax-deferred basis, through contributions to employer-sponsored "qualified plans" (so-called because they satisfy detailed qualifying standards set forth in the Code). The contributions may be made automatically by the employer, or by the employee's electing to forgo current cash compensation in favor of retirement savings. An employee can exclude qualified plan retirement savings from her gross income until she retires and begins to receive distributions from the plan. Like IRAs, qualified plans are subject to statutory ceilings on contributions, although the ceilings are considerably higher than for IRAs. In addition, qualified plans are subject to detailed nondiscrimination rules. Generally speaking, the nondiscrimination rules condition tax deferral for retirement savings of highly-compensated employees on the provision of qualified plan benefits to non-highly compensated employees as well.

It should be clear why many corporate executives prefer to take their deferred compensation in forms blessed by Rev. Rul. 60–31—sometimes referred to as nonqualified deferred compensation—rather than in the form of contributions to IRAs or qualified plans. Unlike IRAs and qualified plans, nonqualified deferred compensation is not subject to any ceiling on the amount of income that can be deferred. And unlike qualified plans, nonqualified deferred compensation is not subject to nondiscrimination rules.[21]

The deferred compensation field remained fairly stable after the issuance of Rev. Rul. 60–31 until Congress enacted § 409A in 2004. This provision, the details of which are monstrously complex even by tax standards, provides for immediate taxability rather than deferral if the amounts payable in the future can be accelerated by the taxpayer-employee or if such amounts can be funded, and hence shielded from the corporation's creditors, in the event of a deterioration of the corporation's financial health. Nonqualified deferred compensation which escapes immediate taxability under § 409A might reasonably be termed "qualified nonqualified deferred compensation," although to the best of our knowledge this terminology has yet to catch on. In any event, it is fair to say that § 409A has taken a significant amount—but by no means all—of the tax fun out of nonqualified deferred compensation.

---

[21] From the point of view of the *employer*, however, there is a distinct disadvantage to nonqualified deferred compensation. An employer may deduct its contributions to a qualified plan in the year in which it makes the contributions, but an employer's deduction for nonqualified deferred compensation is delayed until the year in which the employee receives payment and includes the payment in gross income. This difference is explored in Question 1 in the "Questions and Answers" at the end of this Section.

It may be of some interest—perhaps only archaeological—to ask why the Commissioner should have succeeded so well (in cases like *Lucas v. Earl* and *Helvering v. Eubank:* see 7.01, 7.02) in preventing the assignment of earned income to other taxable *persons,* while largely failing to prevent the assignment of such income to other taxable *periods.* Briefly put, why did the government win in *Eubank,* but lose in *Oates,* when both cases entailed an effort by an insurance agent to minimize the impact of the progressive rate structure through an assignment or restructuring of his renewal commissions? The answer, most probably, is that the question of taxable person was not thought to be constrained by accounting rules to the same degree as the question of taxable period. In *Eubank,* the courts and the Service were at liberty to invent rules of income attribution under the general authority of § 61. Whether the assigned renewal commissions should be attributed to Eubank or to his assignee was not hedged in by fixed accounting principles, and hence the courts were free to regard the question as open. By contrast, the taxpayer in *Oates* could draw support from the cash method itself, which apparently contains no intrinsic distinction between short-term, involuntary deferrals and deferrals which are extended and also prearranged. To tax *both* currently, however, would virtually be to abrogate the cash method of accounting.

More generally, it may simply be that the courts have intuitively favored the idea of self-help income-*averaging*—which does, after all, appeal to one's sense of equity—while viewing income-*splitting* as a dangerous avoidance device and one with a wide potential for mischief. On the other hand, *Oates* involved deferral as well as a challenge to the progressive rate structure, which gave it a potential (subsequently realized) for mischief of a second type, while *Eubank* involved only a threat to progressivity.

(c)   "Calling Off" Constructive Receipt

The constructive receipt doctrine is, of course, an interpretation of the Internal Revenue Code, not a rule of constitutional law. If Congress thinks the doctrine should not apply in a particular situation, it can—and it not uncommonly does—enact a provision making the doctrine inapplicable in that context. Employer-provided free parking at work is generally tax-free under § 132 (1.02), and cash compensation is (obviously) taxable. Absent a special statutory provision, if an employer allowed an employee a choice between parking worth $X and $X of cash compensation, the employee would have to include $X in gross income even if he opted for the free parking (because he was in constructive receipt of the cash). Section 132(f)(4), however, expressly provides that the constructive receipt doctrine does not apply in this situation. The so-called cafeteria plan rules of § 125 make the constructive receipt doctrine inapplicable when a taxpayer is offered a choice between taxable cash and one or more tax-free "qualified benefits." If a taxpayer chooses cash the cash must be included in the taxpayer's gross income, but if the taxpayer chooses the fringe benefit no tax is imposed; it does not matter that the taxpayer had the option to receive cash. Tax-free fringes that may be offered under a cafeteria plan include health benefits, dependent care assistance, and retirement savings.

11.02   Prepaid Expenses

For reasons already made clear, the acceleration of expense deductions normally benefits a taxpayer by permitting her to defer her taxes to later periods. As indicated at 6.02, this factor largely explains why disputes arise between taxpayers and the Commissioner over the scope of the capital expenditure limitation in § 263. If an outlay for certain equipment is treated as an expense under § 162, it is currently deductible and reduces this year's tax. If the outlay is treated as a capital expenditure under § 263, it must be recovered through depreciation over the useful life of the equipment. Taxpayers almost always prefer immediate deduction to deferral.

On the whole, the question of deductible expense or nondeductible capital expenditure is unaffected by the taxpayer's accounting method. Cash and accrual method taxpayers both are required to capitalize the cost of assets having an extended useful life, and to recover such cost through depreciation allowances. A contrary rule, one which permitted cash method taxpayers to deduct currently the full cost of long-lived assets merely because an actual cash outlay had been made, would obviously result in serious distortions of taxable income. Accordingly, despite some increase in record-keeping complexity, cash method taxpayers are no less subject to the capital expenditure limitation than taxpayers using the accrual method.

The same limitation also generally applies to the prepayment of expenses, though there have been occasional lapses in the decided cases and even the administrative rulings. By and large, prepayments of insurance premiums, rents, compensation and the like are currently deductible only to the extent that the "asset" or service so acquired is exhausted during the taxable year. The unused portion of the premiums, rent, etc. is required to be prorated, or amortized, over the years to which the benefit relates.

It is, perhaps, not wholly clear whether § 263, which limits the deduction of expenses otherwise allowable under § 162, applies in a similar fashion to taxes and interest "paid or accrued within the taxable year" under §§ 163 and 164. Arguably, the latter provisions authorize cash method taxpayers to take a current deduction for the items thus *specifically* named even where a substantial prepayment is made. Whether for this or some other reason, the Service at an early date ruled that interest paid in advance for a five-year period by a cash method taxpayer was fully deductible in the year of payment. This ruling, however, invited substantial tax-avoidance through the prepayment of interest on real estate mortgages by high-bracket taxpayers, and as a result, in 1968 the Service revoked its prior position on the ground that the deduction of prepaid interest did not clearly reflect taxable income.[22] Under the later ruling, prepaid interest had to be amortized over the period to which it actually related if the prepayment was for a period of more than twelve months beyond the close of the current year. In 1976 Congress put an end to even this limited concession by adding § 461(g), which requires cash method taxpayers to capitalize all prepaid interest (other than in connection with home mortgage loans) and to deduct such interest ratably over the period of the loan.

Apart from prepaid interest, cash method taxpayers engaged in farming have been permitted, under long-standing administrative regulations, to treat as current expenses a wide variety of costs which other taxpayers would have to capitalize. Although intended merely to simplify the bookkeeping chores of ordinary working farmers, these rules were sometimes converted into lucrative tax-shelter arrangements by high-income individuals—doctors, dentists, movie-stars—who never drove a tractor or milked a cow. Prior to the statutory revisions described below, a brain surgeon, for example, who appeared to be having an especially good year, might have invested in a so-called cattle feeding partnership. The partnership prepaid the cost of the feed for the cattle in the *current* year, allowing the doctor to deduct her share of the prepayment. The cattle were sold in the *following* year, and the doctor then reported her share of the gain. Since her income was lower in the second year than in the first, the good doctor achieved a spreading and deferral of the first year's high earnings. Other syndicated farming shelters were also popular. Thus, deferral *plus* conversion of ordinary income into capital gain was achieved by investing in orchards, vineyards, and the like. Maintenance and other growing costs were currently deductible by the investor, while the later sale of the land and orchard produced a capital gain.

Added to the Code in 1976, and since expanded, §§ 263A and 464 attempt to distinguish between taxpayers who are actively engaged in farming as a business, and taxpayers who passively invest in widely-held farm "syndicates" with a view to exploiting the farm-accounting rules for the purpose of sheltering income derived from

---

[22]   Rev.Rul. 68–643, 1968–2 C.B. 76, 1968–2 C.B. 76. *See also* Asimow, *Principle and Prepaid Interest,* 16 U.C.L.A.L.Rev. 36 (1968).

other sources. Briefly, the provisions mentioned permit farming syndicates to deduct the cost of feed, fertilizer, etc. only when actually consumed. In effect, therefore, deferral through the anticipation of expense deductions is sharply curtailed.[23]

12. The Accrual Method

From an accountant's standpoint, the determination of periodic income is essentially a process of "timing" the recognition of revenue and "matching" against such revenue the expense items which are related thereto. The cash method of accounting makes no scientific effort either to "time" or to "match", because under it the recognition of revenue and expense turns largely on the accidental factor of receipt or disbursement. Subject to the modifications described in the preceding Section, receivables and payables are recognized only when reduced to cash. While this simple method is suitable for individuals rendering personal services, for large corporations and other taxpayers which engage in the sale of merchandise, whether as manufacturers or distributors, and which extend credit to their customers and receive credit from their suppliers, a satisfactory determination of annual income requires the more refined techniques of accrual. Code § 448 generally requires corporations to use the accrual method, although under a 2017 amendment the statutory mandate does not apply to a corporation with average annual gross receipts of $25 million or less. In addition, § 471 generally requires taxpayers engaged in the production or purchase and sale of goods to use opening and closing inventories in computing the cost of goods sold (as explained at 12.03, below)—again with an exception for a business with average annual gross receipts of $25 million or less.

Briefly described, *accrual* is a technique for recognizing revenue items prior to their receipt in cash and for recognizing expense items prior to their actual payment. Thus, accounts receivable—amounts owed to the taxpayer by its customers—and accounts payable—amounts owed by the taxpayer to its suppliers—are both taken into account at the time the obligation becomes fixed, even though payment is not received or made until a later period.

Deferment—which is no less a part of the prescribed technique where ordinary commercial accounting is concerned—is a device for postponing the recognition of revenues received in advance, and of expenses paid in advance, for services to be rendered or goods to be delivered in the future. Suppose, for example, that a lessor receives five years' prepaid rents from its lessee. On the lessee's side, the

[23] The passive loss limitations of § 469, enacted in 1986 and described later in this book (13.02), are not specifically targeted at exploitation of farm-accounting rules, but the § 469 limitations are independently sufficient to make tax shelters of the sort described in the text a thing of the past.

advance rentals are required to be capitalized and prorated over the five-year term. Tax and commercial accounting principles here converge. On the lessor's side, commercial accounting would similarly require that the advance receipt be deferred through credit to a liability account, and then included year-by-year in the lessor's income. As will be seen, however, tax accounting follows a different course at this point. In effect, tax accounting puts the lessor on the cash method for this limited purpose and requires the lessor to include the full prepayment in the year of receipt.

The sections that follow examine three important issues. Section 12.01 takes up the timing and matching of receipts and expenditures by accrual method taxpayers, and in particular the treatment of items that are disputed or uncertain. Section 12.02 gives more detailed attention to the above-mentioned question of deferment, as well as the related topic of reserves for estimated expenses. Finally, 12.03 explains and illustrates the use of inventory techniques in determining the cost of goods sold.

12.01   Recognition of Income and Expenses; Disputed Items

(a)   *Timing of Revenues and Expenditures*

For accrual method taxpayers, the recognition of *income* depends on when the taxpayer's right to receive the item becomes fixed and determinable. In *Lucas v. North Texas Lumber Co.*,[24] the taxpayer, a sawmill operator, gave another concern a ten-day option to purchase its timber lands for a specified price. The option was exercised on December 30, 1916, at which time the taxpayer ceased operations and withdrew its employees from the land. Deeds to the property were delivered to the purchaser on January 5, 1917, and on that date the purchase price was paid and the transaction closed. The taxpayer, on the accrual method, sought to report its profit in 1916, while the Commissioner asserted that the appropriate year for inclusion was 1917. Rates were substantially higher in 1917, a war year, than in 1916. Finding that title to the land did not pass to the vendee until 1917, and that no unconditional liability to pay the purchase price arose until the deeds were delivered, the Supreme Court held that the taxpayer's gain could not be included in the earlier year despite its use of the accrual method.

The *North Texas Lumber* case is generally cited for the proposition that accrual of income is not permitted or required until goods or services have been transferred or performed, even where customers' orders are booked and a binding sale contract has been entered into at a fixed price. Thus, accrual based on contracts for

---

[24]   281 U.S. 11 (1930).

future delivery presumably is improper. On the other hand, the rule as stated has not been applied inflexibly, and accrual of income has been permitted on a contract rather than a "sales" basis where the taxpayer has followed a consistent practice over an extended period of time. It can be argued, indeed, that *North Texas Lumber* was not really an accounting decision at all. The transaction involved a one-time transfer of fixed assets (not a recurring sale of goods), and the issue posed was when such transactions should be regarded as closed. The rule announced—that realization occurs on delivery of the property sold, even though the obligation to deliver became binding in a previous period—is one that probably applies to all casual sales of property, regardless of the seller's accounting method.

Moving to the recognition of *expenses* by accrual method taxpayers, the Supreme Court in *U.S. v. Anderson*[25] confirmed that expense items are to be deducted not when cash happens to change hands, but when "all the events" occur which establish the taxpayer's liability to make the payment and the amount due can be determined with reasonable accuracy. In *Anderson,* the taxpayer, a munitions manufacturer, incurred a special profits tax on munitions manufactured by it in 1916. The tax became due and was paid in 1917, and the taxpayer sought to deduct the tax payment from its income in the later rather than the earlier year. Once again, income tax rates were higher in 1917 than in 1916. The taxpayer argued that taxes do not accrue until they are assessed, and that the assessment date, 1917, was therefore the proper time for deduction. The Court, however, held that the munitions tax must be deducted in 1916. Conceding that taxes technically do not become a *legal* liability until assessed, the Court found, nevertheless, that all the events necessary to fix and determine the taxpayer's obligation had occurred in the earlier period. In an accounting sense, therefore, the taxes had accrued.

Superficially, perhaps, the *Anderson* decision seems inconsistent with the holding in *North Texas Lumber.* If recognition of income had to await the actual delivery of the timberland in *North Texas Lumber,* then perhaps the recognition of expense should have had to await the actual assessment of the munitions tax in *Anderson.* If the all-events test required passage of title to the land, it might also have been expected to require assessment of the tax. Actually, however, the two cases are aimed at somewhat different goals. In *North Texas Lumber* the Court's objective was to establish a practical rule for the *recognition* of revenues by accrual method taxpayers; in general, the decision requires that revenues be recognized when goods are shipped to the buyer, neither earlier nor later. *Anderson,* by contrast,

---

[25]   269 U.S. 422 (1926).

is chiefly interested in *matching* expenses with the particular revenues with which those expenses happen to be associated; the Court's aim was to assure that the taxpayer's gross income and related expenses would be reported in the *same* taxable period. The all-events test was rather a clumsy verbal locution for attaining the two different ends in view, but the results reached by the Court were satisfactory on the whole and are consistent with normal accounting practice.

In *U.S. v. General Dynamics Corp.*,[26] the taxpayer maintained health insurance for covered employees (some 56,000, apparently) through a self-insured program under which it paid medical claims out of its own funds. Employees who had received medical services during the year would file claims for reimbursement under the plan; such claims would then be reviewed for eligibility and coverage by employee-benefit personnel and, if approved, would be paid by the taxpayer in due course. Because there was typically some delay between the time an employee received medical treatment and the time the employee submitted her claim for reimbursement, it always happened that a portion of the current year's reimbursable claims would not actually have been filed with benefit personnel by the year-end and, hence, would not be approved and paid until the following year or perhaps even the year after that. The taxpayer sought to accrue and deduct the full amount paid, due, and estimated to be due for medical services received by its employees during the current taxable year. The amount so deducted included (a) payments actually made and (b) claims approved for payment—the figures for those two categories being known with certainty. Also, however, the accrual included (c) claims not yet filed at year-end but for which a reasonable estimate could be made on the basis of the company's statistical and actuarial experience for prior periods. The government raised no question about categories (a) and (b), but it rejected the company's effort to accrue amounts attributed to category (c) on the ground that, as to the latter, the requirements of the all-events test had not been met.

In a somewhat confusing opinion (and with three dissents), the Supreme Court sustained the government's position under the all-events standard. The Court appeared to accept as reasonable the company's estimate of the dollar amount that its late-filing employees would ultimately become entitled to. Nevertheless, it refused to agree that the fact of liability could be "firmly established" prior to the time that an employee actually filed a claim. Some individuals covered by the medical plan and plainly entitled to reimbursement might simply fail to file their claims, whether

---

[26] 481 U.S. 239 (1987), discussed in Jensen, *The Supreme Court and the Timing of Deductions for Accrual-Basis Taxpayers*, 22 Georgia L.Rev. 229 (1988).

"through oversight, procrastination, confusion over the coverage provided, or fear of disclosure to the employer of the extent or nature of the services received." Such failure, said the Court, was more than a "remote and speculative possibility." Hence, the act of filing must be seen not as a mere technicality or ministerial detail, but as "the last link in the chain of events creating liability for purposes of the 'all events' test."

Actually, and despite the Court's contrary assertion, the possibility that an employee might fail (through oversight, etc.) to file a reimbursement claim does seem pretty remote, or at least quite unlikely, for the obvious reason that anyone who thinks herself entitled to reimbursement—especially for a sizeable doctor's bill—is almost certainly going to ask for it. Rejection of a doubtful claim by the benefit staff following review seems a good deal more likely in a given instance, and one might have thought that if anything qualified as a "last link" it would be the stamp of approval that turned a pending claim into a right to payment. Linkage aside, perhaps the easiest way to explain the *General Dynamics* decision is to say that it follows precedent in refusing to sanction expense accruals on the basis of statistical or actuarial estimates of liability (absent express statutory authorization). As suggested at 12.02, the Code and the decided cases generally deny deduction for additions to reserves for *estimated* expenses, even where the estimate is reasonable and likely to be fairly accurate. Such conservatism in tax accounting can be criticized, but the pattern of legal development in this area— administrative and judicial disallowance, followed in a few specific instances by legislative relief—is quite clear-cut. Though the facts in *General Dynamics* may have been closer to the line of allowability than those present in various earlier decisions, in the end the asserted accrual *was* based on a statistical estimate and for that reason, probably, had to be denied.

(b) Disputed Items

In *North Texas Lumber* and *Anderson* the income and expense items in question were uncontested. The taxpayer's right to receive payment for the sale of land, or its liability to pay the federal munitions tax, and the amounts thereof, were clear. Suppose, however, that a taxpayer's claim to income or liability for expense is subject to dispute. What is the effect of the dispute on its obligation under the accrual method to include or deduct the item prior to payment?

In *Continental Tie & Lumber Co. v. U.S.*,[27] the taxpayer, under legislation enacted in 1920, became entitled to an award from the

---

[27]   286 U.S. 290 (1932).

federal government for losses resulting from government control of its railroad operations during World War I. Actual payment was not made until 1923, however, because it took that long for the Interstate Commerce Commission to promulgate regulations and make a determination of the amount to which the taxpayer was entitled. Finding that the taxpayer's right to an award was "fixed" by the passage of the 1920 legislation, and that data on its books would have enabled it to compute the amount due with reasonable accuracy, the Supreme Court held that the award should have been accrued and reported in 1920 despite the delay in payment.

The *Continental Tie* decision is usually taken to imply a distinction between disputes as to whether an obligation is owing to the taxpayer at all and disputes as to the amount of an obligation conceded to be due. Disputes as to basic liability delay inclusion; disputes as to amount do not, if a reasonable estimate can be made. The distinction is not especially realistic, and probably the better rule would be to require accrual only to the extent of the amount agreed to by the obligor, while permitting delay as to the disputed balance.

The holding in *Continental Tie* can be contrasted with that in *North American Oil Consolidated v. Burnet,*[28] which also involved the inclusion of uncertain income by an accrual method taxpayer. In *North American Oil,* the taxpayer was required to include income at the time it was received in cash despite a very lively dispute over the taxpayer's right to retain it. In *Continental Tie,* the award was required to be accrued prior to payment even though there was uncertainty as to the amount. Taking the two decisions together, the effect is a construction of "accrual" which plainly favors the *earlier* inclusion of uncertain items and in that respect coincides with the tax-collector's convenience. As noted at 10.02, however, the possibility of hardship to the taxpayer has been reduced by the addition to the Code of § 1341, which now affords "transactional" relief where the taxpayer discovers in a later year that she had no right to all or a part of the previously included income.

The general rule governing the accrual of uncertain income— that no inclusion is required as long as the item is unpaid and the other party disputes her basic liability to the taxpayer—has its counterpart on the deduction side. In *Dixie Pine Products Co. v. Commissioner,*[29] the Supreme Court denied the taxpayer's right to accrue unpaid state gasoline taxes in the year incurred, because the taxpayer then contested its liability for such taxes on the ground that the chemical used in its business was not gasoline within the meaning of the state law. Going still further, in *U.S. v. Consolidated*

---

[28]   286 U.S. 417 (1932). The case is discussed at 10.02.

[29]   320 U.S. 516 (1944).

Edison Co.,[30] the Court held that a contested state tax could not be accrued as a deduction even when paid, since all the events necessary to fix the taxpayer's liability would not have occurred until the contest had terminated and the taxpayer's liability was resolved. Congress found the *Consolidated Edison* decision harsh and in 1964 overruled it by adding § 461(f), which provides for the deduction of disputed items in the year paid even though the taxpayer continues to contest her liability after the payment is made. If the taxpayer's liability later turns out to be less than the amount paid, the difference is taken back into income at that time, assuming the earlier deduction resulted in a tax benefit (see 10.03).

A loose end. As indicated, the all-events test is generally taken to mean that an expense item must be accrued when the taxpayer's liability is fixed and the amount is reasonably determinable. But suppose the expense item, though fixed and determinable, relates to services or property that is to be provided to (or by) the taxpayer in a future period. Thus, suppose a company on the accrual method contractually obligates itself to pay another concern $1 million for certain repair and clean-up work that it knows it will require in the future. The work is to be done, and the payment is to be made, 15 years from today. Since both liability and amount are fixed, the all-events test would literally seem to be satisfied.[31] Does this mean that the taxpayer can accrue and deduct the full $1 million in the *current* taxable year even though the work itself is not to be performed and paid for until much later?

Prior to 1984, the answer may well have been yes—in which case the all-events test would have generated a sizeable financial benefit for the taxpayer in question. Assuming a 40% tax rate, the $1 million deduction would be worth $400,000 in current tax savings. Such savings invested at an after-tax rate of 6% for 15 years would grow to about $1 million by the end of that period, and the latter sum could then be used by the taxpayer to meet its obligation under the contract. In effect, the repair work would have cost the taxpayer nothing: by deducting the entire expense in Year 1 (though without actually paying anything until Year 15), the taxpayer would have succeeded in shifting the full cost of the contract to the Treasury. Logic, of course, suggests that if the all-events test did indeed permit an accrual in Year 1, the allowable deduction should have been limited to the *present value* of the future $1 million outlay, or

----

[30]   366 U.S. 380 (1961).

[31]   *U.S. v. Hughes Properties, Inc.*, 476 U.S. 593 (1986); and see *Mooney Aircraft, Inc. v. U.S.*, 420 F.2d 400 (5th Cir.1969), discussed in Gunn, *Matching of Costs and Revenues As a Goal of Tax Accounting*, 4 Va. Tax Rev. 1 (1984).

$400,000. Assuming the same 40% tax rate applied in year 15, the advantage of accruing in advance of payment would then be eliminated. Thus, the tax saving realized by deducting $400,000 today ($160,000) is simply the present value (at 6%) of the tax saving to be realized at the end of 15 years ($400,000); hence, the taxpayer would be indifferent between deducting now and deducting later (it could not, of course, do both). While this solution presumably handles the problem, the difficulty from a purely legal standpoint is that no statutory authority exists for imposing a present-value limitation on accruable amounts.

To prevent avoidance through premature accruals, Congress in 1984 modified the definition of "all-events" by adding § 461(h) to the Code. Section 461(h) provides, in general, that the all-events test shall not be regarded as satisfied until the year in which "economic performance" occurs with respect to an accrual-method taxpayer's liability. Hence, deduction of the $1 million contract obligation would be permitted in Year 15 when the work in question was actually performed, but not in Year 1 when the contract was entered into.

12.02   Advance Receipts and Reserves for Estimated Expenses

An important area of divergence between accounting rules as applied for tax purposes and generally accepted accounting principles involves the treatment of prepaid income. For many years the Treasury has insisted that payments for services to be performed in later years are taxable in the year received even though they are in large part unearned at that time. Generally accepted accounting principles would require that the taxpayer defer the inclusion of advance receipts until the year or years in which the services are performed and the income is actually earned.

The Supreme Court has steadfastly supported the Treasury's position. In *American Automobile Association v. U.S.*,[32] the Court sustained the government's refusal to permit deferment by holding that advance membership dues received by the automobile club were includable in the year of receipt, although the period of an individual's membership almost always extended into the following year. The Court found that the club's allocation of dues on a monthly basis was "artificial" because it bore no necessary relationship to the particular time or times when a member might actually require road services. Accordingly, the club's allocation system did not so clearly reflect income as to be binding on the Treasury. In *Schlude v. Commissioner*,[33] involving prepayments for dancing lessons, the

---

[32]   367 U.S. 687 (1961).

[33]   372 U.S. 128 (1963).

Court again required full inclusion in the year of receipt. The taxpayer had carefully allocated its students' fees to the periods when the dancing lessons, which could be taken at times arranged by the students themselves, were actually given, thus apparently meeting the requirement of accuracy laid down in the *AAA* decision. The Court, however, found the allocation effort still inadequate. Since students who had paid their fees might allow their contract rights to lapse, "the studio was uncertain [at the end of each taxable year] whether none, some or all of the remaining lessons would be rendered."

Though generally regarded as unjustified from an accounting standpoint, the Service's insistence on full inclusion of advance payments has a certain practical merit. Administration is obviously simplified because it is easier to identify the taxable event as the receipt of cash than to work out precise and reliable rules for deferral. In addition, the Treasury is not obliged to wait until later years for its tax collections, in the meanwhile taking an unsecured risk that the taxpayer may ultimately be unable to pay. Here, as at other points in the field of accounting, the Supreme Court has shown itself willing to subordinate equity and accuracy of income measurement to the apparent demands of practical tax administration, though it is notable that the *AAA* and *Schlude* cases were both decided by 5–4 majorities.

Despite its convenience, the tax accounting rule for prepaid income has long been criticized on the ground that it distorts income by requiring inclusion of the unearned portion of a receipt. Advance receipts, it can be argued, are much like loans. While "repayment" is to be made in the form of taxable services, the resulting income ought properly to be deferred until those services have been performed. More serious, perhaps, is the hardship which the taxpayer may suffer by being forced to bunch in a single year income which is actually attributable to two or more taxable periods. Since (as shown below) the deduction of reserves for estimated expenses is not generally permitted, the taxpayer may not offset the prepaid income by related expenses which are expected to be incurred in subsequent years. And even if the taxpayer prepays those future expenses, such prepayment is treated as a deferred expense comparable to a capital expenditure and is required to be prorated over the periods to which it relates. Of course, the hardship from bunching arises when bunching subjects a taxpayer to marginal tax rates higher than the rates that would apply in the absence of bunching. If the taxpayer is always in the top bracket with or without bunching—which is the condition of many individual and all corporate taxpayers under the current tax rate schedules—then bunching does not increase the rate at which income is taxed.

In a few instances, Congress has afforded statutory relief by adding provisions authorizing deferral for specific types of prepaid income. Section 455 permits the deferral of prepaid subscriptions for magazines and other periodicals, and § 456 overcomes the result in the *AAA* case by allowing the postponement of prepaid dues received by membership organizations such as automobile clubs. Also, § 451(c) (enacted in 2017, but codifying prior administrative practice) permits an accrual method taxpayer receiving a payment for services to be performed in a later year (or years) to delay inclusion of the payment until the year immediately following the year of payment. In addition to prepayments for services, the provision applies to other categories of advance payments (but subject to certain statutory exceptions). Apart from §§ 455, 456, and 451(c), the general case law described above presumably still applies.

Very much the same pattern of case-law and statutory development shows up in the area of reserves for estimated expenses. Generally accepted accounting principles normally require that liability reserves be set up to take account of probable expenses which relate to current income but which have not become fixed and unconditional by the close of the taxable year. Tax accounting, on the other hand, with certain limited statutory exceptions, apparently denies a deduction for such reserves. Thus, deductions have been denied for reserves for estimated personal injury claims, for probable maintenance and service guaranties, for estimated refunds, cancellations, and so on. Tax accounting, here, has followed the strict rule that no accrual of expense will be permitted unless the taxpayer's obligation is fixed on the basis of events in existence at the end of the taxable period. The Service, presumably, has been concerned that a more lenient approach would lead to excessive pessimism as to future liabilities in years of high tax rates, and has preferred to forbid the accrual of reserves rather than attempt to deal with taxpayer's estimates on a case-by-case basis.

———

A loose end. Not often has the Commissioner taken such a decisive beating in a tax accounting case as the one he absorbed in *Commissioner v. Indianapolis Power & Light Co.*[34] The *IPL* case had been reviewed by no fewer than 28 judges (including the full Tax Court) by the time it came to a close, yet the Commissioner was unable to persuade even one that his position on the law was correct. Why did he put up such a struggle? The answer, we suppose, is that the legal issue involved—the taxability of customer security deposits—affected a very large number of the country's public

———

[34]   493 U.S. 203 (1990).

utilities, including most particularly local and long-distance telephone companies. The Commissioner's persistence in fighting the *IPL* case is thus presumably to be explained by the sizeable amounts of potentially taxable income that must have been at stake, together, perhaps, with an exasperated sense that form was impeding a true perception of substance.

The rather straightforward question in *IPL* was whether a cash deposit required and received by the taxpayer, an electric utility, from certain of its customers should be regarded as an advance payment for services to be rendered in the future or as a mere security deposit. Ultimately, the issue was one of timing. If viewed as an advance payment, the deposit would be taxable to IPL in the year received under the *AAA* decision but then would be deductible or excludable by IPL in the later year in which it was refunded to the customer or applied against an outstanding bill. If viewed as a security deposit, the deposit would be treated as a loan, in effect, and would become taxable only if and when later applied to the payment of the customer's bill. IPL did not require deposits from all of its customers—only those whose creditworthiness was in doubt—and it was obligated by local law to pay interest to each depositor. On the other hand, the funds deposited were not segregated or set apart in a special account but were presumably added to and used by IPL as part of its general working capital. As of 1975, IPL held something like $1 million in untaxed customers' deposits, and one supposes that the net amount (and hence, in the Service's view, the amount of income being deferred) tended to increase from year to year.

Once a customer had established good credit standing by paying her bills regularly, or on termination of the customer's service, IPL would refund the deposit by check if the customer's account was paid up. In the alternative, at the customer's option, IPL would apply the deposit to any outstanding balance. If the customer's account was delinquent, IPL could of course apply the deposit without the customer's consent. In fact, depositors chose, or were compelled, to apply their deposits to outstanding balances nearly 90% of the time (in whole or part).[35]

Following an earlier ruling, the Commissioner sought to distinguish customer deposits securing the utility's physical property—possible damage to meters, for example—and deposits securing the customer's obligation to make payment to the utility for services rendered. Only the former would be regarded as a "true security deposit," while the latter would be treated as a taxable advance payment. In response, IPL argued that a refundable deposit was just that—a refundable deposit—whether it secured an

---

[35]　88 T.C. at 969.

obligation to compensate for damage to physical property or secured the customer's obligation to pay her electric bills when due.

Affirming a unanimous decision of the Court of Appeals, which had affirmed a unanimous decision of the Tax Court, the Supreme Court held for the taxpayer on the ground that a customer never gave up her legal right to recover her deposit and could always insist upon full repayment in cash (if her bill was paid up). "So long as the customer fulfills his legal obligation to make timely payments," said Justice Blackmun, "his deposit ultimately is to be refunded, and both the timing and method of that refund are largely within the control of the customer." Accordingly, the depositor must be regarded as a creditor and the deposit as a loan. To be sure, only a small minority of customers actually demanded refunds. For most, the deposit ultimately *became* a payment for services by being credited against the monthly bill, and we can assume that those IPL customers whom the company classified as credit risks never thought of their deposits as anything *but* advance payments. It remained true, however, that a customer could recover her deposit if she chose. Some did—not many, but some—and that circumstance turned out to be insuperable as far as the Commissioner was concerned.

12.03   Use of Inventories

Under generally accepted accounting principles, a business which derives profits from the sale of goods must, in determining its income at the end of the year, divide its merchandise costs between those costs which are properly allocable to the current year's operations and those costs which should be deferred to subsequent periods. Formerly, accountants placed emphasis upon the balance sheet showing as the primary objective of inventory pricing, and hence the problem was principally one of valuation. At the present, however, the emphasis is upon income determination, that is, upon the matching of appropriate costs against related revenues. As stated by the American Institute of Certified Public Accountants:

> In accounting for the goods in the inventory at any point of time, the major objective of inventory pricing is the matching of appropriate costs against revenues in order that there may be a proper determination of the realized income. Thus, the inventory at any given date is the balance of costs applicable to goods on hand remaining after the matching of absorbed costs with concurrent revenues.

For tax purposes also, the objective of inventory valuation and inventory identification (that is, the matching of inventory cost against related revenue) is that of clearly reflecting income. Thus, § 471 provides that inventories are to be used whenever they are necessary in order clearly to determine the income of any taxpayer.

According to the Regulations, inventories of merchandise on hand at the beginning and end of every taxable year must be taken in all cases in which the production, purchase or sale of merchandise is an income-producing factor.[36] The use of inventories does not of itself represent a separate and distinct method of accounting. Rather, it is a component of the overall accounting procedure whose essential purpose is to establish the cost of goods sold as a step towards determination of the taxpayer's gross income from business operations.

There are two authorized methods of valuing or pricing inventories for tax purposes. These are (1) the cost method and (2) the use of "cost or market, whichever is lower." As respects the further problem of identifying items included in inventories, the general requirement is that the "first-in, first-out" (FIFO) rule be used. However, taxpayers may also identify inventory under the "last-in, first-out" (LIFO) rule, if a specific election to employ LIFO is made in accordance with the requirements of § 472. FIFO and LIFO are briefly described in the paragraphs following. A comprehensive illustration is provided at the end.

(a) The "First-in, First-out" (FIFO) Method

Where inventory is identified in accordance with the FIFO rule, it is assumed that the goods first acquired are sold first and hence that the goods in the closing inventory are those most recently purchased. In conjunction with FIFO, the taxpayer may utilize either the cost or "cost-or-market" method of inventory valuation. The effects of these methods are summarized below.

1. *Cost.* Under this method, the value of each unit of merchandise is determined on the basis of its actual cost, with additions for freight, handling, and similar expenses. Use of the cost method in conjunction with FIFO may result in fairly wide fluctuations in income, depending on fluctuations in price levels. Thus, profits tend to be greater in a rising market, and in a falling market losses tend to be greater (or profits tend to be less), than where the cost method is tied in with the LIFO formula. The use of "cost" in conjunction with FIFO presents, in many cases, a profit or loss picture which is close to actual results. This is especially so if, as in the case of merchandise subject to deterioration, the goods on hand at the close of the taxable year are in fact those most recently purchased or produced. If the taxpayer's business is one that is characterized by fairly stable prices, the cost method normally recommends itself as being the simplest to use.

---

[36]   As mentioned earlier, however, § 471(c) waives the inventory accounting requirement for businesses with average annual gross receipts of $25 million or less.

2.   *Cost or Market.* Where inventory is valued on the basis of cost or market, whichever is lower, the taxpayer must first determine the cost of items on hand at the closing inventory date and then compare such cost with the market value of identical items on the same date. The lower of the two values is taken as the closing inventory value. For the purpose of subsequent inventories, that closing inventory value will be deemed to be the opening inventory in the succeeding taxable year. Use of the cost-or-market method may be desirable where market prices fluctuate considerably. In the case of a falling market, this method, as compared with the cost method under FIFO, tends to reduce income for the year in question: the value of closing inventory is reduced to market, creating a higher cost of goods sold, which in turn results in a lower gross income figure. However, income for the following year will necessarily be greater than it would be under the cost method, since, as stated, the closing inventory value of one year becomes the opening inventory of the next year.

In the case of a rising market, the use of "cost or market" produces no different result than the simple cost method, since market value is used only when it is lower than cost. Hence, while the cost or market method anticipates losses in a falling market, additional profits are not anticipated in a rising market. The cost or market method may, in general, be used only in conjunction with the FIFO method.

(b)   The "Last-in, First-out" (LIFO) Method

The LIFO method of inventory identification has been available to all taxpayers on an elective basis since 1939. Under LIFO, the taxpayer is permitted to assume that the goods last purchased were the goods first sold, and thus to value his closing inventory as if it were composed of the earliest purchases. There is no requirement that the taxpayer's inventory accounting method match the physical flow of goods; a taxpayer may elect to use the LIFO method even if the taxpayer actually sells its oldest inventory items first. Under LIFO, inventories must be valued at cost. Since the LIFO method assumes that the goods sold during the year are the goods most recently purchased, it has the effect of stabilizing income by minimizing the impact of price level changes upon inventory valuation. Profits are kept down in a rising market, while during a period of declining prices profits are likely to appear where otherwise losses might be shown. In contrast, the use of FIFO, whether in conjunction with cost or with cost-or-market, tends to accentuate profits in a rising market and to reduce profits or increase losses when prices decline. From the taxpayer's standpoint, the LIFO method produces best results during a period of rising prices, unless it becomes necessary to liquidate existing low-cost inventory. In the latter event, the deferred profits representing unrealized inventory appreciation will be "bunched" in the single year of liquidation. The Code has in the past provided limited relief in cases of involuntary liquidations of LIFO inventory due to war conditions, but otherwise simply leaves the taxpayer to assume this risk. As indicated above, for tax purposes LIFO inventory must be valued at cost; the cost-or-market method is not permitted. This, of course, means that an election to employ LIFO would be decidedly inadvisable in a period of declining prices, since the losses inherent in the earlier high-cost inventory would be deferred instead of realized. Efforts to permit the use of LIFO in conjunction with the cost-or-market method have consistently been opposed by the Treasury.

(c) Comparison of Principal Methods

The following example illustrates in simple fashion the difference in gross profits under FIFO (using either the cost method or the cost-or-market method) and under LIFO. It will be noted that the "First Year" involves a rising market and the "Second Year" a falling market for the taxpayer's product. As indicated above, the cost method in conjunction with FIFO tends to accentuate both profits and losses in a sharply fluctuating market. The cost-or-market method under FIFO produces a like result in a rising market, while in a falling market, as compared with the simple cost method, it tends to anticipate inventory losses and hence produces increased losses (or reduced profits). Finally, as compared with the cost and cost-or-market methods under FIFO, the LIFO method produces smaller profits in a rising market as well as smaller losses (or even profits) in a falling market and thus has a stabilizing effect upon income during periods of fluctuating prices.

Assumed Facts

First year:

    Purchases:

(1) 100 units at $50 per unit	$ 5,000
(2) 75 units at $75 per unit	5,625
(3) 125 units at $100 per unit	12,500
	$23,125

    Sales:

200 units at $100 average price	$20,000

    Inventory December 31:

        100 units, with a market value of $110 per unit

Second year:

    Purchases:

(1) 75 units at $100 per unit	$ 7,500
(2) 50 units at $80 per unit	4,000
(3) 100 units at $45 per unit	4,500
	$16,000

    Sales:

225 units at $75 average price	$16,875

    Inventory December 31:

        100 units, with a market value of $35 per unit

Difference in Gross Profits

	FIFO		LIFO
	Cost	Cost or Market	
First year:			
Purchases	$23,125	$23,125	$23,125
Closing inventory	10,000	10,000	5,000
Cost of goods sold	$13,125	$13,125	$18,125
Sales	20,000	20,000	20,000
GROSS PROFIT	$ 6,875	$ 6,875	$ 1,875
Second year:			
Opening inventory	$10,000	$10,000	$ 5,000
Purchases	16,000	16,000	16,000
Total	$26,000	$26,000	$21,000
Closing inventory	4,500	3,500	5,000
Cost of goods sold	$21,500	$22,500	$16,000
Sales	16,875	16,875	16,875
GROSS PROFIT (OR LOSS)	($ 4,625)	($ 5,625)	$ 875

Accounting—Questions and Answers

Returning to the subject of deferred compensation (11.01), the Code makes an important distinction between so-called qualified pension plans—trustee-administered plans that meet strict statutory coverage and benefit requirements and may not discriminate in favor of highly paid employees—and, on the other hand, nonqualified deferred compensation plans that are usually intended to benefit top executives only. Under a qualified plan, the employer is permitted to accrue and deduct its annual plan contributions currently, while inclusion by the employee-beneficiary is deferred until the employee retires and begins receiving cash distributions from the pension trust. In addition, the investment income earned by the trust is tax-exempt. In the case of a nonqualified plan, by contrast, Code Sec. 404(a)(5) allows no deduction to the employer until payment is made to the retired employee and the employee includes the amount paid in her gross income. In effect, deferred compensation is not accruable.

Quite obviously, then, Congress does not intend nonqualified plans of the sort described in Rev. Rul. 60–31 to be treated in the same way as qualified plans. Under plans of both types, the employee includes the retirement benefit when actually received. Under qualified plans, contributions to the plan are immediately deductible by the employer. Under nonqualified plans, the employer can take no deduction until the year in which the deferred compensation is paid in cash and taxed to the employee.

Question 1: Suppose Odette, a highly-paid corporate executive, is given a choice between (a) receiving all of her annual compensation in the current year, and (b) deferring some portion of her compensation until retirement. If deferred, the final payment will include accumulated interest on the deferred amount. Assume that Odette and her employer confront the same marginal tax rate throughout, and that if the compensation is deferred it will be governed by the rules applicable to nonqualified deferred compensation. From a tax standpoint, what advantage would Odette gain by choosing the deferred compensation alternative?

Answer: None whatever, although deferral is normally advantageous to individual taxpayers (see 1.02, above). The reason is § 404(a)(5). In effect, the employer-level tax takes the place of the individual tax and there really is no deferral at all. The result is that Odette's after-tax income at the end of the deferral period will be exactly equal to what it would have been had her compensation been paid currently. To illustrate:

Assume that $20,000 of Odette's salary is either (a) paid to her in the current year or (b) deferred for 20 years (when Odette will retire) and then paid to her together with accumulated interest. Assume also that funds can be invested at a pre-tax interest rate of 10%. Assume finally that Odette and her corporate employer both pay tax at a marginal rate of 35% in all affected periods.

(a) If the $20,000 of salary is paid currently, Odette owes a tax of $7,000 and has $13,000 left to invest at 10%. She receives $1,300 of interest before tax in year 1, pays tax of $455 (35% of $1,300), and is left with $845 after tax. Thus, the after-tax rate of return on her investment is 6.5%. She has $13,845 ($13,000 plus $845) to invest in year 2. By the end of year 20, her total after-tax fund will have built up to about $45,500. Odette's employer can of course deduct the $20,000 in year 1 as a current business expense. The deduction reduces the employer's tax bill by $7,000, so the employer's after-tax cost of paying Odette $20,000 in year 1 is $13,000.

(b) If the salary is deferred for 20 years, Odette's employer is not entitled to a current deduction. The employer takes $13,000 (the amount that would have been its after-tax cost of paying Odette current salary of $20,000), and sets that money aside to fund its obligation to pay Odette deferred compensation in 20 years. As noted in the previous paragraph, a fund of $13,000 invested for 20 years at an after-tax rate of return of 6.5% will grow to about $45,500. In year

20, the employer makes a payment to Odette, the after-tax cost of which equals the $45,500 then in the fund. Because the payment will be deductible to the employer, the employer can make a payment considerably larger than $45,500. More precisely, the amount of the payment is $45,500 / (1 − .35) = $70,000. The employer pays Odette $70,000, the deduction is worth $24,500 ($70,000 × .35) to the employer, and the employer's after-tax cost is thus $45,500—which precisely exhausts the fund. Because the employer can satisfy its obligation to Odette at a year 1 cost of $13,000 in both situations, the employer is indifferent between option (a) and option (b). What about Odette? In (b), Odette receives $70,000 in year 20. She owes tax of $24,500 on that amount, which leaves her with $45,500 after tax in year 20—not coincidentally, the same amount she has in year 20 under option (a). Thus, Odette, like her employer, is indifferent between the two approaches.

To be sure, an executive like Odette would often expect to confront a lower marginal tax rate after she retires than while she is actively employed. If so, there would obviously be an advantage to her in putting off the inclusion to a period in which the lower rate applies, and it is this consideration that motivates deferred compensation plans in many cases. Aside from the prospect of a lower rate after retirement, it is a matter of indifference to Odette and her employer whether she is paid $20,000 in year 1 or $70,000 20 years later, assuming the same tax rate applies to Odette and to her employer. Either way, she winds up with the same old $45,500, no more and no less.

The analysis changes dramatically, however, if the employer's tax rate is significantly lower than Odette's tax rate—as it generally would be under current law, given the top individual rate of 37% and the top corporate rate of 21%. What happens if we rerun the above example, still using 35% as Odette's tax rate, but using 20% as the employer's rate? Nothing changes with respect to scenario (a), under which Odette would have about $45,500 at the end of year 20, except that the employer's after-tax cost of paying Odette $20,000 in year 1 rises to $16,000. Scenario (b), however, changes rather dramatically. The employer takes $16,000 and sets it aside to fund its obligation to pay Odette deferred compensation in 20 years. Because of the employer's 20% tax rate the after-tax rate of return is 8%—a considerable improvement over Odette's 6.5% after-tax rate of return. This difference in the after-tax rates of return on investment is the key to the tax advantage of deferred compensation in this situation. By year 20, the fund will have grown to about $74,560. The employer pays Odette $93,200, at an after-tax cost of $74,560,[37] thus

---

[37]   At the employer's 20% tax rate, the deduction is worth $18,640.

exhausting the fund. Odette pays her 35% tax and is left with $60,580, which is about 33% better than the $45,500 she would have had without the deferred compensation.

In *Albertson's, Inc. v. Commissioner*[38] the taxpayer-employer entered into deferred compensation agreements with a group of top executives under which a portion of their annual salaries would be deferred until retirement or termination of employment. The amounts deferred would be increased each year by an imputed interest factor, so that on the future payout date (but, of course, not before) the executive would receive and include in income the basic amount plus an additional amount reflecting the interest accumulated over the deferral period. As stated, § 404(a)(5) allows an employer no deduction until the deferred compensation is actually paid out and taxable to the employee. Despite that statutory limitation, Albertson's took a current deduction for the annual interest amounts on the ground that "interest", as distinct from "compensation", is not referred to in § 404(a)(5) and is specifically allowable under Code § 163. The claimed deductions, which were disallowed by the Commissioner, totaled more than $660,000.

The Ninth Circuit initially held for the taxpayer, but then, on rehearing, reversed itself and sustained the Commissioner's disallowance. Congress, said the court, plainly intended to encourage employers to institute qualified rather than nonqualified retirement plans for their employees by denying the employer the right to current accrual under a nonqualified plan. If imputed interest could be accrued and deducted currently, even though unpaid and untaxed until a later date, a very large proportion of the deferred compensation amount would in effect escape that restriction. In the case at hand, for example, where payment was deferred for a fifteen-year period at an interest rate of about 15%, nearly half the amount finally received by the employee would be "interest" rather than compensation. If permitted to be deducted by the employer prior to inclusion by the employee, the effect would be to defer the tax on such "interest" for up to fifteen years. Nonqualified plans would then enjoy a substantial measure of the benefits allowed to qualified plans and the intent of Congress would be frustrated. Accordingly, despite the literal wording of the Code provision, current deduction was denied.

Question 2: George Babbitt owned several acres of swampland, which he had purchased several years ago as an investment for $50,000. Last year, when the swampland was still worth $50,000, George donated it to the Zenith Benevolent Society (a § 501(c)(3) tax-exempt organization) and claimed a § 170 deduction of $50,000. The ZBS intended to construct a Museum of the City of Zenith on the

---

[38]   38 F.3d 1046 (9th Cir. 1993), *rev'd on rehearing,* 42 F.3d 537 (9th Cir. 1994).

swampland, but for reasons of both zoning and drainage that plan turned out to be impractical. Although George's donation had been no-strings-attached, the ZBS decided it didn't want to keep the swampland, and so returned it to George this year. Due to a decline in the local real estate market for swampland, the land was worth only $40,000 at the time of its return. How much income, if any, does George have this year as a result of the return of the swampland?

Answer: It's clear that George has income under the tax benefit rule, but it is unclear whether the amount of the income is $50,000 or $40,000. There is a strong argument in favor of $50,000. The idea underlying the tax benefit rule (as applied to George's situation) is to put the taxpayer in the same position as if the contribution had never occurred, to the extent that can be done without violating the sanctity of the annual accounting period. If the contribution had never been made, the decline in value of the swampland would have been unrealized depreciation, and as such would not have been deductible by George. Offsetting the $50,000 deduction with a $50,000 inclusion in the following year approaches that result as nearly as possible, without reopening the earlier year. By contrast, limiting the inclusion to the $40,000 value of the swampland at the time of its return allows George the equivalent of a deduction for the $10,000 decline in value (because the $50,000 deduction exceeds the $40,000 inclusion by $10,000). Despite the strong argument for the $50,000 inclusion, it appears that the IRS would not attempt to tax more than $40,000 in a case such as this.[39]

Question 3: Weird Al was a contestant on the television game show, "Wheel of Jeopardy." He did not win any cash, but he was awarded a five-year supply of candy bars (fair market value, $1,000) as a "lovely going-away prize." Having no desire to eat, sell, or give away the candy bars, Al signed a form (helpfully provided by the show) indicating that he waived his right to the candy bars. Must Al nevertheless include in his gross income the $1,000 value of the candy bars?

Answer: Although the constructive receipt doctrine is usually invoked to determine the *timing* of gross income inclusions, rather than with respect to now-or-never issues, the concept of constructive receipt is broad enough to reach the now-or-never question when a taxpayer declines a benefit that is his for the taking. If Al had asked the show to delay delivery of the candy bars until next year, he would have been taxed on the value of the bars this year under constructive receipt principles. He should be equally in constructive receipt of the candy bars this year if he declines ever to receive them, rather than merely postponing delivery. However, the Service long ago ruled that

---

[39]   *Rosen v. Commissioner,* 611 F.2d 942 (1st Cir. 1980).

a taxpayer in Al's situation could avoid being taxed on the fair market value of the prize by declining to accept it.[40] The Ruling includes no rationale for its conclusion, which is difficult or impossible to reconcile with the constructive receipt doctrine. Despite its technical shakiness, the Ruling reflects an understandable IRS decision to provide relief to prize winners who place low subjective values on their prizes and do not want to pay tax on the prizes' higher fair market values.

---

[40]   Rev. Rul. 57–374, 1957–2 C.B. 69, discussed at 1.02.

Part E

RECOGNITION OF GAINS AND LOSSES—SELECTED ISSUES

Enough has been said about the computation of gains and losses from sales of property to require at this point no more than a brief recapitulation of Code nomenclature. Section 1001(a) provides that "gain or loss" shall be the difference between the "amount realized" from a "sale or other disposition of property" and the taxpayer's "adjusted basis" for the property sold. The term "amount realized" is defined in § 1001(b) to include not only cash but the "fair market value" of any other property received, so that by implication the receipt of consideration in kind is regarded as a realization which generates gain or loss. Section 1011 states that "adjusted basis" means "basis"—usually "cost" as provided in § 1012, but capable of a good many special formulations (see 13.01 next following, for example) depending on the circumstances—as "adjusted" under § 1016. Section 1016 contains a long list of required additions to or subtractions from original cost which are designed to give effect to inclusions, exclusions, deductions or disallowances prescribed by other substantive Code provisions. Of the adjustments listed in the section the most important for the discussion below is that contained in subsection (a)(2), which provides that the basis of depreciable property (such as buildings and machinery) shall be reduced from year to year by the amount allowable as a deduction for "exhaustion, wear and tear, obsolescence, amortization, and depletion."

Having thus determined the amount of gain or loss by simple computation, the next question would be whether or not the gain or loss had been "realized" as a result of the event that occurred. Although the Code says little directly about the realization requirement, it is well understood that "mere" property appreciation or decline is not regarded as a realization of gain or loss. As stated earlier, the income tax is a tax on transactions, not on income as such. Largely because of its ambiguous and artificial character, the realization requirement has generated a good many difficult problems of interpretation. A sampling of these was offered in Section 5, above, and the present Part adds some further illustrations.

Assuming there *is* a realization in the form of a "sale" of property for cash or an "exchange" of one property for another, § 1001(c) then requires that the realized gain or loss be "recognized" (unless otherwise provided) and taken into account in determining the taxpayer's tax liability.[1] While "realization" and "recognition" generally run together, there are a number of transactions which involve a clear realization of gain or loss but for which the Code specifically provides *non*-recognition (sometimes optionally). Leasehold terminations (5.03) and "involuntary conversions" (2.04) are examples that have already been considered. In these and other instances Congress evidently considered that the realization rule or the income definition created hardships when rigorously applied, and it chose instead to protect the gain or the income from immediate recognition or inclusion. In other situations—like-kind exchanges, for example, and certain corporate mergers—the "exchange" is regarded as involving no real alteration in the character of the taxpayer's investment despite a technical or formal change, and again immediate recognition of gain or loss is specifically avoided. In most non-recognition cases, the taxpayer's basis in his original property is carried over to the newly acquired property. The overall effect, then, is a deferral of the gain or loss, rather than total forgiveness or permanent disallowance.

Assuming all of these preliminary considerations are disposed of—*i.e.*, there is a realization of gain or loss and it is not deferred by a non-recognition provision of any sort—the next and final question would be whether the special regime that has been established for *capital* gains and losses is applicable because of the nature of the asset sold. This issue substantially overshadows the others in importance and complexity, and although closely and curiously linked to some of the mechanical questions taken up in this Part, it is simply too extensive to be handled as part of a Part. Hence, our treatment of property sales is carried out in two steps, with the present Part E being given over to realization and recognition questions (largely involving real estate transactions) and Part F being devoted entirely to capital gains and losses.

13. Transactions in Mortgaged Property

Most real estate purchases are financed by mortgage loans, whether obtained from a bank or other institutional lender or from the seller of the property himself if he is willing to hold the purchaser's obligation. The property acquired stands as security for the loan, and in the event of a default in payment of interest or principal by the borrower-mortgagor the lender-mortgagee may foreclose on the security, dispose of it at auction, and apply the proceeds to the debt. Any excess of foreclosure proceeds over the amount due (there rarely is any) is returned to the debtor. Any

---

[1] As indicated at 6.06, losses are deductible only if specific authorization can be found therefor, *e.g.*, in § 165. Losses from the sale of property held for personal use—say the family car—are not allowed; but see discussion at 15.02, below.

deficiency can be enforced against the debtor's other assets if (as would usually be true in the case of a homebuyer) the debtor assumes personal liability for the loan. If no such personal liability is provided for (as noted below, commercial property mortgages are often nonrecourse, meaning that the lender's sole security is the property itself), then the deficiency simply becomes the lender's loss.

The mortgage loan itself is usually repayable—amortizable—in equal installments (monthly, quarterly, etc.) over a stated term of years. As has been noted (2.02), the early payments consist largely of interest on the outstanding principal, while the later payments consist largely of principal itself. If the property-owner sells his property before the mortgage has been fully amortized, the sale proceeds go first to satisfy the mortgage debt—the mortgagee being in the status of a senior security-holder—with only the balance going to the mortgagor, the owner of the equity. In some instances, especially where commercial property is concerned, the new purchaser will simply assume (or take the property subject to) the outstanding mortgage and carry out the established amortization schedule, in which event the residual cash component goes entirely to the equity-owner. The amount received by the equity-owner after satisfaction or assumption of the mortgage would reflect his initial cash investment in the property plus subsequent payments of mortgage principal, plus or minus any change in market value during the period of his ownership.

The subsection that follows raises an important tax question which relates in particular to mortgages on commercial property. In brief, the question is whether an investor who purchases real estate on the basis of a nonrecourse mortgage can take depreciation in the same way, and in the same amount, as if the purchase was entirely self-financed. The answer is affirmative, as will be seen, and on it, to a considerable degree, rests the phenomenon called the "tax shelter."

Mortgages are considered further in connection with the realization requirement at 13.03 and 13.04. The question of what constitutes a borrowing is revived with respect to sale-and-leaseback transactions at 15.01.

13.01   Nonrecourse   Debt   and   the   Depreciation Allowance; The *Crane* Rule

It may have occurred to the reader at various points that debt plays a peculiarly controversial role in the tax law, and this is nowhere truer than in regard to its effect on the depreciation allowance. As suggested just above, many commercial real estate investments—apartment buildings, office buildings, shopping centers—are financed in substantial part by nonrecourse mortgage loans, that is, loans which the investor-borrowers are not personally liable to repay. The investor draws on his own resources for, say, 20% of the purchase price (or construction cost) of the property, and the mortgage lender, perhaps a bank or insurance company, supplies the balance of 80%. The mortgagee can foreclose on the property itself in the event of a default, but it cannot recover against the investor individually. The investor's risk is therefore limited to his equity; he can lose no more than his 20% out-of-pocket investment. If the property falls in value to less than the outstanding mortgage balance and is then foreclosed upon, the unpaid mortgage principal becomes the lender's loss alone.

Under these circumstances, should the investor be permitted to include the amount borrowed in the basis of the property for purposes of computing annual depreciation? Or should his basis be limited to his equity investment, on the ground, presumably, that the investor assumed no personal liability for the mortgage debt? As will be seen, the *overall* allowance for depreciation is the same under either approach. What differs is the scheduling of the allowance—larger in the early years if the mortgage is included in basis, smaller in the early years if it is not—and hence the timing of taxable income. At stake, as usual, is the anticipation or deferral of the property-owner's tax obligations, a factor which is said to be of major importance in promoting real estate investment.

Actually, the Supreme Court pretty well settled the issue more than seventy years ago by holding in the *Crane* case that the "amount realized" by a seller of mortgaged property included both the cash received from the buyer and the face amount of the mortgage to which the property was subject.[2] The seller, it was said, had received a benefit by being relieved of the mortgage indebtedness, and hence her gain was computed by subtracting her basis in the property from the total of the cash received *plus* the mortgage. The Court was not directly concerned with the determination of "basis" under § 1012, or "adjusted basis" under § 1011(a); but the implication was clear and unavoidable. If mortgage indebtedness is included in "amount realized" when property is sold, then it must also be reflected in the seller's "adjusted basis" when acquired. To see why, assume an investor purchases an acre of land for $4,000, paying $1,000 out of his own resources and borrowing the balance of $3,000 on a mortgage. A year later, after $200 has been paid on the mortgage principal, the property is sold for an amount exactly equal to its original purchase price, $4,000, the buyer paying $1,200 in cash and assuming the mortgage balance of $2,800. Under *Crane,* the amount realized by the seller is $4,000, that is, the cash received plus the mortgage assumed by the buyer. Since the seller has obviously realized no gain or loss

---

[2]   *Crane v. Commissioner,* 331 U.S. 1 (1947).

on the transaction, it must be the case that his basis is also $4,000 and includes both cash investment and mortgage balance as well. If the mortgage were excluded from the seller's basis, a taxable gain of $2,800 would result; but this would plainly be improper as there has been no change in the value of the land during his ownership.

The effect of the *Crane* rule on the computation of gain or loss on sale of the property is thus entirely negligible. As long as the mortgage indebtedness is accorded symmetrical treatment, as long as it is dealt with in the same way at both ends of the transaction, the choice between inclusion and exclusion of the mortgage debt is a matter of no importance. As will have been surmised, however, gain or loss on sale is not the only relevant tax calculation. If the property is depreciable (the land mentioned above was not), the choice between inclusion and exclusion directly affects the size of the annual depreciation allowance, and that indeed turns out to be its real significance.

The Court of Appeals' decision in *Parker v. Delaney*[3] will serve as an illustration of what has just been said. Simplifying the facts, the taxpayer had acquired an apartment building in Year 1 with a cash investment of zero but subject to an unassumed mortgage of $273,000. Using the latter figure as his "cost", the taxpayer took depreciation deductions totaling $45,000 during the 10-year period of his ownership and paid $14,000 on the principal of the mortgage. In Year 11 he disposed of the property—actually, he abandoned it to the mortgagee—for no cash but still subject to an outstanding mortgage balance of $259,000 (that is, $273,000 less the $14,000 he had paid back). The taxpayer's adjusted basis for the property at that date was $228,000—$273,000 (original cost) less $45,000 of depreciation. Finding that the mortgage balance represented an "amount realized" in accordance with the *Crane* decision, the court held that the taxpayer had a taxable gain of $31,000—$259,000, the amount realized by the taxpayer, less his basis of $228,000—even though the disposition involved no cash receipt whatever.

In a concurring opinion, Judge Magruder took the trouble to show how the calculation might have been carried out if the *Crane* case had been decided differently. Under a more "natural" reading of § 1001(b), he argued, the "amount realized" in the *Parker* case would properly be *zero* since the taxpayer had received no cash consideration when he quitclaimed the property to the mortgagee. By the same token the taxpayer's basis could not exceed $14,000—his cash payments on the mortgage principal—which would then have to be reduced by the $45,000 that had been allowed to him as depreciation. His adjusted basis would therefore be a negative figure,

---

[3]   186 F.2d 455 (1st Cir. 1950).

($31,000), and when this was subtracted from the amount realized, zero, the resulting positive number, $31,000, would be recognized as taxable gain. The outcome would thus be identical to that arrived at by the court majority, but it would be reached without the artificial construction of "amount realized" which had been resorted to in *Crane*.

To summarize, the alternative calculations in *Parker v. Delaney* are as follows:

		Majority	**Magruder**
1.	Original cost	$273,000	$–0–
2.	Addition to basis	–0–	14,000
3.	Depreciation allowed	(45,000)	(45,000)
4.	Adjusted basis	228,000	(31,000)
5.	Amount realized	259,000	–0–
6.	Gain recognized (5 – 4)	$ 31,000	$ 31,000

Neat, to be sure, but why bother? Why did Magruder go through a recalculation using a different formula when his final result was just the same as the majority's? The answer appears to be this: although compelled in this case to give effect to the $45,000 of depreciation deductions already allowed to the taxpayer in earlier years, Magruder apparently felt that the depreciation should have been limited to the taxpayer's cash investment in the property—that is, to the $14,000 which had actually been paid by the taxpayer to reduce the original mortgage principal. In effect, Magruder thought that the mortgage (for which the taxpayer was not personally liable) should have been excluded from the calculation for all purposes. If this had been done, the taxpayer's total depreciation allowance would have been only $14,000, and his basis as well as the amount realized and gain recognized on disposition of the property would all have been zero. To be sure, the net result is still the same in overall terms: under Magruder's scheme, $14,000 of deductions would offset $14,000 of investment; under the *Crane* rule, $45,000 of deductions were balanced by $14,000 of investment plus $31,000 of taxable gain. But the *timing* of both deductions and the taxable gain is very different. Under Magruder's approach, only $14,000 would be deductible between Years 1 and 10, with nothing taken into income in Year 11. Under *Crane*, $45,000 was deducted between Years 1 and 10, with $31,000 taxed in Year 11. For the usual reason—namely, that tax payments are postponed when deductions are accelerated— taxpayers will generally prefer the *Crane* approach to Magruder's alternative, and it is the *Crane* system which the law applies today.

But (resorting to our usual inquiry) which of the two approaches is correct as an original matter? Should nonrecourse mortgage indebtedness be included in determining the taxpayer's basis for depreciation purposes, or should it be excluded? At this point, a further systematic illustration of the two "rules" may be useful. Judge Magruder's opinion is too brief for us to know exactly what procedure he intended to support, but the one attributed to him below seems consistent with his language and intent. Repeating the illustration used at 6.09(d), assume that the taxpayer purchases an asset—this time a "building"—with a useful life of 5 years and with no expected salvage value. The cost of the building is $4,000 and, for simplicity, assume that the entire purchase price is borrowed from a bank on an 8% mortgage. The annual mortgage payment is $1,000, which is allocated between interest and principal in accordance with the following schedule (some of the numbers are rounded):

Year:	1	2	3	4	5	Total
Interest	$320	260	210	140	70	$1,000
Principal	$680	740	790	860	930	$4,000

Finally, assume that the investor anticipates net rents from the property (he has already found a lessee) of $1,200 a year for the five-year period.

Under an "ideal" system, the investor's annual taxable income would be $1,200 less the sum of (a) the annual interest payment to the bank and (b) the "true" cost of operating the building for the year, otherwise known as "depreciation." As already argued (see 6.09(d)), the correct way of computing annual depreciation is to compare the present value of anticipated cash flows at the beginning of the taxable year with the present value of such cash flows at the end of that year. The difference is the taxpayer's true cost of operation. Under this method of depreciation—previously referred to as the sinking-fund method—the annual depreciation allowance is lower in the earlier years and higher in the later years where anticipated cash flows are level. Annual income follows an inverse pattern. The mortgage amortization schedule set forth above reflects precisely this approach from the bank's standpoint: the repayment of mortgage principal (equivalent to depreciation) starts low and steadily rises, while the interest component (equivalent to income) starts high and steadily declines.

Our real-estate investor is really in the same position as the bank vis-à-vis his own lessee, except that *he* anticipates an annual payment of $1,200. As shown at 6.09(d), the resulting allocation between income and principal recovery is as follows:

Year:	1	2	3	4	5	Total
Income	$627	513	410	295	155	$2,000
Principal	$573	687	790	905	1,045	$4,000

If allowable depreciation followed *this* schedule, the investor's annual taxable income would be higher at the beginning, and lower at the end, of the five-year term. Thus—

Taxable Income—Sinking Fund

Year:	1	2	3	4	5	Total
Net rents	$1,200	1,200	1,200	1,200	1,200	$6,000
Interest	320	260	210	140	70	1,000
Depreciation	573	687	790	905	1,045	4,000
Taxable Income	$307	253	200	155	85	$1,000

How close does either the *Crane* or the Magruder approach come to approximating these "ideal" results?

Under the *Crane* rule the investor's basis for his property is equal to its cost of $4,000 even though the entire purchase price was supplied by the lender. Using the straight-line method of depreciation, the annual depreciation allowance is therefore $800 (5 × $800 = $4,000). The investor's annual taxable income—deducting interest and depreciation from net rents—would then be as follows:

Taxable Income—Crane

Year:	1	2	3	4	5	Total
Net rents	$1,200	1,200	1,200	1,200	1,200	$6,000
Interest	320	260	210	140	70	1,000
Depreciation	800	800	800	800	800	4,000
Taxable Income	$ 80	140	190	260	330	$1,000

The *Crane* rule produces lower taxable income in the early years, higher in the later—although the "ideal" trend is in the opposite direction. The investor's true taxable income in Year 1 is equal to the net cash received after the payment to the bank—$1,200 minus $1,000, or $200—plus the excess of his principal repayment over the cost of operation—$680 minus $573, or $107—for a total of $307. But *Crane* taxes him on only $80, so that $227 of Year 1 income is effectively deferred. The deferral in Year 2 is of $113; in Year 3 it is $10. These deferred amounts are picked up in Years 4 and 5, of course, but in the meanwhile the taxpayer has enjoyed the usual benefit of tax postponement. Furthermore, his annual cash flow for the first three years—$200 a year—is greater than his taxable income in each of those years, a fact which leaves the taxpayer feeling pleased indeed.

By contrast, Magruder's approach—or, at least, the one generally attributed to him—is to include borrowed funds in basis only to the extent of principal actually repaid. Thus, the initial principal repayment of $680 would be recovered over a five-year period at the straight-line rate of $136 a year. Year 2's principal repayment of $740 would be recovered over the remaining four years of the building's useful life at a rate of $185 a year, so that depreciation for Year 2 would be $136 carried over from Year 1 plus Year 2's $185, a total of $321. This would continue until in Year 5 all the unrecovered amounts from the earlier years, plus the entire principal payment made in Year 5, would be deducted as "depreciation." On this scheme, the investor's taxable income would be as follows:

Taxable Income—Magruder

Year:	1	2	3	4	5	Total
Net rents	$1,200	1,200	1,200	1,200	1,200	$6,000
Interest	320	260	210	140	70	1,000
Depreciation	136	321	584	1,014	1,945	4,000
Taxable Income	$744	619	406	46	(815)	$1,000

Magruder's trend—higher taxable income in the early years, lower in the later—is in the same direction as the "ideal," but it is pretty clear that the downward progression from Year 1 to Year 5 is far too steep. Income is being unduly anticipated, depreciation unduly deferred. The proof is that if the taxpayer sold the property at the start of Year 2 he would receive $3,427 from the buyer—*i.e.,* the sum of the present values of the remaining four rental payments. He would then pay the bank the principal he still owed, $4,000 less $680 paid the first year, or $3,320. This would leave a net "amount realized" of $107. The taxpayer's basis, however, would be $544—the $680 paid in, less Year 1 depreciation of $136—so that the sale would actually generate a loss of $437—$544 less $107. It is evident, however, that the "loss" is a bookkeeping artifact. Indeed, the loss of $437 is simply the difference between Magruder's Year 1 taxable income of $744 and the "ideal" Year 1 income of $307. Stated differently, the $437 loss is the difference between the $136 Year 1 depreciation allowed under Magruder's approach and the "ideal" Year 1 depreciation of $573.

All of these dreary numbers really serve to show that the source of the distortion in cases like *Parker v. Delaney* is not the *Crane* rule and the treatment of debt but the failure (or inability) to require an appropriate method of depreciation.[4] Quite obviously, if the sinking-fund method were used, the results under *Crane* would be the same as those of the "ideal" system. Annual income would then be measured accurately, and the inclusion of debt in the taxpayer's basis would be harmless. But since depreciation is overstated in the earlier years (even under the straight-line method), the *Crane* rule seems to open the way to (really, it just does nothing to restrain) the postponement of taxable income. Magruder's approach, by excluding debt from the taxpayer's basis, prevents such postponement—but the corrective is plainly excessive.

A final point (already much discussed at 6.06, above) should be noted. Even if the depreciation allowance is regarded as untouchable, Congress could still (if it wished) achieve results equivalent to the "ideal" by requiring a deferral of the taxpayer's annual interest deductions. Thus, if interest deductions of $227 the first year, $113 the second and $10 the third had to be deferred to the fourth and fifth years, the benefit of anticipating depreciation in the three earlier periods would obviously be washed out. As our illustration implies, however, the law fully recognizes the economic "fact" that the deductible interest component in the taxpayer's annual mortgage payments is higher at the start of the five-year period ($320) than at the end (only $70). The consequence is that the taxpayer gets the best of both worlds: interest deductions are correctly computed (which means higher deductions in the earlier years), while depreciation allowances are incorrectly computed. By contrast, as the reader may recall, the Code sometimes insists on symmetrical treatment of borrowing costs where the asset acquired with the borrowed funds qualifies for a tax preference. Section 265, for example, disallows deductions for interest on funds borrowed to purchase tax-exempt municipal bonds; § 264 does the same in connection with single-premium insurance contracts; § 163(d) restricts the deduction of so-called "investment interest." No similar limitation exists with respect to interest on funds borrowed to purchase depreciable property,[5] although, as already mentioned, permitting depreciation to be overstated is the practical equivalent of exempting a substantial portion of the income generated by such property from tax (or of

---

[4]   See Surrey, McDaniel and Pechman, *Federal Tax Reform for 1976* (1976), p. 19.

[5]   The new limitation on business interest expense deductions imposed by § 163(j) (described at 6.06(a)) may have the effect of limiting the deductibility of interest on amounts borrowed to purchase depreciable property. Unlike the interest disallowance provisions mentioned in the text, however, its application does not depend on the taxpayer having used the borrowed funds to buy depreciable property (or, for that matter, on the taxpayer even owning any depreciable property).

exempting *all* the income, in the case of 100% expensing under § 168(k)).

We do not mean to suggest that the conflict, or difference, between the two deduction schedules is accidental or that Congress is unaware of it. In adopting ACRS—which allows a taxpayer to recover the cost of depreciable property over a much shorter period than the useful life of the property itself—Congress specifically intended to encourage—indeed, to subsidize—investment in plant and equipment. Deferring interest deductions so as to match the deferral of income resulting from over-rapid depreciation would simply be a way of cancelling the subsidy, since most businesses borrow to finance their purchases of plant and equipment. In effect, then, the existing incentive "system" is of a twofold nature: on the one hand, it allows depreciation to be deducted in excess of actual economic cost; on the other, it imposes no corresponding restriction on the deductibility of related interest expense.

Tax shelters represent an extreme example of the twofold system just described. Having permitted the shelter device to spread and flourish to a remarkable degree, Congress finally took decisive action in 1986 by imposing restrictions on the deductibility of so-called passive activity losses. Those restrictions, with related background, are discussed in the following section.

13.02   Real Estate Tax Shelters: The "At-Risk" and "Passive Activity Loss" Limitations

Commencing in the 1960's and continuing at an accelerated pace for some twenty years or so, tax shelters for high-income individuals became a major industry in this country and, in the view of many, a national scandal. Typically through the medium of real estate limited partnerships, top-bracket taxpayers were able, pretty much at will, to reduce their regular tax obligations to very low levels, if not indeed to zero. Public awareness of the tax-shelter phenomenon finally appeared to grow to some degree, and it may be that the willingness of Congress to adopt the 1986 reform legislation after decades of resistance or indifference can in part be traced to a general perception that high-paid people were systematically and habitually avoiding their apparent tax obligations by participating in legally-sanctioned shelter arrangements.

In conventional form, these shelter consisted of highly-leveraged real estate in which individual investors participated as limited partners. The limited partners made initial cash payments to the shelter promoter which were largely absorbed by commissions, fees and similar charges, while the cost of the property itself was financed through a mortgage loan from a bank, insurance company or other institution. The loan was nonrecourse, but, under the *Crane* rule, the limited partners were entitled to treat the borrowed amount as if it were a personal loan and, hence, to include the indebtedness in basis. Rents received by the partnership were then expected to cover mortgage principal and interest requirements plus management fees. Sometimes, but not always, there was a small annual cash return to the investors.

As illustrated below, if a taxpayer is permitted to combine (a) accelerated depreciation and (b) deductible interest on a nonrecourse mortgage loan, the combination inevitably generates substantial "losses" during the earlier years of the enterprise. Such losses are of course tax artifacts. If true economic depreciation were substituted for accelerated depreciation, then, usually, the enterprise would operate at or close to a break-even level—there would be no deductible "loss" to report—and the investment from the standpoint of the limited partners would have little purpose. The same result would arise if (while leaving accelerated depreciation untouched) otherwise deductible interest were deferred or disallowed as under § 265(a)(2). In fact, however, prior to 1986 neither limitation was imposed. Instead, high-bracket taxpayers were enabled (encouraged) to combine tax-exempt income with tax-deductible borrowing and, by so doing, to reduce their taxable income to a minimum. The "loss" resulting from the shelter investment would be offset against income from other sources (chiefly personal services), even though the taxpayer himself would have lost little or nothing in economic terms.

(a) At-Risk

The 1986 Act made a threefold attack on tax shelters—real estate shelters especially—by (1) substantially lengthening the depreciable lives of residential and commercial real estate, (2) partially extending the at-risk requirement (described below) to real estate investment, and most important (3) adopting "passive activity loss" rules which severely limit an individual taxpayer's ability to offset shelter losses against income from other sources. The first of these anti-shelter elements—longer depreciable lives—can be mentioned briefly: under § 168(c), residential real estate is now assigned a 27.5-year and commercial real estate a 39-year recovery period (increased from 31.5 in 1993), as compared with much shorter recovery periods under prior law. Since, as shown at 6.10, accelerated depreciation equals partial tax exemption, the stretch-out of recovery periods reduces the tax benefits that real estate investors have enjoyed in the past.

The at-risk requirement—added to the Code in 1976 and made applicable to all depreciable property *other* than real estate— operates as a further limitation on tax shelters. In effect, § 465 withdraws or dilutes the *Crane* rule by restricting the amount of deductible loss from the ownership of depreciable property to the total amount of the taxpayer's economic investment—the amount he has "at risk." A taxpayer is considered at risk with respect to the cash (or other property) that he has actually drawn from his own resources. Borrowed funds are also deemed to be at risk, but only if the taxpayer is personally liable for the debt or the debt is secured by his personal assets; nonrecourse loans are *not* included in a taxpayer's at-risk amount. The investor cannot deduct any more than the amount placed at risk under this definition, and the amount so deducted reduces his investment correspondingly.

Before the adoption of § 465, tax shelter promotions involved not only real estate but many other kinds of large-scale depreciable assets—airplanes, computers, boxcars, river barges, motion pictures, mining rights, what-not. The shelter elements consisted of the usual dynamic duo—quick depreciation plus deductible interest on nonrecourse indebtedness, with resulting "losses" to the individual investors in the early years. With the adoption of § 465, non-real estate shelters (boxcars, etc.) pretty much lost their appeal. The reason, of course, was that investors would generally be unwilling to assume *personal* liability for shelter debt, which might run to 99% of the entire cost of the property. As stated, however, § 465 specifically omitted real estate from its coverage. For better or worse, Congress was persuaded that the public interest justified special incentives for housing and construction, including the continuation of the *Crane* rule. The real estate industry benefited most handsomely; with equipment shelters effectively ruled out, real estate became, and for some ten years remained, the only shelter game in town.

In 1985, the Treasury proposed that the at-risk rules be extended to include real estate as well as other depreciable property, and in the 1986 Act Congress did extend the rules to real estate, though in a limited manner only. Taxpayers are now treated as being "at risk" with respect to nonrecourse real estate loans from *outside* lenders—banks and other lending institutions; in effect, with respect to conventional institutional financing, the *Crane* rule applies as before and investors are still entitled to include such third-party debt for the purpose calculating deductible losses. With respect to *inside* financing, however—that is, loans made by promoters or by the seller of the property—"at risk" credit is allowed to the buyer-investors only if they are personally liable for the debt. Congress was aware that lender-sellers sometimes make nonrecourse purchase-money "loans" well in excess of the true value of the property sold with no real intention of ever collecting the principal amount of such loans—while investors, with no threat of personal liability, welcome such value inflation as a source of additional depreciation deductions. As noted above, however, once personal liability is required the investor will lose enthusiasm for the scheme just described unless he somehow trusts the lender never to enforce his claim. By contrast, third-party lenders—banks, etc.—are much less likely to make loans that exceed the property's true value and much more likely to seek full repayment of the loan when due. Concerned to prevent abuse of the *Crane* rule, Congress extended the at-risk requirement to promoters' and sellers' loans but, in effect, excluded bona fide third-party financing.

(b) Passive Activity Losses

The most significant step taken by Congress towards eliminating real estate tax shelters was the addition in 1986 of § 469, which segregates losses from so-called "passive activities" (a marvelously oxymoronic term) and bars their use as offsets against income from unrelated sources. As stated, the purpose of shelter investment is to create artificial losses (resulting, largely, from high leverage and over-rapid depreciation) that can be deducted from gross income generally. In limiting the deduction of passive losses to income from similarly "passive" sources, § 469 in effect denies their use as an offset against personal service and other active business income, as well as against "portfolio" income such as dividends, interest and capital gains. The evident consequence is that real property investments of which the chief aim is to generate "losses," but which are otherwise without positive economic value, lost their appeal.

An illustration (oversimplified) may help to show both how conventional tax shelters have been used in the past and how the "passive activity loss" rules now operate to inhibit them. As in 13.01 above, assume that a taxpayer buys a "building" for $4,000, borrowing the entire purchase price from a third-party lender at an interest rate of 8%. The loan, which is nonrecourse, is repayable in equal annual installments of $1,000 over 5 years. Once again, the interest/principal schedule is as follows:

Year:	1	2	3	4	5	Total
Interest	$320	260	210	140	70	$1,000
Principal	$680	740	790	860	930	$4,000

In our earlier illustration, the taxpayer was able to find a lessee who rented the property for $1,200 a year, so that the investment generated a positive annual cash flow of $200 and evidently made sense in purely economic terms. Suppose, however, that we eliminate such economic benefit by stipulating that the lessee will pay rent of only $1,000 a year; in effect, the taxpayer is to serve merely as a pipeline from the lessee to the lender, receiving $1,000 from the former as rent and paying $1,000 to the latter as interest and principal, but netting nothing for himself.[6]

Apart from taxes (and a hope that the property may appreciate) the arrangement is altogether pointless; but if we stir in (a) the *Crane* rule, (b) straight-line depreciation, and (c) annual interest deductions, we will have cooked up a very serviceable little tax shelter. Thus, obviously—

Year:	1	2	3	4	5	Total
Net rents	$1,00 0	1,00 0	1,00 0	1,00 0	1,00 0	$5,00 0
Interest	320	260	210	140	70	1,000
Depreciation	800	800	800	800	800	4,000
Taxable Income/(Loss)	$(120)	(60)	(10)	60	130	–0–

Assuming he expects to have income from other sources and to pay tax at a rate of (say) 30% throughout the five-year period, then— § 469 aside—the taxpayer will save $36 (30% of $120) in taxes the first year by offsetting his "loss" against such other income, $18 the second year and $3 the third—a total tax saving of $57. In all three years the "losses" are artifacts of the tax system; they do not reflect real economic losses. The taxes saved in years 1–3 will have to be repaid in Years 4 and 5, but, as usual, there is a tangible and substantial benefit in deferring to later periods taxes otherwise due currently.[7]

When Year 4 does finally arrive, moreover, the taxpayer (if he is lucky and the property *has* appreciated) may be able to sell the shelter for an amount sufficient to reimburse the tax then due on his built-in gain. Such gain would necessarily be equal to the income

---

[6]   Admittedly—see 6.10(b)—there would be a question as to whether the "lease" qualified as such for tax purposes. It almost surely would if the taxpayer made some equity investment to begin with and had some expectation of a residual value at the end of the term. Adding these factors would complicate the example without really changing the results; however, a *caveat* is in order.

[7]   Familiar question: Why did the lender agree to this deal instead of acquiring the depreciable property directly? The lender, after all, has to report full economic income—$320 the first year, $260 the second, etc.—because he owns a financial asset (the borrower's mortgage note) and receives taxable interest. If the lender had invested in the building instead of the mortgage, his taxable income after depreciation would be only $200 ($1,000 – $800) in the first and each succeeding year. In effect, the lender has permitted the borrower to enjoy the benefit of income-deferral—a total of $190 over years 1–3—instead of claiming that benefit for himself. But why would he do that? The answer—already suggested at 6.03 in discussing *Starr's Estate*—must be that the lender confronts lower tax rates than the borrower under a graduated rate structure or for some reason is wholly or partially exempt from tax. For a consideration— brokerage commission, higher interest rate—the lender is willing and eager to sell his advantageous tax position to the borrower and the borrower is happy to buy it. As always, it takes two to shelter; and as always, the only loser is the Treasury.

previously deferred, that is, $190. Under the rule of *Parker v. Delaney*, the taxpayer, on disposing of the property, would be treated as realizing the remaining mortgage debt—$860 + 930 = $1,790—while his basis would have been reduced to $1,600 ($4,000 − (3 × $800)). Hence his gain (for tax purposes) would be $190 and his tax, as stated, would be $57 at the assumed 30% rate. To recoup the $57 he would need to sell the property for $81.42 above the mortgage debt ($81.42 − (.30 × $81.42) = $57)—in which event the shelter would have worked out very well indeed.

Section 469 effectively eliminates the shelter benefits just described by imposing a kind of quarantine on the so-called "passive activity losses" recorded in Years 1–3. The term "passive activity" refers to any business activity in which the taxpayer does not "materially participate." Rental activities are treated as "passive" (unless, under a 1993 amendment, the taxpayer is engaged in such activities on essentially a full-time basis), and the owner of a limited partnership interest is treated as being engaged in a "passive activity" irrespective of his actual participation. A "passive activity loss"—determined by taking into account all items of deduction attributable to the passive activity, including interest on mortgage indebtedness—is not disallowed, but is deductible only against income from that or another passive activity, with indefinite carryforward. As already emphasized, neither personal service income, nor active business income, nor income from securities investments, is treated as passive activity income, and hence none of these taxable receipts can be offset by shelter "losses". A full-scale segregation is thus accomplished. Tax shelters are banished to a separate schedule, in effect, and are not allowed to mix with other elements of the individual's tax return.

The work-out of all this in our illustrative case should be easy to surmise. Assuming the taxpayer has no other passive activity income, the losses incurred in Years 1–3 will offset nothing in those years but can be carried forward to offset any passive activity income that materializes in subsequent periods—presumably, in Years 4 and 5. Such suspended losses are also deductible if and when the taxpayer disposes of the shelter activity. Thus, as indicated, the taxpayer in our illustration realizes a gain of at least $190—the difference between the unpaid mortgage principal and his adjusted basis—if he disposes of the property at the start of Year 4. Since his prior losses would have produced no tax benefit owing to the "passive activity" restriction, it would be improper to tax his equally artificial gain at that point and the losses then serve to eliminate that gain.

Section 469 bristles with interpretative difficulties—what constitutes "material participation" is only the most obvious[8]—and the Regulations issued by the Treasury are both lengthy and complex. However, as suggested at 6.06 in connection with our discussion of tax arbitrage (of which real estate shelters are simply an example), it is essentially the presence of an exempt income-source—here, over-rapid cost recovery—that is responsible for the problem. Despite the apparent complexity of § 469—the section itself goes on for several pages, and the Regulations are longer still—on balance it has served as a simplification provision. Section 469 has proven to be a very effective deterrent—a sort of "keep out" sign posted in front of potential real estate tax shelters. Given the existence of § 469, taxpayers no longer invest in pre-1986-style real estate tax shelters. To the considerable extent to which the effect of the provision is to deter transactions to which it would apply, no one has to deal with its complexity. The practical effect is actually simplification, because of the elimination of controversies between taxpayers and the IRS over the tax consequences of real estate shelters.

One last reminder may be in order. As just shown, § 469 prevents taxpayers from combining quick depreciation with interest deductions so as to create artificial losses that can be used to offset income from unrelated sources. It does not, however, in any way restrict the "internal sheltering" that was illustrated in the preceding Section. There, the taxpayer, having rented his property to a lessee for $1,200 a year, was able to defer a substantial proportion of his true economic income ($227 in Year 1, $113 in Year 2, etc.) to later periods through a combination of allowable depreciation and interest deductions. Although income is thus understated for tax purposes, § 469, aimed solely at restricting losses, obviously has no application. Put otherwise, § 469 does not increase taxable income by cutting back on the depreciation and interest deductions as such; rather, it *limits* the shelter-effect to the positive income generated by the investment itself.

13.03   Mortgage   of   Appreciated   Property—The *Woodsam* Case

Suppose an investor purchased certain commercial real estate— say a small office building—some years ago at a cost of $100,000. Real estate prices having steadily climbed, the property today has a value of $350,000. The investor, needing money for a wholly separate

---

[8]   Generally the Regulations require a taxpayer to devote at least 500 hours to an activity during the year, in order to qualify as having materially participated in that activity. Reg. § 1.469–5T(a). Seldom will a busy doctor, lawyer, or executive be willing and able to devote that much time to a tax shelter.

purpose, now decides to raise some cash by placing a mortgage on the property. To keep matters simple (even if slightly unrealistic), assume the investor is able to borrow an amount equal to the entire value of the property, that is, $350,000. He is of course prepared to put the property up as security, but he does not wish to be personally liable for the debt or to make any of his other assets available to the lender in case of default. Prospective mortgagees, it turns out, are eager for the business, and the investor is able to obtain the funds he wants by issuing a nonrecourse mortgage. As already explained, if default occurs, the debt can be satisfied through foreclosure of the property itself, but the mortgagee can make no claim for any deficiency against the debtor individually, whatever the value of the other assets in his portfolio.

The mortgage transaction purports to be a loan, of course, and loans (even secured loans) are not usually regarded as realizations. But isn't this situation somewhat different? In view of the absence of personal liability, can't it reasonably be argued that the investor has in fact realized a gain to the extent that the mortgage proceeds exceed his basis in the property? The investor, after all, has withdrawn $350,000 in cash—$250,000 more than his original investment. To be sure, if the property continues to appreciate, he will presumably elect to make the amortization payments on schedule. But if the market shifts around and the value of the property declines, he can simply abandon the property to the lender without personal obligation for the deficiency. The investor has thus terminated his risk on the downside and has converted the property's appreciation into cash. In the worst case scenario—if the building becomes worthless the day after the taxpayer takes out the loan—the taxpayer still gets to keep the $350,000 loan proceeds. Accordingly, why not regard the mortgage transaction as a sale and treat the excess of "amount realized" over basis as a taxable gain?

If this view were accepted, the investor would recognize gain of $250,000 immediately. If the property were sold outright in a later year for, say, $400,000, the investor would have a further taxable gain of $50,000. The entire appreciation would thus have been taxed in two stages: $250,000 at the time the mortgage was issued and $50,000 later on. By comparison, if the mortgage transaction is *not* treated as a realization, then nothing is taxed currently and the gain of $300,000 is deferred until the later year when the property is sold.

This now-familiar contrast between anticipation and deferral suggests that taxpayers would generally resist realization in the circumstances given. In the *Woodsam* case,[9] however, it was the taxpayer who argued *for* realization and the government which

---

[9]   *Woodsam Associates, Inc. v. Commissioner,* 198 F.2d 357 (2d Cir.1952).

successfully opposed it. The reason for the switch in positions, evidently, is that the year in which the mortgage loan was made and the alleged realization took place was barred to the government by the statute of limitations. This, however, did not prevent the taxpayer from arguing that a taxable (but not a tax-collectable) realization had occurred at that point, and that the basis of the property at the time it was subsequently sold—which was the transaction at issue—should be increased to reflect the earlier event. The government—perhaps anxious to avoid a whipsaw in this and in all the similar cases which would at once have been brought forward—argued that neither a realization *nor* a step-up in basis had taken place in the earlier period. The court agreed. Stressing that the mortgagee remained a mere creditor and that the taxpayer as equity-owner would get the benefit of any further property appreciation, the court refused to treat the nonrecourse loan differently from a loan with personal liability; it therefore held that the mortgage was not a "disposition" which produced a taxable gain. As a result, the taxpayer's entire gain was taxed in the year of sale, which was still open under the statute of limitations.

From one standpoint the *Woodsam* case is merely another illustration of the ambiguous nature of the realization requirement. The decision could about as easily have gone for the taxpayer as for the Treasury. A nonrecourse mortgage loan can quite respectably be viewed *either* as (i) a conventional borrowing plus a right in the borrower to "put" the property to the lender (by defaulting on the loan) in the event the value of the property should decline, or (ii) a conventional sale plus a right in the seller to "call" the property (by amortizing the mortgage) in the event the value of the property should rise. Either characterization is plausible, and one suspects that the court may have been led to accept the first and reject the second as much because it found the taxpayer's argument "novel" as because of any fundamental perceptions about the concept of realization. It is true that the realization trigger of § 1001(a) is "the sale or other disposition of property," and that borrowing—even nonrecourse borrowing—against property appreciation does not seem, at first glance, to qualify as a "sale or other disposition" of the property. On the other hand, under the second view described above (of the nonrecourse loan as a conventional sale plus a call option), the nonrecourse borrowing does seem to be the functional equivalent of a sale.

Perhaps the *Woodsam* court was also moved by administrative considerations: a holding for the taxpayer might have obliged the Service to examine the financial condition of all borrowers, even including those who do assume personal liability for their debts. If the borrower's resources are negligible apart from the property pledged, as where the borrower is a corporation with no other substantial assets, the practical effect is roughly the same as if the loan were made on a nonrecourse basis, and perhaps a realization would have to be found in both cases. As suggested at 3.01 in connection with stockholder borrowing, however, the task of distinguishing loans from non-loans is burdensome, and it is no doubt usually best avoided if possible.

At all events, we can now combine the *Crane* and *Woodsam* cases in a single illustration. Suppose a taxpayer purchases an apartment building for $4,000, paying $1,000 out of his own funds and borrowing the balance of $3,000 on a nonrecourse mortgage. The property subsequently appreciates to $10,000 and the taxpayer, as in *Woodsam,* borrows an additional $6,000 by adding that amount to the mortgage. What is the taxpayer's basis for the property? Answer: $4,000. The subsequent borrowing of $6,000 represents untaxed property appreciation and is not included in the taxpayer's basis. That, in effect, is the holding in *Woodsam.* The earlier borrowing of $3,000 is part of his original cost, however, and *is* included in basis under *Crane.* Debt secured by a mortgage is included in the basis of the mortgaged property if—and only if—it is acquisition indebtedness (that is, debt incurred to acquire or improve the property). The $3,000 qualifies as acquisition indebtedness, but the $6,000 does not. If the property appreciated no further and were finally sold for $10,000—the taxpayer receiving $1,000 cash and the mortgage, now $9,000, being assumed by the buyer—the "amount realized" would be the full $10,000. The later as well as the earlier borrowing would be included for this purpose and the taxpayer would recognize a gain of $6,000. The latter outcome is arithmetically correct since the taxpayer has realized a total of $7,000 cash as against an initial cash investment of only $1,000.

Crane and *Woodsam* thus apparently differ in their effect on the computation of basis. Initial borrowing is included in basis under *Crane,* while subsequent borrowing is excluded from basis under *Woodsam* owing to the absence of a taxable realization. In practical effect, however, this difference will often prove illusory. Thus in the illustration just given suppose that the $6,000 subsequently borrowed is invested in a *second* apartment building. The taxpayer will then be allowed depreciation on a total property cost of $10,000— $4,000 for the old property under *Crane,* and $6,000 for the new property *despite* the absence of a realization under *Woodsam.* In effect the limitation described in the preceding paragraph—no step-up in basis without a taxable realization—has been evaded: although the basis of the old property is unaffected by the subsequent borrowing, there is obviously nothing to stop the taxpayer from reinvesting the borrowed funds in another depreciable asset. *Crane* and *Woodsam* thus *both* operate to permit taxpayers to include untaxed capital in property basis—one directly, the other indirectly. From the government's standpoint, therefore, the *Woodsam* case creates (or confirms) a sizeable loophole, and it might very well have been better if the decision had gone the other way.

Indeed, there is irony (of a sort that occurs often in the tax field; see *Taft v. Bowers* at 4.01) in the fact that the government was the *winning* litigant in the *Crane* and *Woodsam* cases. In each case the particular issue concerned the proper method of computing gain on the final sale of property. In *Crane* the government had to argue *for* the inclusion of the purchase-money mortgage in the amount realized by the taxpayer; in *Woodsam* it had to argue *against* the notion that subsequent mortgaging might constitute a realization. The government won in both instances, but the victories have cost it plenty.

One final note on *Woodsam*: Congress is free, of course, to reverse the result in *Woodsam* by enacting legislation providing that borrowing against appreciation is to be treated as a realization event. Although Congress has accepted *Woodsam* as the general rule, it has provided, in § 72(e)(4)(A), that loans under an annuity contract are to be treated as taxable distributions.

13.04   Dispositions of Encumbered Assets—*Tufts* and *Diedrich*

(a)   *Excessively Mortgaged Property*

Despite some ambiguity in the opinion itself, tax commentators have generally felt that the Supreme Court's decision in *Crane* stands for a simple principle of tax-symmetry. If a nonrecourse mortgage is included in the property-owner's basis for purposes of computing annual depreciation, then the unpaid balance of that mortgage must be included as well in determining "amount realized." Put differently, if the tax law treats nonrecourse debt as a real cost when property is acquired, then, to be consistent, "relief" from such debt has to be treated as a real benefit when the property is sold. *Parker v. Delaney* so holds, and notwithstanding Judge Magruder's contrasting view, the general question is now settled beyond argument.

Both in *Crane* and in *Parker v. Delaney,* however, the courts assumed that the property—real estate in each case—had a market value that was at least equal to the amount of the unpaid mortgage at the time the property was disposed of. Even apart from tax-symmetry considerations, therefore, it was more or less reasonable to say that the taxpayer had been "relieved" of the full mortgage debt when the property (subject to the mortgage) was transferred to another. But suppose, in a given case, that the securing property is worth *less* than the mortgage debt. In that circumstance, a taxpayer who is not personally liable would have no economic reason to satisfy the debt in full; threatened with foreclosure, the taxpayer could simply abandon the property to the mortgagee. Paying a lender $100 to retain title to property worth only $90 is hardly sensible as long as the lender's security is limited to the property itself. If the property is disposed of at that point, isn't the measure of "relief", and hence the "amount realized," the lower value of the property rather than the full amount of the debt?

The Supreme Court furnished a negative answer in *Commissioner v. Tufts*,[10] decided in 1983. Rounding and simplifying, the taxpayers in *Tufts* formed a partnership for the purpose of constructing an apartment complex, investing about $40,000 of their own money and borrowing $1.85 million from a bank lender. Their debt was evidenced by a nonrecourse note secured by a mortgage on the building. Over the next two years the taxpayers took depreciation and other deductions of $440,000, which reduced their basis in the building to about $1.45 million. Unable to operate the building profitably, and having repaid none of the loan principal, they sold the property (perhaps at the insistence of the mortgagee) to another investor. The latter paid the taxpayers nothing in cash but took the building subject to the mortgage. On the date of the sale, the fair market value of the property was not greater than the taxpayers' adjusted basis of $1.45 million. Since the value of the property represented the limit of their liability, the taxpayers argued that no more than $1.45 million could be included in "amount realized" and, hence, that no gain should be recognized on the transaction.

Announcing that *Crane* "stands for the ... proposition ... that a non-recourse loan should be treated as a true loan," the Court held that the taxpayers had realized the full unpaid balance of the mortgage debt—$1.85 million—and, accordingly, must recognize a taxable gain of $400,000. The taxpayers, said the Court, had included the loan in their basis "on the understanding" (*i.e.*, for tax purposes) that they had an obligation to repay the full amount. When the obligation was relieved, they necessarily "realize[d] value to that extent within the meaning of § 1001(b)." Accordingly, in determining amount realized, "the fair market value of the property ... becomes irrelevant." In effect, borrowing with personal liability and borrowing without personal liability are to be treated alike for this purpose.

The decision in *Tufts*, as has been said,[11] is entirely unremarkable once the need for tax symmetry is acknowledged, and indeed the final outcome is merely a repeat of the result reached in

---

[10] 461 U.S. 300 (1983).

[11] Andrews, *On Beyond Tufts*, 61 Taxes 949 (1983).

Parker v. Delaney. As in the earlier case, the appropriate measure of gain in *Tufts* was the difference between the deductions allowed, $440,000, and the amount invested by the taxpayers, about $40,000. To be sure, there was an economic loss to someone—the property did fall in value from $1.85 million to $1.45 million. The true loser, however, was not Tufts but the mortgage-lender, which would appropriately recognize the loss if and when it finally foreclosed.

In a concurring opinion, Justice O'Connor proposed another— and in some respects a more coherent—way of analyzing the *Tufts* transaction. Drawing on a thoughtful *amicus* brief, O'Connor suggested that the transfer of excessively mortgaged property might be viewed as a twofold event consisting of (a) a sale of the asset itself, the apartment building, for its actual market value of $1.45 million, and (b) use of the constructive proceeds (again, $1.45 million) to satisfy the taxpayers' debt of $1.85 million. The sale, on this view, would generate *no* taxable gain, because the amount realized by the taxpayers was no greater than their adjusted basis for the building. The debt repayment, however, would result in $400,000 of "cancellation of indebtedness income" in accordance with the rule of the *Kirby Lumber* case (3.02). The *amount* of income to be recognized—$400,000—would be no different from that recognized by the Court majority, but it happens that cancellation of indebtedness income is "ordinary" while gain from the disposition of an apartment building is likely to be capital gain, taxable at a bargain rate. The Court majority conceded that the concurring view might be justified if the issue were considered *de novo,* but it concluded that, under existing authority, the extinguishment of nonrecourse debt must be regarded as part of the property sale itself and could not be viewed as a separate transaction between the borrower and lender.

Imagine a variation on *Tufts* in which the debt is recourse—that is, the taxpayer is personally liable on the debt secured by the mortgage. Because the taxpayer has no substantial assets other than the excessively-mortgaged building, the mortgagee and the taxpayer reach an agreement under which (i) the taxpayer transfers ownership of the building to the mortgagee, thus repaying the debt to the extent of the value of the property ($1.45 million), and (ii) the mortgagee releases the taxpayer for all liability for the remaining amount of the loan ($400,000). According to Rev. Rul. 90–16,[12] the bifurcation approach rejected by the majority opinion in *Tufts* applies in this situation. The taxpayer is treated as (i) selling the property for $1.45 million (which produces no gain, because of the taxpayer's $1.45 million adjusted basis), and (ii) having $400,000 of cancellation-of-indebtedness income (which is excludable under § 108(a)(1)(B) if the

---

[12]   1990–1 C.B. 12.

taxpayer is insolvent). The inconsistency between *Tufts* and Rev. Rul. 90–16 is rather surprising and is difficult to justify, considering that for most purposes the tax system treats nonrecourse and recourse debt identically. One should not lose sight, however, of the fact that both *Tufts* and Rev. Rul. 90–16 produce the correct total amount of income; the only distinction between the two approaches is in the character of that income. By contrast, the approach unsuccessfully championed by the taxpayers in *Tufts* would have understated their income.

A final *Tufts*-related issue—really, a limitation on the scope of the *Tufts* decision—should be mentioned. Having convinced the Court that the original mortgage loan of $1.85 million must be treated as an "amount realized" by the property sellers, is the Commissioner also bound to treat the property buyer—Tufts' vendee—as having an equivalent "cost" of $1.85 million? If so, property having little actual value but subject to large nonrecourse indebtedness (the larger the better, indeed) would become attractive to investors solely as a source of depreciation and accrued interest deductions. Thus, a high-bracket taxpayer might be eager to acquire such property even though he never expected either to realize a penny of rents or to see the property increase in value, and *certainly* never intended to pay off the mortgage debt. His sole aim would be to obtain the tax benefits that derive from the ownership of a depreciable asset whose "cost" for tax purposes would include the full amount of the nonrecourse mortgage. For its part the mortgagee would often be content with small annual interest payments (as stated, no payments on mortgage principal would ever be made), since foreclosure might gain it even less.

Probably, however, where property is *known* to be worth less than the nonrecourse debt at the time the property is acquired, the purchaser's basis should be limited to the lower value figure—$1.45 million in the *Tufts* case. To be sure, *Crane* held that nonrecourse debt is to be treated as a real cost to the purchaser of encumbered property despite the absence of personal liability. But this assumes that the "debt" is real debt—that an investor would, or might, be willing to incur the obligation for objective economic reasons. Quite obviously, however, no one would be willing to pay more for property, or borrow more to buy it, than the property was actually worth. It follows that if (as with Tufts' vendee) the nonrecourse mortgage exceeds the value of the property *when acquired,* such excess should not be regarded as real indebtedness and should not be included in the buyer's "cost."

Assuming (with some support from the decided cases[13]) that the conclusion just stated is correct, what happens when Tufts' vendee sells the property—still subject, say, to the original mortgage of $1.85 million—to yet another purchaser? At that point the rule of symmetry should take hold. Having been allowed a "cost" of $1.45 million, Tufts' vendee should be treated as having realized the same amount on sale, and this would be true even if, by then, the market value of the property had declined still further.

Summarizing, it turns out that the value of property subject to a nonrecourse mortgage is highly relevant in determining a purchaser's "cost" at the time the property is acquired, but altogether irrelevant in determining his "amount realized" when the same property is sold. At acquisition, the question is whether the nonrecourse obligation is or is not true debt, and for this purpose value matters. On sale, the only applicable principle is one of tax symmetry, and for this purpose value is irrelevant.

(b)   Conditional Gifts

The *Diedrich* case,[14] decided by the Supreme Court in 1982, raises yet another question about the application of the *Crane* rule— namely, whether (or how) the rule affects *gifts* of encumbered property. As background, suppose a taxpayer owns stock with a basis of $20 and a value of $100. Pledging the stock as sole security, the taxpayer borrows an amount equal to the appreciation—$80—and then gives the stock, subject to the indebtedness, to another family member. Although gifts are not in themselves realization events, it is obvious here that the taxpayer is partly a giver but partly also a seller. *Tufts* makes it clear that a transfer of encumbered property generates an "amount realized"—just as if the transferee had paid cash instead of taking on the debt—and the courts have had little difficulty in finding, under the facts assumed, that the transaction is a sale as well as a gift.[15] Having invested $20 in the asset transferred, having borrowed $80 in cash with no personal obligation to repay, and having terminated his interest in the asset by conveying it to someone else, the transferor plainly falls within the *Tufts* rule and gain recognition follows. This is true even though the transaction involves family members: as indicated throughout Part C, the Code does *not* employ a systematic notion of family unity—spouses as well as parents and children are viewed as separate persons for tax

---

[13]   *Pleasant Summit Land Corp. v. Commissioner,* 863 F.2d 263 (3d Cir.1988); and see *Franklin's Estate v. Commissioner,* 544 F.2d 1045 (9th Cir.1976). The issue is discussed in Jensen, *The Unanswered Question in Tufts: What Was the Purchaser's Basis?,* 10 Va.Tax Rev. 455 (1991).

[14]   *Diedrich v. Commissioner,* 457 U.S. 191 (1982).

[15]   *Estate of Levine v. Commissioner,* 634 F.2d 12 (2d Cir.1980).

purposes—so that a sale of property by one family member to another is, in general, treated the same as a transaction between strangers.[16]

Though it seems a bit grudging, donors frequently make gifts of property on condition that the donee pay the resulting federal gift tax, which, under § 2502(d), is expressly made a legal liability of the donor. In many cases, presumably, the donee is obliged to sell the property to obtain the necessary funds. Assuming that the donee is in a lower bracket than the donor, however, any gain thereby realized will be taxed at a lower rate than would apply if the donor had sold the property himself to pay the gift tax or had borrowed against the property and then transferred it to the donee subject to the debt. The question, obviously, is whether the conditional gift device actually succeeds in shifting the potential gain to the donee, or whether the "condition"—payment by the donee of the donor's gift tax obligation—turns the gift itself into a taxable event.

In *Diedrich,* the taxpayer made a conditional gift to his children of stock having a basis in his hands of $50,000 and fair market value of $300,000. The federal gift tax, which the children agreed to pay, was $60,000. Resolving a conflict among the circuits, the Supreme Court held that the assumption of gift tax liability by the donees produced a measurable economic benefit to the donor and hence should be regarded as the equivalent of cash consideration. Although the donor's aim was to make a gift—really a *net* gift—it was also his intent, in adding the payment condition, to be relieved of a personal tax obligation. Citing both *Old Colony* and *Crane,* the Court sustained the Commissioner in treating the property transfer as part gift and part sale.

With the Court's approval, the Commissioner calculated Diedrich's gain under § 1001(a) by simply subtracting his property basis, $50,000, from the gift tax obligation assumed by the donees, $60,000. The taxable gain was thus $10,000—an odd result, in a way, because it is less (by a factor of five) than the gain the taxpayer would have recognized if he had sold just enough stock to pay the gift tax himself. Had he followed the latter course, the taxpayer would have had to sell $60,000 worth of stock, which would be one-fifth ($60,000/$300,000) of his total shares. His basis for the shares sold— one-fifth of $50,000—would have been $10,000 and the gain recognized ($60,000 − $10,000) would therefore have been $50,000. In effect, while persuading the Court that part-gift/part-sale was the right way to characterize conditional gifts, the Commissioner used a computational formula—allocating all of the transferor's cost to the

---

[16] Section 267, which disallows losses on transfers of property to specified types of relatives, is an important exception, as is § 1041 (5.04, providing for nonrecognition of gain or loss on transfers of property between spouses or former spouses).

"sale" element—that may still make it advantageous to employ the conditional gift device. Indeed, had the gift tax liability been no greater than Diedrich's basis, there would have been no taxable gain whatever under the Commissioner's formula despite $250,000 of value appreciation in the property transferred.

A loose end. Using the same numbers, what would be the basis of the stock in the hands of Diedrich's donee? Total appreciation was $250,000. Since the donor was held to have recognized a gain of $10,000 on the transfer, the donee's basis just *has* to be a number such that an immediate sale of the stock for $300,000 will generate recognition to the donee of the remaining $240,000 of untaxed appreciation. Sure enough: in the case of part gift/part sale transactions, the Regulations provide that the basis of the property in the hands of the donee shall be the amount paid for the property (here $60,000) or the donor's basis (here $50,000), whichever is greater.[17] It follows that the donee's basis in *Diedrich* is $60,000, and a prompt sale of the stock for $300,000 will indeed produce further taxable gain of $240,000.

Shall we go on? Suppose the donor's basis in *Diedrich* had been $100,000, so that the amount of unrealized appreciation was only $200,000. Since the gift tax liability assumed by the donee, $60,000, would then be less than the donor's basis, the donor would recognize no gain or loss on the transfer; in effect, the donor would simply have recouped a portion of his $100,000 investment. As above, the donee's basis would be the amount paid for the property ($60,000) or the donor's basis ($100,000), whichever was greater. The donee's basis would thus be $100,000 and a prompt sale of the stock for $300,000 would generate taxable gain of $200,000—once again the right result.

13.05   *Estate of Levine*: An Exercise

The *Crane* rule, along with *Woodsam* and related matters, is found by many students to be a bit more challenging than other topics in the tax field, so perhaps an additional illustration of the relevant calculations will be useful. If not actually needed (or if unbearable), the reader can just go on to something else.

In *Estate of Levine*,[18] the taxpayer in Year 1 purchased certain real estate at a cost of $385,485, of which $150,441 was paid in cash and $235,044 was financed by a nonrecourse mortgage. Many years

---

[17]   Reg. § 1.1015–4(a). For transfers made after 1976, the donee's basis would be increased by the proportion of the gift tax that is attributable to the net appreciation in the value of the gift. Code § 1015(d)(6).

[18]   *Estate of Levine v. Commissioner*, 634 F.2d 12 (2d Cir. 1980).

later—call it Year 30—the taxpayer made a gift of the property to a trust for his grandchildren. Between Years 1 and 30 the taxpayer took out additional nonrecourse mortgage loans (the property obviously appreciated in value over that lengthy period), with the result that the total mortgage debt to which the property was subject amounted to $780,000 at the date of the gift.

At various times during the same 30-year period the taxpayer invested $334,452 (cash) in property improvements of a capital nature. More recently, it appears, he made further capital improvements costing $117,716, but that amount was still owing at the date of gift (presumably to contractors) and became a debt for which the donee-trust assumed responsibility. Finally, two smaller deductible items—$5,908 of mortgage interest and $6,857 of assorted repair and maintenance expenses—were also left unpaid, so that each became an obligation of the trust as well.

One more important number: during his 30-year ownership period, the taxpayer deducted depreciation in the total amount of $352,314.

The issue to be decided was whether the gift produced a taxable gain to the taxpayer-donor under the *Crane* rule, and if it did, how much. The gift itself consisted of the taxpayer's equity in the property, *i.e.*, the value of the property less all of the above-mentioned indebtedness. The appraised value of the property was $925,000, while the outstanding indebtedness—$780,000 of mortgage-debt, $117,716 for recent capital improvements, $5,908 of accrued interest and $6,857 for unpaid repair expense—totaled $910,481. Hence, the gift—the value of the equity actually received by the trust—was only $14,519.

The taxpayer cheerfully paid a tiny gift tax on the amount last stated, but contended that he owed the government no more than that. The Commissioner insisted that the taxpayer had realized a taxable gain in the amount of $425,142[19] by reason of the transfer itself and, hence, owed income tax of about $130,000.

The Second Circuit held for the Commissioner. In an elegant if somewhat lengthy opinion by Judge Friendly, the Court found that the indebtedness to which the property was subject represented an "amount realized" by the taxpayer under § 1001(b). Accordingly, even though intended as a gift, the transfer had to be treated—to the extent of such indebtedness—as a "sale" resulting in the recognition of taxable gain.

---

[19] The court, or somebody, made a minor error of addition, resulting in a gain calculation of $425,051.

Judge Friendly's opinion is perfectly consistent with *Crane* and *Parker v. Delaney,* as well as with the Supreme Court's later decision in *Diedrich,* and essentially adds little to those cases. For present purposes, however, it is the arithmetic of the thing that is up for review—how the taxpayer's gain was calculated—rather than the court's willingness to apply the *Crane* rule to a donative transfer.

Following are two ways to reach the right result, the first— "Under the Code"—being a simplified version of the Court's own methodology.

Under the Code:

Adjusted basis (§ 1011):	
Acquisition price	$385,485
Property improvements prior to Year 30	334,452
Recent capital improvements	<u>117,716</u>
	$837,653
Less: Depreciation	<u>352,314</u>
	$485,339
Amount realized:	
Mortgage debt	$780,000
Amount owed for recent capital improvements	117,716
Interest owed	5,908
Repair expense owed	<u>6,857</u>
	$910,481

Taxable gain: $910,481 − $485,339 = $425,142

Simple enough, and quite correct given the commands of *Crane.* But does the result actually reflect a measurable reality, or is it just a legal artifact? Did the taxpayer really "make" $425,142 when everything is taken into account?

The answer to the latter question (one is relieved to be able to say) is yes. As suggested earlier in discussing the *Tufts* decision, the ultimate question is or should be: how much cash did the taxpayer put into the enterprise and how much cash did he take out of it? How much did he invest, how much did he withdraw? The difference between the two, if any, represents "gain" in economic terms, legal details to one side. It is of course important to observe that "withdrawals" includes not only (i) uninvested borrowings, which the taxpayer, in the court's words, "may ... be considered to have 'pocketed,'" but also (ii) amounts deducted (or deductible) by the taxpayer and for which he received (or receives) a tax benefit—here, allowable depreciation plus accrued interest and repair expense. Thus:

<u>Cash Invested/Cash Withdrawn:</u>

Cash Invested:

Acquisition price	$385,485
Less: Original mortgage	235,044
Net cash investment	$150,441

Cash Withdrawn:

Subsequent mortgage total		$780,000
Less: Original mortgage	235,044	
Property improvements prior to Year 30[20]	334,452	569,496
Mortgage proceeds "pocketed"		$210,504
Plus amounts deducted:		
Depreciation	352,314	
Interest owed	5,908	
Repair expense owed	6,857	365,079
Net cash withdrawals		$575,583

Investment gain: $575,583 – $150,441 = $425,142

Actually, the cash invested / cash withdrawn calculation would enable the calculator to reach the right result—taxable gain of $425,142—even if the legal rules were unknown or were hidden behind the veil of ignorance.

———————

A loose end. It may be worthwhile (if a bit obsessive) to raise and answer one last question about the calculation in *Levine.* As noted, in addition to the bank mortgage the trust-donee assumed responsibility for two small unpaid items, viz., accrued interest ($5,908) and assorted repair and maintenance expenses ($6,857). Was Judge Friendly correct in treating those items as (a) deductible by the taxpayer-donor and, hence, (b) includable in amount realized? In so doing, as Friendly acknowledged in a footnote, the Court departed from *Crane,* in which mortgage interest accrued but unpaid at the time of the transfer was *not* added to the transferor's amount realized. The *Crane* Court apparently viewed the accrued interest item as (a) deductible by the transferee-buyer, and therefore (b) not includable by the seller, Mrs. Crane, as part of the purchase price of the property. Who was right? And does it matter?

Answering the second question first, it obviously does (matter). From the transferor's standpoint, deducting the interest and repair

———————

[20]   The $117,716 owed to contractors for "recent capital improvements" resulted in neither an outlay nor an inflow and, hence, can be omitted from the cash invested / cash withdrawn computation.

expense generates an offset against ordinary income, while the corresponding inclusion produces a lower-taxed capital gain. By contrast, the transferee would prefer to take an immediate deduction for those outlays rather than increase basis and recover the amount through annual depreciation. *Levine* supports the first pattern, *Crane* the second. Again, therefore, who was right?

There is certainly a case to be made for the approach of *Levine*. If the donor-transferor borrowed an amount equal to the interest and repair expense from a third party, then paid those items, and then conveyed the property to the donee-transferee subject to the third-party debt, the result would be clear: the payments would be deductible by the transferor, while the debt assumed by the transferee would be included in the transferor's amount realized and added to the transferee's cost. In *Levine* and *Crane* the borrowing comes directly from the transferee (the trust in *Levine,* the buyer in *Crane*) rather than a third-party lender, but arguably that circumstance should have no significance. Under this view, it is as if the transferor had (first) borrowed the amounts in question from the transferee, then paid the interest and repair expense, and then, finally, satisfied his debt to the transferee by transferring the property. Once again, the transferor would take an expense deduction and include the debt in amount realized, while the transferee would add the same amount to basis. On the other hand, there is also a plausible argument that allowing the donor-transferor deductions for expenses he has not actually paid is inconsistent with the cash method of accounting (described in Section 11), assuming he is a cash-method taxpayer (the *Levine* opinion does not specify the taxpayer's accounting method).

13.06   Short Sales and Related Devices

Selling short against the box (as explained below) is a time-honored device by which investors holding appreciated stock were able to cash in their investment gains without triggering a realization for tax purposes. Section 1259, added to the Code in 1997, changed the law by treating the short sale as a taxable realization where the economic effect from the investor's standpoint is indistinguishable from a straightforward sale of his appreciated shares. A series of well-publicized cases in which the short against the box technique was used (shall we say) to excess may have inspired Congress to enact § 1259.

In an ordinary short sale—one that seeks no special tax advantage—an investor who thinks that the market price of a particular stock is going down can direct his broker to sell the stock short at the current market price. Since the investor doesn't actually own the stock, the broker has to borrow the shares from another client's account. The broker then delivers the borrowed shares to the buyer and deposits the proceeds of the sale in the investor's account. The investor can maintain his short position for as long as he likes, meanwhile paying the broker (and through the broker the stock-lender) any dividends that would normally be received on the borrowed shares. At some point, the investor will direct the broker to close out the short sale. The broker then repurchases an equal number of shares in the market, using the fund in the investor's account for that purpose, and returns those shares to the account of the lender. If the stock has gone down as he hoped it would, the investor makes a profit equal to the difference between the original sale price and the lower repurchase price. If the stock has gone up, the investor suffers a loss equal to the difference between the higher repurchase price and the original sale price.

As far as the tax treatment of a short sale is concerned, there is no realization event until the investor closes out his short position and returns the repurchased shares to the stock-lender. Before that date, the investor's cost—whether higher or lower than the original sale price—is not known. The investor recognizes a capital gain or capital loss when the short sale is closed; and since his holding period is measured with respect to the repurchased shares, which are held only momentarily, the capital gain or loss is always short-term.

But suppose the investor actually *owns* shares that are the same as those originally sold. Instead of delivering those shares to the buyer as might normally be expected, the investor elects to make the transaction into a short sale by identifying and delivering borrowed shares. Under prior law, the sale—called a short sale against the box (the "box," we guess, being the investor's vault or safe-deposit box)—was treated in the same way as the ordinary speculative short sale described above. The taxpayer having identified the borrowed shares as the shares originally sold, no gain or loss was realized until the short position was closed out—not by repurchasing stock in the market, but by delivering the shares held in that famous "box." The investor would then, but only then, recognize his capital gain—long-term, of course, because the shares delivered would have been acquired by the investor many years before.

But while the realization rule applied in the same way in both cases, the economic consequences of going short against the box were very different. With a long and a short position in the same stock, the investor could neither gain if the stock went up nor lose if the stock went down. If the stock went up, the long position would gain value while the short position would lose value in the same amount; if down, the reverse. In effect, the investor was out of the market—no further opportunity for gain, no further risk of loss—just as if he had sold the shares in the box in a conventional way.

Under short sale rules, however, as stated, there was no realization and no recognition of taxable gain until the investor actually replaced the borrowed stock with his own stock, which he would do at some future and far-distant date. Meanwhile, if the investor was a person of substantial wealth and large credit, he could borrow virtually the entire cash proceeds of the original sale from his broker and use those funds to diversify his investment portfolio—tax-free.

The 1997 legislation curtailed the tax-deferral advantage just described by treating short sales against the box and equivalent maneuvers as taxable realizations. Under § 1259, if a taxpayer makes a "constructive sale of an appreciated financial position"—typically a short sale against the box—gain is recognized and included in income just as if the taxpayer had sold his appreciated shares for cash.

Section 1259(c) defines the term just quoted to include certain transactions—options, futures, forward contracts—that are equivalent to a conventional short sale against the box, and it further authorizes the Service to write regulations that would classify as a "constructive sale" any other securities transaction having the same economic effect. But even so, and despite the new provision, various "innovative" techniques have been developed by investment bankers that may, and apparently do, enable investors to bail out the cash value of appreciated securities without triggering a realization. These techniques are moderately complex in form (and terminology), but what they boil down to is fairly simple. Instead of selling his appreciated X stock in a straightforward manner and recognizing a large taxable gain, the taxpayer "borrows" an amount equal to the value of the stock from a group of lenders, pledging the stock as *sole* security for the loan. The loan is to be repaid in, say, five years. If at maturity the X stock has gone down in value, the lending group agrees to accept the reduced value of the stock as full repayment of the debt, so that any such decline falls on the lenders alone. If the X stock has gone up, the lenders and the taxpayer share the increase on a predetermined formula. Meanwhile, the taxpayer pays interest at a rate that exceeds the dividend rate on the stock, which makes it worthwhile for the lenders to enter into this purported loan arrangement rather than buying X stock directly on the market.

Has the taxpayer "sold" the stock, in effect, and realized the prior appreciation, or is the "loan" a loan rather than a realization? In favor of "sale" characterization: (a) the taxpayer has received cash equal to the value of the X stock, and (b) the taxpayer's *downside* risk has been eliminated. In favor of "loan" characterization: (c) the taxpayer is obligated to pay annual interest and to repay principal (in some amount) on maturity, and (d) though free of downside risk, the taxpayer has retained a partial interest in any further *upside* appreciation.

So which is it, sale or loan? Given that the taxpayer does retain an economic interest in the X stock by reason of factor (d), existing legal authorities (indeed, the *Woodsam* case itself) appear to support loan rather than sale characterization. Evidently § 1259, which is rather narrowly drawn, has no application.[21] As a result, the taxpayer accomplishes (a) and (b)—that is, converts his X stock to cash in an amount equal to its current market price, and terminates any risk of subsequent decline—without paying a tax on his long-term gain. The taxpayer has certainly experienced a "realization" from an investment standpoint—but not, apparently, for tax purposes.

As a practical matter, arrangements of the sort described require the services of a well-paid investment banker and entail other transaction costs and credit requirements that are beyond the capacity of ordinary investors. In consequence, such arrangements are available only if the taxpayer's appreciated stockholdings are huge.[22]

14. Deferred Payment Transactions

14.01 In General

The tax treatment of deferred payment transactions (*i.e.*, seller financing) has been a vexing problem for the income tax virtually from the beginning. In general, and apart from any specific legislative intervention, sales of property on a deferred payment basis should be treated no differently from sales of property for a single lump-sum payment. The buyer's promise to pay stated amounts in the future—usually represented by notes or other evidence of indebtedness—normally has an ascertainable market value, and this market value constitutes an "amount realized" by the seller. The difference between that amount and his basis would be the measure of the seller's gain or loss. To illustrate, suppose a taxpayer owns an apartment building with an adjusted basis of $20,000 and a fair market value of $100,000. He sells the property to another investor for $10,000 cash and the buyer's $90,000 debt obligation, secured by a mortgage on the building. The debt

---

[21] The legislative history of the provision specifically states that "it is intended that transactions that reduce only risk of loss . . . will not be covered." Senate Report 105–33 (1997).

[22] See, e.g., Salomon, Inc. Prospectus Supplement covering 3,500,000 DECS (Debt Exchangeable for Common Stock), 6 1/4% Exchangeable Notes Due February 1, 2001 (Subject to Exchange into Common Shares . . . of Cincinnati Bell Inc.) Price to Public: $195,125,000. Underwriting discount: $5,845,000. Prospectus dated Nov. 14, 1996.

instrument provides for payment of the $90,000 principal amount of the loan in nine annual installments of $10,000 each. It also provides for annual payments of interest at 12% on the outstanding principal. Assuming that the fair market value of the mortgage is equal to its face amount, the taxpayer would be treated as having realized $100,000 in the year of sale and would therefore recognize and pay tax on his entire gain of $80,000. In effect, the mortgage debt would be viewed as payment for the property sold—the equivalent of cash—and the transaction would be viewed as "closed" even though the greater part of the purchase price is not to be received in cash until later years. Having recognized his gain in full, the taxpayer would hold the mortgage at a basis of $90,000, and the annual mortgage payments made by the buyer would be allocated in part to taxable interest and in part to what would now be a tax-paid capital investment in the buyer's indebtedness.

The "income" definition and the concept of "amount realized" thus make no generic distinction between sales for cash and sales for future payments—in effect, realization does not depend on the medium of exchange. Yet despite this general approach, one cannot help, we think, feeling some uneasiness about the idea of treating a "mere" claim to future payments as the equivalent of money. In the first place, the seller may have difficulty obtaining the funds to pay the tax liability that arises from the sale. Assuming that the $80,000 gain above is taxed at a rate of (say) 30%, the seller would owe a current tax of $24,000. As this exceeds the $10,000 cash down payment received from the buyer in the year of sale, the seller may be compelled to dispose of the mortgage or of other assets, or to borrow himself, to obtain the balance. Such actions may well be costly and contrary to his preference (although, of course, paying taxes is always contrary to one's preference). Second, although a conventional real estate mortgage is easy to value, suppose the deferred payment claim is secured by some relatively unfamiliar type of property—say a patent or a business interest—or is merely a personal obligation of the buyer. Or suppose it is contingent in amount. Since no active market for such claims exists, the danger of an erroneous valuation is obviously considerable and the taxpayer may suffer if the value assigned to the claim by appraisal turns out to be too high.

As might be expected, the tax law has developed a response to both of the problems just mentioned—one a statutory relief provision (the installment sale method), the other a judicial creation (the "fair market value" rule). Both are described in the paragraphs that follow. Where applicable, each enables a taxpayer who has made a deferred payment sale to postpone recognition until the buyer's obligation has actually been reduced to cash. The two postponement schemes operate differently, however, and as will be seen each provides a "solution" that goes somewhat beyond the problem to be solved.

14.02   The Installment Method

Section 453 provides, as a general rule, that gains from deferred payment transactions involving real estate and other investment property shall be spread out proportionately over the entire payment period. More precisely, under § 453(c) the gain taxed in any given year equals the payments received in that year (*i.e.*, a down payment received in the year of sale, or a principal payment on the installment obligation received in either the year of sale or a later year), multiplied by the profit ratio. The profit ratio is the taxpayer's gross profit on the sale (basically, the amount realized on the sale minus the taxpayer's adjusted basis in the asset sold) divided by the total contract price (basically, the amount realized).[23] Letting X stand for the gain taxed in the current year, P for the principal payments received in the current year, GP for the gross profit, and CP for the total contract price, the formula is: $X = P \ (GP/CP)$. P, and therefore X, may change from year to year, but the profit ratio of GP/CP is fixed in the year of sale and never changes thereafter. The effect of the formula is to treat each year's principal payments as a microcosm of the overall transaction. If, by the time the note is fully paid, principal payments (including any down payment in the year of sale) will have consisted of (for example) 40% profit and 60% basis recovery, then each year's principal payments are treated as 40% profit and 60% basis recovery.[24]

In the illustration above, the gross profit is $80,000 ($100,000 amount realized minus $20,000 basis), and the total contract price is $100,000. Thus, the profit ratio is 80%. If the taxpayer receives a $10,000 down payment in the year of sale and a principal payment of $10,000 in each of the following nine years, the taxable gain for each of the ten years will be $10,000 x 80% = $8,000. (If principal payments varied from year to year, then taxable gains would also vary.) By the end of the ten years, the taxpayer will have received total payments—counting both the down payment and the principal payments on the note, but not counting interest payments (fully taxable under § 61(a)(4))—totaling $100,000, will have been taxed on $80,000 gain, and will have been allowed basis recovery of $20,000. Assuming a tax

---

[23]   Section 453 deals with only the tax treatment of payments of *principal* received by the seller. *Interest* payments received by the seller are fully taxable under § 61(a)(4).

[24]   In substance, this is the same as the § 72 formula for separating annuity payments into their income and basis-recovery components, described at 2.02. The only difference—which is purely cosmetic—is that the annuity formula defines the amount of each payment that *is not* taxable, whereas the installment sale formula defines the amount of each payment that *is* taxable.

rate of 30% in all years, the tax on the seller's gain is $2,400 in the year of sale and $2,400 each year thereafter. Cash receipts are thus at all times in excess of the tax due. Taxpayers are free to elect out of the installment method and recognize their full gains in the year of sale, but unless a very special reason exists (*e.g.,* a taxpayer anticipates being subject to significantly higher marginal tax rates after the current year), a taxpayer should not elect out of § 453.

Most commentators applaud the matching of the imposition of tax liability with the receipt of cash accomplished by § 453. It may be worth observing, nevertheless, that the provision, when applicable, actually results in a *reduction* of tax liability and thus has consequences for the taxpayer that are substantive, not merely procedural. If the property seller in the illustration above had sold his building for $100,000 cash, his tax liability of $24,000 would have been payable at once. Having sold on the installment method, his tax is payable at the rate of $2,400 a year over a 10-year period. The present value of the latter obligation, discounted at an after-tax rate of (say) 8%, is only about $16,100. Hence, it can be said that § 453 has effectively reduced the seller's tax by some $7,900.

Whether the section *should* have this consequence can, perhaps, be questioned. The apparently benign object of § 453 is to make it easier for installment sellers to pay their taxes by associating gain recognition with the receipt of cash. In resorting to the technique of income-deferral, however, the section in effect imposes different burdens on taxpayers who otherwise appear to be similarly situated. Thus, property sellers who desire or are willing to invest in their vendee's installment obligations are taxed at one "rate," while those who sell for cash because they prefer to invest the funds received in securities issued by other borrowers are taxed at another and higher rate, everything else being equal. But no reason in policy justifies discriminating between the two sets of investors (nor, perhaps, were the consequences of deferral fully appreciated by Congress when it adopted § 453). Discrimination could be avoided if the successive tax payments carried interest like other "loans"—that is, if the Treasury were treated as a lender entitled to interest on the delayed tax collections—and § 453 relief would then be limited in a way that appears to conform to its goal. The statute does not generally require interest, however, and therefore the installment method serves not merely to associate tax outflows with cash inflows, but also to reduce the installment seller's tax cost in absolute terms.[25]

---

[25]   Under § 453A, a taxpayer who receives installment obligations of more than $5 million from installment sales made in a single year must pay interest annually on the tax deferred by § 453.

14.03   The "Fair Market Value" Rule

The installment method works well mechanically where, as in a conventional real estate sale, the buyer's payment obligations are fixed and determined. If the overall purchase price, the term of the indebtedness, and the amount of the annual payments are all established in advance, calculation of the gain component in each installment is simple and straightforward. But suppose the sale is subject to contingencies so that the price or the payment period is uncertain. The owner of a patent, for example, might transfer his rights to a manufacturer in consideration of the latter's promise to pay a percentage of the sales of the patented article for a stated period of years, but with no fixed maximum amount; or the deal might call for payment of a percentage of sales until a stated total had been reached, but with no fixed limit of time. In *Burnet v. Logan*,[26] as will be seen, the transaction was limited neither in time nor amount—payments were to continue as long as the property, a mine, went on producing revenues for the buyer.

How, if at all, should the installment method be applied in these circumstances? More particularly, how should the seller's basis be apportioned when the total, or the term, or the size of the annual installments is uncertain? In *Logan,* the taxpayer owned stock in a corporation whose principal asset was a fractional interest in a large iron ore mine. In 1916 all of the company's stock was sold to another concern for $2,200,000 in cash—the taxpayer's share was $137,000— plus an agreement to pay the sellers a royalty of 60 cents for each ton of ore taken from the mine. From 1917 to 1920, the years at issue in the case, the taxpayer received payments averaging about $9,000 annually under the royalty contract. The question presented was whether, or to what extent, the annual royalty payments should be included in her gross income.

The government took the position that the 1916 stock sale was a "closed" transaction, a completed disposition of the taxpayer's shares. The royalty contract was found to have a value as of 1916 of $1,900,000 based on the estimated number of tons of ore in the mine and the estimated period (45 years) over which the ore was likely to be extracted. Thus, argued the government, the taxpayer's share of the contract's estimated value (about $120,000) plus her share of the initial cash payment represented the amount realized on the exchange, and the difference between this and her basis for the stock should have been recognized as gain (or loss) in 1916. The royalty contract would then have had a basis in the taxpayer's hands of $120,000, because that was the value assigned to it for the purpose of computing gain (or loss) on the sale of the stock. With an expected

---

[26]   283 U.S. 404 (1931).

payout period of 45 years, each annual royalty payment received under the contract should have been treated as recovery of capital to the extent of $2,667 ($120,000/45), with the balance being included in taxable income. Since royalty payments in the years 1917–20 averaged about $9,000, the included portion of each payment would thus, in the government's view, have been about $6,333.

Holding that nothing was includable in the taxpayer's income for the years in question, the Supreme Court rejected the government's effort at valuation and found that the royalty contract had no ascertainable fair market value when received in exchange for the taxpayer's stock. Although the 1916 transaction was a "sale", the amount realized was indeterminate and the transaction was therefore "not a closed one." This meant (a) that no gain or loss was recognized by the taxpayer in 1916 when the sale took place (the initial cash payment was less than her basis for the stock), and (b) that no income would be taxed to the seller until the annual royalty payments (plus the initial cash payment) exceeded her stock basis, an event which apparently would not occur for a good many years. To be sure, an interest in the same contract had been valued for estate tax purposes on the death of the taxpayer's mother, but in that context a value *had* to be established because the estate tax is imposed once and for all on the occasion of death. Income tax not collected currently can be collected in the future, however, and the Supreme Court therefore decided that it would be better to await the resolution of contingent events than to anticipate them by resort to "estimates, assumptions and speculation." *Logan* has much in common with the 1947 decision of the Tax Court in *Inaja Land* (2.01). Both cases involved uncertainty in the calculation of gain—in *Logan* uncertainty with respect to the amount realized, and in *Inaja Land* uncertainty with respect to the taxpayer's basis in the property sold—and in both cases the judicial response was to adopt a basis-first rule under which no gain would be taxed until all basis had been recovered.

The *Logan* decision thus established that an exchange of property for a contingent payment contract would be regarded as an "open" transaction if the contract claim lacked an ascertainable fair market value. The decision not to recognize gain (or loss) immediately could, perhaps, be defended on the ground that contingent payment obligations are simply too uncertain to value. It is less obvious, however, why the seller should be permitted to defer recognition until his *entire* property basis has been recovered. Suppose the sole stockholder of X Corporation, who has a basis of $250,000 in his shares, sells those shares for $100,000 cash plus 10% of the corporation's profits for each of the next five years. If the 10% payments go along at an annual rate of about $75,000, and if the open transaction treatment of *Logan* applies, the seller will offset his basis against the down payment plus each of the next two years' percentage payments, and thus will report no gain until the fourth year of the six-year contract. From the seller's standpoint this is an even better outcome than that afforded by § 453. While the installment sale election also avoids immediate recognition, it does require that the taxpayer's gain be taken into account ratably as cash installments are received. As noted, § 453 reflects a purpose to relate cash inflows to tax outflows—hence the ratable inclusion. By contrast, *Logan* emphasized the element of risk in the transaction, and responded by deferring gain until the taxpayer's cost had been returned in full.

Long dissatisfied with the *Logan* result, the Treasury in 1980 persuaded Congress to amend § 453 so as to permit contingent payment transactions to be treated as installment sales, with the Treasury itself being authorized to substitute ratable cost-recovery rules for the "front-end" procedure adopted by *Logan.* Thus, in a case in which the payout period is fixed but the maximum amount to be paid is uncertain, the Regulations[27] now require that basis recovery be spread out ratably—that is, equally over the stated payment period. In the example above, one-sixth of the stockowner's $250,000 basis, or $41,667, would be offset against each of the six payments to be received. Where the maximum amount is fixed but the term of payment is indefinite, annual gain recognized and basis recovery will be calculated under the usual § 453(c) formula, using the maximum price to determine the gross profit and the contract price. If, as in *Logan,* both maximum price and payout period are uncertain, the Regulations establish an arbitrary term—15 years—over which basis recovery will be spread. In all such cases, any unrecovered cost will be allowed to the seller as a loss when the contract comes to an end.

Although the § 453 contingent payment Regulations are in most respects an improvement over prior law, it did not take long for tax shelter promoters to devise schemes to exploit ways in which the Regulations diverge from economic accuracy. For an example, see the discussion of "The Offshore Partnership" in "Note: Tax Shelters and Economic Substance."

The above-described rules for applying the installment method to contingent payment transactions do not apply if the taxpayer elects out of § 453. Thus, a taxpayer nostalgic for the basis-first rule of *Logan* could opt out of § 453 in the hope that *Logan* would then apply. This is a risky maneuver, however, because the Regulations warn: "Only in those rare and extraordinary cases involving sales for a contingent payment obligation in which the fair market value of the obligation . . . cannot reasonably be ascertained will the taxpayer be

---

[27]   Reg. § 15a.453–1(c).

entitled to assert that the transaction is 'open.' "[28] If a taxpayer opts out of the installment method, but the fair market value of his contingent payment obligation can be determined (which will generally be the case, according to the Regulations), the taxpayer will not obtain the desired basis-first *Logan* treatment. Instead, the obligation will be valued and the taxpayer will be taxed in the year of sale on his entire gain—a result considerably worse than if the taxpayer had not elected out of the installment method.

15. Non-Recognition Transactions

The Code extends non-recognition to a variety of transactions which would otherwise result in taxable gain or allowable loss. Some of these have already been mentioned (see 2.04, 3.02, and 5.03, for example); others are discussed in the subsections that follow. As usual where gain or loss is required or permitted to go unrecognized, the basis of the property received or acquired is "adjusted" so as to insure that the taxpayer's gain or loss will be picked up later. The effect—as the reader well knows by now—is to postpone tax payment in the case of unrecognized gains, and to accelerate tax payment in the case of unrecognized losses. We need hardly add that taxpayers usually like non-recognition where gain is concerned (though, as in *Woodsam,* recognition and a step-up in basis may sometimes be preferred), but almost always dislike non-recognition when the effect is to defer a loss.

Non-recognition transactions can be divided, very roughly, into three categories:

(1) Continuity-of-investment cases, where non-recognition normally applies to gains and losses alike. Like-kind exchanges of real estate are a major example; corporate mergers (most emphatically not discussed herein; see Preface) are another. In these limited but important situations the Code evidently considers the new investment to be a mere continuation of the old, an alteration in form or identity but not in substance. Hence, the exchange of old property for new, though undeniably a realization, is deemed an inappropriate occasion for final reckoning of gain or loss.

(2) Hardship situations, where non-recognition is usually confined to gains. Leasehold terminations, involuntary conversions, sales of personal residences and various other transactions as to which for one reason or another taxation of gain is thought unusually onerous are to be found in this category. Non-recognition is supplied by way of "relief" in these circumstances and the taxpayer's gain is

---

[28]   Reg. § 15a.453–1(d)(2)(iii).

permitted to be deferred (or, in the case of personal residences, permanently excluded from the tax base).

(3) Tax-avoidance "schemes," where non-recognition applies to losses only. Wash sales—the sale and repurchase of the same security within a 30-day period—and sales of property between family members and other related parties belong to this group. The taxpayer is thought to be manipulating or exploiting the realization requirement by making a spurious disposition of his property, and the Code reacts by disallowing the loss that would otherwise result. In the case of wash sales, § 1091 requires that the security repurchased take the basis of the security sold, so that the loss deduction is postponed until a bona fide disposition is made. In the case of related-party sales under § 267, by contrast, the purchaser's basis for purposes of computing loss is his actual cost rather than the seller's basis. Hence, as with gifts (see 4.02), the loss deduction is permanently disallowed.[29]

The subsections that follow draw a representative from each of the first two categories named above. Like-kind exchanges are discussed in 15.01, and personal residence transactions at 15.02.

15.01   Like-Kind Exchanges

Section 1031(a) provides that gain or loss will not be recognized if real property held by the taxpayer for productive use in a trade or business or for investment is exchanged for other real property (to be held by the taxpayer for business use or for investment) of like kind. Prior to its amendment in 2017, the provision also applied to like-kind exchanges of tangible personal property, and even of some kinds of intangible property, but the 2017 legislation restricted the application of § 1031 to exchanges of real property. The 2017 narrowing was not of great practical significance, because the section's principal application had always been to real estate swaps. (Do such swaps really happen often enough for their tax treatment to be an important topic? Yes, for reasons explained in the "loose end" at the end of this Section.) Gain or loss usually would be considerable in such cases, and there is clearly a realization. At this point, however, the Code chooses to emphasize the continuous character of the taxpayer's economic behavior—still an investor and still in real estate—and treats the exchange as an inappropriate occasion for recognition. Section 1031 is limited to exchanges in kind; recognition cannot be avoided if property is initially sold for cash, even though

---

[29]   Not quite accurate: under § 267(d), if the purchaser later sells the property at a gain, such gain is recognized only to the extent it exceeds the loss disallowed to the original seller.

the proceeds of sale are promptly reinvested in other property of like kind.

The standard policy justifications for § 1031 leave something to be desired. If the idea is that gain should not be taxed as long as one remains invested in real estate, then it would seem that cash sales of real estate, followed by prompt reinvestment of the proceeds in replacement real estate, should also qualify for non-recognition. If the idea is that exchanges should be not be taxed because of problems of valuation (the taxpayer's amount realized on an exchange is the value of the property received, and that value may be open to debate) and liquidity (the taxpayer has received no cash with which to pay the tax), then it would seem that there is just as strong a case for non-recognition for exchanges generally, rather than just for like-kind real estate swaps. Moreover, there is good reason to doubt that valuation and liquidity problems loom large in most like-kind exchanges. As explained below (in the "loose end"), in a great many like-kind exchanges one of the parties would have been perfectly happy to purchase the other party's property for a stated amount of cash. When a party to a like-kind exchange could have received the value of his property in cash, it is difficult to conclude that that party is facing serious problems of either valuation or liquidity. Perhaps the best that can be said in defense of § 1031 is that *some* like-kind exchanges involve genuine valuation and liquidity challenges, and that all three rationales for non-recognition—continued investment in the same sort of property, valuation difficulties, and absence of liquidity—exist simultaneously only in the case of (some) like-kind exchanges.

How is it determined whether the property the taxpayer surrenders in an exchange and the property the taxpayer receives in return are of like kind? The Regulations are extremely lenient. In general, any parcel of real estate—whether ranch land in Montana or a skyscraper in Manhattan—is of like kind with respect to any other parcel of real estate.[30] The effect of the 2017 limitation of § 1031 to exchanges of real property, combined with the long-standing rule that all real property is of like kind with all other real property (apart from a few exceptions of extremely limited application), has been to virtually eliminate the like-kind requirement—despite the fact that the requirement still appears in § 1031(a). In any event, the treatment of all real property as of like kind has helped make § 1031 very popular with owners of business and investment real estate.

The aim of § 1031 is to postpone the recognition of gains and losses, not to forgive them completely. This objective is accomplished, as usual, by requiring that the basis of the old property be substituted

---

[30]   Reg. §§ 1.1031(a)–1(b) and (c).

for the new. If A owns an apartment building with a basis of $60 and a value of $100 which he exchanges for another apartment building of equal value, his basis for the acquired property is the same as that of the property surrendered, $60. The $40 of appreciation that was realized but not recognized on the exchange will be taxed if and when the acquired property is sold for cash or exchanged for dissimilar property. The effect is simply a "rollover" of his original property investment, which can be repeated as often as new opportunities for exchange arise.

Section 1031 does not prohibit the receipt of cash "boot" in connection with a like-kind exchange, and indeed it is likely that some cash is paid in most cases as a way of making up differences in value between the properties exchanged. Postponement is still permitted as to the like-kind element, but gains (though not losses) are recognized to the extent of the cash. If A in the illustration above exchanges his old building worth $100 for a new apartment building worth only $90, and also receives $10 in cash, § 1031 still applies to the exchange but now A recognizes a gain of $10. Under § 1031(d), his basis for the new building is $60: his old basis, $60, plus recognized gain, $10, minus cash received, $10. Thus the unrecognized balance of A's original property appreciation, $30, remains as potential gain to be taxed when the new building is finally disposed of. In effect, A's "investment" has been increased from $60 to $70 because $10 was taxed on the exchange; but $10 is now represented by cash (which necessarily has a "basis" equal to its face amount), while $60 is represented by the new apartment building.

Suppose, in the last example, that A's basis for his original building had been greater than its current market value, say $120. As losses are not recognized under § 1031 (losses are deferred *despite* the receipt of money), the $10 cash would be applied to reduce A's basis for the new building to $110. He would then still have a loss potential of $20 ($90 minus $110), which is equal to the decline in value of the old building.

If property is exchanged subject to a mortgage, § 1031(b) treats the mortgage as money, and gain is recognized to the transferor to the extent thereof. Thus, suppose A purchased the original apartment building for $40 cash, subject to a $20 nonrecourse mortgage. His basis under the *Crane* rule would then be $60. Suppose that the building appreciates in value to $100. If A now exchanges the old building for a new unmortgaged property worth $80 he realizes $100—the value of the new property, $80, plus the $20 mortgage assumed by the transferee. Since the mortgage assumption is treated as money, A would recognize a gain of $20 on the exchange. His basis for the new property would be $60—*i.e.*, basis in the old building, $60, plus the gain recognized, $20, less the "money" received, $20—which properly leaves $20 of appreciation still to be recognized when the new building is sold. While the arithmetic is correct, it is not entirely clear why § 1031 requires recognition of gain in these circumstances. A has withdrawn no cash at any stage, and as the object of the provision is to defer recognition until the original property is converted to money or other dissimilar assets, it would seem consistent for A to recognize no gain on the mortgage transfer and to take the new property at a basis of $40. The section takes a different course, however, and since mortgages are likely to be present in most real estate transactions, the potential for some gain recognition is also likely to be present.

It does not follow, however, that a taxpayer transferring mortgaged property in a like-kind exchange must always recognize some gain. Consideration received in the form of debt relief can be offset by consideration given in the form of either (i) an assumption of a mortgage on the property received in the exchange (or taking the new property subject to an unassumed mortgage), or (ii) cash. To avoid gain recognition, then, a taxpayer receiving boot in the form of debt relief need only make sure that the combination of new debt taken on and cash given equals or exceeds the amount of the debt relief.

Non-recognition may, of course, be undesirable from the taxpayer's standpoint. As noted, losses are not recognized in a like-kind exchange. Thus, taxpayers owning real estate that has declined in value would normally prefer to dispose of their property for cash, recognize their losses, and then reinvest the proceeds in new property at a basis equal to its actual cost. Despite prompt or even simultaneous reinvestment, the intervening cash "step" is apparently enough to avoid the application of § 1031. The Treasury accepts (and will insist where gain has been realized) that a cash sale voids the jurisdictional requirement of the section.

Nevertheless, the government has sought to deny loss recognition in one related context—so-called sale-and-leaseback transactions—despite the existence of an apparent sale for cash. In the leading case, *Jordan Marsh Co. v. Commissioner*,[31] the taxpayer, owner of a large department store, conveyed its real estate—land and building—to certain investors for $2,300,000 in cash, and then entered into a 30-year lease of the same property with the vendees. Claiming that the transaction was an outright sale, the taxpayer sought to deduct as a loss the difference between its adjusted basis for the property and the cash received. The Commissioner disallowed the deduction on the ground that the transaction represented an exchange of like property—a fee interest for a long-term lease—plus

---

[31]   269 F.2d 453 (2d Cir. 1959).

cash to boot. The Regulations under § 1031 provided (and the taxpayer apparently accepted) that a leasehold of 30 years or more was the equivalent of a fee interest. Although plainly contemplating the exchange of a fee in Blackacre for a 30-year leasehold in Whiteacre, the Regulations were not expressly limited to cases involving different properties, and the government could therefore argue that the present transaction also constituted a like-kind exchange.

The court held for the taxpayer and allowed the loss. The price paid for the property by the vendees concededly represented its full fair market value. Moreover, the rentals for which the taxpayer was obligated under the lease were "full and normal," so that the leasehold had no "capital value"—no value in excess of the present value of the rents payable—in the taxpayer's hands. The taxpayer thus received nothing of value apart from the cash, and hence there was nothing to which § 1031 could actually apply. The court concluded that the transaction must therefore be characterized as a "sale" rather than a tax-free "exchange." At all events, the court noted, the "strained" construction given by the government to the word "exchange"—a transfer of property in return for a lesser interest in the *same* property—was unlikely to have been intended by Congress when it adopted § 1031.

But should the government have relied on § 1031 in the first place? Apart from tax consequences, most businesses probably regard leasebacks as an alternative to mortgage financing, a transaction which does not result in the realization of gain or loss. Why, after all, should a company which already owns an asset and wants to continue to use it sell that asset and lease it back? The only possible answer is: to raise capital *without* surrendering the property. In that respect leasebacks and mortgage loans are quite alike: like a borrower, the seller-lessee receives cash up-front and incurs an obligation to make payments of cash in future years; and like a borrower, it remains in possession of the property for an extended period of time. Changes in the value of the property—the ups and downs of the real estate market—are largely borne by the lessee, so that its prior interest in the property cannot really be said to have been terminated, any more than can the interest of a mortgagor.

But, on the other hand, the resemblance to a mortgage loan is not a perfect one. The lease does not go on forever, and if the property can be expected to have some residual value when the lease finally terminates, then that residual value will belong to the buyer-lessor. While a borrower recovers clear title to its property once the loan has been fully amortized, a seller-lessee relinquishes the property to the buyer and has nothing left on termination of the leasehold except an opportunity to renegotiate for an extension of the lease. Undeniably, the reversionary interest—the value of the property when the lease expires—has been transferred by the former owner and now belongs to the buyer-lessor.

Just which of these factors—continued possession of the property or transfer of the reversionary interest—should be regarded as determinative if the issue is framed in terms of "sale or loan" is obviously open to debate. At the least, however, it seems less artificial, less "strained," to put the question in that way than to search for a possible application of § 1031.

The property in *Jordan Marsh* had declined in value. Eager to recognize the loss, the taxpayer argued, successfully, that the leaseback was a "sale," not a like-kind exchange. But suppose the property had appreciated in value, so that "sale" characterization would result in recognition of a taxable gain. Properly advised, the taxpayer would then seek to avoid or minimize its taxable gain by adopting a different transactional structure, to wit, a loan plus a sale of the reverter. Cast in that form, the loan would be non-taxable and only the gain allocable to the sale of the reverter would be subject to tax.

It thus appears that choice of legal structure controls the tax consequences. And that is what we call "tax planning."

A loose end. Suppose F (for farmer) owns a 300-acre cornfield. It used to be way out in the country, but now it is on the edge of an expanding metropolis and its highest and best use is no longer growing corn. F's basis is $100,000. D (for developer) wants to acquire F's property for the development of a residential subdivision. D offers F $1 million. F says no. Why? Because (i) F loves growing corn and (ii) F absolutely refuses to pay tax on $900,000 of land appreciation. As it happens, there are several farms farther out (in what is still the country), the highest and best use of which is still growing corn. For $1 million, one could buy a 1000-acre farm of this sort, every bit as good (as farmland) on a per-acre basis as F's current farm. F tells D that he will swap his cornfield for one or another of these 1000-acre farms if D can persuade any of the owners to sell. Happily, Owner S (i) hates growing corn and (ii) has a high basis for his cornfield.[32] D negotiates with S and finally buys S's cornfield for $1 million. F and D then exchange cornfields. In the end, each party gets what he wants. F gets S's cornfield, D gets F's cornfield, and S gets $1 million.

---

[32]   Both of these facts might be explained by S having recently inherited the farm.

Although the parties have shoehorned this transaction into the form of a like-kind exchange between F and D, one might argue—and once upon a time the Commissioner did argue—that in substance F had engaged in a cash sale followed by a reinvestment, and thus did not qualify for non-recognition under § 1031. In the Commissioner's (former) view, D's transitory ownership of S's property, the purpose of which was merely to achieve a tax-free exchange with F, should be disregarded. In substance (said the Commissioner), D bought F's cornfield directly from F for $1 million cash—following which F used those funds to buy the 1000-acre property from S. F should therefore recognize a $900,000 taxable gain.

While the Commissioner's argument had a certain force, it is not clear why the spin of the triangle had to stop at the Commissioner's number. It is no less plausible to view the transaction as one in which F and S swapped cornfields, one for the other, with S then "independently" selling F's former property to D for $1 million cash. Since (in this version) F would have had no formal connection with the cash transaction between D and S, F's claim to the favorable application of § 1031 would be hard to challenge. And in terms of end result, there is no more reason to characterize the transaction in one way than in the other.

The courts uniformly held for F in these (and like) circumstances, presumably on the ground that F never sought and never received a cash payment from D, and hence satisfied the letter of the like-kind exchange provision.[33] The IRS now concedes that various sorts of three-cornered transactions can qualify as § 1031 exchanges. As a matter of policy, it is questionable whether transactions such as F's should qualify for non-recognition. In our hypothetical, D was willing and able to pay F $1 million cash for F's farm. In fact, from D's point of view that is exactly what happened—D ended up with $1 million less cash and with ownership of F's farm. We know that F's amount realized is $1 million (because D paid $1 million for S's farm and then immediately transferred it to F), and we know that F could have had $1 million cash. Thus, there is no valuation problem, and any liquidity problem F might have was self-inflicted (by turning his back on $1 million cash). In short, the pro-§ 1031 arguments based on valuation and liquidity concerns do not support extending non-recognition to three-cornered exchanges. Nevertheless, it is well-settled that § 1031 applies in F's situation, and in similar situations.

The applicability of § 1031 in three-party settings is what makes the provision of considerable practical importance, rather than a mere curiosity. Simple two-party like-kind exchanges are few; only

---

[33] E.g., *Alderson v. Commissioner*, 317 F.2d 790 (9th Cir. 1963).

rarely do two property owners simultaneously decide that the other's grass is greener. But the availability of non-recognition for three-party transactions means that a taxpayer wanting to sell real estate for cash and reinvest the proceeds in other real estate can achieve the desired results, without recognition of gain, by structuring his transactions as a like-kind exchange rather than as a sale-reinvestment.

Suppose a developer and a landowner would like to do a three-cornered like-kind exchange, but (i) the developer is eager to start building on the landowner's property, and (ii) they are having difficulty locating suitable replacement property for the developer to purchase and transfer to the landowner. If the landowner transfers the land to the developer now, in exchange for the developer's promise to transfer suitable replacement property at a later date (which promise the developer eventually fulfills), does this delayed exchange qualify the landowner for non-recognition under § 1031? In *Starker v. United States*,[34] the Ninth Circuit ruled that § 1031 applied to delayed exchanges. Ultimately, Congress approved *Starker*, subject to certain time limitations. Under § 1031(a)(3), a "deferred exchange" will qualify for non-recognition if the replacement property (S's farm, in the earlier hypothetical) is identified within 45 days of the date on which F transfers his own property (to D), and if the replacement property is received by F within 180 days after F's transfer of his own property.

15.02   Sale of a Personal Residence

Apart from the special relief provision described below, the tax treatment of personal residence transactions is simple and straightforward (as well as illogical). Thus, gain from the sale of a residence is includable in the seller's income (as capital gain) while losses are treated as "personal" and are disallowed. A taxpayer who buys a house for $500,000 and later sells it for $700,000 has $200,000 of taxable gain. If the house were sold for $300,000, the taxpayer's apparent loss would be $200,000, but since a personal residence is neither business nor investment property under § 165(c), the loss would be non-deductible. As shown at 6.07, there are occasional disputes about whether residential property is held for personal use or for investment, but where the seller himself has occupied the residence up to or close to the date of sale the issue will almost always be resolved in favor of "personal."

What may be questioned somewhat more fundamentally[35] is whether the Code calculates gain correctly in the case of residence

---

[34]   602 F.2d 1341 (9th Cir. 1979).

[35]   Epstein, *The Consumption and Loss of Personal Property Under the Internal Revenue Code*, 23 Stan. L. Rev. 454 (1971).

transactions, and whether, by the same token, it is proper to disallow *all* losses from sales of residences on the ground that they are "personal." To see what sort of criticism can be offered, it will be useful to recapitulate—briefly and by illustration—some of what was said earlier (see 1.03 and 7.04) about imputed rents and the depreciation allowance. Suppose a taxpayer pays $500,000 for a personal residence which has an estimated useful life of 25 years. As noted previously, the imputed rental value of the property—make it 12% annually, or $60,000—is excluded from the homeowner's gross income by long-standing administrative rule. At the same time, however, the taxpayer is permitted to take no depreciation on the house because a personal residence does not qualify under § 167 as property used in business or held for the production of income. The depreciation deduction would otherwise be $20,000 a year ($500,000/25) if computed on the straight-line method. The law thus affords the taxpayer a *net* exclusion for imputed rent of $40,000—gross imputed rent of $60,000 less disallowed depreciation of $20,000—and this might be taken as the intended limit of the homeowner's tax preference.

If annual depreciation of $20,000 *were* allowed on the taxpayer's residence, his basis for the purpose of computing gain or loss on sale would of course be adjusted—that is, reduced—by an equivalent amount under § 1016(a)(2). The adjustment, as has been seen, is necessary in order to prevent the taxpayer from receiving two tax allowances for the same expenditure. Thus, the taxpayer's basis at the end of five years would be reduced to $400,000 *if* annual depreciation of $20,000 had been allowed to him over the five-year period. As depreciation is not allowed, however, § 1016(a)(2) does not apply. Hence no adjustment is made to the taxpayer's basis, which remains at $500,000 throughout the period of his ownership. Suppose, then, that the taxpayer sells the house at the end of the fifth year for an amount exactly equal to his original purchase price—that is, $500,000. The property (which is now five years older than when he bought it) has appreciated in value over the period in question, in the sense that $100,000 of decline in value due to wear-and-tear has been offset by $100,000 of increase in value due to market factors. From one perspective, the taxpayer has made a gain of $100,000— the difference between the sale price of $500,000 and the anticipated value of the residence of $400,000. But as his basis is also $500,000, the taxpayer realizes no *taxable* gain even if he gives up homeownership entirely at this point and invests the sale proceeds in other types of assets.

It turns out that a basis adjustment would have been appropriate after all. Although the Code disallows annual depreciation *during* the five-year term, by failing at the same time to reduce the basis of the property to $400,000 it gives the taxpayer a lump-sum basis allowance when the property is sold exactly equal to the depreciation disallowed. This omission results (presumably) from a belief that basis adjustment is solely a corollary to the *allowance* of depreciation deductions. In fact, however, the taxpayer's basis should also be adjusted as a corollary to the *disallowance* of depreciation. Putting the matter another way, consistency of treatment requires that the disallowance of annual depreciation on a personal residence also be reflected in an annual basis reduction, unless for some reason it is intended to reverse the disallowance when the residence is disposed of.

Very much the same sort of comment can be made about losses. Thus, suppose that the taxpayer sells the property for only $300,000 at the end of five years. Although market forces have deprived the taxpayer of $100,000 (again, the difference between the anticipated value of $400,000 and the amount realized of $300,000), the entire loss is disallowed as "personal." Yet, if the purpose of the Code is merely to prevent the taxpayer from deducting the cost of earning tax-free income—which the disallowance of annual depreciation would suggest—the correct approach would be to reduce the basis of the property to $400,000, but then to permit the difference between that figure and the amount realized to be recognized as a capital loss. In brief, the disallowance of "true" losses means that the prior exclusion of imputed rents is to that extent rescinded. By contrast, the non-recognition of "true" gains means that the prior exclusion is to that extent enlarged.

Having foisted these theoretical considerations on the reader, we must now disclose that that § 121 virtually eliminates the taxation of residence transactions by permitting a home seller to exclude up to $250,000 of gain on the sale of a principal residence ($500,000 in the case of a couple filing a joint return), provided that the residence has been owned and occupied by the seller for at least 2 of the preceding 5 years. The $250,000 (or $500,000) exclusion is available for each and every residence sale the taxpayer makes, no matter what the taxpayer's age at the date of sale and no matter how many homes he happens to have bought and sold over the years.

Although it is fair to classify § 121 as a non-recognition provision, it differs from typical non-recognition provisions by providing for permanent exclusion of the gain to which it applies, rather than mere deferral. Exclusion under § 121 does not depend on the taxpayer buying a replacement home. If a taxpayer sells a home at a gain, she may exclude the gain even if she thereafter becomes a renter rather than the owner of another home. In that case, it is obvious that the exclusion is permanent, because there is no replacement property available for deferring the gain. If a taxpayer excluding gain under § 121 does buy a new home, the exclusion is also permanent. The taxpayer's basis in the new home is simply the cost of that new home; the taxpayer is not required to reduce the basis of the new home by the amount of the gain excluded on the sale of the old home.

In periods when home prices are steadily rising, § 121 creates a tax incentive to sell one's home and purchase a similar replacement home in order to obtain a tax-free step-up in the basis of one's residence. Suppose an unmarried taxpayer owns a house with a basis of $300,000 and a current value of $550,000. Her best guess is that the house will continue to appreciate. If she continues to own and live in that home, any additional appreciation will be in excess of the $250,000 ceiling on the exclusion, and thus will be subject to tax when she eventually sells. But if she sells the house now for $550,000 and buys a nearby replacement home for the same price, her basis in the new home will be $550,000 and she will not be taxed on any gain on the sale of the new home unless she sells it for more than $800,000.[36] Of course, this tax benefit comes at a high price in terms of realtor's fees, moving expenses, and the heartbreak of leaving a beloved home (with pencil marks of children's heights on the kitchen doorframe). One imagines that the non-tax costs are high enough that taxpayers seldom pursue this strategy, even in periods of sharply rising home prices.

Section 121 suggests another interesting tax strategy—and this one doesn't even require a hot real estate market. If one is good with tools and doesn't mind living with sawdust, one can buy a fixer-upper, live in it (for at least two years) while fixing it up, and then sell it. Much or all of the gain on sale will be due to the homeowner's "sweat equity" rather than to market changes in the price of housing, and Congress certainly did not design § 121 for the purpose of excluding labor income from the tax base. Nevertheless, the exclusion clearly applies in this situation. If he could figure out a way to deal with the cash flow problem (of getting paid for his labor only once every two-plus years), a dedicated home renovator could legitimately avoid income tax on all his labor income for his entire career.

The current version of § 121 was enacted in 1997. It replaced old § 1034, which provided for deferral rather than permanent exclusion. Section 1034 allowed taxpayers to defer gain recognition on the sale of a residence if, within a two-year period, an amount at least equal

---

[36] There is another potential tax benefit to this "home churning" strategy, relating to the home mortgage interest deduction (7.04). If she wanted to take out a home equity loan on her old house, the taxpayer could not deduct any of the interest on the loan, because it would not be acquisition indebtedness. If, however, she borrows money to buy the new home, the loan will qualify as acquisition indebtedness, and all the interest will be deductible (even if she borrows the entire $550,000 purchase price).

to the proceeds of sale was reinvested in a new residence. In order to preserve the taxable gain potential, the basis of the old residence was carried over to the new. Most taxpayers probably prefer new § 121 to old § 1034, both because the new section simplifies recordkeeping for basis (by making the bases of a taxpayer's former homes irrelevant to the basis of the taxpayer's current residence), and because the new section provides for permanent exclusion rather than deferral. It is not the case, however, that taxpayers always fare better under the new provision than they would have fared under the old. Consider a married couple selling for $1,100,000 a house with a basis of $400,000, and buying a new home costing $1,100,000 (or more). Under § 1034, they could have deferred tax on all their gain; in fact, the old provision had no ceiling on the amount of gain that could be deferred, as long as the new home cost at least as much as the sales price of the old home. Under § 121, however, they must pay tax on $200,000 of their gain. We are not suggesting that any tears should be shed for our imaginary couple, but the general point—that one should not assume that a permanent exclusion provision is more taxpayer-favorable than a deferral provision, without knowing the details of the two provisions—is worth noting.

Recognition of Gains and Losses— Questions and Answers

Question 1: Brangwen owns Glenview, investment property, with a value of $310,000 and a basis of $300,000, subject to a mortgage of $60,000. Rupert owns Harborside, also investment property, with a value of $180,000 and a basis of $140,000. Brangwen and Rupert exchange their properties and Rupert pays Brangwen $70,000 cash (*i.e.*, $250,000, value of Brangwen's property net of the mortgage, minus $180,000, value of Rupert's property, equals $70,000).

Assuming Glenview and Harborside are properties of "like kind" within the meaning of § 1031(a), what are the tax consequences of the exchange to both parties?

Answer: Brangwen realizes a gain of $10,000—$310,000, amount realized, minus her basis of $300,000. Since she received cash "boot" of $70,000 and debt-relief "boot" of $60,000, the $10,000 gain is recognized under § 1031(b). Brangwen's basis for Harborside under § 1031(d) is $180,000: that is, (i) $300,000, her basis for Glenview, reduced by (ii) the sum of $70,000, the cash paid by Rupert, and $60,000, the mortgage Rupert assumed, increased by (iii) $10,000, the gain recognized by Brangwen, equals $180,000. If Brangwen promptly sold Harborside for $180,000 cash, she would recognize no further gain. That is clearly the right result, because all of the gain realized by Brangwen, $10,000, was recognized on the exchange with Rupert.

Rupert realizes a gain of $40,000—$180,000, amount realized, minus his basis of $140,000. (Although Rupert received property with a net-of-mortgage value of $250,000, he received $70,000 of that value in exchange for $70,000 cash; thus, his amount realized with respect to Harborside is only $180,000.) Having received like-kind property only, he recognizes no gain under § 1031(a). His basis for Glenview is $270,000: that is, (i) $140,000, his basis for Harborside, increased by (ii) $70,000, the cash he paid to Brangwen, plus $60,000, the mortgage he assumed, equals $270,000. If Rupert promptly sold Glenview, he would recognize $40,000 of gain ($310,000, amount realized, minus his $270,000 basis). That is clearly the right result, because Harborside had appreciated by $40,000 in Rupert's hands and he recognized no gain on the exchange with Brangwen.

Question 2: Joachim bought General Motors stock on margin some years ago for $75,000, investing $40,000 of his own money and borrowing $35,000 from his broker. At a time when the stock was worth $160,000, Joachim borrowed another $50,000 from his broker and then gave the stock to his daughter, Clavdia, subject to both the initial and the later indebtedness. (The gift did not generate any gift tax liability.) Clavdia subsequently sold the stock for $140,000 and paid off all the debt. What are the tax consequences of these events to Joachim and Clavdia?

Answer: As to Joachim, his basis for the GM stock is $75,000, the $40,000 he paid with his own money plus the $35,000 borrowed from the broker. As the *Woodsam* case shows, the later $50,000 borrowing does not add to Joachim's basis (even if the loan was non-recourse). The gift to Clavdia is treated as a realization under the *Diedrich* case in the amount of the indebtedness taken over by Clavdia, $35,000 plus $50,000, or $85,000. Since the "amount realized" by Joachim, $85,000, exceeds his basis of $75,000, Joachim recognizes a gain of $10,000 on the transfer.

As to Clavdia, her basis for the GM stock is the *greater* of her cost or the donor's basis. Having taken the stock subject to an indebtedness of $85,000, which exceeds Joachim's basis of $75,000, Clavdia has a basis of $85,000. When Clavdia sells the stock for $140,000, she recognizes a gain of $55,000—$140,000, amount realized, minus her basis of $85,000.

Together, father and daughter recognize a total gain of $65,000. This is clearly the right result. Joachim put $40,000 of his own money into the GM investment. He took out $50,000, the amount of his later borrowing, and hence netted $10,000 cash. Clavdia sold the stock for $140,000 but had to pay back $85,000, and hence she netted $55,000 cash. Since the stock was bought for $75,000 and finally sold for $140,000, the net to father and daughter was $65,000 in total.

Question 3: Jock Ewing owned oil land with a basis of zero and a fair market value of $10,000,000. Jock sold the land to his adult son J.R. for no down payment, and J.R.'s promissory note (not secured by the land) for $10,000,000. No principal payments were due on the note until a single "balloon" payment of $10,000,000 due ten years from the date of sale. Twelve months after the sale from Jock to J.R., J.R. sold the land to Cliff Barnes (not a relative of Jock and J.R.) for $11,000,000 cash. What are the tax consequences of these events to Jock and J.R.? *Hint:* Take a look at § 453(e).

Answer: But for § 453(e), Jock and J.R. would be able to use their intra-family installment sale to sell the land outside the family without either family member being required to recognize the bulk of the family's gain. Under the usual operation of § 453, Jock's gain would be deferred until the much later year in which he received the balloon payment from J.R. As for J.R., the installment note would be reflected in his basis (as acquisition indebtedness), so he would realize and recognize a gain of only $1,000,000 on his sale to Barnes. These highly-favorable results would follow from the inconsistent treatment of the $10,000,000 note—as giving rise to immediate basis for J.R., despite not yet having given rise to gain recognition for Jock. Unfortunately for Jock, § 453(e) applies when there is an installment sale between related parties and the related purchaser resells the property within two years of the date of the first sale. Under § 453(e), J.R.'s amount realized on his sale to Barnes is treated as an installment payment from J.R. to Jock, up to the amount due on the note. Thus, J.R.'s sale to Barnes results in a $10,000,000 deemed payment to Jock, triggering recognition of $10,000,000 of gain by Jock under § 453.

Question 4: A wise commentator has written:

> Code § 469 denies to "passive investors" in depreciable real estate a deduction for artificial losses resulting from the combination of deductible interest and overstated depreciation. It is chiefly aimed at preventing such artificial losses from offsetting salaries, fees and other personal service income. It does not (speaking generally) prevent an equivalent tax benefit from being realized by taxpayers who can finance the investment by drawing on their own, rather than borrowed, resources.

A favorite uncle of yours has read the quoted statement but admits he really doesn't understand it. Aware that you are taking an excellent tax course, he asks you for help. Using the "tax shelter" illustration on p. 356, explain the wise man's observations to your uncle.

Answer: In the example on p. 356, the taxpayer-mortgagor would (in the absence of § 469) be able to defer $190 of otherwise taxable personal service income from years 1, 2 and 3 to years 4 and 5. The investment itself is of course pointless in economic terms ($1,000 in, $1,000 out) apart from the shelter effect. As shown, § 469 obliterates the shelter by "suspending" the taxpayer's artificial losses in years 1–3 and allowing those losses to be deducted only when equally artificial income materializes in the two later years.

But suppose the taxpayer finances the investment by using his own resources rather than borrowing from a bank-lender. To do that the taxpayer sells an investment that he now owns. That investment (let's conveniently suppose) is a five-year mortgage loan, one that generates taxable interest income to the taxpayer-investor in exactly the same amounts as the interest paid to the bank by the shelter-buyer at p. 356; that is, $320, $260, $210, $140 and $70 in years 1–5, respectively. Keeping everything on a par, the taxpayer realizes $4,000 from the sale of his present investment (the mortgage), invests the $4,000 in a "building," and rents the property to a tenant for five years at the same rental of $1,000 a year. Results under the Code:

Year:	1	2	3	4	5		Total
Net Rents	$1,000	1,000	1,000	1,000	1,000	=	$5,000
Depreciation	800	800	800	800	800	=	4,000
Taxable income	$ 200	200	200	200	200	=	$1,000

But of course the taxpayer's "true" income—by which we mean his economic benefit from year to year—can really be no different from the interest paid to the bank in the main-text illustration, *i.e.*, $320, $260, $210, $140 and $70. The taxpayer has switched from a financial asset (the mortgage) to a tangible asset (the "building"), but, as already much discussed, the rate of cost-recovery—whether we call it amortization (of a mortgage loan) or depreciation (of a building)—should also be the same; that is, $680, $740, $790, $860 and $930 in years 1–5, respectively. In effect, the taxpayer has simply taken the bank's place as financier.

So, is the taxpayer happy? He is. In fact, just as happy in his own quiet, unassuming way as the shelter-buyer was before the enactment of § 469, except that in *this* taxpayer's case it is investment income that is being deferred rather than personal service income. Thus—

Year:	1	2	3	4	5		Total
Economic income	$320	260	210	140	70	=	$1,000
Taxable income	200	200	200	200	200	=	$1,000
(Deferred income)/ "Phantom income"	($120)	(60)	(10)	60	130	=	–0–

Conclusion: § 469 prevents taxpayers from combining depreciation with interest deductions to create artificial losses that can otherwise be used to shelter income from unrelated sources. It does not, however, in any way restrict the "internal sheltering" just illustrated, because it does not reduce the overstated depreciation allowance that is the source of the deferral. The effect is to restrict the "sheltering" to investors who are self-financed. The same benefit is denied to those who would borrow to make the investment—and who, having personal service income only, would then offset their artificial losses against salaries and fees.

If still interested, your uncle can find discussion of the same point in connection with municipal bond interest at p. 174.

Question 5: Gordon owns 1,000 shares of stock of Greed, Inc. (a publicly traded corporation), in which he has a basis of $5 million. Sadly, the shares are currently trading at only $1 million. Gordon thinks Greed stock is poised for a rebound, so he wants to continue the economic substance of ownership. He would also, however, very much like to be able to claim a $4 million capital loss deduction on the stock.

(a) What will be the tax result if Gordon exchanges his Greed shares for an equal number of identical Greed shares owned by another investor?

(b) What will be the tax result if, instead of an exchange, Gordon sells his Greed shares for $1 million and a week later purchases an equal number of identical shares for $1.1 million (the Greed stock having appreciated 10% during the week)?

(c) Suppose the numbers are reversed—Gordon's basis in the stock is $1 million and the stock's current value is $5 million. Gordon wants the economic substance of continued ownership, but he also wants to recognize (and thus pay tax on) his $4 million gain this year, in advance of an expected increase in the long-term capital gains tax rate next year. Could Gordon sell his shares this week, repurchase identical shares next week, and achieve his tax goals (gain recognition at this year's lower capital gains rate and a stepped-up $5 million basis in the replacement stock)?

Answer: (a) This will not work. According to Reg. § 1.1001–1(a) (first sentence), an exchange constitutes a realization event only if the properties exchanged "differ materially either in kind or in extent." Because an exchange of identical assets does not qualify as a realization event, Gordon will not be able to deduct his $4 million loss.

(b) The Regulation cited above applies only to exchanges. A sale for cash qualifies as a realization event, even if the taxpayer later purchases identical replacement property. However, § 1091 provides for nonrecognition by a taxpayer who sells property at a loss and within a sixty-one day period centered on the day of sale acquires "substantially identical" replacement property. This provision would apply to deny Gordon a deduction for his $4 million realized loss. Under § 1091(d), Gordon's basis in the replacement stock will be $1.1 million (his basis in the old stock, increased by the $100,000 excess of the cost of the replacement property over the sale price of the original property). Thus, his loss deduction is deferred rather than permanently disallowed.

(c) The sale is a realization event, and the nonrecognition rules of § 1091 apply to losses but not to gains. Therefore, we think Gordon's plan should achieve the desired result of triggering tax at this year's lower capital gains rate. There may be some chance, however, that the IRS could claim that the loss was disallowed under the sham transaction doctrine or the step transaction doctrine.

Question 6: Homer and Marge, a married couple, bought and moved into their new house (the first home either had ever owned) on January 1 of the current year, having paid $500,000 for the house. They thought they would live in the house for decades, but a few months later Homer received a too-good-to-turn-down employment offer from a nuclear power plant in a distant city. He accepted the offer and they put their house on the market. Exactly eight months after they bought and moved into the house, they sold the house and moved out. Because the Springfield residential real estate market was (for some strange reason) dramatically overheated, they were able to sell the house for $620,000. How much gain, if any, must they recognize on the sale?

Answer: Section 121(a) ordinarily requires that taxpayers have owned and lived in a residence for at least two years, in order to qualify to exclude gain on the sale of the residence. However, § 121(c) waives the two-year ownership and use requirement if the sale is "by reason of a change in employment" (among other acceptable reasons). In that case, § 121(c)(1) provides that the $500,000 ceiling on excludable gain must be reduced. The reduced ceiling amount is $500,000, multiplied by the ratio of eight months to two years. Thus the ceiling is $500,000 x (1/3) = $166,667. Because their gain is below even the reduced ceiling, it is all excluded from their gross income.

Part F

CAPITAL GAINS AND LOSSES

16. Introduction

16.01   Some History; Repeal and Reinstatement

At the moment, the top marginal tax rate on most income ("ordinary" income, in the jargon of the Code) is 37%, but the top rate on most long-term capital gains is only 20%. A long-term capital gain is gain on the sale or exchange of a "capital asset" which the taxpayer has held for more than one year. Capital assets are defined by § 1221 in a manner that covers most assets held for investment; shares of stock and land held for appreciation are classic examples. Apart from a few years following the enactment of the Tax Reform Act of 1986, our law has consistently awarded a "preference" to long-term capital gains, either by exempting a portion of such gains from tax or by taxing such gains at a bargain rate. In 1986, Congress reduced the top marginal rate for individual taxpayers to 28%, and simply repealed the preferential treatment of capital gains. The effect of the latter step was to require capital gains to be included in gross income in full and to tax such gains at the same top rate—28%—as income from ordinary sources. The element of "preference" thus disappeared entirely. Congressional tax-writers were of course aware that the preponderance of capital gains goes to high-bracket taxpayers; with the top individual rate cut nearly in half, it was felt that the "need" (as the Senate Committee put it) to maintain a reduced rate for capital gains no longer existed and, hence, that ordinary income and capital gains could be taxed alike.

Despite repeal of the capital gain preference, Congress kept in place all of the complex definitional and computational paraphernalia described in the Sections following, so that taxpayers were still required to distinguish *capital* gains and losses from *ordinary* gains and losses. A major reason for retaining (instead of wiping out) the whole burdensome statutory scheme was that Congress thought it important to protect the revenues by restricting the deductibility of capital *losses*. As noted much earlier (5.01, 5.05), the realization—and hence the timing—of investment gains and losses is largely voluntary: a taxpayer can sell his property this year, next year, or never. Because only *realized* gains are subject to tax, a permission to offset investment losses against ordinary income would prompt taxpayers to realize their losses immediately while postponing the realization of their gains, with possibly damaging consequences to the fisc. Thus, a taxpayer owning stock X which has appreciated in value by $100,000 and stock Y which has declined in value by $100,000 (and whose net worth is therefore unchanged) might well elect to sell Y but retain X and use his Y loss to eliminate tax on his salary or business income. To prevent this outcome, the 1986 Act continued the prior law restriction contained in Code § 1211. In effect, realized capital losses can be offset only against realized capital gains (plus $3,000 of ordinary income). The Y loss thus produces a significant tax benefit for the taxpayer only if and when he realizes the X gain (or of course any other capital gain).

The equalization of ordinary income and long-term capital gain rates under the 1986 Act, and the elimination of the capital gain preference, did not last very long. The current top rate on most long-term capital gains (20%) is slightly more than half the top marginal rate on ordinary income (37%). Under Code § 1(h) the tax rate on net capital gain (*i.e.*, the excess of net long-term gain over net short-term loss) depends on the amount of the taxpayer's taxable income. To the extent a taxpayer's net capital gain, when combined with the taxpayer's other taxable income, would not result in taxable income of more than $77,200 (joint return), $51,700 (head of household), or $38,600 (single taxpayer), the gain is not taxed. To the extent a taxpayers' net capital gain would result in taxable income higher than the relevant above amount, but lower than $479,000 (joint return), $452,400 (head of household), or $425,000 (single), the gain is taxed at 15%. Any remaining gain is taxed at 20%.[1] Suppose, for example, an unmarried taxpayer has $800,000 of taxable income, consisting of $600,000 of ordinary income and $200,000 of net capital gain. She would subtract her net capital gain and compute the tax— under her § 1 tax rate schedule, featuring a top rate of 37%—on her remaining income of $600,000. Because the $200,000 of net capital gain, when metaphorically stacked on top of the taxpayer's $600,000 of ordinary income, is entirely above the $425,800 threshold for the 20% rate, all $200,000 of gain is taxed at 20%. The taxpayer's total tax is the sum of the tax on $600,000 at ordinary income rates and the 20% tax on $200,000. Most corporate dividends are also taxed at the rates applicable to net capital gain. Technically, however, dividends continue to be classified as ordinary income, with the result that they cannot be offset by capital losses.

The capital gains preference differs from the norm for a few special asset categories. Under § 1(h), gains from the sale of so-called collectibles—jewelry, antiques, fine art—continue to be taxed at the old 28% rate (or the taxpayer's marginal tax rate on ordinary income, whichever is lower). Section 1202 provides that "qualified small business stock" gets a 50% (or, in some cases, 75% or 100%) gain

---

[1]   All dollar thresholds in the text are for 2018; the thresholds will be adjusted for inflation in later years.

exclusion. Finally, gains on sales of depreciable real estate—§ 1231 property—are taxed under a special regime, which is described at 18.02, below.

Whether the capital gain preference is wise or unwise as a matter of national economic policy has been debated by tax specialists for decades, and perhaps the safest thing to say is that the question is debatable. What cannot be denied, however, is that the decision to treat capital gains in a special way adds substantially to the complexity of the federal income tax. The effect of this is felt by students, who are obliged to devote much more study time to the material that follows than might otherwise be required, by practicing lawyers, who must tirelessly engage in "planning" their clients' transactions so as to maximize capital gain and minimize ordinary income, and by the Internal Revenue Service itself, which has the task of policing the relevant statutory distinctions. According to a Service publication, that particular task—determining when capital gain treatment is appropriate and when it is not—has absorbed more administrative time and effort on the part of government personnel than any other *single* feature of the Internal Revenue Code.

Wise or otherwise, the capital gain preference comes at a high cost to the system.

16.02   Legislative Purpose

With only one brief intermission, preferential treatment for capital gains has been a major feature of the federal income tax since 1922. Generally speaking, it applies to long-term gains from sales of investment property and permits those gains to be taxed at substantially lower rates than the rates that apply to "ordinary" income.

How can this longstanding tax concession be explained? What justifies the special treatment of investment gains? Curiously in view of its significance to the revenues, the capital gain preference has never received a systematic exposition in any official source. Congressional committee reports, debates, etc., contain little on the subject of underlying policy, apart from occasional references to "fairness," "incentives" and the like. Some of the policy justifications offered by commentators for the capital gains preference have obvious weaknesses. For example, it is sometimes argued that a capital gains rate preference is needed to prevent "bunching"—that is, taxation of income at an inappropriately high marginal tax rate when capital gains accrued over many years are realized in a single year. Under the current rate structure, however, the top marginal rate of 37% kicks in at a relatively low income level, with the result that most taxpayers with substantial capital gains are in the 37% bracket every year. Obviously, "bunching" is not an issue for a taxpayer who is in the 37% bracket every year. And even if relief from "bunching" were in order, an income-averaging system (see 10.01) for capital gains would provide much better-targeted relief than a rate preference. It is also sometimes claimed that the capital gains preference serves in lieu of adjusting basis to reflect inflation. The notion seems to be that taxing too much gain (by taxing inflationary gain as well as real gain) at too low a rate (the capital gains rate) might happen to produce the same result as taxing the right amount of gain (real economic gain) at the right rate (the taxpayer's marginal rate for ordinary income). Of course, it would be the sheerest coincidence if the two wrongs happened to produce a right. If the inflation concern warrants a statutory remedy, the obvious fix is to adjust the basis of capital assets for inflation and then to tax the real gain (if any) at ordinary income rates.

The only justification for the capital gains rate preference that stands up at all well to scrutiny is the justification based on the so-called Laffer curve (named after the economist Arthur Laffer, who did not discover the phenomenon illustrated by the curve, but who did explain it to Ronald Reagan). The idea is that, for any type of tax, it is possible to construct a Laffer curve which shows how much revenue the tax would raise if imposed at various rates. Increasing the rate of tax has two countervailing effects on revenue. Raising the rate obviously increases the revenue raised on what remains in the tax base, but increasing the rate also shrinks the tax base by discouraging taxpayers from engaging in the taxed activity. At first, as the rate increases above zero, the increasing rate effect is larger than the shrinking base effect, and revenue increases. Eventually, however, a revenue-maximizing rate is reached (the top of the Laffer curve); if the rate is increased above that rate the shrinking base effect will be more significant that the increasing rate effect, and revenue will fall. The moral is that, although Congress does not necessarily want to impose tax at the revenue-maximizing rate, it certainly does not want to impose tax *above* the revenue-maximizing rate (unless the point of the tax is to discourage the taxed behavior, as might be true for a tax on, say, alcohol or tobacco).

What does all this have to do with the capital gains preference? The location of the top of the Laffer curve for a particular type of tax depends on the extent to which taxpayers respond to increasing tax rates by reducing the taxed activity. It turns out that high rates of tax do not greatly discourage taxpayers from working; the top of the Laffer curve for an income tax on labor income is well above 50%. Realizations of capital gains, however, are much more sensitive to the tax rate—basically because simply holding onto appreciated property is generally a more attractive option than not working. Economists debate the location of the top of the Laffer curve for capital gains, but it is surely much lower than the top of the Laffer curve for labor income. If Congress wanted to impose a top marginal rate on ordinary income that was at or below the top of the Laffer curve for labor income, but above the top of the Laffer curve for capital gains, there would then be a strong case for a capital gains rate preference as necessary to avoid taxing capital gains at higher than the revenue-maximizing rate. Although the Laffer curve argument for a capital gains preference would be powerful if the top marginal rate were 50% or higher, with a top marginal rate of 37% the case for a preference seems less than overwhelming.

The absence of a clearly articulated set of policy objectives for the capital gains preference has been criticized by many.[2] Among other things, it has apparently kept Congress from setting up a detailed and explicit statutory classification system for capital assets. Unsure of its own goals, Congress has provided an incomplete picture of what belongs in the class of "capital assets," leaving to the courts and the Service the task of developing the further content of that term through case-by-case analysis. As the discussion in Section 17 will show, this effort has largely been directed at *limiting* the scope of the capital asset definition—a difficult undertaking without clear statutory guidance—and most would agree that it has not worked out as well as might be wished.

In *Burnet v. Harmel*,[3] the Supreme Court stated that the purpose of the capital gains preference was "to relieve the taxpayer from . . . excessive tax burdens on gains resulting from a conversion of capital investments, and to remove the deterrent effect of those burdens on such conversions." The Court presumably had two problems in mind, both arising from the act of "conversion" or realization. The first is the aforementioned "bunching" problem. Although, as noted, bunching concerns are not very significant given the modest extent of rate progression under current law, bunching concerns loomed larger in earlier decades when tax rate schedules were much more aggressively progressive.

The second problem alluded to in *Harmel*—usually referred to as the "locked-in" effect—is evidently forward rather than backward looking. Thus, suppose an investor who owns an appreciated asset identifies another investment property which seems to offer higher returns than the one he now holds. Apart from the effect of taxation, the investor would sell his existing property and reinvest the proceeds in the new, higher-yielding asset whose existence and potential he has presumably spent time and money to discover. But,

---

[2]   See Surrey, *Definitional Problems in Capital Gains Taxation*, 69 Harv.L.Rev. 985 (1956).

[3]   287 U.S. 103 (1932).

on the other hand, if he sells his appreciated property he has to pay an immediate tax on the gain. If he holds it, however, that tax can be postponed indefinitely—even death does not result in a taxable realization. As a result, the higher expected yield from the new property has to be reduced, in effect, by the tax cost of disposing of the old, and when this calculation is made it may turn out that the new opportunity is not sufficiently profitable to make the switch worthwhile. The taxpayer is thus locked into his existing investment by the prospect of a tax on the sale, and his capital is deprived of the mobility which it ought ideally to possess. The connection with the Laffer curve argument is apparent. Faced with the prospect of a capital gains tax if he sells his appreciated asset, the taxpayer decides not to sell, and the government collects no capital gains tax from him.

Once again, therefore, the capital gains preference operates to mitigate the "deterrent" effect of the realization rule by making it less costly for those who own appreciated property to switch into other assets when their investment judgment dictates that they should, and in that respect the mobility of capital is improved.

Assuming that *Harmel* was correct, or largely correct, in its summary of the goals that Congress had in mind when it adopted the capital gain rules, does either objective really justify the preference in its present form? As noted, the "bunching" rationale for a capital gains preference is extremely weak at the moment, given the rate structure of the current income tax. The "mobility of capital" argument is more plausible as a justification for tax relief, but it still is unclear why a rate differential is an appropriate way to respond to it. If one takes seriously the notion that taxing property gains "deters" investors from transferring capital to more profitable uses, then the correct response would seem to lie in one of two mutually exclusive directions. Thus, (a) we could refrain from taxing property gains *at all* if the taxpayer promptly reinvests the proceeds of sale in other long-lived assets. Under this approach, the taxpayer would be permitted, in effect, to roll over his capital investments free of tax. As with like-kind exchanges (15.01), his original basis would be continued in the new investment property, and the deterrent effect of gain taxation would be removed entirely.[4] In the alternative, (b) we could tax property gains at ordinary rates *as they accrue,* without waiting for an act of realization. The taxpayer would then obtain no advantage from postponing the sale of his appreciated property, because the annual appreciation (or decline) would be taxed (or deducted) at the year-end anyway. There would thus be no reason to

---

[4]   See Blum, *Rollover: An Alternative Treatment of Capital Gains,* 41 Tax L. Rev. 383 (1986).

refrain from switching investments if better opportunities came along.

As compared with either of these "extreme" solutions—roll-over or annual accrual—the capital gains rate preference seems a weak and inadequate compromise. Capital gains were and are still subject to a substantial (even though reduced) measure of taxation; hence realization, which is at the heart of the problem, continues to deter the making of individually and socially desirable investment choices. At the same time, taxpayers who do realize capital gains get the benefit of the reduced rate of tax even when the gain is *not* reinvested and the proceeds of sale are expended on consumption. Reinvestment is not a condition of the capital gain preference; hence the preference is not confined to those who do actually reinvest their profits.

Regarding capital losses, the present treatment—for the most part, permitting capital losses to offset only capital gains—is also a function of the realization requirement. As noted earlier, because only realized gains are subject to tax, a permission to deduct losses from other income would encourage taxpayers to realize their losses immediately while postponing the realization of their gains, with a resulting loss to the revenues. The restricted deductibility of capital losses, however, means that less successful investors—those who experience more losses than gains on a lifetime basis—are compelled to make a tax sacrifice for the benefit of more successful investors. The latter get the advantage of postponing their gains *until* realized, while the former "pay" for this advantage by forgoing a full deduction for their losses even *when* realized.[5]

A loose end. Lacking any better opportunity, this may be the place to point out that the federal income tax in a sense discriminates against savers, as compared with consumers, by imposing what some would call a *double* tax on savings. Income, however derived, is taxed to an individual *once* when he earns or receives it. If the amount that remains is expended on consumption goods—food, lodging, entertainment, etc.—no further tax is imposed on the individual with respect to that original receipt. If, however, the individual chooses to "expend" his after-tax income on shares of stock, corporate bonds or other assets which produce further income, then that further income will of course be subject to a further tax. Savers are thus taxed *twice*; consumers only once.

---

[5]   See Warren, *The Deductibility by Individuals of Capital Losses under the Federal Income Tax,* 40 U.Chi.L.Rev. 291 (1973).

To illustrate: Assume C and S, individuals, live in a country which at present imposes no income tax whatever. Each earns $1,000. C, a consumer, chooses to expend his $1,000 on a vacation. S, a saver, expends his $1,000 on a 6% bond with a view to receiving annual interest of $60 to use in future periods. Since they live in a tax-free world, both individuals get what they want for the same dollar expenditure.

Now assume that their country adopts an income tax of 50%. How much must C and S earn in order to acquire, respectively, a $1,000 vacation and a $60-a-year income stream? As to C, the answer is obviously $2,000. Since the vacation is not a deductible expense, it has to be purchased out of after-tax income. With the new 50% income tax in force, C will have to earn $2,000 in order to have $1,000 left for his annual trip to Florida. But what about S? The bond purchase *also* is not deductible—taxpayers are no more allowed to deduct amounts expended on "savings" than they are amounts expended on "consumption." At the same time, however, the interest on S's bond will *itself* be subject to the 50% income tax. In effect, earnings devoted to the purchase of an income-stream, *and* the income-stream itself, are *both* included in income. This means that S will actually have to earn $4,000 in order to be in the same position that he occupied before the new tax was enacted. Thus the $4,000 would be reduced by the 50% tax to $2,000. The $2,000 that remained would then be used to buy a 6% bond yielding interest of $120 a year. The $120 of annual interest would *also* be taxed at the 50% rate, leaving a net after-tax income-stream of $60. In this sense, therefore, while C the consumer is required to earn only $2,000 because he pays the 50% income tax just once, S the saver is required to earn $4,000 because his savings are subjected to a double imposition.[6]

Does all this provide any justification for a capital gains preference? Not in any explicit way, certainly. In the first place, as already observed, the capital gains preference applies without regard to whether gains are expended on consumption goods or reinvested in other capital assets. Hence the preference is not confined to savers. It is the *source* of the income—realized capital appreciation—rather than the destination of the proceeds which attracts the favored treatment. Second, and by the same token, the preference is not available for savings generally. Taxpayers whose income derives from personal services are taxed on such income at the full ordinary rates even if they spend none of it and save it all. Once again, source

---

[6]   A now-classic exchange of views on this topic appears in Andrews, *A Consumption-Type or Cash Flow Personal Income Tax*, 87 Harv.L.Rev. 1113 (1974), and Warren, *Fairness and a Consumption-Type or Cash Flow Personal Income Tax*, 88 Harv.L.Rev. 931 (1975). And see Fried, *Fairness and the Consumption Tax*, 44 Stan.L.Rev. 961 (1992).

is the determining criterion. Personal service income is always taxed at ordinary rates no matter what expenditure choice the taxpayer then elects to make. Finally, the capital gains preference is not available for income *streams* from investment assets (with the important exception of dividends). In the example in the preceding paragraph, the capital gains preference is of no help to S because the interest she receives is ordinary income, not capital gain.

Still—and conceding that the point is more intuitive than rational—we suspect that there remains in the minds of many a dim sense that capital appreciation is not truly "income". If so, the feeling may ultimately trace to a hunch that capital gains, more often than not, are held back from the ordinary flow of consumption expenditure and reinvested in new or additional income-producing assets. Perhaps, then, favored treatment represents an oblique and unsystematic response to the problem of discrimination illustrated in the comparison of C and S, above. If capital gainers are also savers— typically, if not always—then maybe the capital gain preference is intended to mitigate the double-tax on savings by treating such gain as if it lacked the taxable characteristics of "income."

16.03   Mechanics of Computation

The computation of tax on capital gains and losses, though detailed, is reasonably straightforward and can be summarized fairly briefly. To begin with, § 1222 divides capital gains and losses into two classes—long-term and short-term. Long-term gain or loss is defined to mean gain or loss from the sale or exchange of capital assets held for more than one year; short-term gain or loss refers to gain or loss from the sale of capital assets held for one year or less. Net long-term gains are treated "preferentially"; net short-term gains are simply taxed at ordinary rates.

For individual taxpayers, the long-term capital gain preference takes the form of special low rates of zero, 15%, and 20%, applicable in lieu of the § 1 rates on ordinary income. The relevant Code provision is § 1(h), the basic rules of which were described above (16.01). For another example of the application of these rules, imagine a married couple with ordinary income of $50,000 and net capital gain of $750,000. The tax on the $50,000 of ordinary income is determined under the usual rules of § 1, as if the $50,000 were the taxpayers' only income. Notionally stacking the capital gain on top of the ordinary income, and using the income thresholds for 2018 (set forth at 16.01), the first $27,200 of capital gain ($77,200 minus $50,000) is taxed at the rate of zero, the next $401,800 ($479,000 minus $77,200) is taxed at 15%, and the remaining $321,000 ($800,000 minus $479,000) is taxed at 20%.

In general, capital losses can be offset only against capital gains. Any excess or unused capital loss for the current year can be carried forward to subsequent taxable years without time limitation. In order to minimize recordkeeping where the unused capital loss is relatively small, § 1211 permits individual taxpayers to offset capital losses (whether short-term or long-term) against ordinary income up to $3,000 annually.

The calculation of short-term and long-term capital gains and losses is carried out through the "netting" procedure set forth in § 1222. The section begins by distinguishing short-term from long-term gains and losses by reference to the one-year holding period. It then directs the taxpayer to net the gains and losses in each category separately. If one category shows a net loss and the other a net gain, the net loss and the net gain are netted against each other. This means that short-term loss may offset long-term gain or, equally, that long-term loss may offset short-term gain. There are then these possible outcomes:

(1)   Net gains in both categories, in which case the net short-term gain is taxed at ordinary rates, while the net long-term gain is dealt with under § 1(h) and is generally subject to the 20% rate limitation;

(2)   Net losses in both categories, in which case the net losses are combined and can be offset against up to $3,000 of ordinary income (with unlimited carryforward);

(3)   Net loss in one category and net gain in the other, in which case the loss in the former category (whether short or long) is offset against the gain in the latter category (whether short or long). Having combined the two categories—

(a)   If there is an excess of short-term gain over long-term loss, the excess is a short-term gain and is taxed at ordinary rates;

(b)   If there is an excess of long-term gain over short-term loss, the excess is a long-term gain and is generally taxed at a rate of 15% or 20%;

(c)   If the net loss in either category exceeds the net gain in the other, the excess (loss) is offset against $3,000 of ordinary income, with unlimited carryforward.

By way of simple illustration, assume that the taxpayers, a married couple, have salary income of $150,000. The taxpayers have also realized a long-term capital gain of $55,000, a long-term capital loss of $10,000, and a short-term capital loss of $5,000, all from the sale of securities. Assume finally that the taxpayers take the standard deduction. Their tax liability for the year (using the 2018 standard deduction amount and tax rate schedule) would be determined as follows:

Salary		$150,000
Long-term capital gain	$55,000	
Long-term capital loss	(10,000)	
Net long-term capital gain	$45,000	
Net short-term capital loss	(5,000)	
Net capital gain (§ 1222(11))		40,000
Gross income		$190,000
Standard deduction, $24,000		(24,000)
Taxable income		$166,000
Taxable income reduced by $40,000 net capital gain		$126,000
Tax on $126,000 under § 1(a)		$19,599
Tax on net capital gain under § 1(h) (15% of $40,000)		6,000
Total tax liability		$ 25,599

Without the § 1(h) rate-limitation the taxpayers' total tax liability would be $28,419, so the saving for the year is $2,820—not an insignificant amount for the taxpayers in question.

So much for mechanics, on to strategy:

If the reader has ever had an investment account with a brokerage company, she almost certainly will have received a "Year-End Tax Planning" letter of which the aim is to alert her to the possibility of saving taxes by realizing gains and losses on securities in her portfolio. The strategic alternatives are fairly numerous and depend on which categories of gains and losses have already been realized during the taxable year and which categories remain unrealized. As a kind of self-administered test, assume that an investor has already realized $10,000 of long-term gain during the current taxable year. She also has in her portfolio $10,000 of unrealized long-term loss on stock X, and $10,000 of unrealized short-term gain on stock Y. She has decided, as a matter of investment judgment, to sell both stock X and stock Y, but she does not care whether she sells one or both just before the end of the current year or just after the start of the new year. From a tax standpoint, what should she do?

The answer, of course, is that she should hold on to both stocks until the current year ends, and sell both after the new year begins. If she sold both stocks before the end of the current year, the long-term loss on stock X would offset the long-term gain already realized, and the investor would be left with a short-term gain on stock Y, which would be taxed at ordinary rates. The same would be true if she sold stock X this year and sold stock Y next year, except that the short-term gain would be taxed a year later. If she sells both X and Y in the new year, however, the long-term loss on X will offset the short-term gain on Y. The gain realized in the current year is then taxable without offset, but since it is of the long-term variety it qualifies for the 20% rate-limitation under § 1(h) and the investor can congratulate herself for her shrewd year-end maneuvering.

17. Judicial Development of the Capital Asset Definition

17.01   General Comment

As the sections that follow will suggest, the Supreme Court has played an unusually active role in developing—more often limiting—the scope of the capital asset definition. With some exceptions, the Court's effort over the years has been to narrow the category of transactions qualifying as sales of capital assets and thereby to prevent that category from occupying a larger part of the tax universe than seemed consistent with congressional intent. The need for judicial activism in this area resulted, in part, from the curious, upside-down way in which the Code itself defines the term "capital asset." Thus, § 1221 *begins* with the broad assertion that "capital asset means property held by the taxpayer (whether or not connected with his trade or business)." The key word in this phrase obviously is "property", a word which contains no inherent or intrinsic limitations, and which, therefore, could be understood to embrace rights, claims and interests of any and every description. Taken literally, the statute seems to contemplate a world that includes nothing *but* capital assets, and speaks as if all transactions and dealings qualified for capital gain or loss treatment. To be sure, eight classes of property—among them, business inventory and salary claims—are at once excluded from the definition of a capital asset, thus, in effect, being typed as "ordinary." Yet the existence of these specific exclusions, which appear in §§ 1221(a)(1)–(8), seems to strengthen the possibility that all *non*-excluded items may be swept into the capital asset category.

Plainly, however, Congress did not intend that the federal income tax should primarily be a capital gains tax. The capital asset definition was meant to apply to investment property—primarily securities and real estate—which is capable of appreciating in value over an extended period of ownership. Other kinds of assets or claims, especially those that do not customarily reflect long-term changes in value, are expected to be covered by the "normal" operation of the income tax and to be taxed at customary rates. In the latter category would be recurring income of all sorts, whether from business, services or investment itself, as well as a nearly limitless variety of income items that do not fit so neatly into familiar compartments. In effect, if congressional intention is the guide, then ordinary income should be the general rule and capital gain should be the exception.

This Section considers some of the major cases in which the courts have undertaken to interpret the capital asset definition. Consistent principles have not always been easy to articulate, because the original aim of Congress in enacting the capital gain provisions is nowhere set forth in comprehensive terms. As the quotation from *Burnet v. Harmel* suggests, however, the courts have assumed that the capital gains preference was intended chiefly to serve as an averaging and anti-lock-in device. It has also been assumed that income from business or professional activities, as well as recurring investment income such as royalties, interest and rents, are to be viewed as falling *outside* the favored category. But while these assumptions are necessary and plausible, their implementation in particular cases often has been difficult. As in the income-attribution field, the courts have been compelled to invent and manipulate doctrinal concepts in order to reach results which they could regard as consistent with legislative intent. The concept of "property" has sometimes been utilized to this end, as has the notion that some kinds of economic interests are merely a "substitute for future ordinary income." In addition, since capital gain or loss is described in § 1222 as resulting from the "sale or exchange" of a capital asset, ordinary or capital treatment occasionally has turned on whether a particular transaction qualified, or failed to qualify, as a "sale or exchange." Judicial opinions are frequently opaque, however, and in that respect they reflect the courts' uncertainty about underlying legislative goals.

17.02   Everyday Business Activities

The profits and losses realized by a business enterprise through the sale of its products to customers are obviously *ordinary* profits and losses. This is true whether the enterprise is a corporation, taxable at the 21% rate set forth in § 11, or a partnership or proprietorship whose net income or loss is taken into account directly by the individual partners or proprietor. Everyday business income, together with wages, salaries, dividends, interest and rent, accounts for the great bulk of taxable income, and it plainly falls outside the category of capital gain or loss. Section 1221(a)(1), discussed in some detail at 18.01, makes this conclusion clear by excluding business "inventory" from the capital asset definition, thus insuring that day-to-day merchandise transactions will have no claim to capital gain treatment. Real and depreciable property used in business—land and buildings, machinery and equipment—is likewise denied capital asset status by § 1221(a)(2). As will be seen at 18.02, however, these so-called fixed assets are subject to a special regime under § 1231, which does permit capital gain in limited measure.

But what about other kinds of business assets—securities, leases, franchises, trade-names, "goodwill" and other intangibles—which do not fit neatly within the excluded classes of "inventory" or of real and depreciable property, but which also may be a source of gain or loss to the enterprise? Section 1221 says nothing directly about these residual items, so that at least one approach would be to view the catch-all clause as conferring capital asset status on all of them more or less by default. The test, quite simply, would be whether the asset in question—say, a franchise or a license—is specifically excluded by § 1221(a)(1) or § 1221(a)(2). If not, then even though the asset is used in business, and even though business activity commonly yields ordinary gains and losses, the gain or loss in this instance must be capital because the asset literally constitutes "property" within the terms of § 1221.

The Supreme Court has tackled the issue in question—whether business assets not specifically excepted from the capital asset definition are, as a consequence, necessarily within it—in two widely separated decisions, *Corn Products Refining Co. v. Commissioner,*[7] decided in 1955, and *Arkansas Best Corporation v. Commissioner,*[8] decided in 1988. The former, as will be seen, was a sort of *tour de force* in which the Court substantially expanded the category of *non-*capital assets to include property acquired for a purpose integral to the taxpayer's everyday business, even though not squarely within a statutory exception. The latter, in contrast, may be read as a somewhat embarrassed attempt, inspired by three decades of unhappy experience with the former, to refocus the problem in narrower terms.

In *Corn Products* the taxpayer was a large manufacturer of corn starch, syrup, sugar and related products. It typically accepted orders from its customers under which shipment of merchandise was to be made within 30 days at a set price. Since its storage facilities were limited, the taxpayer was sometimes obliged to purchase raw materials in the spot market, and on occasion, when weather conditions had caused a sudden increase in spot prices, it evidently

---

[7]   350 U.S. 46 (1955).

[8]   485 U.S. 212 (1988).

found that customers' orders could only be filled at a loss. To deal with this problem, the company embarked on a regular program of buying corn futures—contracts which entitled it to purchase a fixed amount of corn at a future date at a fixed price. If the price of corn thereafter rose, the company would be protected: it could either take delivery under the futures contracts if it had an actual need for raw materials, or else sell the contracts at a gain and reimburse itself for any increase in the spot market price.

In 1940 the taxpayer realized a gain of $680,000 from the sale of futures contracts; in 1942 it sustained a loss of $110,000. Finding that the taxpayer had a "business" as distinguished from an "investment" purpose in purchasing the corn futures, the Supreme Court held that the gains (and losses) were ordinary and hence taxable at the regular corporate rate. The futures, in the Court's view, had played an "integral part" in the taxpayer's business by protecting it "against a price increase in its principal raw material and [assuring] a ready supply for manufacturing requirements." Profits and losses arising from the "everyday operation of the business" must be regarded as ordinary, therefore, because Congress did not intend to award preferential treatment to transactions that are a "normal source of business income."

As noted, the Court rejected the taxpayer's argument that the corn futures were entitled to capital asset status merely because they qualified as "property". That term, it said, must be narrowly construed. At the same time, the Court appeared to concede that the futures were neither "inventory" in a conventional sense nor stock-in-trade within the meaning of what is now § 1221(a)(1). In effect, therefore, by a strong handling of the statute, the Court *created* a class of property—property acquired for a purpose integral to the taxpayer's business—which it found to be constructively excepted from the capital asset definition. The Court did not say that *all* business assets must be treated as ordinary, and presumably the reference to "everyday" operations was intended to imply a distinction between recurring transactions and others. It did, however, apparently establish that the statutory exceptions were not exhaustive and that in cases not covered by a specific exception the question of "capital or ordinary" could not be answered without additional analysis of the taxpayer's purpose or intent.

Though *Corn Products* was undoubtedly correct in outcome, emphasizing the taxpayer's motive for acquiring property led to much uncertainty in application. The treatment of securities—stocks, bonds and the like—proved especially troublesome. In *Commissioner v. Bagley & Sewall Co.*,[9] for example, the taxpayer entered into a

---

[9]   221 F.2d 944 (2d Cir. 1955).

construction contract with a foreign government for the manufacture of certain machinery, and was required under the contract to deposit U.S. Government bonds as security for its performance. The taxpayer purchased the bonds for this purpose at a cost of $820,000 and then, immediately after completing the contract, resold the bonds at a $15,000 loss. The court of appeals held that the loss was allowable in full as a deduction from ordinary income. Although the bonds were obviously "property", the factual background made it clear that their purchase "was a reasonable and necessary act in the conduct of [the taxpayer's manufacturing] business," and that "no investment was intended." Accordingly, the taxpayer was upheld in treating the $15,000 bond loss as "a deductible business expense [under § 162], or business loss [under § 165], properly taken in the instant year since that was the first time the reason for holding the bonds disappeared and the extent of the loss could be accurately measured." Dissenting, Judge Frank argued that the exceptions in § 1221(a)(1) *et seq.* were exclusive, that the court had no power to broaden those exceptions through "judicial amendment," and, hence, that the taxpayer's loss should have been treated as a capital loss offsettable solely against capital gains.

Subsequent cases, most of them involving stock or other securities acquired to achieve a business goal of some sort, tended to apply the *Corn Products* rationale quite broadly. In *Booth Newspapers*,[10] for example, ordinary loss treatment was allowed where the taxpayer, a publisher, sold the stock of a newsprint manufacturer which it had originally purchased during a paper shortage in order to secure a long-term source of supply. The court found the stock to be a non-capital asset on the ground that the taxpayer had a "business purpose" in making the original purchase, although the same result might have been reached by characterizing the stock as a substitute for raw materials and hence as "inventory" under § 1221(a)(1). Other decisions have carried the business purpose rationale to more surprising lengths. Thus, an ordinary loss result was reached where the taxpayer originally bought securities in another firm in order to have access to new technologies,[11] and, in yet another case, where a holding company's purpose in acquiring the stock of a subsidiary was to protect its own business reputation.[12] In these and like decisions, the stock or securities, though lacking the close relationship to current inventory that was present in *Corn Products* itself, were found to have been purchased for business rather than investment reasons and for that reason alone were held to have ordinary status under the rationale employed in *Corn*

---

[10] *Booth Newspapers, Inc. v. U.S.*, 303 F.2d 916 (Ct.Cl.1962).

[11] *Schlumberger Tech. Corp. v. U.S.*, 443 F.2d 1115 (5th Cir. 1971).

[12] *Campbell Taggart, Inc. v. U.S.*, 744 F.2d 442 (5th Cir. 1984).

Products. In a few instances where the securities finally sold at a loss had been held for an extended period of time, the courts denied ordinary loss treatment on the ground that the taxpayer's original business purpose had later been displaced by a purpose to hold for investment; in other cases (prior to *Arkansas Best*) the courts attempted to distinguish between securities acquired for the purpose of protecting the taxpayer's existing business (ordinary) and acquisitions aimed at expanding into new business areas (capital). Some courts, also, found themselves enmeshed in the difference between "predominant" and "substantial" business motivation, with the outcomes in particular cases turning on highly tenuous elements of proof. Once again, the emphasis on motive and intent made it difficult to insure uniform administration of the capital gain and loss provisions where business taxpayers were concerned.

The administrative problem was aggravated, from one standpoint, by the fact that the *Corn Products* "rule" was regarded as a "rule of law" available to taxpayers as well as the government and applicable to gains and losses alike. Not surprisingly, therefore, as just suggested, most of the litigated cases involving an application of the *Corn Products* doctrine were cases in which the security or other asset was disposed of at a *loss.* Asserting that the property was acquired for business-related rather than investment-related reasons, the taxpayer reported the loss as a deduction from ordinary income. When the very same property appreciated, on the other hand, the taxpayer was likely to find that investment motives were predominant and to report his profit as a capital gain. Had the bonds in *Bagley & Sewall* gone up, for example, the gain would almost surely have shown up as a routine capital gain on the taxpayer's return, where only a very sharp-eyed revenue agent would have thought of challenging it. Hence, ironically, the *Corn Products* doctrine served chiefly as a justification for ordinary loss treatment; rarely did it produce ordinary treatment on the gain side. Tax lawyers refer to this general phenomenon—of taxpayers taking inconsistent positions at the expense of the fisc—as whipsaw, and *Corn Products* produced one of the worst (from the government's perspective) whipsaw problems in the history of the income tax. It is ironic that the problem resulted from a case that the government won. *Corn Products* and its aftermath is a classic illustration of what the late Martin Ginsburg (a leading tax lawyer and tax professor) labeled the "law of Moses' rod": "Every stick crafted by the government to beat on the head of a taxpayer will, sooner or later, metamorphose into a large snake that will bite the Commissioner on the hindpart."[13]

---

[13]   Ginsburg, *The National Office Mission,* 27 Tax Notes 99 (1985).

In view of these difficulties, many commentators suggested that the Court would have been better advised had it reached the result it did in *Corn Products* on a narrower ground; namely, that the corn futures were merely a substitute, or "surrogate", for the taxpayer's principal raw material. Had the Court followed this simpler course, one important consequence would have been to permit the Service to insist that assets be "included in inventory" at the time of their original purchase if the taxpayer intended to claim ordinary treatment thereafter. In effect, taxpayers would have been required, as a matter of tax accounting, to declare the status of the asset—whether ordinary or capital—when it was initially acquired, rather than after it had been disposed of. Gains and losses would then have been treated alike and "optional" or hindsight classification would have been foreclosed.

More than anything else, perhaps, it was the "potential for . . . abuse"—the taxpayer asserting that its original motive had been investment-related when the property was later sold at a gain, but business-related when it was later sold at a loss—that led the Supreme Court in *Arkansas Best* to declare (after thirty-odd years) that its *Corn Products* opinion had been misunderstood and that the prevailing interpretation was "too expansive."

In *Arkansas Best,* the taxpayer, a holding company, in 1968 acquired as an investment 65% of the stock of a commercial bank. The bank did reasonably well at first but beginning in 1972, as the local real estate market declined, the bank developed financial difficulties and was classified as a "problem bank" by federal examiners. During the "problem" period, which extended through 1974, the taxpayer (together with other shareholders) contributed substantial amounts of capital to the bank and received additional shares. The taxpayer sold the greater part of its bank stock in 1975 and, as a result, reported and claimed deduction for an ordinary loss of about $10 million. The Tax Court, purporting to apply *Corn Products,* held that the bank stock purchased by the taxpayer *prior* to 1972 had been acquired with an "investment" goal in view—*i.e.,* the taxpayer thought the stock was undervalued and would appreciate—while the stock acquired through capital contribution *after* 1972 had been acquired "exclusively for business purposes"—*i.e.,* to preserve the taxpayer's business reputation by preventing the bank (of which the taxpayer was the controlling shareholder) from failing. It followed, on this view, that the taxpayer's stock loss was a capital loss to the extent attributable to the pre-1972 shares, but ordinary to the extent attributable to the shares acquired during the later period.

Rejecting the Tax Court (and affirming the Eighth Circuit), the Supreme Court held that *all* of the taxpayer's bank stock, whenever acquired, was a capital asset and that no portion of the taxpayer's loss could be treated as ordinary. The Court expressly disapproved the expansive interpretation that *Corn Products* had received in *Booth Newspapers* and other lower court cases. Justice Marshall admitted, or conceded, that the opinion in *Corn Products* may not have made clear whether the ordinary-income result "was based on a narrow reading of the phrase 'property held by the taxpayer' [in § 1221], or on a broad reading of the inventory exclusion of [§ 1221(a)(1)]." Now, however, and in order to resolve any uncertainty on that score, the Court was prepared to assert that *Corn Products* should properly have been interpreted as "involving an application of § 1221's inventory exception" rather than an effort "to create a general exemption from capital-asset status for assets acquired for business purposes." While the corn futures were not "actual inventory," they were plainly a part of the taxpayer's inventory-purchase program and as such were mere substitutes or surrogates for the corn inventory itself. It followed that the *Corn Products* "doctrine" could be of no benefit to the taxpayer in *Arkansas Best*. The bank shares were not in any sense inventory in the taxpayer's hands—the taxpayer was obviously not a dealer in securities—and hence the taxpayer's loss, whether attributable to the shares acquired for investment or to the shares acquired for a business-related purpose, was a capital loss.

Having overruled the *Booth Newspapers* line of decisions, at least as to rationale, *Arkansas Best* presumably also rejects the reasoning in *Bagley & Sewall* and requires that we approve Judge Frank's dissenting view instead. The question would not (or would no longer) be whether Bagley & Sewall had acquired the bonds for a business rather than an investment purpose. Rather, the pertinent question would be whether the loss was in some way a surrogate or substitute for a business expense—presumably the cost of procuring a performance bond—that would otherwise be allowable under § 162. Pretty plainly, it was not. To be sure, a contractor that undertakes a large construction project would almost always be required to post a bond in order to secure its performance obligations under the contract. The bond would normally be obtained from a surety company to which the taxpayer would pay an insurance premium, such premium being deductible as an ordinary and necessary business expense. But if, in lieu of a surety bond, the taxpayer posts security of its own, using its own capital for that purpose and acting as a self-insurer, then it seems fair to say that the taxpayer has earned the insurance premium for itself. In effect, the taxpayer has both "paid" (to itself) and "received" (from itself) an imputed premium, the two steps together simply producing a wash as far as the taxpayer's return is concerned. The customary bond-premium outlay associated with contract performance is thus effectively taken account of for tax purposes by being treated as an imputed payment and an imputed receipt. Hence an ordinary deduction on the ground that the company's loss was functionally equivalent to a business expense would not be justified.

Putting it differently, the loss sustained by the taxpayer in *Bagley & Sewall* was the result of a chance decline in the Treasury bond market and had nothing to do with the cost of performing the contract as such. While the bonds were admittedly acquired for a business-related reason, *Arkansas Best* makes it clear that "business purpose" no longer serves as the operative criterion. That being so, capital rather than ordinary loss treatment would (now) appear to have been appropriate.

In 1999 Congress added § 1221(a)(7) to the Code, excluding "hedging transactions" from the definition of capital assets. As defined by the statute, "hedging transactions" include inventory-substitute hedges similar to the hedge involved in *Corn Products*. As interpreted by the Regulation,[14] the term also extends to certain other types of hedges, including hedges "to manage risk of interest rate or price changes or currency fluctuations with respect to borrowings" of the taxpayer. In contrast with *Corn Products*, the provision does not expose the government to the risk of whipsaw, because it provides that a hedging transaction is treated as generating ordinary income or loss only if it is "clearly identified" by the taxpayer as a non-capital transaction before the close of the day on which the taxpayer entered into the transaction.

17.03   Substitute for Future Income

(a)   Carved-out Interests; Hort *and* Lake

Suppose a taxpayer buys a parcel of undeveloped land for $100, with the expectation that the future rental income (received, say, from a fishing and hunting club) will be $8 a year. Subsequently, fishing and hunting having grown in popularity, the annual rent expectation goes up to $10, and the land itself appreciates to $125. If the taxpayer now elects to sell the land, he will, of course, recognize a $25 gain, and since land, normally, is a capital asset, the gain will be taxed as capital gain. On the other hand, if the taxpayer chooses to hold the land and receive the annual rent, he will have $10 a year of ordinary income. The rent will be included in his income without an offset of basis, moreover, because the tax law, which follows accounting concepts here, does not permit the cost of land, securities,

---

[14]   Reg. § 1.1221–2.

or other non-wasting assets to be recovered until the property is finally disposed of.

All this, of course, is well understood. Whatever the merits from a policy standpoint, the Code makes a sharp distinction between gain that is realized on a sale of property and income received in the form of periodic yield. The former is taxed as capital gain, the latter as ordinary income. In formal and practical terms the distinction is an easy one to administer, because the difference between selling a parcel of land and retaining the ownership is obvious on its face.

But suppose the above landowner attempts to steer a middle course. Not wanting to sell his land, but needing cash for current expenses, he sells to another investor his right to receive the annual rent from the land for the next five years. At an appropriate rate of discount—say 8%—the present value of $10 a year for five years is $40, and that is what the taxpayer gets from the vendee. In return, the taxpayer notifies his tenant to pay over all rents to the vendee until the five-year term has ended.

How should the $40 payment be taxed? The question—which has a wicked odor of fruit-and-tree about it—is really not very difficult, because the risk of wide-scale tax avoidance if the "sale" were allowed to qualify as a capital transaction has simply been too great to bear. Thus, suppose the transaction *were* treated as a sale of a capital asset. The result, presumably, would be three-fold: (a) The taxpayer would be entitled to offset a proportionate part of his $100 basis against the proceeds of sale. Since the five-year rents right represents 40/125ths of the total value of the land, its "basis" would be 40/125ths of $100, or $32, and the taxpayer's gain on the transaction would be only $8, *i.e.*, $40 minus $32. (b) The $8 gain would be treated as capital gain. And (c), the taxpayer's remaining basis for the land would be reduced to $68—$100 minus the $32 already recovered. If the land were still worth $125 at the end of the five-year term and were then sold, the taxpayer would recognize a further capital gain of $57, *i.e.*, $125 minus $68. Total income from the land investment over the five-year period would thus have been $65—rent prepayment of $40 plus sale price of $125, less $100 original cost—and *all* of it would have been taxed as capital gain.

Plainly, however, if these outcomes were adopted by the law, all taxpayers owning income-producing property would be free (and, in effect, encouraged) to convert their ordinary investment income into capital gain by selling, or discounting, such income in advance of payment. Once the period covered by the advance sale had passed, the property-owner could *again* dispose of the future income for a term of years, and again report the "gain" as capital. By this process of anticipation (in itself a distortion of normal behavior), periodic investment income could be converted into capital gain contrary to the evident intent of Congress.

Arguably, also, the status of the taxpayer in the illustration above is closer to—"more like"—that of an investor who retains his land and receives his rent payments in the normal way than it is to one who sells his property outright. Again assuming that the land continues to be worth $125 when the five-year period covered by the advance sale is over, the picture that emerges is as follows: Immediately prior to the advance sale the taxpayer owns land with a market value of $125. Immediately after the advance sale he owns $40 cash plus a reversionary interest in the land worth $85 ($125 less $40). The reversionary interest then rises in value year-by-year, until, at the end of the fifth year, the taxpayer resumes full ownership of the land, which *still* has a value of $125. The $25 of appreciation that was present at the beginning of the five-year period thus remains *unrealized*; in addition, the taxpayer has enjoyed a periodic economic "gain" through the annual increase in the value of his reverter.

In these respects, the advance-seller's position is similar to that of the "normal" rent recipient: both own appreciated property at the end of the five-year term, and both have enjoyed a periodic addition to wealth. Presumably, therefore, both should be treated alike. In fact, as the *Hort* and *Lake* cases suggest, the courts *would* treat both alike, with the single exception that the advance-seller, having chosen to convert his right to future rents to current cash, would be taxed in the year the advance payment was received instead of at annual intervals. It might, indeed, be better to avoid even this dissimilarity, and to allow the advance payment to be taxed on a prorated basis over the five-year period. The rules of tax accounting (see 12.02) generally do not permit the deferral of cash receipts, however, and while this rigidity in accounting practice may be regrettable, it is not a matter that can be dealt with through the capital gain provisions except at the risk of considerable tax avoidance.

In *Hort v. Commissioner*,[15] the taxpayer inherited a building, of which the main floor had been leased to a bank for a period of 15 years at an annual rental of $25,000. Subsequently, when the lease still had some 13 years to run, the bank notified the taxpayer that it wished to terminate its occupancy. Office rents had declined sharply by reason of the Depression, and in any event the bank no longer found it profitable to maintain a branch in the taxpayer's building. After negotiations, the taxpayer agreed to cancel the lease in consideration of a cash payment by the bank of $140,000.

---

[15]   313 U.S. 28 (1941).

The taxpayer reported a *loss* from the transaction of $21,000. The lease (in his view) had a separate basis of $257,000, which was said to be the discounted value of the rents due from the bank for the 13 years remaining. The amount realized on the cancellation was calculated to be only $236,000, *i.e.*, the cash payment of $140,000 plus $96,000 representing the *reduced* rental value of the premises for the same 13-year period. Rejecting this approach, the Commissioner not only disallowed the loss, but treated the $140,000 payment as ordinary income.

In a brief opinion, the Supreme Court sustained the Commissioner in all respects. Cancellation of the lease, it said, "involved nothing more than the relinquishment of the right to future rental payments in return for a present substitute payment and possession of the leased premises." Since those future rents would have been taxed as ordinary income if received in the normal course, the "substitute" payment could be treated no differently. As respects the claimed loss, moreover, the Court concluded that it would not be consistent to allow the taxpayer a separate basis for the lease. If the taxpayer had suffered an economic injury because of the lease cancellation, that injury "would become a deductible loss only when its extent had been fixed by a closed transaction," that is, by a sale of the underlying real estate itself.

While the "substitute for future income" language is in some respects overbroad (because the sale price of any investment asset depends on the present value of the expected future income stream from the asset), the Court's intention in *Hort* is reasonably clear. Quite simply, the Court's aim was to deny (a) capital treatment, and (b) an offsetting basis, to one who disposes of a right to future income which has been carved out of a larger estate. In effect, the sale of an income right, unaccompanied by a disposition of the underlying property, results in ordinary income to the seller equal in amount to the entire proceeds of the sale.[16] The "substitute" language, in the view of most commentators, was merely a shorthand way of asserting that carved-out interests do not qualify as capital assets and do not absorb any portion of the taxpayer's property basis.

The *Hort* decision is generally cited as the leading and definitive authority for the carved-out interest rule. Yet it might be noted that the case itself involved the *cancellation* of a lease by the lessee rather than the sale of a lease to a third party, and it can be argued that the

---

[16] However, § 1286(b)(3) (enacted long after *Hort*) requires a taxpayer who "strips" a bond (*i.e.*, sells the right to receive some interest payments on the bond, while retaining the bond itself) to allocate his basis in the bond between the rights sold and the rights retained (in proportion to the values of the rights sold and the rights retained), and to offset against the sales proceeds the basis allocated to the rights sold. The provision applies only with respect to debt instruments.

former transaction, as compared with the latter, really does not present quite the same compelling case for ordinary treatment. Where a lease is sold by the lessor to a third party, the amount received by the seller must be a substitute for future rental payments that would otherwise be taxed at ordinary rates. In practical effect, the transaction is equivalent to the sale of an account receivable, *i.e.,* the rent due under the lease. The buyer simply acquires the right to receive a series of cash payments, and hence the amount he pays the seller for that receivable will be the same whether rents have gone up or down in the market and whether the lease is burdensome or advantageous to the lessee.

A payment for cancellation, by contrast, involves the vacating of the premises by the original lessee—the lease has plainly grown burdensome—with the lessor then presumably re-leasing the premises to another party at a lower figure and reporting the new rental-stream as ordinary income. The payment received by the lessor can thus be identified as, and really cannot be anything but, a premium attributable to a change in the market value of the leased premises. In effect, Hort's lease went up in value because rents dropped, just as a bond goes up in value when interest rates fall. If the bank repurchased or redeemed its own previously issued *bonds* at a premium—the bondholder recovering his original principal plus the premium amount—the bondholder's gain would be a capital gain. Arguably, the bank's act in repurchasing or cancelling its lease (which, from the bank's standpoint, is just another kind of IOU) should be viewed in equivalent terms: the lessor likewise recovers his original principal (the leased premises) plus a premium for giving up the lease (in *Hort,* $140,000). If a bond-redemption generates capital gain to a bondholder, why not a lease-redemption to a lease-holder? In essence, the two seem quite alike. But whatever the strength of this position, the Supreme Court in *Hort* obviously viewed the sale and the cancellation of a lease as indistinguishable for tax purposes— equally to be regarded as an act of carving-out—and it is clear at present that lease-cancellation payments are ordinary income to a lessor.

In *Commissioner v. P.G. Lake, Inc.,*[17] the Supreme Court extended the rule of the *Hort* case to transactions involving mineral properties—perhaps the one field in which sales of carved-out interests do commonly serve as a device for financing acquisition and exploitation activities. In *Lake,* the taxpayer-corporation owned the working-interest in two oil leases. In exchange for the cancellation of a debt, it assigned to its creditor a right to receive the sum of $600,000 out of the proceeds of future sales of oil. The parties anticipated that

---

[17]   356 U.S. 260 (1958).

the payout would take about three years, a period substantially shorter than the useful life of the working-interest itself. The Fifth Circuit found the assignment to be a sale of a capital asset on the ground that the assigned oil-payment right constituted an "interest in land" under local law. The Supreme Court reversed. "The substance of what was received," the Court said, "was the present value of income which the recipient would otherwise obtain in the future. In short, consideration was paid for the right to receive future income, not for an increase in the value of the income-producing property."[18]

As in *Hort,* the quoted language is broader than it needed to be, because the Court's aim, again, was merely to assure that carved-out interests would be treated as ordinary. Thus, capital gain treatment would presumably have been sustained if the life of the oil-payment and the life of the working-interest had been coterminous, since then the fatal element of carving-out would have been absent.

(b) Sale of a Life Estate

As suggested, the issues raised in *Hort* and *Lake* have an element of fruit-and-tree about them, and it is not surprising to discover that the Supreme Court found it useful in those cases to draw analogies from the older income-attribution cases. Thus, *Hort* cites *Horst,*[19] and *Lake* draws heavily on *Clifford, Horst, and Schaffner.* The reason is fairly plain. In the income-attribution cases, the Court's aim was to prevent property-owners from shifting tax to lower-bracket donees through short-term assignments of income. In *Hort* and *Lake,* the aim was to prevent the conversion of ordinary income into capital gain through use of a similar device. In both areas, though for somewhat different reasons, the Court sought to block what it regarded as a subversion of Congressional intent, and in both the preventive rule was one which required that the underlying property be completely disposed of (whether through gift or sale) before the desired tax benefit would be allowed.

In one well-known instance, however, this practice of placing reliance on the income-attribution cases proved slightly disastrous. In *McAllister v. Commissioner,*[20] the taxpayer sold her life estate in

---

[18]   Section 636—added to the Code after the *P.G.Lake* decision—would treat the $600,000 paid to the creditor as the repayment of a mortgage loan. The repayment would be ordinary income to the taxpayer, but it would be taxed periodically, that is, year-by-year, until the full amount was repaid.

[19]   The similarity of the names of the taxpayers in *Hort* and *Horst,* combined with the analytical connection between the two cases, has been a source of confusion for generations of law students and tax practitioners (and even, to tell the truth, tax professors). In a better world, at least one of the two taxpayers would have had some other name.

[20]   157 F.2d 235 (2d Cir. 1946).

a testamentary trust to the trust's remainderman for $55,000 cash. Asserting that her basis in the life estate, computed actuarially, was about $63,000, the taxpayer reported a capital loss from the sale of $8,000. Much as he had in *Hort,* the Commissioner disallowed the loss and treated the entire $55,000 as ordinary income.

With one dissent, the Second Circuit held for the taxpayer. Judge Clark, for the majority, reasoned that the issue "reduce[d] itself to the question whether the case [was] within the rule of Blair v. Commissioner . . ., or that of Hort v. Commissioner. . . ." In *Blair,* he noted, the Supreme Court had held that the gift of a life estate represented "the assignment of a property right in a trust." Hence, the donee rather than the donor was taxable on the trust income received thereafter. *Blair,* said Clark, was "indistinguishable from the present case," because here, as there, the taxpayer transferred her entire interest in the property. By contrast, had Mrs. McAllister attempted to sell the income for a few years only—had she, as in *Hort,* engaged in a carving out—the transaction would be viewed as mere income anticipation, and the Commissioner's position would be sustained.

Dissenting, Judge Frank argued that the *Blair* decision was not determinative: the fact that the *donor* of a life estate was held not taxable under § 61(a) on trust income received by the donee did not, in his view, establish that the *seller* of a life estate was to be treated as having disposed of a capital asset within the meaning of § 1221. *Hort* rather than *Blair* was the relevant authority, he thought, because the sale of a life estate, like the cancellation of a lease, "resemble[d] the advance payment of dividends, interest, or salaries." As in *Hort,* the sale was merely a substitute for future income, and hence the proceeds should have been taxed at ordinary rates.

Once again, it is important to emphasize that there were really *two* issues before the court in *McAllister:* (1) whether Mrs. McAllister could report a *loss* from the transaction, and (2) whether in any event the life estate was a capital asset in her hands. As stated, Judge Clark resolved both questions favorably to the taxpayer, because the absence of a carving-out convinced him that the case was controlled by *Blair.*

The decision in *McAllister* almost certainly was wrong. To see why, it will be useful to remind ourselves of the rules that govern the taxation of trust income where the life-tenant *retains* her life estate and receives annual distribution from the trust in a "normal" manner. As indicated at 4.02, under the "system" approved by the Supreme Court in *Irwin v. Gavit,* the life tenant is taxed on *all* the trust income during the term of the trust, and is *not* allowed an offset for amortization. The remainderman, on the other hand, includes nothing in his income either annually or on the termination of the trust. At the death of the life-tenant, the remainderman takes over the trust property at a basis equal to its full basis in the hands of the trustee, just as if the remainderman had been the sole legatee. To illustrate, assume that a decedent leaves property in trust (life estate to A, remainder to B) with a basis and value at death of $100,000. The property is expected to yield income of $8,000 a year. Based on A's life-expectancy (say 12 years), the present value of her interest in the trust is $60,000; that of the remainderman $40,000. Under *Gavit*, A will include the full $8,000 of trust income every year throughout her lifetime. B will include nothing, and when the trust terminates at A's death B will take the trust property at a basis of $100,000. The *Gavit* "system" is thus one in which the exclusion for gifts and bequests—and hence the *entire* basis in the property—goes to the remainderman alone. All the taxable income—and hence *none* of the basis—goes to the life tenant.

Apparently unaware of *Gavit*, the court in *McAllister* disregarded the system just described insofar as the life-tenant was concerned. The decision, in effect, permits A to take credit for a proportionate share of the basis of the trust property where the life estate is *sold*, but does (and of course can do) nothing to limit the remainderman's claim to the full basis of the property when the trust terminates. The result is an *over*-recovery of basis. If A sells her life-estate for $60,000 immediately after the decedent's death, she has no gain or loss under *McAllister* because her basis for the life-estate is held to be $60,000. When the trust terminates, B's basis for the trust property under *Gavit* becomes $100,000. Thus, 160% of the property's basis will ultimately be recovered by its beneficial owners, which is obviously an erroneous outcome.

The error becomes even clearer when one observes that the effect of *McAllister* is to eliminate entirely a substantial proportion of the taxable income of the trust. This follows from the fact that the *purchaser* of the life estate (in *McAllister* the remainderman himself) is entitled to amortize his cost over the expected term of the interest he has purchased—12 years in our illustration. The purchaser stands apart from the relationship between the life-tenant and remainderman; he is an "unrelated" investor who has actually laid out $60,000 for a wasting asset, and that outlay is properly recoverable by him through amortization deductions totaling $60,000 over 12 years. In overall terms, therefore, $60,000 of trust income will be taxed to *nobody*.

The *Blair* case, of course, did not entail the same consequence. While the donee of the life estate became taxable on the trust income (no doubt at a lower marginal rate than the donor), the Supreme Court did not suggest that the life estate acquired a basis in the donee's hands by reason of the gift, or that any change occurred in the normal operation of the *Gavit* rules. Income-shifting was approved in *Blair* because of the absence of a carving-out, but this holding had, or should have had, no bearing on the treatment of amounts realized on *sales* of life estates. In emphasizing *Blair* and overlooking *Gavit,* Judge Clark simply fastened on the wrong income-attribution rule.

A similar set of observations can be made about the second question raised in *McAllister*—whether the life estate was a capital asset in the hands of the life tenant. Even if Judge Clark had gotten the basis problem right—which would have meant giving the life tenant a basis of zero—it would have been inconsistent with *Hort* and *Gavit* to treat the proceeds of sale as capital gain. The aim of *Gavit,* really, is to simplify the taxation of trust income by treating the life-tenant and the remainderman as if they were one individual. Under *Hort,* if an individual property-owner sells an income interest for a term of years but retains the underlying property, the proceeds of sale are taxable as ordinary income because the transaction is viewed as a carving-out. By plausible analogy, the same should be true if a life estate is sold separately from the remainder, because *Gavit* integrates the life-tenant and the remainderman for tax purposes. If, however, the life estate is held to be a capital asset, then, in effect, the ordinary income thrown off by the trust will be $60,000 less than it should be, and a clear advantage arises in creating split interests in property as compared with outright gifts or bequests.

The *McAllister* problem was finally dealt with by Congress in 1969 through the addition to the Code of § 1001(e). Curiously, however, § 1001(e) is limited to the basis aspect: the subsection provides that for purposes of computing gain or loss, a term interest in property shall have no basis in the hands of a donee or heir, except where the sale of the term interest is part of a transaction in which all beneficial interests are disposed of. No change was made as respects the capital asset status of the life estate, however, so that if the illustrative transaction took place now, the taxpayer would presumably have $60,000 of capital gain. Apparently, Congress was persuaded that sellers of life estates (often, perhaps, older people) would suffer hardship if the proceeds of sale were taxed all in one year as ordinary income, and having corrected the computation of basis, was willing to continue favored treatment as respects the resultant gain.

(c)   Other Contract Rights

Right or wrong, the *Hort* and *McAllister* decisions show that the courts do not treat all transactions involving contract claims alike. In *Hort,* the element of carving-out led to ordinary treatment; in

McAllister, the assumed absence of that element led to capital gain. In other cases, especially when employment rights are concerned, the courts have sometimes resolved definitional issues by finding that the contract sold or cancelled lacked or possessed the status of "property"; in still others, the factor of "sale or exchange" has been seen as critical. Overall, the treatment of contract rights is exceedingly untidy; the decided cases are hard to line up in a consistent fashion, and judicial reasoning is often unclear. Much of the blame belongs to Congress. Here, as in the *Corn Products* area, the need is for a detailed statutory classification which effectively separates capital from non-capital transactions. Uncertain of its own goals in the capital gain field, however, Congress has largely preferred to leave the matter to the courts.

Leasehold interests. As already noted in connection with *Hort,* a *lessor* normally has ordinary income on the sale or cancellation of a lease. *Hort,* obviously, was a case in which rental values had *fallen* after the lease was entered into; the lease had grown onerous to the lessee, who paid the lessor a cash sum to be free of it. But suppose that the real estate market had moved in the other direction, that rental values had increased, and that the rental called for in the lease had become a bargain by current standards. The lease would then have been economically burdensome to Hort, the lessor. If Hort had paid $140,000 to the lessee for the cancellation of the lease, or if the lessee had sold its rights to occupy the building to a third party, would the lessee have had ordinary income also? The answer, apparently, is no. The courts have held, as to *lessees,* that the sale or surrender of a lease results in capital gain.[21] In the lessee's hands, it is said, the leasehold is a substantial interest in real estate, not merely a claim to future income. Whereas the amount received by Hort, a lessor, for cancellation of the lease was held a substitute for future rents, the amount paid to a lessee for surrendering *its* interest in a lease is regarded as received in exchange for a property right which qualifies as a capital asset.

As usual, however, distinctions based on the "substitute for ordinary income" doctrine are not very satisfying. A lessee who is the beneficiary of a favorable lease enjoys a saving of annual rents which will be reflected in higher net income from the business operations conducted on the leased premises. Since rentals are otherwise fully deductible, the saving is merely an addition to the ordinary income which the lessee will realize through occupancy. If this benefit is bought up by the lessor, or is sold to a third party, the payment received is as much and as clearly a "substitute for future income" as

---

[21]   *E.g., Commissioner v. McCue Brothers & Drummond, Inc.,* 210 F.2d 752 (2d Cir.1954). And see Code § 1241.

the payment that is made to a lessor when the fact-pattern is reversed.

Probably, though, the "substitution" doctrine is nothing more than judicial shorthand, just as is the fruit-and-tree doctrine in the income-attribution field. The real, or at least the best, reason for distinguishing between lessors and lessees resides in the presence (in one case) and the absence (in the other) of the familiar element of carving out. Once again, a lessor who disposes of his interest in a lease *still* owns the underlying income-producing property—land or building—after the disposition. He therefore retains the ability, on the expiration of each successive lease, to *repeat* the process of making an advance disposition of his right to future rentals. If such advance dispositions were accorded capital gain treatment, then all of the property-owner's ordinary rental income could be converted into capital gain. By contrast, a lessee owns only cash following the disposition of a lease, and thus lacks the opportunity to again dispose of his rights in the same leasehold. The tax law reflects this difference, in effect, by treating the leasehold as a mere substitute for ordinary income when it is the *lessor* who sells or surrenders the lease. Where the *lessee* is concerned, however, the leasehold turns out to be substantial "property."

In the *Metropolitan Bldg. Co.* case,[22] the taxpayer was both a lessee of certain property in Seattle—the University of Washington being the lessor—and a sublessor of the same property. Olympic, Inc., a hotel operator, was the sublessee. Both the head lease and the sublease had only two years to run. Wanting to lease the property directly from the University (at a much higher rent and for a much longer term), Olympic paid Metropolitan $137,000 to terminate both the sublease between it and Metropolitan and Metropolitan's lease from the University. The question was whether that payment should be treated as ordinary income under *Hort*—payment to a sublessor from a sublessee—or capital gain under the authorities cited above— payment to a lessee for the sale of a lease. The correct result, fairly obviously, is capital gain. Metropolitan's entire interest in the leased property was terminated, and unlike the lessor in *Hort* it had nothing left to use, dispose of or re-lease to another subtenant. Reversing the Tax Court, the Ninth Circuit so held on the ground that "the transaction constituted a bona fide transfer . . . of the leasehold in its entirety,"[23] rather than a carved out substitute for future rents.

---

[22]   282 F.2d 592 (9th Cir. 1960).

[23]   Three-cornered transactions of this sort can be somewhat ambiguous. Was the issue raised by the government in *Metropolitan Bldg.* the right one? Arguably, (i) the payment by Olympic to Metropolitan was really for the benefit of the University, because it enabled the U to terminate Metropolitan's lease without drawing directly on its own resources; accordingly, (ii) that payment should be treated as a prepayment

Employment contracts, agencies, distributorships, etc. Suppose the manager of a baseball team is dismissed by his club at the end of the first year of a two-year contract. The contract calls for a salary of $1,000,000 a year, and the manager, after negotiation, agrees to accept $300,000 for releasing the club from its remaining obligation. Is the $300,000 payment capital gain, or is it ordinary income?

The courts have held consistently that payments made to an employee for the surrender of his employment contract are ordinary.[24] Although the decisions sometimes rest on the ground that the contract cancellation is not a "sale or exchange," or that an employment contract is not "property," it seems likely that the courts have been influenced chiefly by the feeling that employment and personal service is simply not an appropriate context for capital gain. Possibly, also, there is an analogy between the position of the baseball manager in the illustration above and the position of a lessor of real estate. The manager receives a payment for cancellation of his contract because his services are now worth less to the club than when the contract was entered into, but he is also free to accept similar employment elsewhere. In *Hort,* the lessor received a premium from his lessee because rental values had declined, and, again, was free to re-lease the property to another tenant. If ordinary income was required to be recognized in *Hort* (for reasons relating generally to the carved-out interest limitation), perhaps the same principle justifies ordinary treatment for employees (*i.e.,* lessors of services) when an employment contract is terminated. It would also seem to follow that if an employ*ee* is like a less*or,* then an employ*er* is like a less*ee.* Hence, if the baseball club sold a player's contract to another team for cash, presumably its gain would be capital.

Once we leave real estate leases and employment agreements, however, the treatment of contract termination payments becomes uncertain. It has been held, for example, that amounts received by a taxpayer on the transfer of an agency contract giving the taxpayer an exclusive right to represent a popular singer were ordinary. Viewing the agency agreement as essentially similar to an employment contract, the Tax Court found that the right to represent a client was not a capital asset.[25] The Fifth Circuit, on the other hand, has held

---

of rent from Olympic to the U, and then a payment of the same amount from the U to Metropolitan. Metropolitan would still get capital gain, and the U, being a tax-exempt entity, would be indifferent. Olympic, however, would have to amortize the prepayment of rent over the lengthy term of the new lease, a much longer period than the two years remaining on the old leases. So viewed, the real issue in the case would have been the amount of Olympic's annual amortization allowance, not the taxpayer's capital gain.

[24]   *E.g., McFall v. Commissioner,* 34 B.T.A. 108 (1936).

[25]   *General Artists Corp. v. Commissioner,* 17 T.C. 1517 (1952), affirmed 205 F.2d 360 (2d Cir. 1953).

that the sale of a right to service mortgage accounts by collecting payments and performing other duties on behalf of the mortgage-holder, an insurance company, did entail the transfer of a capital asset.[26] The court apparently felt that the service contract was a major structural element of the taxpayer's business, and not merely a right to earn employment income. Code § 1241 specifically provides that the cancellation of a distributorship agreement shall be treated as a "sale or exchange" in cases in which "the distributor has a substantial capital investment in the distributorship." Although the section deals only with the sale or exchange requirement, it was evidently Congress' intent to afford capital gain treatment when a distributorship involving a significant outlay by the taxpayer is sold or terminated. The proper treatment of contracts which cannot easily be classified as employment contracts, but which do not meet the capital investment test of § 1241, is thereby left in doubt.

Among the most interesting of the many decisions in the contracts field is *Commissioner v. Ferrer*.[27] As a matter of incidental history, the Second Circuit prior to *Ferrer* had distinguished fairly sharply between real-estate leases and other contract rights. Thus, as noted earlier, the court found capital gain upon a lessee's surrender of its lease to the lessor, but also found ordinary income upon the cancellation of an exclusive distributorship,[28] the sale of exclusive agency rights,[29] and the termination of an exclusive right to buy the output of a coal mine. In the last of these cases, *Commissioner v. Pittston Co.*,[30] the court held that the taxpayer's contractual right to acquire the mine output at a predetermined price lacked the quality of a substantial property interest, in part because the taxpayer's sole remedy would have been in money damages had the mine owner elected to breach the contract by selling coal to third parties. In this respect, the court said, the taxpayer's status differed from that of a lessee whose rights in the leased premises are enforceable in equity and thus constitute an interest in the property itself. A dissenting opinion argued that the output contract was the equivalent of a lease of the mining property and, hence, should have been treated as a capital asset.

The "substantial property" test was also stressed in *Ferrer*. The taxpayer, a well-known actor, had entered into a dramatic production contract with the author of a novel called *Moulin Rouge*. The contract gave Ferrer (1) the right to produce and present a play based on the novel, (2) the right to veto any disposition of movie rights prior to the

---

[26] *Nelson Weaver Realty Co. v. Commissioner*, 307 F.2d 897 (5th Cir.1962).

[27] 304 F.2d 125 (2d Cir. 1962).

[28] *Commissioner v. Starr Brothers*, 204 F.2d 673 (2d Cir.1953).

[29] *General Artists Corp. v. Commissioner*, supra note 25.

[30] 252 F.2d 344 (2d Cir. 1958).

time the play had run for a specified period, and (3) the right to receive 40% of any motion picture proceeds if the play was in fact produced and the movie rights were sold thereafter. Before a play could get underway, however, Ferrer received an offer from John Huston to do a movie based on *Moulin Rouge* in which Ferrer would play the lead. As part of the deal, Huston insisted that Ferrer consent to either "an annulment or conveyance" of the dramatic production contract between himself and the novelist. Ferrer agreed and entered into a new contract with Huston. Under the new contract, Ferrer was to receive a salary for performing the role of Toulouse-Lautrec, plus a stated percentage of the motion picture distribution profits. The latter was said to be in consideration for the surrender by Ferrer of the original dramatic production contract. In 1953, in addition to the salary, which he reported as ordinary income, Ferrer received $180,000 as his percentage of the distribution profits. The issue in the case, simply, was whether the percentage payment should be treated as ordinary income or capital gain.

The Tax Court found as a fact that the percentage payment was *not* mere personal service income, but had truly been received in exchange for Ferrer's assignment of the dramatic production contract. The contract, in turn, was held to be a capital asset, and hence the entire payment was treated as capital gain. On appeal by the Commissioner, the Second Circuit declined to reverse the lower court's findings on the personal service issue. It did, however, reassess the character of the contract rights which Ferrer had acquired and then released, by treating each as a separate economic interest in the novel. On this basis, the court decided that right (1)— the right to produce a play—was analogous to a lease of the story property, Ferrer being the lessee, because equitable relief would have been available had the contract been breached; and that right (2)— the veto power—was equivalent to an "encumbrance" which equity would also protect if necessary. However, as to right (3)—the right to share in the proceeds of any sale to the movies—the court found that this element did *not* rise to the status of an "equitable interest" in property, but merely represented a claim to "a percentage of certain avails . . . as further income from the lease of the play." Right (3), in the court's view, was comparable to the right of a lessee to receive from his lessor "a percentage of what the lessor obtained from other tenants attracted to the building by the lessee's operations"; in effect, the movie rights would become valuable if the play was a success. Since such percentage payments would be ordinary income to the lessee if received during the term of the lease, a sale of the lessee's right thereto for a lump-sum payment produced ordinary income as well. Accordingly, rights (1) and (2) were given capital asset status, while right (3) was held to be ordinary. The case was then remanded to the Tax Court for an allocation of the percentage money among these several interests.

Judge Friendly's opinion in *Ferrer* is skillfully devised and plausible. Even so, one can question whether it was truly appropriate to treat each of the taxpayer's contract rights as a separate unit, instead of viewing the contract, as the Tax Court had, as one single economic interest. Suppose, to use the court's leasehold analogy, that a lessee is entitled to occupy certain premises for a term of years. The lease provides for a stated annual rental, but provides also that this stated rental is to be reduced by payment to the lessee of a percentage of the rents received by the lessor from other tenants in the same building. In exchange for a lump-sum, the lessee now surrenders his entire leasehold interest, including his right to rent reduction payments. It seems quite clear that such a transaction would produce capital gain. There might be doubt about the result if the lessee sold off the right to percentage payments by itself and retained the lease, but where the leasehold is disposed of as well there seems to be no reason to deny capital gain treatment once it is conceded that a lease is a capital asset. In *Ferrer* the "lessee" retained nothing, and certainly the right to share in the motion picture proceeds was a part of the overall lease arrangement, not an independently acquired interest. It is difficult to see, therefore, why right (3) should have been carved out of the basic contract and treated as if disposed of for a separate consideration when that was simply not the case, except as this construction may have been necessary to reach the desired result.

One suspects that at bottom this complex decision reflects an unstated compromise which traces back to the basic issue of personal services. Constrained by the Tax Court's negative finding on that question, the court nevertheless managed, through a deft manipulation of the lease analogy, to sustain the Commissioner in treating a portion of the percentage money—probably the major proportion—as ordinary income. Actually, the simplest, and probably the most nearly accurate, view of the facts in *Ferrer* was that the entire percentage payment represented a reward for Ferrer's services as an actor. Had Ferrer declined to take the lead in the movie, Huston most probably would have made no deal with him whatever. The fact that Ferrer also had some control over the story-property may have meant that he could ask somewhat more for his services than otherwise. Fundamentally, however, the entire receipt was compensation—or, at least, income from the taxpayer's trade or business—and quite probably all of it should have been lumped together with Ferrer's salary and found to be ordinary in the first instance.

Lottery winnings. In the *Maginnis* case,[31] the taxpayer, his wife and three sons won a total of $23 million in the Oregon state lottery. The Maginnises' share was $9 million, payable in 20 annual installments of $450,000. After receiving annual payments for a few years, Mr. & Mrs. M sold their right to the remaining installments to a third-party investor for a lump sum of $3,950,000. The taxpayers reported the lump-sum payment as long-term capital gain. The Commissioner insisted that the payment was ordinary income.

Affirming the district court, the Ninth Circuit held for the Commissioner. The characteristics of a capital gain, said the court—namely, substantial "investment" and long-term "appreciation"—were absent in the case of lottery winnings (or, presumably, any lucky number prize). Had the taxpayers received their payment from the State, whether as a lump sum or in installments, such payment or payments would be ordinary income—if for no other reason, because cashing in a lottery ticket is not a "sale or exchange" of a capital asset. Selling the claim to a third party could not, in itself, convert what would otherwise be high-taxed ordinary income into low-taxed capital gain. The Court was slightly troubled by the well-worn capital gain paradox—that selling an appreciated investment asset gets capital gain treatment even though the gain reflects the present value of a future stream of ordinary income—but ultimately concluded that a corporate bond and a lottery ticket are two different things, the former being an investment, the latter a mere gamble.[32]

Probably right, though not so easy to rationalize in terms of doctrine. The elements of "investment"—the cost of the lottery ticket, or maybe a fistful of lottery tickets—together with "appreciation" in the value of the ticket itself, are really not lacking if you take the quoted terms literally. One alternative, we suppose, would be to treat the lottery payoff as an annuity issued by the State of Oregon. The present value of the State's obligation—make it $4 million for convenience—would be the "amount realized" in exchange for the winning ticket. That amount could be taxed as capital gain over the 20-year payout period at a rate of $200,000 a year. The $250,000 excess of the annual $450,000 payment over $200,000 would be ordinary interest income, likewise taxable on an annual basis.

In the end, perhaps, the question reduces to whether or not Congress intended "bets" to be treated as "property held" under § 1221(a). Did it? Whom should we ask?

---

[31] *U.S. v. Maginnis,* 356 F.3d 1179 (9th Cir. 2004).

[32] The issue of capital gains treatment for sellers of rights to future lottery payments has been much litigated in recent years, with the government winning consistently. *E.g., Womack v. Commissioner,* 510 F.3d 1295 (11th Cir. 2007); *Watkins v. Commissioner,* 447 F.3d 1269 (10th Cir. 2006); *Lattera v. Commissioner,* 437 F.3d 399 (3d Cir. 2006); *Davis v. Commissioner,* 119 T.C. 1 (2002).

17.04   Fragmentation and Imputed Interest

With one exception (Judge Friendly's opinion in *Ferrer*), up to this point the issue of capital gain or ordinary income has been presented on an all-or-nothing basis. The futures contracts in *Corn Products* either were, or weren't, capital assets; the lease-cancellation payment in *Hort* either was, or wasn't, a "return of capital." By contrast, in the cases next discussed the property disposed of appears to possess elements that are mixed, to be neither wholly capital nor wholly ordinary. Under such circumstances, will the law require the asset to be fragmented into separate components for the purpose of characterizing the taxpayer's gain or loss, or will it insist on a finding that the property is either one thing or the other, but not both? This curious question is considered here in two contexts: first, the sale of an entire business—a "going concern"—whose assets include both capital and non-capital items; and second, the disposition of a security or other claim whose value includes an accrued or "imputed" interest factor. These two situations do not exhaust the fragmentation problem, however, and the same or a similar problem will be seen to arise again in later sections.

(a)   Sale of an Entire Business

In *Williams v. McGowan*,[33] the taxpayer sold a hardware business which he owned and operated as a sole proprietor. The assets of the business included cash, inventory, accounts receivable, and fixtures and other depreciable property. The sale resulted in an overall net loss which the taxpayer reported as ordinary. The Commissioner sought to treat the loss as capital, however, on the ground that the hardware "business", viewed as an entity, was a capital asset. Speaking through Judge Learned Hand, the Second Circuit upheld the taxpayer. Section 1221, Hand noted, specifically broke the elements of a business down into separate categories, such as stock-in-trade and depreciable assets. This, he reasoned, showed that Congress meant to "comminute" the business into fragments, and that it did not regard "the whole" as a capital asset. Since, apparently, the hardware business included ordinary assets only, the loss that resulted from the sale was held to be an ordinary loss. Dissenting, Judge Frank argued that it was artificial and unrealistic to carve up the transaction into distinct sales of separate properties. "Where a business is sold as a unit," he said, "the whole is greater than its parts. Businessmen so recognize; so, too, I think did Congress." In effect, therefore, while Hand viewed the separate classification of business assets as mandatory, whether those assets were sold piecemeal or as part of a sale of the entire concern, Frank

---

[33]   152 F.2d 570 (2d Cir. 1945).

regarded the "business" as distinguishable from its component parts and viewed the entirety as qualifying "property."

Just where Williams' loss came from is not made clear in the court's opinion, but at least one possibility is that his store's inventory—hammers and nails and nuts and bolts—had declined in value relative to its cost. Assume that was so. From a policy standpoint, would it be sensible to distinguish for capital gain or loss purposes between a bulk sale of inventory to a single purchaser and day-to-day over-the-counter sales at retail? The obvious purpose of § 1221(a)(1) is to assure that the gross profit from daily business transactions is treated as ordinary. In the case of a retailer like Williams, "gross profit" would be the difference between the wholesale cost of the storekeeper's inventory and the price he charges his customers—otherwise known as the retailer's markup. Net operating income consists of gross profit less selling costs. Thus, Williams buys hammers and nails in bulk from his supplier, displays the stuff on his dusty shelves, and sells it to people who walk in and out of the store all day making small purchases. The price to customers is expected to cover the firm's inputs—rent, utilities, salaries, etc.—and also reward poor Williams for his capital investment and for the tedious hours he spends standing behind the counter answering questions.

Should § 1221(a)(1) apply in the same way when Williams makes a bulk sale of his inventory and terminates his business? There is no retail markup on a bulk sale. If the statutory aim is to assure that the gross profits realized by a dealer are ordinary, doesn't that purpose lapse when the dealer sells his entire inventory to another dealer? The latter will of course resell the goods to *his* retail customers and add a retail markup of his own. Although Williams may have suffered a loss (the year was 1940, still a Depression year), the same transaction would no doubt have produced a substantial gain given wartime scarcities had he waited and sold his inventory after the start of World War II (the start, that is, from the American perspective). Litigating positions would then be reversed. Williams would argue that the gain bore no relationship to his status as a dealer and hence should be treated as capital gain, just as would the sale of pork bellies or any other "commodity" that rose in value. The Commissioner would assert that the statute makes no such distinction—inventory is "inventory" in the hands of a dealer whether sold in bulk or otherwise. The court did not discuss the issue in quite these terms, having somehow found a better precedent in Roman law. However, the opinion does appear to reject the idea of treating the assets sold as "unitary", even within a single category. Presumably, therefore, the court did not, or would not, regard the bulk-sale feature as making any difference.

We might note that the same question—in reverse, but still the same question—has arisen with respect to real estate acquired and held for long-term investment, but then much later subdivided and sold in piecemeal fashion to individual homebuyers. Is the seller's gain capital gain because the property was originally acquired for investment, or is it ordinary income because the property was finally sold to retail customers in the ordinary course of business? Does the investor become a dealer because of the way he finally disposes of the property? Or does he remain an investor no matter how he disposes of it? That issue, which has been litigated fairly extensively, is discussed, at 18.01, below.

The requirement of "comminution," which was approved in *Williams*, tends to complicate the bargaining between the seller and the buyer of a business, because it usually means that they must agree not only on an overall purchase price for the company, but also on the specific allocation of that purchase price among the assets sold. This is important to the seller for the obvious reason that the allocation governs the amount of ordinary income he has to recognize on the sale; it is important to the buyer because it determines his basis for the assets acquired and hence his own potential for future ordinary income. To the extent the purchase price is allocated to non-capital assets—typically inventory—the seller's ordinary income is increased while the buyer's is reduced; to the extent allocated to depreciable assets, the seller may get some capital gain under § 1231 (discussed at 18.02(a)), but also some ordinary income under the depreciation recapture rules of §§ 1245 and 1250 (18.02(b)), while the buyer has a higher basis for computing depreciation; to the extent allocable to goodwill, the seller gets capital gain treatment and the buyer gets an asset whose cost (under § 197, discussed at 6.11) is amortizable over a 15-year term; finally, to the extent allocable to a non-depreciable asset such as land, the seller gets capital gain while the buyer is left with a cost that will not be recoverable until the asset itself is sold. The interests of the two parties are thus in some respects adverse, a factor that may make agreement more difficult to reach. On the other hand, the need to agree upon an allocation protects the government from the danger that seller and buyer will attempt to take inconsistent positions, which, in a given case, might otherwise eliminate the ordinary income component on both sides. The freedom of the parties to agree on the allocation of the purchase price of a business is restricted by § 1060 and the Regulations thereunder, which feature a moderately elaborate set of rules designed to prevent the parties from using allocations not reflective of economic reality. Under § 1060(a), an allocation agreed to by the parties is "binding on both the transferee and transferor unless the [IRS] determines that such allocation . . . is not appropriate."

(b) Bond Discount and Imputed Interest

Suppose a corporate borrower issues a five-year bond for $620. The bondholder is entitled to no interest payments during the five-year term but on redemption at maturity the corporation agrees to pay the holder $1,000. As a formal matter, it can be argued that the $380 difference between the issue and the redemption price is "property appreciation" and should be taxed as capital gain, but, really, the argument is almost too weak to require refutation. The original issue discount of $380 represents compensation to the bondholder for the use of the borrowed funds and simply takes the place of annual interest payments. Recognizing this, § 1271—which otherwise treats gain or loss on sale or retirement of a bond as capital gain or loss—provides in effect that original issue discount shall be taxed to the bondholder as ordinary interest income. Section 1272 requires, further, that the bondholder accrue such interest annually—rather than deferring it until maturity or sale—even though the holder may be an individual who is on the cash method of accounting. As respects the latter rule, the controlling analogy is to accrued interest on a savings account, which is taxed to the depositor each year whether withdrawn by him in cash or left to accumulate.

The same analogy should answer the question of *how much* interest is accruable by the bondholder annually. The implicit rate of return to the bondholder in our example is 10%, *i.e.,* $620 invested at a 10% constant rate of interest (compounded annually) will grow to $1,000 at the end of five years. By accepting a discount bond instead of insisting on annual interest payments, the bondholder—like a savings account depositor who leaves his annual interest in the account—is really increasing the principal amount of his loan from year to year. Thus, the original loan is $620. At 10%, interest for Year 1 is $62. Since the latter amount is left in the borrower's hands instead of being withdrawn, "principal" increases to $682 at the start of Year 2 and interest for that year is about $68. For years 3, 4 and 5 the accrued interest amounts would be $76, $83 and $91, respectively, with the total of all such annual accruals, plus the original issue price of $620, necessarily equaling the redemption price of $1,000.

Given the tax law's historical reluctance to grapple with the everyday miracle of compound interest, it may surprise some to learn that § 1272(a)(3)—added in 1982 at the urging of the Treasury—actually does require a "scientific" calculation of annual interest in connection with original issue discount bonds (*i.e.,* $62 in Year 1, $68 in Year 2, etc.). Prior to 1982, the relevant Code provision used a straight-line calculation, which, in our example, would produce level annual interest accruals of $76 ($380/5 years). Since the straight-line method inevitably *overstated* interest in the earlier years, the corrected method would appear to be more favorable to bondholders. For the same reason, however, it is *less* favorable to borrowers: the latter were previously permitted to compute their accrued interest expense on the same straight-line basis and thus take larger deductions in the earlier years than their true interest cost. But why, then, should the Treasury have sought the change? Wouldn't all this more or less balance out from the standpoint of the revenues? Hardly. Before 1982, original issue discount bonds were usually sold to tax-exempt entities, such as employee pension plans, or to lenders having unused loss carryovers or otherwise lacking in "tax appetite." Allowing the borrower to anticipate its interest deductions under the straight-line method was thus often harmless to the bondholder, which could, indeed, expect to receive a somewhat higher interest rate from the borrower as consideration for joining in the scheme. As has been seen (*e.g.*, 6.03(c)), any distortion in the timing of income and deductions can be converted into financial benefits for *both* parties to the relevant transaction, provided that one of the parties is exempt or unprofitable, or confronts a lower tax rate than the other.

Yet another legislative change should be mentioned. Prior to 1984, the ordinary treatment provided for by § 1272 applied only to discount in the *original* issue price of a bond. If discount developed because of later market fluctuations, redemption of the bond at par resulted in capital gain. Thus, suppose a bond originally issued for its par value of $100 dropped to $90 because of a rise in prevailing interest rates. An investor who bought the bond in the market for $90, and then simply held the bond until maturity and received $100 from the issuer, had a $10 capital gain. In effect, bond discount resulted in ordinary income only if the interest element was built into the issue price by the borrower.

Plainly, however, a distinction between market discount and original issue discount makes little sense in economic terms. Thus, the difference between the taxpayer's $90 purchase price (in the example just given) and the $100 he receives when the bond matures is "interest" as far as he is concerned. The taxpayer's aim is to pay $90 now for a promise to receive $100 later, and it doesn't matter to him (taxes aside) whether he buys the bond from another investor or from the bond-issuer directly.

The 1984 Act changed the treatment of market discount bonds so that investors are now required to report market discount as ordinary income when the bond is disposed of, whether through sale or redemption at maturity. Under § 1276(a), the reportable amount is limited to the gain realized on such disposition, so that no interest would be imputed if the bond mentioned in the preceding paragraph were finally sold for less than the investor's $90 purchase price. Original issue discount, by contrast, is accruable annually, presumably because the issuer itself will be amortizing the discount through annual interest deductions.

The Code sections just discussed—§§ 1271 *et seq.*—apply to bonds, debentures, notes and other conventional debt instruments. With respect to claims of a less formal character that are not covered by those sections—for example, a claim to a legacy or to unpaid fees or commissions—the courts have generally held that settlement or collection does not constitute a "sale or exchange."[34] The definitions of the various sorts of capital gains and losses in § 1221 all require a "sale or exchange" of a capital asset. This is narrower than the "sale or other disposition" standard for realization of gains and losses under § 1001(a). If a taxpayer disposes of a capital asset in a manner not constituting a "sale or exchange"—abandonment of worthless property is an obvious example—the gain or loss is generally not capital because of the absence of a "sale or exchange."[35] There is no obvious policy rationale for limiting capital gain and loss treatment to "sales or exchanges," and it is (apparently) only because of poor drafting that § 1222 refers to "sales or exchanges" rather than "sales or other dispositions." Nevertheless, the courts have felt compelled to give effect to the statutory language, and to hold that the disposition of a capital asset does not produce capital gain or loss if the disposition is not a "sale or exchange."

As a result of the "sale or exchange" requirement, if an investor purchases a claim (*e.g.*, to a legacy or to an unpaid commission) at a discount, any gain realized when the obligor makes payment will be treated as ordinary income.[36] The courts' theory in cases of this sort is that the taxpayer's claim is merely "extinguished" when it is satisfied by the obligor; no "exchange" occurs because the obligor himself acquires no property other than relief from the obligation. This application of the sale or exchange requirement is obviously rather wooden, but perhaps it here serves as recognition of the imputed interest element in the creditor's gain. As with discount bonds, such imputed interest can be identified as the difference between the purchase price of the claim and the amount finally received from the obligor.

In an effort to avoid ordinary income in these circumstances, taxpayers have sometimes resorted to a sale of the purchased claim

---

[34] *Fairbanks v. U.S.*, 306 U.S. 436 (1939).

[35] Several provisions waive the "sale or exchange" requirement in certain situations. For example, § 165(g) provides that the loss resulting from a security becoming worthless is a capital loss, despite the absence of a "sale or exchange."

[36] *E.g., Pounds v. U.S.*, 372 F.2d 342 (5th Cir.1967) (settlement of a purchased commission claim held ordinary income).

to a third party just prior to its collection. In *Jones v. Commissioner,*[37] the taxpayer purchased a remainder interest in a trust from the original remainderman. After the life-tenant's death but prior to actual distribution of the trust property, the taxpayer resold the remainder to another. Apparently, he feared that receipt of the trust property through distribution by the trustee would fail to qualify as a "sale or exchange." Conceding that the remainder (like any other "security") was a capital asset, the court held that despite the sale to a third party the taxpayer must recognize as ordinary income the implicit interest which had accrued on his investment. In effect, the accrued interest element was regarded as a non-capital component of the gain. The court therefore remanded the case to the trial court for the purpose of determining what portion of the total gain should be regarded as ordinary and what portion should be treated as capital.

The proceedings on remand are unreported, but perhaps the following would be illustrative. Assume that the trust in the *Jones* case owned property worth $100,000 when initially created; that the life-tenant had an actuarial life expectancy of five years; and that Jones immediately purchased the remainder for $75,000. Viewing the remainder as analogous to a discount bond, the anticipated interest element is obviously $25,000 over the five-year period, or $5,000 a year on a straight-line basis. Suppose, however, that the life-tenant died after only *two* years, and suppose also that the trust property—say real estate—had risen in value by that time to $120,000. We could now identify three elements of gain: (a) interest of $10,000 (*i.e.*, $5,000 × 2 years); (b) a mortality gain of $15,000; and (c) pure property appreciation of $20,000. Assuming the "sale or exchange" requirement was satisfied, the *Jones* decision apparently contemplates that (a) would be taxed as ordinary income, and (c) as capital gain. As to (b), the proper treatment is less clear. Since Jones was a casual investor and not an insurance company, however, the probability is that it, too, would be treated as capital gain.

17.05   Recurring Receipts

As noted in connection with the *Hort* case, the law distinguishes in a basic way between gain realized on a sale of appreciated property and periodic income such as dividends, interest and rents. The former, of course, is capital gain, the latter ordinary income. In *Hort,* the Court had to decide whether the sale of a carved-out income interest was "more like" a sale of appreciated property or "more like" the receipt of ordinary rent. The decision to treat the carved-out interest as ordinary was dictated, essentially, by a fear that recurring

---

[37]   330 F.2d 302 (3d Cir. 1964).

investment income would otherwise become convertible—pretty much on a wholesale basis—into low-taxed capital gain.

The cases discussed in this subsection—especially *Commissioner v. Brown*[38]—also involve the problem of differentiating between property appreciation and recurring income. Here, however, the issue concerns the *method* by which the purported sale has been effected, rather than the intrinsic nature of the asset disposed of. It is conceded that the property is a capital asset; what is questioned is whether the *transfer* qualifies as a sale. If, for example, the purported sale price is to be paid out in installments over an extended period of years, and if the payments themselves are contingent on the income to be derived from the property transferred, there may be legitimate doubt as to whether the transaction is a "sale" or merely a species of lease or profit-sharing arrangement. As a technical matter, capital treatment requires a "sale or exchange" (as discussed at 17.04); and in any event the philosophy of the capital gain preference assumes a completed disposition of the property in question. Accordingly, a finding that the transfer falls short of being a complete disposition normally means ordinary income to the transferor.

The discussion of *Brown,* which follows next, examines the "completed disposition" standard in the context of contingent-payment transactions. As will be seen, the Supreme Court has been liberal in characterizing such transactions as "sales". The *Carter* case, discussed thereafter, raises the further question of how the "fair market value" rule, established by the Court in *Burnet v. Logan* (14.03), relates to the treatment of the payments received. It turns out that "open" transactions—those in which a fair market value for the buyer's obligation *cannot* be ascertained—are treated more favorably than transactions that are deemed to be "closed". A brief consideration of the merits of this distinction concludes the section.

(a) Contingent Payments

A transaction in which property is to be paid for out of income to be derived from the property itself obviously presents a borderline problem under the "sale or exchange" requirement. From a policy standpoint, the capital gain preference seems to be intended, in part, to afford relief to taxpayers who are compelled to report in a single taxable year property appreciation which has accrued over an extended period of years. In addition, perhaps, the lower capital gain rate is designed to free taxpayers to shift investments in accordance with economic considerations by easing the impact of the taxable realization when appreciated property is sold. But if the property is transferred in exchange for future payments that will be spread out

---

[38]   380 U.S. 563 (1965).

over a number of years, and if, in addition, those payments are contingent on the income-producing capacity of the property itself, then neither element of "policy" seems readily applicable. Assuming that the taxpayer's gain is deferred (whether through use of the installment method under § 453 or because of other applicable rules of realization) until the payments are received, the effect is to produce a kind of homemade averaging of income which renders doubtful the need for further relief through a reduction of the applicable rates. Further, as the taxpayer is to be paid out of future income from the property transferred, it seems doubtful whether a "shift" from one investment to another really can be said to have occurred.

These objections to permitting capital gain treatment for deferred payment transactions—and especially for *contingent* deferred payment transactions—are not inconsiderable. But whatever their force, the fact is that neither Congress nor (for the most part) the courts have found them determinative. Thus, reporting gain on the installment basis under § 453 does not affect the seller's right to treat that gain as capital if the property sold is a capital asset. The installment method is *not* conditioned on a taxpayer's willingness to accept ordinary income from a transaction that would otherwise produce capital gain. The same is true where deferral of gain results from the taxpayer's use of the cash method of accounting or from the operation of the so-called fair market value rule. As with installment reporting under § 453, the justification for deferral—lack of ascertainable value, or the cash method of accounting—stands apart from the taxpayer's entitlement to capital gain.

Transactions in which the purchase price is payable out of income have been treated in the same way, on the whole, despite the obvious element of continued risk to the seller. Thus, after much litigation, the Commissioner finally agreed (and § 1235 now expressly provides) that the transfer of a patent in exchange for the transferee's promise to pay royalties based on production of the patented article is a sale that qualifies for capital treatment, even though royalty payments are to continue over the entire useful life of the patent. Capital gain has also been approved where corporate stock was sold for amounts which were to be measured by the dividends payable on the shares over a stated period of years,[39] or even by the net profits of the business. It is, of course, well arguable that such transactions should be distinguished from those in which the buyer's obligation is independent of the income from the property transferred, with only the latter type being viewed as a sale or exchange. But, on the other hand, the difficulty of establishing a fixed

---

[39] *Estate of Marshall v. Commissioner,* 20 T.C. 979 (1953).

price for patents, closely held businesses, and other non-marketable assets is probably considerable in many cases—the property may lack a prior earnings record or be subject to other substantial uncertainties. Often, therefore, such property can be sold only on a contingent-payment basis. If such arrangements were automatically treated as non-sales, the effect would be to disqualify property of this character from capital gain treatment simply because of its inherent riskiness.

In *Commissioner v. Brown*, the taxpayer sold his stock in a lumber company to a charitable organization. The purchase price was $1,300,000, payable $5,000 down and the balance within ten years out of the earnings of the lumber company. Following transfer of the stock to the charity, the assets of the company were leased back to an operating company managed and controlled by Brown himself. The operating company paid its profits over to the charity as deductible "rent", and the charity then paid the greater part of such rents to Brown as the purchase price of his stock. Once the entire purchase price was paid, the operating assets would belong to the charity. The figure of $1,300,000 was found to be a fair valuation for the lumber business.

Rejecting the Commissioner's contention that the transaction could not be a "sale" because the risks of the business remained with the seller, the Supreme Court held that the disposition of the taxpayer's stock was "complete," and that the amounts received were entitled to be treated as capital gain. The Court recognized that because the buyer was a tax-exempt charity no corporate tax would be owed on the earnings of the business. As a result, the purchase price could be paid out more rapidly than if the buyer were merely another taxable entity. In effect, as Justice Harlan pointed out in a concurring opinion, the charity had acquired the residual value of the lumber business by allowing the taxpayer to "use" its tax-exemption until the $1.3 million figure had been reached. In the Court's view, however, this factor did not alter the legal conclusion that property may be "sold" for tax purposes, even when the purchase price is payable out of the future earnings of the property itself.

So-called bootstrap sales to charity, of the sort exemplified in *Brown*, were substantially curbed by Congress in the Tax Reform Act of 1969. Section 514, which was added by the Act, provides, in effect, that unrelated income from debt-financed property shall be taxed to the charity as ordinary business income. This means that tax-exempt organizations are in no better a position than taxable entities when they seek to buy property out of their own future income. Since the income is now taxable to the charity, it can neither pay a higher price nor effect a quicker payout than other buyers. The Reform Act did not reverse the Court's determination that contingent-payment transactions will generally qualify as sales, however, and hence the status of such transactions continues to be controlled by *Brown*.

(b) Open Transactions

As noted at 14.03, the Supreme Court in *Burnet v. Logan* held that contingent-payment transactions do not result in immediate recognition of gain to the transferor if the fair market value of the transferee's obligation is uncertain; and further, that gain is not to be recognized until the payments received exceed the transferor's basis for the property transferred.[40] The *Brown* decision makes the additional point that such transactions will satisfy the "sale or exchange" requirement necessary for capital gain treatment, even when the property is to be paid for out of its own income.

These two sets of rules have produced a very favorable outcome when applied in combination. In *Commissioner v. Carter*,[41] the taxpayer was the sole stockholder of a corporation which was engaged in the oil brokerage business. The corporation was liquidated in 1942 and distributed to the taxpayer, together with other assets, certain brokerage contracts entitling it to commissions on future deliveries of oil. The value of the contracts was conceded to be unascertainable because the amount of the commissions to be received was contingent on various future events. Under Code § 331, the surrender of stock in a corporate liquidation is treated as a "sale or exchange" by the stockholder. Accordingly, the 1942 liquidation produced a capital gain because the value of the other assets distributed exceeded the taxpayer's basis for her stock.

In 1943, the taxpayer received $25,000 under the brokerage contracts. As to this later receipt, the Commissioner asserted that ordinary treatment was appropriate. The liquidation, he argued, had been completed in 1942; hence, the later payments could not be deemed to have been realized from the prior sale or exchange. Such later payments (in the Commissioner's view) were independent of the liquidation, and were therefore merely "commission income" taxable at ordinary rates.

The court of appeals held for the taxpayer, largely on the authority of *Burnet v. Logan*. The court reasoned that the "open" transaction rule of *Logan*—which applies where the property received lacks an ascertainable value—meant that the liquidation itself should be treated as an ongoing and continuing event. The

---

[40] As also noted at 14.03, however, the "open transaction" treatment of *Burnet v. Logan* is available today only if (a) the taxpayer opts out of the installment method of § 453, and (b) the transaction qualifies as one of the (in the words of the Regulations) "rare and extraordinary cases involving sales for a contingent payment obligation in which the fair market value of the obligation . . . cannot reasonably be ascertained."

[41] 170 F.2d 911 (2d Cir. 1948).

commission payments were thus attributable to the original "exchange," and hence qualified as capital gain. It would be "most unjust," the court said, to tax the commissions as ordinary, since, if the contracts *could* have been valued originally, that value would have been treated as realized from the liquidation. In effect, then, the taxpayer was entitled both to defer reporting her gain until the commission payments were actually received, and to report all such payments as gain from the "sale or exchange" of her shares, a capital asset.

Since the court in *Carter* stressed the comparison, we should ask just what the result would have been if the brokerage contracts *had* had an ascertainable value at the time of the liquidation. In *Waring v. Commissioner*,[42] the taxpayer, on the liquidation of his wholly-owned corporation, received a licensing agreement which entitled the corporation to receive royalties from a third party for the right to use the name "Waring" in connection with the sale of electric blenders. The taxpayer valued the contract at $300,000 and reported a capital gain on the excess of that amount over his stock basis. Upholding the Commissioner, the court found that the act of valuing the agreement *closed* the liquidation. Accordingly, royalties received by the taxpayer in subsequent years first were offset against his "tax-paid" basis for the licensing contract, that is, $300,000. After that, though, any further payments were taxable as ordinary income, because those further payments were not related to the prior sale or exchange.

In effect, then, in *Waring* the corporate liquidation produced (a) immediate recognition of capital gain, and (b) subsequent ordinary income for payments in excess of the value assigned to the licensing agreement. By contrast, in *Carter* the results were (a) no immediate recognition, and (b) subsequent capital gain.

These contrasting outcomes put more pressure than seems desirable on the initial question of ascertainable fair market value. Instead of letting such substantial tax differences turn on an accidental factor, it might be better (contrary to *Waring*) to permit contingent payment arrangements to produce capital gain whether or not the contract right or other claim is capable of being valued when received. The imputed interest rules of §§ 483 and 1274 preserve some ordinary treatment in any case, and perhaps the only operative requirements that should apply to the remainder of the gain realized by the transferor are the capital asset and the completed disposition requirements. As respects the latter especially, it may be that the *Brown* decision goes too far in permitting contingent-payment transactions to qualify as sales or exchanges. This, however, appears to be a determination which bears a rational

---

[42]   412 F.2d 800 (3d Cir. 1969).

relationship to the capital gain preference, even if its present substance is debatable. By contrast, the distinction between "open" and "closed" transactions seems capricious and is essentially unrelated to any positive policy concept in the field.

The 1980 revisions to the installment method of § 453 (14.02 and 14.03) have lessened the significance of *Carter* and *Waring*. Today, a taxpayer would find himself in a situation governed by one case or the other only if the taxpayer elected out of the installment method. If a taxpayer selling a capital asset for contingent payments does not elect out of § 453, gain will be taxed under the installment method as contingent payments are received. Each contingent payment will be treated as consisting of three elements: (1) basis recovery, as determined under the § 453 Regulations governing contingent installment payments (described at 14.03), (2) an imputed interest element determined under the original issue discount Regulations,[43] and (3) capital gain (equal to the total amount of the contingent payment, reduced by the sum of the first two elements). A taxpayer considering electing out of § 453 in the hopes of qualifying for open transaction treatment under *Burnet v. Logan* and *Carter* should bear in mind the warning of the Regulations that open transaction treatment applies only in "rare and extraordinary cases . . . in which the fair market value of the [contingent payment] obligation . . . cannot reasonably be ascertained."[44] If the taxpayer opts out of § 453 and it is eventually determined that his is not a "rare and extraordinary case," then he will find himself in the not-very-attractive tax situation of Mr. Waring.

———

A loose end. One word more on *Carter*. There is, we think, a better way to frame the tax issue in *Carter* than by struggling with the open/closed transaction question. The right to the oil brokerage commissions had of course been earned by the corporation in earlier years through its regular business activities, and no doubt any expenses associated with those activities—telephone, travel, office expense—had been deducted by the corporation when incurred. It is clear, therefore, that Mrs. Carter was the assignee of another taxpayer's (the corporation's) earned income. Mrs. Carter herself had nothing to do after the corporation was liquidated but wait for the commission payments to roll in.

In the *Eubank* case (8.02), the Supreme Court held that the assignor of a right to receive future renewal commissions remained taxable on those commissions despite having assigned the right to a

———

43 Reg. § 1.1275–4(c).
44 Reg. § 15a.453–1(d)(2)(iii).

family trust prior to payment. *Eubank*, in effect, was simply an extension to deferred service income of the fruit-and-tree rule of *Lucas v. Earl*. Would a corporate assignor be treated the same way as Mr. Eubank, and would liquidation be treated the same as a gift in trust? The answer to both questions, one would think, is yes. If so, it would follow that the brokerage commissions should properly have been regarded as ordinary business income and taxed to the corporation itself despite the "anticipatory" assignment to Mrs. Carter occasioned by the liquidation.

Taking this approach, the open/closed transaction issue, along with the underlying valuation problem, disappears. As transferee of the corporation's assets, Mrs. Carter was properly responsible for its debts, including federal taxes, and would be required, as transferee, to pay the corporation's regular income tax even though the corporation had ceased to exist as a legal entity. The effect would then be the same as if the liquidation had been postponed until all the commissions were received and the corporation paid its tax directly, with the balance of its assets, *after* tax, distributed to Mrs. Carter as capital gain.

18. Sales of Business Property

The tax law in effect divides business assets into three categories. The first consists of so-called current assets, in particular inventory and accounts receivable, which are expressly excluded from the class of capital assets by § 1221(a)(1) and § 1221(a)(4). As indicated at 17.02, the inventory exclusion was interpreted (in *Corn Products* as subsequently refined by *Arkansas Best*) to embrace commodities futures and other securities which, though not actually part of the taxpayer's stock-in-trade, are a surrogate for the taxpayer's basic raw materials or "an integral part of [its] inventory-purchase system"; non-capital status for inventory hedges (and some other types of hedges as well) is now expressly provided for by § 1221(a)(7), enacted in 1999. The second category consists of fixed assets—plant and equipment—which are likewise excluded from the class of capital assets by § 1221(a)(2) but for which a special tax regime is established under § 1231 and related provisions. Finally, as our earlier discussion of *Williams v. McGowan* should suggest (17.04), a third category of intangible property rights, of which the most important example is business goodwill, must also be inferred. These residual rights become capital assets more or less by elimination. Since they are not excluded by specific provision (or by judicial interpretation), they fall within the general language of § 1221, under which "capital asset" is defined to mean "property held by the taxpayer (whether or not connected with his trade or business)." As far as business property is concerned, then, the only assets that qualify as "pure" capital assets are those few that belong to this last, residual category.

We concern ourselves in this Section with the Code's treatment of stock-in-trade and real or depreciable property used in business. From the standpoint of litigation and administrative controversy, § 1221(a)(1), the stock-in-trade exclusion, has been by far the more troublesome of the two. The recurring question there has been whether the taxpayer's relationship to particular property is that of a "dealer"—one who is systematically engaged in buying and selling such property—or merely that of a casual "investor." This tiresome characterization problem has been, and remains, one of the more actively litigated issues in the entire capital gain field. By contrast, relatively few interpretative questions have arisen under § 1221(a)(2). Presumably, one has little difficulty in simply identifying property as "real or depreciable." On the other hand, from the standpoint of Code mechanics, the treatment of depreciable property such as buildings and equipment is far more detailed and extensive than that of stock-in-trade. Here, the question of policy has been how to integrate the capital treatment which § 1231 accords to gains from the sale of such assets with the annual allowance for depreciation, the latter being a deduction from ordinary income.

Section 18.01, next following, takes up the standards developed by the courts in distinguishing between "dealers" and "investors" for the purpose of § 1221(a)(1). Section 18.02(a) summarizes the treatment of real or depreciable property under § 1231, and section 18.02(b) describes the so-called depreciation recapture rules, which appear in §§ 1245 and 1250.

18.01   Property Held for Sale to Customers

As indicated, § 1221(a)(1) specifically excludes business merchandise from the capital asset definition. The cans on the grocer's shelf, the coal in the mine-owner's mine, the ships in the shipbuilder's yard, all are ordinary assets in the hands of a taxpayer whose business is to buy, dig, or produce those items for sale to customers. Section 1221(a)(1) uses no fewer than three statutory phrases to describe this kind of asset—"stock in trade," "inventory," and "property held by the taxpayer primarily for sale to customers in the ordinary course of his trade or business." However, since the last of the quoted phrases is the broadest and least technical of the three, it has largely swallowed up the first two and has been chiefly relied on by the Commissioner in his frequent efforts to draw borderline transactions into the ordinary income category.

The great majority of litigated cases under § 1221(a)(1) have involved real estate, and perhaps one way to open up the subject is to ask just why this should be so. Why should land and buildings, more often than other kinds of property, appear to occupy an ambiguous status? Why shouldn't corporate securities (on the one hand), or shirts and socks (on the other), have generated an equal volume of controversy?

As respects shirts and socks, at least, the answer is fairly clear. Those handy items, and indeed everything else in the category of consumption goods, are sold almost exclusively by professional dealers—*e.g.,* stores—for whom the status of the property as simple inventory is never questioned. Household durables—cars and washing machines—are sometimes sold by the consumer himself (more often traded-in), but the isolated and occasional nature of such transactions, as well as the prior household use, makes it clear that the requisite "business" context is lacking. Ambiguous cases do of course arise; nonprofessionals sometimes purchase unusual consumption items (stamps, antiques) for resale, and in such event they may be viewed as dealers if their activities are extensive. But on the whole, consumption goods which are dealt in by professionals are dealt in *only* by professionals, and the applicability of § 1221(a)(1) is immediately clear.

What about corporate securities? Although stocks and bonds are typically held for investment, a very active stock-market speculator may engage in many transactions in the course of a year, trading hundreds of thousands or even millions of dollars' worth of shares, and devoting all of his time and energy to that single activity. In common understanding, stock market speculation is his "business". Yet, apart from professional underwriters and securities dealers, persons who trade on the stock market, no matter how actively, can be perfectly confident that their gains and losses will be treated as capital. The reason is that the words "to customers," which were added to § 1221(a)(1) in 1934 in order to prevent ordinary loss deductions in the declining market of that period, have also served to assure capital treatment for gains in the rising markets of later eras. In effect, individuals who buy and sell securities, usually through a broker, are not considered to be one another's "customers" within the meaning of the statute. As respects securities, therefore, the only condition that the taxpayer needs to satisfy to get preferential treatment is the holding-period requirement. If stocks or bonds are held for more than one year, any gain or loss is long-term gain or loss. No distinction is made between occasional investors and active traders, other than the statutory distinction between long- and short-term transactions.

The same construction has *not* been applied to real estate (or other property). Any person to whom land or buildings are sold is a "customer" of the seller, so that the question of ordinary or capital treatment depends on whether the property is held "primarily for sale," and on whether the taxpayer's conduct amounts to a "business." The reason why the "customers" requirement has been applied one way for securities and another way for other property may reside in the impersonal nature of the securities market. More probably, however, it is simply that Congress has been understood to have intended that language to be confined to the situation at which it was directed eighty years ago, namely, trading in securities.

The result is that those who "trade" actively in real estate are treated just like professional real estate dealers, while only "investors" in real estate qualify for capital gain. There is thus a need to distinguish between "traders" and "investors." By contrast, the category of "trader" is virtually irrelevant in the field of conventional merchandise because, as a practical matter, the only functioning category is that of "dealer." And it is irrelevant as respects securities because "traders" and "investors" are treated alike.

In determining whether real estate is held "primarily for sale . . . in the ordinary course of . . . business," the courts have emphasized the frequency and continuity of the taxpayer's dealings, the length of time the property was held, the presence or absence of development activities such as subdividing and installing utilities, the extent of the taxpayer's selling effort, and so on. The decided cases are too individual to usefully generalize about, and the "listing of factors" approach is probably the best that can be done by way of making relevant factual distinctions.

Many of the cases in this field involve gain which is traceable both to long-term property appreciation *and* to business activity. Thus, the taxpayer, having long ago acquired a substantial tract of land, now decides to dispose of the property. He finds, however, that the best, or perhaps the only, way of doing so is to subdivide the tract and sell off the units to individual buyers. A portion of the overall gain will then be attributable to historical appreciation and a portion to the "business" of subdivision and development. Neither full capital gain nor full ordinary income is correct in the circumstances, but the courts, lacking authority to fragment the taxpayer's gain, are compelled to opt for one or the other, with the preponderance of the "liquidation" cases coming out on the capital gain side.[45]

When the taxpayer's subdivision and development activities are substantial enough to convert the land from a capital asset to a non-capital asset, the tax results can be striking. Suppose our taxpayer owns undeveloped acreage in which she has (to keep the numbers simple) a basis of zero. A developer has offered her $4 million for the land. If she sells to the developer, she will have $4 million of long-

---

[45]   *E.g., Curtis Co. v. Commissioner,* 232 F.2d 167 (3d Cir.1956); compare *Biedenharn Realty Co. v. U.S.,* 526 F.2d 409 (5th Cir.1976), finding ordinary income.

term capital gain, taxable at 20%. After paying tax of $800,000, she will be left with $3.2 million. Alternatively, she could do the development work herself, subdividing the property and selling off individual lots for single-family homes. Let's suppose (unrealistically, but again to keep the numbers simple) that she would incur no expenses in developing the property, and that she could sell the lots for a total of $5 million. It would seem that she should seriously consider becoming a developer, since there is an additional pre-tax profit of $1 million to be made. But what will be the effect on her tax liability? If her development activities convert the land into a § 1221(a)(1) asset, then *all* the gain—*not* merely the last $1 million of gain attributable to her development efforts—will be taxed as ordinary income. Assuming the entire $5 million gain is taxed at 37%, her tax will be $1.85 million, and she will be left with only $3.15 million after tax—which is, shockingly enough, $50,000 less than her after-tax result if she sells the property *for $1 million less* to the developer. Her pre-tax profit goes up by $1 million if she develops the property herself, but her tax goes up by $1.05 million. In effect, her marginal tax rate on the $1 million of development profit is 105%.

What is going on here? How can her marginal tax rate be 105%, when the top rate on ordinary income is only (so to speak) 37%? The answer is that the additional tax of $1.05 million has two components: (1) a tax, at the rate of 37%, on the $1 million development profit (a tax of $370,000), and (2) an increase from 20% to 37% in the tax rate on the $4 million of long-term appreciation (increasing her tax by 17% of $4 million, or $680,000). Her development activities do not merely generate a 37% tax on her development profit; they also convert her long-term investment profit from capital gain to ordinary income, increasing the tax on that long-term gain by $680,000. This is an example of what tax professionals sometimes refer to as a "cliff effect"—a situation in which a relatively small change in the taxpayer's economic situation produces a disproportionate change in the taxpayer's tax bill. For the most part, Congress has designed the income tax to avoid cliff effects. The most important example of an avoided cliff effect is the operation of the tax rate schedule of § 1. If a taxpayer in the 12% bracket works a few hours of overtime, generating enough income to break into the 22% bracket, only the last few dollars of income are taxed at 22%; the taxpayer still gets the benefit (relatively speaking) of the 12% and 10% brackets with respect to the rest of his income. As the real estate development example demonstrates, however, the income tax is not devoid of cliff effects—and this particular cliff effect is dramatic indeed. One would think there should be a rule permitting a taxpayer in the developer's situation to bifurcate her gain into $4 million of long-term capital gain and $1 million of ordinary income, but there is no such provision.[46]

"Dual purpose" cases have raised problems similar to those raised by the "changed purpose" cases. In *Malat v. Riddell*,[47] the taxpayer owned an interest in a parcel of land which had been acquired either for the purpose of sale or for development as rental property, whichever should prove to be more profitable. Ultimately, because of problems relating to zoning and financing, the taxpayer gave up on the entire idea and sold his interest in the venture. Reversing the court of appeals, which had held the taxpayer's gain ordinary on the ground that "resale" had been a substantial reason for the original purchase, the Supreme Court held that the word "primarily" must be construed as "principally" or "of first importance," and remanded the case for further findings under that standard. On remand, the trial court found that the taxpayer was entitled to capital gain, because the "principal" purpose of the land venture had been to develop the property for rental, with resale being a second-best alternative. Since the taxpayer's gain, presumably, was traceable to property appreciation rather than development and sales activities, the final outcome seems not unreasonable in the circumstances.

If a taxpayer's real estate (or other property) is *not* regarded as stock-in-trade, its classification then depends on whether it is "used in the taxpayer's business"—for example, as a warehouse or factory building—or is merely held for investment. If the latter, the taxpayer's gain or loss is of course capital under the general language of § 1221. If the property is used in trade or business, on the other hand, it is specifically excluded from capital asset status by § 1221(a)(2). This, however, means that the gain or loss will be governed by the special and, in a sense, even more favorable rules of § 1231, which are described in the subsection next following. As will be seen, § 1231 treats net gains from the sale of § 1231 assets as capital gain (subject to a rather mild depreciation-recapture requirement in the case of real estate, and to a more substantial recapture requirement in the case of tangible personal property), while treating net loss as *ordinary* loss. Hence, a further (though considerably simpler) sub-classification of the property must be made even after the § 1221(a)(1) question has been resolved.

---

[46]   A taxpayer may be able to accomplish a self-help bifurcation of gain by selling the undeveloped land to a corporation which she controls, and then having the corporation develop the land. There are, however, several difficulties involved in this self-help approach.

[47]   383 U.S. 569 (1966).

18.02   Fixed Assets: Real and Depreciable Property

(a)   Section 1231

Land, buildings, and machinery—assets which accountants classify as "fixed"—are dealt with by the tax law in a curious, asymmetrical fashion. Under § 1231, gains and losses from the sale of real and depreciable property used in the taxpayer's business are swept into a special category. If recognized gains from the sale of such property exceed recognized losses for the taxable year, the gains and losses are all treated as long-term capital gains and losses. But if recognized losses exceed recognized gains, then the gains and losses are treated as ordinary. The effect, quite simply, is to treat net gain from dispositions of fixed business assets as long-term capital gain, while treating net loss from such transactions as ordinary loss deductible from ordinary income.

Although the adoption of § 1231 was prompted by special wartime conditions which long ago ceased to be relevant, Congress chose to continue this peculiar capital-gain-but-ordinary loss regime over the ensuing decades, and there has been little legislative interest in changing it. The explanation, in part at least, is that Congress has wished to encourage the replacement of, and to spur investment in, depreciable plant and equipment.

Apart from incentive effects, an argument can be made that asymmetrical treatment is actually correct as a matter of tax policy (depending, of course, on a willingness to accept capital-ordinary distinctions to begin with). Thus, on the gain side, it can be argued that sales of fixed assets, as opposed to stock-in-trade, are really extraordinary transactions which involve the disposition of a part of the business itself. They do not occur in the regular course of operations, and any gains—perhaps on sales of business real estate— would often represent appreciation that has accrued over an extended period of time. As respects losses, although symmetry would be expected normally, in the present context we find ourselves dealing mostly with *depreciable* property (land being the exception), rather than corporate stock or the like. If the property were retained by the taxpayer for the remainder of its useful life, an ordinary loss would be allowed, in effect, through annual deductions for depreciation. The same would be true if the property were simply abandoned or scrapped without being sold at all. Since investment in depreciable property, thus, is recoverable through an offset against ordinary income, the result, arguably, should be no different when allowable depreciation is anticipated by the sale of the property at a loss. To be sure, this justification does not serve very well where land is concerned, because land is non-depreciable. However, the alleged difficulty of allocating the purchase price of real estate between land

and buildings when both are sold together has evidently convinced Congress that it would be too burdensome to insist on separate capital loss treatment for the land component.

Suppose the owner of a single residential property rents it out continuously for a period of years and then sells the property at a loss. Is the modest rental activity a "trade or business" so that the loss is "ordinary" under § 1231, or is the loss a capital loss from the sale of property held for investment but not used in "business"? Prompted, perhaps, by the fact that such property becomes "depreciable property" once it has been rented out—and that depreciation is a deductible expense—the Tax Court has held that § 1231 does apply and that the loss is "ordinary."[48] Presumably, the same would be true of any depreciable asset that generates gross income, even if "business" classification otherwise seems awkward.

(b)   The Recapture Principle

Since § 1231 permits capital treatment for gains from sales of *depreciable* property, the provision creates a special problem with respect to the depreciation allowance. The problem has been rendered acute by the adoption of accelerated depreciation rules (and even more acute in the case of immediate expensing of most tangible personal property under § 168(k) in 2018 through 2025). Thus, annual depreciation is a deduction from ordinary income, and the amount deducted is subtracted from the taxpayer's property basis. If the value of the property at a given date exceeds its adjusted basis—if the depreciation allowed for tax purposes has been greater than the actual decline in the property's value—then a sale of the property will produce a gain, and the gain under § 1231 will be capital (or would be capital, but for the recapture rules described below). This means that the prior deductions from ordinary income will have been transmuted into capital gain through sale. While Congress *might* desire to sanction this highly advantageous combination of tax benefits as a way of encouraging investment in depreciable property, from the standpoint of tax policy it seems improper for taxpayers to receive capital treatment on the sale of business assets, the cost of which has been recovered out of ordinary income. Other instances of the same phenomenon—*e.g.*, the deduction of interest on funds borrowed to purchase growth stocks—have been noted previously.

To deal with this problem, the Code since 1962 has limited the ability of property owners to combine ordinary depreciation deductions with capital gain by requiring the "recapture" of all or a portion of the depreciation when the property is sold. Under § 1245— which, roughly speaking, applies to depreciable property other than

---

[48]   *Hazard v. Commissioner,* 7 T.C. 372 (1946).

real estate—a taxpayer's gain on the sale of his property is taxed as ordinary income to the full extent of his prior depreciation deductions. In effect, a balancing inclusion is required to the extent that the proceeds of sale exceed the taxpayer's *adjusted* basis, but do not exceed his *original* basis for the property. To illustrate simply, if an asset purchased for $10,000 were depreciated to $6,000 and then sold for $9,000, the gain of $3,000 would be "recaptured" as ordinary income. If the same property were sold for $11,000, the first $4,000 of gain would again be ordinary under § 1245; the remaining gain of $1,000 would be capital gain under § 1231, subject to the netting rules of that provision.

Section 1250 (added in 1964) applies the recapture principle to real estate, but its effect is weaker than that of § 1245. Generally described (and omitting many details), § 1250 recaptures only the excess of depreciation actually taken over the depreciation that would have been allowed under the straight-line depreciation method. Recapture under § 1250 thus applies to the excess of accelerated over straight-line depreciation, whereas § 1245 extends recapture to all depreciation previously allowed. Straight-line depreciation is required with respect to all real property acquired after 1986, with the result that recapture under § 1250 applies only to property placed in service before that date. Suppose a taxpayer buys a building (after 1986) for $1 million and properly claims depreciation deductions totaling $400,000 over several years, thus reducing her adjusted basis in the building to $600,000. If she then sells the building for $750,000, her gain of $150,000 will not be recaptured under § 1250 (because the building was depreciated using the straight-line method). However, her $150,000 capital gain (assuming the gain turns out to be capital after the application of the netting rules of § 1231) will be "unrecaptured § 1250 gain"— basically, gain on the sale of depreciable real estate that would be recapture gain if § 1245, rather than § 1250, applied to buildings. Under § 1(h), "unrecaptured § 1250 gain" is taxed at 25%, rather than the usual long-term capital gain rate of 15%.

19. Personal Services

There ought to be, and on the whole there is, less legal ambiguity about the status of personal service income under the capital gain rules than about any other category of receipts. This follows from the fact that capital gain always requires a disposition of "property." Once claims for wages, salaries and fees are specifically excluded from the capital asset definition—a result apparently achieved by § 1221(a)(4)—there is little in the way of "characterization," "motive," "relationship" or the like that is left to argue about. The status of other kinds of gains and losses varies to some extent from taxpayer to taxpayer; real estate transactions, for example, may be either capital or ordinary depending on whether the taxpayer is a dealer or an investor. But personal service income is always ordinary, because personal services inevitably lack the essential characteristic of "property."

This is not to say, however, that interpretative problems have been wholly lacking. While the difference between personal service income and gain from the sale of property is normally clear, if the discussion at 8.02 is recalled it should not be difficult to foresee that line-drawing problems will arise with respect to the status of self-created property rights such as patents, copyrights and similar interests. Are these intangibles to be viewed as "property" because, like a share of stock, they are embodied in a legal certificate, have an extended useful life, sometimes entail an outlay of capital, and can be sold for a consideration by the original owner or his successors? Or are they to be regarded as personal service claims because they relate so closely to the expenditure of time and talent by their creators? Fortunately in one sense, the treatment of self-created intangibles is now largely resolved by specific Code provisions. As will be seen at 19.02, self-created patents, copyrights, and artistic creations are specifically excluded from the capital asset definition by § 1221(a)(3).

The problem of services-or-property can be framed more generally. Since service income is ordinary while property gain is capital, there has been an incentive for highly-paid individuals to find devices by which personal rewards can be transmuted into property rights. The *Ferrer* case (17.03(c)) was an illustration of this: to a degree the taxpayer actually succeeded in converting his income from acting services into gain from the sale of a contract claim, such claim being viewed as "property" and hence a capital asset.

The property-service distinction has also been exploited—to a considerable degree with express congressional approval—by yet another group of highly paid individuals, namely, corporate executives. Unable to escape the status of "employee", corporate executives have sought, where possible, to convert their salaries into property ownership through the medium of stock options and related devices. The treatment of employee stock options, which has a lengthy statutory and case-law history, is briefly reviewed in the Section following.

19.01   Employee Stock Options

Suppose the taxpayer, a corporate executive, is granted an option by his employer to purchase 1,000 shares of the employer's stock at $5 a share. The option is exercisable at any time within the next three years, but it is not transferable to others and can be exercised only if the taxpayer is then still an employee of the company. In Year 1, when the option is granted, the stock is quoted at $6 a share—that is, $1 a share above the option price.

The taxpayer actually exercises the option in Year 2. By that time, however, the market value of the stock has jumped to $30, so that by exercising the option the taxpayer acquires property with a value of $30,000 for a cash investment of only $5,000. Assume that he holds the stock itself for further appreciation, and then in Year 3 sells the entire 1,000 shares for $32,000. Plainly, the taxpayer has made an overall profit of $27,000—the difference between the $32,000 realized on selling the shares and his $5,000 cash investment. The question that arises, essentially, is whether any portion of that gain should be viewed as ordinary compensation from his employment.

In *Commissioner v. Lo Bue*,[49] which involved a similar set of facts, the Supreme Court reversed a finding by the Tax Court that no portion of the gain was ordinary. The Tax Court had held that the purpose of the option grant was to give the taxpayer a "proprietary interest" in his employer and not to compensate him for his services. Observing that "the company was not giving away something for nothing," the Supreme Court found that it was simply "impossible" to view the stock option arrangement as anything but compensation. The measure of such compensation, moreover, was the difference between the option price and the market value of the shares at the time the option was exercised. This, said the Court, had been the uniform Treasury practice for decades.

Concurring in part and dissenting in part, Justice Harlan agreed with the Court majority that the Tax Court's "proprietary interest" exemption should be rejected. He argued, however, that the appropriate measure of ordinary compensation was the value of the options at the time they were granted rather than the spread between option price and stock value at the time of exercise. Whatever that earlier value may have been, said Harlan, it was *that* amount which represented the taxpayer's income from employment, and it was *then* that the taxpayer received ordinary compensation from his employer.

Using the figures in our initial illustration, the difference between the majority and the dissenting approach in *Lo Bue* is quite considerable, even though both agreed that the option was a compensatory device. Thus, the majority would find no income in Year 1 despite the fact that the value of the stock in the illustration then exceeded the option price by $1 a share. In Year 2, however, the majority would treat the difference between stock-value and option price—$25,000 in the illustration—as ordinary compensation. The employee would then become an investor with respect to the shares

---

49   351 U.S. 243 (1956).

acquired, and would hold those shares at a basis of $30,000 (*i.e.*, $25,000 included in income plus the $5,000 purchase price). When the stock was sold in Year 3 for $32,000, the taxpayer would realize a further gain of $2,000. This, of course, would be taxed as a capital gain.

Under Harlan's approach, as stated, the option would be valued and taxed at the time it was granted in Year 1. Since the option was worth at least $1,000, that amount (at least) would be included as ordinary compensation for that year.[50] No further income would result from the exercise of the option in Year 2, however, because that event would be regarded as a purchase rather than a realization. The taxpayer's basis for the shares acquired would then be $6,000— $1,000 included in income in Year 1 plus the $5,000 stock purchase price—and when the shares were finally sold for $32,000 in Year 3, a capital gain would be recognized of $26,000.

In effect, then, total income—$27,000—would be the same under either approach (indeed, it would be the same even if the Tax Court's view had been adopted). The choice between the two approaches makes a considerable difference, however, in the timing of taxation and in the character (ordinary or capital) of the income. Neither approach is reliably more taxpayer-favorable than the other; which is more taxpayer-favorable in a particular case depends on the value of the stock in each of the three years.

Is there a right or a wrong in all this? Ultimately, the conflict between majority and dissent appears to have turned on a question of fact—namely, whether the options granted to LoBue did, or didn't, have an ascertainable market value at the date of grant. The majority seemed to concede that if the options could have been valued in Year 1, then that value would indeed have been the measure of the taxpayer's ordinary compensation, with all further gain being capital. "But this," it said, "is not such a case. These . . . options were not transferable and LoBue's right to buy stock under them was contingent upon his remaining an employee of the company until they were exercised." Harlan, by contrast, would have found that when LoBue "received an unconditional option to buy stock at less than the market price, he received an asset of substantial and

---

[50] Actually, the option would certainly be worth more than $1,000. To see why, consider an option that is "at the money" at the time of granting—for example, an option to buy stock currently trading at $5,000 for $5,000. The option has value despite being merely "at the money," because it gives the option holder the right to any future appreciation in the stock (during the term of the option) without exposing the option holder to the risk that the stock may decline in value. For ease of illustration, however, the discussion in the text assumes the value of the option at the time of granting is simply the amount by which it is then "in the money"—$1,000 in the example.

immediately realizable value, at least equal to the then-existing spread between the option price and the market price."

As usual, it is somewhat irritating to find substantial tax differences turning on the presence or absence of an ascertainable market value. In fact, however, the difficulty may be unavoidable. If (as the *Lo Bue* majority found) the option lacks an ascertainable value when granted, then, apparently, the only practical alternatives are (a) to accept the Tax Court's position that there is no compensation whatever, a difficult view to maintain when the transaction involves an employer and employee, or (b) to conclude that nothing of a taxable nature has occurred until the employee receives property that does have a measurable dollar value, but then to view *that* as a receipt of taxable compensation. Absent a fair market value for the options at the date of grant, there is, perhaps, no escape from the conclusion that exercise is the taxable event. And once again, since an employment relationship is involved, it is well-nigh "impossible" to regard the resulting income as anything but ordinary. On the other hand, the weakest feature of the majority opinion in *Lo Bue* is the unsupported finding that the options were in fact without an ascertainable value. As Justice Harlan suggested, the tax rules could at least treat as ordinary income in Year 1 the amount by which the option is "in the money" at the time it is granted, even if it is considered impractical to value the "option privilege" (*i.e.*, the ability of the option-holder to benefit from appreciation in the stock, without being at risk of a decline in the stock's value). The Court is far from persuasive on this point, and indeed the issue appears to have taken Justice Black (the author of the majority opinion) somewhat by surprise.

Code § 83—which applies to stock options other than the "incentive" options covered by § 421, mentioned below—adopts as a "general rule" the position expressed by Justice Harlan in *Lo Bue*. The section provides that if an employee receives a nonforfeitable option which has an ascertainable fair market value at the date it is granted, that value (less any price paid for the option itself) constitutes ordinary income to the employee at that time. Hence, no further income will be recognized when the option is exercised. When the shares acquired are finally sold, the difference between the sale price and the taxpayer's stock basis will be taxable as capital gain. But if no value for the options can be ascertained at the date of grant, *and* if the option is not "in the money" at the time it is granted,[51] then, generally, the tax results will be those approved by the majority in *Lo Bue*—that is, ordinary income at the date of exercise.

---

[51]   If the option is "in the money" at the time of the grant, it is considered deferred compensation subject to the monstrously complex anti-deferral regime of § 409A.

Code § 422 creates a special class of so-called "incentive" stock options which enjoy preferential status when certain restrictive conditions are met. These conditions, set forth in § 422, include a requirement that the option price be at least equal to the market value of the underlying stock at the time the options are granted (*i.e.,* that the option not be "in the money" at the time of granting) and that the stock itself be held for at least two years after the date of grant and one year after the date of exercise. If the statutory conditions are satisfied, then neither the grant nor the exercise of the option results in taxable income to the employee (in which event no business expense deduction is allowed to the employer). Gain will be recognized when—that is, deferred until—the stock is sold. As in the Tax Court's version of *Lo Bue,* such gain will then be taxed as capital gain and the employee will have no ordinary compensation whatever.

Section 422(d) limits the value of stock with respect to which incentive stock options can be exercised to $100,000, which means that high-paid company executives generally opt for non-incentive (sometimes called "non-statutory") options for which there is no such limitation.

19.02   Patents, Copyrights, and Self-Created Property

Regarded as a problem *de novo,* the proper treatment of patents and copyrights seems clear. If we take as a fixed premise the idea that personal service income is ordinary, then the income received by an inventor or an artist from the transfer of a patent or copyright fairly plainly belongs to the class of ordinary receipts. The principal element of value in either case derives from personal effort, and the mere fact that the patent or the copyright constitutes a legally protectable interest can hardly disguise the primary nature of the taxpayer's personal contribution. To be sure, patents (though generally not copyrights) may sometimes entail a commitment of capital in the form of an outlay for materials and equipment. In consequence, it can be argued that "investment" also plays a role in the development of patented innovations and, hence, that the capital and ordinary components should both be given recognition when the patent is disposed of. But a practical basis for making such a division would be exceedingly hard to formulate unless arbitrary rules of allocation were employed. Moreover, the same sort of problem exists elsewhere (indeed, everywhere) in the capital gain field; thus, investing in corporate shares involves both capital and an exercise of personal skill and judgment, yet no effort is made to "impute to the factors" where gain from the sale of stock is concerned. If, then, considerations of feasibility require an all-or-nothing determination in this as in other areas, one's intuition is that patents and copyrights should both be regarded as ordinary.

However, for many years—from 1950 through 2017—the Code treated self-created patents more favorably than self-created copyrights. Since 1950, § 1221(a)(3) has specifically excluded taxpayer-created copyrights and artistic property from the capital asset definition. There was no similar provision for self-created patents, with the result that under the peculiar structure of § 1221— everything is a capital asset except for those asset types specifically excluded—self-created patents qualified as capital assets.

The exclusion of self-created copyrights and artistic property, which was added in 1950, was intended to assure that all copyrights and similar property would be treated as noncapital, whether created by a professional or by an amateur. Prior judicial and administrative decisions—of which the best known involved a lump-sum sale of his war memoirs by General Eisenhower—had permitted amateur authors to report as capital gain the proceeds from the sale of their *first* published work (after which, presumably, they became professionals). Section 1221(a)(3) overcomes this interpretation and imposes ordinary treatment on amateur and professional authors (artists, etc.) alike. However, § 1221(b)(3), added to the Code in 2006, permits the creator of a musical composition to elect to treat the composition (or a copyright in the composition) as a capital asset. It is not immediately apparent (to put it mildly) why creators of musical works should be privileged over writers, painters, and sculptors. No doubt on this question (as is true of so many questions), a page of history is worth a volume of logic.[52]

The favorable treatment of self-created patents came to an end with the tax legislation of 2017. As amended in that year, § 1221(a)(3) now denies capital asset status to any taxpayer-created "patent, invention, model or design (whether or not patented), a secret formula, or process," in addition to the copyrights and artistic creations already covered by the subsection. The moral for anyone who is desperate to achieve capital asset status for self-created intellectual property? Write a song.

Apart from patents and copyrights, the sale of a personal service business—say an accounting or a medical practice—may also generate a question of services-or-property. The consideration paid for a professional practice might be allocable partly to the seller's covenant not to compete—that is, his agreement to refrain from practicing his profession for a given number of years or in a defined area—and partly to the goodwill of the business. Goodwill, in this context, would apparently refer to the seller's reputation and

---

[52] See Brody Mullins, *Music to Songwriters' Ears: Lower Taxes—Country Artists' Group Presses Lawmakers to Slash the Levy on Lyrics*, Wall Street Journal, Nov. 29, 2005.

following among his clients, customers or patients. Payments for non-compete agreements, generally, are viewed as ordinary. If an advance bonus for services to be performed in the future results in ordinary income, then a payment to refrain from such performance should be treated similarly. As to professional goodwill, however, while this "asset" could easily be regarded as a personal attribute of the seller akin to the use of his name, the courts have held that if the seller's practice is actually transferable to another practitioner for a consideration, then the thing transferred must have an independent existence which entitles it to be regarded as "property". Hence, evidently, payments allocated to professional goodwill will qualify for capital gain treatment.

In *Miller v. Commissioner*,[53] the widow of the famed orchestra leader received a payment from Universal Pictures in connection with the making of "The Glenn Miller Story." The amount paid, more than $400,000, was in consideration for the taxpayer's granting to the company an "exclusive right" to produce a motion picture "based upon the life . . . of Glenn Miller." Rejecting her claim to capital gain, the court of appeals found that Mrs. Miller had no "capitalizable" property interest in the reputation of her deceased husband. Although the $400,000 plainly had been paid for something—presumably, the possibility that Mrs. Miller did have a protectable interest had seemed plausible to Universal—the court found no supporting authority in state law for the proposition that a decedent's heirs may inherit a right to his public image. Accordingly, the Commissioner was upheld in treating the payment as ordinary income.

Weakly reasoned in its reliance on state property concepts, Judge Kaufman's opinion also seems a little rough on Mrs. Miller. It is true, as the court noted, that if Miller himself had sold his "story" to the movies during his lifetime, the proceeds of such sale would have been ordinary. Since Miller was in the entertainment business, payment for an "appearance," whether in person or by proxy, would clearly be a return to personal effort. His widow, however, was in quite a different status. She, in effect, had acquired by inheritance (or at least Universal thought so) an "enterprise" called "Glenn Miller." While it could be argued that a sale of movie-rights alone was a kind of carving-out (there might also have been book rights, rights to the Glenn Miller "sound," etc. that went with the name), it seems likely that the only economic interest of any real value that remained after Miller's death was the right to do a movie of his life. The fact that this interest was ill-defined or uncertain under state law seems irrelevant in view of the transaction that actually took place between

---

[53]   299 F.2d 706 (2d Cir. 1962).

the parties. What should have counted, one supposes, was the circumstance that the thing conveyed—call it an inchoate right or contingent chose in action, if you like—had been acquired by inheritance rather than through the taxpayer's personal efforts. No element of services pertained as far as Mrs. Miller was concerned, and hence her claim to capital gain treatment was really fairly strong.

A loose end. Private equity fund managers typically receive "two and twenty" packages as compensation for their fund management services—cash equal to two percent of the value of the assets under management, plus a twenty percent interest in the profits of the private equity partnership. Although the two percent portion is taxed as ordinary income (as one would expect), under the partnership tax rules of Subchapter K of the Code (mercifully beyond the scope of this book), the profits interest generally qualifies for long-term capital gain treatment—despite the fact that the result is glaringly inconsistent with the general rule that compensation for services is taxed at ordinary income rates. The current tax treatment of these twenty percent "carried interests" has been forcefully criticized,[54] and it is possible that one of these days Congress will amend Subchapter K to require ordinary income treatment. It is also entirely possible, of course, that Congress will continue to do nothing in this area.

Capital Gains and Losses—Questions and Answers

Question 1: Higgle, Barter & Truck (HBT), a partnership, operates a large tire and auto parts store on premises leased from Bluehill Shopping Center. A clause in HBT's lease, which still has eight years to run, prohibits Bluehill from renting shopping-center space to any competitive retailer. Bluehill now wants to rent substantial space to Sears, a national chain which sells tires and auto parts along with other products. HBT at once brings an action against Bluehill and obtains an injunction prohibiting Bluehill from entering into a lease with Sears.

HBT and Bluehill then engage in negotiations. In the end, Bluehill pays HBT $200,000 and HBT releases all of its rights under the injunction, which frees Bluehill to rent to Sears.

Is the $200,000 payment received by HBT from Bluehill ordinary income or capital gain?

Answer: Capital gain, apparently, assuming the *Ferrer* case has authority as precedent. In *Ferrer*, the court reasoned that a lessee

---

[54] See, e.g., Fleischer, *Two and Twenty: Taxing Partnership Profits in Private Equity Funds*, 83 N.Y.U. L. Rev. 1 (2008).

(more precisely, a party in a position analogous to that of a lessee of real estate), whose lease included a right to exclude competitors, could treat that right as an "equitable interest" in the leased premises and therefore as substantial property. As such, in the court's view, it was a capital asset within the definition of § 1221(a). Since HBT would have deducted its annual rents, it presumably has a zero basis in the lease restriction (as well as in its rights under the injunction), so that the entire $200,000 is recognized as gain. That gain, however, as stated, would be taxable to the partners at the preferential capital gain rates.

Could it be argued that the transaction involved a "carving-out"—a sale by HBT of just one profitable feature of its larger lease, and hence a "substitute for future ordinary income"? Not really. Once the lease restriction is treated as a separable equitable interest in the property, the fact that HBT transfers and conveys that interest for the entire term of the lease probably eliminates the "substitute . . ." characterization. Section 1241 treats the cancellation of a lease by a lessee as an "exchange" and thus presumably intends the lease to be treated as a capital asset in the lessee's hands. While the section refers to "a lease," not a separable right in a lease, there is no indication that Congress meant to withdraw from the capital asset definition any lesser interest that would otherwise qualify as such under "common law" principles.

Question 2: In the *Azar Nut Co.* case,[55] the taxpayer, located in El Paso and in the business of packaging nuts of all kinds, entered into a two-year employment agreement with Frankovic, a highly-regarded executive with experience in the nut-packaging field. Frankovic, uneasy about having to buy a new family house in El Paso, insisted that Azar promise to buy back the new house for an amount not less than F had paid for it if F's employment should not be renewed at the end of the two-year term. Azar agreed. Sure enough, Azar dismissed F at the end of the two-year term and, as required, bought F's house for $285,000, which was equal to F's purchase price. Azar tried at once to resell the house but evidently found no one willing to pay $285,000 for it. Finally, after peddling it around for more than eighteen months, Azar sold the house for only $185,000, taking a $100,000 loss on the deal. Azar never attempted to rent the house and never used it in its nut-packing operations.

Is Azar's $100,000 loss deductible as either an ordinary business expense under § 162(a) or an ordinary loss under § 165(a), or is it a long-term capital loss under § 1222(4) (and hence useless to Azar, which has no capital gains)? As stated, the house was never "used in

---

[55] *Azar Nut Co. v. Commissioner*, 931 F.2d 314 (5th Cir.1991), *aff'g* 94 T.C. 455 (1990).

the trade or business" by Azar, so the loss would not qualify as ordinary under § 1231(a)(2).

Answer: Had Azar sold the house immediately for $185,000, it would, we think, be clear that the $100,000 loss was in effect job-termination or severance pay, taxable to F and deductible by Azar as an ordinary and necessary business expense under § 162(a) (or, if you like, as a business loss under § 165(a)). If Azar had paid F $100,000 in cash at the time he left the firm (F having sold the house himself for $185,000), the payment would certainly be a deductible business expense. The *Arkansas Best* decision makes it clear that a mere "business motive" is not sufficient to take an asset out of the capital asset category under § 1221, but the Supreme Court presumably had no intention of converting business expenses into capital losses merely because the expenditure takes the slightly indirect form that it did in the *Azar* case. A case like *Bagley & Sewall* would probably be put in the capital loss category after the *Arkansas Best* decision, but on analysis (see p. 421) the bond loss in that case had no valid claim to being classified as a business expense and can easily be distinguished from the situation in *Azar*.

What the taxpayer needs to carry the day here is appraisal evidence showing that the house was worth only $185,000 at the time F left the company. Having held the house for another eighteen months, there is the possibility that Azar could have sold it for more than $185,000 when F departed, but chose not to do so in the hope that the market value would rise. At that point (arguably) Azar became an investor, or at least a speculator, and the house itself became a capital asset. If in fact the value went further down over the eighteen-month period, then that further decline would presumably be a capital loss.

But in any case eighteen months is a fairly short period of time and Azar did attempt to sell the house the moment F moved out. Accordingly, the $100,000 should be allowed under § 162(a) or § 165(a) as an offset against ordinary income.

Convinced? See the decision cited in the footnote.

Question 3: Jim Hawkins, a game young lad, has been running errands for a disreputable looking guest at his father's small hotel, where Jim works as a bellboy. The guest is very fond of Jim, tips him generously, and apparently regards Jim as a sort of nephew. Fearing that he is about to die of cirrhosis of the liver, the guest one day hands Jim an oilskin packet. "Jim," says he, "You've been a great help to me and I appreciate it. Yo-ho-ho, I'm out of money but here's something to reward your loyal services and your friendship. Guard it carefully." A month later the disreputable guest drops dead of thundering apoplexy. Jim at once opens the packet and finds that it contains a hand-drawn map of a small island located somewhere off the Spanish coast. At the bottom of the map are scrawled the words: "X Marks The Spot. Capt'n Flint His Treasure." Not sure what to do with it, Jim hides the map in his room at the bottom of an old underwear drawer.

The year following is a sad one for the Hawkins family. Jim's father passes away after a short illness and the hotel slides into bankruptcy, leaving Jim's mother in a state of near destitution. Hoping to divert her a bit, Jim gives his mother the oilskin packet as a souvenir of happier times. Ms. Hawkins one day shows the oilskin packet and its contents to Mr. Trelawney, a wealthy neighbor. Having studied the map with great interest, Trelawney offers to buy it from Ms. Hawkins for $25,000 cash. She gladly accepts.

What are the tax consequences of these events to Jim and Ms. Hawkins?

Answer: Debatable. Maybe this question belongs to Part C (Attribution of Income), but we think the choice-of-taxable-person and capital gain issues run together in this instance.

A lot depends on the relationship between Jim and Capt'n Flint. If Flint gave Jim the oilskin packet as an act of love, then the transfer should qualify as a "gift" under § 102(a) and nothing would be includable in Jim's gross income. In a later year Jim gives the packet to Ms. Hawkins—obviously a "gift"—and Ms. Hawkins sells the thing to Trelawney for $25,000 in cash. Jim's basis for the map is unclear under § 1015(a). According to that subsection, "If the facts necessary to determine the basis in the hands of the donor [in this case, Capt'n Flint] are unknown," then the basis in the hands of the donor "shall be the fair market value of such property . . . as of the date . . . at which . . . such property was acquired by such donor. . . ." Let's suppose the best estimate of the fair market value of the map as of the crucial date is zero. If so, Ms. Hawkins would therefore have a basis of zero as well, and would recognize a $25,000 gain when she sold the map to Trelawney. Her holding period would include Flint's holding period (not merely Jim's) under § 1223(2) and would certainly exceed one year.

Is the map a capital asset in Ms. Hawkins' hands? Section 1221(a)(3)(C) removes from the capital asset definition "a . . . letter or memorandum, or similar property" held by a taxpayer (Ms. H) whose basis is determined by reference to the basis of "a taxpayer whose personal efforts created such property." The aim of the Code, obviously, is to treat as ordinary income the sale of untaxed, self-created intellectual property (copyrights, etc.), whether "such property" is sold by the creator or by his donee. Does that provision cover the treasure map? We wouldn't think so. Flint (an honest taxpayer, one hopes) presumably included the treasure in his gross income—or if he didn't, he should have. The map merely represents a set of instructions as to how to retrieve the treasure and is otherwise valueless. If the map was a "gift" from Flint to Jim and from Jim to her, and if her basis in the map is zero, it appears that Ms. H has $25,000 of long-term capital gain.

But was it a "gift" from Flint to Jim? Arguably, Jim earned the map by reason of his energetic services as a bellboy. It was, in effect, a tip. With no way to determine its value, Jim included nothing in gross income at the time he received the oilskin packet. But we know from the Supreme Court's decision in *Earl* that personal service income is not assignable for tax purposes, and we know from *Eubank* that the service-performer continues to be taxable even though, by reason of accounting or other realization rules, such income was not included by him in the year it was earned. Personal service income is of course "ordinary." Taking this view of the matter, the sale proceeds of $25,000 would be taxed not to Ms. H but to Jim himself, and not as capital gain but as ordinary income. Ms. Hawkins would then take a basis equal to Jim's basis—$25,000—and would have no gain to recognize on the sale to Trelawney.

Question 4: You own undeveloped land, which you bought as an investment many years ago at a very low price (let's call it zero). A developer who wants to turn the land into a neighborhood of single-family homes has offered you $10 million for the land, and you are seriously considering the offer. You are also considering going into the real estate development business yourself, in which case you would divide the property into individual lots and sell the lots for an anticipated total of $15 million. Let's assume, unrealistically, that you would incur no development expenses. Let's also assume, almost realistically, that any capital gain you realize would be taxed at 20%, and that any ordinary income would be taxed at 37%. Do you sell the land to the developer, or do you develop it yourself?

Answer: This problem raises the same issue as the real estate development example at 18.01, but the difference in the numbers makes a difference in the result. Here, if you sell to the developer you will clear $8 million, after paying tax of $2 million. If you develop the property yourself, and if your development activities convert the property to a § 1221(a)(1) asset in your hands (as activities on this scale almost surely would), your tax would be $5.55 million (37% of $15 million), and you would clear $9.45 million after tax—which is, of course, $1.45 million more than if you sold to the developer. Developing the property yourself increases your pre-tax income by $5 million and increases your tax liability by $3.55 million. That amounts to an effective marginal tax rate of 71%—which is impressively high, but still below 100%. Whether it is worth going to the effort of generating another $5 million of pre-tax profit, only to have the government take 71% of that profit, is a question the answer to which only you can determine.

Question 5: Stanley owned a piece of heavy equipment which he used in his construction business (a sole proprietorship). He had purchased the equipment several years ago for $20,000. After having (properly) claimed ACRS deductions totaling $7,000 (assume neither § 168(k) nor § 179 applied), his adjusted basis in the equipment is now $13,000.

(a)   What will be the tax result to Stanley if he now sells the equipment for $10,000?

(b)   What if he sells the equipment for $15,000?

(c)   What if he manages (surprisingly) to sell the equipment for $22,000?

(d)   What if the asset in question is not equipment, but a building (for which Stanley had been claiming straight-line ACRS), and Stanley sells it for $22,000?

Answer: (a) Stanley will realize a § 1231 loss of $3,000, which will be an ordinary loss if the result of the § 1231 netting process is a loss.

(b)   Stanley will realize a gain of $2,000, which will be ordinary income under the ACRS recapture rules of § 1245. (Basically, gain on the disposition of a § 1231 asset is recaptured as ordinary income to the extent of the lesser of (i) the amount of the gain or (ii) the amount of ACRS deductions previously claimed on the asset.)

(c)   Stanley will realize a gain of $9,000, of which $7,000 will be ordinary income under § 1245 and $2,000 will be § 1231 gain (taxable as capital gain if the result of the § 1231 netting process is a gain).

(d)   Stanley will again have $9,000 of gain, but this time nothing will be recaptured as ordinary income, because the more lenient rules of § 1250 will apply in lieu of § 1245. Thus he has $9,000 of § 1231 gain, which will be capital gain if the § 1231 netting produces a gain. The $7,000 of gain attributable to ACRS deductions will, however, be treated as "unrecaptured § 1250 gain," taxed at 25% rather than at the usual rates for long-term capital gain.

Question 6: Euphoric State University unintentionally conferred tenure on Professor Bumble, pursuant to a university rule under which a professor is deemed tenured if he has taught at the university for more than six years without the university having formally reviewed his performance. Tenure is an assurance of lifetime employment with the university (barring major misconduct or incompetence on the part of the professor, or financial distress on the part of the university). In the years after Bumble received tenure, Euphoric State became increasingly dissatisfied with his performance, although his performance was not so poor as to support revocation of tenure for cause. Eventually Euphoric State and Bumble agreed that he would resign his tenured appointment in exchange for a one-time payment of $300,000 from the university. Bumble is hoping that the $300,000 will be taxed as long-term capital gain on the sale of a zero-basis capital asset (his tenure). Will his hopes be realized or dashed?

Answer: Almost certainly dashed. The facts are closely based (believe it or not) on those of a 1983 Tax Court decision, *Foote v. Commissioner*.[56] Following a long line of cases holding that payments made to an employee for the surrender of her employment contract are ordinary income because the right to continued employment is not a capital asset, the Tax Court held that Bumble's tenure was not a capital asset. Courts in this area appear to be following an intuition that capital gain treatment is simply inappropriate in the employment context. For good measure, the Tax Court in *Foote* also held that the tenure buyout did not satisfy the "sale or exchange" requirement for capital gain treatment, because the tenure was extinguished rather than transferred.

---

[56]　81 T.C. 930 (1983).

AFTERWORD

If the reader has the strength to look back at the materials discussed in this book, he or she might become aware that there are three major systemic problems—problems fundamental to the income tax as a whole—which the Code, the cases, and the Internal Revenue Service are obliged to confront at many points. Seeing this may help some students to organize the materials more easily and perhaps resist confusion.

The first such problem is obvious; the second pretty much so; the third is sometimes hidden and a bit harder to observe. We exaggerate only slightly when we assert that most, if not quite all, of the interpretative issues that arise under the particular Code provisions that have been examined—though they may seem scattered and diverse—can actually be subsumed under one or another of the systemic problems to which we now refer.

Systemic Problem #1: Business or Personal. The distinction between business-related expenditures and expenditures that are "personal, living, or family expenses" is vital in calculating an individual's taxable income. But as the reader knows by this time, there is no easy formulaic device that will enable one to make the necessary distinction, chiefly, we suppose, because individuals are free to characterize their activities in a self-serving way and because a person may in fact be engaged in business and personal activities at one and the same time. The so-called business lunch is an obvious example.

If one goes back to such cases as *Pevsner, Hantzis,* and the Cardozo decision in *Welch v. Helvering,* one is pretty much forced to conclude that distinguishing "business" from "personal" can never be done in a wholly convincing way and never with complete finality. The courts of appeals decided the first two cases for the government, but both decisions were reversals of the Tax Court, a majority of whose putative tax experts actually found for the taxpayers. In *Welch* the great judge simply couldn't help treating the taxpayer's expenditures as falling into both categories at once, being "necessary for the development of the [taxpayer's] business" but also akin to the restoration of "a family name that is clouded by thefts committed by an ancestor." The *Welch* opinion is generally regarded as a muddle, yet there may be some truth to the notion that the taxpayer's motives in repaying the creditors of his bankrupt predecessor (a family business started by "an ancestor," *i.e.,* his father) were indeed of two sorts.

475

The same business-personal question arises on the gross income side and accounts for the decades-long struggle by Congress and the Service to cope with employee fringe benefits. *Benaglia* is an obvious example, *Kowalski* is another. Breakfast, lunch and dinner meet a highly personal need and generate personal satisfaction. Presumably, however, what you eat, how much you spend, and in whose company, may be forced upon you by business considerations rather than being a matter of personal choice. If so, perhaps the personal benefit should be valued at less than retail cost, perhaps much less, perhaps even zero in some cases. On the other hand, a good meal and a soft bed (in a luxury hotel) *could* be viewed as additional compensation for a job well done, whatever the limitations on choice and personal preference. The dissenting judges in the *Benaglia* case evidently thought so.

Recognizing that the line between business and personal expenses has to be drawn somewhere, a number of fairly lengthy Code sections—§§ 119, 132, and 274, among others—bravely attempt to do just that, in some cases by imposing dollar limitations on the amount deductible or excludable, in others by denying deductions for broad categories of expenditures (such as "entertainment," in 2018 and later years). Those provisions inevitably present interpretative questions of their own, however, and leave taxpayers some room to resolve doubts in their own favor.

Systemic Problem #2: Realization and Deferral. A taxpayer who can find some legal means of deferring his tax obligation will have succeeded in reducing that obligation in absolute terms. As the reader well knows, the present value of a dollar in tax that can be paid a year from now (or, better yet, ten years, or fifty years) is substantially less than a dollar in tax that has to be paid today. The difference is simply measured by compound interest on the deferred liability. Apart from parents and grandparents (as the old saying goes), the United States is the only lender that is generally willing to make interest-free loans.

This familiar "timing" problem—when gross income can be deferred, and when deductions can be accelerated—shows up everywhere and lies at the root of many of the cases and statutory provisions that appear in our discussion. The litigation in *Crane* and *Tufts* and (by extension) the Code treatment of "at-risk" investment and "passive activity losses" are familiar examples. The crucial issue in the *Crane* area was whether annual depreciation is to be calculated with respect to the entire cost of the property acquired, including amounts borrowed, or only with respect to the taxpayer's equity investment. The Court having decided—perhaps unwisely—in favor of "entire cost," Congress and the Internal Revenue Service spent decades fighting off the consequences, with that effort culminating, finally, in the enactment of Code section 469, a provision of impressive complexity.

The realization requirement itself, first fixed in place by *Eisner v. Macomber*, is responsible for the segregation of capital gains and losses and probably also at some level for the tax-preferred status of long-term capital gains. This in turn generates the definitional problems so labored in Part F. In a slightly subtler way, the home mortgage interest deduction can be traced to the difficulty, or impossibility, of treating the imputed value of home occupancy as "realized" by the homeowner, leading in turn to discrimination between those who own their homes and pay deductible mortgage interest and those who pay nondeductible rent. Finally, realization is a major issue in the corporate merger field, of which our discussion of like-kind exchanges under Code § 1031 provides a foretaste.

Realization and deferral of tax was a leading theme in Part A. As suggested in the Note at p. 489, the effect of the realization requirement is to convert our income tax into a kind of hybrid tax system, in which consumption tax elements—the exemption or partial exemption of investment income—can be found as well as income tax elements.

Systemic Problem #3: Tax Arbitrage. Any financial arrangement in which inflows (income) and related outflows (expense) are treated asymmetrically meets the definition of "tax arbitrage" (in tax jargon). The municipal bond illustration at 6.06, in which excluded income would be combined with deductible interest (but for § 265), is the simplest illustration of an arbitrage, but the same problem arises at many other points in one form or another. As suggested in connection with the tax treatment of original issue bond discount at 17.04(b), the arbitrage problem often appears in a two-party setting. Prior to Code amendment, corporate issuers of original issue discount bonds were permitted to deduct the discount on a straight-line basis, which meant deductions in the early years substantially in excess of actual interest cost. On the same straight-line basis, investors were required to include in income more interest than they imputedly received. But since many investors in original issue discount bonds were tax-exempt organizations—*e.g.*, universities—the benefit to the issuers resulted in a harmless detriment to the investors. The two together could thus create (and divide) a tax saving at the Treasury's expense. The enactment of Code sections 1271 and 1272 brought this two-party arbitrage to an end, but only after it had been exploited for many years to the parties' mutual advantage.

Choosing cases more or less at random, *Haverly, Knetsch,* and *Whipple,* though they arise under different Code provisions and present different problems of statutory construction, are all essentially tax arbitrage decisions. The question posed was whether economic income that was tax-excluded (as in *Haverly*), or tax-deferred (as in *Knetsch*), or tax-preferred (as in *Whipple*), could be matched with a full deduction from ordinary income for related expenditures—the very definition of an arbitrage. The answer, in each case, was no.

The decisions just mentioned suggest that the courts themselves may be alert to tax arbitrage even without the aid of a specific provision like section 265. But not always. The *Tufts* case, mentioned above, though decided for the government, presents a kind of long-range arbitrage, which Justice O'Connor's concurrence was intended to prevent. In *Tufts* the taxpayers took depreciation deductions on their property and then disposed of the property when it was worth substantially less than the outstanding nonrecourse mortgage. The Court held, in effect, that the taxpayers were obliged to treat the previously deducted depreciation as a taxable gain. But the balancing inclusion was taxed as long-term capital gain, not as ordinary income. As a result, the taxpayers were allowed to take in tax-preferred income (the capital gain) with one hand while deducting ordinary expense (annual depreciation) with the other. No doubt aware that an arbitrage was underway, O'Connor argued that the gain should be treated as debt-cancellation income, and hence classified as ordinary. But the majority did not agree. And perhaps rightly so, since Congress could have shut down this particular arbitrage opportunity by conforming the § 1250 recapture rules for buildings to the stricter § 1245 recapture rules for tangible personal property, but Congress chose not to do so.

Having said all this, the question that remains is whether the foregoing helps or hurts the student reader struggling to master these (previously) unfamiliar materials. Helps, we think. Can't hurt (we hope).

Often, and to the surprise of many students, the income tax course turns out to be among the best and most successful in the entire law-school curriculum. One reason for this is that the questions raised in the course are fairly specific, and there are right answers as opposed to wrong ones.[1] Courses of broader scope, by contrast, often suffer from a certain undergraduate malaise. Approached as a set of technical constructs (and apart from the weight of statutory detail), the tax course is relatively easy to teach

---

[1]   It may also help that students frequently come to the income tax course with the assumption that the material will be hopelessly complex and incredibly boring, and are pleasantly surprised when the material turns out to be (a) for the most part, manageable, and (b) actually rather interesting, at least in places.

and understand. Our effort has been to assist in that direction by making the technical issues easier still.

Note

WHAT IS THE TRUE VALUE OF A TAX PREFERENCE?[1]

Brief reference has been made at various points to so-called tax preferences—the exemption for municipal bond interest, for example, or the exclusion of imputed rents from owner-occupied residences, or the phenomenon of accelerated depreciation. Quite obviously, such preferences permit taxpayers who own "preferred" assets to receive income free of tax, or subject to a lower-than-normal effective rate of tax. Not wanting to complicate matters in the main text, we have made little effort to show in detail how these preferences relate to a progressive rate structure but have simply left the reader to infer that the value of tax exemption for $1 dollar of income is equal to $1 times the taxpayer's marginal tax rate. While this is true as far as it goes, it probably doesn't go far enough. Tax preferences exist in a dynamic market, which means that they, like other valuable goods, are the object of competitive bidding. An asset—say a municipal bond—that yields tax-*exempt* dollars is bound to be worth more to investors than an asset—say an ordinary corporate bond—that yields the same number of *taxable* dollars. Because in the final analysis investors are interested in *after*-tax income, they will certainly be willing to pay more for a tax-exempt income-stream than a taxable one, everything else being equal.

The vital question is, how *much* more? Paying a premium for a tax advantage obviously reduces the value of the advantage to the payor. The higher the cost of an exempt asset as compared with the cost of an equivalent taxable asset, the *less* the value of the exemption to the buyer. Indeed, if the premium were high enough, the value of the exemption would dwindle to the vanishing point.[2] Once again, therefore, the important question is: how *much* of a premium do investors have to pay when they buy an asset that enjoys a tax preference?

Perhaps this issue is best approached by trying to answer a simpler question first. Let's assume that we have a progressive tax

---

[1] This Note—which is intended to be explanatory and illustrative—explains and illustrates by reference to the pre-1986 rate schedule rather than the current rates for two reasons. First, computations are simpler—50% is a handier number than 37%; second, the outcomes and comparisons are more dramatic if the rate structure is steeply progressive. The implication, of course, is that the "true value" of a tax-preference would indeed tend towards zero if we had a single-rate tax system and gave up the idea of progression altogether.

[2] See Bittker, *Tax Shelters and Tax Capitalization—or, Does the Early Bird Get a Free Lunch?*, 38 Nat'l.Tax J. 416 (1975).

system and that the rates themselves (as was true before the 1986 Act) rise from a minimum of zero (on amounts covered by the standard deduction) to a maximum of 50%. Under these circumstances, will individual taxpayers all be willing to pay the same amount for an asset that produces ordinary taxable income—a corporate bond, for example—irrespective of their particular bracket rates? Or will high-bracket taxpayers be willing to pay more, or less, for the bond than low-bracket taxpayers? If the income tax were proportionate—say a flat 25% rate for everyone—we would feel pretty confident that the after-tax value of an income-stream would be the same for all investors, and hence that everybody would be willing to pay the same price for the bond just mentioned. But what happens to asset prices when a progressive tax system is introduced, with some investors paying tax at one rate and some at another?

The answer is: nothing. Assuming that financing costs (interest paid to a bank or other lender for funds borrowed to purchase the bond) are deductible, the value of a bond that yields taxable income is the same to a 50% taxpayer as it is to a 20% taxpayer. Going further, the value of the bond to all investors under a progressive tax system is the same as it would be under a proportionate tax system— indeed, it is the same under a progressive (or proportionate) tax system as it would be if there were no income tax at all. The reason, briefly, is that if financing costs are deductible, the reduction in income caused by an income tax (at *whatever* rate) is offset by a precisely proportional reduction in the after-tax rate at which the income stream is capitalized.[3] It follows that a 50% taxpayer, a 20% taxpayer, and a 0% taxpayer (such as a charity) will all place the same value on any particular investment.

An illustration may help to make the point. Suppose that a fully taxable corporate bond is expected to yield $100 a year in perpetuity. Assume that, apart from any tax considerations, the expected income stream would be capitalized at a rate of 12%. Under the usual formula for determining the present value of a perpetuity (see Appendix *infra*), the value of the bond would be $100/.12 = $833. Will the bond have a different value to a 50%, a 20% or a 0% taxpayer?

---

[3]   Thus, in valuing an investment, if the income-stream is reduced by tax, then the capitalization rate must also be applied on an after-tax basis. "Capitalization rate" is just another name for the rate of interest at which an investor can borrow to finance the purchase of the asset she wants to own. Since interest on a loan is normally deductible, the applicable capitalization rate equals the interest rate *after* allowing for the deduction. As shown in the arithmetical illustration below, if the interest rate *before* tax is 12% and the investor is in the 50% bracket, the interest rate *after* tax, and hence the capitalization rate, is 50% of 12%, or 6%.

	After-tax Earnings	After-tax Capitalization Rate	Present Value	
50% taxpayer:	$100(1 − t) = $50	.12(1 − t) = .06	$\frac{\$50}{.06}$	= $833
	where t = 50%			
20% taxpayer:	$100(1 − t) = $80	.12(1 − t) = .096	$\frac{\$80}{.096}$	= $833
	where t = 20%			
0% taxpayer:	$100(1 − t) = $100	.12(1 − t) = .12	$\frac{\$100}{.12}$	= $833
	where t = 0%			

Surprise! The progressive income tax has no effect whatever on the price that investors in different tax brackets will pay for the same capital asset. The bond is worth $833 to everybody.

But now suppose that Congress, for reasons of national policy, decides that it would like to encourage investors to put more money than they otherwise would into a certain type of investment, say bonds issued by low-income housing developers. In effect, Congress wants more of the nation's savings devoted to investments of this particular sort, because it believes that low-income housing deserves a boost. Accordingly, Congress amends the Internal Revenue Code to provide that the income from such bonds shall be exempt from tax. *Now* what happens to investors in different brackets and to the value of the asset? The twofold answer is (a) that the value of low-income housing bonds will rise substantially, and (b) that 50% taxpayers will pay more for such bonds than will taxpayers at any lower bracket-level. Indeed, if the market works perfectly, it should be the case that 50% taxpayers will acquire *all* the low-income housing bonds that are issued by developers. To illustrate—

	Earnings (Tax-free)	After-tax Capitalization Rate	Present Value
50% taxpayer	$100	.12(1 − t) = .06	$100/.06 = $1,667
20% taxpayer	$100	.12(1 − t) = .096	$100/.096 = $1,042
0% taxpayer	$100	.12(1 − t) = .12	$100/.12 = $833

So, whereas a fully taxable bond has the same value to all taxpayers no matter what their tax bracket, a tax-exempt bond is worth more to high-bracket taxpayers than to those in lower brackets. And since the exemption has its greatest value for taxpayers in the highest bracket, it should follow that the newly-issued housing bonds will be taken over *entirely* by the members of that class. In the illustration above, the 50-percenters are willing to pay as much as $1,667 for the bonds. No lower-bracket investor would find it advantageous to match that price, and hence the 50% group will presumably buy all the housing bonds that are available.

In view of these effects, does the enactment of the tax exemption impair tax equity? Are similarly situated taxpayers being treated alike, or is there now an element of undue favoritism in the system? The answer is that *if* everything worked out as neatly as shown above, the system would contain no favoritism whatever. From the standpoint of "horizontal equity," the proper test is whether after-tax returns are the same for taxpayers who are in the same tax bracket and who make identical dollar investments, one in an exempt asset, the other in a taxable asset. In the case above, an investment of $1,667 in the *exempt* bond yields $100 a year—both before tax and after tax—for a 50% taxpayer. The same dollar investment in an equivalent *taxable* bond by another 50% taxpayer yields 12% of $1,667 = $200 before tax, and 50% of $200 = $100 after tax. Hence, two taxpayers in the same tax bracket come out the same whichever bond they buy. Once again, the taxable bond yields $200 pre-tax, while the exempt bond yields only $100. But the non-exempt investor pays a tax of $100 while the exempt investor pays no tax. The buyer of the taxable bond carries out Congress' will by paying $100 in tax; the buyer of the exempt bond carries out the same legislative will by paying no explicit tax, but by enduring an "implicit tax" of $100 ($200 − $100) in sacrificed yield. After tax (whether actual or implicit), each investor winds up with the same $100.

What about "vertical equity"? Is the prior relationship between high-and low-bracket taxpayers maintained, or is there some loss in progressivity because of the bond exemption? Again, *if* everything works out as neatly as described above, the progressivity of the rate structure will be unaffected. Thus, a 20% taxpayer who invests $1,667 in a taxable bond yielding $200 will pay a tax of $40 (*i.e.*, 20% of $200). As already shown, a 50% taxpayer who invests the same amount in an exempt bond pays an "implicit tax" (in the form of sacrificed yield) of $100. The ratio $40/$100 is the same as the ratio 20%/50%, so that the vertical relationship between high- and low-bracket taxpayers is preserved despite the tax exemption.

Finally, what about "efficiency"? Is Congress achieving the goal it had in view when it enacted the preference? Are low-income housing developers receiving *all* the dollars that the Treasury is giving up? The answer is yes. If our top-bracket taxpayer had invested $1,667 in a taxable bond paying annual interest of $200, the taxpayer would have had an after-tax return of $100, the bond issuer would have had a borrowing cost of $200, and the government would have collected $100 tax. When the taxpayer instead purchases an exempt bond for $1,667, the taxpayer pockets the same $100 return as in the case of the taxable bond, but the bond issuer's borrowing cost is reduced to $100 and the government collects no tax. The entire $100 of tax revenue given up by the government inures to the benefit of the bond issuer, in the form of a decreased cost of borrowing; the taxpayer serves only as a conduit for the delivery of the subsidy from the government to the issuer of the bond. To be sure, $834 ($1,667 − $833) of resources are being drawn into low-income housing investment that would not go there if the legislated preference were absent; in effect, $1,667 is being "forced" into the exempt bonds whereas normal market operations would allocate only $833. But this is the *intended* result; it is a product of legislative design. Congress *means* to interfere with the market in precisely the degree indicated.

The rather striking conclusion that can be drawn from this discussion is that, under ideal conditions, tax preferences—exemptions of income derived from designated investments—are both efficient (given the legislative aim) *and* equitable. Thus, the enactment of an exemption for low-income housing bonds means that those bonds will be issued at a higher price than taxable bonds of equivalent yield. Moreover, all such bonds should pass into the hands of 50%-bracket taxpayers, because the exemption has the greatest value to them and they will (or should) outbid all investors at lower bracket levels. As a result, the beneficiaries of the exemption should be the bond issuer and, ultimately, those who reside in the low-income housing, because the higher issue price of $1,667 will precisely offset the benefit of the tax-exemption to the bond-purchaser. This is as it should be, of course, because it is those concerned with low-income housing who are *supposed* to benefit under the Congressional scheme.

Unfortunately for all this heady analysis, in the real world it appears that tax preferences are *not* fully capitalized. It is a familiar observation, for example, that state and local bonds (the interest on which is exempt from tax under § 103) are frequently purchased by individuals and corporations paying tax at *less* than the topmost rate. Put differently, the yield on exempt municipal bonds is customarily higher (*i.e.,* closer to that of fully taxable corporate bonds) than it would be if all such bonds were bought up by top-bracket taxpayers who paid a price equal to the full value of the exemption to *them*. Apparently, the volume of municipal bonds is too large—the credit needs of state and local governments are simply too great—for all such securities to be absorbed by taxpayers in the highest bracket. In addition, Code § 265(a)(2) specifically disallows deductions for interest on amounts borrowed to purchase municipal bonds (see 6.06), which means that top-bracket taxpayers are limited to financing such purchases out of their own resources and cannot use borrowed money for that purpose. For these and other reasons, municipal bonds have to be priced so as to appeal to taxpayers in lower brackets as well. In effect, the issue price of the bonds has to be low enough to produce a yield attractive to taxpayers who fall *below* the topmost tax bracket. At the same time, of course, such bonds can and will be purchased by taxpayers who *are* at the highest bracket level. Issuers of tax-exempt bonds cannot price discriminate in the manner familiar to (for example) purchasers of airline tickets. If bond issuers have to offer an interest rate high enough to attract, say, taxpayers in the 25% bracket, they will have to offer the same interest rate to taxpayers in the 37% bracket, even though that interest rate creates a windfall for the top-bracket taxpayers.

Although this state of affairs may sound more democratic, the ironic fact is that the sale of municipal bonds to taxpayers below the 50% bracket renders the preference afforded by such bonds both inequitable *and* inefficient. This can be confirmed by returning to our numerical illustration. If, for example, the low-income housing bonds have to be sold (in part) to 40% taxpayers, then the issue price of those bonds cannot be more than $1,389:

	Earnings (Tax-free)	After-tax Capitalization Rate	Present Value
40% taxpayer	$100	$.12(1 - t) = .072$	$1,389

But recall that 50%-bracket taxpayers would be willing to pay as much as $1,667 for these same bonds. Since the bonds have to be issued at $1,389 in order to clear the market, however, it is pretty plain that 50% taxpayers are going to enjoy a windfall. Instead of having to invest $1,667 to obtain a net yield of $100, they need invest only $1,389 and can use their saving of $278 for other things, including additional investment. Hence, 50% taxpayers who purchase the bonds for $1,389 now get a *real* tax benefit, of which the present value is $278. In addition, and relatedly, the cost to the federal government of enacting the tax subsidy for housing bonds is now greater than the benefit that is actually realized by developers and residents of low-income housing. Compare the results when a top-bracket taxpayer pays $1,389 for a taxable bond paying $167 annual interest (*i.e.*, 12% interest) with the results when a top-bracket taxpayer pays $1,389 for a tax-exempt bond paying $100 annual interest. In the case of the taxable bond, the taxpayer's after-tax return is $83.50, the bond issuer's borrowing cost is $167, and the government collects $83.50 tax. In the case of the tax-exempt bond, the taxpayer's after-tax return is $100, the bond issuer's borrowing cost is $100, and the government collects no tax. Of the $83.50 of forgone tax revenue, $67 goes to the bond issuer in the form of lower borrowing cost ($167 − $100), but $16.50 goes to the top-bracket taxpayer in the form of a higher investment return ($100 − $83.50).

Our initial question—"What is the true value of a tax preference?"—can now be answered. If the market for tax-exempt assets worked perfectly—if *all* tax-preferred income-streams wound up in the hands of the highest-bracket taxpayers—tax preferences on the whole would be valueless to their holders and harmless to the rest of us. The preferences would operate efficiently in achieving particular legislative goals, in the sense that all the benefits would go to the intended beneficiaries; and they would leave intact the horizontal and vertical relationships that one regards as equitable.

Apparently, however, the market for tax preferences does not work perfectly; all exempt assets do *not* come to rest in the hands of top-bracket taxpayers. As a result, there is some loss of tax equity as among taxpayers, and likewise some inefficiency from the government's standpoint. How much of each is difficult to say.

The inequities and inefficiencies described above occur when (1) taxpayers must compete in the market for a limited supply of tax-favored assets, and (2) the tax preference takes the form of an exclusion or deduction, so that the preference will have different values to taxpayers facing different marginal tax rates. If either of these conditions does not obtain, then the analysis developed above does not apply.

The first condition does not obtain if the tax preference attaches to the taxpayer himself, rather than to a particular type of asset. In that case, the "implicit tax" (*i.e.*, the reduced pre-tax rate of return on tax-favored assets), so central to the above analysis, does not exist. For example, tax exemption for the investment return on Roth IRAs (5.06) depends on the taxpayer's satisfying the Roth IRA eligibility requirements, not on the nature of the investment assets put into the Roth IRA. Because a taxpayer investing in a Roth IRA does not have to compete with other potential investors for a limited supply of tax-favored Roth IRA assets, the price of Roth IRA assets is not driven up by the tax preference, and there is no implicit tax. A practical implication of this observation is that it would be foolish to purchase tax-exempt municipal bonds for one's Roth IRA. The interest rate on the municipal bonds would reflect the usual implicit tax on tax-favored assets, but the § 103 exemption would be of no value to the investor (because the income would have been exempt in any event, under the rules governing Roth IRAs).

The second condition does not obtain if the tax preference attaching to a particular type of asset is invariant—that is, of equal value to all potential investors, regardless of their particular tax situations. In a tax system with a graduated rate structure, a preference in the form of an exclusion or deduction cannot be invariant. However, a refundable tax credit based on the ownership of a tax-favored asset can easily be designed to be invariant.[4] An invariant refundable credit would have an identical value to taxpayers in the 50% and 40% brackets (for example). As a result, the windfall that accrues to 50%-bracket taxpayers when an asset with an exclusion (or deduction) preference must be marketed to 40%-bracket taxpayers would not occur in the case of an invariant refundable credit. Because of this feature of refundable credits, a strong case can be made that all tax incentives for socially beneficial activities should be in the form of refundable credits.[5]

---

[4]   If the amount of the credit is a function of the taxpayer's adjusted gross income (or any other tax attribute of the owner of the tax-favored asset), then the tax preference is not invariant, despite the fact that the preference is in the form of a credit (rather than an exclusion or deduction).

[5]   Batchelder, Goldberg and Orszag, *Efficiency and Tax Incentives: The Case for Refundable Tax Credits*, 59 Stan. L. Rev. 23 (2006).

Note

INCOME TAX, CONSUMPTION TAX, FLAT TAX

"No income tax is really just, from which savings are not exempted," wrote John Stuart Mill in *Principles of Political Economy*. Often quoted and much debated, Mill's notion, in simplest terms, was that *unless* savings are exempted from tax, those who choose to save their income are taxed twice, while those who choose to expend their income on consumption are taxed only once. The point can easily be explained by example. Assume we live in a tax-free world and that C (for consumer) and S (for saver) both earn $1,000 in wages this year. C chooses to consume the whole $1,000 currently; S chooses to save the $1,000 and invest it in a 1-year 10% bond, because she prefers to have $1,100 to consume next year. The arithmetical relationship between C and S—between the decision to consume this year (C) and the decision to consume next year (S)—is obviously 1 to 1.1. Now suppose Congress enacts a 40% income tax so that C and S both have to pay a tax of $400 on their current wages, leaving each with $600. Once again, while C chooses to consume her after-tax $600, S elects to save by investing in a 1-year 10% bond, expecting to have $660 for consumption in the year following. But will she? Plainly not if the interest on her bond is taxable, as of course it would be under a conventional income tax (and is under Code § 61). S will have to pay a tax of $24 on the $60 of bond-interest and will have only $636 ($660 − $24) available for consumption in the second year. The 1:1.1 relationship that prevailed in the tax-free world becomes 6:6.36 in the post-tax world, *i.e.*, 1:1.06. At least arguably, S has been taxed twice on the same bond investment. Much vexed, S may simply grind her teeth and sulk, or she may decide to become a consumer like C and give up being a saver. At all events, Mill condemns the outcome as not "really just." Others, to be sure, have disagreed.

Without worrying for the moment about the meaning of "justice" in this context, it is useful to note that the extra tax on savers could be eliminated, if we wished to eliminate it, in either of *two* ways. First, and most simply, we could amend the tax law to provide that *all* investment income (meaning interest, dividends, rents and capital gains) should be exempt from income tax. Since "income" can derive from only two sources, labor and investment,[1] the income tax would then apply to personal service income alone. In other words, the income tax would become a wage tax. C and S would both be taxed

---

[1]   Apart from the rare genuine windfall, which neither of the authors has ever been fortunate enough to experience.

on the $1,000 earned in Year 1, but the $60 of interest received by S in Year 2 would be received tax-free. S would then have $660 in Year 2 instead of only $636, and the injustice that Mill claimed to perceive would be overcome.

Our present income tax actually follows this course in the special case of municipal bonds, the interest on which is excluded from gross income by Code § 103. Of course the specific legislative purpose of exempting municipal bond interest was not to placate S, but to subsidize state and city borrowing costs. The effect, however, at least in form, is to limit the tax on savings (if invested in municipals) to a single imposition, and in that way to put C and S on a parity. Another example of an exemption for capital income is the interest earned on a life insurance or annuity contract, which, as noted at 2.03, is permitted to be accumulated tax-free under the Code. As with municipal bonds, the effect is to relieve from the so-called double tax individuals who choose to save in this medium. Yet another example of the limited adoption of wage tax principles in the Internal Revenue Code is the permanent exemption for the investment return in Roth IRAs (5.06).

The alternative device by which the extra tax on savers could be eliminated, though perhaps less exposed and obvious, is equally effective and has the same consequence as a straightforward bond interest exemption. If the tax law allowed S to *deduct* her bond investment in Year 1 and pay tax only when the amount invested is withdrawn for consumption—Year 2 in our example—the extra tax would disappear and the relationship between C and S would return to what it was in the pre-tax world. Thus, if S could deduct her $1,000 bond investment as if it were a current business expense, she would pay no tax whatever in Year 1 and would have $1,100 available for consumption in Year 2. If the $1,100 were withdrawn from savings in Year 2 and then taxed at the 40% rate, the tax in Year 2 would be $440 and S would have $660 left for spending just as above. Under this approach the income tax would be replaced by a consumption tax; consumption spending would be subject to tax, but savings would not.

Once again, our present income tax law has certain equivalent features. Quick depreciation rules (including instantaneous depreciation, in the case of 100% expensing under § 168(k)), which permit taxpayers to accelerate the recovery of investment in equipment and real estate, are one important example. Allowing the postponement of tax on unrealized investment appreciation is another. Deferring tax on pension plan contributions (or on regular— *i.e.*, non-Roth—IRAs; see 5.06) is yet another. In each of these instances, present law permits investors to deduct (or exclude) their savings in determining their annual taxable income. The consequence, as just shown, is to treat the yield on such savings as tax-exempt.

To summarize: The income tax is a tax system that has two parts. First, it taxes personal service income (wages, salaries, fees, etc.) when earned. Second, it taxes wealth—which represents the amount saved and invested by the taxpayer after first paying tax on her earnings—by including dividends, interest, rents and capital gains in gross income. If we wished to eliminate the wealth-tax element, we could do so in either of two ways. We could simply treat all income from capital investment as tax-exempt, and tax wages only. In the alternative, we could allow all investments to be deducted currently, and tax spending only. Either technique would place Consumer and Saver on an "equal" footing from a tax standpoint, in the sense that the arithmetical relationship between the two would be the same in the post-tax world as it was in the pre-tax world.

Eliminating the so-called extra tax on savings (assuming we wished to do that) could be accomplished at a single stroke by replacing our present income tax with a retail sales tax, a revenue raising device now much relied upon by states and municipalities. In New York City, for example, the tax is at a rate of 8.875% on retail sales and services (with exemptions for food, medical services, etc.). It has been suggested by some that enactment of a sales tax at the Federal level might be a good idea as well.[2] If we took that step— actually replaced our income tax with a national sales tax—then, whatever else might be said about that decision, the effect, as suggested, would be to treat consumers and savers alike. Consumption would be taxed, but savings and investment would be subtracted from the tax base. With a sales tax in place, C, who spends her $1,000, would pay a tax in Year 1 of $400.[3] S, who saves her $1,000 and spends nothing in Year 1, would owe no tax whatever. In Year 2 when she consumes those savings plus $100 of interest, S would pay a tax of $440. The relationship between C and S would then be 1:1.1—just as it was in the pre-tax world—and J.S. Mill (among others) would evidently regard the result as equitable.

---

[2]   Boortz and Linder, *The FairTax Book* (2005).

[3]   A minor computational complexity results from the fact that income taxes are calculated on a tax-inclusive basis (*i.e.*, the amount of the tax is included in the tax base), whereas retail sales taxes are calculated on a tax-exclusive basis (*i.e.*, the amount of the tax is not included in the tax base). Under a 40% income tax, in Year 1 C earns $1,000, pays $400 tax (40% of $1,000), and is able to consume $600. To replicate these results under a tax-exclusive retail sales tax requires a higher nominal tax rate. Thus, for C to devote her entire $1,000 of Year 1 earnings to consumption and to the tax on that consumption, C would purchase goods at the (pre-tax) cost of $600, and would pay tax of $400, determined by applying a tax rate of 67% to her purchases of $600.

The same analysis (though perhaps a little harder to see) applies to yet another well-known revenue device. Very many other countries impose and collect their sales taxes at the business level rather than the consumer level through the medium of a value-added tax (VAT). VATs and retail sales taxes are essentially alike (apart from point of collection) and indeed any comprehensive retail sales tax can be replicated by a VAT—and vice versa. The aim of both, quite simply, is to tax households on their consumption expenditures. The retail sales tax is collected from the retailer at the point of final sale to the consumer; the VAT is levied on producer firms rather than households, and on the "value added" at each stage of production. The VAT is said to be superior to a retail sales tax from the standpoint of enforcement; also, being a bit less out in the open, it is usually given a broader base of application.

As the reader is probably aware, sales taxes (retail or firm-level) are often objected to on grounds of regressivity. Low-income households must spend most or all of their annual earnings on food, rent and other consumption items, while upper-income households may choose to spend a portion of their earnings on consumption and save the balance. Hence a sales tax, which cannot as a practical matter be graduated,[4] hits the poor harder in percentage-of-income terms than it does the rich. To most though perhaps not all observers, that result appears distinctly unfair. The question, then, is whether those (like the redoubtable Mill) who think that the income tax is unjust to savers can contrive a tax system that (a) limits the tax base to consumption and excludes savings, but also (b) avoids the objectionable regressivity feature as well.

There are two methods of implementing a progressive consumption tax. One method is based on the Flat Tax proposal—a proposal that received a great deal of attention during the 1996 presidential campaign.[5] Succinctly stated, the Flat Tax is simply a VAT with an exemption for a limited amount of wages. The Flat Tax plan has two integrated parts: (1) a so-called Business Tax that is collected from firms (whether or not incorporated), and (2) an Individual Compensation Tax that is collected from individual wage-earners. Taken together, the bases of the two parts of the Flat Tax are the same as the base of a VAT. Both taxes would be imposed at the same rate, say 20%. However, an exemption for the first $Y of their wage income ($36,000 for a family of four under one version of the plan) is allowed to individual taxpayers. In effect, therefore, low-wage households are relieved of the Individual Compensation Tax

----

[4]   For an extremely funny fictional account of Illinois' disastrous 1977 experiment with a progressive retail sales tax (to repeat, this is fiction), see David Foster Wallace, *The Pale King* 194–97 (2011).

[5]   Hall and Rabushka, *The Flat Tax* (2d ed., 1995).

entirely and regressivity is mitigated. The same effect cannot be achieved under a standard VAT, because the VAT (or a retail sales tax) is imposed on the sale of products and does not take the consumer's income level into account. Although the developers of the Flat Tax proposal advocate taxing all wages above the exemption level at a single ("flat") rate—a point so important to them that they named the tax after its rate, rather than (as in the case of every other sort of tax we can think of) after its base—the wage tax component of the proposal could, of course, accommodate a graduated rate structure of any desired degree of progressivity.[6]

The other method of implementing a progressive consumption tax more closely resembles the current income tax. It would be possible to convert the income tax to a consumption tax while retaining a great deal of the architecture of the current system. Start from the observation that *Income = Consumption + Savings,* or $I = C + S$. This follows from the fact that there are, basically, only two things one can do with one's income—spend it on current consumption, or save it. Thus, income defined in terms of sources (the left-hand side of the equation) necessarily equals income defined in terms of uses (the right-hand side of the equation). Subtracting S from both sides of the equation, and switching the sides, we find that $C = I - S$. Thus, the income tax would become a consumption tax if all savings were deductible—which could be accomplished simply by amendment to the rules in § 219 restricting the ability of taxpayers to make deductible IRA contributions. If all taxpayers were able to make deductible contributions to savings accounts, in unlimited amount and for any purpose, the income tax would become a consumption tax. When a taxpayer took money out of his savings account to spend on consumption, that spending would be subject to the consumption tax.[7] In terms of the consumption tax formula, $C = I - S$, spending out of savings (*i.e.*, dissaving) is negative savings, and thus increases the consumption tax base for the year of negative savings.[8] Converting the income tax to a consumption tax of this kind—sometimes referred to as a "cash-flow tax"—could be accomplished while leaving huge portions of the current Internal Revenue Code intact, including the graduated tax rate schedules of § 1. This is, of course, the second of the two devices, described earlier in this *Note,* for equalizing the tax treatments of C (consumer) and S (saver).

---

[6]   Bradford, *What Are Consumption Taxes and Who Pays Them?*, 39 Tax Notes 383 (1988).

[7]   This is consistent with the taxation of IRA distributions under current law.

[8]   Debt-financed consumption is also a form of negative savings, and as such is also subject to tax under the $C = I - S$ formula.

Which brings us back to the wage tax, the first of the two devices for equalizing the tax treatments of C and S. A wage tax is not a consumption tax, but (as the analysis of the situations of C and S has shown) under certain conditions the two types of taxes will produce equivalent economic effects. If we are going to consider ways of making the tax system fairer to the likes of S (on the assumption that the current system is unfair to S), shouldn't a wage tax be among the options? Of course, the federal government already has a wage tax—the payroll tax devoted to financing Social Security and Medicare—but the idea here would be to repeal the income tax while increasing the rate (or rates) and expanding the base of the payroll tax. In terms of analogies to the current income tax, instead of building on the treatment of regular (deductible) IRAs, as would a cash-flow tax, a wage tax would build on the treatment of Roth IRAs.

For whatever reason, proposals to replace the income tax have focused on various methods of taxing consumption; no proposal to replace the income tax with an expanded wage tax has attracted significant attention. Should such a proposal attract interest in the future, it is worth briefly noting two respects in which cash-flow ($C = I - S$) and wage tax treatment do *not* produce equivalent results. First, the two types of taxation will not produce equivalent results if the applicable tax rates are different under the two systems. For a particular taxpayer, the results will not be the same under the two systems if the taxpayer's marginal tax rate is different in the year in which she earns income (the taxable year under a wage tax) and the year in which she consumes (the taxable year under the cash-flow tax). Second, the two types of taxation have very different effects on taxpayers who have wealth at the time the systems are introduced. If a taxpayer has wealth at the time a wage tax is introduced, she can thereafter spend out of that wealth without being subject to tax. By contrast, if a taxpayer has wealth at the time a consumption tax is introduced, later spending of that wealth will be consumption (dissaving) and will be taxable under a cash-flow tax.

A stimulating debate should follow at this point as to which of the two eligible taxing regimes—income or consumption—has the better claim to fairness and equity. We prefer to evade that issue, however, and in lieu of further discussion respectfully refer the reader to the very worthy materials cited on p. 410 at note 6.

Note

TAX SHELTERS AND
ECONOMIC SUBSTANCE

In the 1990s and early 2000s, the tax system suffered from a plague of tax shelter devices promoted by major accounting and investment banking firms, often with the active support of some of the best-known law firms in the nation.[1] The plague seems now to have ended—not for any one reason, but for a rather complicated combination of reasons (described below). While the tax shelter phenomenon lasted, the cost to the Treasury—that is, to the rest of us—in taxes never collected was horrendous.

These tax shelters were intended to shield the taxpayer from paying tax, otherwise due and payable, on income from unrelated sources.[2] Typical would be income in the form of executive compensation—perhaps resulting from the exercise of non-statutory stock options, as in the *Lo Bue* case (19.01)—or gain from the sale of a closely held business. In one case the authors are aware of, stock options exercised by an executive generated $200 million of ordinary compensation income; in another, the sale of a computer company produced capital gain of twice that amount for family stockholders. The taxpayers in both cases were willing, eager and easily persuaded to pay fees (in the millions) to promoters who assured them that their regular tax obligations could—legally and without financial risk—be eliminated or reduced to a minimum through investment in a tax shelter devised by the promoters themselves.

From the taxpayer's standpoint there was little to lose (apart from fees) by investing in a tax shelter scheme *provided* that the only consequence, if the scheme unraveled, was payment of taxes that would have had to be paid anyway (plus interest on those taxes). So why not give it a try? The outlook would have been a lot more chancy—often prohibitively so—if the taxpayer also had to confront the risk of civil penalties for understating his income, penalties that might, depending on circumstances, run as high as 75% of the tax due. In many cases, probably most, that danger would have rendered the tax shelter unsalable. The solution to this awkward problem was

---

[1]   For a very readable in-depth account of the tax shelter phenomenon, from inside some of the most deeply involved law and accounting firms, see Rostain & Regan, *Confidence Games: Lawyers, Accountants, and the Tax Return Industry* (2014).

[2]   We may be tempting fate by describing tax shelters in the past tense. The tax shelter industry appeared dead after the enactment of the passive loss rules (13.02) in 1986, but it returned with a vengeance only a few years later. We are not quite convinced that tax shelters are (in the words of the Munchkin coroner) "really most sincerely dead" this time either.

for the promoter to furnish to the taxpayer (at the taxpayer's expense) an opinion of independent tax counsel whose considered conclusions on the legal status of the tax shelter were presumably entitled to respect. Usually running to forty or fifty pages of heavily footnoted legal analysis, such opinions invariably stated that in the event of a challenge by the government the taxpayer's position was "more likely than not" to be upheld by the courts. The phrase "more likely than not" apparently meant that there was at least a 51% chance of success in any future litigation, although, to be sure, by implication, there might also have been a 49% chance of failure. But whatever the outcome, the effect of such an opinion, or so it was hoped, was to immunize the taxpayer from the danger of civil penalties. If unlucky enough to be audited, the taxpayer could honestly assert that he sought the opinion of reputable counsel and was assured thereby that the shelter scheme was consistent with the requirements of law.

Some high-standing law firms steadily declined to furnish such opinions; others, with bills to pay, did not.

More than a score of tax shelter schemes were actively promoted and sold to high-income taxpayers in the 1990s and early 2000s. Some were deferral schemes, others were income elimination schemes; both, of course, were designed to generate substantial tax savings for the shelter investor. Shelter plans were always complicated and detailed—much documentation and many interconnected steps on the way to tax paradise. This complexity in itself provided the taxpayer with protection of a sort by discouraging and possibly confusing an examining revenue agent if an audit took place.

But not the reader. Below are two quite typical shelter "strategies" that should be fairly easy to follow. The first strategy was intended to benefit an executive with valuable stock options, the second a seller (as it happens a corporate seller) of a very successful business. As we hope the two examples will suggest, the shelters of the 1990s and 2000s were more varied in their design than the pre-1986 leveraged real estate tax shelters shut down by the enactment of the passive loss rules of § 469 (13.02). Although the passive loss rules were an effective "silver bullet" aimed at the heart of pre-1986 shelters, it was not clear than any such one-shot response to these newer shelters could succeed.

The Executive Compensation Solution

Jones, an important executive employed by X Corporation, a public company, holds *Lo Bue*-type (*i.e.*, non-"incentive") stock options entitling him on exercise to buy 100,000 shares of X stock at $10 a share. X stock is now selling at $100 a share on the New York

Stock Exchange. Jones' options will expire in one week, hence Jones is bound to exercise them promptly. Acting on the advice of his well-respected tax advisor, Jones sells his options to his son, Junior, for an unsecured non-negotiable 30-year promissory note in the face amount of $9 million, the net value of the options. The unsecured 30-year note is a balloon note, meaning that the principal amount, $9 million, is to be paid by the buyer/obligor (Junior) at the end of the 30-year period, not before. Junior at once exercises the options, paying X $1 million (having been given that sum by his generous father) and receiving 100,000 newly-issued X shares from the company. Over the next few days, Junior sells the X shares for $10 million.

Income tax results? According to Jones' tax advisor, (i) Jones recognizes no income on the sale of the options to his son, and (ii) Junior recognizes no income on either his exercise of the options or his sale of the X shares. "Wonderful!" cries Jones. "What a great country this is! But how can it be?" The advisor explains:

As to result (i), Jones, like almost all individual taxpayers, uses the cash method of accounting. An arm's-length sale of the options for cash or other property of value would result in immediate recognition of ordinary income, just as would a straightforward exercise of the options. However, the Regulations under § 83 (since amended) provide that a cash method taxpayer does *not* recognize income on receipt of an unsecured promissory note until the note is paid. Under the Regulations, evidently, an unsecured note is a "mere promise to pay in the future" and is not deemed the equivalent of cash in the hands of a cash method taxpayer. Hence the sale to Junior has no present tax consequences to Jones.

As to result (ii), Junior's basis for the options will be equal to the face amount of the same note, viz., $9 million. Under general tax rules (see pp. 345–353, above), the basis of property paid for with debt (even non-recourse debt) is the same as it would be if purchased for cash. It follows that when Junior exercises the options, paying X $1 million, his basis for the X stock then issued to him will be $10 million, which of course includes the $9 million he "paid" his father. Since he sells the stock almost at once for the same $10 million, he reports no gain on the sale.

To be sure, Jones (or his estate) will have to report $9 million of ordinary income when Junior finally pays off the note at the end of 30 years. But Jones is glad to wait. If Jones exercised the options himself, he would of course be taxable on $9 million at the time of exercise, *i.e.*, today. At a combined federal and state tax rate of (let's say) 40%, Jones would owe a tax of about $3.6 million under the *Lo Bue* case. But the same tax deferred for 30 years has a present value of only about $360,000, assuming a discount rate of 8%. So, in present value terms, Jones saves more than $3 million by selling his stock options to his son.

Not bad. That unnamed tax advisor is certainly entitled to a fee for his good advice. Would 10% of the tax saving be fair? For good measure, the advisor supports his advice to Jones with a "more likely than not" legal opinion from a well-known law firm. And of course there are many other Joneses in the world to whom the same advice (and the same legal opinion) should be very welcome. The advisor even has an appealing name for his program. He calls it the Executive Compensation Solution.

In Notice 2003–47,[3] the IRS announced that it would challenge the 30-year deferral of Jones' option income—result (i)—by insisting that Junior's note constitutes an "amount realized" notwithstanding Jones' use of the cash method of accounting, or, in the alternative, by arguing that the transaction between Jones and Junior is not bona fide and lacks a business purpose. Perhaps *Lucas v. Earl* would also have a role to play.

As far as we know, only one taxpayer has chosen to litigate this issue.[4] The reason others have not, we would guess, is that they are not willing to incur the litigation costs and take the risk of civil penalties that a losing struggle in the Tax Court would entail. Instead (again, a guess), the vast majority of taxpayers who bought the ECS scheme (those, at least, who were audited or otherwise identified) have chosen to settle with the Commissioner for the tax due plus interest, the Commissioner having promised to waive penalties as a way of encouraging settlement.

The Offshore Partnership

As described at 14.03, Congress in 1980 extended installment sale treatment to cases like *Burnet v. Logan*, in which an asset is sold for an amount that is contingent on future events—in the case itself, the sale of a coal mine for a royalty payment per ton of coal mined over the life of the mine itself. Under the old *Logan* rule, the seller's basis would be fully recoverable before the seller recognized any income from the transaction. Section 453(j)(2) authorized the Treasury to devise a ratable recovery rule that would apportion basis recovery over the entire payout period, with each annual payment treated as part income and part basis recovery. When promulgated

---

[3]   2003–2 C.B. 132.

[4]   *Verizon Bus. Network Servs. v. Day-Cartee*, 103 AFTR 2d 1654 (S.D. Miss. 2009), *vacated and remanded*, 379 Fed. Appx. 404 (5th Cir. 2010) (in an opinion in connection with a lawsuit between employer and employee, court noted that the employee's ECS case is pending in Tax Court; as of this writing no *Day-Cartee* Tax Court opinion has appeared).

by the Treasury, the Regulations required, in the case of contingent payments with no maximum stated amount but with a fixed payment period, that the taxpayer's basis be recovered on the straight-line method over the payment period. If the taxpayer sold his right to contingent payments before the end of the payment period, any unrecovered basis would be taken into account in the year of sale.

As described, the ratable cost-recovery rule seems a reasonable solution to the awkward contingent payment problem posed by the *Logan* case. But what the Regulations failed to anticipate was that so-called tax-planners would treat the rule as an invitation to create an avoidance scheme of the most egregious and transparent character. In *ACM Partnership v. Commissioner*,[5] the tax planning was done by one of the nation's great financial institutions, Merrill Lynch, and the taxpayer to which the avoidance scheme was sold was a major consumer products company, Colgate-Palmolive, maker of soap and toothpaste and other articles of personal hygiene.

Colgate had earlier realized a large taxable gain on the sale of a subsidiary. The object of the tax plan was to create a deductible "loss" that could be carried back and offset against that gain,[6] thus eliminating the tax otherwise due.

Briefly described (rounding all the numbers and omitting many details), the plan went like this:

1. Colgate and Merrill Lynch entered into an offshore partnership with a Dutch bank, Algemene Bank Nederland, to which the parties made the following capital contributions (in millions):

	Capital Investment	Partnership Interest
Dutch Bank	$140	80%
Colgate	$ 33	19%
Merrill Lynch	$ 2	1%
Totals	$175	100%

2. In the same year, the partnership

(A) bought $175 million of notes issued by Citicorp, and then *immediately*

(B) sold the Citicorp notes to other investors, receiving from the latter (i) $140 million in cash, plus (ii) installment notes payable quarterly over the five-year period following (the LIBOR notes).

---

    5   157 F.3d 231 (3d Cir. 1998), *cert. denied,* 526 U.S. 1017 (1999).

    6   Code § 1212(a) (allowing a corporation to carry back a capital loss to the three years preceding the loss year).

The dollar amount of each quarterly payment was not fixed, but would vary from quarter to quarter depending on the prevailing interest rate for short-term interbank loans—the so-called London Interbank Offer Rate (LIBOR)—a rate that changes slightly from day to day to reflect loan demand and other market conditions. Overall, the LIBOR notes were expected to generate $35 million, but it could be a little more or it could be a little less depending on LIBOR over the five-year term of the notes.

3.   Shortly thereafter, the Dutch Bank received a cash distribution from the partnership equal to its original capital investment—$140 million—and was eliminated as a partner. Merrill Lynch also got back all but a few hundred thousand dollars of its original capital investment. This left Colgate with a 99% interest in the partnership and Merrill Lynch with a 1% interest.

4.   In the next year, the LIBOR notes were sold by the partnership for roughly $35 million in cash, following which the partnership in effect distributed virtually all of its assets to Colgate and Merrill Lynch, the sole remaining partners. Colgate got back just about the same amount it put in (less, of course, large fees paid to Merrill Lynch and the Dutch Bank), which is exactly what it expected.

Pointless? Completely—except for the anticipated tax consequences. The partnership treated the sale of the Citicorp notes as a contingent installment sale within the Regulations under § 453(j)(2)—the "contingency" being the quarterly fluctuations in LIBOR during the five-year payout period. By reason of such fluctuations the payments to be received by the partnership would vary from quarter to quarter. Hence the *total* amount to be received over the entire six-year period—the year of sale and the next five years—was uncertain, *i.e.*, "contingent" on the LIBOR from time to time prevailing.

Assuming (as the tax-planners intended) that the contingent installment sale rules applied, the partnership's basis in the Citicorp notes would be recoverable ratably (against the $140 million cash payment in the year of sale and against the principal payments on the LIBOR notes) over the six-year period in equal amounts of $29.167 million a year, *i.e.*, $175 million (cost of the Citicorp notes) divided by six years equals $29.167 million. In the year of sale, therefore, the partnership had a gain of $140 million (cash received) less $29.167 million, or about $111 million. Only 19% of that gain, about $20 million, was allocated to Colgate by reason of its 19% interest in the partnership, and only $1 million was allocated to Merrill Lynch. The remainder, roughly $90 million, was allocated to the Dutch Bank, which, being a foreign entity, paid no taxes to the United States on income from non-United States sources.

In the following year when the LIBOR notes were sold, the partnership—now consisting of Colgate's 99% interest and Merrill Lynch's 1% interest—offset its entire remaining basis, about $146 million ($175 million basis in the Citicorp notes, less the $29.167 million basis recovered in the year of the initial sale), against the sale price of $35 million. The result was a "loss" of about $111 million, of which 99%, or $110 million, was allocable to Colgate (and $1 million to Merrill). Taking into account the $20 million of gain that it realized in the first year when the cash payment of $140 million was received, Colgate had a net deductible loss of $90 million ($110 million minus $20 million) to carry back against the taxable gain previously realized on the sale of its subsidiary. The "loss," of course, was solely a function of the ratable cost-recovery rule, not of any actual market disaster.

In summary, the Dutch Bank gained $90 million and Colgate lost $90 million. In fact, neither partner gained or lost anything. Same for Merrill Lynch.

Too good to be true? Yes, but just barely. Affirming the Tax Court, the Third Circuit in a 2–1 decision disallowed Colgate's purported $110 million loss (and eliminated its earlier $20 million gain).[7] The overall partnership arrangement—and in particular, the purchase and immediate resale of the Citicorp notes—lacked "economic substance" in the court's view, and as a consequence, under settled law, must be disregarded for tax purposes. "In order to be deductible," the court observed, "a loss must reflect actual economic consequences sustained in an economically substantive transaction and cannot result solely from the application of a tax accounting rule. . . ." The dissenting judge argued, more or less typically, that the loophole, if there was one, should be left for Congress to close.

The majority opinion in *ACM Partnership* bears a close resemblance to the 1960 *Knetsch* decision (discussed at 6.06(b)), in which the Supreme Court disallowed phantom interest deductions under a sham annuity contract. There, as here, the absence of an economic or commercial purpose apart from tax-saving was fatal to the scheme. Undeterred, Colgate's tax-planners thought it worthwhile to try the sham-transaction game again, largely in the hope of baffling the courts and the Service or (better yet) getting by without an audit. And they nearly did.

---

[7]   157 F.3d at 260.

The End of Shelters (For the Moment)

In the first few years of the new millennium, the IRS appeared to be in serious danger of losing the tax shelter war. Although most courts paid lip service to the economic substance doctrine—under which a transaction lacks economic substance, and so is disregarded for tax purposes, unless the transaction had a realistic potential for producing a non-tax profit, and the taxpayer entered into the transaction for substantial non-tax business purposes—some courts found economic substance almost everywhere they looked. In addition to winning a significant portion of the litigated cases,[8] taxpayers "won" an unknown—but surely significant—number of cases simply because the IRS never detected their shelters. By 2006, however, IRS Commissioner Mark Everson was able to tell a Senate panel, "No longer are abusive tax shelters being marketed by top level accounting firms,"[9] and that statement remains true as of this writing. So what happened? The demise of tax shelters (at least for the time being) seems to have been caused by the combination of four factors.

The first factor was the end of the tax shelter "audit lottery." Reg. § 1.6011–4(a), promulgated in 2003, requires a taxpayer who has participated in a "reportable transaction"—a term defined broadly enough to include almost all marketed tax shelters—to file a "reportable transaction disclosure statement" with the IRS. Although there was initially no penalty for failure to comply with the disclosure requirement, Congress fixed that problem in 2004 by enacting § 6707A, which imposes substantial penalties on taxpayers failing to file reportable transaction disclosure statements. In addition, § 6111 requires tax shelter promoters to disclose their shelters to the IRS, and § 6707 provides penalties for noncompliant promoters. The disclosure requirements appear to have been quite effective. Today, few if any tax shelters succeed merely because the IRS never becomes aware of the shelters.

The second factor was a change in the outcomes of the litigated cases. Until the middle of the last decade, the scorecard in litigated tax shelter cases was fairly even; taxpayers had prevailed in a significant percentage of the reported cases. Sometime around 2005, however, the IRS began winning nearly every case, and the government's winning percentage has remained extremely high ever since. The IRS claims, no doubt with some reason, that it got better at litigating shelter cases over time, and that its improved record reflects its improved litigation strategies and techniques. We cannot

---

[8]   E.g., *Compaq Computer Corp. v. Commissioner*, 277 F.3d 778 (5th Cir. 2001).

[9]   Everson, *Everson Testimony Calls for "Fundamental" Reform to Deal With Tax Gap*, Tax Notes Today, Sept. 27, 2006, 2006 TNT 187–36.

help suspecting, however, that there may also have been a change in judicial attitudes toward tax shelter cases. Perhaps as judges came to realize that tax shelters posed an existential threat to the federal income tax, they became less willing to allow taxpayers to slip through the Code's alleged loopholes.

A dramatic third factor was the government's decision to bring felony charges against accountants and lawyers promoting especially egregious tax shelters. Although the number of tax professionals prosecuted was small relative to the number of tax professionals who were engaged in tax shelter promotion, and although not all the defendants were convicted, the prosecutions seem to have had a remarkably chilling effect on the entire tax shelter industry. Given the fact that more than a few tax shelters were being upheld (until the middle of the last decade) in civil litigation, it may be surprising that the government was able to obtain criminal convictions in some shelter cases. The apparent explanation is that some tax shelter promoters were not content with extremely aggressive interpretations of the tax laws; they also fraudulently misrepresented the facts of their shelter transactions. A jury might never convict based on a difference of opinion between the promoter and the government over the scope of the economic substance doctrine, but backdated documents (for example) are a different matter.

Finally, taxpayers who settled their cases with the government on unfavorable terms sued their tax shelter promoters for malpractice. Almost all the tax shelter malpractice cases were resolved by settlement or arbitration, so there is very little information in the public record about the resolutions of the cases. However, informed scuttlebutt indicates that tax shelter malpractice cases have been numerous and costly for defendants. In combination with the other three factors described above, the threat of malpractice claims appears to have been sufficient to persuade accounting firms and law firms to abandon the business of tax shelter promotion, at least for the moment.

Economic Substance

As in *ACM*, the Commissioner often resorts to "lack of economic substance" as a way of making the point that the transactions in question were entered into solely or chiefly for the purpose of avoiding taxes. Before 2010, almost all courts viewed "economic substance" as a legal requirement, one that the taxpayer had to satisfy in order to sustain the sought-for tax benefit, even though that requirement did not appear in the Code itself. In 2010 Congress codified the economic substance doctrine by enacting § 7701(*o*). The timing of the codification is a bit ironic. Having pondered codification while the tax shelter storms were raging, Congress finally enacted § 7701(o) in the calm after the storms. At least the provision will be waiting if the tax shelter industry reappears one day.

Under the new provision, if a judge decides the economic substance doctrine is "relevant" in a particular case, the transaction will be treated as possessing economic substance only if (1) it "changes in a meaningful way (apart from Federal income tax effects) the taxpayer's economic position," and (2) "the taxpayer has a substantial purpose (apart from Federal income tax effects) for entering into such transaction." The first requirement involves an objective analysis of the economics of the transaction, while the second looks to the subjective motivation of the taxpayer. Whether each requirement is satisfied will usually depend on whether the transaction had a realistic potential of producing a meaningful pre-tax profit.

Obviously, it does not follow from codification of the doctrine that the government will now prevail in every case in which it asserts that a tax shelter lacks economic substance. For one thing, courts remain free to decide that the doctrine is not "relevant" in particular situations. The legislative history offers a non-exhaustive list of types of transactions to which the doctrine should not be relevant. The basic idea is that the doctrine should not apply in any situation in which Congress clearly contemplated taxpayers' entitlement to the tax benefit at issue, even in situations where economic substance might be lacking. To take an obvious example, the IRS could not use the doctrine to deny the § 103 tax exemption for municipal bond interest income on the grounds that a taxpayer had no non-tax reason for purchasing municipal bonds paying interest exempt from tax under § 103, instead of purchasing corporate bonds bearing a higher rate of taxable interest.

The second reason the government will not necessarily prevail in every case involving the codified doctrine is that the existence of economic substance is—at least in some cases—very much in the eye of the beholder. Under the codified doctrine, as under the earlier judicial doctrine, just how much "substance" is necessary, and just what "substance" consists of, are questions that have to be decided case-by-case. Most tax shelters do include the remote possibility that the taxpayer can make money on his investment *if* all the contingencies fall out in his favor. And of course it is not a court's business to decide whether the taxpayer was wise or foolish to invest in a long-shot. On the other hand, the new statute does provide that a transaction has economic substance based on its profit potential only if "the present value of the reasonably expected pre-tax profit from the transaction is substantial in relation to the present value of the expected net tax benefits that would be allowed if the transaction were respected."

All in all, it seems fair to say that codification of the doctrine does not change things very much. It does put an end to the occasional court declaring that the judge-made version of the doctrine violated the separation of powers,[10] but that was a fringe position even before codification. It also clarifies a few aspects of the doctrine. For example, it resolves a split in the circuits as to whether the two-prong test for economic substance was conjunctive or disjunctive—in other words, whether a taxpayer had to satisfy both prongs of the test in order to prevail (the conjunctive version), or whether it was enough for the taxpayer to satisfy just one prong or the other (the disjunctive version). Under the codified doctrine, the test is unmistakably conjunctive. There is less to this issue than meets the eye, however, because courts almost never render split decisions on the two prongs; in virtually every case, a transaction either satisfies both prongs or satisfies neither.

The most significant aspect of the 2010 economic substance legislation is probably the enactment of a 20% penalty (increased to 40% in the case of a transaction not adequately disclosed by the taxpayer) under § 6662 for an understatement of tax attributable to a "disallowance of claimed tax benefits by reason of a transaction lacking in economic substance." The significance lies in the fact that this is a genuinely strict liability penalty; the penalty applies even if the taxpayer had "reasonable cause" for the understatement and "acted in good faith." What this means, of course, is that no tax shelter opinion letter from a law firm, no matter how gold-plated the letter, can protect a taxpayer from the new penalty.

Codification of the economic substance doctrine was not, of course, the only possible legislative response to the tax shelter plague. Arguably, it might have been better for Congress to enact a blunt prohibition against the recognition of non-economic losses and other tax benefits unless such recognition is clearly consistent with congressional intent. The loss claimed to be deductible in *ACM* would be disallowed on the ground that there was, in fact, no such loss and, of course, no showing of any favorable legislative intent. The economic substance doctrine would be irrelevant on this approach: no loss, no deduction, without regard to economic substance or the taxpayer's alleged expectation of a nontax benefit.[11] Legislation enacted in 2017 takes a halting step in this direction. Under § 461(*l*), an individual taxpayer can deduct business losses against no more

---

[10] *Coltec Indus., Inc. v. United States,* 62 Fed. Cl. 716, 756 (2004), *vacated and remanded,* 454 F.3d 1340 (Fec. Cir. 2006), *cert. denied,* 549 U.S. 1206 (2007).

[11] Chirelstein and Zelenak, *Tax Shelters and the Search for a Silver Bullet,* 105 Colum. L. Rev. 1939 (2005).

than \$250,000 (\$500,000 in the case of a joint return) of nonbusiness income. The provision is effective in 2018 through 2025.

Appendix A

PRESENT VALUE

This book has used the concept of "present value" and "discounting to present value" at many points. The excerpt below (reprinted with permission) explains the concept and supplies the relevant Tables.

Exercise: An investor expects to receive (i) a lump-sum payment of $5,000 at the end of year 3 plus (ii) a 20-year annuity of $1,000 a year, the first payment to be received at the end of year 4. What is the present value of the investor's expectations, assuming a discount rate of 10%?

Answer: $10,146. Do you agree? If not, write the authors.

ALCHIAN AND ALLEN,
UNIVERSITY ECONOMICS
205–209 (2d ed. 1967).

The *more distant* the deferred service (or income, or goods), the *lower* its present price. A dollar deferred two years is worth less today than a dollar deferred one year, if the rate of interest is positive. At an interest rate of 6 percent, the current price of $1 deferred a year is 94 cents—the amount that will grow at 6 percent in one year to $1. This is given by the formula

$$p_1 \;=\; \frac{A}{(1+r)} \;=\; \frac{\$1.00}{(1+.06)} \;=\; \$.943.$$

To get the present price for $1 deferred *two* years, simply repeat the above operation. If $1 deferred one year from now is now worth 94 cents, then deferring the dollar an additional year again reduces its present value by the same proportion. For two years, this is .943 × .943 = .890. A dollar due in two years is worth 89 cents today.

This same relationship can be expressed by noting that at 6 percent per year 89 cents will grow in one year to 94 cents, and then in the second year the 94 cents will grow to exactly $1. This can be expressed in form

$$p_2 \,(1+r)\,(1+r) = A.$$

where p_2 represents the amount now that will grow at the 6 percent annual rate of interest to $1, the amount A, at the end of the two-year period. Solving for p_2, we get

507

$$p_2 = \frac{A}{(1+r)(1+r)} = \frac{A}{(1+r)^2} = \frac{\$1.00}{(1.06)^2} = \$.890.$$

Two years' discounting is measured by the factor $1/(1.06)2 = .890$; three years of discounting is obtained by multiplying the future amount due in three years by $1/(1.06)3 = .839$. The present value of $1 deferred t years from today is obtained by use of the factor $1/(1.06)t$. Multiplying the amount due at the end of t years by this present-value factor gives the present value (or present price, or discounted value) of the deferred amount, A, due in t years. A set of these present-value factors is given in Table 13–1 for various rates of interest and years of deferment. The present-value factor decreases as t is larger: the farther into the future the amount due is deferred, the lower is its *present* value.

TABLE 13–1
Present Value of $1: What a Dollar at End of Specified
Future Year Is Worth Today

Yr	3%	4%	5%	6%	7%	8%	10%	12%	15%	20%	Yr
1	.971	.962	.952	.943	.935	.926	.909	.893	.870	.833	1
2	.943	.925	.907	.890	.873	.857	.826	.797	.756	.694	2
3	.915	.890	.864	.839	.816	.794	.751	.711	.658	.578	3
4	.889	.855	.823	.792	.763	.735	.683	.636	.572	.482	4
5	.863	.823	.784	.747	.713	.681	.620	.567	.497	.402	5
6	.838	.790	.746	.705	.666	.630	.564	.507	.432	.335	6
7	.813	.760	.711	.665	.623	.583	.513	.452	.376	.279	7
8	.789	.731	.677	.627	.582	.540	.466	.404	.326	.233	8
9	.766	.703	.645	.591	.544	.500	.424	.360	.284	.194	9
10	.744	.676	.614	.558	.508	.463	.385	.322	.247	.162	10
11	.722	.650	.585	.526	.475	.429	.350	.287	.215	.134	11
12	.701	.625	.557	.497	.444	.397	.318	.257	.187	.112	12
13	.681	.601	.530	.468	.415	.368	.289	.229	.162	.0935	13
14	.661	.577	.505	.442	.388	.340	.263	.204	.141	.0779	14
15	.642	.555	.481	.417	.362	.315	.239	.183	.122	.0649	15
16	.623	.534	.458	.393	.339	.292	.217	.163	.107	.0541	16
17	.605	.513	.436	.371	.317	.270	.197	.146	.093	.0451	17
18	.587	.494	.416	.350	.296	.250	.179	.130	.0808	.0376	18
19	.570	.475	.396	.330	.277	.232	.163	.116	.0703	.0313	19
20	.554	.456	.377	.311	.258	.215	.148	.104	.0611	.0261	20
25	.478	.375	.295	.232	.184	.146	.0923	.0588	.0304	.0105	25
30	.412	.308	.231	.174	.131	.0994	.0573	.0334	.0151	.00421	30
40	.307	.208	.142	.0972	.067	.0460	.0221	.0107	.00373	.000680	40
50	.228	.141	.087	.0543	.034	.0213	.00852	.00346	.000922	.000109	50

Each column lists how much a dollar received at the end of various years in the future is worth today. For example, at 6 percent a dollar to be received ten years hence is equivalent in value to $.558 now. In other words, $.558 invested now at 6 percent, with interest compounded annually, would grow to $1.00 in ten years. Note that $1.00 to be received at the end of fifty years is, at 6 percent, worth today just about a nickel. And at 10 percent it is worth only about .8 of one cent, which is to say that 8 mills (.8 of a cent) invested now would grow, at 10 percent interest compounded annually, to $1.00 in fifty years. Similarly $1,000 in fifty years is worth today $8.52, and $10,000 is worth today $85—all at 10 percent rate of growth. . . . Why not make that investment? Formula for entry in table is $p = A/(1 + r)^t$.

FUTURE AMOUNTS CORRESPONDING TO GIVEN PRESENT VALUES

Instead of deriving present values of future amounts, we can derive for any annual rate of interest the future amount that will be exchangeable for any present value. How much will $1 paid now purchase if the future amount is due in one year, or in two years, or in three years? At 15 percent per year, $1 will be worth $1.15 in one year. And at 15 percent for the next year, that $1.15 will in turn grow to $1.32. Hence, $1 today is the present price or value of $1.32 in two years. In terms of our formula, this can be expressed

$$p_2 (1 + r)(1 + r) = A.$$

$$\$1 (1.15)(1.15) = \$1 (1.32) = \$1.32.$$

If the future amount is deferred three years, the term (1.15) enters three times, and if deferred t years, it enters t times. For three years, the quantity (1.15) is multiplied together three times, denoted $(1.15)^3$, and equals 1.52. Therefore, in three years $1 will grow to $1.52. In general, the formula is

$$p_t (1 + r)^t = A$$

for any present payment, p_t, that is paid for an amount A available t years later. The multiplicative factor $(1 + r)^t$ is called the *future-value* (or *amount*) *factor*. Values of this future-amount factor for different combinations of t and r are given in Table 13–2.

TABLE 13–2

Compound Amount of $1: Amount to Which $1 Now Will Grow by End of Specified Year at Compounded Interest

Yr	3%	4%	5%	6%	7%	8%	10%	12%	15%	20%	Yr
1	1.03	1.04	1.05	1.06	1.07	1.08	1.10	1.12	1.15	1.20	1
2	1.06	1.08	1.10	1.12	1.14	1.17	1.21	1.25	1.32	1.44	2
3	1.09	1.12	1.16	1.19	1.23	1.26	1.33	1.40	1.52	1.73	3
4	1.13	1.17	1.22	1.26	1.31	1.36	1.46	1.57	1.74	2.07	4
5	1.16	1.22	1.28	1.34	1.40	1.47	1.61	1.76	2.01	2.49	5
6	1.19	1.27	1.34	1.41	1.50	1.59	1.77	1.97	2.31	2.99	6
7	1.23	1.32	1.41	1.50	1.61	1.71	1.94	2.21	2.66	3.58	7
8	1.27	1.37	1.48	1.59	1.72	1.85	2.14	2.48	3.05	4.30	8
9	1.30	1.42	1.55	1.68	1.84	2.00	2.35	2.77	3.52	5.16	9
10	1.34	1.48	1.63	1.79	1.97	2.16	2.59	3.11	4.05	6.19	10
11	1.38	1.54	1.71	1.89	2.10	2.33	2.85	3.48	4.66	7.43	11
12	1.43	1.60	1.80	2.01	2.25	2.52	3.13	3.90	5.30	8.92	12
13	1.47	1.67	1.89	2.13	2.41	2.72	3.45	4.36	6.10	10.7	13
14	1.51	1.73	1.98	2.26	2.58	2.94	3.79	4.89	7.00	12.8	14
15	1.56	1.80	2.08	2.39	2.76	3.17	4.17	5.47	8.13	15.4	15
16	1.60	1.87	2.18	2.54	2.95	3.43	4.59	6.13	9.40	18.5	16
17	1.65	1.95	2.29	2.69	3.16	3.70	5.05	6.87	10.6	22.2	17
18	1.70	2.03	2.41	2.85	3.38	4.00	5.55	7.70	12.5	26.6	18
19	1.75	2.11	2.53	3.02	3.62	4.32	6.11	8.61	14.0	31.9	19
20	1.81	2.19	2.65	3.20	3.87	4.66	6.72	9.65	16.1	38.3	20
25	2.09	2.67	3.39	4.29	5.43	6.85	10.8	17.0	32.9	95.4	25
30	2.43	3.24	4.32	5.74	7.61	10.0	17.4	30.0	66.2	237	30
40	3.26	4.80	7.04	10.3	15.0	21.7	45.3	93.1	267.0	1470	40
50	4.38	7.11	11.5	18.4	29.5	46.9	117	289	1080	9100	50

This table shows to what amounts $1.00 invested now will grow at the end of various years, at different rates of growth compounded annually. For example, $1.00 invested now will grow in thirty years to $5.74 at 6 percent. In other words, 5.74 due thirty years hence is worth now exactly 1.00 at a 6 percent rate of interest per year. . . . The entries in this table are the reciprocals of the entries in Table 13–1; that is, they are the entries of Table 13–1 divided into 1. . . . Formula for entries in table is $A = 1(1 + r)^t$.

For example, at 6 percent in five years, the future-amount factor is 1.34, which means that a present payment of $1 will buy, or grow to, the future amount $1.34 at the end of five years. Notice that the entries in Table 13–2 are simply the reciprocals of the entries in Table 13–1.

PRESENT CAPITAL VALUE FOR SERIES OF FUTURE AMOUNTS

If there is a sequence of amounts due at future times, we can find a present value for this series of amounts. Just as we add up the costs of individual items in a market basket of groceries, we add up the present values of each of the future amounts due. That sum is the present value of the whole series of amounts due at various future dates.

This series might be compared with an oil well that each year on December 31 spurts out one gallon of oil that sells for $1. To simplify the problem, let's first suppose that the series of dollars (spurts of oil) continues for only two years. If the interest rate is 6 percent, the present value of $1 deferred one year is 94 cents (see Table 13–1, column of .06 rate of interest for one year); and the present value of $1 due in two years is 89.0 cents (see the same table, same column, but now read the entry for year 2). The sum of the present capital values of both amounts due, the one in one year and the other in two years, is the sum of 94.3 cents and 89.0 cents, which is $1.83. To say that the rate of interest is 6 percent per year is equivalent to saying that you can exchange in the market $1.83 today for the right to receive $1 in one year *and* another dollar in two years.

Suppose the sequence is to last three years, with three $1 receipts. The aggregate present value is augmented by the present value of the dollar due in the third year. At a 6 percent rate of interest, this extra dollar has a present value of 83.9 cents (see Table 13–1). Therefore, the present value of the three-year series is $2.67 (given in Table 13–3). We have noted that this present value of a series of amounts due is called the *capital value* of the future receipts. Capital value is the current *price* of the rights to the stream (series) of receipts.

Some technical jargon will be convenient for subsequent analyses. The sequence of future amounts due is called an *annuity*, a word that suggests *annual* amounts. A two-year sequence is a two-year annuity. The term "annuity" denotes the series of annual amounts for a specified number of years. A person who has purchased the right to a stream of future annuities or amounts due—for example, his pension benefits—is sometimes called an *annuitant*.

TABLE 13–3

Present Value of Annuity of $1, Received at End of Each Year

Yr	3%	4%	5%	6%	7%	8%	10%	12%	15%	20%	Yr
1	0.97 1	0.96 0	0.95 2	0.94 3	0.93 5	0.926	0.909	0.890	0.870	0.833	1
2	1.91	1.89	1.86	1.83	1.81	1.78	1.73	1.69	1.63	1.53	2
3	2.83	2.78	2.72	2.67	2.62	2.58	2.48	2.40	2.28	2.11	3
4	3.72	3.63	3.55	3.46	3.39	3.31	3.16	3.04	2.86	2.59	4
5	4.58	4.45	4.33	4.21	4.10	3.99	3.79	3.60	3.35	2.99	5
6	5.42	5.24	5.08	4.91	4.77	4.62	4.35	4.11	3.78	3.33	6
7	6.23	6.00	5.79	5.58	5.39	5.21	4.86	4.56	4.16	3.60	7
8	7.02	6.73	6.46	6.20	5.97	5.75	5.33	4.97	4.49	3.84	8
9	7.79	7.44	7.11	6.80	6.52	6.25	5.75	5.33	4.78	4.03	9
10	8.53	8.11	7.72	7.36	7.02	6.71	6.14	5.65	5.02	4.19	10
11	9.25	8.76	8.31	7.88	7.50	7.14	6.49	5.94	5.23	4.33	11
12	9.95	9.39	8.86	8.38	7.94	7.54	6.81	6.19	5.41	4.44	12
13	10.6	9.99	9.39	8.85	8.36	7.90	7.10	6.42	5.65	4.53	13
14	11.3	10.6	9.90	9.29	8.75	8.24	7.36	6.63	5.76	4.61	14
15	11.9	11.1	10.4	9.71	9.11	8.56	7.60	6.81	5.87	4.68	15
16	12.6	11.6	10.8	10.1	9.45	8.85	7.82	6.97	5.96	4.73	16
17	13.2	12.2	11.3	10.4	9.76	9.12	8.02	7.12	6.03	4.77	17
18	13.8	12.7	11.7	10.8	10.1	9.37	8.20	7.25	6.10	4.81	18
19	14.3	13.1	12.1	11.1	10.3	9.60	8.36	7.37	6.17	4.84	19
20	14.9	13.6	12.5	11.4	10.6	9.82	8.51	7.47	6.23	4.87	20
25	17.4	15.6	14.1	12.8	11.7	10.7	9.08	7.84	6.46	4.95	25
30	19.6	17.3	15.4	13.8	12.4	11.3	9.43	8.06	6.57	4.98	30
40	23.1	19.8	17.2	15.0	13.3	11.9	9.78	8.24	6.64	5.00	40
50	25.7	21.5	18.3	15.8	13.8	12.2	9.91	8.30	6.66	5.00	50

An annuity is a sequence of annual amounts received at the end of each year. This table shows with each entry how much it takes today to buy an annuity of $1 a year at the rates of interest indicated. For example, an annuity of $1 a year for twenty years at 6 percent interest could be purchased today with $11.40. This amount would, if invested at 6 percent, be sufficient to yield some interest which, along with some depletion of the principal in each year, would enable a payout of exactly $1 a year for twenty years, at which time the fund would be completely depleted. And $1,000 a year for twenty years would, at 6 percent compounded annually, cost today $11,400, which is obviously 1,000 times as much as for an annuity of just $1. Formula for entry is $p = [1 - (1 + r)^{-t}]/r$.

How about a four-year annuity? The fourth year's $1 has a present value of 79.2 cents, which, when added to the present value of a three-year annuity of $1 a year, gives $3.46. A five-year annuity would have a present value of $4.21, because the dollar received at the end of the fifth year is now worth 74.7 cents. Proceed to the end of ten years, and you will find that the present capital value of a ten-year annuity of $1 each year is $7.36.

If we extended the series to twenty years (still with $1 at the end of each year) at 6 percent per year, the present capital value would increase to $11.40. Notice that the *present* value of the *last half* of that series (the ten amounts due in the eleventh through the twentieth years) is only $4.04 (= 11.40 − 7.36). At a 6 percent interest rate, $4.04 *today* will buy you $1 a year for ten years, beginning at the end of the eleventh year from now.

Table 13–1 gives the present value of each separate future payment in the annuity. For convenience, Table 13–3 gives the present value of annuities of various lengths, where the payment *at the end* of each year is $1. Looking at that table under the 6 percent interest rate, you will find that the present capital values for the *sum* of the discounted amounts due in the preceding examples are the entries in the rows for one, two, three, four, five, ten, and twenty years. Look at the entry for two years at 6 percent. It is the sum of .943 and .890, based on the data of Table 13–1. For an annuity lasting fifty years, the entry is 15.8—which means that a fifty-year annuity of $1 per year, with the first payment coming at the end of one year, has a present capital value of only $15.80 (at 6 percent).

Even an annuity that lasted forever (called a *perpetuity*), or for as long as you and your heirs desire, would have a finite capital value—namely, $16.67.

A second thought will remove the mystery from the fact that an infinitely long series of $1 amounts due yearly has a finite (limited) price today. To get a perpetual series of payments of $1 every year, all one has to do is keep $16.67 on deposit in a bank, if he can get 6 percent per year. Every year the interest payment of $1 can be taken out, and this can be done forever. In effect you pay $16.67 today to purchase an infinitely long sequence. But you can also see that the first fifty years of receipts (a fifty-year annuity) has a present value of $15.80. Hence, the remaining infinitely long series of $1 receipts, beginning fifty years from now, is worth today only about 87 cents. Distant events have small present values!

TABLE OF CASES

INDEX

References are to Pages

519